I

In Search of Christian Unity

IN SEARCH OF CHRISTIAN UNITY

A History of the Restoration Movement

Henry E. Webb

STANDARD PUBLISHING
Cincinnati, Ohio   30-88579

Sharing the thoughts of his own heart, the author may express views not entirely
consistent with those of the publisher.

Library of Congress Cataloging in Publication Data:

Webb, Henry, E.
    In search of Christian unity : a history of the Restoration Movement /
Henry E. Webb.
        p.   cm.
Includes bibliographical references.
ISBN 0-87403-768-9 (Case)
ISBN 0-87403-769-7 (Paper)
1. Restoration movement (Christianity)—History. 2. United
States—Church history.   I. Title
BX7315.W333 1990
286.6—dc20   90-30921
                                                                CIP

Contents

101190

Why Another History?

Every new generation of Christians needs to confront its religious heritage. In some manner, either formally or informally, the beliefs and practices that have been handed on need to be scrutinized afresh. The presuppositions implicit in the heritage need to be examined. Claims need to be measured against accomplishments. Above all, aims and purposes need to be appraised, embraced, modified, or rejected. Occasionally, this can involve a painful and embarrassing process, but it must be exercised if the religious heritage is to remain vital. Passive acceptance of preformulated ideologies seldom generates dynamic religious commitment. On the other hand, careful scrutiny of the faith of the fathers can lead to personal ownership and commitment to one's heritage.

The work of the historian is indispensable to this enterprise. Any satisfactory appraisal of the present must explore the past and bring into focus such factors as originating impulses, influencing phenomena, and inherent tendencies. The religious communion whose story is traced in this work has been examined by historians for more than a century, and excellent historical accounts have been produced. In light of this fact, it might plausibly be asked, "Is there need for another history of the religious communion variously known as the Disciples of Christ, the Restoration Movement, or the Christian Churches?" Simply to raise the question is to call forth at least two reasons for such an effort.

One factor in the need for a new history rises out of the very practical consideration that many of the works of earlier historians are no longer available to today's students. Most have been out of print since many years ago. They are available for library use but cannot function for classroom text purposes, and they are largely unavailable to churchmen who long to learn more about their religious heritage. The reprint services of the movement have not republished the older histories, probably because they are "out of date" so far as meeting the needs of contemporary students is concerned.

How does a history book, which treats past events, become "out of date"? There are several answers to this question, two of which are of obvious concern to contemporary students. One of these is that history is continuously being made and any work that deals with the history of a contemporary subject must be constantly updated. Obviously, the Roman Empire isn't making any new history (although new information and insights are constantly coming to light), but histories that treat living subjects are daily becoming obsolete. Most of the published histories of the religious fellowship under study focuses on the nineteenth century.[1] Little information pertaining to the twentieth century is in print.

Another consideration mandating a new treatment of the history of the movement is the change of perspective in contemporary historiography. Today's historians are much more aware of the complex nature of the train of historical events than were the writers of a generation or more ago. Religious movements may be conceived in terms of doctrinal upheavals, institutional developments, or ideological thrusts. However, the trend in modern historiography is to recognize that sociological and cultural dynamics are very significant factors in church history, especially in the United States where no established church exists and religious pluralism is so very persuasive. Some critics of contemporary historiography insist that too much importance is currently being placed on sociological factors. This writer makes no claim of being a social historian but considers social and cultural considerations too important to ignore completely. The movement under study developed in one of the most interesting and dynamic epochs in American history, and the relationship between the genius of the movement and the milieu of its development is at once meaningful and fascinating.

The Problem of Terminology

A major problem with which I have wrestled extensively for many years concerns terminology to be employed. Consistency in the use of terms would seem to be essential; yet it is almost impossible to maintain without causing misunderstandings. Terms that were widely current in the nineteenth century became freighted with connotations arising from twentieth-century controversies. The only alternative to this dilemma would be to employ new labels. This J.D. Murch did when facing this problem several decades ago. However, the employment of designations such as "Leftist," "Centrist," and "Rightist" not only oversimplifies the issues and thus distorts the fairness to the Puritans, it must be recognized that "religious freedom" constituted no part of their objective. Their "errand into the wilderness"[1] was a mission to plant the true religion in the only place where they could be free from the strictures imposed by Charles I and the Anglican establishment. Theologically, they were Calvinist. Their religious zeal and their beliefs differed sharply from those of the Virginia colonists to the South or the Pilgrim Separatists to the North. Religious diversity was characteristic of American life from its very beginning.

Once begun, the stream of settlers on the eastern seaboard continued unabated for three centuries. Colonial charters were obtained by trading companies (Carolina), by enterprising proprietors (Pennsylvania), and even for philanthropic purposes (Georgia). The people who came to America brought their faith with them, and the faith of these settlers was very diverse. In addition to English settlers, there were Dutch, Swedes, Germans, and some Jews.

Most of the colonies had an established church, Rhode Island and Pennsylvania being conspicuous exceptions. Generally speaking, the southern colonies were officially and predominantly Anglican. The New England colonies were Puritan, and the middle colonies were a mixture of many types of Protestantism. Here one might find in addition to Puritan Calvinists and Anglicans some who claimed to be Baptists, Quakers, Lutherans, Reformed, Presbyterians, Catholics, and an interesting collection of small sects, many of which emphasized the communal aspect of early Christianity.

It was in Puritan New England that the religious dimension of life was most intense. Generally speaking, the communities were more populous and the congregations were larger than in the middle or southern colonies. Here the first colleges in North America were established to provide, in good Calvinistic tradition, for an educated ministry as the necessary foundation for an enlightened society. The Puritan ideal of the godly community is ambitious beyond human capacity, and it contained the seeds of its own destruction. Combining the concepts of a totally Christian citizenry (hence the baptizing of every child at birth) with the concept of the church's consisting of the "called" who are experiential Christians with genuine Christian deportment, the Puritans in reality were seeking the union of two mutually irreconcilable aims.[2] Frustration was inevitable. Religious life in the Puritan colonies declined perceptibly by 1660. The records of the synods of New England display a dreary succession of lamentations about the spiritual condition of the area.[3] Second- and third-generation Puritans had not experienced the trauma involved in a decision to forsake their homeland and venture forth on a journey into the unknown in an effort to establish a godly society. Accordingly, their religious devotion was not quite as intense as that of the early settlers. It seems that their energies were increasingly claimed

Chapter Two

Religion in Early America

Antecedents of the Frontier Awakening

From the beginning of American history, religion has played an important role. Religious motivations were responsible for the migration of a major portion of the earliest permanent settlers to the New World. To be sure, other factors were also involved; motives are seldom single. Attractive economic possibilities beckoned settlers to the New World, and, for some few, there was the lure of sheer adventure. But many of those who came to the early settlements were seeking a new way of life and a more satisfactory religious situation. Freedom from religious opposition very often became an important part of the better way of life they were seeking.

The British crown was much less concerned about maintaining religious uniformity in its American colonies than was the French government. Consequently, the English colonies became a haven for persecuted dissenters. This was a blessing that would be denied to French dissenters who would have liked to come to Canada or Louisiana. The English colonies saw several varieties of Protestantism planted in their midst from the very beginning. Jamestown, settled in 1607 under a charter granted to the Virginia Company, was provided an Anglican chaplain. But the Pilgrims, arriving in Massachusetts a decade later, would have nothing of Anglicanism. As dissenters and Separatists from the Church of England, they established their own church in Plymouth, which recognized no ties with the Church of England. Within the next decade, many hundreds of Puritans settled in Boston and the surrounding area intent upon establishing a "godly commonwealth" in the New World. They have often been criticized for seeking freedom to worship as they believed they ought while denying this freedom to others (like Roger Williams and Ann Hutchingson) who disagreed with them in theology or practice. In all

43

history of the movement, but it also implies a schematic arrangement that hardly does justice to those with whom Murch finds himself in disagreement. For these reasons, this terminology has not
appealed to scholars, and it is not employed in the present work.
This leaves unsolved the problem of how to discuss the serious differences in understanding that have risen within the movement in the
more than one and one-half centuries of its history. There is urgent
need for some means of referring to the various bodies within the
total framework of the movement that is at once specific, non-pejora-
tive, and widely accepted. The difficulties in meeting such criteria
are patent when questions such as the following are posed: Are we
dealing with a movement or a Movement; a denomination or a
Denomination, or neither? Should those involved be called "disciples"
or "Christians" only? Collectively, do we have churches, or *a* church,
or *the* church? And how are we to understand such labels as cooperative, independent, anti-organ, and non-progressive, to list only a
few? The theological implications of the above are sufficient to pre-
cipitate a heated discussion almost any time adherents of one of
these positions open the subject. Yet, despite the fact that all of these
terms are largely unsatisfactory, and that they carry a certain emotional charge in some quarter of the movement, it is inevitable that
they be employed. Suitable options simply have not been found.

Certain basic rules of composition seem to impose themselves
upon the problem and greatly influence the rationale for adopting a
given terminology. One is that whenever a term is employed as a
proper name (proper not necessarily in the sense of appropriate, but
only in reference to a specific identity), it should be capitalized.
Thus, whenever reference is made to a specific, identifiable group of
disciples of the Lord, the term will be Disciple. It was thus employed
by Alexander Campbell. Similarly, when reference is made to this
particular religious movement initiated for the purpose of restoring
Biblical Christianity as the means of reuniting the divided body of
Christ, it must be cited as the Restoration Movement. Whether or
not a denomination was thereby formed depends entirely on the
meaning one assigns to the term.[2] Etymologically, the term simply
means to name something, and, in this sense, it was employed by the
very conservative Moses E. Lard.[3] However, it often is employed to
designate well-structured, readily-identifiable religious bodies that
accept the principle of separate churchly existence. Whether or not
the term is appropriate for the subject under study in the volume
will not be decided to everybody's satisfaction in this or any other
volume. Care will be exercised to use the term so as not to give conscious offense. As an example, the term Disciples Denomination is
readily acceptable to that portion of the movement that established
headquarters in Indianapolis, Indiana, and thus it may be used of
this body without objection. The rest of the movement dislikes the

term; hence its use will be avoided when referring to it. A similar treatment of the term *brotherhood* will be followed. The term will be capitalized when referring to a specific body, usually the denomination known as the Disciples of Christ.

How shall the remaining portion of the movement be designated? That portion whose desire for separate existence was officially recognized in the federal census of 1906 prefers to be designated as "Churches of Christ," even though hundreds of congregations that do not share their aversion to the use of musical instruments in worship are also known by that name. After 1906, the designation "Churches of Christ" will refer exclusively to this "non-instrumental" body.

It is the segment of the movement that, since 1927, has related to the North American Christian Convention that is the most difficult to designate. The nearest thing to an official title that can be cited is The Undenominational Fellowship of Christian Churches/Churches of Christ.[4] Obviously, such an accolade is too cumbersome to have any practical utility. The common designation is "Independent," referring to the fact that, since 1926, if not earlier, those churches so designated have chosen to conduct missionary activity independently of the United Christian Missionary Society. There are obvious objections to the use of the term; the implications attaching to it are undesirable. For this reason, an attempt has been made by some to use the term "Direct Support Christian Churches/Churches of Christ." This designation has not gained popular support, probably because of the fact that the rather narrow focus it places upon missionary methodology is not an adequate basis for identifying a religious fellowship, especially one that subscribes to the principles of this body. An attempt has been made to label this body "Church of Christ Number Two,"[5] but this is also more pejorative than descriptive and has not found any appreciable acceptance.

In the light of these considerations, it seems that a certain arbitrariness in the choice of terms is inevitable. Furthermore, it would appear that popular usage, while not always logical nor consistent, has the advantage of being more readily understood. It is not without misgivings (nor considerable consultation with other historians of the movement) that I have yielded to popular usage of terms and adopted the following arrangement that appears to me to be required by the historical circumstances: (1) Terms will be used in the several chapters in a manner consonant with the way they were used during the period of time the particular chapter embraces. Thus, prior to the union of 1832, the churches of the Stone following will be design- to form a fellowship that is distinguished largely by its aversion to using musical instruments in worship, the designation "Churches of Christ" will be reserved for this body. (4) Similarly, after the separation beginning in 1927, the designation "Disciples of Christ" will be used to refer to the denomination with headquarters in Indianapolis, Indiana. (5) The remaining portion will be designated as "Christian Churches" and sometimes merely as "Independents."

It may be argued that this is confusing, especially to one who is being introduced to the history of this people. The objection is valid and can be countered by pointing out that "this is the way that it happened." Popular terminology is not always accurate, but it communicates. Voltaire pointed out that the Holy Roman Empire was neither holy, Roman, or an empire, but everybody knew what the term meant, and it would have been futile to attempt to introduce a more accurate cognomen. It is not the province of the historian to adjust the facts of history to make them fit into a rational or consistent pattern. Rather it is incumbent upon him to relate, explain, and interpret historical data as it developed, with all its irrationality and inconsistencies. This is the only defense that can be cited for the acknowledged terminological ambiguities that will be encountered. It is doubtful, however, if any other defense is necessary.

The Matter of Perspective

Fortunately, the myth of scientific and purely objective historiography so dear to the Enlightenment has been exploded in this century. No historian has ever written wholly objectively; such is beyond human capability. It is no great merit for a historian to be candid about his perspective (some may call it bias) in the writing of history; the fact is that it is impossible to conceal one's point of view. This work inevitably reflects the author's lifelong identity with the movement under study, his sympathy with its objectives, pride in its achievements, and disappointment with its foibles. While genuinely committed to the necessity of basing Christian faith and practice upon firm Biblical ground (in this sense, restoration of New Testament Christianity), no attempt is made in this work to trace "the true church" down through the centuries. Since the first century, the church has always numbered within its ranks genuinely devoted saints; and, paradoxically, it has always been in need of reform. The author's reluctance to use such terms as *apostate, heresy,* and *infidel* should not be construed to mean that the writer is indifferent toward the various doctrinal and other differences encountered in this study. Much has emerged in the history of the movement with which this author has little sympathy. However, any desire to write tpolemic history is emphatically disclaimed, and it is the author's hope that the temptation to indulge in such unworthy historiography has been resisted. It is the intent to state opposing positions honestly and fairly within the limits of the brevity that the work imposes. In some cases, the treatment of viewpoints that the author does not endorse have been submitted to the scrutiny of persons subscribing thereto. Whether the objective of fairness has been achieved to an appreciable degree must be left, in last analysis, for the reader to decide.

Limitations

Few are more aware of the limitations imposed by the scope of the work than the writer himself. Because the aim is comprehension, important details are neglected or omitted altogether. It is hoped that the work will prove useful to students and churchmen who are seeking an overview of the history of the movement and a greater awareness of their religious heritage. Every person who is already familiar with much of this history or who has a particular institutional interest at heart will be disappointed by the brevity with which his particular interest has been treated. Hopefully, this defect will be compensated in part through footnotes and bibliographical references. Responsibility for determining what items are included and what is omitted rests with the author, who regrets but cannot escape the practical limitations of the work.

Personal Acknowledgments

The author is pleased to acknowledge his indebtedness to his many teachers and colleagues who have contributed insights that are reflected in this work. To attempt to name these scores of persons would be unwise. However, one name stands out preeminently. Dr. Dean E. Walker, the author's mentor in several ways, possessed a grasp of the nature of the Stone-Campbell Movement and an extensive participation in its history that was equaled by few and surpassed by none. To this master teacher, the author is profoundly in debt.

End Notes

[1]For example, LeRoy Garrett, *The Stone-Campbell Movement* (Joplin: College Press, 1981), uses approximately 80% of his text to deal with persons and events of the nineteenth century.

[2]For a discussion of this issue, see James B. North, "Are We a Denomination?" *Christian Standard,* March 18, 1979, p. 4.

[3]Moses E. Lard, ed., *Lard's Quarterly,* 1866, p. 335.

[4]This designation was adopted by the *Yearbook of American Churches* in 1971 at the suggestion of the Commission on Chaplaincy Endorsement.

[5]The term has been used primarily by A.T. DeGroot in several published works. See *Church of Christ Number Two* (Fort Worth: published by the author, 1956).

Chapter One

Mandate of the Movement

The Tragedy of Division in the Church

The epoch-making public ministry of Jesus of Nazareth reached its climax in a series of events that centered in Jerusalem and culminated at Calvary. His voluntary sacrifice completed His mission in the overall purpose of the Father (John 19:30). The agony of Calvary was crowned with the glory of the resurrection, which transformed the despair of His followers into a dynamic hope and inspired in them a dedication to His cause that no force on earth could crush. With the words of His Commission ringing in their ears, His followers went forth to make disciples of all nations (Matthew 28:19, 20).

But what would become of these disciples? Would they carry forth His purpose of reconciling all men to God? Or would they go their separate ways, dissipate their energies in pursuit of their own ends, and thereby cause the great purpose to which He had given His life to fade into oblivion? Even as Jesus contemplated His own suffering, this was a matter of major concern to Him. He addressed an impassioned prayer to the Father on behalf of the subsequent unity of His disciples (John 17:20, 21). In the centuries that have followed, relatively few of His followers seem to have taken this prayer very seriously.

In the course of human events, every community becomes the focus of two types of forces. There are cohesive forces that serve to bind individuals together in a group. These unifying factors may be imposed from without or arise from within. Without them, there can be no community. But there are also divisive forces at work in every community. These arise from a variety of sources and tend to nullify the cohesive factors and fracture the community. When the cohesive factors are more significant, the community remains united. When the divisive factors become more significant than the cohesive forces, division is the result. The Lord recognized the inevitability of this

17

process that is inherent in group dynamics and prayed that His followers would remain sufficiently committed to the unifying dynamic in the overall purpose of God to ensure that the divisive forces rising out of human nature would be sublimated. This would be a reasonable expectation from the redeemed, who are counseled to seek first the kingdom of God (Matthew 6:33). Unfortunately, such was not to be the case as history unfolded.

It should not be surprising that divisive factors can be found in the church. Redeemed humans are still human and, though they have access to resources that can overcome base human tendencies, they are still subject to a vast array of human foibles. Jesus never expected humans to become superhuman. He did hope that His followers would be able to order their priorities so that the will of their Father would prevail over human limitations and base ambition.

Divisive factors soon appeared within the body of disciples that came into being on the Day of Pentecost. Three thousand, soon five thousand, and more were united by a common faith and hope in the risen Jesus Christ. Although they possessed neither formal organization nor institutional resources, their unity expressed itself powerfully in table fellowship, in the fellowship of prayer, and in the very tangible fellowship of shared possessions (Acts 4:34, 35). It was in the latter area where dissension first appeared. The minority of the fellowship, who were of Hellenic background, began to complain about their treatment at the hands of the Hebrew majority (Acts 6:1-7). Already the ugly specter of social and national differences was surfacing in a community in which there was to be no bond or free, Jew or Greek, because Christ had reconciled all of them to the Father and had thereby made them one in a more significant brotherhood. The wisdom of the apostles counseled the group to rectify any unintentional injustice by the selection of seven spiritual men to ensure that the needs of the Greek Christians were met. It is noteworthy that all of the men who were chosen bear Greek names, thus testifying to the willingness of the apostles to admit the brethren of Greek background into full and equal fellowship with the whole body. Subsequent problems of ethnic difference have had less satisfactory endings.

Racial and national differences often give rise to convictions and hostilities that are very deeply rooted in the human psyche. These convictions and hostilities are frequently fortified by allegiance to highly valued and cherished institutions. Such was the case with the loyalty of many of the Palestinian Jewish Christians to the law of Moses and the institutions of Israel. They accepted Jesus Christ as the Messiah who was to fulfill the aspirations of the chosen people of Israel but insisted that His people were to be marked by fidelity to the law and the temple. Indeed, the Jewish Christians continued to frequent the temple (see Acts 2:46) and persisted in observing the Jewish dietary code. (Note the difficulty with which Peter, the leader of the apostles, surrendered his commitment to the dietary code: Acts 10:13-16; Galatians 2:11-14.) Such uncompromising adherence to distinctive Jewish, Old Covenant institutions would have reduced the mission of Christ to that of a Jewish reformer, and Christianity would have become merely a reformed sect of Judaism.

More than any other, it was the apostle Paul who saw the implications of God's purpose in Jesus Christ. Having been convinced by his Damascus Road experience that the narrow Pharisaism of his early years was not in keeping with the divine purpose, he ultimately opened his eyes to the realization that, in Jesus Christ, God was calling all men to reconciliation with himself. This conviction involved Paul in the two major enterprises that were to consume the remainder of his days. One was a series of far-reaching missionary journeys that would take him deep into Gentile areas with the good news that the true and living God seeks to save all men regardless of race or nationality. This salvation is accomplished not by adherence to the religion of Israel, but through faith in Jesus Christ. His faithful and fruitful mission was crowned by martyrdom in that citadel of Gentile power and worldly culture, Rome. But this mission involved him in the other major enterprises of his life, the proclamation of the gospel of Jesus Christ against those who would confine its scope to Jews and proselytes alone. For Paul, this was an unceasing battle. He journeyed, preached, and wrote extensively in behalf of the gospel for *all* men. He was dogged at every turn by "Judaizers," men who would not concede that God could operate among men except through the law. Many of Paul's letters reflect this controversy, and it was the subject of an apostolic conference in Jerusalem (Acts 15). It led to personal slander of the apostle[1] and was the major cause of his arrest in Jerusalem and susequent incarceration (Acts 21:17-36). But his efforts were not in vain. The vision of what the Father of all mankind sought to accomplish in Jesus Christ was planted in a score of Gentile congregations in the empire, each of which was to be a beachhead for the confrontation with pagan culture. Paul's basic understanding of the ultimate purpose of God in the world was beautifully set forth for the benefit of future generations in his epistle to the Ephesians. Near the end of a rich life, the seasoned and mature apostle summarized his Christian philosophy (cosmic understanding) in chapters 1—3 and pointed out some of the practical implications in chapters 4—6.

Early Gentile Christianity

The church was rescued from narrow Judaistic sectarianism, but at heavy cost. As Christianity increased among the Gentiles, many of those who were zealous for the law lapsed back into Judaism. Although the church had begun among the Jews, the majority of its numbers by the end of the first century were Gentile. The significance of Jerusalem as a center of Christian activity steadily declined until, after the city's destruction in A.D. 135, it scarcely ranked as a center of influence, and the religion of Jesus Christ was almost exclusively Gentile.

Because the religion of Christ is the fulfillment of the religion of the Old Testament, both Jew and Christian were impoverished when the church and synagogue became isolated institutions. Gentile Christians were deprived of the rich understanding of the meaning of their faith that is provided by an in-depth appreciation of the Old Testament, an understanding that would have greatly assisted them in the second and third centuries in their struggles with paganism. Similarly, Jews were deprived of the fulfillment of the hope of Israel because they learned about Jesus only from those synagogue teachers who had repudiated Him. Meanwhile, pagans could not help but be confused at the specter of two bodies of people who worship the same God but shun each other. Such is the nature of schism. It impoverishes all parties.

When, in fulfillment of the divine purpose as set forth in the Great Commission, the church launched forth into the Gentile world, it entered a veritable whirlpool of religious forces that soon threatened to tear it apart. Religious life in the pagan empire was vigorous and diverse. Any and every kind of doctrine and practice could be found, and there were scores of teachers whose speciality lay in their ability to synthesize a wide variety of religious views into a single system. By cleverly adjusting the meaning of terms, they were able to absorb the most diverse viewpoints into their systems. Though rather varied, these composite and strange religious systems are known as Gnosticism. The systems are quite complex and cannot be treated at length here. They generally incorporate a few very significant presuppositions toward which Christian terms can be bent: the eternal conflict between good and evil, the fundamental nature of matter as evil, the supremacy of one God who presides over an array of lesser spiritual beings, angels, principalities, powers, and the like, and the basic conflicts of flesh (evil) and spirit (good). Claiming superior wisdom and special insight, the Gnostic teachers were ready to reinterpret Christianity and absorb it into their systems. The God of the Old Testament was rejected because He created matter. Jesus (good) could not have had a physical body (flesh is evil), so the incarnation was denied. Having only a spiritual body, He could not really die, thus eliminating the atonement. But the language of the New Testament that refers to the warfare with the flesh and matter was utilized to give credence to the Gnostic reinterpretation of the faith.[2]

The threat Gnosticism posed to the survival of Christianity was more serious than anything that the Roman government could present. The danger is reflected in the New Testament itself (1 Timothy 6:20; 1 John 4:2, 3). The church met this threat in three ways: (1) It defined its creed. The so-called Apostles Creed was designed to affirm precisely what the Gnostics denied. (2) It affirmed its canonical writings, thereby limiting the effectiveness of the numerous spurious writings that circulated Gnostic views. (3) It greatly enhanced the authority of the bishop to define the true teaching of the church.

The process created schisms. Gnostic sects were spun-off from the church, some surviving for two centuries. But the main body of Christians, now called the "catholic" church, survived. A respected church historian noted that, by the end of the second century, the church was quite different from the apostolic fellowship. Whether it could have survived the tremendous Gnostic crisis without certain adaptations can be seriously questioned.[3]

Another serious division in the second-century church originated in Asia Minor. A group of devout Christians became distressed over what they understood as the increasing worldliness of the church. The hope of the imminent return of Jesus, which marked the early church, had waned with the passing of the decades. Concurrently, much of the enthusiasm had declined, and the special gifts of the Spirit seemed to be less evident. A man named Montanus led an effort to revive the hope of the early return of the Lord. Joined by two "prophetesses," he managed to generate considerable enthusiasm and some wild excesses.[4] His followers became very puritanical and austere, the more so as their enthusiasm increased. An effort was made to revive the disappearing spiritual gifts, especially tongues. The main body of Christians was unimpressed, which unsurprisingly caused Montanus and his followers to regard them as calloused and unspiritual. Ungracious judgments were made that resulted in an ugly schism that persisted for several centuries in Asia Minor and North Africa. Both groups were the poorer for this schism. The church needed the vigor and devotion of the Montanists and the Montanists needed the stability that came from being related to the main body of Christians.

It is generally believed that times of hardship and persecution serve to unify the followers of Christ as their common bonds become more apparent and their need for mutual support becomes more critical. But one of the most persistent schisms in the church arose while the most severe persecution was at its height. Carthage, in North Africa, was the center of a very large Christian community. It was made up of a large native (Berber) majority and a Roman minority. The Berbers were poor, not well educated, and socially inferior to the Romans. The latter was not only the ruling class, but dominated the economic and social life of the province as well. The Romans also dominated the church through the bishop, who was elected from their numbers. Racial tensions between the two factions were intensified by the personal ambitions of leaders and, in 311, a rival bishop was elected who championed the Berber interests. The church in Carthage divided. Of course, the real reasons for the conflict were not admitted. The racial cause of the schism was obscured behind trumped-up theological issues so that each side accused the opposing faction of being "unorthodox." Unlovely schism was represented as a noble effort to preserve the faith. Here was a technique that was to prove useful in numerous subsequent cases. Perhaps it was legitimate in several instances. In North Africa, however, the faith was dealt a dreadful blow by those who were claiming to defend it. The result was a struggle that, for bitterness, has seldom been rivaled.[5]

The third century of Christian history provides us with the beginnings of a controversy that was to grow into the most serious division in the ancient church. The problem arose out of the teachings of several brilliant men of wide learning in the Hellenistic culture that prevailed in the Roman Empire. They were, quite naturally, using the thought forms of Hellenism to give expression to their faith in Jesus Christ. Christians have always held that Jesus Christ is God. They have also held, true to their Jewish background, that God is one. Believers have often struggled to explain how, if Jesus Christ is God, there would not thus be two Gods. And if the Holy Spirit is also a Person in the Godhead, how then would it be possible to avoid tritheism? Space prevents recounting the several ingenious theories that have been advanced to avoid this dilemma.[6] Certainly one of the more sophisticated is that advanced by the learned Alexandrian presbyter, Arius. He solved the problem to the satisfaction of many by affirming that Jesus was God; but unlike the Father, He is not eternal. Before "God created the heaven and the earth," He created His only Son. From this perspective, Arius could affirm virtually any statement in the Scriptures.

This explanation appeared to be rational, and it soon gained a significant following. Strong opposition was registered by Athanasius, destined to become bishop of Alexandria and lifelong crusader for what came to be known as Nicene orthodoxy. He insisted that the Son must be eternal with the Father, else He could not procure our salvation. Constantine, the first Christian emperor of Rome, was at a loss to know how to handle an issue that threatened to divide the church, which he had hoped would help to unify and solidify his empire. He summoned all of the bishops of the empire to come to Nicea at government expense to settle the issue. In A.D. 325, more than three hundred bishops met in Nicea and, after long debate, adopted the Creed of Nicea. It incorporated terms that were not only non-Biblical, but also were not understood by most of those present or by the vast majority of Christians in the empire. Government sanction was given to this definition of orthodoxy and those who dissented were anathematized.

Not only are the dynamics of the Council of Nicea subject to serious criticism (the emperor, though unbaptized himself, was the most influential factor in the decision), but it is obvious that the creed utilizes thought categories that derive from Greek philosophy and are quite foreign to the Hebrew-Christian tradition. The creed did not unite the church; it further divided it. Human formulas that have as their object the definition of orthodoxy function as theological fences to exclude dissenters and narrow the fellowship of Christ. Thus, they are poor bases for the preservation of fellowship and unity.

The Arian schism was long-lived and bitter. Centuries were to pass before Arians were persuaded or forced to come back into the orthodox church. Many fell victim to the Mohammedan advance. This controversy was soon followed by a series of Christological controversies that fractured the ancient church and made the Christian regions of the Near East an easy prey for the conquering armies of Islam. Territories lost to the crescent of Mohammed have not been reclaimed by the cross to this day.

Medieval Divisions

A work of this nature must necessarily overlook many important movements in the history of Christianity. However, the great East-West schism that is dated at 1054 is one that cannot be overlooked. The Christianity of Western Europe had developed along somewhat different lines from that of the East, and after a thousand years these differences were quite pronounced. The language of the church in the West was exclusively Latin (of a poor quality) whereas the liturgy in the East was Greek or a vernacular. The West had evolved an episcopal structure that provided for some degree of papal authority, although this was by no means well defined or widely respected. The East had no such counterpart. There were no serious efforts to reconcile these differences because they really did not matter all that much. However, when conflicting political conditions arose, it did not take long to effect mutual excommunication. Although recently Pope and Patriarch have embraced each other as brothers in Christ, the removal of the excommunication after more than nine hundred years appears too radical a step to contemplate. Although most people in either faction would be at a loss to explain just why these two bodies are at odds, the bodies remain separate. Meanwhile, both branches of these followers of Jesus Christ have been confronted by the militant followers of Marx and Lenin, whose intent was to bring about their elimination as speedily as possible.

Thus far, a series of schisms has been recounted without confronting a very legitimate question: Is schism always wrong? Are there any circumstances in which schism is the lesser of two evils? Does fidelity to Jesus Christ require that we part company with those who would make shipwreck of the faith? What does the Bible teach on this subject? It will be found that the answer may be very complex. Few would hold that schism is never justified. The problem will be treated at greater length in chapter 2.

One of the most obvious examples of the problem is found in a celebrated medieval schism involving the Waldensians. Peter Valdez, a rich cloth merchant who lived in Lyons, France, was much impressed by an itinerant preacher who used the Scriptures in the vernacular. Believing he had been called of God, Peter made provision for the care of his family and then sought permission from his bishop to preach. Unfortunately, the church of this area was having difficulty with a heretical group that fused Christianity with ancient pagan thought. Known as Cathari (the Pure), they made heavy use of parts of the Scriptures to entice Christians to their position. For this reason, the Third Lateran Council (Rome, 1179) had restricted the use of the Scriptures in the hands of laymen. Regarding Peter as an uninstructed layman rather than a heretic, the bishop denied his request for permission to preach. Peter considered the bishop's prohibition as the voice of man against the voice of God, so he defied the authorities and began to preach. This was followed by excommunication. The rift thus created widened to mutual recriminations and eventual warfare between Peter's growing numbers and the majority authority. Waldo's schism, while regrettable, can be seen as preferable to yielding to the strictures of a church that forbids preaching from the Bible. The Waldensians were persecuted and driven to refuge in the Alps. They have survived to this day, being the largest and oldest non-Roman-Catholic Christian body in Italy. One cannot help but sympathize with the Waldenses nor avoid the conclusion that the medieval church was much impoverished by the loss of these people with their deep dedication to Jesus Christ and their strong evangelical emphasis.

Another medieval schism began in England and reached its most tragic climax in Bohemia. John Wycliffe (1338-1384) lived in a period when the church was acutely in need of reform. He is remembered today for translating the New Testament into English. His challenge to the greed of the high clergy came to be used by self-serving noblemen until his cause was largely ruined in England. But it was carried to Bohemia (modern Czechoslovakia) by students. There it found fertile soil. John Huss (1373-1415) led the movement that demanded reform in the church. Called to appear before the Council of Constance (1414-1417) and promised safe-conduct by the Emperor, he was arrested, condemned, and burned at the stake for heresy.

Civil War followed in Bohemia. Thousands died in a struggle in which personal and political motives soon became intertwined. A part of Huss's followers were persuaded by concessions made at the Council of Basel in 1433 to return to the church of Rome. The remainder suffered bitter persecution. The Moravian Church of today traces its ancestry to these followers of John Huss.

Reformation Divisions

The major eruption in western Christendom came in the sixteenth century. Again, deep religious convictions entwined with more mundane social, political, and economic motives. Martin Luther, whose Biblical studies led him to conclude that his church had obscured the faith dimension of Christianity by its system of merits based on good works, initiated a series of events that culminated in the major division in Western Christendom. Rallying behind three themes: salvation by faith, the sole authority of the Scriptures, and the priesthood of every believer, German Protestants could not accommodate to the demands of Rome. Western Europe had never acknowledged that there would be more than one church; but, for the first time in fifteen hundred years, the Empire, in the Peace of Augsburg of 1555, recognized two churches. Emperor Charles V, the most powerful emperor in the history of the Holy Roman Empire, was powerless to prevent this split and abdicated the throne rather than be party to the Peace settlement that would formally divide the church. Actually, the church had divided many times before, but always the dissidents were considered to be heretics and without legal rights. The Peace of Augsburg was the first recognition of legitimate legal rights for two different bodies of the followers of Christ, each of which denied legitimacy to the other. By this date, however, a number of other divisions had already developed in the western European church. The English church declared itself independent of Roman authority in 1534 and, except for a brief formal reunion under Mary Tudor two decades later, has continued as a separate body to this time. National and economic factors played a large role in this schism.

John Calvin (1509-1564), whose logical exposition of Christian doctrine causes many to consider him to be the father of Protestant systematic theology, and whose lucid commentaries on the Scriptures won the attention of men of every nation, spent the major part of his adult life in the Swiss city of Geneva. This city came to be a place of refuge for persecuted Protestants from many lands. Exerting much influence on the government of the city, though never holding any public office, Calvin sought to create in Geneva a Christian commonwealth, an earthly counterpart to the kingdom of God. His influence was far-reaching. He is truly the international reformer. The national churches in Scotland and the Netherlands are basically Calvinist, as were the Puritans in England and the Protestants of Bohemia and Hungary. While these peoples developed no sense of unity among themselves, the differences that separated them were more national than theological.

By far the most schismatic movement in the sixteenth-century Protestant Reformation is found among the heterogeneous sects generally referred to as the Anabaptists. Their basic conviction that the church is a gathered fellowship of regenerate believers in covenant led them to reject both infant baptism and the concept of the state church, a concept that had prevailed in Christendom for twelve hundred years. Their history is marked by dreadful persecution and many martyrs. The concept of religious individualism (separation of church and state), so dear to Americans, is largely their bequest to modern society. Every "free church" (congregational) movement in Christendom is in their debt. This understanding of the nature of Christianity has had fewer problems in generating personal commitment to Jesus Christ than it has had in conceiving that the church of Christ is one or imagining how that unity could be expressed. But if the Anabaptists could be considered the radicals of the sixteenth century, it must be conceded that the future would see many of their views widely accepted, especially in the New World, resulting in hitherto undreamed-of diversity and pluralism. The growth of religious separatism saw a corresponding decline in the concept of the unity of the followers of Christ. Modern times have seen much greater importance placed on individual liberty than on Christian unity. The New World was settled just as this transition was beginning to develop.

Religious Diversity in the New World

When the New World was discovered (1492), there was but one church in western Europe. When serious settlement began a century later, there were many. Most of the New World settlements came from two Roman Catholic nations, Spain and France. The former was to impose its religion and culture on the entire continent south of the Rio Grande River. (Brazil is closely related through the Portuguese.) France sought to dominate North America before the fortunes of war confined her influence to Canada and the Louisiana Territory. The Dutch and the English managed to establish themselves on the Atlantic shores between these two major Roman Catholic powers. The English territories soon became havens for religious refugees. This use of the colonies was tolerated by the English monarchy because it helped to solve a domestic problem and it tended to create an English buffer against French and Spanish expansion in the New World. The Dutch were eliminated from the area in 1664 with the seizure of New Amsterdam.

Except for the short-lived effort of the Puritans of Massachusetts Bay to create and maintain a holy commonwealth, religious diversity marked the English settlement. To be sure, every colony except Rhode Island and Pennsylvania had an established church, and the way of the dissenter was not always easy, but no colony succeeded in suppressing dissent after Roger Williams's conflict with the Boston authorities and his subsequent successful effort in Rhode Island. While France and Spain prevented heretics (Protestants) from migrating to their colonies, the great variety of persons who migrated to the English colonies in the first century after 1609 made religious uniformity quite impractical. We may generalize and note that the New England colonies were predominantly Puritan, the Middle colonies were mixed, and the Southern colonies were largely Anglican in composition. Actually, by 1700, no one group of Christians was sufficiently strong to impose its ways on any single colony. Religious pluralism was a fact of life in the English colonies and, consequently, religious liberty in some degree was a practical necessity to the survival and prosperity of the colonies. The demand for religious liberty was voiced by the numerous dissenting sects in the colonies and was augmented by the Deists in the eighteenth century for very different reasons.[7]

Before the Revolutionary War, the larger religious bodies in the English colonies were Puritans (Congregationalists), Presbyterians, Anglicans (including Methodists who did not become separate until 1784), Baptists, German and Dutch Reformed, and Lutherans. Also to be found, though in smaller numbers, were Roman Catholics, Quakers, Mennonites, Moravians, and several communal groups such as the Shakers.

Contrary to popular opinion, the Revolutionary era was not a period of religious vitality. The Great Awakening of 1736-1750 had spent its force. Deism had been introduced from English and French thinkers and displaced Christianity in the thinking of many Americans. Students of this period of American history generally estimate that only about ten percent of the population held membership in a church. This does not mean that the culture of the time was not heavily influenced by Christian concepts, but it does indicate that the influence of the gospel through the church was quite minimal. It was further weakened by the multiplicity of divisions among this ten percent of the people. Tragically, every one of Europe's major divisions had been transplanted to the new nation. The origins of these divisions were largely European and had little significance for Christians in the New World. They would persist, proliferate, and weaken the cause of Christ for the centuries to come. In 1789, the thirteen colonies, whose geography, climate, and economic interests were quite diverse, united to form the United States of America. This new nation grew rich and powerful by developing the potential that the New World had to offer. This federal union did not destroy the individuality of the different states and regions; rather, it proved that such diversity could enhance the bounty of the whole nation. With pride, Americans would be able to say, *"E pluribus unum* (out of many, one)." It remained to be seen whether the followers of Christ in the New World would be able to do the same and whether they could find the unity that would simultaneously exalt Christ and enhance His name while respecting the integrity of individual commitment. Could Christians *e pluribus* seize the unprecedented opportunity provided by a New World to find *unum?* Or would it be *plurissimus?* Only a strong aversion to division could prevent the latter. Unfortunately, such an aversion was not to be found in a land where individual freedom was highly prized. Many Christians, though not all by any means, failed to comprehend the implications of continuous division. It seemed to matter little to most Americans of the period that Christians were wasting their resources duplicating facilities in some areas while the gospel was unheard in others, that preachers often spent more time seeking to convert other followers of Christ than they did to convert nonbelievers, that religious hostility often involved a practical denial of the very gospel in whose behalf the hostility was maintained, and that the church, which the Lord had intended should be a unifying force among men, was actually serving quite the opposite end. The sectarian approach to Christianity has become such a normal feature of American church life that the Biblical plea for the unity of Christ's church sounds radical and illusory to the average Christian of this day. The contemporary church needs to reconsider the easy peace that it has made with a condition that was abhorrent to the Lord of the church. No more incisive commentary on the evil nature of the denominational Christianity that evolved in the American religious experience can be found than that which was expressed by the late H. Richard Niebuhr.

> Denominationalism in the Christian church is . . . an unacknowledged hypocrisy. It is a compromise, made far too lightly, between Christianity and the world. Yet it often regards itself as a Christian achievement and glorifies its martyrs as bearers of the Cross. It represents the accommodation of Christianity to the caste-system of human society. It carries over into the organization of the Christian principle of brotherhood the prides and prejudices, the privilege and prestige, as well as the humiliations and abasements, the injustices and inequalities of that specious order of high and low wherein men find the satisfaction of their craving for vainglory. The division of the churches closely follows the division of men into the castes of

national, racial, and economic groups. It draws the color line in the church of God; it fosters the misunderstandings, the self-exaltations, the hatreds of jingoistic nationalism by continuing in the body of Christ the spurious differences of provincial loyalties; it seats the rich and poor apart at the table of the Lord, where the fortunate may enjoy the bounty they have provided while others feed upon the crusts their poverty affords.

Denominationalism thus represents the moral failure of Christianity. And unless the ethics of brotherhood can gain the victory over this divisiveness within the body of Christ it is useless to expect it to be victorious in the world. But before the church can hope to overcome its fatal division it must learn to recognize and to acknowledge the secular character of its denominationalism.[8]

The process of transplanting every European sect to the fertile soil of the New World, where it would both multiply and divide profusely, inevitably would challenge some brave voice to question its wisdom and its fidelity to the Lord of the church. Such a cry came in the early nineteenth century. It was not without precedent. Throughout Christian history, the concern for a united church had never entirely disappeared. In a day of easy acceptance of the divisive forces that nullify the Lord's prayer for the unity of His people and render futile the apostolic plea for such a church, it is well that a brief summary should be made of those efforts that have sought to reserve the unity of Christians or to reconstruct broken fellowship. Surely the Lord's blessing on the peacemaker applies as well to those who assuage theological and ecclesiological conflict as to those who seek to overcome civil conflict. The history of Christianity has not been entirely that of strife and schism. There have been many noble disciples of the Lord who have taken seriously His deep longing that His people should be one "that the world may believe" (John 17:21) that He is Savior. They have recognized that the greatest obstacle to fulfilling the Great Commission is not materialism, Communism, or rationalism, but a divided Christendom.

Efforts to Preserve Unity in the Early Church

The plea of the Lord of the church for the unity of His people has often been muted in the church, but it has never been completely silenced. Nobody has ever claimed that Jesus intended to build a plurality of churches. All of the teaching of the Bible on the subject of the church presupposes its unitary nature. Paul, who pioneered as a missionary to the Gentiles, insisted that there should be but one church in which there was no Jew-Gentile distinction. He went to great lengths to preserve the bonds of fellowship with the Jewish Christians while he worked at the same time to create Gentile churches. He gathered funds for the poor saints in Jerusalem (Acts 11:29; 1 Corinthians 16:1; Galatians 2:9, 10) and, at great personal risk, delivered these gifts to Jerusalem (Acts 21:7-15). Indeed, it was his determination to maintain unity with Jewish Christians that led to his imprisonment in Jerusalem (Acts 21:17-34) and his long journey to Rome to appear before Caesar. When he wrote to the churches in the vicinity of Ephesus to plead for Christian unity, he was himself a prisoner of the forces then at work to divide the church.

Unity in the early church expressed itself in a remarkably broad fellowship and a network of communication between churches. Letters were freely exchanged and the writings of the apostles were shared. Texts were reproduced so that eventually most of the major congregations possessed copies of both the canonical and non-canonical writings. Congregations demonstrated concern for and support of other congregations in times of peril or need.[9] The church was a brotherhood; it was the family of God, truly "catholic"[10] in its scope.

Preservation of the unity of the early church was no easy task—as the unfortunate schisms and excommunications recounted above illustrate. The Greco-Roman world pulsated with rival religious forces and the early church inevitably was confronted with numerous challenges. The New Testament itself reflects the anguish of the Judaistic controversy, which threatened a rift between the churches of Palestine and those of the West, and the growing Gnostic problem, which has been noted already. In the face of these fracturing forces, it was crucial to keep ever before the body of Christians the ideal of Christ for a united following and the unity of His church. Precisely how the unity of the church is manifest has been one of the vexing questions that has confronted Christians ever since the days of the apostles. Generally, Christians have held that the focus of the church's unity is found in its faith,[11] but there are various understandings of how this unity is manifested. Many early Christians saw in Paul's instructions to the elders of Ephesus (Acts 20:16-38) a very prominent role for the elders in the matter of preserving the body of Christians intact. At the beginning of the second century, the elder/bishops were actually represented as the successors of the apostles.[12] This suggestion had wide-reaching consequences by the end of the century. Confronted with a serious schism midway in the following century, Cyprian, bishop of Carthage, affirmed that the unity of the church is manifested in the unity of the bishops. He declared:

> The bishop is in the Church, and the Church is in the bishop; and if any one be not with the bishop, he is not in the Church, . . . the Church, which is orthodox and one, is not cut nor divided, but is

indeed connected and bound together by the cement of the priests who cohere with one another.[13]

Nobody in the third century was more zealous to maintain the unity of Christendom than Cyprian of Carthage. Whatever criticism may be offered with respect to Cyprian's concept of the nature of the unity of the church, one cannot fault his understanding of the need for the church to preserve its unity in the face of the worst persecution by the Roman government that the church would ever endure. Cyprian himself would be numbered among the martyrs. The focus that he gave to the unity of the church as a unity inhering in the church's episcopate would have far-reaching consequences beginning with the next century.

State-enforced Unity

It is interesting that the strongest advocate for and promoter of Christian unity in the fourth century would not be a cleric but a layman, the Emperor Constantine. Having come to the throne as victor in a long civil war, the first Christian emperor of Rome was anxious to find an ideological basis for the unification of his realm. He had witnessed the futility of persecuting Christians and, at a critical moment in his own life, had embraced the cross. It is quite possible Constantine had been so deeply impressed by the constancy of the Christians under persecution that he thus became convinced that Christianity was not only the true religion, but that it would be the faith of the future. He was willing to make whatever adjustments were necessary to make the new faith the ideological core of his empire.[14] But if the new faith were to be useful as a cohesive force in an empire that abounded with divisive factors, it was crucial that the church be united itself. Schism within the church would be a serious political liability. An ugly schism in North Africa came to the emperor's attention when he attempted to favor the church there with a generous gift. Were there two churches of the one Lord to be found in North Africa? Such a condition could not be tolerated either on theological or political grounds. If the emperor did not understand the former, he certainly knew the implications of the latter. But what to do? If the church consists of the bishops, one might assemble the whole church by bringing together all of the bishops.[15] When the assembled bishops reached a decision on any given matter, their voice was understood to be the voice of the whole church. Accordingly, Constantine summoned the bishops in the portion of the empire over which he was then sovereign to meet, at government expense, in Arles, in southern France, in 314. The Donatist problem[16] was submitted to this body for consideration and judgment with the full expectation that all parties would comply with the decision of the bishops. When the Donatists, who lost their case, refused to comply with the majority, they found themselves in defiance not only of the church but of the state as well. The ugly spectacle of Christian persecuting Christian set in a scant two years after the conversion of the first Christian emperor. Here we have the first example of a pattern that would dominate the history of the church for more than a millennium and would claim the lives of untold thousands. The unity of the church would be maintained by the power of the state and often by the force of arms. While division in the body of Christ is devastating, it is questionable whether unity by force is preferable.

When Constantine conquered the eastern half of the Empire in 324, he found the church there torn by a much more serious conflict involving the relationship of the Son to the Father. Employing the technique used with limited success at Arles, Constantine summoned all of the bishops of the Roman Empire to meet at Nicea, near his new capitol on the Bosphorus. This gathering of 318 bishops (only six were from the West) theoretically represented the entire church. When it formulated the famous Creed of Nicea of 325, its ecclesiastical prestige was reinforced by the authority of imperial edict. The orthodox faith was articulated in a fixed formula, and dissenters were banished from the empire. This was the first ecumenical council (council of the whole church), the forerunner of many later ones that created numerous creeds for the purpose of precisely defining orthodoxy. The unity of the church demanded acceptance of the creed.

The greatest theologian of the ancient church in the West, Augustine of Hippo, wrestled mightily with the problem of the church's unity. North Africa abounded with Donatist schismatics whose claims to apostolic succession were as good as those of the larger church and whose puritanical life-style was, if anything, morally superior to that of the majority party. In one of his more widely known tracts, Augustine repeated Cyprian's phrase: *Salus extra ecclesiam nulla est* (outside the church there is no salvation). By a specious argument, he so defined the church as to exclude those followers of Christ who opposed him. Here we see a technique that became widespread in succeeding centuries. The unity of the church was maintained by excluding as heretics and aliens from the household of faith all who refused to comply.[17] Not only was the catholicity of the church thereby maintained, but the door was opened for the most savage treatment of dissent. Augustine himself found Scriptural foundation for the employment of force against heretics in Luke 14:23[18] and gave approval to the savageries of the Theodosian Code against heretics. Throughout the Middle Ages, feudal society rested upon a theoretical, uniform church-state ideal. Under these conditions, the unity of the church was maintained by imprisonment, torture, and even death. Nonetheless, the number of religious dissenters was significant.

The visible unity of Western Christendom was shattered by the Protestant revolt of the sixteenth century, when state enforcement of church unity broke down in feudal Germany. A complex combination of forces made this inevitable. It is possible to discern economic, political, social, and religious motives working in different combinations and to varying degrees to produce the extensive changes in Christendom that resulted. Luther led a revolt that in earlier centuries would have been crushed. He was fortunate to enjoy the protection of a powerful prince in his defiance of an Emperor whose many responsibilities elsewhere prevented his dealing effectively with the German situation.

Generally, the reformers deplored the division of the church. Efforts were made to avert the fragmentation of the body of Christ, especially in the 1540s, but all were in vain.[19] Similarly, some efforts were made to prevent the fragmentation of the Protestant community,[20] but sociocultural and theological considerations could not be overcome. Luther's embrace of individualism at Worms in 1519 ("unless I can be proven wrong . . . I will not recant") and of nationalism (in the tract of 1520: *To the Christian Nobility of the German Nation*) destroyed the idea of a universal church and forced him to seek unity on confessional grounds. Protestants resorted to the formulation of creeds as grounds for the unity of the church. Numerous creeds were produced in the sixteenth and successive centuries, none of which could serve as unifying forces within Protestantism. In fact, creeds often became barriers to Christian unity. Protestantism rushed headlong and unchecked into endless and confusing schism. Numerous voices, among them Hugo Grotius and Ruppert Meldenius of the Netherlands, and English churchmen such as Richard Baxter, Edward Stillingfleet, and Bishop Usher, were raised against the schismatic tendencies. Successive decades demonstrated that the cohesive forces in Protestantism could not withstand the intense pressure to divide.

Pleas for Unity in the New World

The opening of the New World to European colonization raised a serious question for the churches. Would the settlement of America witness the transplanting of every European sect to the New World, or would Christians avail themselves of the opportunity to make a fresh start and strive to bring into being a church that could appeal to all believers because it was truly Biblical, hence truly catholic and reformed? It is amazing how many immigrants to the New World hoped that the latter could happen. The chapters that follow relate the story of one significant effort to achieve this end. However, it would be an injustice were no mention made of some of the other voices in the New World that were raised in behalf of greater unity among Christ's followers.

The foremost evangelist of the Great Awakening in the days prior to the Revolutionary War was George Whitefield. He often spoke to his audiences in terms that deplored sectarianism. Once, when preaching from the balcony of the old courthouse in Philadelphia, Whitefield exclaimed:

> Father Abraham, who have you in heaven? Any Episcopalians? "No." Any Presbyterians? "No." Any Baptists? "No." Any Methodists, Seceders, or Independents? "No, no!" Why, who have you there? "We don't know those names here. All who are here are Christians." Oh, is that the case? Then, God help me! And God help us all to forget party names, and to become Christians in deed and truth.[21]

The tireless and self-sacrificing Count Ludwig von Zinzendorf, founder of the Moravian body, came to America and sought to fuse all of the German immigrants into one fellowship. These limited efforts to achieve a greater degree of unity within one ethnic group were frustrated by those Lutherans whose devotion to the Augsburg Confession caused them to question the Count's orthodoxy. Similar efforts within other ethnic communities to cope with the tendency toward fragmentation were likewise unsuccessful.

Quite apart from these efforts for greater Christian cohesion, which may be understood to have arisen out of evangelical concern, was an impulse for Christian unity that recommended itself to English and American churchmen on what might be seen as more of a rational than an evangelical basis. John Locke's little book, *The Reasonableness of Christianity*, presented such a platform. He deplored the pointless and often obscure speculations that could be found in the numerous creeds, and insisted that simple confession of the Messiahship of Jesus coupled with repentance for sins was all that the early church required for salvation.[22] The accretions of Christian history were set aside by Locke as superfluous. Christianity was portrayed as a simple matter of belief of facts set forth in the Scripture and compliance with concepts that are also found in the Biblical record. This understanding of the nature of Christianity, simple, reasonable, and ethical, would appeal to the rationalistic tendencies of the eighteenth century and find a warm reception in that wing of the Anglican Church that had been influenced by Deism. Nor was such an understanding of the nature of the Christian religion without spokesmen in America. James Madison, D.D., the president of William and Mary College, addressed the convention of the Protestant Episcopal Church of Virginia in 1786, pleading,

> Would to God, those dissensions which too much abound amongst Christians, could at this moment be banished from amongst us! Would to God, instead of those variances that often arise from subjects with which obedience to the doctrine of Christ is by no means connected, that, union and church fellowship could everywhere be established. . . .
> Abandon those idle controversies, those "dotings about questions and strifes of words," those "perverse disputings" which have too long occupied the minds of Christians, and which serve only to excite "envy, strife, railings, evil surmisings," shameful to the professors of a religion whose basis is universal charity.[23]

Turning to the creedal bases of fellowship, which were almost universally considered to be the essential component of Christian unity, Madison declared,

> I will then venture earnestly to recommend to all Christians to reject every system, as the fallible production of human contrivance, which shall dictate articles of faith, and adopt the Gospel alone as their guide. Am I not sufficiently warranted, my brethren, in this recommendation? I trust there is scarce any one amongst us who will object to a recommendation of this nature, whether we attend to the fallibility, the ignorance, the prejudice of men, or to the truth, wisdom, and perfection of the Author of our divine religion.
> I will take the liberty to advance a general proposition, the evidence of which, I persuade myself, may be established by the most incontestable proofs. The Proposition is indeed simple and plain; it is, "That those Christian societies will ever be found to have formed their union upon principles the wisest and the best, which impose the fewest restraints upon the minds of their members, making the Scriptures alone, and not human articles or confessions of belief, the sole rule of faith and conduct."
> It is a maxim, self-evident to every one, and which was held sacred by the fathers of Protestantism, "That the Scriptures contain all things necessary to salvation, and are the sole ground of the faith of a Christian." This maxim, the basis of the reformation, and which is acceded to by all Protestants, is alone sufficient, independent of what experience hath taught, to induce every Protestant church, to reject all systems of belief, unless conceived in the terms of Scripture, not only as unwarrantable, and in the highest degree oppressive to the rights of private judgment, but as presumptuous, and as casting an unworthy reflection on the Scriptures themselves.[24]

He then focused on what he considered to be the basic core of the Christian religion by declaring, "Those things alone should be held as *essentials,* which our Lord and Master, hath fully and clearly expressed, and which therefore cannot require the supposed improvements and additions of men."[25]

He concluded this unusual address by suggesting:

> To promote the great event before mentioned, it is also the particular duty of a Christian church to frame their mode of public worship upon a plan so liberal, so free from all matter of theological disputation, so truly scriptural, that all who call themselves Christians may come to the same communion, and there join in what the "spirit of prayer inspires," in that adoration pure which God likes best.[26]

These views, expressed thirty years before Thomas Campbell came to America, were thoroughly consistent with Enlightenment thinking. Persons of this mentality could find neither pride nor comfort in a divided Christendom. It remained only for a dynamic movement to appear among a people whose ties to traditional sectarian bodies were minimized by a new environment to issue a clear call for reform along these lines to evoke a ready response. Such a call came in the *Declaration and Address.* The movement came to be known as the Reformation of the Nineteenth Century.

The Plea for Restoration—
Promise and Problems

The need to recapture the beauty, simplicity, and effectiveness of the dynamic church reflected in the New Testament is a conviction shared to some extent by all generations of Christians. It is sometimes expressed as "reformation" and more recently as "renewal." Often, however, this need is described with more explicit focus on the church of the first century as "restoration."[27] The concept of restoring some vital reality that has been lost or obscured is very old. It characterized several medieval movements whose understanding of the pure church would be strange to our thinking. It was a prominent idea among the Anabaptists. Michael Servetus, whom Calvin's Geneva burned at the stake for denying the doctrine of Trinity, wrote a book titled *Restitution of Christianity.* William Penn was the author of a small book, *Primitive Christianity Revived.* The Scottish reformer James A. Haldane published a volume, the title of which, in part, was: *A View of the Social Worship and Ordinances Observed by the First Christians, Drawn from the Scriptures Alone.* Numerous other examples of attempts to restore in some way the Christianity reflected in the New Testament could be cited. In the history of Christianity, there have been few so bold as to publicly advocate dispensing with the Biblical base for their beliefs and practices. The great majority of followers of Christ have sought to justify their views by reference to the Scriptures.

However, the serious challenge to the ideal of restoration is encountered at the point of defining exactly what is to be restored. A brief glance at the many books and pamphlets appealing for some type of restoration discloses the fact that there is a bewildering variety of understanding of precisely what should be restored. Some have focused their concern for restoration on the church as an institution. Others have emphasized doctrines and sacraments while some others, more influenced by Pietism, see the need for individual holiness as the focus of restoration.[28] Precisely which of these concerns should be the focus of efforts for restoration and how they relate to contemporary culture and society is a subject for almost endless discussion. Quite obviously, the Christianity of the New Testament was related to the life and culture of the first century. It would be neither possible nor desirable to restore all of this. But how does one extricate "Christianity" from the first-century cultural setting in which it is found? The distinction between essential Christianity and its cultural expression is not easily discerned or universally accepted. The New Testament does not define or otherwise specify "essential" Christianity. What it presents is a dynamic faith functioning effectively in a sociocultural situation somewhat different from that which presently prevails in the modern western world. However, the task of identifying the timeless, enduring realities of the Christian faith within its setting in the time period of the first century cannot be avoided or neglected. The great variety of insights and viewpoints about the nature and goals of restoration should not lead to the conclusion that the ideal is impossible of achievement. Rather, the plethora of insights only indicates that the goal of restoration is greater and more complex than what might first have been presumed. A.T. DeGroot sensed this when he wrote, "The restoration of primitive Christianity is an operation so grand in scope and so demanding in patient seeking of precious truth that Disciples of Christ may be proud even to be among the noble company of those who have engaged in this task."[29]

The Restoration Movement, whose history is presented in this volume, could be viewed as simply another in the long series of restoration efforts in the history of the church. To do so would be to miss its uniqueness and do it a grave injustice. Generally, movements of this type have viewed restoration as a desired end in itself. The movement under study has rather viewed the restoration of New Testament Christianity as an effective means for the achievement of another end, namely the unity of the fractured body of followers of Christ. Thus, while other restoration efforts sought primarily to be "right" in God's sight, regardless of how many others were "wrong," the movement under study did not come into being with such disregard for the rest of the "erring" followers of Christ. Rather, it sought to be Biblically faithful because it held that such Biblical fidelity is the only viable basis on which to appeal to other followers of Christ to achieve the unity for which the Lord of all Christians earnestly prayed. It has often been alleged that the concept of restoration is inevitably sectarian.[30] The restoration effort under study is unique in that it sought earnestly for a genuine catholicity.[31] It made a serious appeal for unity on the basis of the effort to restore New Testament Christianity. Thus it sought to unite two very different and often antagonistic objectives. The account that unfolds will provide illustrations of the difficulty of this task and will reflect the relative success which this movement has achieved in realizing its aim.

End Notes

[1]Several references can be cited. See especially 1 Corinthians 4, 5, 10—12.

[2]The literature on Gnosticism is extensive, and recent findings have led to new evaluations of the nature of Gnosticism. The earlier viewpoint is well expressed by Philip Schaff, *History of the Christian Church* (Grand Rapids: Eerdmans, 1959), Vol. II, pp. 444ff. More recent understanding is found in Robert Grant's *Gnosticism and Early Christianity* (New York: Harper & Row, 1966), and Hans Jonas, *Gnostic Religion* (Boston: Beacon Press, 1963).

[3]W.W. Walker, *A History of the Christian Church* (New York: Scribner's Sons, 1959), p. 60.

[4]Eusebius, *Ecclesiastical History,* V:16:7.

[5]For a good brief discussion, see F.J. Foakes-Jackson, *History of the Christian Church to 461 A.D.* (Cambridge: Deighton, Bell, & Co., 1947), pp. 290-292. For a fuller treatment, see the anti-Donatist works of Augustine.

[6]See Augustine, *De Trinitate.* For a good brief summary, see Walker, op. cit., pp. 67-71.

[7]For an excellent discussion of this subject, see Sidney Meade, *The Lively Experiment* (New York: Harper & Row, 1963).

[8]H. Richard Niebuhr, *The Social Source of Denominationalism* (New York: Meridian, 1957), pp. 6, 25. Niebuhr traces the causes of division among Christians to sources quite different from those understood in the religious body that is the subject of this study. The significance of Niebuhr's insights is increasingly being recognized.

[9]For a good discussion, see A. Harnack, *The Mission and Expansion of Christianity,* Vol. I, p. 180ff.

[10]The term means "universal" and was first employed early in the second century by Ignatius of Antioch to refer to the totality of the one body of Christ. *Ad Smyrna,* VIII: "Wherever Jesus Christ is, there is the Catholic Church." A.C. Coxe, translator, *The Ante Nicene Fathers* (Grand Rapids: Eerdmans, 1950).

[11]Paul urges the Christians in Ephesus to "keep the unity of the Spirit through the bond of peace" (Ephesians 4:3).

[12]See especially the epistles of Ignatius of Antioch.

[13]Cyprian, *Epistle LXVIII:8*. E.W. Wallis, translator, *Ante Nicene Fathers,* Vol. V (Grand Rapids:Eerdmans, 1951), pp. 374, 375.

[14]It must be remembered that the emperors had previously been worshiped as "gods." Thenceforth, such would not be possible. This was a serious blow to imperial prestige, which required a new definition if the emperor were to enjoy religious sanction for his person. This he found in an interpretation derived from Romans 13:1-7.

[15]This was the contention of Cyprian of Carthage (see above) and was widely accepted. It is the presupposition that underlies the authority of the ecumenical councils.

[16]See above, end note 5. The schismatic body was called Donatist after their leader and second bishop, Donatus.

[17]Augustine, 61:2.

[18]His exegesis of Jesus' phrase "Compel them to come in" in the parable of the banquet was taken to mean that Jesus approved the use of force. While such an interpretation is not acceptable today, its unquestioned acceptance for many centuries provided justification for imprisonment, torture, and execution of thousands of "heretics." It was the theoretical basis for the Inquisition (Augustine, *De Corrections Donatissarum,* 24).

[19]A series of conferences (Hagenau and Worms, 1540; Regensburg, 1541) were held, largely at the behest of Emperor Charles V. They reached an impasse over the question of authority.

[20]See Ruth Rouse and Stephen C. Neill, *A History of the Ecumenical Movement* (London: S.P.C.K., 1954), pp. 42-60, for a good summary.

[21]Edward S. Ninde, *George Whitefield, Prophet—Preacher* (New York: Abingdon Press, 1924), p. 188.

[22]John Locke, *The Reasonableness of Christianity* (Chicago: Henry Regnery Co.). See especially pp. 163-170.

[23]James Madison, *Sermon* (Richmond: Thomas Nicolson, 1786), p. 7. Compare this platform with the Chicago Lambeth Quadrilateral of 1888 (cf. Rouse & Neill, op. cit., p. 265).

24Ibid., p. 8.

25Ibid., p. 11.

26Ibid., p. 15.

27Some have insisted upon a distinction between "reformation" and "restoration" (cf. Alexander Campbell, "A Restoration of the Ancient Order of Things," a series of thirty-two essays in the *Christian Baptist* beginning February 7, 1825). Others have insisted that the distinction cannot be sustained. The terms are often used by leaders of the movement interchangeably.

28Alfred T. DeGroot discusses this problem in *The Restoration Principle* (St. Louis: Bethany Press, 1960). He holds that restoration is valid only when "defined in essentially spiritual terms" (p. 8), which he undertakes to do in chapter 8, "What Should be Restored?" (p. 165). However, his answers have much more bearing on attitudes and spirit than Biblical substance, leaving many searchers for meaningful Christian faith somewhat adrift.

29Ibid., p. 183.

30See, for example, ibid. More recently, this view has been advanced by LeRoy Garrett, op. cit., p.11.

31For a good discussion, see Fred Norris, "Apostolic, Catholic, and Sensible: the Consensus Fidelium," *Essays on New Testament Christianity*, C. Robert Wetzel, ed., (Cincinnati: Standard, 1978), p. 15.

in exploiting the possibilities of the New World, commercial and otherwise. Increasing secularism caused the Synod of Boston to note in 1669, "That God hath a Controversy with His New England People is undeniable, the Lord having written His displeasure in dismal Character against us."[4] It cataloged a list of thirteen areas of notable spiritual decline and recommended a re-emphasis on the covenant and a tightening of discipline. However, a full generation was to pass before a notable reversal of religious lethargy can be discerned.

The reversal was dramatic and became what is known today as the Great Awakening. This was not an event but more of a series of revivals—a movement lasting for a number of years, if not decades, proceeding generally from New York and New England southward and profoundly altering the pattern of church life and theology in America. Most historians date the beginning of the Great Awakening with the activities of Theodore Frelinghuysen, a Dutch Reformed pastor with pietistic backgrounds, who arrived in New York in 1720 and began to emphasize the devotional life and a zealous type of lay participation in church activity. The dynamic thus generated spread slowly to affect other congregations. An Irish immigrant pastor, William Tenet, was touched by the new zeal and began training his own sons and several other young men in a "Log College" in Neshaminy, Pennsylvania, for this type of ministry.

Meanwhile, remarkable spiritual activity was developing in New England under the preaching of Jonathan Edwards.[5] The intellectual Edwards read his carefully reasoned sermons from prepared manuscripts with telling effect. Sinners trembled at the prospect of judgment. Hundreds were added to the church, and the moral climate of Northampton, Massachusetts, was visibly changed.

The incipient revival was greatly reinforced and extended by the arrival of George Whitefield, an associate of John Wesley. Whitefield, who arrived in America in 1740, had initiated a remarkable awakening in England by his dynamic preaching. A tireless worker who often preached five or six times daily, Whitefield itinerated relentlessly until he literally spent himself preaching the gospel. Thousands were added to the churches before the Awakening exhausted itself in New England and moved into the Middle and Southern colonies, where it continued for several more decades under second-generation leadership.[6]

It was inevitable that the kind of religious expression often seen in the Great Awakening would produce a severe reaction. Nothing quite like it had ever been witnessed in Christian history. Emotional excess was particularly conspicuous in the work of one of the prominent revivalists, James Davenport, but it was not absent from most of the revival efforts. The revival proved to be divisive in its effect upon the church. Two basic kinds of opposition surfaced. There were the old-school Calvinists whose understanding of the doctrine of election was outraged at what appeared to them to be an outright appeal to free human response to the gospel. They opposed any evangelistic effort *per se* and were often dubbed "Old Lights" as opposed to the "New Light" revivalists who were willing to adjust their Calvinism to the needs of the hour. Apart from these ministers was another school of thought that opposed the seeming triumph of the emotional factor over the rational. Governed by a primarily intellectual understanding of the nature of Christianity, these men, led by Charles Chauncey of Boston's prestigious First Church, denounced the revival and moved steadily in the direction of Unitarianism. In the post-revival period of reaction and controversy, European Enlightenment thought and its religious counterpart, Deism, was firmly planted in America.

A Period of Religious Decline

It is generally recognized that the years immediately before and after the American Revolution were the poorest of any period in American history for the church. Reliable statistics of church membership for this period are lacking, but the best estimates are that less than ten percent of the population were members of any church.[7] In addition to controversies arising out of the Great Awakening and the reaction to it, the advances of Deism were creating major problems for the church.

Deism was the rational religion of the eighteenth century. It is not to be confused with atheism. Its god was the Creator-god, author of the laws of nature, but not necessarily the God of the Bible. Deists were by no means consistent in their attitude toward Christianity. Some, like George Washington, made easy reconciliation of Deistic and Christian concepts. Others, like Benjamin Franklin and Thomas Jefferson, had little time for the church themselves, but they considered it to be socially useful. A few, like Thomas Paine, were hostile to Christianity. The period of the Revolutionary War was the heyday of Deism in America.[8]

The cause of Christianity was greatly harmed by the Revolution also. War, with its killing, its plunder, and its appeal to the baser human instincts, never advances the aims of Christ. Furthermore, the war left the churches in a state of confusion and disarray. Several had looked to the mother country for leadership and guidance and were "orphaned" by the severance of the ties with Europe.

Gradually, the churches determined that they would need to form some kind of national organizations within the new nation. This was done by the Methodists at the celebrated "Christmas Conference" in Baltimore in 1784, with the blessing of the aged John Wesley. The

Anglicans who, as might be expected, suffered most severely during the war because of divided loyalties, met in a General Convention in 1785 in Philadelphia to constitute the Protestant Episcopal Church. Presbyterians organized a General Assembly in 1789. The following year saw the pope name John Carroll to be the first Roman Catholic bishop in the United States. The last decade of the eighteenth century was not a period of conspicuous growth, but it was a period of religious organization in the new nation.

Bringing the scattered colonial congregations together into denominational organizations on a national scale was not done easily. Severe tensions surfaced, especially among the Episcopalians, Lutherans, and Methodists. Schism resulted among the Methodists. Francis Asbury, whom John Wesley sent to America to establish the Methodist Church in the new nation, quickly assumed episcopal authority, much to the dismay of a group of rugged frontiersmen in Virginia and North Carolina. Objecting to concentration of authority in the bishop, which included the exclusive right of assignment of ministers to their charges, they sought to create an appeal process. When this failed, they withdrew under the leadership of James O'Kelly. In 1792, at Lebanon Church in Surrey County, Virginia, the dissenters organized the Republican Methodist Church. Two years later, at the suggestion of Rice Haggard, they voted to adopt the name "Christian." At the same time, they voted to take the Bible as their only creed.[9] Despite these alterations, however, the group remained essentially Methodist in faith and practice.

Meanwhile, the nation was on the move. War clouds were forming in Europe because of the French Revolution, and immigrants were flocking to the New World. An abundance of good, cheap land was available between the Appalachian Mountains and the Mississippi River. As the war in Europe intensified, trade with Europe slackened and a depression struck the seaboard states. This set in motion a veritable flood of settlers seeking to find new homes and opportunities on the western frontier. The Mohawk Valley was the northern gateway to the West (Ohio). Others came to Pittsburgh and floated down the Ohio River with their families and all of their belongings, settling eventually in or near one of the many Ohio, Kentucky, Indiana, or Illinois landings that soon grew to be busy towns. Still others came in wagons down the Shenandoah Valley of Virginia or across the mountains of North Carolina to find the trail that Daniel Boone had blazed through the Cumberland Gap into the rich bluegrass region of Kentucky. This westward stream of people was to continue with but a few interruptions for a century.[10] A hearty people were carving a new nation out of the wilderness. The land available for settlement was more than doubled in 1803 when Napoleon, needing money for his wars against Great Britain, sold the Louisiana Territory to the United States for $15,000,000.

Much has been written about the nature and character of the frontiersman. To survive on the frontier required a special kind of person. Lacking the conveniences and readily available supplies
afforded by the East, the frontiersman quickly learned to make do
with what was available. He learned to be resourceful, inventive,
creative, self-reliant, persistent, and courageous. Social amenities
were generally absent. He was often blunt and forthright, even
crude. He cared little for distinctions of birth or family lineage, but
had immense respect for practical performance. He was generally
uninhibited, self-sufficient, accustomed to hard work, and at home
with danger and suffering. A culture was evolving on the frontier
that would be the dominating influence in the development of the
new nation.[11]

Religiously, the frontier left much to be desired. The hardy pioneer
was not known for his piety. There was little in the way of law and
order. The clearing of land and building of houses was the most pressing need. There was little time for building churches. Two other factors impeded the religious development of the frontier. One of these
was the absence of roads necessary for the gathering of Christians.
Most roads were little more than tracks that were impassible in bad
weather. Bridges were few, and a swollen stream could prevent travel altogether. Except in towns, church participation on the frontier
was limited to a few months of the year. Another factor in the religious poverty of the frontier was the lack of effective plans or
resources to evangelize the new territory. Denominations were just
beginning to form organizations and were not yet ready to send significant numbers of competent ministers or evangelists to the frontier. As a result, religious life on the frontier languished. The frontier
was ripe for revival when the nineteenth century opened. The
revival began in 1801 and reached its zenith in August of that year
in a place called Cane Ridge, in Bourbon County, Kentucky, where
Barton W. Stone was the minister of a rural Presbyterian church.

Stone and the Frontier Awakening

Barton W. Stone was born on Christmas Eve in 1772 in Port
Tobacco, Maryland. Shortly thereafter, his father died, leaving his
mother to rear a large family. Together with a number of servants,
the family moved to Pittsylvania County in the Virginia backwoods.
Young Barton witnessed the outbreak of the War of Revolution and
his older brother's departure for service in the Revolutionary Army.
He also heard the roar of cannon in the battle between General
Green and Lord Cornwallis some thirty miles distant.[12] His early
schooling was taken under "a very tyrant of a teacher who seemed to

take pleasure in whipping and abusing his pupils."[13] Nonetheless, Stone was an eager student and subsequently enrolled in David Caldwell's Academy in Guilford, North Carolina (near Greensboro). There he determined "to acquire an education or die in the attempt."[14] Caldwell's school proved to be an excellent choice, offering the finest opportunity for learning to be found in the area. Stone's intention was to prepare for the reading of the law.

The religious affiliation of the Stone family was with the Church of England. When national independence was gained, many of the clergy returned to England, and the vicinity where the Stone family dwelt was invaded by Baptist and Methodist preachers. Religious conflict was soon generated, much to Stone's confusion and dismay. His entry into David Caldwell's Academy brought him into contact with yet another denominational emphasis, the Presbyterian Church and Calvinism. Caldwell had studied at Princeton and was no stranger to revival efforts linked to the earlier Great Awakening. The academy was alive with religious activity, so much so that, at one point, Stone seriously considered removal to another school "for no other reason than that I might get away from the constant sight of religion."[15] The course of his thinking was changed by

Barton Warren Stone (1771-1844) pastor of the Cane Ridge Church (1796-1812), leader in the great revival in 1801, and editor of the *Christian Messenger* (1826-1837, 1839-1844).

the hell-fire and brimstone preaching of James McGready, a Presbyterian revivalist who was to have great influence on Stone a decade or so later. McGready's fiery preaching convinced Stone that he was lost. He described the anguish of his soul himself:

> I resolved from that hour to seek religion at the sacrifice of every earthly good, and immediately prostrated myself before God in supplication for mercy.
>
> According to the preaching, and the experience of the pious in those days, I anticipated a long and painful struggle before I should be prepared to come to Christ or, in the language then used, before I should get religion. This anticipation was completely realized by me. For one year I was tossed on the waves of uncertainty—laboring, praying, and striving to obtain saving faith—sometimes desponding, and almost despairing of ever getting it.

The doctrines then publicly taught were, that mankind were so totally depraved that they could not believe, repent, nor obey the gospel—that regeneration was an immediate work of the Spirit, whereby faith and repentance were wrought in the heart. These things were portrayed in vivid colors, with all earnestness and solemnity . . . but it was God's own sovereign time, and for that time the sinner must wait.[16]

Agony led to despondency and apathy as Stone waited in vain for a religious experience. The turning point came in 1791, when William Hodge's preaching on the love of God awakened Stone's religious sensitivities to the possibility that God would not turn away those who earnestly seek Him. The agony was past, the future was unclouded, and Stone completed his studies at the academy with nothing more than the typical financial worries to trouble him. Upon completion of his studies, Stone confided to Dr. Caldwell his desire to preach, but confessed that he had no assurance of a divine call. His kindly mentor relieved his apprehensions by advising him that a desire to glorify God and save sinners by preaching should not be suppressed, and he encouraged him to submit a discourse on a given text to the next meeting of the Presbytery. In 1793, he was a candidate for ministry with the Orange, North Carolina, Presbytery and was assigned a course of study in divinity in preparation for licensing. Previously, Stone's attention had been focused on the Bible alone, and he confessed that his "mind had remained happily ignorant of and undisturbed by polemic and obscure divinity."[17] The doctrine of the Trinity was particularly incomprehensible. Fortunately for him, his examiner before the presbytery was Henry Patillo, who sensed and probably shared Stone's problem with the doctrine of Trinity and skillfully guided the examination of the candidate so as to avoid a controversy over the subject. Stone was licensed to preach.

While awaiting the granting of his license to preach, Stone had visited his mother in Georgia. Following an illness that lasted several months, he was chosen to be professor of languages at nearby Succoth Academy, a Methodist institution operated by Hope Hull. John Springer, a nearby Presbyterian minister who befriended the young teacher, managed to keep alive Stone's desire to preach. During his single session at the academy, Stone proved to be an effective teacher, was able to repay his debts, and received his license to preach. With a fellow licentiate, he was commissioned to ride and preach in lower North Carolina, a district where there was serious religious decline. The experience was devastating for Stone's companion, who concluded that he was not suited for the work of ministry and abandoned the effort. Stone was similarly affected but resolved to try his effectiveness in Florida. The first Sunday en route to Florida brought him to a chance encounter with a pious old lady who convinced him that he was simply playing the part of a Jonah running away from his duty and that he ought to head over the mountains westward to the frontier of Tennessee. Stone crossed the mountains into Virginia and journeyed down the Shenandoah Valley into Tennessee. Leaving Knoxville in the company of two men, Stone had a brush with the Indians who were still numerous in the forests and was abandoned by his companions on the trail when his horse lost a shoe and could not keep pace. Arriving at a settlement near Gallatin, Tennessee, he happily met two fellow students and resolved to travel on with one of them, John Anderson. They traveled through the Cumberland area about Nashville, "which at that time was a poor little village hardly worth notice."[18] Gradually, they made their way northward into Kentucky. By the end of 1796, Anderson decided to winter near Lexington, and Stone was invited to stop with two small frontier congregations, Cane Ridge and Concord, in nearby Bourbon County. Concluding that a settled ministry was more productive than an itinerant one, Stone accepted the invitation of the two churches to be their settled and permanent pastor, though he had not yet been ordained. The next year, he was persuaded by the Transylvania Presbytery to travel to Charleston, South Carolina, to seek funds for a college for Kentucky.[19] Aside from a harrowing escape from Indians, the most memorable event of the journey was a confrontation with "slavery in more horrid forms than I had ever seen it before."[20] Stone determined henceforth to oppose this cruelty.

An important event in Stone's life occurred in 1798 when the time of ordination approached. Realizing that the examination would center in the Westminster Confession of Faith, Stone undertook to study the document. He was greatly troubled at what he read. He had not resolved his problem with the doctrine of Trinity, and he found further difficulty accepting the doctrines of election, reprobation, and predestination found in the confession. Stone confided in Dr. James Blythe and Robert Marshall (who would later be an associate) that he held out very little hope of passing the examination. They encouraged Stone to face the examiners. Stone, himself, describes the event:

> I went to the Presbytery, and when the question was proposed, "Do you receive and adopt the Confession of Faith, as containing the system of doctrine taught in the Bible?" I answered aloud, so that the whole congregation might hear, "I do, as far as I see it consistent with the Word of God." No objection being made, I was ordained.[21]

Frontier Presbyterians were notoriously lax by Eastern standards. Elsewhere, such a reply would surely have been probed to ascertain whether the qualification sheltered some doctrinal aberration, as indeed it did relative to the doctrines of Calvinism. The difficulties did not take long to surface. The implications of the doctrines of total depravity and election weighed heavily on the young minister, whose "mind was continually tossed in the wave of speculative divinity."[22] He ultimately abandoned Calvinism outright. His experience was by no means unusual on the frontier; the hardy, self-reliant pioneer found it difficult to believe that he was helpless to do anything that would affect the nature of his eternal destiny.

Aside from theological problems, Stone's mind was troubled by the state of religion on the frontier. Apathy was widespread, and the influence of Christianity was on the decline. The young pastor was searching for a way to revitalize frontier religion when he learned of a remarkable awakening on the Kentucky-Tennessee border and resolved to investigate it. A journey through the wilderness brought him to Logan County, Kentucky, where he found a large gathering of people encamped on a prairie and giving eager attention to the powerful evangelical preaching of James McGready and the McGee brothers. The vigorous preaching produced spectacular results. Stone had never before seen its like. When convicted of sin, strong men fainted and lay motionless for hours. Recovering, they would rise to speak eloquently of their joy and gratitude for salvation. Stone examined the proceedings critically before concluding it was the work of God. He returned to Cane Ridge impressed, perplexed, and encouraged. Evidently, he preached with renewed vigor the following Sunday because, to everyone's surprise, the same happenings occurred at Concord. A revival of five days ensued as word spread rapidly through the countryside. An eyewitness describes the event:

> I proceeded next morning to Concord, ten miles distant, where a sermon was preached, at which several became affected and struck down. The exercises continued all night. This was the first occasion that shewed the necessity of performing out of doors. The number being so great, the Lord's Supper was administered at a tent. A great solemnity appeared all day. A number were struck down; on the whole occasion about 150. The exercises continued from Saturday till Wednesday, day and night, without intermission. The appearance itself was awful and solemn. It was performed in a thick grove of beachen timber; candles were furnished by the congregation. The night still and calm. Add to that, exhortations, praying, singing, the cries of the distressed, on account of sin; the rejoicing of those that were delivered from their sin's bondage, and brought to enjoy the liberty that is in Christ Jesus; all going on at the same time. About 4000 persons attended, 250 communicated; twelve waggons [sic] had brought some of the people with their provisions, and from distant places. This was the first occasion that shewed the necessity of encamping on the ground; the neighbourhood not being able to furnish strangers with accommodation; nor had they a wish to separate.[23]

Stone interrupted his preaching briefly in midsummer of 1801 to marry Elizabeth Campbell, daughter of Col. William and Tabitha Campbell, on July 2. The newly married couple made a brief trip to Muhlenburg County, then hastened back to Cane Ridge where a great gathering was planned. This was but one of several such outdoor meetings in the area, but it would be the largest and most influential. A contemporary, Col. Robert S. Patterson, writes:

> On the first Sabbath of August, was the sacrament of Kainridge, [sic] the congregation of Mr. Stone. This was the largest meeting of any that I have seen; it continued from Friday till Wednesday. About 12,000 persons; 125 wagons; 8 carriages; 900 communicants; 300 were struck.[24]

Estimates of the number of persons attending vary considerably. No accurate count was made. People came and went so that the total number was not present at any one time. The sight must have been wondrous to behold. By day, a dozen preachers used stumps for pulpits and proclaimed their message to hearers who found a comfortable hearing in the shade in the woods. One could sample the preaching and move from one spot to another until an appealing sermon could be found. Word of the strange happenings spread rapidly and kindled excited discussion. Little mention is made of the group's singing, but it must have been impressive. There were numerous horses, cows to provide fresh milk, and live chickens to provide eggs. At night, hundreds of camp fires lighted the area as families cooked their meals in the open and then bedded down under the stars. The frontier provided little in the way of social outlet to the scattered

The old Cane Ridge Meeting House in Bourbon County, Kentucky, constructed in 1791 of massive blue ash logs. It served a congregation until 1922. Still erect, it is probably the largest single-room log building in the nation.

families, and it is only reasonable to assume that this gathering afforded opportunity for the settlers to swap stories, share information on cures for illness of both humans and livestock, exchange pointers on planting and harvesting, and discuss a dozen other matters of interest. But the main interest was religion, and two items in particular are to be noted about this gathering that would have important consequences: the matter of the "unusual manifestations" and the great sense of unity arising from the absence of any denominational emphasis.

The unusual manifestations were convincing to many, baffling to others, and offensive to yet others. The controversy they engendered would be long and caustic. Barton W. Stone seems not to have promoted such manifestations, nor did he condemn them. He did categorize them, as follows:

(1) The falling exercises, common to believers and unbelievers alike, wherein the victim would give a loud shriek and then fall to the floor, remaining unconscious for an undetermined time.
(2) The jerks, usually the violent backward and forward movement of the head, although sometime the entire body convulsed.
(3) The dancing exercise, usually preceded by the jerks. This came to believers and occupied them until they collapsed from exhaustion.
(4) The barking exercise. This was a variety of the jerks where the person grunted or gasped audibly in the process. It was so named by a contemptuous person who observed a man so convulsed leaning on a tree. He described him as "barking up a tree," the apparent origin of that expression.
(5) The running exercise was peculiar to unbelievers who, feeling something unusual seizing them, attempted to run away, but were felled.
(6) The singing exercise. This was the most impressive of all to Stone. His description follows:

> The subject, in a very happy state of mind, would sing most melodiously, not from the mouth or nose, but entirely in the breast, the sounds issuing thence. Such music silenced everything and attracted the attention of all. It was most heavenly.[25]

It would be a mistake to see the Cane Ridge meeting only in terms of the unusual manifestations. The fact is that many people were led to embrace the Christian faith, and the effects were seen in many communities. Not only was interest in church life quickened, but community life was improved and lawlessness and immorality declined. There is no doubt that the series of revivals is subject to serious criticism, but this should not obscure the positive results, which were considerable.

Perhaps the most significant impact made by the revival was one that was neither planned nor anticipated. In the enthusiasm of preaching, singing, and fellowship, there was little sectarian consciousness. Only a very small portion of the frontiersmen were theologically sophisticated enough to be able to discern doctrinal or creedal distinctions in the preaching at Cane Ridge. These were further obscured by the excitement caused by the exercises. The auditors were eager to hear the Bible and, in this context, sectarian distinctions were matters of little import. The indelible impression of the singleness of purpose and intent of the vast gathering at Cane Ridge would linger long in the minds of many present and express itself in Stone's passion for unity, which he frequently described as his "polar star."[26]

The Reaction

Revival efforts such as the frontier awakening were generally divisive, and the events of 1801 proved not to be an exception. Criticism, which was quick to surface, can be categorized into three general types.

First, there were those who were offended at the various manifestations and the uncontrolled emotion. Such religious exercises destroyed a rational understanding of the gospel. In contrast to the enthusiasm of the revivalists, Stone could speak disparagingly of the "iceberg style"[27] of the opponents, who seemed only to lecture on theology.

Second, the informal and unstructured nature of the camp meeting encouraged preaching by unordained laymen. This was not a problem for Methodists and Baptists, whose church polity allowed such activity; but it met with opposition from Presbyterians because it violated their concepts of ministry.

The most serious objections, however, centered in the theological position the revival preaching reflected, which violated the doctrines of the Westminster Confession of Faith. The preaching of the revival effectively rejected the doctrines of election and depravity. Stone summarized the theological perspective of the preaching at the Cane Ridge Meeting as follows:

> The distinguishing doctrine preached by us was, that God loved the world—the whole world, and sent his Son to save them, on condition that they believed in him—that the gospel was the means of salvation—but that this means would never be effectual to this end, until believed and obeyed by us—that God required us to believe in his Son, and had given us sufficient evidence in his Word to produce

faith in us, if attended to by us—that sinners were capable of under-standing and believing this testimony, and of acting upon it by com-ing to the Saviour and obeying him, and from him obtaining salvation and the Holy Spirit. We urged upon the sinner to believe *now*, and receive salvation—that in vain they looked for the Spirit to be given them, while they remained in unbelief—they must believe before the Spirit or salvation would be given them—that God was as willing to save them *now*, as he ever was, or ever would be—that no previous qualification was required, or necessary in order to believe in Jesus, and come to him—that if they were sinners, this was their divine warrant to believe in him, and to come to him for salvation—that Jesus died for all, and that all things were now ready. When we began first to preach these things, the people appeared as just awakened from the sleep of ages—they seemed to see for the first time that they were responsible beings, and a refusal to use the means appointed, was a damning sin.[28]

It is quite clear from Stone's summary that the Revivalists were preaching doctrines unacceptable to orthodox Presbyterians, who took the Westminster Confession seriously. The spirit of unity that most of the participants experienced at Cane Ridge from the fact that they all read from the same Bible, sang the same hymns, prayed to the same God, and exalted the same Christ was soon shat-tered by charges placed against one Presbyterian minister, Richard McNemar, before the Synod of Kentucky. Four other Presbyterian ministers, including Stone, made common cause with McNemar and stunned the hostile synod by withdrawing from its jurisdiction. The synod, sensing that their actions may have been abrupt, appointed a committee to counsel with the five. The influential David Rice urged that the Westminster Confession was really a bulwark against infi-delity and atheism, but the five were unconvinced. The synod there-upon dismissed them from the ministry and sent letters to their respective churches declaring their pulpits vacant. The result was to throw the Presbyterian churches of the area into confusion. Stone, who had emancipated his slaves, was unemployed and thenceforth dependent on his labor as a farmer to support his small family. He worked until late into the night, coaxing from the soil a meager income. He preached whenever opportunity provided to those in the area who gave support to his stand.

The five discharged ministers—Robert Marshall, John Dunlavy, Richard McNemar, John Thompson, and Barton W. Stone—proceed-ed to organize a separate body, which they called the Springfield Presbytery (named after a village in Ohio located near Cincinnati). Their reasons for doing so were published in a pamphlet entitled *The Apology of Springfield Presbytery*. In it, the objections to the doc-trines of election and foreordination were detailed, and a general rejection of all creeds of human devising was affirmed. Interestingly, the Methodist Church in Virginia found the attack on the Calvinistic doctrines useful and reprinted the *Apology,* deleting, however, the position disavowing all human creeds. A brief pamphlet war followed.

The history of the Springfield Presbytery was to be brief, lasting only from September, 1803 until June, 1804. New ideas were spreading in the minds of the frontiersmen, and these would inevitably produce new alignments. It was quite clear to some of the men of the Springfield Presbytery that they had formed a new sect, which was contrary to their intent and certainly not in harmony with the unity they had known at Cane Ridge. When the Presbytery met at Cane Ridge in June of 1804, the ministers were joined by Rice Haggard, the man who a decade earlier had persuaded the Republican Methodists at Mt. Lebanon, Virginia, to adopt the name "Christian" as the Biblically approved title for the followers of Jesus Christ.[29] A lively discussion ensued concerning the future of the Springfield Presbytery, which resulted in a decision to dissolve it. The body published an interesting document, *The Last Will and Testament of the Springfield Presbytery,* which was signed by the five constituting ministers and David Purviance, who had joined them. The text is reproduced below:

The Presbytery of Springfield, sitting at Cane-ridge, in the county of Bourbon, being, through a gracious Providence, in more than ordinary bodily health, growing in strength and size daily; and in perfect soundness and composure of mind; and knowing that it is appointed for all delegated bodies once to die; and considering that the life of every such body is very uncertain, do make and ordain this our last Will and Testament, in manner and form following, viz.:

Imprimis. We will, that this body die, be dissolved, and sink into union with the Body of Christ at large; for there is but one Body, and one Spirit, even as we are called in one hope of our calling.

Item. We will, that our power of making laws for the government of the church, and executing them by delegated authority, forever cease; that the people may have free course to the Bible, and adopt the law of the Spirit of life in Christ Jesus.

Item. We will, that candidates for the Gospel ministry henceforth study the Holy Scriptures with fervent prayer, and obtain license from God to preach the simple Gospel, with the Holy Ghost sent down from heaven, without any mixture of philosophy, vain deceit, traditions of men, or the rudiments of the world. And let none henceforth take this honor to himself, but he that is called of God, as was Aaron.

Item. We will, that the church of Christ resume her native right of internal government—try her candidates for the ministry, as to their soundness in the faith, acquaintance with experimental religion, gravity and aptness to teach; and admit no other proof of their authority but Christ speaking in them. We will, that the church of Christ look to the Lord of the harvest to send forth laborers into his harvest; and that she resume her primitive right of trying those who say they are apostles and are not.

Item. We will, that each particular church, as a body, actuated by the same spirit, choose her own preacher, and support him by a free will offering, without a written call or subscription—admit members—remove offenses; and never henceforth delegate her right of government to any man or set of men whatever.

Item. We will, that the people henceforth take the Bible as the only sure guide to heaven: and as many as are offended with other books, which stand in competition with it, may cast them into the fire if they choose; for it is better to enter into life having one book, than having many to be cast into hell.

Item. We will, that preachers and people, cultivate a spirit of mutual forbearance; pray more and dispute less; and while they behold the signs of the times, look up, and confidently expect that redemption draweth nigh.

Item. We will, that our weak brethren, who may have been wishing to make the Presbytery of Springfield their king, and wot not what is now become of it, betake themselves to the Rock of Ages, and follow Jesus for the future.

Item. We will, that the Synod of Kentucky examine every member who may be suspected of having departed from the Confession of Faith and suspend every such suspected heretic immediately; in order that the oppressed may go free, and taste the sweets of gospel liberty.

Item. We will, that Ja— —, the author of two letters lately published in Lexington, be encouraged in his zeal to destroy partyism. We will, moreover, that our past conduct be examined into by all who may have correct information; but let foreigners beware of speaking evil of things which they know not.

Item. Finally we will, that all our sister bodies read their Bible carefully, that they may see their fate there determined, and prepare for death before it is too late.

Springfield Presbytery: L.S.
June 28th, 1804:

Robert Marshall
John Dunlavy
Richard McNemar
B. W. Stone   Witnesses
John Thompson
David Purviance

The authorship of the document has been attributed to Stone, whose viewpoint it surely expresses. Recent evidence, however, seems to point to McNemar as the author.[30] The signers disclaimed human creeds, sectarian names, and human organizations, and expressed a desire to "sink into union with the body of Christ at large." Such was not to be for this body. Already, the cohesion of the body was being tested, and it would soon vanish entirely. Three Shaker missionaries arrived from the East and began to make inroads into the fellowship of the Christians. McNemar and Dunlavy were early converts, the latter eventually becoming one of their ruling elders. The ascetic and communal life-style of the Shakers succeeded in luring many converts into their ranks, and Stone was forced to labor hard to check their growth. Meanwhile, Marshall and Thompson, who were hesitant about signing the *Last Will and Testament* because they feared it would dissolve ties between ministers, were having second thoughts about their severance from the main body of Presbyterians. Questions about the atonement, baptism, church government, and the Trinity led them to conclude that the liberties of a fellowship based on the Bible alone could be dangerous. They began to feel the need for a doctrinal anchorage, especially in view of the Shaker inroads and the generally unsettled state of frontier religion. Accordingly, they made their rather humiliating submission to the Synod of the Presbyterian Church and were received back into its ranks on October 9, 1811. Of the original five, only Stone remained. By this date, however, others had subscribed to the aims stated in *The Last Will and Testament*, and the movement had grown to such proportions that the defection of Marshall and Thompson made little difference to its progress.

Stone's Theological Struggle

In the years when Stone bore heavy responsibilities for leadership of the growing religious movement, he faced several personal crises. In 1809, his only son died, and, in May of 1810, his wife died, leaving him with four small daughters. A year and a half later, he remarried, then settled briefly in Tennessee, returned after a year to teach briefly in Georgetown, Kentucky, established the church there, and then embarked on a period of evangelizing and church planting in Kentucky, Ohio, and Indiana.

In the midst of his sorrows and his personal problems, Stone's mind was wrestling with two of the most challenging concepts in Christian theology, the doctrine of the atonement and the subject of the Trinity. Stone had been taught the widely accepted theory that Christ died to make satisfaction for the wrongs that mankind

committed against God. In the more extreme form in which it was
often presented by frontier revivalists, God was pictured as an angry
deity who could only be appeased by blood. Stone not only objected to
such a representation of the Heavenly Father, he also held, as indeed
had many before him, that such a theory of satisfaction contradicts
Biblical teaching about grace. If the debt of sin is paid, then nothing
is forgiven. If satisfaction has been made, there is no grace. Thus,
Stone dismissed the traditional explanation of Christ's death as un-
Biblical. How, then, did Stone understand Christ's death on the
cross? He considered a view advanced by some Methodists of his
acquaintance, that Jesus died to reconcile the Father to lost men.
But his study of the Bible led him to conclude that "the death of
Jesus is never represented as having any effect on God, or his love;
but on man the whole effect of it is passed."[31] Stone finally settled on
the conviction that the effect of Christ's death is upon man, a position very similar to the moral influence theory expressed in the
twelfth century by Abelard. He was vigorously attacked for his views
by orthodox Presbyterians who asserted that Stone had reduced
Christ's death to a martyrdom and limited its results to naturalistic
efforts. If the death of Christ brought reconciliation, the arguments
over the proper theory of His death caused alienation. Stone ultimately recognized what the church has historically called the "mystery" of the atonement and urged that discussion of the subject be
confined to Scriptural language.[32]

The second doctrine that troubled Stone's mind was the Nicene
formulation of the relation of the three persons of the Godhead, pop-
ularly known as the Trinity. The term is not found in the Bible; it is
a Latin term coined at the start of the third century by the North
African theologian, Tertullian. The concept for which it stands, namely that the one God exists in three Persons who are coequal, coessen-
tial, and coeternal, was given dogmatic sanction at the Council of
Nicea in A.D. 325. Since then, advocates of any other formula to
describe the relation of the Father, Son, and Holy Spirit have been
considered heretical by the main body of Christendom. Denial of this
formula has sometimes been a capital offense, as is seen, for example, in the case of Michael Servetus. The precise nature of Stone's
views are not altogether clear. He believed that Jesus Christ was the
Son of God, but not God in the same sense as the Father. His position
seems to be similar to that of Arius, whom he disavowed (and probably didn't understand). He held, with John's Gospel, to the preexis-
tence of Christ, but denied the eternality of Christ. He would affirm
any Biblical statement about the Son, but failed to read "Trinity" into
any of them. He was attacked by Thomas Cleland in a bitter pamphlet barrage that began in 1814 and lasted a decade. Fortunately
for Stone, the frontier was not given to burning at the stake those
who questioned the dogmatism of Nicea, and few who objected to

Stone's theological formulas could question his dedication to Jesus Christ as Lord or his devotion to His cause. Years later, Alexander Campbell would counsel Stone to avoid useless speculations.[33]

Meanwhile, the frontier settlements were expanding as the tide of settlers continued to move across the Appalachians. The Christians were aggressively evangelistic, and congregations both grew and multiplied. From his farm near Georgetown, Kentucky, Stone constructed a school, trained numbers of young men for ministry, traveled widely and preached, and began the publication of the *Christian Messenger,* a monthly designed to provide a sense of cohesion to the growing movement.[34] It was published from November 1826 until Stone's death in 1844, except for several brief interruptions. John T. Johnson, a Reforming Baptist minister of Georgetown, Kentucky, was associated with Stone as coeditor for two years before Stone's move to Illinois. The journal is an invaluable treasure of information about the editor, the churches of the area, and the issues of the times.

Two years before the beginning of the *Christian Messenger,* Stone met Alexander Campbell, whom he later acknowledged as "the greatest promoter of this reformation of any man living."[35] Campbell's name had been widely known in Kentucky since 1823 when he had debated W.L. McCalla and subsequently traveled in the state. In the same year, Campbell began publication of the *Christian Baptist,* which enjoyed circulation among the Baptists of Kentucky. In September, 1824, on his second tour of Kentucky, Campbell came to Georgetown and met Stone. The similarity of their objectives was immediately apparent. Their acquaintance grew through editorial correspondence and through association of their followers in the same communities. It was logical that the two groups, each seeking the unity of Christians, should unite. Their platforms for seeking unity were almost identical: the teaching and example of the Bible. Their understanding of what this implied involved some problems, which will be explored in a subsequent chapter along with an account of the merger.

At this point it is appropriate to attempt an appraisal of the nature of the movement for which Stone was the major spokesman. The Christians of the frontier had developed a homogeneity that was largely a synthesis of the religious forms found on the frontier. Born of the frontier revival, they would continue to employ revival techniques involving the mourner's bench and a strong emotional appeal. Upon leaving the Presbyterian Church, they renounced synods and became congregationally autonomous in church government, but they found it useful to hold regular "conferences." Speaking of these, Stone wrote in 1826:

> Our sole business is to confer together on the state of religion among the churches, to arrange our appointments so as to supply the

churches which may need our aid in preaching, administering the
ordinances, and attending to the ordination of elders, to worship
together, to strengthen the bonds of union, and to encourage each
other in the work of the Lord.[36]

These early Christians were paedobaptists. Robert Marshall seems
to be the first among the early leaders to consider the propriety of
baptism of believers by immersion. It was the consensus that the
matter be left to individual judgment. In June, 1807, Stone (himself
unimmersed) immersed David Purviance, thus introducing the
practice among the Christians. Eventually, the immersion of believers became almost the sole practice among the Christians so that
Stone could say in 1826, "Now there is not one in five hundred
among us who has not been immersed."[37] Following the union with
the Campbell-led movement, the Christians seemed to have little difficulty in adopting Campbell's understanding of Christian baptism.

The history of the Christians associated with Barton W. Stone
merges with that of the Disciples, who were associated with Thomas
and Alexander Campbell, in 1832, and is related in chapter 4 of the
present work. The major credit for success of the merger of the
Christians and Disciples belongs to Stone. He labored in behalf of
the merger in Kentucky until 1834 when he moved to Jacksonville,
Illinois, unable to resist the westward tide. Many Kentuckians were
settling Illinois and lands west of the Mississippi. Stone's aim was to
evangelize the territory and eventually establish a Christian college.
He was also attracted to the anti-slavery situation in Illinois. The
last decade of his life was spent in traveling to preach and establish
churches in Indiana, Illinois, and Missouri. In 1841, Stone suffered a
paralyzing stroke. He died in Hannibal, Missouri, on November 9,
1844, while returning home from preaching at the Missouri State
Annual Meeting. In 1847, his body was placed in the cemetery at
Cane Ridge, where hundreds of visitors come to view the old log
church and recall the events of 1801. In 1957 a beautiful shelter was
erected over the old meeting house to protect it from the elements. A
full-time curator resides nearby, and a museum on the site houses
Stone memorabilia.

End Notes

[1]"Errand to the Wilderness" is the title of an election sermon on the Puritan mission preached by Samuel Danforth in 1670. It was adopted as the title of a very fine monograph by Perry E. Miller (Cambridge: Harvard University, 1956).

[2]For a good discussion of this conflict, see Alan Simpson, *Puritanism in Old and New England* (Chicago: University of Chicago Press, 1955), pp. 19-38.

[3]See Smith, Handy, and Loetscher, *American Christianity: An Historical Interpretation With Representative Documents* (New York: Scribner, 1960), Vol. I, pp. 197-229, for a brief treatment of this period. For a more extensive treatment, see Perry E. Miller, *The New England Mind: From Colony to Province* (Cambridge: Harvard University, 1953).

[4]"The Necessity of Reformation," text found in Smith, Handy, and Loetscher, op. cit., pp. 205-216.

[5]A great interest has developed in recent years in the work of Jonathan Edwards, often called "America's greatest theologian," and abundant literature has been produced. Recommended are Ola E. Winslow, *Jonathan Edwards* (New York: Macmillan, 1940), Perry E. Miller, *Jonathan Edwards* (New York: Sloan, 1949), and, more recently, Conrad Cherry, *The Theology of Jonathan Edwards: A Reappraisal* (Garden City: Doubleday [Anchor Books], 1966).

[6]For more information on the Great Awakening, see Edward Gaustad, *The Great Awakening in New England* (New York: Harper, 1957); W.W. Sweet, *Religion in Colonial America* (New York: Scribner, 1942).

[7]Smith, Handy, and Loetscher, op. cit., Vol. I, p. 517. Winthrop Hudson suggests that church membership was probably about 7% of the population, but he warns against misinterpreting such statistics that reflect a period before the requirements for church membership were so fully relaxed. At this time, the number attending worship was generally three times the membership (Winthrop Hudson, *Religion in America* [New York: Scribner, 1973], p. 129).

[8]An interesting account of a confrontation between the Deistic students of Yale University and the evangelical President Timothy Dwight is described by Jerold C. Brauer, *Protestantism in America* (Philadelphia: Westminster Press, 1965), pp. 102-104.

64 *Religion in Early America*

[9]W.E. MacClenny, *Life of Rev. James O'Kelly* (Raleigh: Edwards and Broughton, 1910) pp. 116-117. Some years later, the churches of the O'Kelly Christians in Virginia and North Carolina became troubled about baptism, due largely to the influence of Alexander Campbell's writings. Many adopted the name Christian Baptists (Ibid., p. 159). As this group spread into Tennessee, they tended to identify with the Christian movement led by Barton W. Stone.

[10]For a graphic description, see W.W. Sweet, *The Story of Religion in America* (New York: Harper, 1959), pp. 298-303.

[11]The interesting thesis of Frederick J. Turner, set forth in *The Frontier in American History* (New York: Holt, 1921), is still a matter of controversy among historians. Cf. George Rogers Taylor, ed., *The Turner Thesis Concerning the Role of the Frontier in American History* (Boston: D. C. Heath, 1949).

[12]John Rogers, *Biography of Elder Barton W. Stone, Written by Himself; With Additions and Reflections by Elder John Rogers* (Cincinnati: J.A. & U.P. James, 1847), p. 2.

[13]Ibid., p. 3.

[14]Ibid., p. 6.

[15]Ibid., p. 7.

[16]Ibid., p. 9.

[17]Ibid., p. 13.

[18]Ibid., p. 22.

[19]Probably the initial efforts for what later became Transylvania College, the first college west of the Appalachians.

[20]Rogers, op. cit., p. 27.

[21]Ibid., p. 30.

[22]Ibid.

[23]Smith, Handy, and Loetscher, op. cit., Vol. I, p. 567.

[24]Ibid., Vol. I, p. 569.

[25]Rogers, *op. cit.*, pp. 41, 42. John Rogers, biographer of Barton W. Stone and himself a witness to exercises, after serious reflection on their validity was moved to reject them as evidence of Divine approbation. He concluded, "We have seen that to regard them as tokens of the divine favor is of the essence of fanaticism—that to suppose they are divine attestations of the truth of any dogma, is the most consummate nonsense, not to say, presumption" (p. 384).

[26]William West observes: "Stone's idea of Christian unity, though advanced for its time, failed to approximate the modern ecumenical idea of church unity, because his stress was primarily on the individual." William Garrett West, *Barton Warren Stone: Early American Advocate of Christian Unity* (Nashville: Disciples of Christ Historical Society, 1954), p. 210.

[27]Rogers, op. cit., p. 43.

[28]Ibid., pp. 44, 45.

[29]Charles C. Ware, *Barton Warren Stone* (St. Louis: Bethany Press, 1932), p. 141.

[30]West, op. cit., p. 77.

[31]Rogers, op. cit., p. 58.

[32]Stone, *Christian Messenger,* Vol. IX, 1835, p. 233.

[33]Campbell's letter to Stone on the Doctrine of Trinity, *Christian Baptist,* Vol. V, No. 3 (October 1, 1827).

[34]The *Christian Messenger* was reprinted by College Press, Joplin, Missouri, in 1978, in fourteen volumes.

[35]Rogers, op. cit., p. 76.

[36]Stone, *Christian Messenger,* Vol. I, 1826, p. 140.

[37]Ibid., p. 267.

Chapter Three

Thomas Campbell

The nineteenth century will always be known in American history as the century of the great immigration. The land whose western limits were scarcely known at the beginning of the century was transformed by its end into a unified nation bordering two major oceans and spanned by telegraph wires and transcontinental railroads. Most of the millions who tilled its fertile fields and populated its towns and villages were immigrants who had first set foot in the new land within that very century. Many of these first-generation Americans would leave an indellible mark in shaping the new national culture. In religion, few would have greater impact than an Irishman of Scotch ancestry who came to the new world in the first decade of the nineteenth century.

Thomas Campbell, eldest son of Archibald Campbell, was born on February 1, 1763, in County Down, Ireland. Archibald's ancestry was Scotch, but he had migrated to Northern Ireland for reasons not altogether clear. He was reared a Roman Catholic, served in the British Army in the Battle of Quebec, and, upon his return to Ireland, abandoned the Roman church in favor of the Church of England. He was firmly attached to this church, and determined "to serve God according to act of Parliament."[1]

Thomas and his three younger brothers were given an excellent classical education in a military school near their home in Newry.

Thomas Campbell (1763-1854), author of the *Declaration and Address* and father of Alexander Campbell.

This would serve Thomas well in future years, first as a student and then for many years as a teacher. Also, as a young man, he developed a religious sensitivity that the "cold formality of the Episcopal ritual, and the apparent want of piety in the Church could not satisfy."[2] He ultimately transferred his interest to the Presbyterian Church, a move that required a considerable shift theologically. It involved accepting the doctrine of divine election and the need to know some kind of experience as a special evidence of one's calling. Thomas agonized over this matter until, one day, he had such an experience wherein

> he felt a peace diffuse itself suddenly throughout his soul, and the love of God seemed to be shed abroad in his heart as he had never before realized it. His doubts, anxieties, and fears were at once dissipated, as if as by enchantment.[3]

He would later have cause to question the validity of such an experience, but the immediate effect was to incline young Thomas to enter the ministry, a goal by no means pleasing to his father. Prior to entering into the ministry, however, he spent several months teaching school in an impoverished community south of Newry and another period as a teacher in the nearby town of Sheepbridge. Here he so impressed a wealthy Seceder Presbyterian that he offered to finance Thomas's studies in the university. Having finally won the reluctant consent of his father, young Thomas embarked in 1783 for Glasgow. The university there was enjoying a period of influence as a notable seat of learning. It had successfully integrated the rational methodology of the Enlightenment, popular in the English universities, with the Christian faith that had too often been abandoned in English and continental institutions. Enlightenment thought had been given a skeptical direction by the Scottish philosopher, David Hume, who had become famous for his denial of the reality of miracles, although that by no means represents the heart of his philosophical skepticism. At this period, the University of Glasgow was the seat of the labors of Thomas Reid and his illustrious student, Dugald Stewart. The common sense school of philosophy was formulated to counter Hume's skepticism.[4] Both Thomas and Alexander Campbell's orientation toward life in general, and to the study of the Bible in particular, would be profoundly conditioned by Scottish common sense philosophy.[5]

The university course required three years of study. After graduating, Campbell entered the seminary of the Seceder branch of the Presbyterian Church for a five-year period of theological study. Actually, this training required only eight weeks per year, spent under the personal tutelage of Dr. Archibald Bruce at Whitburn, midway between Glasgow and Edinburg. Presumably, Campbell spent most of the remainder of the time in Ireland studying and teaching school. During one of these periods in Ireland he courted, and in 1787 married, Jane Corneigle of County Antrim, the daughter of a French Huguenot family of deep piety. On September 12, 1788, their first child was born. They named him Alexander. In 1791, Thomas completed his preparatory studies and submitted to the examination for licensing as a minister of the church. He served small churches while earning his livelihood primarily by teaching.

Ministry at Ahorey

It was in 1798 that Thomas Campbell moved his family, consisting now of a son and two daughters, to a newly established rural congregation at Ahorey. To appreciate the challenge that confronted Thomas Campbell, it is necessary to gain some idea of the state of the Presbyterian Church at this time and to note something of the political and social conditions of the community.

The hardy Scots manifested a vigor and dedication in their religious activities that stands in marked contrast to the more placid attitudes of the English. Religious controversies often assumed serious proportions and evoked passionate responses. By the close of the eighteenth century, a number of controversies had divided the Church of Scotland. Thomas Campbell may properly be identified as an Anti-Burgher, Seceder, Old-Light Presbyterian. A brief description of these classifications and the controversies to which they refer gives an insight into the condition of the church in Scotland and Northern Ireland.

Since medieval times, the feudal lords of Scotland determined the choice of the priests of their parishes, a practice that was not entirely eliminated by the Protestant Reformation in Scotland, despite the fact that it was a violation of the Presbyterian doctrine that the congregation should call its own minister. Parliament passed (1709) the Act of Security, which protected the right of the Presbyterian Churches to call their ministers, but this protection was withdrawn shortly after by the Patronage Act, which restored the ancient privileges of the landowners. A series of vain protests followed before the majority of the Scottish churches seemed to acquiesce. Ebenezer Erskine and his brother, Ralph, led a minority of the more evangelically inclined churches to secede in 1733.[6] By 1747, this Seceder Church was torn over whether or not its members could take the oath required of those who would become burgesses. The oath required that one who would serve the community as burgess support "the religion presently professed within the realm." The stricter sentiment held that this referred to the non-Seceder Church and, thus, a member of the Seceders could not subscribe to the oath. This position came to be known as Anti-Burgher, and it was embraced by Ebenezer Erskine's son-in-law and Ralph Erskine's son, who proceeded to excommunicate their elders. Subsequently, a dispute arose over the proper interpretation of the twenty-third chapter of the Westminster Confession, which deals with the power of the magistrates. This divided the Anti-Burgher, Seceder Presbyterian Church into New Light and Old Light factions. The latter faction was led by Alexander Bruce, Thomas Campbell's teacher of theology. Obviously, the Presbyterians in Scotland at this time were much more concerned about dogmatic orthodoxy than they were about the unity of the church. One would have to be very well informed doctrinally to avoid trespassing on some cherished dogma and thereby incur the risk of excommunication.

This unfortunate condition was made even more ridiculous when it was transported to Ireland, where the political situation was different and the divisive issues had no relevance. The established church in Ireland at this time was Anglican, and there was no question about the propriety of professing adherence to it. Consequently, there was no dispute over the oath of the burgess and no point of maintaining the Burgher/Anti-Burgher division. Thomas Campbell saw clearly the futility of perpetuating divisions in a situation where the original causes had lost all meaning. This insight became one of the basic convictions of his life: namely, that it was both foolhardy and sinful to perpetuate meaningless division in the body of Christ. Accordingly, he sought to unite the two parties of the Seceder Church in Ireland and was sent to Glasgow to plead the matter before the General Synod in Scotland, but to no avail. His efforts, however, bore fruit later. The two parties united in 1820, thirteen years after Campbell had migrated to America.

Theological division was only a part of the strife that the irenic young minister was to confront at Ahorey. Equally serious was civil strife in Ireland. The island had been conquered by Cromwell, and the northern portion had been settled by many Scottish Protestants. The central and southern portions were, and still remain, solidly Catholic. The old religion became the basis of Irish patriotism and sheltered movements for rebellion and independence. Pitted against the Catholic majority was the Protestant Society of Orangemen. A lodge of this fraternity existed in County Armagh from 1795. Roman Catholics were frequently terrorized and could seldom find redress by recourse to the law. In addition, the Society of United Irishmen, another secret organization, appealed to many of the residents of the area and contributed to the civil turmoil. An intense dislike of the strife generated in the community by these societies led Thomas Campbell to adopt an attitude of opposition to all secret societies, which he passed on to his son.

A growing family forced Thomas Campbell to abandon his effort to subsidize his meager ministerial salary by small-scale farming and move to the nearby village of Rich Hill in 1805. In a time when there were no public schools, ministers often served as private instructors. With three sons and four daughters, Thomas Campbell had the beginnings of a school in his own household. The school that he conducted at Rich Hill supplemented the income from the church and launched Campbell on a career that would engage his energies for many years in America. Alexander Campbell, who had been tutored by his father since early childhood, was soon pressed into service as an associate.

Scotch Independents

Rich Hill was an exciting place for the Campbell family. Here was found a congregation of Scottish Independents (Congregationalists). Thomas Campbell often returned home from his Sunday morning services at Ahorey in time to attend the evening service of this congregation.[7] The practice of attending services of another denomination was called "occasional hearing" and was permitted, but not encouraged, by the Seceder Church. Campbell befriended the local pastor and availed himself of the opportunities to hear some of the celebrated preachers of the day. Among them was the noted evangelist Roland Hill, friend of George Whitefield of Great Awakening fame.

It is important to note something of the emphases that were to be encountered in the Rich Hill congregation, though the extent that these were to have any influence on Thomas and Alexander Campbell

The Presbyterian Church building at Ahorey, North Ireland, where Thomas Campbell served as pastor prior to coming to America in 1807. It still houses an active church.

is a matter of dispute. One of the earliest of the Scotch Independents was John Glas, who forsook the Presbyterian Church in 1728 and founded independent churches in most of the large towns in Scotland. He emphasized the importance of restoring the New Testament church. His work was more fully developed by his son-in-law, Robert Sandeman. Sandeman taught a plurality of elders, mutual exhortation of members, and weekly Communion, which may have led Thomas Campbell to urge in vain that Presbyterians should commune more frequently than twice yearly.[8] Most significantly, however, was Sandeman's understanding that faith is belief in the testimony about Christ rather than the result of some supernatural act performed on the elect. Precisely how much emphasis on this understanding of faith was to be found at Rich Hill cannot be determined, but it is certain that this view of faith was expressed by Thomas Campbell shortly after his arrival in America.

Another important influence at Rich Hill was a wealthy layman named James Alexander Haldane. He and his older brother, Robert, led an evangelistic movement that sought to restore New Testament practices. The Haldane brothers disapproved of the formalism of the Church of Scotland and became alarmed over the spread of rationalistic theology. They devoted their wealth to promoting a warm, evangelistic type of preaching and to building tabernacles to present this ministry. They encouraged lay preaching and supported a school in Glasgow to train laymen for ministry. Eventually, the Haldanes would practice weekly Communion and the immersion of believers within the congregations they established in Scotland. These churches later were numbered among the Scotch Baptists.[9]

Thomas Campbell met James A. Haldane and heard him preach at Rich Hill. It was the Haldanes who financed the evangelistic tour that brought Rowland Hill to Rich Hill. In 1797, James Haldane was instrumental in organizing the "Society for the Propogation of the Gospel at Home," and Thomas Campbell gave this evangelistic agency his support. The Haldane insistence on congregational autonomy and a plurality of elders in every congregation influenced Campbell's thinking at this time. They emphasized simple evangelical Christianity and placed little importance on "the sectarian necessities and constraints of party-preachers."[10] The Rich Hill congregation was much more directly under the influence of the liberal, gracious spirit of the Haldane movement than the more contentious and controversial Sandemanian effort.

Another preacher at Rich Hill, whom Thomas Campbell was to hear and with whom he was to engage in serious religious discussion, was the eccentric John Walker. He resigned a promising clerical and teaching career out of the conviction that all Christians should share in ministry and, thus, there should be no professional clergy. Hostility to a professional ministry has appeared with varied intensity since Luther's emphasis on the priesthood of all Christians. John Walker's was one of many voices that was raised in Protestant circles complaining about clerical domination.

The open attitude of the Rich Hill congregation stood in striking contrast to the theological rigidity of the Seceder Church. The Rich Hill congregation respected individual conscience and permitted a freedom for holding personal opinions that Thomas Campbell found quite appealing. These people seemed to be spared those conflicts that were managed and orchestrated by ecclesiastical bodies existing above the congregation. For the Rich Hill Independents, there simply was no extra-congregational authority. Subsequent experience with ecclesiastical tribunals would recommend this arrangement to Thomas and Alexander Campbell, at least for a time. The impressions that the Rich Hill congregation made on Thomas Campbell strongly influenced his thinking in the New World, not only with reference to liberty of opinion, but also on the matter of church polity.

While the Campbells' residence in Rich Hill lasted less than three years, ideas and patterns of religious activity were encountered that would have major consequences in their later religious thinking. Actually, this residence was ended because of Mr. Campbell's declining health, due no doubt to the demands of ministering to a rural congregation while conducting a flourishing school in the town, and to a climate that was often harsh. In one period of serious illness, Thomas Campbell's physician recommended a long rest, perhaps a sea voyage. Eighteen-year-old Alexander disclosed that he intended to migrate to America when he became of age and suggested to his father that he would take charge of the school at Rich Hill if his father would make an exploratory trip to America. If he found conditions favorable, the whole family could join him in the New World; otherwise he could return. One of the members of the Ahorey church had relatives who had migrated to Washington, Pennsylvania, and wished to join them but feared to make the journey alone. It was thus decided that the elder Campbell should accompany the young woman to Pennsylvania. He embarked from Londonderry on April 8, 1807, and, after an unusually brief transatlantic voyage of thirty-five days aboard the sailing vessel *Brutus,* arrived in Philadelphia as spring was breaking. Coming to the New World in pursuit of improved health proved to be a very fortunate decision, for Thomas Campbell lived to be ninety years of age; he died in 1854.

The Challenge of the New World

It was a happy circumstance for Thomas Campbell on arrival in Philadelphia to find the Anti-Burgher synod in session in that city.

He presented his credentials, was warmly received, and assigned to the Chartiers Presbytery in western Pennsylvania, which was his destination and the location of many of his friends who had immigrated previously. The journey of 350 miles to the frontier town of Washington, made by stage or wagon, was a punishing ordeal, but Campbell arrived in time for the meeting of the Chartiers Presbytery on June 30 and July 1 and was assigned a preaching circuit. Educated ministers were scarce in frontier presbyteries and were shared by several congregations.

With seriousness of purpose and a heart of compassion, Thomas Campbell began to minister to the spiritual needs of the frontier settlements. These were quite unlike North Ireland communities; there were fewer people but a great number of religious affiliations, including several types of Presbyterians who would not permit intercommunion. Because church law did not permit Communion to be celebrated without the presence of an ordained minister, and because ordained ministers generally were not plentiful on the frontier, many Presbyterians had not shared the Lord's Supper for a long period of time. Thomas Campbell's desire to minister to the spiritual needs and promote the Christian nurture of the wider community was to mean trouble in a matter of a few months.

Contrary to what might be supposed, religious tolerance was not common on the frontier. Animosities generated in the Old World had been exported to the New, although they generally had little or no relevance. The immediate occasion for trouble in Campbell's case stems from a Communion service at Cannamaugh, a sparsely settled community above Pittsburgh, at which he was assisted by William Wilson, a fellow Seceder minister. Wilson took offense at Campbell's preparation sermon in which he deplored the existence of division and party spirit in the church and suggested that all who felt disposed should feel free to share in the Supper without respect to party differences. Although he expressed no dissent to Campbell at the time, Wilson lodged a complaint with the presbytery against Campbell upon his return. Shortly after, another minister, John Anderson, refused to keep an appointment with Campbell because of the latter's departure from orthodox positions. The presbytery determined to investigate. Richardson suggests that the real cause of the trouble that followed was jealousy of Campbell's popularity and superior abilities, a suggestion given some credence by the presbytery's abrupt and inconsiderate handling of the matter. For reasons not completely understood, Thomas Campbell was not given a fair hearing before the Chartiers Presbytery. It is interesting to note, however, that the formal charges brought against Campbell made no reference to the incident involving the Lord's Supper to which Richardson refers. Actually, the formal charges, which were extracted from the minutes of the presbytery and synod and published by William Herbert Hanna,[11] disclose a long and complex proceeding about some very serious theological concerns that represent a considerable departure from standard Presbyterian doctrine. The charges were drawn up by a committee made up of John Anderson and several of his students. He had been the theological mentor for the presbytery and had guided a number of the ministers through their preparation and ordination. The indictment charged Thomas Campbell with the following seven offenses:

1. Taught that a person's appropriation of Christ to himself as his own Savior does not belong to the essence of saving faith, but only to a high degree of it.

2. Asserted that a church has no divine warrant for holding Confessions of Faith as terms of communion.

3. Asserted that it is the duty of ruling elders to pray and exhort publicly in vacant congregations.

4. Asserted that it is permissible to hear ministers that are in stated opposition to our testimony.

5. Asserted that our Lord Jesus Christ was not subject to the precept as well as the penalty of the law in the stead of His people or as their surety.

6. Asserted that man is able in this life to live without sin in thought, word, and deed.

7. Preached in a congregation where a minister was settled without any regular call or appointment.[12]

Campbell replied in writing to the above charges, but his defense was not considered satisfactory to the presbytery, which suspended him. He then decided to take the matter to the synod, which met in Philadelphia in May, 1808. The reader who wishes to trace the rather lengthy proceedings step by step should consult W.H. Hanna's narrative. Considerable time was given to deliberation over the problems posed by the charges against Campbell. The last three charges were dropped. In regard to the first four charges, if they actually represent heresy, as the synod was inclined to believe, Campbell was guilty. The point of the first complaint is that Campbell would not insist that saving faith must necessarily include some type of mystical or emotional experience, which Presbyterians at that time regarded as evidence of election. The second charge may very possibly have referred to conclusions Campbell had reached from fellowship enjoyed at Rich Hill, which was enjoyed beyond the limits imposed by creedal uniformity. The truth of the matter was that Campbell could no longer honestly limit the definition of Christ's church to the confines of the Westminster Confession of Faith. The third charge involves the distinction usually made in that day between "ruling elders" (laymen) and "teaching elders" (clergy). Campbell's understanding of the priesthood of believers led him to acknowledge without hesitation that he thought it advisable for elders to pray and exhort in public worship when no minister was available. The fourth charge indicates that Campbell was no longer sectarian. He candidly admitted:

> I believe that in the present broken and divided state of the church, when Christians have not an opportunity of hearing those of their own party, it is lawful for them to hear other ministers preach the gospel where the publick [sic] worship is not corrupted with matters of human invention.[13]

It was the judgment of the associate synod that Mr. Campbell's departures from Presbyterian usages were not of such nature to warrant suspension but rather of sufficient gravity that he should be censured. The decision was to "rebuke and admonish." Campbell was asked whether he would consent to this, and, after one brief objection, he yielded.

The rebuke having been duly administered by the moderator, the whole matter was to have ended. Campbell was assigned preaching appointments in Philadelphia for the next two months and then sent back to the Presbytery of Chartiers without liability. Commenting on the treatment of Campbell by the associate synod of North America, W.E. Garrison observed:

> Nothing could exceed the courtesy and fairness with which Mr. Campbell had been treated by the Synod. Its findings of fact, in regard to his views and their divergence from the standards and practices of the church were accurate. If it erred . . . it was an error that leaned toward charity.[14]

As much could not be said for the attitude of the Presbytery of Chartiers. When Campbell returned to western Pennsylvania in the summer of 1808, cleared of the charges which the presbytery had lodged against him, he found himself to be *persona non grata*. No church was available to him; he was effectively ostracized. It was evident that Campbell's breadth of spirit and his concept of faith combined to exclude him from the narrow confines of that frontier Presbyterian Church. Essentially a man of peace, Campbell found himself to be the object of much hostility. One wonders if, had his family not been preparing to join him in the New World, he might have been tempted to abandon this frontier and return to Ireland. But he had written the family the previous January instructing them to plan to join him, and they were completing their preparations for the journey at sea at the very time that Thomas Campbell found it necessary to make a formal withdrawal from the Presbyterian ministry. His letter of withdrawal was received by the presbytery on September 13, 1808. All of the churches of the presbytery were accordingly notified of the departure of Mr. Campbell from their ministerial ranks.

Even so, Thomas Campbell was at no loss for opportunities to preach. He had many friends in the area, some of whom he had known in Ireland, and they were very sympathetic to his plight. The frontiersmen respected integrity of character and personal dedication, both of which they saw in Campbell. They failed to appreciate the actions of the presbytery, which suggested to them the kind of religious persecution that was out of place in the New World. Homes were opened for preaching services. When the weather was favorable, meetings were held out of doors. Soon a considerable number of friends and neighbors shared his interest in de-emphasizing creedal conflicts and pursuing unity on the basis of the teaching of the Bible. With no intention of establishing a separate denomination, the group began to consider how they might advance the cause of Christian unity. It was agreed that this might best be done through the formation of an organized body with the promotion of Christian unity as its primary aim. After much discussion, consensus was reached on the proposition: "Where the Scriptures speak, we speak, where the Scriptures are silent, we are silent." Concern was expressed about whether this principle would lead to abandonment of infant baptism. At the time, Thomas Campbell was uncertain, but he thought it would not. Convinced of the validity of the principle, however, he was willing to subject baptismal practice, and any other practice of the church, to scrutiny as to its validation by the Scriptures. In the meantime, an organization was formed on August 17, 1809. It was named the Christian Association of Washington, Pennsylvania. Thomas Campbell was charged with the task of writing a statement outlining the aims of the association, a labor that occupied the major part of his time for the next six weeks. It resulted in the most important literary product of his life and, very probably, the most influential single document in the history of the Disciples, the *Declaration and Address*. Other members of the association undertook to construct a simple log meetinghouse at a convenient and accessible place where two roadways intersected. The building was also to serve as a common school. This was a fateful step because, although the association anticipated only two meetings per year, the members found themselves gathering weekly at various places where Thomas Campbell could be found expounding the Scriptures. Those who attended these gatherings became increasingly estranged from their congregations and, in the normal course of events, it could only be a matter of time before the gathering would consider itself to be a *de facto* church. It actually happened in May of 1811.

The Declaration and Address

The *Declaration and Address of the Christian Association of Washington* was completed and ordered to be printed on September 7, 1809. It came from the press of the local newspaper in the form of a fifty-six page booklet in December, 1809. The work consists of four parts. The *Declaration* (three pages) outlines the aims and procedures of the association. The *Address*, the most significant section (eighteen pages), sets forth an eloquent plea for the unity of the followers of Christ and incorporates the thirteen propositions that have merited the serious consideration of Christians who were and are concerned with the divided state of the church. Then follows an appendix (thirty pages), which explains several topics in the *Address* in greater detail and speaks to some possible objections. Finally, a brief postscript (three pages) offers some suggestions for future developments.

Unfortunately, the contents of the *Declaration and Address* are not widely known today. This is true, in part, because of the length of the work, but even more because of the style of early nineteenth-century composition, which many contemporary readers find somewhat awkward. While it is not feasible to reproduce the entire document here, certain portions that are especially significant must be noted and several generalizations attempted. The serious student of the movement will want to consult the entire document,[15] and will find the commentary by Dean Frederick Kershner[16] to be helpful.

The text of the *Declaration* stated unequivocally that the association had no intention of ever becoming a church.[17] How, then, did Campbell conceive the function of the association? Evidently, he hoped similar associations would be formed in every community and that these would generate such a demand for Christian union on a Biblical basis that the sectarian advocates would see the follies of creedal division and yield to the wisdom of creating in the New World a new beginning for the church and a glorious new day in the history of Christianity. To this end he issued the following appeal in the *Address:*

> We call, we invite you again, by every consideration in these premises. You that are near, associate with us; you that are at too great a distance associate as we have done. Let not the paucity of your number in any given district, prove an insuperable discouragement. Remember Him that has said, "If two of you shall agree on earth as touching anything that they shall ask, it shall be done for them of my Father who is in heaven: for where two or three are gathered together in my name, there am I in the midst of them." With such a promise as this, for the attainment of every possible and promised

good, there is no room for discouragement. Come on then, "ye that
fear the Lord; keep not silence, and give him no rest till he make
Jerusalem a joy and a praise in the earth." Put on that noble resolution dictated by the prophet, saying, "For Zion's sake will we not
hold our peace, and for Jerusalem's sake we will not rest, until the
righteousness thereof go forth as brightness, and the salvation
thereof as a lamp that burneth." Thus impressed, you will find
means to associate at such convenient distances, as to meet at least
once a month; to beseech the Lord to put an end to our lamentable
divisions; to heal and unite his people, that his Church may resume
her original constitutional unity and purity, and thus be exalted to
the enjoyment of her promised prosperity, that the Jews may be
speedily converted, and the fullness of the Gentiles brought in. Thus
associated, you will be in a capacity to investigate the evil causes of
our sad divisions; to consider and bewail their pernicious effects;
and to mourn over them before the Lord—who hath said: "I will go
and return to my place, till they acknowledge their offense and seek
my face." Alas! then, what reasonable prospect can we have of being
delivered from those sad calamities, which have so long afflicted the
Church of God; while a party spirit, instead of bewailing, is everywhere justifying the bitter principle of these pernicious evils; by
insisting upon the right of rejecting those, however unexceptionable
in other respects, who cannot see with them in matters of private
opinion, of human inference, that are nowhere expressly revealed or
enjoined in the word of God. Thus associated, will the friends of
peace, the advocates for Christian unity, be in a capacity to connect
in larger circles, where several of those smaller societies may meet
semi-annually at a convenient center; and thus avail themselves of
their combined exertions for promoting the interests of the common
cause. We hope that many of the Lord's ministers in all places will
volunteer in this service, forasmuch as they know it is his favorite
work, the very desire of his soul.[18]

This hope was doomed to disappointment. No other association of
this kind was ever formed. Since the objective of the association was
the destruction in due time of the whole denominational structure, it
is not surprising that the members of the association were not welcomed enthusiastically in the various denominations where they
were to carry on their work of reform.

In 1810, Thomas Campbell gathered two congregations in nearby
communities consisting of people who were mostly of Presbyterian
background. Having no desire to be isolated from Christian fellowship (How could one advocate reform when he was isolated?) and
urged by his friends, Campbell applied for ministerial communion
with the Burgher Synod of Pittsburgh. The application was denied
and the aims of the Christian Association were cited as one of the

reasons. Robert Richardson comments: "For a party to have admitted
to its bosom those who were avowedly bent on the destruction of partyism would, of course, have been perfectly suicidal."[19]

The incident posed a problem: can proponents of undenominational Christianity advance their cause without becoming a denomination? This issue would have to be faced over and over again in the
years to come.

A second item of note in the *Declaration* is the repeated reference
to "simple evangelical Christianity" coupled with such phrases as "a
pure Gospel ministry" and "that simple original form of Christianity
expressly exhibited upon the sacred page; without attempting to
inculcate anything of human authority, of private opinion, or inventions of man. . . ." Such statements reflect the conviction that the
church of the day was burdened with a yoke of tradition that was not
only useless but even detrimental to the accomplishment of its purpose as envisioned by the Master.

The *Address* opens with a powerful indictment of the divided state
of the church. Campbell noted the harmful consequences in terms of
the weakening of the message of Christ, the confusion of unbelievers,
the unlovely spirit of contention, the crippling of the missionary
thrust, and the violation of the express will of Christ; matters that
are visible to every generation of Christians. The depth of his
anguish over this state of affairs is disclosed in the following impassioned words:

> What awful and distressing efforts have those sad divisions pro-
> duced! What aversions, what reproaches, what backbitings, what
> evil surmisings, what angry contentions, what enmities, what
> excommunications, and even persecution!! And, indeed, this must,
> in some measure, continue to be the case so long as those schisms
> exist: for, saith the apostle, where envying and strife is, *there* is con-
> fusion and every evil work. What dreary effects of those accursed
> divisions are to be seen, even in this highly favored country, where
> the sword of the civil magistrate has not as yet learned to serve at
> the altar. Have we not seen congregations broken to pieces, neigh-
> borhoods of professing Christians first thrown into confusion by
> party contentions, and, in the end, entirely deprived of Gospel ordi-
> nances: while, in the mean time, large settlements and tracts of
> country remain to this day entirely destitute of a Gospel ministry,
> many of them in little better than a state of heathenism, the
> Churches being either so weakened with divisions that they cannot
> send them ministers, or the people so divided among themselves
> that they will not receive them. Several, at the same time, who live
> at the door of a preached Gospel, dare not in conscience go to hear
> it, and, of course enjoy little more advantage, in that respect, than
> if living in the midst of heathens. How seldom do many in those

circumstances enjoy the dispensations of the Lord's Supper, that great ordinance of unity and love. How sadly, also does this broken and confused state of things interfere with that spiritual intercourse among Christians, one with another, which is so essential to their world; so divided in sentiment, and, of course, living at such distances, that but few of the same opinion, or party, can conveniently and frequently assemble for religious purposes, or enjoy a due frequency of ministerial attentions.[20]

Churches in the Reformed/Presbyterian tradition have always regarded church discipline as one of the marks of the true church. With almost prophetic insight, Campbell sensed the fact that a divided church could not be a disciplined church. The ultimate result would be dilution of membership to a degree that would be destructive of Christian character and witness.

And even where things are in a better state with respect to settled Churches, how is the tone of discipline relaxed under the influence of a party spirit; many being afraid to exercise it with due strictness, lest their people should leave them, and, under the cloak of some specious pretense, find refuge in the bosom of another party; while lamentable to be told, so corrupted is the Church with these accursed divisions, that there are but few so base as not to find admission into some professing party or other. Thus, in a great measure, is that Scriptural purity of communion banished from the Church of God, upon the due preservation of which much of her comfort, glory, and usefulness depend.[21]

But he saw a great and unusual opportunity to correct these ills, an opportunity the like of which had not existed for centuries. In America, the land where men had triumphed over Europe's oppressive heritage and created a new form of civil government that did not interfere with the church, it would be possible to reform the church simply by returning to pristine Biblical practice. By this means, the old inherited European schisms could finally be buried.

Thus, the major burden of the *Address* is the possibility of achieving Christian union in the new nation. Campbell boldly advanced a platform for Christian union: the Bible alone. He assumed, and with good reason, that all of the churches in America accepted the Bible as basic to their beliefs and respected the authoritative nature of its teaching. He concluded, therefore, that the cause of division rested in human additions to the Bible in the form of interpretations (creeds) and practice (traditions). This being the case, the solution to the problem that destroyed the effectiveness of the gospel was for all to abandon these human inventions and unite on the basis of the Bible alone. In the words of Campbell:

It is, to us, a pleasing consideration that all the Churches of Christ which mutually acknowledge each other as such, are not only agreed in the great doctrines of faith and holiness, but are also materially agreed as to the positive ordinances of the Gospel institution; so that our differences, at most, are about the things in which the kingdom of God does not consist, that is, about matters of private opinion or human invention. What a pity that the kingdom of God should be divided about such things! Who, then, would not be the first among us to give up human inventions in the worship of God, and to cease from imposing his private opinions upon his brethren, that our breaches might *thus* be healed? Who would not willingly conform to the original pattern laid down in the New Testament, for *this* happy purpose? Our dear brethren of all denominations will please to consider that we have our educational prejudices and particular customs to struggle against as well as they. But this we do sincerely declare, that there is nothing we have hitherto received as matter of faith or practice which is not expressly taught and enjoined in the word of God, either in express terms or approved precedent, that we would not heartily relinquish, so that we might return to the original constitutional unity of the Christian Church: and, in this happy unity, enjoy full communion with all our brethren, in peace and charity.[22]

Following an eloquent plea for men of good will to join in the quest for Christian union, Campbell proceeded to lay down thirteen propositions for consideration and discussion. This is the most significant portion of the document. Campbell takes particular pains to note that the propositions are not a creed, either by intent or by nature. While the propositions are not excessively long, it is not necessary to reproduce them in their entirety here. Their content may be summarized as follows:

1. The first is the most famous of the propositions and is reproduced in full:

That the church of Christ upon earth is essentially, intentionally, and constitutionally one; consisting of all those in every place that profess their faith in Christ and obedience to him in all things according to the scriptures, and that manifest the same by their tempers and conduct, and of none else as none can truly and properly be called christians [sic].

2. That, although the church of Christ must exist in separate congregations that are geographically distinct and removed from one another, there ought to be no division in its fellowship or any fraternal rupture.

3. That only those matters "expressly taught and enjoined upon them, in the word of God," may be tests of fellowship or articles of faith among Christians.

4. That

> ... the New Testament is as perfect a constitution[23] for the worship, discipline and government of the New Testament church, and as perfect a rule for the particular duties of its members; as the Old Testament was for the worship, discipline and government of the Old Testament church.[24]

5. That no human authority has power to make laws for the church or alter what has been given in the New Testament.

6. That inferences and deductions from the Scriptures, no matter how compelling or logical they may seem to be to persons making them, must never become tests of fellowship or a part of the creed of the church.

7. That theological systems have a legitimate place in the life of the church but they ought not to be made terms of communion because they are of human construction and hence involve human reason and because they are beyond the grasp of many in the church.

8. That salvation does not depend on theological acumen but on recognition of one's need of Jesus Christ, profession of faith in Him, and obedience to Him. This should suffice for membership in the church.

9. That all who have complied with the above should recognize each other as Christians and love each other as brethren and members of the same body.

10. That division among Christians is anti-Christian, anti-Scriptural, unnatural, and productive of evil and confusion.

11. That division is caused by neglect of the will of God and the arrogance of human beings who have assumed unwarranted authority in the church.

12. That all that is needed to reform the church is to return to the Biblical norm of admission of members and discipline of the membership, to develop a ministry that is faithful to the Bible, and to restore the divine ordinances to their intended function.

13. That those matters that the church does not find provided in the Scriptures and thus adopts out of her own wisdom should be recognized as "expedients" so that, should subsequent wisdom counsel alteration of such things, no division would result.

It has been noted that the propositions are the most significant portion of the *Declaration and Address* as far as subsequent developments are concerned. The remainder of the *Address* is given to a plea for all Christians to seek the unity of the church. It is a plea based on the good sense and wisdom of the body of Christian people. There is no suggestion that the desired end could be achieved by any means short of the development of a common mind and general will to take advantage of the freedom in the New World to accomplish what was denied to the church in the Old World, namely Christian unity. This common sense appeal would characterize the advocacy of the "plea" in the decades to follow.

The appendix is given to further elucidation of points in the *Address* and a discussion of questions and objections Campbell anticipated would be raised by the *Address*. He was especially concerned that some might conclude that his repudiation of the theological formulas and creedal definitions as grounds for fellowship be considered as "Latitudinarianism." He argued for the adequacy of the Bible as a standard to govern the Christian enterprise and cautioned against the prevailing disposition to pass judgments against brethren in matters pertaining to human opinions. Harboring no illusion that all Christians would ever see everything alike, Campbell suggested that a wider degree of liberty in the church could prove spiritually profitable.

> But that all members should have the same identical views of all Divinely revealed truths, or that there should be no difference of opinion among them, appears to us morally impossible, all things considered. Nor can we conceive what desirable purpose such a unity of sentiment would serve, except to render useless some of those gracious, self-denying, and compassionate precepts of mutual sympathy and forbearance which the Word of God enjoins upon His people. Such, then, is the imperfection of our present state. Would to God it might prove, as it ought, a just and humbling counterbalance to our pride! Then, indeed, we would judge one another no more about such matters.[25]

The publication of the *Declaration and Address* failed to evoke any notable response. Thomas Campbell took pains to circulate copies to the ministers of the area, but there is no evidence of any significant reaction. The impact of this document was reserved for future decades.

The postscript was written several months after the publication of the *Declaration and Address* and incorporates suggestions growing out of the first meeting of a committee of twenty-one members of the Christian Association. Two steps were projected to promote the cause: (1) preparation of a "catechetical exhibition of the fulness and precision of the holy scriptures upon the entire subject of christianity," as recognition of the fact that "doctrinal exhibitions" are "highly expedient" when not used as tests of Christian fellowship, and (2) a monthly magazine to detect and expose the "various anti-christian enormities, innovations, and corruptions, which infect the christian church." Neither suggestion was actualized.

Problems Posed by the Declaration
and Address

How may the *Declaration and Address* be regarded after the passing of almost two centuries? Contemporary readers are quick to discern certain problems in the document that merit attention. One problem rises out of the Protestant Reformation and is evident in Campbell's opening paragraph of the *Declaration,* where he makes a strong affirmation of the right of private judgment.

> From the series of events which have taken place in the churches for many years past, especially in this Western country, as well as from what we know in general of the present state of things in the Christian world, we are persuaded that it is high time for us not only to think, but also to act, for ourselves; to see with our own eyes, and to take all our measures directly and immediately from the Divine standard; to this alone we feel ourselves Divinely bound to be conformed, as by this alone, we must be judged. We are also persuaded that as no man can be *judged* for his brother, so no man can *judge* his brother; every man must be allowed to judge for himself: as every man must bear his own judgment—must give account of himself to God. We are also of the opinion that as the Divine Word is equally binding upon all, so all lie under an equal obligation to be bound by it, and it alone; and not by any human interpretation of it; and that, therefore, no man has a right to judge his brother, except in so far as he manifestly violates the express letter of the law.[26]

It is immediately apparent that if each person "must be allowed to judge for himself" the meaning of revealed truth found in Scripture, the result could be a plethora of interpretations with equal validity, confusion confounded. How is such hermeneutical anarchy to be avoided? Rome avoids it by vesting authority to define the doctrine of the church in the bishop, ultimately in the Bishop of Rome, who, since 1871, is regarded as infallible when speaking "ex cathedra" on matters of faith and morals. Protestants, unwilling to resort to such authority, relied on creeds, which they regarded as the commonly accepted distillate of the truth found in the Scriptures. They were aware of the ancient criterion of true interpretation of Scripture set forth in the sixth century by Vincent of Lerins, which holds that the church must regard as true that which has been believed "always, everywhere, and by all men" (*Semper, ubique, et ab omnibus*). They regarded the content of the creeds that they accepted as consistent with the beliefs of the church from the very beginning and, thus, "truly Catholic."[27] But Protestantism's numerous creeds were obviously in conflict with each other. Furthermore, there were various interpretations of the creeds. Thus, the result of private interpretation is unbounded chaos and division upon division, which has been the story of Protestantism. Is there no alternative to the authoritarianism of the Roman Papacy on the one hand or the confusion of Protestantism on the other? To the Campbells, both father and son, there is. Whereas each man must come to his own understanding of the truth of God, no man is free to create his own interpretation of Scripture without regard for the understanding of the scholarship of the church through the centuries. Both Campbells had great confidence that the Scriptures were given to be understood by the application of normal human reason and principles of intelligent understanding. In later years, Alexander Campbell would often quote: *"Vox populi, vox dei"* (the voice of the people is the voice of God), not in the sense that the majority was always right, but that the overwhelming consensus of the thoughtful scholarship of the church *(the consensus fidelium)* must be respected in the search for truth, as it is unlikely that all of the people could be wrong all of the time. Dean Kershner comments:

> The first consideration which it is necessary to keep in mind in order to understand the doctrine of authority embodied in the *Declaration and Address* is the belief of its author in the substantial infallibility of what may be called "the common mind." Both Thomas and Alexander Campbell believed in a universal common reason which makes possible unity of thought on the part of individuals. This common reason or common mind, when applied to the Scriptures, would necessarily yield the same interpretation and in this way guarantee unity of thought and action. Both of the Campbells rejected the idea that any individual judgment with regard to the Scriptures should be considered authoritative, but they were assured that the judgment of the common mind or the universal reason could not be mistaken. Hence the Scriptures, interpreted as above indicated, constituted for them an infallible and universal authority.[28]

Thus, from its inception, the appeal of the Restoration Movement was not grounded in some esoteric new truth, as was the case with Mormonism or Christian Science in later years. Rather, its appeal was genuinely catholic. The right of each individual to do his own thinking is respected, but no individual is granted license to write off the best thinking of the consecrated minds of the church over the centuries. Here is an important balance between traditionalism and extreme individualism. When taken seriously, this balance encourages creative initiative in the pursuit of truth while at the same time providing an effective constraint against the tendency toward sectarian exclusiveness.

A second problem is posed by the *Declaration and Address* when it declares that the purpose of the Christian Association is to promote "simple evangelical Christianity" and "to support a pure gospel ministry that shall reduce to practice that whole form of doctrine, worship, discipline and government, expressly revealed and enjoined in the Word of God."[29] But when it comes to defining precisely what that simple evangelical Christianity is, it is found to be anything but a simple task. It had been pointed out that Campbell presupposed "that it is possible to define a simple evangelical Christianity, with a definite body of doctrine and a definite program of ordinances, worship, and government for the Church."[30] Such an assumption is seriously questioned by scholars of the New Testament today. In practice, every theology and every form of polity seeks Biblical justification. Despite the difficulties, the ideal of Biblical authenticity remains. Biblical scholarship of the past hundred and fifty years has provided an abundance of insight into the lives of the early Christians and into the cultural complexities of the various early Christian congregations. However, this has not destroyed the conviction shared by scholars of many different perspectives that the Biblical ideal is the rightful goal toward which the efforts of churchmen everywhere should strive.[31] Contemporary observers might want to state the aims that Campbell set forth for the association in somewhat different words, but the fundamental ideal of seeking Biblical sanction for the activities of the church remains largely unaltered. This is not to obscure the difficulties involved in pursuing the ideal; it is to affirm the necessity of espousing the ideal and recognizing the Biblical criteria on which all efforts in Christ's name must ultimately be evaluated.

A third problem arises out of the method that the *Declaration and Address* recommends for realization of the desired unity, namely restoration. It is often pointed out that restorationist emphases have been divisive, not unitive.[32] The theme of unity through restoration led Thomas Campbell to employ such phrases as "conform to the model and adopt the practice of the primitive church expressly exhibited in the New Testament" or "the New Testament is as perfect a *constitution*"[33] (italics not in the original). This language implies that there is a particular pattern for the church that can be found in the New Testament and can be reproduced in contemporary times. While the subscribers to the *Declaration and Address* are generally agreed as to the importance of fidelity to the New Testament for guidance in the life of the church, there has been no unanimity on any of the models or patterns of the church that have been discerned by students of the New Testament. Indeed, it must be acknowledged that efforts to enforce legalistically any particular pattern of organization or procedure have led to serious strife. Campbell's words must be understood for what he meant them to imply, and this can only be determined in the light of his subsequent conduct and that of his son and heir. To do so relieves these phrases of the rigid and uncompromising legalism that some, who have taken the phrases out of context and absolutized them, have espoused.

Many persons, then, have found genuine validity in the plea for restoring the faith and practices of the early church while also being aware of certain factors imposed by cultural differences between the the first century and now. These differences impose serious limitations on precisely what can and ought to be restored. It is possible to choose not to recognize these cultural differences, but it is not possible to escape them. Ultimately, the problem of the nature of the authority of Biblical example and precedent, *vis-a-vis* contemporary culture, must be faced by every serious student of the Scriptures. Campbell's plea for Protestantism to take its timeworn slogan *"sola Scriptura"* more seriously was timely and relevant.

A fourth problem that contemporary Christians discern with the *Declaration and Address* involves an insight that is of comparatively recent development. It can be pointed out that Thomas Campbell saw the causes of division in the body of Christ as primarily doctrinal, whereas divisions are now seen by many as primarily social in nature. Campbell could point to "human opinions" that were incorporated into creeds and imposed on the followers of Christ as the cause of the fractured fellowship of the church. Modern historians tend to regard the significant differences in the church to be more socioeconomic than doctrinal in nature.[34]

Before reaching any judgment on this problem, careful students will take care to avoid the anachronism of imposing judgments from the twentieth century on a situation prevailing at the beginning of the nineteenth. The fact of the matter is that the sharp socioeconomic stratification that modern industrialism has imposed on society and culture simply cannot be found on the American frontier at the beginning of the nineteenth century. Society was much more homogeneous than it is now. If Campbell's analysis may be criticized from today's perspectives as too simplistic, it must also be noted that he should not be faulted for failure to anticipate the impact of industrialization yet a century ahead. In fact, Thomas Campbell was acutely aware that political and other cultural factors were at the base of many of the church's schisms. He had encountered this in the Burgher/Anti-Burgher split in Ireland and was aware that this schism had been transferred to the United States where it was also irrelevant.

Very candidly, the seeker for unity in the body of Christ today must recognize the fact that, as society has become more complex, socioeconomic factors have both multiplied and intensified. Such candor does not invalidate Campbell's plea for his own times; it simply brings the problems of schism into clearer focus in our own times.

Before moving on from the *Declaration and Address,* several other items ought to be noted. One of these is the deliberate alteration of a well-known slogan to which Campbell must have given much thought. Rupert Meldenius,[35] a seventeenth-century German theologian who was repelled by the jangling theological controversies of Lutheran scholasticism, wrote an appeal for peace and unity in which he incorporated a phrase that would be oft quoted: *in necessariis unitas, in non necessariis libertas, in utrisque* (or *in omnibus*) *caritas.* (In essentials unity, in non-essentials liberty, in all things charity.) Meldenius undertook to define what was essential to be the New Testament, the early church, and the Augsburg Confession. Thomas Campbell was aware that the attempt by Meldenius or any other person to define what were the "essentials" was in effect drawing up a *de facto* creed. He wrote:

> We dare neither assume nor propose the trite indefinite distinction between essentials and non-essentials, in matters of revealed truth and duty: firmly persuaded that whatever may be their comparative importance, simply considered, the high obligation of the Divine authority revealing, or enjoining them, renders the belief or performance of them absolutely essential to us, in so far as we know them.[36]

Campbell thereby bypassed the temptation to delineate the "essentials" (that which is of the "essence" of Christianity) on which one is judged to be or not to be a Christian. The slogan was subsequently altered to say: "In faith, unity; in opinion, liberty, in all things, love." Though the former form is still used, the latter version is a more accurate representation of the position expressed in the *Declaration and Address.*

It is important, especially in the light of subsequent misunderstandings, to appreciate Campbell's position with respect to creeds. While denouncing their use as tests of fellowship and, thus, as the cause of divisions in the body of Christ, Campbell recognized that "theological exhibitions" have value for "the edification of the church," and that "the great system of Divine Truths (theology) and defensive testimonies in opposition to prevailing errors"[37] (apologetics) have their legitimate place in the church. In other words, a church that rejected an official creed should not be an amorphous entity devoid of theological perspective or depth. On this point, Campbell was explicit:

As to creeds and confessions, although we may appear to our
brethren to oppose them, yet this is to be understood only in *so far*
as they oppose the unity of the church, by containing sentiments not
expressly revealed in the word of God; or by the way of using them,
become the instruments of a human or implicit faith: or, oppress the
weak of God's heritage: where they are liable to none of these objections, we have nothing against them. It is the *abuse* and not the *law-
ful use* of such compilations that we oppose. [Italics in original.][38]

Thomas Campbell would have deplored two unfortunate conditions
of later years and denied that his disavowal of creeds as tests of
Christian communion had any reference to either tendency. These
are (1) the kind of empty reductionism that makes Christ, in some
vague, emotional sense, the least common denominator in a denominational union that denies the importance of the nature and content
of faith, and (2) the kind of anti-intellectualism that regards theological inquiry as extraneous to faith and resorts to simple proof texting
to solve life's problems with little regard for the contextual fabric
that gives meaning to any text. It can be shown that, where a carefully considered theological framework does not exist, the vacuum is
filled with some form of popular folk theology accepted unconsciously
and uncritically, and reinforced with randomly selected proof texts.
Such an alternative never appealed to Campbell as an acceptable
option to the creeds.

Some Presuppositions of the Declaration
and Address

In conclusion, note should be made of some of the presuppositions
of the *Declaration and Address*. These are many, and only the more
obvious ones can be discussed. Primary among the presuppositions is
the authority of the Scriptures in all matters pertaining to both the
life of the individual Christian and the body of Christians, the
church. In the case of the latter, it should govern both teaching (doctrine) and practice (ecclesiology). This idea was largely unchallenged
in 1809, but it has been severely questioned in this century.
    A second presupposition is that it is possible to discern "simple,
evangelical Christianity" without an admixture of "human opinion."
This kind of thinking was typical of the Enlightenment background
of Campbell's education, but it oversimplifies the problem by obscur-
ing what is quite evident to scholars of this day; that is, the subjective aspect of the human perspective. Today's student is fully aware
that no person is free from his or her own personal perspective and

bias. In fact, recent tendencies go so far in the opposite direction as to bring into question the possibility of serious communication between persons because words allegedly mean what the hearer determines their meaning to be. Such tendencies ultimately resolve themselves into such extreme individualism as would render useless the preaching of the gospel or question the possibility of communicating the faith.

A third presupposition, one that also arises from Enlightenment orientation, concerns the appeal to reason and common sense as the means for extracting "truths" from the Scriptures that would provide the incontrovertible basis for Christian union. Such a methodology was congenial both to the general intellectual climate of Thomas Campbell's day and to his own educational experience at Glasgow. It recommends itself to many of Campbell's followers at the present time, but it is clearly at variance with the more emotional religion that is attractive to the masses. Some have claimed that Campbell's method of Biblical hermeneutics leads to an intellectual religion that neglects the emotional dimension of Christianity altogether. This is not necessarily the case, but the criticism is widespread, especially in those circles where much emphasis centers upon religious experience.

Finally, it should be recognized that Campbell assumed that it would be possible to extract from the Scriptures a "simple, original form of Christianity,"[39] and, further, that "by simply returning to the original standard of Christianity, the profession and practice of the primitive church, as expressly exhibited upon the sacred page of the New Testament,"[40] the problem of divisions in the church would be solved. Thus, the postscript to the document suggests one of the tasks of the association should be to undertake the preparation of

> a catechetical exhibition of the fulness and precision of the holy scriptures upon the entire subject of christianity—an exhibition of that complete system of faith and duty expressly contained in the sacred oracles; respecting the doctrine, worship, discipline, and government of the christian church.[41]

Such an ambitious project was never undertaken, although Alexander Campbell's *Christian System* three decades later would approach its purpose. In more recent times, scholars have generally given up hope of finding a "simple, original form of Christianity" because they have recognized that such efforts usually reflect the conscious or unconscious presuppositions of the investigator. Indeed, this is clearly the case with Thomas Campbell, whose Enlightenment mode of thinking presupposed a primordial excellence that commends restoration.[42]

To cite some of the presuppositions of the *Declaration and Address* and note some of the problems that contemporary scholarship finds therein is not to discredit the document or to invalidate its main theme. The pressing need within Christendom today is for a unified witness with convincing power sufficient to cope with the secularized culture that has engulfed, and threatens to smother, the fragmented body of Christ. Furthermore, although the hermeneutical problems may be serious, it appears that no effort in behalf of Christian unity will be able to show much progress unless it can be seen to rest firmly upon a Biblical foundation.

The Brush Run Church

Armed with an amibitious program, the little body of Christians comprising the Christian Association of Washington, Pennsylvania, set themselves to undertake a herculean task. They published their document, built a meeting house, and waited for things to happen. Nothing did. Thomas's family had arrived in America, and young Alexander, having decided for the ministry, placed himself under his father's tutelage. Members of the association, not particularly welcome in the denominations whose existence they had come to question, met for worship at the log building they had erected. It soon became clear to them that it was one thing to advocate a "simple, original form of Christianity"; it was a greater challenge to give expression to the ideal in a functioning congregation. Accordingly, on May 4, 1811, the association constituted itself a church with Thomas Campbell as elder. Four deacons were chosen and Alexander was licensed to preach. This action fixed the ecclesiological pattern of the group squarely within a congregational polity. No outside authorization or consent was sought or deemed to be necessary for this act. Congregational theory holds that a body of believers is free to constitute itself into a church by its own intent, deriving its authority to do so directly from Christ.[43] In so doing, they set a precedent. Thenceforth, and until comparatively recent times, all of the churches in the Campbellian tradition have operated on a congregationally autonomous polity.

As a church, the little Brush Run congregation had no formal connection with any religious body. This was not to continue for long, primarily because the group was not characterized by a sectarian viewpoint that would cause them to believe that they were the only "true Christians" and henceforth privileged to exist in isolation from others. In fact, the very opposite idea prevailed; they longed for unity. A second factor that led them into a larger fellowship developed somewhat unintentionally when the members began to accept immersion as the Biblical form of baptism. When the group first enthusiastically approved the principle "Where the Scriptures speak, we speak; and where the Scriptures are silent, we are silent,"[44] the suggestion was put forward by "a shrewd Scotch Seceder," Andrew Munro, that it would mean the end of infant baptism.[45] At the time, Thomas Campbell, evidently unaware of the implications of the position, doubted that this would be the case. Considerable discussion followed during the next several months. The situation was brought to the point of decision early in 1812 when the first grandchild was born. Consistent with the newly adopted principle of fidelity to the Scriptures rather than traditional creeds or practices, Alexander undertook a serious, in-depth study of baptism as presented in the Bible. He examined the Greek usage of *baptizo* and concluded that it could mean only one thing—to immerse. The examples that he found in the New Testament confirmed this conclusion. Accordingly, he made arrangements with a Baptist preacher who lived nearby to baptize, not the infant daughter, but the parents. En route to the house of this preacher, one Matthias Luce, he stopped at his father's house and was surprised to learn that his sister, Dorothea, had been troubled about her baptism for some time and desired to be immersed. In the discussion of the matter with their father, they were surprised to meet with no serious objection, his only concern being that the occasion should be publicly announced in advance to the congregation at Brush Run. Wednesday, June 12, was selected as the day for baptism; the place, the deep hole in Buffalo Creek. When the group assembled, not only Alexander Campbell and his wife, but Thomas and his wife, and three other persons were prepared to be baptized. All were immersed into Christ by Mr. Luce upon simple confession of faith in Jesus Christ and without any recitation of an experience of conversion or an act of admission by a congregation.[46] These seven, in addition to three others whom Thomas Campbell had previously immersed at their own request, meant that ten of the members of the Brush Run Church had been immersed. At the next meeting of the congregation, thirteen more persons requested immersion and subsequently others followed so that soon "the great majority of the church speedily consisted of immersed believers, upon which, the other individuals who had been in the association abandoned the cause, being unwilling to follow the reformatory movement any further."[47]

The adoption of immersion was viewed as the logical and necessary consequence of the principles articulated in *The Declaration and Address*.[48] Alexander Campbell's thorough study of the subject equipped him to be an effective advocate of believer's baptism by immersion in the subsequent debates. This largely determined the position of the movement on this subject for the greater part of the century to follow.

The initiative that young Alexander displayed in taking this position on baptism caused his biographer to make this significant observation:

From the moment that Thomas Campbell concluded to follow his son in relation to baptism, he conceded to him in effect the guidance for the whole religious movement. As for himself, it was evident that he had previously accomplished his special mission in propounding and developing the true basis of Christian union.[49]

Thenceforth, Alexander was the undisputed leader, the man of decision, the person who could see how to cast into action the ideals that Thomas had spelled out.

Affiliation With Baptists

The adoption of immersion created a strong affinity with the Baptists in western Pennsylvania. They were relatively few in number and welcomed the prospect of reinforcement to their cause. As contacts with Baptists increased, the suggestion was made that the Brush Run Church unite with the Baptists as a member-congregation of the Redstone Baptist Association. Discussion followed over a period of more than a year. The agreement on the subject and form of baptism tended to obscure some very serious differences that were to emerge later and wreck this fellowship. However, bearing in mind that the purpose of the association was unity, not division, and having no desire for isolation, the decision was made to apply for membership in the Redstone Baptist Association. Thomas Campbell was pleased because the Brush Run Church was no longer an isolated body, but an accepted part of a larger body of the followers of Christ. This relieved his fear of creating yet another division in Christendom.[50] The Brush Run Church confronted the Redstone Association with an unusual problem. The Baptist Churches of the association had adopted the strongly Calvinistic Philadelphia Confession of Faith as the basis of their fellowship. The Brush Run Congregation was strongly opposed to such creeds. Accordingly, the Brush Run application for membership was accompanied by a long statement detailing their opposition to creeds and indicating their sole attachment to the Scriptures. A minority in the association, mostly preachers, opposed the admission of the Brush Run Church, but the majority prevailed. However, this relationship which began in 1813, would become increasingly difficult to maintain and would finally be terminated in 1825.[51]

Early in 1814, Thomas Campbell moved the larger portion of his family westward to the vicinity of Zanesville, Ohio. Thenceforth, he would remain active in the work of the reformation, but his role would be what his biographer terms "an able assistant" to the more vigorous work of his gifted son. The Ohio residence was brief, and he returned to Pennsylvania, where he spent the greater part of his remaining years assisting in the conduct of Buffalo Seminary, preaching and itinerating widely in the Western Reserve, and writing. He lived to see his family well established in the New World and the religious movement that he had initiated become a significant movement on the frontier. He witnessed the origin of a very influential journal and college under the leadership of his illustrious son. In 1835, his wife died, but Thomas lived an active life until January 4, 1854, a month short of his ninety-first birthday. The rather poor minister who came to America forty-six years earlier to seek improved health was rewarded abundantly beyond his power to hope or imagine.

End Notes

[1]Robert Richardson, *Memoirs of Alexander Campbell* (Philadelphia: Lippincott, 1868), Vol. I, p. 24. The words are Richardson's. An invaluable source of information on Thomas Campbell is found in Alexander Campbell's *Memoirs of Elder Thomas Campbell* (Cincinnati: Bosworth, 1891.)

For a good, more recent biography of Thomas Campbell, see Lester G. McAllister, *Thomas Campbell: Man of the Book* (St. Louis: Bethany Press, 1954).

[2]Richardson, op. cit., Vol. I, p. 22.

[3]Ibid., p. 23.

[4]For a brief but still useful account of this philosophic encounter, see Noah Porter, "Thomas Reid," *The Story of Scottish Philosophy*, David S. Robinson, ed. (New York: Exposition Press, 1961), pp. 118-150.

[5]The University of Chicago historians of the movement tend to place primary importance upon the influence of John Locke on both father and son. Frederick Kershner, Dean Walker, and the old Butler School of Religion school held that the Campbells reflect Scottish common-sense philosophy. For a detailed study of this issue, see James C.V. Emond, *A Consideration of the Thesis: There Was a Scottish "Common Sense" Thought Influence Relative to Alexander Campbell"* (Milligan College, TN: Emmanuel School of Religion, unpublished M.A.R. thesis, 1974).

[6]Richardson (op. cit., Vol I, p. 53) mistakenly assigns leadership of the secession move to Alexander Erskine. However, the correct designation is Ebenezer Erskine. Cf. McNeil, *The History and Character of Calvinism* (New York: Oxford University, 1954), pp. 356, 357.

[7]Richardson, op. cit., Vol. I, p. 61.

[8]Ibid., p. 69.

[9]See Henry C. Vedder, *A Short History of the Baptists* (Philadelphia: American Baptist Publication Society, 1907), pp. 223, 224.

[10]The description is that of Richardson, op. cit., Vol. I, p. 74.

[11]William Herbert Hanna, *Thomas Campbell, Seceder and Christian Union Advocate* (Cincinnati: Standard, 1935), pp. 39-43.

[12]Condensation of the charges by McAllister, op. cit., p. 78. For the full text, see Hanna, loc. cit.

[13]Hanna, op. cit., p. 48.

[14]W.E. Garrison, and A.T. DeGroot, *The Disciples: a History* (St. Louis:Christian Board of Publication, 1948), p. 138.

[15]The *Declaration and Address* has been reprinted many times.
Some of the more recent reprints are as follows: Indianapolis: International Convention of Disciples of Christ, 1949; Birmingham, England: the Berean Press, 1951; St. Louis: Bethany Press, 1955; Lincoln: Lincoln Christian College Press, 1959. Many editions omit the *Postscript,* which was not written when the *Declaration and Address* was first published.

[16]Frederick D. Kershner, *The Christian Union Overture* (St. Louis: Bethany Press, 1923).

[17]Thomas Campbell, *Declaration and Address* (St. Louis: Bethany Press, 1955), p. 25.

[18]Ibid., pp. 51, 52.

[19]Richardson, op. cit., Vol. I, p. 330.

[20]T. Campbell, op. cit., p. 28.

[21]Ibid., p. 29.

[22]Ibid., p. 34, 35.

[23]The tendency to view the New Testament as a "constitution" was part of the mentality of the early nineteenth century, which had a preoccupation with constitution making, according to Ronald Osborne, *The Reformation of Traditions* (St. Louis: Bethany Press, 1963), pp. 269, 270. The widespread use of this analogy led to an unfortunate legalistic method of interpreting the New Testament by later Disciples.

[24]The distinction between Old and New Testaments, suggested here, will be further elucidated by Alexander Campbell in his debate with John Walker in 1820, much to the displeasure of some of the Baptists whose cause he was defending. Many people at this date held to a "level Bible" concept; applying texts from either Testament to the church and making little, if any, distinction as to their Biblical context.

[25]T. Campbell, op. cit., p. 81.

[26]Ibid., p. 23.

[27]For a good discussion of this problem, see Kershner, op. cit., pp. 41-45.

[28]Ibid., p. 44. Here the influence of the Scottish common sense school of Thomas Reid and Dugald Stewart is easily discerned.

[29]T. Campbell, op. cit., pp. 24, 25.

[30]Garrison and DeGroot, op. cit., p. 149.

[31]A recent example is seen in the work of the Roman Catholic scholar Hans Kung. See *The Church* (New York: Sheed and Ward, 1967), especially the section on "The Fundamental Structure of the Church," pp. 107-260.

[32]See A.T. DeGroot, *The Restoration Principle* (St. Louis: Bethany Press, 1960). Also Garrett, op. cit., p. 10.

[33]T. Campbell, op. cit., p. 34.

[34]This is a twentieth-century trend by some historians who are impressed with the findings of Max Weber and Ernst Troeltsch in Germany. The latter's thesis, found in his *Social Teaching of the Christian Churches* (New York: Macmillan, 1931), has been adapted to the American scene by H. Richard Niebuhr, *Social Sources* (op. cit.), which has had wide influence on American religious historiography, especially that coming out of Yale University.

[35]Meldenius is a Latinized pseudonym for Peter Meiderlin (1582-1651). The phrase, found in his *Paroenesis* (1626), was quoted in Richard Baxter's *The True and Only Way of Concord of All the Christian Churches* (1680). Paul Johnson traces the phrase to the irenic Roman Catholic humanist George Cassander, who lived in Cologne in the 1560s (*A History of the Christian Church* [New York: Atheneum, 1977], p. 319).

[36]T. Campbell, op. cit., p. 36.

[37]Ibid., p. 46.

[38]Ibid., p. 59.

[39]Ibid., cf. Proposition V.

[40]Ibid., p. 77.

[41]The postscript was written after the December 14, 1809, meeting of the association and hence was not included in the original publication of the *Declaration and Address*. For this reason it is often not included in reprints. It may be found in 1908 Centennial reprint.

[42]For further consideration of this serious problem, see Richard T. Hughes, and C. Leonard Allen, *Illusions of Innocence, Protestant Primitivism in America, 1630-1875* (Chicago: University of Chicago Press, 1988).

[43]For a good discussion, see Smith, Handy, and Loetscher, op. cit., Vol. I, pp. 82ff. Note especially "Principles and Foundations of Christian Religion, 1605," by Henry Jacob, for the congregational concept of the church.

[44]Cf. Richardson, op. cit., Vol. I, p. 236.

[45]Ibid., p. 238.

[46]The service of baptism was no hurried event, nor was it a brief appendage to a service of worship. Thomas spoke at length of the reasons why he reached the decision to be immersed and was followed by a discourse on the Biblical teaching on baptism by Alexander. The meeting lasted seven hours. One of those present, Joseph Bryant, had to leave the gathering shortly after it began to attend a muster of soldiers for the War of 1812 against Great Britain. He attended to his military duties and returned in time to hear an hour's preaching and witness the baptisms.

[47]Some later Disciples have criticized the adoption of immersion as a retrogression. C.C. Morrison commented, "The fact is, and it can hardly be disputed by anyone who will face the full content of *The Declaration and Address,* that the Brush Run Church, in adopting the policy of immersionist exclusiveness, lapsed back that far into sectarianism ("The Essential Plea of the Disciples," *Christian Century,* April 25, 1912, p. 393). W.H. Garrison is less caustic in his evaluation when he notes:
> The adoption of immersion as an essential item in the proposed platform for union radically changed the program of the movement and its relation to the churches which were to be united. It had begun with the idea that all the churches had a common core of belief and practice which would have adequate basis of union if they would discard the divisive human opinions which they had woven around it. But now the reformers could no longer say, as Thomas Campbell had said in the *Address,* that all the churches are "agreed in the great doctrines of faith and holiness" and "as to the positive ordinances of Gospel institution: and that our differences, at most, are about the

things in which the kingdom of God does not consist." The achievement of union was no longer a matter of simply persuading the churches to unite upon things that they already held. Now, it was necessary to persuade them also to accept one positive ordinance, which only the Baptists believed to be commanded in the New Testament (Garrison and DeGroot, op. cit., pp. 160, 161).

[48]Richardson, op. cit., Vol. I, pp. 401, 402. Robert Richardson's evaluation is quite to the contrary of those noted above. Far from seeing the adoption of immersion as an impediment to the success of the movement, he tended to view it as a catalyst. Commenting on Thomas Campbell's comparative indifference to the question of baptism, he observes:

It is perhaps useless to speculate as to what might have been the result of the reformatory movement initiated by Thomas Campbell had he continued to insist upon the loose views he had previously entertained upon the subject of baptism. It is extremely doubtful if his well-meant efforts could ever have made any considerable impression upon the religious community at large (p. 400).

[49]Ibid., p. 401.

[50]Ibid., p. 458.

[51]There is confusion as to the exact date when the Brush Run Church was admitted into the Redstone Baptist Association. Richardson fixes the date at 1813 (Ibid., p. 438), but the minutes of the Redstone Baptist Association indicate that the church was admitted in 1815.

Chapter Four

Alexander Campbell: Early Years

Alexander Campbell, eldest son of Thomas and Jane Corneigle Campbell, was born on September 12, 1788, in County Antrim, Ireland. His father was a minister whose meager income needed to be supplemented by teaching, so it was quite natural that Alexander should come under his father's tutelage. Indeed, except for a brief period at an academy conducted by his uncles and a year spent at the University of Glasgow, his own father was his constant teacher and guide. As Alexander matured, he was able to assist his father in the school and, when Thomas left for America, Alexander, at the age of eighteen, was left in charge of the Academy at Rich Hill. Furthermore, in the absence of his father, Alexander shared with his mother the responsibility for caring for his sisters and two younger brothers until the family could be reunited in the New World. When the summons came for the family to join their father in America, they embarked on the perilous transatlantic voyage on October 1, 1808. A journey on the North Atlantic in a small sailing vessel late in the year was hazardous at best. A week after departure, the little ship was caught in a storm and driven on the rocks near the shore of the Isle of Islay off the coast of Scotland. In the crisis, the crew proved to be less than competent, and the passengers, mostly Irish-Catholic immigrants, were gripped with terror. Having been tossed about by the winds, the ship came to rest on a reef whose sharp rocks penetrated the hull. Since it was after 10:00 P.M. when the ship stuck fast, the peril was complicated and the fears compounded by darkness. After cutting the masts to allow the badly listing ship partially to right itself, there was nothing to do but sit out the black night amid the gale and crashing waves with the hope that dawn would break before the ship did. With the coming of day, the passengers were transferred to the shore with difficulty but no loss of life. The people of the island were friendly and hospitable, and the passengers were assisted in returning to the ill-fated *Hibernia* to recover such personal belongings as were not already washed overboard. Alexander's care in recovering and drying his books caught the attention of the chief owner of the island, Laird Campbell, and he subsequently took great interest in the youth.

Decision for Ministry

The harrowing shipwreck experience had the effect of clarifying Alexander Campbell's sense of the significant values of his life. Finding himself on the brink of death, he saw more clearly than ever before that there were matters of eternal importance compared to which much of human interest loses its significance. Where once a number of possibilities for his life's vocation claimed the consideration of the youth standing on the threshold of adulthood, all but one disappeared into the blackness of the stormy night of October 7 and 8, 1808. Standing on the slanting, storm-swept deck of the doomed ship, nothing seemed more important to him than preaching the gospel. He resolved that he would devote his life to the ministry. This was a firm, personal decision; Alexander Campbell never considered it to be a supernatural, divine "call."

Any attempt to continue the journey to America before spring of 1809 appeared to be unwise, so the decision was made to spend the winter in Glasgow. Alexander rejoiced at the opportunity of attending the university where his father had studied. Also, in Glasgow there was the prospect of dialogue with Greville Ewing, an eminent teacher who conducted a training school for lay preachers. Indeed, Campbell was furnished a letter of introduction to Greville Ewing by one of the residents of the Isle of Islay, and, when they arrived in Glasgow, Ewing proved to be most helpful in finding suitable lodging for the stranded family.

The university soon absorbed young Alexander's time. He plunged into the study of Greek, logic, and philosophy, and he continued his reading of French and English literature. A normal day began at 4:00 A.M. and ended at 10:00 P.M. His rather detailed diary (written in Latin) reveals that he read widely in an amazingly broad field.[1] That he developed a certain philosophic perspective while at the university seems to be beyond question, but the precise nature of this perspective is much disputed. It is fairly safe to say, however, that he was much impressed with inductive logic and empiricism.

Perhaps even more significant to the growing mind of the young prospective minister than the university studies were certain influences in the religious life of Glasgow to which he was exposed. Greville Ewing became a trusted friend and a stimulating source of religious ideas. Ewing had left the Presbyterian Church in 1800 and identified with evangelistic endeavors sponsored by James A. and Robert Haldane and spearheaded by the celebrated evangelist, Rowland Hill. The wealthy Haldane brothers built a number of tabernacles in major Scotch cities, and the congregations that gathered in them were constituted as Scotch Congregational Churches. The shortage of preachers for these congregations led to the opening of a school in Glasgow, which was conducted by Ewing. Students would gather at Ewing's house and engage in lively theological discussions, and Alexander Campbell often joined these parleys. In addition to conducting the school, Ewing preached in the Glasgow tabernacle, where Alexander regularly attended the Sunday evening service, the morning worship hour having been spent at the Seceder Presbyterian Church.

The discussions with Greville Ewing concerned exciting developments in the religious life of Scotland, and these raised all kinds of questions in the virile mind of the young inquirer. The writings of John Glas, who four decades earlier had launched a movement to separate the church from the control of the civil government and had emphasized the necessity of restoring the practice of primitive Christianity, had been introduced into Ewing's seminary. Glas's followers, subsequently led by his son-in-law Robert Sandeman, had emphasized weekly Communion and a plurality of elders. Some of these "Glassites" or "Sandemanians" accepted immersion and became the nucleus of the old Scotch Baptists.

Thus, the evangelical concern of the Haldanes and Rowland Hill, which had produced a Scotch Congregationalism, divided when the Haldanes accepted immersion. Young Alexander Campbell was caught in the midst of two streams. At the university and at the Seceder Church, he encountered the standard Reformed theology of the Westminster Confession variety. But in his associations with Greville Ewing and the Haldanes, he encountered very different concepts of church government, doctrinal authority, and ministry. These Scotch Independents placed very little importance on creeds and much weight on the Scripture and the examples of the early church. As Independents, they were not bound by the actions of synods or general assemblies. Robert Richardson, Campbell's associate and biographer, was convinced that the impact of the discussions in the Ewing circle on the growing mind of the young Campbell was considerable.[2] This was demonstrated in a spiritual crisis in the spring of 1809 when the time for the semiannual Communion of the Seceder Presbyterian Church arrived. All of Alexander's family loyalties were with this church, and he had no desire to separate from the body that had claimed the devotion and service of his father and had likewise nurtured him. But he could no longer give the Seceder Church his allegiance because he had concluded, not easily or willingly, that it did not represent the church of Christ as seen in the

New Testament. In this troubled state of mind, he obtained from the elders of the Seceder Church the necessary token that would admit him to Communion. On the appointed Sunday, he attended the service, but he hesitated until the last table of communicants before going forward. At last he went forward, depositing the metal token on the plate and departing without communing. Thus, "he renounced Presbyterianism for ever."[3]

Family Reunion in America

The university term having been completed in May, Alexander Campbell spent the months of June and July tutoring the children of several wealthy families in a nearby village. In August, passage was was obtained on an American vessel, and the family embarked for the New World. To the perils of the sea were added the uncertainties of those maritime conflicts arising from the Napoleonic wars that were shortly to involve the United States in the war of 1812. The two month's voyage was safely concluded despite some harrowing storms that tore away part of the ship's rigging and some leaks that required that passengers as well as crew take turns at the pumps. The ship landed in New York on September 29, 1809, and the family proceeded to Philadelphia, where arrangements were made to travel the last 350 miles over the mountains to Washington, Pennsylvania, by wagon. When they were ten days into their journey, they were surprised to meet Thomas Campbell on the road. He had intercepted them en route, bringing fresh horses to make the remainder of their journey easier. There was a joyful reunion of the family.

During the period of the family's separation, both father and son had experienced serious changes in their Christian understanding, and neither was aware of the spiritual pilgrimage of the other. With some caution and with measured phrases, Thomas Campbell disclosed to the family that he had parted from the Presbyterian Church and was associated with a body of believers who sought the abandonment of human creedal barriers to the unity of the followers of Christ and were pursuing a course of Christian activity on the principle: *Where the Scriptures speak, we speak; where the Scriptures are silent, we are silent.* Alexander was thrilled to learn of these developments and considerably relieved of his apprehensions as he recounted to his father the story of his own convictions about the need to follow the Bible examples more closely than the tradition of the Presbyterian Church would permit. Independently of each other, father and son had reached very similar conclusions. Alexander was shown the printer's proofs of the *Declaration and Address* and heartily endorsed the aims and proposals therein. He was delighted to observe his father's enthusiasm for the reformation that he was proposing. Alexander resolved to join in pursuing vigorously the aims of the Christian Association.

Once the family was settled, Alexander entered upon studies to equip himself for his life's greatest endeavor. His father again became his tutor and guide. A routine was adopted that provided for an hour each day to be given to the study of Greek, another to Latin, and a half hour to Hebrew. Two hours were devoted daily to study of a text of the Bible in the original language, and additional time was allotted for church history. In addition to spending six hours daily in his own study, three more hours were given to tutoring a friend and his own sisters. Such a heavy routine of study was unusual on the western Pennsylvania frontier, and the youthful Scot attracted the attention of some of the more observing of the settlers, including the publisher of the local newspaper, *The Reporter*. Soon Alexander was contributing a series of articles commenting on life and events in the community and published under a pseudonym. Thus began rather inconspicuously what was to be an extensive and highly influential publishing career.

Beginning of Ministry

Meanwhile, the rigorous study regimen was complemented by the activities of the Christian Association, many of whose members assembled every Lord's Day. The number of people who learned about the aims of the association and endorsed its purposes increased almost weekly. In the Spring of 1810, Alexander was asked to speak briefly to the congregation following a sermon by his father. This was the younger Campbell's first attempt at public address, and the response was so favorable that he was asked to deliver a full sermon. On July 15, he preached to a group that had assembled in a grove, taking for his text the closing portion of the Sermon on the Mount. It was apparent to all present that this youth of twenty-two was destined to be an outstanding public speaker. The warm response of the congregation was reassuring to the youth, and it confirmed his judgment that he must devote his life to the proclamation of the good news of Jesus Christ.

Immediately, the young preacher was asked to address gatherings of interested Christians, usually in the out-of-doors or in private homes. In the year following his first sermon, he preached 106 sermons. His sermons were marked by logical arrangement, exhaustive analysis of the Biblical text, and clarity of expression. His father was his mentor and took pains to ensure that young Alexander developed a good homiletic method.[4]

The interest that the Christian Association was generating in and around Washington, Pennsylvania, was causing a problem. By intent, the association was not to be a church, as the *Declaration and Address* had explicitly stated. There was no desire to add yet another to the already excessive supply of religious parties within Christendom. Actually, the purpose of the Association was to create a movement to work within existing bodies to bring about reform and thereby achieve Christian unity. As a body, the association was to meet only semiannually. But practical necessity required another course. Thomas Campbell was unwelcome in the Presbyterian Church because of his lack of enthusiasm for the creed. The same could be said for the others who endorsed the views expressed in the *Declaration and Address.* The result was that they found themselves meeting for fellowship and worship not semiannually but weekly. The group was taking on the character of a church, a distant body of people who were not in fraternal relations with any other body, an anti-party party. This caused Thomas Campbell great distress. How could he plead for the union of Christians when he was in fellowship with nobody? At the encouragement of a ministerial colleague, he sought fraternal relations with the non-Seceder branch of the Presbyterians but was rebuffed. There was nothing else to do but recognize the fact that the weekly fellowship was in reality a church. Accordingly, and contrary to its original intent, the Christian Association of Washington, Pennsylvania, constituted itself a church in May, 1811, as noted in chapter 3. Thomas Campbell was appointed elder and Alexander was licensed to preach. Four deacons were chosen and, on the following Lord's Day, the first Communion service was held.

This was a momental step because it reflected certain important presuppositions in the thinking of the group. One had to do with the nature of "church." They acted on the assumption that a church can come into being when a body of believers intends so to constitute itself; that it is not dependent upon recognition from any governmental or ecclesiastical body but is *ipso facto* body of Christ by self-constitution. This is consistent with the old Anabaptist understanding of the church, and it fit perfectly into the freedom of the American frontier. Also implicit in this action was the concept that a local body was competent as the whole church of Christ and thus could not only select but also license and ordain its ministry without recognition or approval from other congregations. This concept of the adequacy of the congregation to exercise all of the functions of the church would become a basic characteristic of the reform efforts that eventually would stem from this beginning, to the considerable distress of some of its later adherents.

A month after the association became a church, on June 16, 1811, the congregation met for the first service in an unfinished log building located near Brush Creek. Alexander Campbell preached the first sermon. There were thirty-eight members. The worship services and weekly Communion resembled those of the Scotch Independents (Haldanes) who had been so important a factor in the Campbells' thinking to this point.

The reluctance of Thomas Campbell to take the step of bringing a separate church into being has already been noted.[5] The question has frequently been raised since: Was this a mistake? Did the movement become a denomination by this act? Two very important factors would suggest a negative answer to these questions. The first is the fact that a very real bond of faith and purpose had made of these people a viable religious community. This fact alone does not justify a separate congregational existence. All kinds of common interests may bind Christians into subgroups within any given congregation. But when a denomination becomes hostile to one of its subgroups within and refuses to tolerate its existence or sustain fraternal relations, there remains little in the way of alternative to constituting a separate identity. This was the reality that the Christian Association confronted.

The second factor that suggests the wisdom and necessity of separate existence is more positive in nature. Here was a group of people with a distinct plea, namely to create a truly catholic type of Christianity (restoration of simple, primitive faith and practice) and offer this as the basis for reuniting the broken body of Christ. But it is one thing to talk about this aim; it is something else to exemplify it. The time had come for ideas to become concrete, for propositions to be made actual and be proven realistic. Who can fault these people for the very natural longing to demonstrate the truth that they espoused? It is easy to be critical of the nonsectarian sect or the anti-denomination denomination,[6] but it is much more difficult to justify a plea that is never implemented or to prescribe a more viable course of action in these circumstances.

In the fall of 1810, while delivering some books that Thomas Campbell had offered to loan Mr. John Brown, a neighbor, Alexander Campbell met Margaret Brown. A courtship developed, which led to marriage on March 12, 1811. A year and a day later, their first child was born.[7] This event precipitated the examination into the Biblical concept of baptism previously noted (chapter 3) and the congregation's adoption of immersion as the Biblical mode. The initiative in this was taken by Alexander and, henceforth, in Richardson's judgment, the leadership of the movement rested primarily with the younger Campbell.[8] Alexander Campbell was ordained by the Brush Run congregation on January 1, 1812.

Following his marriage to Margaret Brown, Alexander Campbell lived on a farm belonging to his father-in-law. When many members of the Brush Run Church made plans to move west to Ohio in the Spring of 1814, Mr. Brown, not wanting to see his only daughter move away, deeded the farm to Alexander as an inducement for his family to remain at Bethany. To his study and preaching endeavors, Campbell added the care and management of this farm, an enterprise at which he was to prove so successful financially that he was able throughout his life to carry out an earlier resolution never to accept any compensation for preaching the gospel. The original house, which Alexander Campbell enlarged several times, has been preserved to the present day.

The Brush Run Church was located in the open country several miles from any town. Some of its members had moved to Charlestown (now Wellsburg, West Virginia) on the Ohio River. They had been meeting in the courthouse and, at Campbell's suggestion, they undertook the construction of a church building. On a tour of the East to collect money for this building, Campbell made friends of many of the religious leaders in that part of the country. The Brush Run Church no longer exists, so the church at Wellsburg is the oldest congregation of the Restoration Movement.

Early in 1818, Alexander Campbell opened a school in his home. It was designed primarily for young men in the hope that they could be enlisted to forward the cause of reforming the churches, but young women were also enrolled. Buffalo Seminary flourished for a number of years but never accomplished all that Campbell had hoped. Thomas Campbell was engaged to assist in the school when he returned from Kentucky in 1819. He had been conducting a thriving school there when he learned that the laws of the state forbade him to teach or otherwise address slaves except in the presence of white witnesses. He found slavery in Kentucky so repugnant that he returned to Brooke County, Virginia, where slavery, though legal, was rare and comparatively humane.[9]

Difficulties With the Baptists

The circumstances that led Alexander Campbell to undertake a serious and extensive study of baptism in the New Testament, and the subsequent immersion of many of the members of the Brush Run Church leading to the affiliation of the Brush Run congregation with the Redstone Baptist Association, has been previously noted (chapter 3). Campbell was impressed by the Baptist people because they seemed eager to study the Bible, but he had a very low opinion of the Baptist clergy because they appeared to be ignorant and bigoted.[10] There were ministers in the association who were discerning enough to recognize that many of Campbell's views were not standard Baptist, and they set out to expose his heresy. Smoldering discontent came to a head at the annual meeting of the Redstone Association at Cross Creek in August, 1816. Steps had been taken to exclude Alexander Campbell from the program, much to the dislike of some of the constituency who wanted to hear him. However, when one of the scheduled preachers became ill, Campbell was asked to step in, and the demand was so insistent that he could not be excluded. The young preacher spoke directly to the issues that had been quietly discussed, and he preached one of his most famous sermons.[11] The "Sermon on the Law" was an exposition of Romans 8:3, in which Paul says: "For what the law could not do, in that it was weak through the flesh, God sending his own Son in the likeness of sinful flesh, and for sin, condemned sin in the flesh" (King James Version). Herein Campbell pointed out that Paul used the term *law* to represent the Mosaic Covenant, which was inadequate to save men and had thus been displaced by a New Covenant. This New Covenant was mediated by Jesus Christ and is the basis of the Christian religion. Thus, a distinction was drawn between the Old and New Testaments that the Baptist preachers of that day were not accustomed to making. They were irritated by some of Campbell's conclusions, particularly the suggestion that Christians are not bound by the laws of the Old Testament and that ceremonies and customs and holy days found in the Old Testament provide no warrant for Christian custom or practice. (Here Campbell anticipated the positions he would take in his first debate on baptism.) This seemed to some like stark antinomianism. How could Sunday worship be maintained if the fourth commandment were no longer binding? What would happen to the morals of the nation if the Decalogue were undermined? It mattered little to them that Campbell had observed that "whatever was excellent in the Law" was incorporated into the kingdom of Christ. The law-keeping mentality of some of the Baptist preachers would not hear the message of the text.

These men were further offended by Campbell's conclusion that "there is no necessity for preaching the law in order to prepare men for receiving the gospel."[12] For generations, Calvin's followers had accepted his idea that the continuing function of the law was to convict men of sin and acquaint them of their lost estate.[13] This generated a steady barrage of hell-fire and brimstone sermons on the frontier. But Campbell noted that Jesus Christ commissioned His disciples to preach to mankind the good news and to teach them what He had commanded. Campbell further observed that, in all of the sermons in the book of Acts, there is "not one word of law-preaching in the whole of it . . . not one precedent of preaching the law to prepare their hearers, whether Jews or Gentiles, for the reception of the gospel."[14]

Few people today would disagree with the theses of the "Sermon on the Law," so it is difficult for the contemporary mind to understand the shock waves the sermon created in the Redstone Baptist Association. Cries of heresy were heard, and an attempt at formal condemnation was being planned for the next annual meeting of the association. Henceforth, many churches were closed to Alexander Campbell, and every effort was made by a small group within the association to limit and counteract his influence.

At the same meeting of the Redstone Association at which Alexander Campbell preached the "Sermon on the Law," Thomas Campbell presented an application from a small congregation in Pittsburgh for admission into the association. Like the Brush Run Church, this congregation had disavowed any creedal basis of fellowship in favor of the simple New Testament confession of faith. The application was rejected because it was "not presented according to the constitution of the Association" which required a creedal statement. Commenting on this, W.E. Garrison observed: "The Brush Run Church had been accepted on a 'Bible alone' basis, but it [the Redstone Association] seems to have felt that one such church was all that the Association could stand."[15]

Alexander Campbell (1788-1866), primary leader of the reformation in the nineteenth century, editor of the *Christian Baptist* (1823-1830) and the *Millennial Harbinger* (1830-1866), first president of the American Christian Missionary Society, and first president of Bethany College.

The persistent efforts of the orthodox Baptist faction in the Redstone Association to brand Alexander Campbell with the label of a heretic made for continuing unpleasant situations. The printed *Sermon on the Law* was used as the basis for heresy charges that were advanced annually in the Redstone Association. The anti-reform antagonists were persistent and, by 1823, were confident that they were strong enough to dislodge Campbell. But Campbell preempted their plot by transferring his church membership to the church at Charlestown. This congregation was affiliated with another Baptist association and hence was no longer within reach of the Redstone opponents. Most of the congregations belonging to the Mahoning Baptist Association were found in Ohio and seemed to be much less committed to fixed Baptist dogma than those of Redstone.

The Campbell-Walker Debate

No small cause of the agitation against Alexander Campbell within the Redstone Association arose, curiously, from his success in defending the immersionist position in his first debate, held at Mt. Pleasant, Ohio, in June of 1820. The Baptists of that vicinity had been active in persuading an unusual number of Presbyterians to be immersed, and the Presbyterian minister reacted with a series of sermons in defense of infant baptism. In the course of the discussions that followed, John Walker, the Presbyterian minister, issued a challenge to the Baptist minister, or any other person whom he might choose, to debate the subject of baptism. Feeling himself to be unequal to the challenge, the Baptist minister appealed to Alexander Campbell to defend the Baptist position. Doubting whether such a debate would be useful in furthering the cause of truth, Campbell was reluctant to consent. But the appeals were urgent and repeated, and he finally agreed. Mt. Pleasant, Ohio, was only twenty-three miles from Campbell's home.

The terms of the debate were agreed and the first topic to be discussed was the fundamental one of who is a proper *subject* for baptism. This was to be followed by a discussion of the proper *mode* of baptism. Each speaker was to have forty minutes, and the debate was to continue as long as there was interest in it or until the moderators concluded that enough had been said.

John Walker set forth his position in his opening statement:

> I maintain that baptism came in the room of circumcision; that the covenant on which the Jewish Church was built, and to which circumcision is the seal, is the same with the covenant on which the Christian Church is built, and to which baptism is the seal; that the Jews and the Christians are the same body politic under the same lawgiver and husband; hence the Jews were called the congregation of the Lord; and the Bridegroom of the Church says, "My love, my undefiled is one"—consequently the infants of believers have a right to baptism.[16]

Campbell was quick to challenge the presupposition behind this statement, namely that there is no significant difference between the Old Covenant and the New Covenant. This supposition sees Christianity merely as an extension of Judaism and reverts often to the law to find legal basis for Christian dogmas or practice. Such a viewpoint, though scarcely to be found today, was widespread and popular in the early nineteenth century. It was especially characteristic of Calvinistic bodies such as Presbyterians and Baptists, who emphasized God's immutable, divine decrees. Hence, Sunday worship was justified by the Sabbath law and customs of the Jewish nation while Christian morality was justified by an appeal to the Decalogue. This type of thinking tended to see baptism as a Christian extension of Jewish circumcision and thus a symbolic act of admission into spiritual Israel. This was the heart of Walker's argument, and it led him to insist that infants were proper subjects of baptism and hence must have been included in the four cases of "household" baptism in the New Testament.

The view of the Bible that tends to obliterate the distinction between the two Testaments was first challenged by Johannes Coecceius and Witsius in the seventeenth century in Holland. They abandoned the Calvinist doctrine of the unchangeable nature of divine law and recognized that divine law actually does change because the Bible sets forth several successive covenants, each of which is unique and manifests its own characteristics. These covenants are not unrelated, but they are different. Covenants were made with Noah, Abraham, Moses, and finally the one made by Jesus Christ. The thesis of the epistles to the Galatians, the Romans, and the Hebrews could be cited to indicate that Christians are not under the law. Consequently, any argument that is based upon an analogy with a custom that prevailed in another covenant is without validity as a basis for a Christian institution. The meaning and purpose of baptism must be located within the context of the New Covenant and not understood as an extension of a rite of Judaism. Of course, Alexander Campbell was quick to note that circumcision included no reference to forgiveness of sin or the promise of the Holy Spirit,[17] both of which were promised in baptism.

Walker seemed not to know how to deal with Campbell's devastation of his thesis except to reaffirm it. This gave Campbell opportunity to reiterate the basic distinctions of the covenants. When Walker cited quotations from the church fathers to support paedobaptism, Campbell pointed out that there was no record of the practice for the first 150 years of Christian history, and the earliest mention of it was by Tertullian (c. 216), who disapproved. This gave Campbell an opportunity to elaborate on the need for a reformation of the churches that would eliminate traditions for which no precedent could be found in the Bible.

Eventually, the debate turned to the second topic—the proper mode of baptism. Here Walker affirmed that pouring and sprinkling were Scriptural modes of baptism, that "in water" may be rendered "with water," the instrumental use of εν (en), and that βαπτιζω (baptizo) did not necessarily mean "to dip" because it is used in some places in the sense of "to wash." Campbell responded to this argument by citing a number of lexicographers and commentators, including a number of paedobaptists, to establish the meaning of this Greek word. He went on to insist that the church has no authority to alter the "form" of a positive ordinance because the form or act is the very thing that is commanded. Man's duty is not to rationalize, but to obey.

The debate was a new experience for Alexander Campbell, and he hastened to publish it. It is important to note the impact of this debate both on the public and on Campbell himself. On the latter, Richardson notes:

> During the progress of this discussion he seems to have become more and more favorable to such methods of public disputation—a result partly due, perhaps, to the easy triumph over his opponent, and his growing consciousness of the possession of powers peculiarly adapted to such encounters, but still more to the conviction that they afforded a favorable means of diffusing amongst the people a knowledge of those religious principles to which he was himself devoted.[18]

Campbell closed the debate with Walker by issuing a challenge to any paedobaptist minister to debate the subject of baptism.[19] The interest aroused by the discussions soon exhausted the first edition of 1,000 copies of the debate, and 3,000 additional copies were printed. Publication was opening up a wider audience to the young reformer, and he found that it was an inviting means of expanding the scope of his influence.

The impact of the debate on others varied greatly. Most of the Baptists believed that their cause had been gloriously upheld. But a few, the ones who found fault when the same views were set forth in the Sermon on the Law, recognized that this young reformer was not standard-brand Baptist. They redoubled their efforts to expel him from their association.

The debate had introduced Alexander Campbell into a new community of Baptist churches and preachers. Among the latter, two were anxious to hear more from the stimulating young thinker, particularly on the matter of the succession of the covenants. Adamson Bently and Sidney Rigdon, of Warren, Ohio, came to Bethany in the summer of 1821. They engaged Campbell in conversation all night, advised him of the organization of the Mahoning Association, and urged him to visit the churches, assuring him of their enthusiastic interest. He had also become acquainted with some Haldanian Scotch Baptists in Pittsburgh, where his father had ministered. A small congregation had formed there under the guidance of George Forrester, an immigrant from Scotland who conducted an academy in Pittsburgh. Forrester had made a convert of another Scotch immigrant, a graduate of the University of Edinburg named Walter

Scott. Scott was persuaded to assist Forrester in conducting the academy in Pittsburgh, and, when the latter drowned, Scott found himself heir to both the school and the ministry of the little congregation. One of the pupils of the school was Robert Richardson, who was destined to make a significant contribution to later developments of the movement as physician, professor of chemistry at Bethany College, editor, and biographer of Alexander Campbell. Scott's restless, inquiring mind led him to explore with a consuming interest the insights and understandings of Alexander Campbell. The two men, in many ways quite different, became fast friends and respectful co-laborers. Walter Scott was to contribute immeasurably to the success of the Restoration Movement by providing the essential features of its evangelistic methodology. More of this will be detailed in chapter 5.

The Christian Baptist

As has been previously noted, the debate with John Walker and its subsequent publication caused Alexander Campbell to see the wider possibilities of promoting the reform of Christianity through the press. He conceived the idea of a periodical and decided to name it the *Christian*. Walter Scott advised him to incorporate the name "Baptist" into the title if he hoped to circulate it among the Baptist churches; hence the title: the *Christian Baptist*. The prospectus stated the policy of the periodical as follows:

> The "Christian Baptist" shall espouse the cause of no religious sect, excepting that ancient sect "called Christians first at Antioch." Its sole object shall be the eviction of truth and the exposing of error in doctrine and practice. The editor, acknowledging no standard of religious faith or works other than the Old and New Testament, and the latter as the only standard of the religion of Jesus Christ, will, intentionally at least, oppose nothing which it contains and recommend nothing which it does not enjoin. Having no worldly interest at stake from the adoption or reprobation of any articles of faith or religious practice, having no gift nor religious emolument to blind his eyes or to pervert his judgment, he hopes to manifest that he is an impartial advocate of truth.[20]

The *Christian Baptist* was given to a scathing exposé of what its editor conceived to be the accumulated debris of centuries of Christian history. The chief object of his denunciation was the clergy with its presumed dignities, privileges, and usurpations of the honor and power that rightfully belonged to Christ. He portrayed the clergy as money-hungry and vainglorious in a series of five articles in the first volume of the periodical.[21] A biting satire of the clergy appeared under the heading, "The Third Epistle of Peter."[22] He ran a series of articles on "A Restoration of the Ancient Order of Things,"[23] in which he examined the existing state of religion and compared it to the church in the New Testament, finding the former sadly lacking. He examined the various creeds and found reasons to reject all of them. Some of his bitterest invective was reserved for an innovation that was gaining currency among frontier denominations at that very time—the missionary society. Although he would later change his mind about them, the first volume of the *Christian Baptist* portrays these societies as clever devices to extract funds from the faithful in callous disregard of the missionary method found in the New Testament.[24]

The reformatory zeal displayed by the youthful editor of the *Christian Baptist* has been characterized as iconoclastic by one Disciple historian, who also notes, "Mr. Campbell was not the last among the Disciples who could be courteous in speech but vitriolic in print."[25] One reader of the journal called Campbell's attention to the fact that: "Forbearance is certainly a christian [sic] grace, strongly recommended by both precept and example, in the word of God" and noted that the very capable editor was "as a man, in private circles, mild, pleasant, and affectionate; as a writer, rigid, satirical, beyond all the bounds of scriptural allowance."[26]

Campbell accepted the criticism in good grace, acknowledged its validity, and simply noted that "if the apostles were on earth now, and were to write on the present state of things in christendom, their writings would appear to be very different in spirit from those which they wrote when first declaring God's philanthropy in the gift of his Son."[27]

The wide circulation of a periodical as critical as the *Christian Baptist* had an unsettling effect on the Baptist churches.[28] The later volumes of the publication contain letters that indicate a growing hostility on the part of many Baptists, which reached its climax in separation from the Baptists and cessation of publication of the *Christian Baptist* with its seventh volume in July of 1830. Prior to this date, however, there were several important developments that deserve mention.

While on a visit among Baptist churches in Kentucky in 1824, Alexander Campbell met Barton W. Stone, leader of the "Christians" of Kentucky. The similarity of interest was noted by both men. Two years later (1826), Stone began publication of the *Christian Messenger* and, the following year, initiated editorial correspondence with Campbell on the doctrine of Trinity. Campbell wisely turned aside from lengthy discussion by noting that the doctrine of Trinity, like its Arian counterpart, was neither Scriptural nor rational.

The Campbell-McCalla Debate

In May of 1823, while preparing the first issue of the *Christian Baptist*, Alexander Campbell received a letter from W.L. McCalla, a Presbyterian minister in Augusta, Kentucky, who accepted the challenge to debate the subject of baptism, which Campbell issued at the close of the debate with Walker. A lengthy and sometimes harsh correspondence ensued before the terms were settled for the debate, which was to be held in Washington, Kentucky, near Maysville, in October, 1823. The Ohio River was the main artery of transportation into the frontier regions in that day, but the river level that fall was too low for steamboat navigation. Campbell, then, was obliged to travel three hundred miles on horseback to reach the site. Sidney Rigdon accompanied him and served as a recorder of proceedings, anticipating their publication.

From the beginning of the discussion, Campbell made it quite clear that the meaning and purpose of baptism were to be found, not in the Old Testament, but in the New. He then proceeded to demonstrate from the New Testament that faith was a prerequisite for baptism. But whereas the Walker debate had centered on the subject and mode of baptism, the debate with McCalla focused on the purpose of baptism. Campbell could not overlook the fact that baptism in the New Testament is closely associated with remission of sins. In a very significant statement, to which he would later refer and which would be indelibly impressed on his followers, Campbell argued that a close tie must inevitably be recognized between baptism and the whole matter of salvation.

> I know it will be said that I have affirmed that baptism saves us. Well, Peter and Paul have said so before me. If it was not criminal in them to say so, it cannot be criminal in me. When Ananias said unto Paul, "Arise and be baptized, and wash away thy sins, calling upon the name of the Lord," I suppose Paul believed him and arose and was baptized, and washed away his sins. When he was baptized, he must have believed that his sins were now washed away in some sense that they were not before. For, if his sins had been already, in every sense, washed away, Ananias' address would have led him into a mistaken view of himself, both before and after baptism. Now, we confess that the blood of Jesus Christ alone cleanses us who believe from all sins. Even this, however, is a metaphorical expression. The efficacy of his blood springs from his own dignity and from the appointment of his Father. The blood of Christ, then, really cleanses us who believe from all sin. Behold the goodness of God in giving us a formal token of it, by ordaining a baptism expressly "for

the remission of sins." The water of baptism, then, formally washes away our sins. The blood of Christ really washes away our sins. Paul's sins were really pardoned when he believed, yet he had no solemn pledge of the fact, no formal acquittal, no formal purgation of his sins until he washed them away in the water of baptism [italics in original].[29]

The debate continued for seven days, during which McCalla sought to strengthen his cause by charging Campbell with subverting morality and undermining the Sabbath, an obvious reference to the latter's views on the separation of Jewish and Christian covenants. He also charged that Campbell was opposed to sending the gospel to the heathen, which Campbell quickly denied. At one point, McCalla was reprimanded by the moderator for using slanderous language. The debate did much to win popular support for the practice of believer's baptism,[30] and both Campbell's influence and the circulation of the *Christian Baptist* were greatly increased in Kentucky and southern Ohio. Campbell, who had entered the arena of debate with reluctance, was now persuaded that public debates were a valuable "means of propagating the truth and of exposing error."[31] Thereafter, wherever Alexander Campbell traveled and spoke, an audience was assured. From this time until the end of his life, he would be "in journeyings often," and his circle of associates as well as his reputation would grow. Important new acquaintances included Philip S. Fall of Louisville, John T. Johnson of Georgetown, and the itinerant evangelist "Raccoon" John Smith.

The Nature of Faith

In addition to writing irritating articles on the matters of clergy-domination of the churches and the un-Biblical nature of missionary societies, the editor of the *Christian Baptist* addressed himself to another subject of controversy on the frontier: the matter of religious experience as evidence of conversion. Here Campbell was touching the nerve center of popular frontier revivalism. The prevailing practice of evangelizing the scattered settlements required a hell-fire type preacher to prey upon the emotions of the hearers, exhorting them to cast themselves on the mercy of God at the mourner's bench and there await the sign of their redemption, which was identified with deep emotional trauma. Such evangelistic methods were common to both Calvinist and Arminian denominations. They differed in their interpretations of what was happening and why, but they all used the same means and sought the same end in the frontier revivals. Campbell fearlessly called into question the validity of such religious experience as a mark of conversion[32] and prerequisite to baptism. He insisted that feelings and emotional experiences could be misleading and ephemeral, and such provides no adequate basis for faith, pointing rather to the witness of the Biblical record as the sufficient and only adequate foundation for the Christian faith. In doing this, however, he alienated many who were impressed with popular revivalism. But he won the confidence of thoughtful persons to whom the weakness of such techniques had become painfully apparent. Campbell's rejection of popular revivalism, however, was not merely a repudiation of a technique of crowd manipulation that preyed on the emotionally unstable and produced conversions that were likewise superficial and correspondingly unstable. Campbell's rejection of frontier revivalism was rooted in his understanding of the nature of faith itself. He understood faith to be a matter of responsible judgment that a person makes on the basis of evidence that he confronts. His position was clearly set forth in the first volume of the *Christian Baptist*.

> Evidence alone produces faith, or testimony is all that is necessary to faith. This is demonstrably evident in every case; and therefore the certainty felt is always proportioned to the character of the testimony produced. Faith is capable of being greatly increased in many instances; but only in one way, and that is, either by affording additional evidence, or by brightening the evidences already produced.—To exhort men to believe, or to try to scare them into faith by loud vociferations, or to cry them into faith by effusions of natural or mechanical tears, without submitting evidence, is as absurd as to try to build a house or plant a tree in a cloud.
>
> . . . .
>
> The term *faith* is used in the Bible in the commonly received sense of mankind, and the faith which we have in the testimony of God differs from that we have in the testimony of men in this one respect only—that as men may be deceived, and may deceive others, so the confidence we repose in their testimony, in some instances, may be very limited; but as God cannot be deceived himself, neither can deceive others, so the confidence we have in his testimony is superior to that we repose in the testimony of men; and as the word comes to us in demonstration of the Holy Spirit, or attested to us by the supernatural gifts which accompanied the testimony of the original witnesses; so it affords the highest possible evidence, and therefore produces the greatest confidence.[33]

Faith thus is primarily a rational process. It comes when one who has heard the word of Christ is led to certain conclusions about Him, based on the evidence provided. Such a concept of faith did not win

the approval of those who held that faith was a gift of God reserved
for those whom God elected for salvation but who were otherwise
too depraved to believe. It recognized no agony or trauma, only an
open mind and a readiness to exercise it. It presupposed that all
men, though sinful, were possessed with sufficient cognitive capacity to recognize truth and sufficient volitional power to make responsible conclusions and act thereupon. Such presuppositions were
based on an empirical epistemology.[34] Campbell held that all human
knowledge is derived from sensory perception, including man's
knowledge of the divine truth that is the foundation of faith. His
position is clearly articulated in the following excerpt from the 1828
Christian Baptist.

> The inlets of all human knowledge are the five senses. Reflection
> upon the ideas thus acquired gives birth to new ones, akin, however,
> to those received by sensation. Imagination may now combine these
> ideas without any restraint but its own power. It may associate
> those ideas with, or without regard, to natural fitness, congruity, or
> consistency. It may create a Polyphemus or a Centaur; but it cannot
> create an idea perfectly new. As human skill and human power may
> new modify, but cannot create a particle of matter; so the imagina-
> tion may vary or new modify the ideas acquired by sensation, but
> cannot create a new one.[35]

Campbell's empirical concept of faith places great emphasis upon
the historical nature of revelation and upon the Bible as the trust-
worthy record of the revelatory events. This predetermined his
approach to the Scriptures as well as the nature of his preaching. It
meant that all who shared this view would not only seek a reformation of the church *per se* but would advocate a new understanding of
the nature of faith, a new concept of evangelism, and a new view of
the Bible. It is no wonder that some of the more discerning Baptists
held that Mr. Campbell was not true to their heritage and ought
therefore to be expelled. By the close of 1828, events were moving
rapidly toward that end. Within two years, virtually all of the ties
with the Baptists would be severed.

Separating from the Baptists was more of a process than an
event. Serious doctrinal differences had surfaced, but whether these
were of such weight as to warrant schism is another matter.[36] Few
Baptists today would hold positions seriously different from those
advocated by Alexander Campbell, a vocal minority to the contrary
notwithstanding. Personal animosities and a persistent effort at
heresy hunting bore its fruit, and the consequent breakdown of personal relationships rendered continued Christian fellowship impractical. The initiative in separation generally rested with the orthodox
Baptists in the various associations, and the technique was often

that of adopting resolutions that pronounced "anathemas" on certain viewpoints as justification for excluding the undesired congregations. Such actions were not generally in keeping with historic
Baptist principles, but they were effective at this time. Accordingly,
ten churches in the Redstone Association excluded thirteen congregations in 1825.[37] The Tates Creek Association in Kentucky followed suit when ten churches expelled sixteen reforming
congregations. Perhaps the most widely known case is that of the
Beaver Association of western Pennsylvania, which adopted a resolution of excommunication of the reforming Mahoning Association,
spelling out several "errors." Campbell called these charges "a tis-
sue of falsehoods."[38] This action set a pattern that was followed by
several other associations, some of which modified the Beaver
Anathema or added to the charges. Acrimonious conflict was bearing its inevitable fruit in schism. Soon the reformers could no longer
be considered to be Baptists. Campbell found that the followers of
Jesus were called "disciples" in the Bible and readily accepted this
term to refer to the reformers.

Trouble with the more sectarian orthodox Baptists did not curtail
Alexander Campbell's amazing productivity during these years. At
least four important events claim attention in the later years of the
decade. The first of these is the publication in 1826 of a new version
of the New Testament. As a competent scholar of the Greek New
Testament, Campbell was acutely aware of two weaknesses of the
widely used King James text. Despite its literary beauty, Campbell
realized that it was not easily understood because the idiom of
English expression had changed in the intervening centuries, and
scholarship had provided a much more accurate Greek text than
that from which the King James was translated.[39] Campbell relied
heavily on translations that had been made earlier by the Scottish
scholars Dr. George Campbell (Gospels, 1789), James MacKnight
(epistles, 1795), and Philip Doddridge (paraphrase, 1739-1756).
These works were checked with the Greek text of Griesbach (1796).
Campbell was not interested in novelty; rather he sought accuracy.
He was particularly troubled by the fact that most of the translations then in use tended to obscure the meaning of certain crucial
words by "transliterating" rather than translating them. Particularly notable were terms like *baptize, deacon,* and *presbyter.* He undertook to translate these terms and the resultant version contains
phrases such as, "Reform and be each of you immersed," and, "He
who believes and is immersed will be saved"; John the Baptist is
called "John the Immerser."[40] Such changes were offensive to the
paedobaptist community and, coupled with changing the King
James's *thees, thous,* and other seventeenth-century forms to a
more contemporary style, aroused a storm of criticism.[41] Nonetheless, the work went through six editions by 1838 in America, several

printings in London, and one in Wales. The new version of the New Testament demonstrated that Campbell was a competent linguist, text critic, and translator, and one who was years ahead of his time in the context of the American frontier. When Bible societies were organized to print and distribute the Scriptures on a wider scale, Campbell gave them his hearty support.

As concerned as Alexander Campbell was for genuinely Biblical Christianity, he could not help but be offended by many of the popular but rather crude hymns that found their way into the churches. This has been a problem almost from the very beginning of the practice of hymn singing, and efforts have been made in previous centuries to "clean up" church music.[42] In 1828, Campbell undertook to publish a hymnbook in which un-Biblical concepts would be excluded. He apologized that the hymnbook contained only 125 hymns, explaining that, after a search of many European and American selections, he "could find but very few songs adapted to the genius of the Christian religion and pure speech."[43] The effort was not a huge success. Good hymns are not often preferred above popular but superficial tunes. The past two centuries have produced many hymns and gospel songs, but congregations seldom discriminate when it comes to hymnody. Doctrines set to music are sung even though they would be noticeably offensive if spoken. Campbell's concern for worship set a good example. The search for hymns of both theological and musical merit is a persistent one.

The Campbell-Owen Debate

A third major undertaking by the youthful reformer in the latter years of the twenties was a debate with the British socialist Robert Owen in which Alexander Campbell sought to defend the Christian religion. Robert Owen was a successful industrial tycoon and philanthropist with genuine concern for the improvement of the conditions of the poor. Convinced that man was largely a creature of his environment and concerned to improve the life-style of the two thousand employees in his textile mill, Owen introduced numerous innovations such as improved, company-built dwellings, company-operated low-price stores, and company-sponsored nurseries—measures that are often considered paternalistic today but were regarded as philanthropic in that day. New Lanark became a model community, and Owen's success there caused him to conclude that all of society could be revamped by eliminating the capitalist system. In the depression following the Napoleonic Wars, Owen gained a significant following, but his influence was checked in 1817 when he declared war on organized religion. Owen sought to abolish religion, marriage, and private property. Popular reaction in England caused him to despair that the government would ever adopt his plans for reorganizing society into functioning communes, so he turned his attention to America. In 1824, he purchased the Rappite colony of some twenty thousand acres on the Wabash River in Southern Indiana from the German religious sect that had founded it. Here he endeavored to establish the ideal community in the pure, uncorrupted environment of the New World. Certain that his utopian socialist experiment would flourish, Owen named it New Harmony. However, the heterogeneous collection of settlers fell into such strife over the meaning of their ideals that the settlement was soon dubbed "No Harmony." Convinced that his followers had abandoned his principles, yet undaunted in his conviction of their essential rightfulness, Owen founded three other colonies and persisted in advocating his social formulae along with his religious hostility. The latter involved repeated challenges to any reputable minister to debate the matter of the worth of the Christian religion. Owen issued his challenge as follows:

> I propose to prove, as I have already attempted to do in my lectures, that all of the religions of the world have been founded upon the ignorance of mankind; that they are directly opposed to the never-changing laws of our nature; that they have been and are the real source of vice, disunion and misery of every description; that they are now the only bar to the formation of a society of virtue, of intelligence, of charity in its most extensive sense, and of sincerity and kindness among the whole human family, and that they can no longer be maintained except through the ignorance of the mass of the people and the tyranny of the few over that mass.[44]

Alexander Campbell could not allow such a challenge to go unmet, although other ministers chose to ignore it. He accepted Owen's challenge, and, at a meeting in Bethany, the two men agreed to hold the debate in Cincinnati, Ohio, April 13-21, 1829. A stenographic report was to be made and the proceedings were to be published.[45] The debate attracted wide attention and hundreds attended, some coming from as far as New York, Pennsylvania, and Virginia. The event was conducted with proper decorum and in good spirit, but it was hardly a debate. In his second speech, Owen introduced his "Twelve Laws of Nature" and spent the remainder of his time extolling them. Neither Campbell nor the moderator could force him to discuss the issues in the challenge. Richardson observes: "It soon became evident, indeed, that Mr. Owen *could* not reason, that he had no just perception of the relations between proposition and proof, and that it was vain to expect from him any logical discussion of the points at issue."[46] Campbell, therefore, gave himself to a defense of the claims of Christianity and an exhibition of the beneficial effects of the religion of Christ upon mankind. In one masterful speech of twelve hours duration, he presented the prophetic and historical evidence for Christianity and then subjected Owen's "godless" system to devastating scrutiny.

At the conclusion of the debate, the audience was asked to register its sentiments, and hundreds rose to indicate their confidence in the Christian religion while only three rose to register opposition. The widespread publicity that the debate generated cast Alexander Campbell in the role of the defender of religion against godless attack, and the consummate skill with which he had set forth the beauty of apostolic Christianity enhanced Mr. Campbell's reputation enormously. Furthermore, it gave him a platform from which to expound effectively the merits of Biblical and early Christianity. Campbell made no effort to defend contemporary sectarianism. In fact, he conceded its faults. Even Mr. Owen had to qualify his earlier denunciations by admitting that his references were to Christianity "as at present taught."[47] Thereafter, Mr. Campbell was heard with great respect almost everywhere he traveled.

The Virginia Constitutional Assembly

The same year that Alexander Campbell undertook to defend the Christian religion in debate with Robert Owen saw him make his only foray into the civil-political realm. The state of Virginia undertook to adopt a new constitution, and Campbell sought and won election as a delegate to the Constitutional Convention in Richmond. His motive was to strike a blow toward the eventual ending of slavery in the Old Dominion.[48] His only hope of accomplishing this was to enlarge the suffrage in the state so as to break the political stranglehold held by the slave-owning aristocracy of the coastal counties with their great tobacco-producing plantations. Campbell fought gallantly, lost every encounter, and came home with a clear conscience, the respect of friend and foe alike, and little else. He had done battle with "the greatest array of political talent and reputation that had been assembled since the Federal Constitutional Convention of 1787."[49] Former Presidents James Madison and James Monroe, Chief Justice John Marshall, and John Randolph were all supporting the privileges of the slave-holding oligarchy. The opposition was overwhelming, but Campbell reasoned and pleaded to the limit of his strength to democratize the government of the state.[50] Three more decades and a bloody war would be required to accomplish what reason and Christian humanitarianism were not permitted to achieve in the proud Old Dominion.

It should not be overlooked that, in the midst of greatly enlarged activity and multiplied responsibilities, Alexander Campbell suffered an acute personal loss. On October 22, 1827, his wife died following a long struggle with tuberculosis. Realizing the terminal nature of her illness, Margaret Campbell was concerned that her children would be provided maternal care, so she requested her husband to marry her best friend, Miss Salina Bakewell. Campbell gave his consent and the next year fulfilled the promise and entered into a happy union that was to last until his own death almost four decades later.

Note has previously been made of the action of several Baptist associations in expelling churches deemed to be influenced by "Campbellite" views of reform. Such actions were considered by many congregations to represent an arbitrary and unwarranted exercise of power. The result was that the very concept of an "association of churches" was called into question. It occurred to some that no Biblical precedent could be found for such a body, and this judgment was reinforced by every report of hostile action in a Baptist association. The overwhelming consensus in the Mahoning Baptist Association was in favor of its dissolution. This was done in 1830 at the meeting in Austintown, Ohio, despite Campbell's reluctance. Henceforth, the meeting would be an annual gathering for worship, fellowship, reporting, and planning for cooperative activity. A similar step was subsequently taken by other Baptist associations, and this action is generally considered as the symbolic act that dissolved the last tie with the Baptist churches.[51] Richardson notes, "The system of annual meetings thus intended was afterward generally adopted by the churches in various districts throughout the different States."[52] Henceforth, the reformed churches would be entirely congregationally governed while at the same time maintaining voluntary fellowship with each other.

End Notes

[1]Richardson, op. cit., Vol. I, pp. 137-146.

[2]Ibid., Vol. I, p. 176.

[3]Ibid., Vol. I, p. 190.

[4]Richardson (ibid., Vol. I, p. 324) observes:
He [Thomas] would admit of no fanciful interpretations or far-fetched applications, but desired constantly that the discourse should be strictly confined within the range of the ideas presented in the passage. In regard to this point, he differed from many of his fellow ministers . . . who often wandered widely from the text, and made it rather a motto for some speculation of their own, than a Scripture theme to be discussed and enforced.

Among the many publications concerning Alexander Campbell's preaching, the reader will find the following particularly helpful: Alger, M. Fitch, Jr., *Alexander Campbell: Preacher of Reform and Reformer of Preaching* (Austin: Sweet, 1970) and Granville Walker, *Preaching in the Thought of Alexander Campbell* (St. Louis: Bethany Press, 1954).

[5]See chapter 3 for the original purpose of the Christian Association of Washington, Pennsylvania.

[6]This is the assessment made by Roland Bainton in his article, "Alexander Campbell and Christian Unity," *The Sage of Bethany*, P.E. Gresham, ed. (St. Louis: Bethany Press, 1960), pp. 81-94.

[7]Margaret Brown Campbell died on October 22, 1827, a victim of tuberculosis. She was the mother of eight children, five of whom survived her.

[8]Richardson, op. cit., Vol. I, p. 401.

[9]Ibid., Vol. I, pp. 494-502.

[10]An evaluation in his own words may be found in ibid., Vol. I, pp. 438-441.

[11]The text of the sermon was not written until after its delivery. It was distributed in pamphlet form. Thirty years later, it was reprinted in the *Millennial Harbinger* of 1846, pp. 493ff.

[12]Richardson, op. cit. Vol. I, p. 477.

[13]John Calvin, *Institutes of the Christian Religion*, II:vii:2.

[14]Richardson, loc. cit.

[15]Garrison and DeGroot, op. cit., p. 164.

[16]James Wilson, *Infant Sprinkling Proved to Be a Human Tradition; Being the Substance of a Debate on Christian Baptism Between Mr. John Walker, a Minister of the Secession, and Alexander Campbell, V.D.M., a Regular Baptist Minister* (Steubenville: 1820), p. 9.

[17]Richardson (op. cit., Vol. II, p. 20) notes that this passing reference to the purpose of baptism is Campbell's first recognition of what later "assumed so conspicuous a position in the restoration of the primitive gospel."

[18]Ibid., Vol. II, p. 29.

[19]Without question, the necessity of a public defense of believer's baptism forced Campbell to consider the wider implications of the subject, and this so impressed him that he would, in two subsequent debates and in a great many other ways, employ his great skill to combat paedobaptism. Richardson notes:
> He could not be content with the simple and common theme, that "infant sprinkling is a human tradition." He could not confine his thoughts merely to the validity or invalidity of that ordinance, as was customary. He must take a wider view, and believing that this "human tradition carnalized and secularized the Church," "introduced an ungodly priesthood into it" and "prevented the union of Christians," he could well affirm it to be "injurious" to religious "society." And not only so, but knowing that the confounding of the Jewish and Christian institutions which it required led to national religious establishments, and filled the clergy with an eager thirst for political power, and that persecutions had generally proceeded from Paedobaptist parties, he would assert still further that it was "injurious" to political "society" and inimical to public liberty.
>
> In the frankness and fearlessness of his independent spirit, he, from this time forward, held himself in readiness, accordingly, to meet within the lists of public discussion any worthy champion who might appear in opposition to the truths he taught, or in defence of popular religious error (Ibid., Vol. II, p. 30).

[20]Ibid., Vol. II, p. 50.

[21]*Christian Baptist,* Vol. I, No. 3-7 (October 6, 1823; November 3, 1823; December 4, 1823; January 5, 1824; February 2, 1824).

[22]Ibid., Vol. II, No. 12 (July 4, 1825).

[23]Ibid. The series ran intermittently through thirty-two essays, beginning in Vol. II, No. 7 (February 7, 1825), and concluding in Vol. VII, No. 2 (September 7, 1829).

[24]The very first essay in the *Christian Baptist* included a condemnation of missionary societies, p. 15. Other negative discussions in Volume I may be found on pp. 40-45, 62, 63, 157-162. (All page numbers cited from the Gospel Advocate reprint, 1955.)

[25]Garrison and DeGroot, op. cit., p. 175.

[26]R.B. Simple, *Christian Baptist,* Vol. III, No. 9 (April 3, 1826).

[27]Campbell, Ibid.

[28]See a letter from a Baptist editor in Vol. V, No. 1 (August 6, 1827), who notes that Campbell's rejection of creeds in favor of his understanding of the "conceived order" is a *de facto* creed. Campbell denied (ibid.).

[29]Richardson, op. cit., Vol. II, pp. 81, 82. Note a certain similarity to Calvin's view on this point (*Institutes,* IV: xv. 1, 22).

[30]Richardson notes that, at the time of this debate, Campbell had reached the full understanding of the design of baptism, but that it was "reserved for Walter Scott, a few years later, to make a direct and practical application of the doctrine, and to secure for it the conspicuous place it has since occupied among the chief points urged in the Reformation." (Ibid., Vol. II, p. 84.)

[31]Ibid., Vol. II, p. 90.

[32]*Christian Baptist,* Vol. II, pp. 174ff, pp. 221ff; Vol. III, pp. 147ff (Gospel Advocate reprint).

[33]Ibid., Vol. I, No. 9 (April 5, 1824).

[34]Campbell was philosophically in sympathy with the Enlightenment. The influence of John Locke is apparent, but is probably not as directly determinative as the Chicago school (i.e., the Disciples Divinity House) insisted. Rather, this had been tempered by the realism of Scottish

Common Sense Philosophy of Thomas Reid and Dugald Stewart. (See Robinson, op. cit.)

[35]A. Campbell, "Essays on Man in His Primitive State," *Christian Baptist,* Vol. VI, No. 4 (November 3, 1828); p. 95 in the Gospel Advocate reprint.

[36]A useful analysis of this question is presented by W.E. Garrison; Garrison and DeGroot, op. cit., pp. 201-205.

[37]Richardson, op. cit., Vol. II, pp. 165. However, the minutes of the Redstone Association do not support Richardson's claim here. They note that four churches were excluded in 1826.

[38]Ibid., Vol. II, pp. 323. For Campbell's reaction see *Millennial Harbinger,* 1830, pp. 174, 261; 1843, p. 4.

[39]For a good study of Campbell as a translator and critic, the reader is referred to Cecil K. Thomas, *Alexander Campbell and His New Version* (St. Louis: Bethany Press, 1958).

[40]The advisability of such translation is questioned by Owen Crouch in a thought-provoking article on the significance of Greek suffixes appearing in the *Christian Standard,* July 15, 1950, p. 10; July 22, 1950, p. 13.

[41]For a review of the various kinds of criticism of *The Living Oracles,* see Thomas, op. cit., chapter 3.

[42]Probably the most widely known was the reform of Pope Gregory I (590-604), who excluded offensive music from the worship service. Many other efforts have followed.

[43]*Christian Baptist,* April 7, 1828—Vol. V, No. 9 (p. 224 in Gospel Advocate reprint).

[44]Reproduced in Richardson, op. cit., Vol. II, pp. 240, 241.

[45]Campbell published the debate and an edition was also published in London. Later editions were published under the title, *Evidences of Christianity: A Debate Between Robert Owen and Alexander Campbell* (Cincinnati: American Christian Publication Society, 1852).

[46]Richardson, op. cit., Vol. II, p. 274.

[47]Ibid., Vol. II, p. 284.

48Garrison and DeGroot, op. cit., p. 200.

49For an insightful analysis of Campbell's role in the Convention, see Robert O. Fife, "Alexander Campbell's Role in the Virginia Constitutional Convention" (unpublished paper delivered at Bethany College Restoration History Conference, July 21, 1977). See also Harold L. Lunger, *The Political Ethics of Alexander Campbell* (St. Louis: Bethany Press, 1954), pp. 75-104.

50"What business had I in such matters?" he wrote his friend, William Tener of Londonderry, in 1830. "I will tell you. I consented to be elected because, first, I was desirous of laying a foundation for the abolition of slavery. . . ." Cited by Louis Cochran, "Drama of Alexander Campbell," Gresham, ed., op. cit., p. 72. See also Campbell, "The Crisis," *Millennial Harbinger,* 1832, p. 86.

51It was a "pivotal event," according to Eva Jean Wrather, *Creative Freedom in Action,* (St. Louis: Bethany Press, 1968), p. 9. She adds,
> The dissolution of the Mahoning Association, in truth, marked a watershed. Two issues of major import were decided there, decided for generations of Disciples of Christ yet unborn.
> The first was dramatic, immediate. Before the dissolution the Reformers were Baptists; afterwards they were Disciples—for good or ill, a separate communion. For some two years before the Austintown meeting certain Baptist associations had been expelling reform churches. After the Mahoning dissolution there was no turning back the tide of separation, and within another two years the division was complete.
> The second issue decided that day stands revealed, in the long court of history, as a watershed in the Reformers' concept of the nature of church government. It marked a major shift from the associational principle to radical independency. At the critical moment of their emergence into a new communion, the congregations of Mahoning left themselves with no center of authority, no system for concerted action.

52Richardson, op. cit., Vol. II, p. 329.

Chapter Five

Associates in Reform

By 1830, it was apparent to religiously informed persons on the frontier of the United States that a dynamic new movement was emerging and that this force, calling for a united effort to reform the churches, would have great appeal to thoughtful and earnest Christians. That Alexander Campbell, of Brooke County, Virginia, was the leader of the movement was generally recognized by the common use of the label "Campbellite," which was staunchly rejected by those involved in the reform effort. The ever-widening circulation of the *Christian Baptist* and the publicity arising from three debates had made Campbell's name and his views familiar in hundreds of households. But it would be a mistake to conclude that the growth of the movement was the work of one man, or that the influence that propelled it emanated from one source only. Indeed, it is no reflection on the leadership of Alexander Campbell to recognize that, without the comradeship and support of a number of capable men, his own efforts would have produced little. It is the purpose of the present chapter to examine the contribution of some of these men.

Walter Scott

"Among the helpers and fellow-laborers of Alexander Campbell the first place in zeal and ability must be awarded to Walter Scott,"[1] at least in the opinion of Scott's chief biographer, William Baxter. Many others would concur. The genial Scott was born in Dumfreeshire, Scotland, October 31, 1796, of the same clan that included Sir Walter Scott. Though of moderate circumstances, his parents managed to give him a university education at Edinburg. Being devout Presbyterians, they hoped that he would enter the ministry. However, upon graduation, he heeded the suggestions of an uncle to emigrate to New York, where he became a Latin tutor in a classical academy. Reports of the inland country led him to yield to the western call and journey by foot to Pittsburgh, where he found similar employment in an academy conducted by George Forrester, a fellow Scot of Baptist persuasion who convinced his young associate of the need to take the Bible as his sole authority in religion. Scott undertook a serious study of baptism in the Greek New Testament, was immersed, and became involved with the little body of Haldanean Baptists that Forrester had gathered.

The tragic drowning of George Forrester shortly thereafter left the work of church and school as Scott's responsibility, a burden that he took very seriously. By chance, a pamphlet on baptism published in 1820 by a small congregation in New York City fell into his hands. It was written by Henry Errett, father of Isaac Errett, and dealt with the design of baptism in terms of remission of sins. Scott was consumed with a desire to know more. He closed the school, walked from Pittsburgh, Pennsylvania, to New York City, located the congregation, and was profoundly disappointed in what he found. He discovered that the congregation lacked appreciation for the truth they had espoused and was without vision, preoccupied with trivial matters, and afflicted with the kind of petty legalism that sometimes blights the "Bible only" position. Heeding an appeal to return to Pittsburgh and the tutelage of some promising youth, Scott walked back, stopping en-route to visit small Baptist churches in New Jersey, Baltimore, and Washington, D.C. Despondent, Scott confessed that, upon arrival in Washington, he "went to the Capitol, and, climbing up to the top of its lofty dome, I sat myself down, filled with sorrow at the miserable desolation of the Church of God."[2]

This proved to be the darkness that preceded the dawn. Thereafter, events quickly led Scott to a new challenge that would claim his best energies for the remainder of his life. Having walked the nearly 300 wilderness miles from Washington to Pittsburgh, he took residence with the Richardson family, whose son Robert he was engaged to tutor. He also resumed the ministry of the little congregation that had come to be known as "Kissing Baptists" because they had adopted the practice of greeting each other in this fashion and of washing feet (seeking to heed Romans 16:16 and John 13:14 respectively).

Shortly after Scott's return from his New York journey, in the winter of 1821-1822, he met Alexander Campbell. An immediate affinity was discernible. Both men had been educated for the Presbyterian ministry, both had consciously forsaken the Westminster Confession of Faith in favor of a strictly Biblical approach to faith, and both were deeply disturbed by the deplorable condition of the churches as they then observed them. The two men supplemented each other's gifts and talents admirably.[3] Campbell, Scott's elder by some eight years, was to be the great religious statesman who would give direction to the movement, but it would be Scott above all others who would give practical impetus to the movement. This he did by developing a new type of evangelism that ultimately enlisted thousands as it was employed by an ever-increasing number of frontier evangelists.

The close personal ties between Alexander Campbell and Walter Scott led Campbell to seek the counsel of Scott regarding the publication of a journal. It was Scott's suggestion to name this journal the *Christian Baptist,* as noted in chapter 4. Campbell accepted the suggestion, and Scott was a frequent contributor, publishing his articles under the pseudonym "Phillip."[4]

In 1826, Walter Scott moved from Pittsburgh to Steubenville, Ohio. The following year, Alexander Campbell stopped to persuade Scott to attend the annual meeting of the Mahoning Baptist Association, which was to meet that year in New Lisbon, Ohio. Scott was reluctant because he was not a member of a church that belonged to the Mahoning Association, but Campbell was persistent. It was a fateful meeting. The Mahoning Association was not prospering. Reports at the meeting indicated that the member churches represented had a total of thirty-four baptisms and thirteen additions otherwise. There had been thirteen excommunications. Deaths and withdrawals had reduced the net gain for the fourteen churches to sixteen members. This was a dismal report at a time when the population was expanding rapidly. Obviously, something needed to be done to revitalize these churches. The association decided to engage an evangelist. A committee was appointed to select a suitable person, and the unanimous choice fell upon the guest at the meeting, Walter Scott. Scott accepted the challenge.

Two themes were prominent in Scott's understanding of the Christian religion to this point, and both were to emerge in his new venture in evangelism. One of these was the importance of the restoration of the gospel and the church of the first century. He had contributed a series of four articles to the first volume of the *Christian Baptist* under the title: "On Teaching Christianity." These articles suggest that Scott understood restoration more as an end in itself than a means of achieving the end of Christian union. The latter note is hardly discernable in Scott's thought to this point.[5] George Forrester's long hours of discussion with the youthful Scott had left a lasting impression of the necessity of restoration of the New Testament faith.

The other engrossing concept in Scott's thinking at this time was the exaltation of Jesus, the Messiah. For several years, he had been convinced that "the great central idea of the Christian religion is the Messiahship; that Jesus is the Christ, the Son of the living God"; a proposition around which, in his estimation, "all other truths revolve as planets around the sun." This theme developed into Scott's major literary effort, a book entitled *The Messiahship or The Great Demonstration,* published in 1859. The two themes would converge in Scott's unique work as an evangelist in the Mahoning Association.

In order to appreciate Scott's contribution to evangelism, it is necessary to note the nature of frontier revivalism. The "Second Great Awakening," as it is frequently called, quite often centered in the camp meeting, as at Cane Ridge. The first objective of the preacher in such a meeting was to convict the hearer of his sinful condition. Thus, much of the preaching was of the hell-fire type. A student of this period of American life has commented on revival preaching of this era as follows:

> Throughout the revival preaching there are two main themes. The first and predominant one is the imminent danger of hell, . . . the destructiveness of sin, the evilness of man, the wrath of God, and the impossibility of man achieving salvation through his own actions. The other side of their message was the love of God in Christ, His atoning death (described in gory detail as the result of your sins), which if accepted, would relieve the load of sin and guilt, result in a godly life and prepare the person for the beauty and glory of heaven.[6]

Samuel Jennings, a contemporary of the camp meetings, made it clear that he believed the form of preaching was as important as the content when it came to getting the desired results:

> The most learned lectures may be delivered to any man, or set of men, for years together, and yet if that kind of energy which urges to immediate practice be wanting, all will be vain. The tenor of the Gospel to be successful is "now is the accepted time, now is the day of salvation." And the minister of the gospel, to be successful, must show by every word and every gesture that he feels it so. He must "know the terror of the Lord," and act consistently with the deepest sense of it or he will never effectually persuade men.[7]

The convicted sinner was expected to agonize before the Lord at the mourner's bench, where he entreated the Lord to be merciful and save him. Such anguish could continue for several hours before the Lord would respond with some miraculous "assurance of pardon."[8] At this moment, it was held that God bestowed the "gift" of saving faith upon the penitent sinner. The whole process was highly emotional and often quite devoid of substantive content. Skilled practitioners of revivalist arts became very adept at manipulation of frontier crowds and frequently produced spectacular results. Revivalistic methods were employed primarily by Methodists, Baptists, and Presbyterians, accounting in large measure for the rapid growth of these denominations. While Methodists (Arminians) and Baptists and Presbyterians (Calvinists) differed widely in their explanations of the happenings at the revivals, all employed the same methods and produced similar effects.

The young evangelist whom the Mahoning Baptist Association had employed to dispel the prevailing lethargy and inspire growth in the churches of the area was ill-suited by education or disposition to engage in American frontier evangelism of the mourner's bench variety. Nothing in his educational experience at the University of Edinburg would recommend frontier revivalism. His own espousal of reformatory attitudes came about as a result of the study of the Bible, to which he had been directed by George Forrester. And an analysis of the four articles which he provided for the *Christian Baptist* in 1823 and 1824 indicates that he had rejected revivalist techniques. He had reached the conclusion that faith is not the product of God's electing grace bestowed upon whomever His inscrutable will chooses to save, but rather the acceptance by man of claims that have been made by Jesus Christ that are supported by adequate evidence. In Scott's own words written earlier for the *Christian Baptist:*

Walter Scott (1796-1861), associate of Alexander Campbell in the work of reform and editor of *The Evangelist* (1832-1844). Scott developed the distinctive evangelistic method widely utilized by Churches of Christ in the nineteenth century.

There is but one authorized way of making Christ known to man, in order that they may believe and be saved. . . . the great fact to be believed in order to be saved, is, that he is the Son of God; and this being a matter-of-fact question, the belief of it as necessarily depends upon the evidence by which it is accompanied, as the belief of any other fact depends upon its particular evidence. . . . to preach the gospel is just to propose this glorious truth to sinners, and support it by its proper evidence.[9]

Commenting further on the method of apostolic preaching, Scott notes:

> They [the apostles] first proposed the truth to be believed; and secondly, they produced the evidences necessary to warrant belief; and thirdly, if any seemed to despise the gospel, or resist the Holy Spirit, i.e. the evidence afforded by the Holy Spirit in gifts, miracles, and prophecy, then they warned the despisers of the consequences, and thus freed themselves from the blood of all men.[10]

Quite obviously, Scott could not be expected to move in the typical pattern of contemporary evangelism because he was operating from a different theological orientation than that of the contemporary revivalists. The suggestion has been made that Scott's views were formed along empirical lines by his discovery of the writings of John Locke in the library of George Forrester in Pittsburgh.[11] Actually such a displacement of Calvinist theology by Lockian empiricism was rather widespread at this time. It remained for Scott to work out its implications for evangelism on the American frontier. These implications soon became apparent once Scott undertook seriously the work of evangelism. W.E. Garrison has noted that Scott's evangelistic thought was

> utterly unlike the Great Western Revival, which had stirred Kentucky and Tennessee a generation earlier and out of which had emerged the western branch of the "Christian" church. His was no frenzy of emotion, but a blending of rationality and authority, and appeal to common sense and simplicity. It assumed the absolute authority of the Bible, which almost no one doubted; and it asserted man's rational ability to understand what he ought to do and why, and his moral ability to do it.[12]

The Baptist church at New Lisbon, Ohio, quickly availed itself of the services of the newly-appointed association evangelist and scheduled a series of discourses by the "eloquent stranger."[13] From the first Sunday, the house was thronged. Scott's first message was a reflection of his understanding of the Christian faith. He expounded on Matthew 16:16, the good confession, affirming that it expresses the foundation of the Christian religion. Scott noted that those who accepted this truth as proclaimed by the apostles were admonished to repent and be baptized and then were promised the forgiveness of sin and the gift of the Holy Spirit. He invited all who believed to respond in the same manner. From the audience, a highly respected Presbyterian, delighted to discover somebody with a concept of faith similar to his own, pressed forward to make public confession of faith and express a desire to be baptized in that apostolic fashion. That afternoon, in the presence of a large gathering, William Amend was immersed in a nearby stream. The event stirred great interest and considerable controversy in the town of New Lisbon. In the next several weeks, scores followed the example, and Scott's services as an evangelist were sought by other congregations in the area.

Scott and some of his associates interpreted the event at New Lisbon as a new Pentecost wherein the gospel was restored to the church that had been reforming itself. Scott's biographer, William Baxter, comments:

> This event, which forms an era in the religious history of the times, took place on the 18th of November, 1827, and Mr. Amend was, beyond all question, the first person in modern times who received the ordinance of baptism in perfect accordance with apostolic teaching and usage.[14]

Alexander Campbell never concurred in this judgment. Indeed, Campbell's own understanding of faith and his adoption of immersion had influenced his method of proclamation in a similar fashion some years earlier. After laboring strenuously in the cause of reforming the church for almost two decades prior to this event, it was quite difficult for him to accept this date as the precise time of the restoration of the gospel.

Scott's evangelism introduced a closer identification of baptism and the remission of sins than had been evident in the thinking of Stone or the Campbells. Scott often spoke of baptism "for" the remission of sins,[15] and he agreed with a friend who said:

> I have for some time thought that the waters of baptism must stand in the same position to us that the blood of sacrifices did to the Jews. The blood of bulls and of goats could never take away sins, as Paul declares, yet when offered at the altar by the sinner, he had the divine assurance that his sins were forgiven him. This blood was merely typical of the blood of Christ, the true sin offering to which it pointed prospectively; and it seems to me that the water in baptism, which has no power in itself to wash away sins, now refers retrospectively to the purifying power of the blood of the Lamb of God.[16]

Such a view of baptism has never lacked for advocates, even to the present time. Some ministers insist upon expressing it in every baptismal act. Alexander Campbell had discussed the design of baptism at length in his debate with McCalla in 1823. He had offended Baptists by the close association he had made between baptism and the forgiveness of sin. However, he hesitated to go so far as to affirm, with Scott, that baptism was performed as the means of securing the remission of sins. Speaking of another situation, Richardson notes:

> Mr. Campbell greatly disapproved the practice of making such issues, and of using such strong and unguarded expressions as the "power of remitting sins" and "washing away sins in baptism." "These," said he, "have been most prejudicial to the cause of truth, and have given a pretext to the opposition for their hard speeches against the pleadings of the Reformers." The habitual use of such expressions he thought also calculated to lead men to overlook or disparage that faith in the sacrifice of Christ from which alone baptism derived its efficacy. On this account, in baptizing persons, he used only the simple formula, "Into the name of the Father and of the Son and of the Holy Spirit," and forebore adding to it, like Mr. Scott and others, the expression "for the remission of sins." "When any doctrine," said he (Mill. Harb. for 1832, p. 299), "is professed and taught by many, when any matter gets into many hands, some will misuse, abuse and pervert it. This is unavoidable. We have always feared abuses and extremes."[17]

Thus, Campbell's understanding of baptism was somewhat intermediate between that of the Baptists, who admitted no relationship between baptism and the remission of sins, and of Scott, who identified the two. Campbell tended to insist that the grace of God that resulted in sin's forgiveness was operative upon the confluence of several vital factors and that to focus upon only one of these was a serious over-simplification that produced a distortion of reality and truth.

None would deny, however, the effectiveness of Scott's new approach to evangelism nor question the fact that it contributed enormously both to the growth of the reformation of the nineteenth century and to the metamorphosis of the Mahoning Baptist Churches into Churches of Christ. At the conclusion of his first year of work, Scott was able to report to the churches of the Mahoning Association meeting in Warren, Ohio, in August of 1829, that the membership of the churches had more than doubled. Six new churches had been established, and "ministers from several sects have embraced the ancient gospel and preached it with great success."[18] The messengers from these churches were so pleased with Scott's work that they voted to reappoint him for the next year and to engage William Hayden to assist him in the evangelistic enterprise.

Such spectacular growth as Scott produced was beyond the imagination of the analytic, reflective mentality of Alexander Campbell. Accordingly, he requested his father to visit the site of Scott's labors and observe Scott's efforts. The elder Campbell had never observed anything to compare with the popular reception that Scott's reasoned appeal to the common-sense mentality of ordinary, intelligent people was receiving. He reported that Scott won disciples for Christ "by simply and boldly stating the ancient gospel, and insisting upon it; and then by putting the question generally and particularly to males and females, old and young. Will you come to Christ and be baptized for the remission of sins and the gift of the Holy Spirit?"[19] He paid Scott the tribute of having demonstrated how to implement the potential that was latent in their own insights. He wrote enthusiastically:

> We have long known the former (the theory), and have spoken and published many things *correctly concerning* the ancient gospel, its simplicity and perfect adaptation to the present state of mankind, for the benign and gracious purposes of his immediate relief and complete salvation; but I must confess that, in respect to the *direct exhibition* and *application* of it for that blessed purpose, I am at present for the first time upon the ground where the thing has appeared to be *practically exhibited* to the proper purpose. [Italics in original.][20]

It was during Scott's first year of evangelism that he developed what was to become widely known (though somewhat altered) as the "five-finger exercise." Riding into a village in southern Ohio, he encountered a group of small children who were leaving a school. He engaged them in conversation and then said: "Children, hold up your left hands." When all had done so, he continued: "Now beginning with your thumb repeat what I say to you: Faith, repentance, baptism, remission of sins, gift of the Holy Spirit—that takes up all your fingers." After this was repeated several times, he sent the children home to announce to their parents that "a man will preach the gospel tonight at the school house, as you have it on the five fingers of your hands."[21]

It is important to note not only the content of the five-finger exercise but also the sequence of the five components. Herein is seen the uniqueness of Scott's method of evangelism and its deviation from normal frontier revivalism. The usual pattern would be somewhat as follows: action of the Holy Spirit, repentance, faith, remission of sins, baptism. The differences between the two methods would generate endless discussion and controversy that reflect Calvinistic vs. empirical presuppositions.[22] Scott's five-finger exercise would have lasting effects on subsequent reformation evangelism and theology, especially as this relates to the nature of preaching, the meaning of baptism, and the role of the Holy Spirit. Scott's sermons, addressed primarily to the common sense of his

hearers, centered on the claims of Jesus, the evidence that the New
Testament provides to sustain these claims, and the implications
that such claims had for the thought and life of every human being.
In contrast to the doctrine of election, Scott's evangelism presupposed that every normally intelligent person could weigh the evidence for Christianity and make a rational decision based on such
evidence. A positive decision was understood as "faith" and was not
contingent upon divine intervention to any degree. Having decided
favorably on Jesus' claims, the consequent obedience to the instructions of Jesus would lead to the promised salvation. All of this is
reminiscent of Covenant or Federal theology, a Puritan modification of Calvinism that would make it palatable to the American
temper.[23]

The evangelistic enthusiasm that Scott aroused soon demanded
the participation of others. William Hayden[24] joined the effort in
1828, soon to be followed by Adamson Bentley and Marcus
Bosworth. When the Mahoning Association met in Austintown,
Ohio, in 1830, more than 1,000 converts were reported. Hearing
that the Redstone Association had taken adverse action against the
Reformers and "had pursued a very arbitrary course, with regard
to churches and individuals who could not accept fully all that was
required by the Creed and Articles of Faith,"[25] Scott took the lead
in questioning the legitimacy of such organizations. It was at this
meeting that the Mahoning Association, finding no Biblical precedent for a body possessed of such authority as the Redstone and
Beaver Associations exercised, dissolved itself,[26] as noted in chapter 4 above. Thus, an important precedent with far-reaching consequences was set. This action determined the totally congregational
polity of the reformation. It was Scott's, not Campbell's, decision
that prevailed and, in the judgment of William Baxter, "freed the
Disciples from the last vestige of human authority, and placed
them under Christ, with his Word for their guide."[27] This judgment
was not shared by others who were present. Alexander Campbell
managed to retain an annual fellowship meeting of these churches,
but cooperation was quite limited. A.J. Hayden characterized the
ensuing years as follows:

> The twenty years succeeding is the period of our anarchy. During
> this time we had no concert, regular or irregular, stated or inciden-
> tal, if we except some ineffectual efforts to bring a better order into
> existence. The great saving power was the yearly meeting system.
> This, serving as a bond of union, was a powerful support to the
> cause. These meetings were the conservation of the churches. They
> were aggressive, adding multitudes of converts. By diffusing a gen-
> eral, personal acquaintance, they cultivated a strong tie of brother-
> hood. Yet with all their benefits, which were neither few nor weak,

they were not organic. They sent out no missionaries; they called for no reports; they performed no action for the churches, nor for the systematic diffusion of the gospel. They came as a cloud with blessings, poured out their treasure of good, and departed.

During these years many attempts were made to form cooperations. They were failures. The cry of priest-craft, or sectarianism, was alone sufficient to blast the effort for order.[28]

Thenceforth the Disciples would have a problem deciding how to handle the process of inter-congregational cooperative action and especially how to handle the institutions that inevitably develop through such cooperative action. This is not to say that the decision was inappropriate. But it must be recognized that, by avoiding one set of problems, they became involved in another set. Which of the sets of problems is least objectionable is the church-polity question that has been debated for centuries and about which the Bible sheds less light than was formerly thought to be the case.

The years of extensive travel and exhausting preaching took their toll on Scott's health and stamina. In 1832, he moved to Cincinnati and, shortly thereafter, to the nearby village of Carthage, Ohio. In an effort to sustain the evangelistic activity he had generated, he began publication of a monthly journal that was appropriately titled *The Evangelist*. Here he associated briefly with Dr. Robert Richardson, his former pupil who was now a physician in Carthage and served as assistant editor of the journal. *The Evangelist* was published through 1838. In 1836, Scott was elected the first president of Bacon College in Georgetown, Kentucky, the first school to be organized by the Disciples. He served less than a year and was succeeded by David S. Burnett.

In 1844, Scott moved his family to Pittsburgh, Pennsylvania, where he began publication, with Robert H. Forrester, of the *Protestant Unionist*. As a representative of the Allegheny City Church, he attended the gathering in Cincinnati, Ohio, in 1849, that created the American Christian Missionary Society and was elected third vice president. Shortly thereafter, he moved to Mays Lick, Kentucky, where most of his remaining days were spent. He died there on April 23, 1861, shortly after the beginning of the Civil War.

Second only to Scott's influence as an evangelist is his contribution as an editor and author. His most notable literary achievement was the publication two years before his death of *The Messiahship or Great Demonstration*.[29] Herein, Scott sought to raise Christ above creed or sect and to present Him as the reconciler of all mankind.

Scott's later years, like Campbell's, were troubled by the controversy over slavery and the approaching Civil War. Both men were

adamantly opposed to slavery; neither were abolitionists. Sensing
the enormous problems that emancipation involved, Scott was at
first inclined to favor colonization and the cause of Liberia. As it
became apparent that this would not be practical, Scott searched
his mind and exhausted his imagination for a solution, all in vain.
He was perplexed, and his death in 1861 mercifully spared him the
anguish of the bloodbath that followed.

Sidney Rigdon

Not everybody who espoused the cause of reforming the church by
adherence to Biblical precedents would remain committed to the
same understanding of what restoration of Christianity entailed.
Mention has already been made of two of Stone's original associates
who returned to the Presbyterian Church and of two who joined the
Shakers. Among Campbell's associates, Sidney Rigdon must be
mentioned if only because of his subsequent importance in the
development of Mormonism. Born in 1795 in western Pennsylvania,
reared on a farm, educated largely by his parents, he was converted
and licensed to preach by the Baptists. He began his ministry in
Ohio but transferred to a small church in Pittsburgh, Pennsylvania,
in 1821. With Adamson Bentley, his brother-in-law, he made a visit
to Bethany to discuss certain items they had read in Campbell's
publication of his debate with Walker. The entire night was spent in
discussion, and by dawn the two had become convinced of the merits
of reformation. He later labored in Mantua, Mentor, and Kirkland,
Ohio, urging his hearers to reject creeds and base their faith solely
on the Bible, which he tended to approach very literally. A crisis
occurred in 1828 in Warren, Ohio. Expounding on the need to
restore the Christianity of the New Testament, Rigdon focused on
Acts 2:45 and extolled the need to set up a Christian community of
possessions similar to that in Jerusalem. Alexander Campbell, who
was present, took issue and argued in a lengthy discourse that this
type of arrangement was peculiar to that particular situation and
was not reflected in any other congregation mentioned in the New
Testament. Rigdon was chagrined, embarrassed, and embittered
toward Alexander Campbell, which, no doubt, played at least a par-
tial role in his defection from the reformation. It must be remembered that communal concepts of the church were widely accepted
at this time.[30] Rigdon may well have concluded that Campbell was a
halfway reformer, and he proceeded to establish a "common stock
society" in the congregation at Kirkland, Ohio.

In October, 1830, Joseph Smith's first four Mormon missionaries
arrived in Ohio. After a brief encounter with them, Rigdon claimed

to have had a "revelation" assuring him that the Book of Mormon was to be believed.[31] Much excitement followed, which resulted in the conversion of the Kirkland congregation to Mormonism. Many who had become convinced of the need to restore the church to its pristine purity were also convinced that such a restored church should have a divine sanction in the form of some supernatural manifestation.[32] The Disciples disavowed contemporary miracles but the Mormons claimed to perform them. This made a decisive difference to some people.

The subsequent career of Sidney Rigdon, the Mormon, is not relevant to this study beyond noting that he became a trusted aid of Joseph Smith, an unsuccessful rival of Brigham Young for the leadership of the Mormons after Joseph Smith's assassination in Carthage, Illinois, a teacher in the Mormon "university" in Nauvoo, Illinois, and a founder of the Mormon community in Independence, Missouri. Rebuffed in his bid for Mormon leadership, Rigdon returned to Pittsburgh and established a church there. He died in New York in relative obscurity.

John T. Johnson

The initiative for bringing about the union of the Reformers of western Pennsylvania and Ohio with the Christians of Kentucky and Tennessee (see chapter 6) can be traced primarily to John T. Johnson. A cultured, mild-mannered but resourceful ex-lawyer, he was a mature adult before he was converted to Christ. Born near Georgetown, Kentucky, in 1788, he grew up on a frontier farm at a time when Indian depravations were a hazard. As a lad of thirteen, he attended and years later could claim "a most vivid recollection of the great revival of 1801."[33] Convinced of the need to become a Christian, he was, according to the prevailing Calvinism of the frontier, left to wait for some mystical experience that indicated God's election. Twenty years would pass before he "made a profession of religion during the summer of 1821, and joined the Baptist Church at the Great-Crossings."[34] In the meantime, he had graduated from Transylvania University, studied law and been admitted to the bar, served as an aid to General William Henry Harrison in the War of 1812 against Great Britain, served several years in the Kentucky legislature, and made and lost a small fortune. Following his conversion, he served two terms in Congress (he supported Jackson in the congressional settlement of the hung electoral college in 1825), was appointed judge of the Kentucky Court of Appeals, and then terminated a promising political career to take up a more challenging one. He had learned of the reform efforts of

Thomas and Alexander Campbell to unite the people of God. The *Christian Baptist* circulated freely in Kentucky, and the Baptist Churches were alive with discussions about the propriety of creeds, and the like. As the Baptists began to take measures to exclude the "Campbellites," Johnson formed a congregation in keeping with the reform position. This was in the spring of 1831. Johnson was forty-two years of age, and he determined to devote the remainder of his days to advancing the cause of unity on the basis of the Bible alone.

Meanwhile, Barton W. Stone had moved to Georgetown and established the Christian Church there. The two men realized the similarity of their aims and the need to join forces. Stone invited Johnson to become co-editor of the *Christian Messenger,* a position he occupied for three years until Stone moved to Illinois. Stone later commented about Johnson:

> We lived together in Georgetown, and labored and worshiped. We plainly saw that we were on the same foundation, in the same spirit, and preached the same gospel. We agreed to unite our energies to effect a union between our different societies. This was easily effected in Kentucky, and in order to confirm this union, we became co-editors of the Messenger. This union, irrespective of reproach, I view as the noblest act of my life.[35]

John T. Johnson gave himself primarily to the evangelization of the growing frontier for the remainder of his life. He traveled widely and established many churches. But he was careful to avoid the image of the typical frontier revivalist who preyed on the emotional sensitivities of his hearers. A contemporary minister noted:

> He may be thought, by those who do not know him, a "revivalist." Such he is not—at least not in the usual meaning of the term revivalist, *but the farthest from it imaginable.* There is no cant, no affectation—his speech being merely earnest conversation. It never enters his mind to play the orator. His addresses are characterized by devotion to the teaching of the New Testament, by *obvious sincerity* and an all-pervading desire for the salvation of his hearers. [Italics in original.][36]

Johnson was instrumental in establishing Bacon College (named after Sir Francis Bacon, advocate of inductive logic) in 1836 in Georgetown. A friend and supporter of this venture through all its vicissitudes and successive moves, he joined Walter Scott, first president, in editing the *Christian* in 1837. He also published the *Gospel Advocate* beginning in 1834.

The cause of evangelism so captured John T. Johnson's thinking that he began to plead with the churches to cooperate in doing what they could not do separately. His words, penned in 1842, have a contemporary ring to them:

> Can we get along without consultation and co-operation? If we can, there is no need of congregations. Every divine dispensation of God's goodness, Patriarchal, Jewish and Christian, has been distinguished by consultation and co-operation. At the very commencement of the christian kingdom, the apostles were in consultation and co-operation. The history in the Acts of Apostles, is a continuation of the same, together with the consultation and co-operation of the congregations. . . . It is a very easy matter for a congregation to say, We will pay a special sum for the support of an evangelist. It is as easy for the congregations in a county to meet, and appropriate what they have resolved to raise and pay. And it is just as easy to collect and pay the amount quarterly.
>
> If the evangelist would be faithful, let him make written reports every month, while his labors are fresh in his recollection; and let him deposit in the treasury of the co-operation, every cent he receives from abroad, that he may be guarded against receiving more than is his due. The crisis calls for action.[37]

Thus, "cooperations" were born, which would develop into State Missionary Societies. They were responsible for establishing hundreds of congregations in the nineteenth and early twentieth centuries.

Johnson's travels in behalf of the evangelistic cause of the movement continued with advancing years, and his interest in the development of additional resources of the expanding religious body grew with his expanding vision. He saw the need for a home for orphan girls and became an associate of Dr. L.L. Pinkerton in founding the Midway, Kentucky, home and school. He was quick to see the value of education for young people and was a founder of the Kentucky Christian Education Society.[38] He sensed the inadequacies of the King James translation of the Bible and was active in the Revision Association,[39] of which he was a vice president. Throughout the years, he gave encouragement to Bacon College and its efforts to educate young men to preach to gospel. It would be difficult to overestimate the influence of John T. Johnson on the growth of the movement in Kentucky and the western frontier. He died in Lexington, Missouri, in 1856.

"Raccoon" John Smith

No figure in the history of the Disciples movement so dramatically represents the frontier portion of the movement as John Smith.

The cause had its share of well-educated leaders, but the role of the vigorous, self-educated frontier evangelist who could speak the idiom of his pioneer neighbor because he rose from the same soil should not be overlooked. "Raccoon" John Smith was typical of hundreds of such preachers of many denominations who combed the frontier in the nineteenth century. He got his unusual nickname from his own typical introduction of himself:

> I am John Smith, from Stockton's Valley [Kentucky]. In more recent years I have lived in Wayne, among the rocks and hills of the Cumberland. Down there, saltpeter caves abound, and raccoons make their homes.[40]

Born on October 15, 1784, in Sullivan County, Tennessee, Smith was reared in a rigidly Calvinistic family of frontier Baptists. The death of his father in 1803 turned Smith's thoughts to religion. Persuaded that he ought to become a Christian, he was equally convinced that there was nothing he could do to effect his conversion. Since God gives the gift of faith to the elect, he must await some unusual sign that he was so favored. He agonized for days, often in a secret place of prayer in a nearby thicket. He was near the point of despair when suddenly he experienced a sense of relief, which his brother convinced him was the longed-for evidence of conversion. But doubts returned and he had to confess that the earlier experience was only an illusion. His pious mother could only comfort him with "you must wait the Lord's time."[41] In desperation, he attended a meeting at which some who had had saving experiences were to relate them to the church. He went away disgusted with what he had heard. Eventually, he was persuaded simply to relate the story of his anguished quest to the church, which he did on December 26, 1804. Such was the esteem in which Smith was held that the church voted that "the experience just related is a work of grace,"[42] and Smith was accordingly baptized the next day. Shortly thereafter, he was encouraged to preach, but he had been taught that a special call from the Lord was a necessary prerequisite. Thus, frontier Calvinism enforced a second frustration and caused further introspection as he yearned for some evidence of a call to preach. In due time, he yielded to the urging of friends and was ordained to the Baptist ministry upon pledging his adherence to the Philadelphia Confession of Faith. He preached the doctrines of this confession (viz. total depravity, predestination, perseverance, etc.),[43] although some of these were being seriously questioned among Baptists of that time. However, it was a personal tragedy that demolished Smith's adherence to this form of Calvinism.

Seeking more fertile land to farm, Smith moved his family to the vicinity of Huntsville, Alabama, in 1814. In January of 1815, while away from home on a preaching mission, his log cabin burned and two of his small children perished in the fire. Smith was tormented by the thought that these children might be of the non-elect and hence might be suffering the anguish of eternal fire. His woes were multiplied shortly after this tragedy by the death of his wife and an almost fatal bout with what was probably pneumonia. It was an impoverished, discouraged, theologically troubled John Smith who retraced his way back to Stockton's Valley in Kentucky. As his strength returned, he resumed his preaching, but he could never again resume the rigid Calvinism of many of his Baptist colleagues. He had abandoned the Philadelphia Confession for all practical purposes. For several years, he was adrift on a sea of confusion.

This was Smith's frame of mind when he came across a copy of the *Christian Baptist*. He devoured it, thrilled by the suggestion that one could be a Christian without belonging to a particular religious party; that followers of Christ need not subscribe to abstract propositions framed by theological synods or conform to prescribed practices of ecclesiastical courts. He read with much sympathy, in the light of his own conversion, that it was not according to the gospel to require an "experience" of salvation prior to coming to saving faith. While pondering the radical implications of what he had read, he learned that the editor, Alexander Campbell, was coming to Flemingsburg, Kentucky, in the spring of 1824. Smith journeyed to meet him and spent several days in serious discussion of the views that Campbell was propounding. He was especially concerned about the "experiences" of conversion. Although many of the Baptists in his region were manifesting hostility against the gentleman Reformer from Virginia, Smith found Campbell to be

Home of "Raccoon" John Smith, frontier preacher in Kentucky and leader in the union effort in 1831-32. Typical of the dwellings on the frontier, this cabin is witness to the harsh realities of life in that era.

consistent, honest, and Biblically oriented. Smith began to plead the cause of reformation. Naturally, this evoked opposition from those who were committed to the doctrines of the confession. Smith was a very effective evangelist, and his practice of baptizing scores of people into Christ without the consent of any church or without the usual examinations to ascertain that they had been born of the Holy Spirit was particularly offensive to Baptist churches.[44] He also encouraged converts in several frontier communities to organize churches on the basis of the Scriptures as their only creed. A rupture with orthodox Baptists was inevitable, but Smith was of such constitution that hostility only intensified his activity. The sympathy of his second wife was such that she took over complete responsibility for management of the farm, thereby freeing him to devote his full energies to evangelism. Many of the Baptist churches in Kentucky began to repudiate the confession and vote out their covenants. Some changed their name to Church of Christ.[45] Some congregations divided. Associations responded by taking measures to exclude Reformers and the congregations that they represented.

Meanwhile, John Smith had come to know Barton W. Stone and to manifest an interest in the efforts of the Christians to avoid sectarianism. His Baptist adversaries in 1830 were quick to brand the "Stonites" as "Arians," and the excommunicators in the Bracken Association charged that the Reformers, whom they proceeded to cast out, "would not have been satisfied until they had brought into the churches, and to the communion table, every thing that professed faith in Jesus Christ, and had been baptized for the remission of sins, regardless whether they were *Arians* or anything else."[46]

It would require two years of discussion for Smith and the rest of the Reformers to understand that Stone's rejection of a "doctrine of the Trinity" did not imply that he denied the divinity of Christ, that his rejection of a "theory" of atonement (obviously a human construct) did not involve denial of the fact of atonement, and that his practice of what would be called "open-communion" might be more consistent with a plea for Christian unity and less sectarian than what the Reformers had been willing to consider. Smith became a catalyst in the merging of the two reformation forces in 1832. He served as one of the messengers who, with John T. Rogers, visited the churches of both groups to urge union. His remaining years were fruitful in evangelism. He died in Missouri on February 26, 1868, and was buried at Somerset, Kentucky.

To take particular note of a few men who worked closely with Alexander Campbell in the reformation effort in the early nineteenth century should not obscure the fact that many others fulfilled significant leadership roles. Samuel Rogers and his son, John

T. Rogers, labored effectively in Ohio, Indiana, and pioneered in Missouri. Among Samuel Rogers' converts was Benjamin Franklin, who was an effective leader in the next generation of Reformers. Jacob Creath, Sr., and his son, Jacob Creath, Jr., were effective leaders in Kentucky, Tennessee, and Missouri. Aylette Raines, whom some disliked because of opinions he held about "Restorationism"[47] but whom Campbell insisted should be accepted as a brother, labored fruitfully in central Kentucky. Many others could be named whose labors on the Western Reserve and in Kentucky in the decades of the twenties and thirties caused the idea of reform to take firm root in the fertile soil of frontier America.[48]

End Notes

[1]William Baxter, *The Life of Walter Scott* (Cincinnati: Bosworth, Chase and Hall, 1874), p. 15. A useful condensation of this 450-page work was done by B.A. Abbott and released to mark the centennial of Scott's paper, *The Evangelist*, in 1926: *Life of Elder Walter Scott* (St. Louis: Bethany, 1926).

Scott became the tutor of Robert Richardson, and useful insights into his life may be gleaned from the latter's *Memoirs of Alexander Campbell.* An excellent biography of Scott was published by Dwight Stevenson, *Voice of the Golden Oracle* (St. Louis: Bethany Press, 1946). A compendium of Scott's doctrinal thinking has been compiled by John Neth, *Walter Scott Speaks* (Milligan College, TN: Emmanuel School of Religion, 1967).

[2]Baxter, 1926, op. cit., p. 29.

[3]Richardson undertakes to make such a comparison of the two, op. cit., Vol. I, pp. 510-512.

[4]The pseudonym suggests that Scott's relationship to the editor was similar to Phillip Melancthon's supportive role in Luther's reform efforts.

[5]That Scott became concerned for Christian unity and saw restoration in the light of this goal is seen most clearly in the fact that he named the periodical that he published late in life (1844-1849) the *Protestant Unionist.*

[6]Howard Jost, *Religious Structures in the Great Revival, 1799-1805* (Chicago: University of Chicago, unpublished paper, March 18, 1969), p. 12.

[7]Lorenzo Dow, *The Dealings of God, Man, and the Devil: as Exemplified in the Life Experience, and Travels of Lorenzo Dow, in a Period of Over Half a Century; Together With His Polemic and Miscellaneous Writings, Complete* (Cincinnati: Applegate & Co., 1848), p. 262.

[8]Numerous studies have been made of frontier revivalism. The reader is referred to Bernard A. Wiesbarger, *They Gathered at the River* (Boston: Little, Brown, & Co., 1958), and Whitney R. Cross, *The Burned Over District* (Cornell University Press, 1950) as good examples. The life and early career of Charles Grandison Finney illustrate nineteenth-century revivalism.

[9]Scott, "On Teaching Christianity—No. IV" *Christian Baptist,* Vol. I, No. 7 (February 2, 1924).

[10]Ibid.

[11]See William E. Tucker and Lester G. McAllister, *Journey in Faith* (St. Louis: Christian Board of Publication, 1975), p. 130.

[12]Garrison and DeGroot, op. cit., p. 44.

[13]The description is that of William Baxter, 1926, op. cit., p. 44.

[14]Baxter, 1926, op. cit., p. 47. J.D. Murch seems to concur by naming his chapter on Scott: "Walter Scott and the *Gospel Restored,*" op. cit., p. 97.

[15]The Greek preposition *(eis)* in Acts 2:38 may be rendered "for" or "unto." Its implication is result, not cause. See J.H. Thayer, *A Greek-English Lexicon of the New Testament* (New York: American Book Co.), 1889, p. 183f, for a fuller discussion. See also W.F. Ardnt and F.W Gingrich, *A Greek-English Lexicon of the New Testament and Other Early Christian Literature* (Chicago: University of Chicago, 1952), p. 228f.

[16]Baxter, 1926, op. cit., p. 54.

[17]Richardson, op. cit., Vol. II, p. 288.

[18]Scott's report is found in full in A.S. Hayden, *A History of the Disciples in the Western Reserve* (Cincinnati: Chase & Hall, 1875), pp. 171-173.

[19]Baxter, 1926, op. cit., p. 65.

[20]Ibid. W.E. Garrison (op. cit., pp. 180-192) concurs in this appraisal, suggesting that, except for Scott, there might be no need to write a history of the movement.

[21]Ibid., pp. 81, 82. Cf. Richardson's account (op. cit., Vol. II, p. 208) of the origin of Scott's five-point analysis of the gospel.

[22]For a good discussion of the differences in evangelistic methods, see William T. Moore, "The Old Evangelism and the New," *A Comprehensive History of the Disciples of Christ* (New York: Revell, 1909), pp. 659-681. It would be incorrect to conclude that Scott was only interested in "head religion." Following the custom of his day, he frequently utilized the services of an "exhorter" to move people to action following his own address.

[23]For a good discussion of this, see Perry Miller, op. cit., pp. 48, 49.

[24]Hayden's "forte was the singing of gospel songs." W.E. Garrison, *Christian Unity and Disciples of Christ* (St. Louis: Bethany Press, 1955), p. 90. Hayden, a Baptist who was an early subscriber to the *Christian Baptist,* abandoned Calvinism when he heard Walter Scott preach in 1827. He was an effective evangelist in Ohio until his death in 1863.

[25]Baxter, 1926, op. cit., p. 91.

[26]A. Campbell, "Mahoning Association," *Millenial Harbinger,* 1830, p. 414-416.

[27]Baxter, 1926, op. cit., p. 93.

[28]Hayden, op. cit., p. 462.

[29]Walter Scott, *The Messiahship or Great Demonstration* (Cincinnati: H. Bosworth, 1859).

[30]See Charles Nordhoff, *The Communistic Societies of the United States* (New York: Schocken Books, 1965).

[31]William A. Linn, *The Story of the Mormons* (New York: Russell & Russell, 1963), p. 123.

[32]Ibid., p. 126. See also Smith, Handy, and Loetscher, op. cit., Vol. II, p. 80.

[33]John Rogers, *Biography of Elder John T. Johnson* (Cincinnati: published by the author, 1861), p. 13.

[34]Ibid., p. 20.

[35]Ibid., pp. 27, 28.

[36]Ibid., p. 329, Letter of Dr. L.L. Pinkerton.

[37]Ibid., p. 194.

[38]Ibid., p. 349.

[39]Ibid., pp. 394-400. An address before this association in St. Louis, Missouri, indicated his grasp of textual and translation problems at a time when the science of textual criticism was in its infancy.

[40]John A. Williams, *Life of Elder John Smith* (Cincinnati: R.W. Carroll, 1870), p. 115. Williams's biography is the most adequate work on John Smith, though a very popular biographical work has been provided recently by Louis Cochran, *Raccoon John Smith* (New York: Duell, Sloan & Pearce, 1963).

[41]Ibid., p. 62.

[42]Ibid., p. 64.

[43]For a summary of his dogmatic views, see ibid., pp. 89, 90.

[44]Ibid., p. 219.

[45]Ibid., pp. 291ff. Smith's reasons for leaving the Baptist Church are given on pp. 293-295 of this work.

[46]Ibid., p. 428—quoted by the author without further references.

[47]The term was used to refer to what is now known as Universalism.

[48]A brief but useful resumé of biographical data on the early leaders is found in John W. Wade, *Pioneers of the Restoration Movement* (Cincinnati: Standard, 1966).

Chapter Six

Launching a Movement

The leaven of reformation had permeated the frontier Baptist community to such an extent that the leadership of several Baptist associations concluded that excision was the only effective solution. Expelled congregations began to adopt the name "Church of Christ," for which they found Biblical sanction in Romans 16:16. Individually, they spoke of themselves as "disciples," also on Biblical grounds (cf. Acts 11:26). Their enemies often referred to them as "Campbellites," a name that was uniformly repudiated because of its obvious sectarian character.

The Millennial Harbinger

The close of the decade of the 1820s witnessed a realignment of religious positions so that the continued publication of the *Christian Baptist* was deemed inappropriate. No longer were the majority of its readers considered to be Baptist. Nor was it useful to direct the attention of the readers to activities and developments within the Baptist fold. A new journal was needed, one that could be free to explore the possibilities inherent in the changed situation, a journal that would be more positive and more creative. Accordingly, the *Christian Baptist* was terminated at the end of its seventh year (Campbell held that the Biblical seven signified completion)[1] and replaced by the the *Millennial Harbinger,* the first number of which appeared in January 1830.

The prospectus for the new periodical defined its aims in no uncertain terms:

> This work shall be devoted to the destruction of Sectarianism, Infidelity, and Antichristian doctrine and practice. It shall have for its

object the development, and introduction of that political and religious order of society called THE MILLENNIUM, which will be the consummation of that ultimate amelioration of society proposed in the
Christian Scriptures.[2]

The significance of the name of the journal should not be overlooked. It means "Herald of the Millennium." The title reflects
Campbell's deep conviction that the preaching of the pure Word of
God would produce the true church and, thereby, eventually affect
society to such a degree as to transform it into that blessed condition envisioned in the prophets and implied in the phrase *kingdom
of God*. This kind of social optimism, which may sound strange to
the ears of a more cynical generation, was widely accepted in the
nineteenth century. It reflected Campbell's deep faith in the power
of the gospel to meet both the individual and the social needs of
mankind. Thus, Campbell's millennialism was far removed from
present-day premillennialism.[3]

Millennial views were very much a part of the American scene at
this time. These ranged from a secular utopianism to revivalist apoc-
alypticism. One of the more prominent and engaging forms of premillennialism was that of William Miller, a Baptist farmer from New
York, who predicted the return of Christ in 1843-44. Campbell devoted a series of articles to the excitement generated thereby, with the
intent of proving by Miller's own presuppositions that his dates
could not be correct. Campbell's understanding of the arrival of the
happy epoch was based on a gradual change in human culture as it
is brought into harmony with the will and purpose of God through
preaching. As early as 1830, he wrote: "To introduce the last and
most beneficial change in society, it is only necessary to let the
gospel, in its own plainness, simplicity, and force speak to men."[4] He
had great confidence in the potential of redeemed men to realize the
hopes implicit in the ideal of the kingdom, but not before the whole
of mankind was won to Christ. In 1848, he wrote:

> This may yet be regarded comparatively as a dark age; compared
> not with the past, but with the future. For my own part, though so
> much enlightened compared with past ages, I must regard the pre-
> sent age as dark in anticipations of the future.[5]

With confidence in the transforming power of the gospel to produce
a just and harmonious society, Campbell could look hopefully to a
constantly improving future. He believed that the freedom of the
New World, the technological developments that were occurring with
amazing rapidity, and the development of industrial resources all
would combine to produce a society that would realize the hopes
associated with the millennium.[6] Consequently, although Campbell

could write a twenty-six-article series on "The Coming of the Lord,"[7] he did not see the event as imminent, and he disdained the practice of making converts on the fears that could be generated by preaching a doctrine of the near return of Christ.[8] Nor did the doctrines of the return of the Lord assume any prominence in the evangelistic preaching of Walter Scott.

The *Millennial Harbinger* increased the impact that the reformer from Bethany was making in the Western Reserve and the upper South. Coupled with the vigorous evangelism of Walter Scott, "Raccoon" John Smith, and scores of other frontiersmen, the "reform" movement spread widely. A correspondent of the *New York Baptist Register* expressed alarm over the growth of the movement, writing:

> Mr. Campbell's paper, and their vigorous missionary efforts, are making great achievements. It is said that one half of the Baptist churches in Ohio have embraced this sentiment and become what they call, "Christian Baptists." It is spreading like a mighty contatagion [sic] through the Western states, wasting Zion in its progress. In Kentucky, its desolations are said to be even greater than in Ohio.[9]

Movements Similar and Different

Inevitably, this reform movement became increasingly aware of the similarities of the "Christian" movement. Campbell visited Georgetown, Kentucky, in 1824. and met Barton Stone. In 1826, Stone began publication of the *Christian Messenger*, and the occasion shortly presented itself for editorial correspondence. The subject of the Trinity provided the initial exchange. Stone suggested that Campbell's trinitarian views violated his own principle of rejecting human opinion. Campbell reassured Stone that no theological formula was satisfactory or capable of being an adequate criterion of Christian fellowship, urged him to avoid the kind of speculation that had led others to brand him Arian or Unitarian, and assured him of fraternal acceptance so long as he was willing to pray to Christ as God and affirm what the Scriptures testified about the Son.[10]

The evangelistic efforts of the Christians caused them to cross paths with Walter Scott and his colleagues of the Mahoning Association. Warm friendships developed, and the similarities of the aims of the two groups immediately became apparent. Mutual awareness augmented the editorial correspondence and led to a growing conviction among both bodies that their mutual concern for the unity of Christ's followers made it incumbent that they explore the possibility of union. There were difficulties. These may be discerned in at least five significant areas in the life of the church.

1. The Name

Ever since the dissolution of the Springfield Presbytery in 1804, Stone had used the name *Christian* to designate both the church for which he preached and the individual member of the church, citing Acts 11:26, "The disciples were called Christians first at Antioch." Campbell acknowledged the appropriateness of the name "Christian" but expressed concern that it had been employed in a sectarian sense and declared: "We shall choose the *older* name, *'disciple;'* and recommend to all the brotherhood to be called not *'Christians,'* but *'the disciples of Christ.'*"[11] But Campbell's reasons never impressed Stone or any of his followers, so the issue of the name has never been resolved, causing a certain amount of confusion of identity to those not well acquainted with the movement.

2. Baptism

Alexander Campbell's understanding of baptism had been carefully formulated by serious Bible study and refined by two formal debates and endless discussions of the subject. Actually, his views were what might be considered "High Church" and "sacramental." He insisted on a serious attitude toward baptism because he could not, on the basis of what the Bible said, dissociate this act of faith from the gracious forgiveness of man's sin. Stone, on the other hand, assigned no such significance to baptism. Although the Christians had adopted immersion of believers as the proper mode of baptism and almost all of their people had been immersed, they seem not to have seen it as a condition of salvation or made it a condition of church membership. In what was typical of the frontier, they seem to have adopted the practice without too serious an inquiry as to its meaning. Accordingly, Stone alluded to Campbell's "peculiar views of immersion," which he deemed "sectarian," and suggested that if the disciples insisted on making these

> peculiar views of immersion a term of fellowship, it will be impossible for them to repel, successfully, the imputation of being sectarians, and of having an authoritarian creed (though not written) of one article at least, which is formed of their own opinion of truth; and this short creed would exclude more christians from union than any creed with which I am acquainted.[12]

Stone's criticism was prophetic, anticipating the thinking that in subsequent years would lead some to the practice of "open membership." But it was Campbell who knew where he stood on the meaning of baptism. He acknowledged the truth of Stone's observation, but his commitment to restoring New Testament meaning to this significant act forbade him to compromise. Stone, on the other hand, had not been able to harmonize his practice and preaching of baptism with his understanding of Biblical teaching on the subject. It was inevitable that he would move in the direction in which Campbell had led and within a few years this would be the position of the united movement.

3. The Lord's Supper

Reformers from the beginning of the Brush Run Church had been observing the Supper weekly. But in restraining access to the table, they had imitated the Baptist practice of closed Communion.[13] They were hostile, at first, to the Communion customs of the Christians. Campbell went so far as to suggest that "the apostles were commanded to teach only the immersed to do and observe all the things which the Lord commanded,"[14] thus jusifying the exclusion of the unimmersed from the Supper. The Christians were not accustomed to weekly Communion, and their more ordered concept of church government led them to question the propriety of holding the Supper except under the supervision of an ordained minister.[15] However, when they did hold a Communion, it was not "closed" to those outside their ranks. These differences, though implying significant theological variations, were soon dissolved into the common practice of weekly Communion under the presidency of "elders" and open to all believers. This solution was congenial to frontier individualism wherein the Supper (in contrast to baptism) was regarded as primarily a matter between the worshiper and God in which none was "either invited or debarred." It was also a very concrete expression of rejection of creeds that tended to "fence the table" by excluding from fellowship those who did not subscribe to their formulations. And it was an overt manner of expressing what one of the popular slogans of the movement affirmed: "Not the only Christians, but Christians only" by opening what has historically been the symbol of fellowship in Christ to all who believe in Him regardless of their views on matters of "opinion." This implication of open Communion was lost on many who were so conditioned by the individualism in American culture that the fraternal dimension of the Supper was obliterated. But it did trouble some who saw clearly the Biblical implications of the Supper in which table fellowship reflects close personal ties and the Supper itself as the act that symbolizes the unity of the body, among other things, and is hence a "communion" of the community.[16] Their difficulties were not so great as to afford any obstacle to the merging of the two bodies. A practical uniformity of understanding soon emerged.

4. Evangelism

Less troublesome was the difference between the Reformers and the Christians on the matter of how persons became Christians. The Christian movement was born in the frenzy of the frontier revival and generally employed revivalist techniques, often including the mourner's bench. There was more inclination to focus conversion on an experience.[17] Reformers, on the other hand, followed the evangelistic techniques pioneered by Walter Scott in which the conversion of a sinner was much less emotional and more a matter of hearing, believing, and obeying the gospel. The latter method was often criticized as "head religion" and reproved for ignoring the role of the Holy Spirit in conversion. Its defenders insisted that the Holy Spirit worked in and through the preached Word in winning hearers to Christ and the new evangelistic method actually eliminated only the abuses that were erroneously attributed to the Spirit. The appeal of the new evangelism to the good judgment and common sense of the average, intelligent sinner presupposed his ability to act responsibly toward the good news. This approach was widely accepted by the unchurched frontiersman, who often appreciated it as a welcome option to the emotional frenzy that characterized frontier revivalism and repulsed many sincere seekers of the truth. It would not be correct to infer that Scott's evangelistic method entirely displaced the revivalism of the Christians, but, in the ensuing synthesis, it was the predominating influence.

5. Church Order

The two groups held dissimilar concepts of church order. The Christians had a more precise concept of ministry and, as may be expected from their Presbyterian background, looked favorably upon formalized inter-congregational relations. They operated within a "conference" rather than on the basis of a strict congregational polity. The Reformers, on the other hand, emerged in the independent Brush Run Church, which, within a single congregation, chose its own officers, licensed a man to preach, and managed its own affairs totally on a local basis. While it is true that the Brush Run Church became a member of a Baptist Association, its experience with that body was such as would not recommend that type of extra-congregational authority. Alexander Campbell transferred to the Wellsburg Church, which belonged to the Mahoning Association. Here the sentiment against any ecclesiastical body above the local congregation was so strong that the association dissolved itself in 1830. Campbell himself had misgivings about this and shortly thereafter began a series of articles on the necessity of cooperation between the churches.[18] But the prevailing sentiment among the Reformers was that there was no extra-congregational authority to be found in the New Testament and none was to be accepted in any form. It would take a century and a half and require a massive promotional effort before one segment of the Campbell-Stone heirs could be persuaded to accept a formalized, extra-congregational authority.[19]

Such total congregationalism caused Campbell some hesitation as the subject of union with the Christians was suggested. He raised questions as to the manner in which a union between such groups could be effected.[20] Campbell was more a thinker than a man of action. His analytical mind led him to anticipate in advance the significance of actions he might be tempted to take. But while he was hesitating and contemplating, others were ready to act. A will to unite had been generated in Kentucky and doubts arising in Bethany would not be able to check it. Both Campbell and Stone had set into motion forces in behalf of the unity of believers that would not easily be restrained. The action centered in Georgetown and Lexington, Kentucky. Barton W. Stone, John T. Johnson, and "Raccoon" John Smith were the leading advocates of action on the matter of union. The *Christian Messenger* of January, 1832, carried the following announcement:[21]

UNION OF CHRISTIANS

We are happy to announce to our brethren, and to the world, the union of Christians in fact in our country. A few months ago the Reforming Baptists (known *invidiously* as Campbellites) and the Christians, in Georgetown and the neighborhood, agreed to meet and worship together. We soon found that we were indeed in the same spirit, on the same foundation, the New Testament, and wore the same name, *Christian*. We saw no reason why we should not be in the same family. The Lord confirmed this by his presence; for a good number was soon added to the church. We agreed to have a four days meeting on Christmas in Georgetown, and on New Year's Day at Lexington for the same length of time. A great many Teachers and Brethren of both descriptions assembled together and worshipped together in one spirit and one accord. Never did we witness more love, union, and harmony, than was manifested at these meetings. Since the last meeting we have heard of the good effects. The spirit of union is spreading like fire in dry stubble.

The process of uniting two bodies of people who were without any type of supra-congregational structure empowered to act in behalf of and commit the individual congregations was not an easy one. Largely, it came down to a matter of convincing each congregation of the basic rightfulness and Christian propriety of the proposed merger. To accomplish this task, "Raccoon" John Smith of the Disciples and John Rogers of the Christians were appointed to "ride together through all the churches of both descriptions, which contributions are to be deposited together with Brother John T. Johnson as treasurer and distributor."[22] These efforts were augmented by editorial endorsement from the publications. The *Christian Messenger* carried articles in favor of the union by Stone, Johnson, and Smith.[23] The

Millennial Harbinger was cautious at first but soon came to full support of the effort, as did Walter Scott's *Evangelist.*

The process of union was consummated with much success chiefly because there was so much to recommend it. Despite the differences previously noted, the similarities were much more significant in the minds of the congregations, and these similarities were to prove the basis of genuine community. Chief among them were (1) a desire for unity among the followers of Jesus Christ as the necessary condition for accomplishing His purposes, (2) an aversion to creeds and theological systems as divisive, *per se,* and a desire to ground faith in "the pure word of God," (3) a dislike of ecclesiastical structures above the congregational level, and (4) an evangelical spirit that sought the conversion of every person to "simple evangelical Christianity." Vigorous prosecution of the union by editors, evangelists, and preachers was sufficient to cause most congregations in those towns and villages where both groups existed to initiate conversations toward merger.[24] Both groups took care to avoid the suggestion that one "joined" the other. To be sure, the actual process of merging was not without difficulties on the local level, but the will to unite generally prevailed. When Barton W. Stone moved to Jacksonville, Illinois, in 1834, he found two congregations, Church of Christ and Christian. He refused to unite with either until they had united themselves. The merger of the two groups was most successful in Kentucky and Tennessee,[25] where virtually the entire number of churches of both groups joined. Not so for the Atlantic coastal area where "Christian" churches existed that were little influenced by Barton W. Stone. These congregations of the O'Kelly movement and churches of "Christians" in New England remained aloof, objecting primarily to "Campbellite" emphasis on immersion, though this was not their only problem with the merger.[26] Remaining separate, these congregations would unite in 1931 with a branch of the Congregational Church, and, in 1957, this Congregational-Christian Church would merge with the Evangelical and Reformed Church to become the United Church of Christ. Some of the Christian churches in New England had become infected with Unitarian sentiments, and Alexander Campbell, who avoided Trinitarian verbalism but thought in those terms, could not countenance union with those who failed to embrace the full divinity of Jesus Christ.[27]

Cooperatives for Evangelism

Growth generates enthusiasm and produces its own dynamic. As congregations flowed together, augmenting each other's numerical strength, a new sense of urgent mission gripped the movement for

Christian unity on the basis of the New Testament. There were many communities untouched with the "plea" for Biblical unity, communities that would be won to sectarianism by the efforts of the several denominations that had already organized to send evangelists into the frontier. The situation called for a vigorous and determined evangelism directed to both the numerous unchurched and the adherents of the older sects. The original team of Rogers and Smith was expanded in Kentucky to four separate efforts. The situation counseled the formation of "cooperatives" wherein several congregations in a given area undertook to support the efforts of an evangelist who sought to organize new congregations of Christians-only. Alexander Campbell had urged the churches toward this type of cooperation since 1831. Kentucky and Indiana took the lead in forming local or district "cooperatives,"[28] and other states followed in subsequent decades.

Even more significant than the efforts of the cooperations to support evangelism in the expanding frontier were the efforts of countless individuals who were committed to the aims and ideal of the movement. Many were farmer/preachers, like Barton W. Stone, whose living came from the soil but whose efforts on the weekend were directed toward calling believers together to "break bread," sometimes in homes, if possible in a simple "meeting house" constructed of logs, and occasionally in a one-room schoolhouse. The decades prior to the Civil War were restless times and Americans were on the move westward. Countless congregations of Christians-only were gathered by the initiative of committed laymen who convinced their neighbors of the folly of reproducing the often meaningless schisms of their old communities in the virgin territory of mid-America. It simply made sense to all who believed in Jesus Christ to unite their efforts to build His church. Thus, in a very real sense, the merger of 1832 created a "people's movement" that was relevant to the times. Such movements are hard to stop. The movement experienced great growth.

It should be borne in mind that this was the age of Jackson, a time when the frontier was seething with activity and beginning to exert itself in national affairs. Much has been written about the frontier[29] and its influence upon the movement.[30] The frontiersman was independent and self-sufficient. He was impressed by "common sense" solutions to his problems. He loved simplicity and was fond of direct action. He was little impressed with traditions, constituted authority, or social amenities. The simplicity of the plea to cut through accumulated theological jargon and proceed directly from the pure Word of God to establish self-governing, independent congregations made much sense. Such a congregation could be formed solely upon local initiative without permission from, or obligation to, any ecclesiastical authority, and it could offer unlimited opportunity for development of the creative potential within the local community. Since the frontier was largely without class stratification, the appeal reached a large percentage of the population by mid-century. By this time the movement was clearly a major force on the frontier.

The United States was overwhelmingly Protestant in the nineteenth century, but the beginnings of massive immigration from Roman Catholic countries could be discerned in the third and fourth decades. This gave rise to anti-Catholic feeling and caused widespread interest in Alexander Campbell's fourth debate, this time against Archbishop John B. Purcell of Cincinnati, Ohio, in 1837. This was the only time in the history of North America that a prelate of Purcell's rank would engage a Protestant in debate. Campbell attacked the Roman Church on the ground that it was not catholic, apostolic, or holy, but rather that it is a sect devoid of Biblical foundation, that many of its doctrines—such as that of purgatory, indulgences, transubstantiation, and supererogation—are immoral in tendency and injurious to society; that it is the Babylon of Revelation; and that it is essentially anti-American. When this debate was completed, the proceedings were published[31] and Campbell was widely acclaimed as the defender of the Protestant cause. Henceforth, Campbell and his brethren were regarded not as religious agitators but more and more as advocates of orthodox Christian teaching.

Colleges

While the evangelistic efforts and the many publications of the movement were by far the most conspicuous evidences of its vigor, other important resources were developing. As early as 1833, a charter was granted for a college to be opened in New Albany, Indiana, but nothing materialized from this effort. Three years later, the first of many colleges that the movement was to spawn opened its doors in Georgetown, Kentucky. It was actually a spin-off from the existing Baptist college, and its emphasis was on cultural breadth. The fact that it was named for Francis Bacon, the father of the inductive method, reflects the type of scientific thinking valued by its founders. Walter Scott was named president of the college and was succeeded after a one-year term by David S. Burnet. Scott evidently did not find the fund-raising pressures to his liking. Bacon College was moved to Harrodsburg, Kentucky, in 1839 and, after a troubled existence of a decade, became one of the progenitors of the reorganized Transylvania University.

Education was too much a part of Alexander Campbell's heritage for him to resist the opportunity to establish a college. He had opened a school for boys in his own home in 1818, but, within five years, it proved to be a disappointment. In 1839, he began a series of articles in the *Millennial Harbinger* in which he set forth his ideas on education.[32] Sensitive to the fact that education is derived from the home and the church as well as the school, Campbell outlined a rather elaborate scheme for what would appear to be a communal-type institution dedicated to the nurture of youth from seven years through college. A family house would shelter children from seven to fourteen years of age (in that day boarding schools were not uncommon). From primary school through college, emphasis would center

The old Bethany meeting house. In 1852 this building replaced a smaller, stone structure erected in 1831. It served the Bethany congregation until 1910. A. Campbell and many other early leaders of the movement preached here.

"Old Main," designed from a building at the University of Glasgow, it replaced an earlier structure destroyed by fire in 1857. The building is listed in the National Registry of Historic Places. It has been beautifully restored by a generous grant from the state of West Virginia.

on Biblical instruction and its bearing upon secular literature, nature, and art. The moral development of youth would be a primary concern.[33] The institution would be located in a rural place "not convenient to any town or place or rendezvous." (Those who have visited Bethany College generally agree that none of Mr. Campbell's aims were more fully realized than this.) Acknowledging that this was a long-cherished dream, Campbell disclosed that he had waited until he was reasonably assured that Bacon College had been successfully launched before proceeding with his plans. Now past his fiftieth year and having devoted his energies to writing, preaching and lecturing, sheep-raising, and publishing, he was ready "to bestow much personal labor, without charge," in the establishment and supervision of a great dream. He would begin with the establishment of the college; the primary school would follow. He was ready to provide the land and many thousands of dollars. He sought the counsel and support of his brethren.

A charter was secured for Bethany College in 1840, and the doors were opened in 1841. President Campbell taught moral philosophy and lectured at the daily early-morning chapel. A group of illustrious colleagues was soon gathered, including Robert Richardson, W.K. Pendleton, Robert Milligan, and others who would inspire a generation of leaders committed to the reform of Christianity. Young men were eager to study at Bethany, and parents were willing to sacrifice in order that their children might study with the famous Mr. Campbell. Campbell's skill as an administrator and his wide range of travels and contacts with people of influence insured the survival of the college through many trying periods, including a disastrous fire that destroyed the main building and library on the night of December 10, 1857. Classes were interrupted for only one day. The work of rebuilding began in earnest despite a national depression and the forebodings of a terrible civil conflict. In the decades that followed, Bethany College would provide a steady supply of leaders for a movement that was making a powerful impact on the American religious scene.

The concept of a Biblically-centered broad education embracing the arts and sciences developed under Campbell's guidance. It profoundly influenced the development of many other educational institutions of the Disciples. These were not long in coming. Tolbert Fanning opened Franklin College near Nashville, Tennessee, on January 1, 1845. It emphasized intellectual, moral, and physical education, the last of which was supplied by work on the farm on which the school was located. The venture received Campbell's endorsement and encouragement.[34] The outbreak of war in 1861 closed the school and its building was used as a barracks, first for the South and later for the army of the North. It reopened for a short period following the war.

A decade following the founding of Bethany College, the Western
Reserve Eclectic Institute was opened at Hiram in Portage County,
Ohio. The auspicious name was suggested by Isaac Errett. A.S.
Hayden was named president, and 102 students enrolled for classes
in the fall of 1850. The next year, James A. Garfield enrolled as a
student, launching a meteoric career that would see him become a
graduate, a preacher, a professor, president of the institute, and
state senator by 1860—and President of the United States by 1881.

Schools and colleges soon began to appear where resources were
insufficient and planning was inadequate. Naturally, many were
short-lived. Among those that survived are Northwestern Christian
University (now Butler) in Indianapolis (1855), Kentucky Female
Orphan School (now Midway College; 1849), Eureka College (1855),
Abingdon College (later merged with Eureka) in Illinois (1854), and
Christian University (now Culver-Stockton College) in Canton, Missouri (1855). In many cases, these colleges would not merit the designation today, but they represented heroic efforts to provide needed
education on the frontier prior to the Civil War.

While busily engaged in the development of Bethany College,
Alexander Campbell took time for his fifth and final debate. The subject of baptism was much discussed in Kentucky and constant
inroads were being made into the ranks of the Presbyterians in that
state. Accordingly, the synod of Kentucky wanted a competent, public defense of infant baptism and so arranged for a debate between
N.L. Rice of Paris and Alexander Campbell on the proper subject,
action, and mode of baptism. Careful preparations were made for the
meeting in Lexington, Kentucky, November 15 to December 1, 1843.
Henry Clay was engaged as moderator. Four hours daily for sixteen
days were devoted to the discussion. The published record constituted a volume of 912 pages of small print, which enjoyed an enormous
sale for its day.[35] There soon followed several more immersions of
those who had been sprinkled in infancy. Mr. Campbell's discussion
of baptism in this volume remained as the most thorough treatment
of this subject in print until recent times.

Missions—David S. Burnet

A vigorous and growing religious movement such as the one under
scrutiny could not avoid being influenced by contemporary religious
developments. Most of the Protestant denominations had responded
to the extension of Western European colonial powers in Asia, India,
and Africa by organizing missionary societies to Christianize these
lands. So vigorous and widespread were these efforts that Kenneth
Scott Latourette designates the period between the end of the

Napoleonic wars and the beginning of World War I as "the great century" for missions.[36] Although Alexander Campbell had condemned missionary societies in his *Christian Baptist*[37] period, the practicality of an alternate method of carrying the gospel to foreign regions had yet to be demonstrated. Disciples had formed "cooperations" to do evangelistic work at home, and the conviction gained strength with each passing year that something similar ought to be done to project the message abroad. Reflecting upon the growing interest in foreign missions, J.H. Garrison observed:

> The birth of a conscience on the subject of foreign missions had furnished a motive for the calling of the first convention and the organization of the American Christian Missionary Society, second only to the pressure of immediate domestic needs and the growth of a group consciousness seeking expression.[38]

Precisely how such foreign work could be accomplished was another matter. Alexander Campbell was of the opinion that some type of representative assembly would be the appropriate body to launch a project for the whole Brotherhood.[39] However, in spite of recognizing the need for a general convention,[40] he took no initiative to organize such an assembly. Meanwhile, as Campbell was setting forth reasons for organization in the pages of the *Millennial Harbinger,* David Burnet was launching the organizations in Cincinnati that eventually served to bring together a body of persons ready to act.

David S. Burnet was born on July 6, 1808, in Dayton, Ohio. When he was eight, the family moved to Cincinnati. His father became mayor of the city in 1821, and David, at thirteen, served as clerk in his father's office. One uncle was a judge and U.S. Senator, and another uncle was the first president (provisional) of the Republic of Texas. The family was wealthy and aristocratic, and David, who began the study of law in 1821, seemed destined for a career in politics and statecraft.

The Burnet family was prominent in the Presbyterian Church. When David was sixteen years old, he became involved in the developing Sunday-school movement and began a serious study of the Bible. On his own, he concluded that baptism was properly done by immersion and applied to the Baptists for baptism without ever subscribing to any Baptist creed or confession. Intelligent and articulate, Burnet soon came to be known as "the boy preacher" among Baptists, who encouraged him to exercise his natural gifts as a speaker. This seems to have infuriated his aristocratic family, which sought to interfere with his inclination for preaching by obtaining for David an appointment to West Point Military Academy.[41]

When the scholarship was turned down, the family was furious. The next year, David Burnet met Alexander Campbell. In 1827, when twenty years old, he became the pastor of a Baptist church in Dayton, Ohio, a congregation so permeated with the reform views set forth in the *Christian Baptist* that it changed its name to Central Church of Christ in 1829, rejecting all written articles of faith.[42] This was the second congregation to declare itself separate from Baptist fellowship; the first was Christian Chapel, a congregation Burnet helped to organize at Eighth and Walnut Streets in Cincinnati in 1828 and one that was destined to enjoy an illustrious history. In 1830, Burnet married Mary Gano, the youngest daughter of Major General John S. Gano, one of the founders of Covington, Kentucky. They had no children.

Cincinnati was at the crossroads of the nation in 1830. An important river port on the great waterway to the west, the completion of the Miami Canal in that year linked it with the Great Lakes so that it became the terminal for an artery to the north while just across the river lay roads through Kentucky to the south. The previous year, Alexander Campbell and Robert Owen picked Cincinnati as the site for their debate, and Lyman Beecher came to Cincinnati in 1830 to help launch a new Presbyterian denomination and establish Lane Seminary. Cincinnati had an irresistible attraction to D.S. Burnet and would be the site of his most fruitful labor as an editor and an organizer.

Burnet's relationship with Alexander Campbell was always one of respectful admiration, but there were some trying experiences. In 1833, Burnet made an extensive evangelistic tour of the Atlantic seaboard states from Virginia north in company with Alexander Campbell. Convinced that there was need for insights that had been published in the *Christian Baptist*, Burnet undertook in 1835 to publish a one-volume edition of the seven-volume series, deleting news items, correspondence, and personal items while reprinting editorials and essays.[43] In 1836, he launched the *Christian Preacher*, which he edited for five years. The next year, he accepted the presidency of Bacon College in Georgetown, Kentucky, the first of many colleges to be established by the Disciples. He succeeded his friend Walter Scott and held the post for two years. When the college trustees decided to move the school to Harrodsburg, Kentucky, Burnet returned to Cincinnati and opened a girl's school with the forbidding name of Hygeia Female Academy.

It was during the decade of the 1840s that David Burnet made what he would later judge to be "the most important act of my career."[44] His reference was to three organizations that he was largely instrumental in launching. The first, known as the American Christian Bible Society, the purpose of which was "to put into the hands of every human being the Bible, without note or comment,"[45] was announced in 1845. Campbell, no doubt concerned lest the new effort jeopardize contributions to fledgling Bethany College, reacted negatively toward this effort. Four reasons were cited by Campbell for taking what must have appeared to his readers to be an unexpected position: (1) He doubted "the propriety of any institution being got up . . . without a general understanding some way obtained of the concurrence and support of the whole brotherhood in the scheme. This is always essential to its claims upon them [sic]."[46] (2) The Baptist Bible Society was achieving the same purpose effectively, thus rendering the new effort superfluous. (3) Cooperation with the Baptists would help to maintain good relationships with them. (4) The giving level of the churches was not sufficient to sustain both the society and "our infant Colleges yet unable to stand alone."[47] While the fourth reason probably provides the clue to Campbell's reaction, the first reason left him vulnerable to Burnet's retort:

> Was there a convention of the churches to establish Bethany College, the claims of which must now be heard, and until they are heard the Society must die in despair? The Society, composed of some hundreds, cannot ask aid to their brethren; but Bethany College, called into being by one brother, may.[48]

To this, Campbell could respond only by falling back to a semantic ploy, namely that he had not presumed to call Bethany the *American Christian College*,[49] a manifestly weak reply that Burnet could have easily disposed of by pointing out that, regardless of the name, Campbell was indeed seeking nationwide support for Bethany College, and that was the very point of the issue.

The organization in 1846 of the Sunday School and Tract Society, later renamed the the American Christian Publication Society, was Burnet's second venture in practical promotion. Both organizations held their annual meetings, thenceforth called "anniversaries," on contiguous dates. This move did not improve relations between the Bethany and the Cincinnati leaders, but they were sufficiently cordial to permit them to consider an invitation that both visit the churches in England. They traveled to New York City together, but Burnet did not undertake the journey overseas. Relations deteriorated the next year when Campbell, always opposed to secret societies, noted that Burnet was to address a cornerstone ceremony for a new Masonic Hall in a town near Cincinnati. He challenged Burnet to an explanation.

Such was the situation when the third organization came into being: the American Christian Missionary Society (A.C.M.S.). Various editors had expressed a desire for a more comprehensive organization based on a wider representation than had been developed to date, and it seemed appropriate that the anniversary of the Bible and tract societies in Cincinnati would be the most likely time and place for the messengers of the churches to convene. On October 24-28, 1849, 156 delegates from one hundred churches in eleven states gathered in Cincinnati, Ohio. They came with different ideas. Some had been formally designated as "delegates" to represent their congregations in the deliberations in Cincinnati, while others just came because of their interest in supporting the missionary enterprise. The latter represented nobody but themselves. A lively discussion ensued over the nature and character that the assembly was to assume, and it became obvious that the only feasible solution would be to regard all present as delegates. Any other course would have excluded the majority of those present. Thus, the gathering became a mass meeting of interested individuals rather than a body of representatives of churches that could claim a quasi-official status. The assembly proceeded to create the American Christian Missionary Society.

It is important to understand the nature of a "society" and precisely how the society concept provided a happy solution to the problem of doing overseas mission work. A society is a single-purpose organization of interested individuals. This was a favorite device in the nineteenth century, which saw societies created for all kinds of purposes, both religious and otherwise. Bible societies, mission societies, and temperance societies vied with literary societies, historical societies, animal protection societies, and societies to combat diseases. All appealed for the interest and support of individuals who subscribed to their worthy purpose and were willing to dedicate a portion of their time and means to promote the aims of the given society. Since the purpose was specific and carefully and clearly defined, the area of a society's activity was limited. Thus, a society supported by individuals and created specifically to do mission work was not considered to be a threat to congregations that were zealous to maintain their independence. The structure of membership in the A.C.M.S. clearly reflects this composition. Individuals joined the society; congregations did not. Different types of membership were provided, ranging from ten dollars per year for an individual to twenty dollars for a life membership and one hundred dollars for a life directorship. More than two thousand dollars was subscribed in this manner, and an additional three thousand dollars was pledged to the new society by the end of the meeting.[50]

Though not present, Alexander Campbell was far too prominent to be overlooked in the selection of the first president and, doubtless, his support too critical to the success of the venture to permit the selection of another for the office. Burnet graciously accepted a vice presidency, although the responsibility of presiding over the earlier sessions and giving continued guidance to the new organization fell largely to him simply because Campbell's commitment to Bethany College compromised his usefulness to the society. Burnet was elected president after Campbell's death in 1866, but died in 1867 before he completed his first term. In 1856, the Publication Society and the Bible Society were absorbed by the Missionary Society.

From its inception, the A.C.M.S. faced two serious challenges. The first, having theoretical implications, dealt with the question of the legitimacy of a society *per se*, whereas the second, more practical in nature, centered in the matter of insuring the integrity of the society as a missionary agency by resisting the ever-present pressure to have the society act on resolutions dealing with matters extraneous to its original purpose. On both scores, serious trouble would arise that would wreck the society in less than two decades.

It was not long before the question was raised as to whether or not the matter of carrying out the Great Commission belonged rightfully to the church and was wrongfully transferred to a society consisting of those individuals who chose to interest themselves in this aspect of the Lord's work. Jacob Creath, Jr.[51] called for a convention to discuss the legitimacy of societies.[52] The elders of the church in Connellsville, Pennsylvania, clearly stated the case when they declared emphatically: "The church is the only missionary society and can admit no rivals." This has continued to be the position of those churches in the movement that are noted for rejection of musical instruments. This position involves a number of hidden presuppositions: namely, that (1) the New Testament provides not only an objective to be accomplished, but a specific method for accomplishing the objective, which method is valid and unalterable in every age and culture, and (2) that an auxiliary such as a society is something outside of and wholly apart from the church. Failure to achieve a satisfactory resolution of these issues would lead to division in years to come.

A second challenge faced by the infant society, namely the preservation of its integrity by resisting extraneous issues, proved to be a difficult matter from the very beginning.[53] Resolutions were passed urging Lord's Day observance and the organization of Sunday schools in every congregation. Churches were also advised to use care in their recognition of preachers, an indication that the new movement was facing a problem with unworthy, vagrant preachers. But numerous other matters in which different persons wanted an expression of opinion were ruled out of order. The presiding officers could hardly have been unaware of the hovering cloud of the slavery issue that would burst above the assembly as it had done four years earlier in the Baptist Missionary Convention. The society could not hope to survive if it did not adhere closely to its original purpose. Failure to respect this reality in 1863 caused the society no end of trouble following the Civil War.

The immediate purpose in the creation of the American Christian Missionary Society was to evangelize the world with the New Testament message. Dr. James T. Barclay, a classical graduate from the

University of Virginia and medical graduate of the University of Pennsylvania, offered himself for missionary service. Dr. Barclay owned the Jefferson estate at Monticello, Virginia. He was a cultured gentleman who was committed to the aims of the movement and was anxious to extend its influence abroad. The society's original subscription in Cincinnati grew to a sum sufficient to send Dr. and Mrs. Barclay to Jerusalem in 1850.

The choice of Jerusalem as the site for the first missionary efforts resulted from enthusiasm that was not guided by the understandings now provided by studies in the contemporary field of missiology. It was suggested that inasmuch as the gospel was preached beginning in Jerusalem that the logical and Biblical place to begin the propagation of the restored gospel would also be Jerusalem.[54] At the time, no questions were raised as to whether conditions then prevailing in the city were favorable to the planting of a New Testament church or what kind of sustaining support would be required to insure the success of the effort. Dr. Barclay was to learn in his four-year residence there that the ruling Turkish Moslems are among the most difficult peoples to convert, and that the

James T. Barclay, M.D. (1807-1874), the first missionary sent out by the American Christian Missionary Society. His efforts in Jerusalem (1850-1854) were terminated when support was withheld because Dr. Barclay had been a slave owner.

Roman, Greek Orthodox, and Jacobite representatives of Christianity were not only fanatic devotees to their respective causes, but were so hostile in their rival claims to the sacred shrines that the Moslem Turks were often required to intervene to maintain peace. The only enduring consequence of the mission was Dr. Barclay's book, *The City of the Great King,*[55] which gave to the people of America an insight into contemporary Jerusalem and its environs in a day when this area was far away and enshrouded in mystery.

Dr. Barclay returned to America in 1854 to find that he had become the center of one of the society's several controversies. He returned to Jerusalem in 1858 to work amid discouraging circumstances until forced to come home because of lack of funds in 1861. The slave issue had been heating up with each passing year, and Northern abolitionists learned that Dr. Barclay had owned slaves on his Monticello plantation. But the society had already projected a second venture, one that had greater appeal to the North. One of the options that seemed to have credibility to opponents of slavery in the 1850s was the resettlement effort to purchase slaves and return them to Africa. This resulted in the creation of Liberia on the west coast of Africa. Alexander Cross, a Kentucky-born slave, was purchased, educated, and sent to Liberia in 1854 to evangelize there. But his death from fever two months after his arrival terminated this effort.

The society partially offset the criticism of Northern anti-slavery enthusiasts for sending Dr. Barclay overseas by selecting an abolitionist, J.O. Beardsley, to begin a work in Jamaica. Beardsley sailed for Jamaica in 1858 amid great enthusiasm. Although this effort was briefly interrupted as a result of the society's difficulties following the Civil War, it was reopened in 1876 and ultimately produced a permanent result.

The fortunes of the infant missionary society were largely determined by national developments relating to the issue of slavery. It suffered from the hostilities related to the Civil War and never recovered, as will be noted in chapter 8. It would be one of the factors that, after the war, produced schism in the movement that sought the unity of the followers of Christ.

Associates in Leadership

While there is no question that Alexander Campbell was the leading thinker who gave shape and direction to the Disciples from the time of the merger with the Christians in 1832 until the outbreak of the Civil War in 1861, it would be a gross injustice to overlook some of the others whose labors and leadership contributed to the growth of the movement.

William K. Pendleton

Closely associated with Alexander Campbell for more than a quarter of a century was William K. Pendleton. Born in Louisa County, Virginia, in 1817, the son of Col. and Mrs. Edmond Pendleton, of English descent, W.K. studied law at the University of Virginia. His parents became enthusiastic advocates of the reform through reading the *Christian Baptist* and the *Millennial Harbinger*. He was baptized by Alexander Campbell in 1840, married successively Lavinia Campbell (1840), and Clarinda (1848). He was elected vice president of Bethany in 1845 and assumed, in addition to lecturing, much of the administrative responsibility of the college. He was also a major contributor to the *Millennial Harbinger*, of which he was made co-editor in 1846. Thus, in the two major responsibilities of Campbell's activity, W.K. Pendleton provided the dependable assistance that enabled Campbell to travel extensively and engage in his numerous other activities. He succeeded Campbell as the second president of Bethany in 1866. In many ways, Pendleton was an example of the Bethany ideal. He was broadly educated, cultured, and a man respected for his faith and character.[56] He died in 1899 and is buried in God's Acre at Bethany.

Robert Richardson

Another close associate of Alexander Campbell was his biographer, Robert Richardson. Son of an eminent Pittsburgh family, Richardson was placed under the tutelage of Walter Scott, through whom his family was introduced to the Campbells and the reforms that they were fostering. When Richardson completed medical studies, he settled in Carthage, Ohio, probably to be near Walter Scott, who had located in this community near Cincinnati and was publishing the *Christian Messenger* at the time. In 1836, Alexander Campbell persuaded him to move to Bethany, where he built a home known as Bethphage and assisted in editing the *Millennial Harbinger*. In many ways, he complemented Campbell through his careful attention to detail and his irenic spirit. He and W.K. Pendleton were the first to be elected to the faculty when Bethany opened in 1840, Richardson serving as professor of chemistry[57] as well as physician to the community.

Richardson was a frequent contributor to the *Millennial Harbinger*. In 1853, he published *Principles and Objects of the Religious Reformation*,[58] which had appeared serially in the *Harbinger* in 1852. He insisted that the reformation was based on simple principles and sought to counter tendencies toward a heartless legalism. This resulted in an editorial battle with Tolbert Fanning, editor of the *Gospel Advocate,* in 1857. This foreshadowed the division that followed the Civil War. Fanning, the opponent of the A.C.M.S., held that Richardson and Pendleton came to exercise an unwarranted influence over Campbell during the latter's declining years. Richardson is best remembered as Campbell's biographer.

End Notes

[1]Campbell gave more than the usual significance to numbers, placing a special value on the number seven. Not only did he bring the *Christian Baptist* to a conclusion after its seventh volume, but he published the *Millennial Harbinger* in five series of seven volumes. In 1865, when Campbell was no longer functional, W.K. Pendleton reverted to the standard enumeration and designated the volume No. XXXVI rather than begin a new series.

[2]Alexander Campbell, ed., *Millennial Harbinger*, Vol. 1, No. 1, (January 4, 1830), p. 1.

[3]A century later, this question would pose a divisive issue for noninstrument churches of Christ. Whether or not Campbell may properly be classified as postmillennial (cf. Wayne Hensley, *The Rhetorical Vision of the Disciples of Christ—A Rhetoric of American Millennialism* [Minneapolis: University of Minnesota, unpublished Ph.D. thesis]) is open to some question of definition. Campbell's article, "The Coming of the Lord," in the *Millennial Harbinger*, 1841, p. 97-104, suggests a postmillennial viewpoint.

[4]Alexander Campbell, "An Oration in Honor of the Fourth of July," *Millennial Harbinger*, 1830, p. 309. See also *Popular Lectures and Addresses* (Philadelphia: James Challen & Son, 1863), p. 377.

[5]Alexander Campbell, "Baccalaureate Address," *The Millennial Harbinger*, 1848, p. 427.

[6]An interesting perspective on Campbell's millennial views is presented by Richard Hughes, who sees a shift of forms in Campbell about 1841. Prior to this date, Hughes sees Campbell's hopes resting on the restored church. Subsequent to 1842, Hughes suggests that Campbell reflects civil millennialism, the conviction that the American nation would realize the millennial hopes. As the Civil War approached, Campbell was forced to modify these views. Cf. Richard T. Hughes, "From Primitive Church to Civil Religion: the Millennial Odyssey of Alexander Campbell," *Journal of the American Academy of Religion*, March 1976, p. 87.

[7]*Millennial Harbinger;* the series began in January, 1841, and continued through October, 1843. A particularly interesting discourse is found in the (March) 1841 volume, pp. 97-104.

[8]"The Coming of the Lord—No. XVI," *Millennial Harbinger*, 1842, pp. 259-265.

[9]"Campbellism," *Vermont Chronicle,* quoted in *Millennial Harbinger,* 1830, p. 117.

[10]See Richardson, op. cit., Vol. II, pp. 201-204.

[11]Alexander Campbell, "The Name Christian," *Millennial Harbinger,* 1830, p. 373. See also *Millennial Harbinger,* 1831, pp. 385-396. Interestingly, Thomas Campbell preferred the name "Christians." See Richardson, op. cit., Vol. II, p. 371.

[12]Barton W. Stone, *Christian Messenger,* May 28, 1828. Reprinted also in *Millennial Harbinger,* 1830, pp. 370, 371.

[13]Campbell's closed Communion reasoning may be found in the *Millennial Harbinger,* 1830, pp. 473-475. See also 1831, pp. 391-393.

[14]Alexander Campbell, "The Christian Messenger," *Millennial Harbinger,* 1830, p. 474. For additional discussion, see John A. Gano, "The Lord's Supper," *Christian Messenger,* 1831, pp. 30-32, and editor's comment—ibid., p. 32.

[15]Richardson, op. cit., Vol. II, p. 384. This threatened the union at its outset. See *Millennial Harbinger,* 1832, pp. 191, 192.

[16]See, for example, 1 Corinthians 10:17. For an example of one man wrestling with this problem, see Moses E. Lard, "Do the Unimmersed Commune?" *Lard's Quarterly,* Vol. I (Georgetown: by the author, 1864), p. 41.

[17]This may be seen in the reports from the churches that are found in the *Christian Messenger.*

[18]"The Co-operation of Churches," *Millennial Harbinger,* 1831, pp. 235-238, 241-246, 435-441; 1832, pp. 201, 202, 244-250, 382-384. Two of the articles in the series (II and III) bear Walter Scott's pseudonymn, "Philip," and two (V and VI) are "correspondence between A.B.G. and F.W.E."

[19]See discussion on Restructure, chapter 16.

[20]Alexander Campbell, "Reply on Union, Communion, and the Name Christian," *Millennial Harbinger,* 1831, p. 389.

[21]*Christian Messenger,* Vol. V, No. 1, pp. 6, 7.

[22]Ibid.

23John Smith's assessment of the critical issues in the merger effort is worthy of examination. See *Christian Messenger,* Vol. VI, No. 3, pp. 87-91.

24Barton W. Stone relates how the merger of existing congregations in Illinois came about. See Stone, *Biography,* op. cit., p. 78.

25W.A. Harper, *The Genius of the Christian Church* (Elon College, NC, 1929), p. 40. The author indicates that a very large portion of the Christian churches in Illinois and Missouri also entered the union with the Disciples.

26For a discussion of Stone's futile efforts to bring the Christians of the East into the union, see William G. West, *Barton W. Stone: Early American Advocate of Christian Unity* (Nashville: Disciples of Christ Historical Society, 1954), pp. 189-202.

27In 1846, Alexander Campbell expressly repudiated a union overture from the Pennsylvania Christian (Unitarian) Conference, on the grounds that those who denied the divinity of Jesus Christ were not to be considered Christians (*Millennial Harbinger,* 1846, p. 222).

28It is beyond the scope of this work to detail the development of the movement on a state level. A good summary of these efforts may be found in Garrison and DeGroot, op. cit., or in the many individual state histories cited in the bibliography. In 1833, Campbell wrote an article for the Disciples of Christ for *The Encyclopedia of Religious Knowledge* in which he estimated that the Disciples numbered at least 100,000 in the United States alone. This figure is much too large for this date in the history of the Disciples. See *Reprints of Disciple Documents,* No. 1 (Lexington: The College of the Bible, 1951), p. 7.

29Frederick Jackson Turner greatly influenced American historiography by his epoch-making address at the Chicago World's Fair in 1893, in which he maintained that the frontier was the dominating factor in the development of the American nation.

30See, for example, William Moorehouse, *The Restoration Movement: The Rhetoric of Jacksonian Restorationism in a Frontier Religion* (Bloomington: University of Indiana, unpublished Ph.D. thesis, 1967). See also W.E. Garrison, *Religion Follows the Frontier: a Diary of the Disciples of Christ* (New York: Harper & Bros., 1931).

31Alexander Campbell and John B. Purcell, *A Debate on the Roman Catholic Religion* (Cincinnati: J.A. James and Co., 1837).

32*Millennial Harbinger,* 1839, pp. 233, 234, 279, 280, 446-451. The final article cited disclosed Campbell's intention to establish Bethany College.

33See John L. Morrison, *Alexander Campbell and Moral Education* (Stanford University: unpublished Ph.D. thesis, 1966).

34Alexander Campbell, "Our Colleges," *Millennial Harbinger,* 1846, p. 386.

35Alexander Campbell and N.L. Rice, *A Debate . . . on the Action, Subject, Design, and Administrator of Christian Baptism* (Lexington: A.T. Skillman & Son, 1844).

36Kenneth Scott Latourette, *A History of the Expansion of Christianity* (New York: Harper and Row, 1941). Volume IV is titled *The Great Century in Europe and the United States of America.*

37The first article of the first edition began what was a frequently repeated diatribe against missionary societies. See Vol. I, p. 11; also pp. 37, 63, 64, 158, 180. (Page numbers cited from the Gospel Advocate reprint, op. cit.)

38J.H. Garrison, *Religion Follows the Frontier* (New York: Harper, 1931), p. 190.

39Campbell's views on "Church Organization" were set forth in a series of five articles: *Millennial Harbinger,* 1849. pp. 90-93, 220-224, 269-271, 271-273, and 459-463.

40*Millennial Harbinger,* 1848, p. 711.

41The most adequate biography of David S. Burnet is by Noel L. Keith, *The Story of David S. Burnet: Undeserved Obscurity* (St. Louis: Bethany Press, 1954).

42Ibid., p. 29.

43This useful volume was reprinted by College Press, Joplin, Missouri, 1983.

44Letter to W.T. Moore, February 28, 1867, quoted in Keith, op. cit., p. 187.

45D.S. Burnet, et. al., "Address," *Millennial Harbinger,* 1845, p. 371.

46Alexander Campbell, "Remarks," Ibid., pp. 372, 373.

47Ibid., p. 373.

48D.S. Burnet, "American Christian Bible Society," Ibid., p. 453.

49Alexander Campbell, "Strictures on the Above [i.e., Burnet's article]," Ibid., p. 457.

50See "The Convention of Christian Churches," *Millennial Harbinger*, 1849, pp. 689-695 for a report and Campbell's reaction.

51The biography of Jacob Creath, Jr., was written by P. Donan, *Memoir of Jacob Creath, Jr.* (Indianapolis: Religious Book Services, n.d.).

52Benjamin Franklin, ed., *Proclamation and Reformer*, 1849, p. 283. This periodical published a lively discussion of the issue in 1849 and 1850. Its editor was generally favorable to the society at that time. He eventually became a bitter opponent.

53Grant K. Lewis notes in his history of the A.C.M.S., "Sometimes subjects were brought before it that were divisive and embarrassing to a missionary society. Ofttimes matters of vital interest to the churches were ruled out of order as not germane to Christian missions" (*The American Christian Missionary Society* [St. Louis: Christian Board of Publication, 1937], p. 155).

54Campbell commended the decision: "Let us, then, 'begin at Jerusalem,' and place our first foreign missions as near the site of her temple and her altar, as is possible" (*Millennial Harbinger*, February, 1850).

55James T. Barclay, *The City of the Great King* (Philadelphia: J. Challen and Sons, 1858).

56W.T. Moore, who knew him personally, esteemed him as "perhaps the best representative man among the better educated class of the Disciples" (op. cit., p. 421).

57The science building at Bethany College bears Richardson's name. A good biography of Richardson is that written by Cloyd Goodnight and Dwight E. Stevenson, *Home to Bethphage* (St. Louis: Christian Board of Publication, 1949).

58See H. Eugene Johnson, *Simple Principles, Robert Richardson's Reformation* (Tampa: published by the author, 1977) for an analysis of this brief publication.

Chapter Seven

Alexander Campbell: Unrivaled Leader

For a quarter of a century prior to the outbreak of the Civil War, Alexander Campbell was the unquestioned leader of the new religious movement that was coalescing in the American West. So overwhelming was his influence in shaping the posture and directing the thinking of the Disciples that a brief portrait of the man and his role in the events of his day is fully justified. Although the fellowship of the Disciples did not provide any ecclesiastical authority beyond the level of the local congregation, Alexander Campbell wielded remarkable influence as lecturer, editor, and educator. He was generally called "Elder" and frequently addressed as "Bishop," terms Campbell understood to be synonymous.

Alexander Campbell was possessed with enormous physical and mental energies. He stood 5' 11" tall, lean and straight. His piercing blue eyes, clear voice with a remnant of a Scottish accent, and poised bearing commanded the attention of audiences whenever he spoke. W.E. Garrison describes him as

> a cultured gentleman—scholarly, urbane, courteous, and eloquent. He was a man trained in the classics, a student (though not a graduate) at an ancient European university, bookish in his tastes, widely read in history and literature, familiar with the standard books in philosophy and theology, polished (though admittedly redundant) in his literary style and no less polished though perhaps a little ponderous in his manners, sensitive to the amenities of good society, and appreciative of the luxuries of "gracious living" when he became able to afford them. In short, he was a "gentleman" by every standard except that of hereditary wealth—and that standard had no standing on his side of the Atlantic.[1]

Alexander Campbell was a man of many interests, all of which must be considered if one is to gain an adequate appreciation of the contribution he made to the religious life of developing America. Following the merger with the Christians of the Stone movement in 1832, leadership of the combined group fell increasingly to Campbell. It required that he be away from home and family for long periods of time. In journeyings often, he covered great distances on horseback and river steamers. The Ohio River was the highway into the West, and the Campbell home was located only a few miles from the river port at Wellsburg. Only in his later years did the railroad make its entrance as an important passenger carrier.

Alexander Campbell's extensive travels were not underwritten by any "expense allowance"; indeed, the costs were never derived from any salary he received from any church. He resolved as a virtually penniless youth that he would take no money for preaching the gospel[2] and he never forsook this decision, although he was often solicitous for Bethany College.

It is appropriate to note that Alexander Campbell was a very successful businessman. The farm, the gift of his father-in-law shortly after his marriage to Margaret Brown in 1811, was wisely managed and enlarged. He developed fine herds of Merino sheep and served as president of a national wool growers association. He invested in land in several states on the frontier, which was probably the source of most of his wealth. At his death, he was one of the wealthiest men in the new state of West Virginia, leaving an estate valued by his executors at some $200,000, a considerable sum in terms of monetary value of that day. This does not take into account the gifts of land and personal funds made to Bethany College. The management of farms, sheep, and land-holdings was only a sideline activity, but it made possible a whole range of activity at no cost to the churches that benefited from them.[3]

Alexander Campbell: Editor and Publisher

It was as editor and publisher that Alexander Campbell reached most people. His viewpoints and insights printed in the *Millennial Harbinger* were widely circulated and read with respect. To encourage dissemination of knowledge in the expanding republic, the federal government provided generous postal subsidies for periodicals. These Campbell fully availed himself of when he was appointed Postmaster at Bethany. The *Millennial Harbinger* was published regularly from 1830 until 1870,[4] although its circulation was severely restricted during the Civil War. Campbell is listed as the sole editor until 1846. The demands of ever-widening activity coupled with a

"desire to give to the work something more of the character of a FAM-
ILY MAGAZINE, to interest and instruct the young members of our
churches"[5] led Campbell in 1846 to appoint W.K. Pendleton to the
post of assistant editor. In 1848, possibly because of Campbell's long
absence occasioned by his voyage to England, the name of Robert
Richardson appears with Pendleton's as co-editor. Subsequently, the
name of A.W. Campbell (brother) and Robert Milligan appear. Isaac
Errett's name appeared in 1861. By this time, Campbell's health was
in serious decline. The volumes for 1863-1865 were edited by W.K.
Pendleton, and the last five volumes, published after Campbell's
death, were edited by Pendleton and Charles Louis Loos.

To the modern reader, the *Millennial Harbinger* would have little
appeal. But in an age when the average household was not deluged
attractive and technically sophisticated printed material, the
Harbinger's arrival was anticipated and its monthly offering of news,
comments, essays, and correspondence was devoured. Campbell's
style was formal and repetitious, verbose and sometimes circuitous,
but his ideas were clear and expressed with confidence. He treated
his subjects rationally and often with evident sarcasm. He was devastating as a disputant, persuasive as an expounder of what he considered to be be simple, Biblical truth, and a relentless critic of the
follies of the denominations. All of this was appealing to an age that
relished debates and placed a premium on confrontational discourse.

The century following the inauguration of the *Millennial
Harbinger* in 1830 was the era of greatest influence for religious
journalism. The postal system provided cheap distribution, and the
printed page did not have to compete with radio, motion pictures,
and television for the attention of men's minds. But if the access to
the minds of men was simple, the demands of production were heavy.
Campbell's editorial work was only one of several responsibilities
that claimed his energies. Before daybreak, in all kinds of weather,
Campbell would betake himself to his windowless, hexagonal study[6]
a hundred feet from his home and write his editorials, essays, and
replies in longhand prior to a busy day in the classroom and the college president's office or the management of the farm. His productivity was enormous and the routine was demanding because he was
responsible for supervising, composing, printing, and mailing. He
was both editor and publisher.

Alexander Campbell: Educator

After 1840, Bethany College claimed a large portion of Campbell's
time and energies. He was both president and professor, lecturing on
the sacred Scriptures and on moral philosophy. The day at Bethany

began with chapel at 7:00, at which Campbell generally lectured.[7]
He had well-defined convictions about the nature and purpose of
education. In anticipation of the founding of Bethany, he wrote:

> *The formation of moral character, the culture of the heart,* is the
> supreme end of education, or rather is education itself. With me
> *education* and *the formation of moral character* are identical expres-
> sions. An immoral man is uneducated. The blasphemer, the profane
> swearer, the liar, the calumniator, the duellist, the braggadocia, the
> peculator, &c. &c. are vulgar, barbarous, and uneducated persons.
> But such is not the popular opinion. Why? Because, as De Fellen-
> berg avers, "the formation of character by means of schools—i.e. by
> means of systematic discipline and instruction, is a new thought.
> Schools were first established for other purposes; and when estab-
> lished, the formation of character was not an element in their sys-
> tem—*nor is it so yet."* This statement, which certainly is true,
> deserves the gravest reflections of the gravest men; and is, to my
> mind, a justifiable reason—an imperious demand for the *new insti-
> tution* to which we are calling the attention of Christians and phi-
> lanthropists of every name. We contemplate a scheme in which the
> formation of the physical and intellectual man shall not be neglect-
> ed, but which shall be always held in subordination to the moral
> man. In which, in one word, the formation of moral character, the
> cultivation of the heart, shall be the Alpha and the Omega, the radi-
> cal, regulating, and all-controlling aim and object in all the literary
> and scientific studies, in all the exercises, recreations and amuse-
> ments of children and youth.[8]

Decades before the expression "education for the whole man" was
heard among educators, Campbell insisted that education must
address the broader needs of man and provide useful insights into
those areas of life that pertain to decision-making and responsibility
to society. Campbell's convictions about education were rooted in
Enlightenment thinking, which was generally optimistic about the
possibilities inherent in human nature. He saw education as the
means of unlocking these possibilities. Such a conviction was well-
nigh universal in nineteenth century America, and it accounts for
the great number of colleges that were founded by the Protestant
churches during that era. "Vocational training" was hardly considered to be a proper concern for a college and consequently was granted little place in the curriculum. The focus was on the development
of the mind and its embellishment through encounter with the great
ideas and issues that emerge in human life. Campbell insisted that
divine revelation must be a central part of this encounter because its
content is crucial to the goal sought, namely the development of the
mature Christian character.[9] Such character would be rationally

competent, morally sensitive, and culturally refined. The educated person would think clearly, construct his life according to the ethic of Christ, and exhibit the grace and refinement of the best of social standards. Such a fusion of the heritage of both Athens and Jerusalem was an ambitious undertaking that is not popular in the twentieth-century secular view of education. It is sometimes criticized for encouraging cultural elitism, but it served as the ideal for scores of institutions for higher education founded in later years by the intellectual heirs of Alexander Campbell. It is still espoused by some of them today.

Alexander Campbell: Responsible Citizen

Consistent with Alexander Campbell's philosophy of education and his Enlightenment understanding of the possibilities of human development[10] was his understanding of the democratic state. An ardent admirer of Thomas Jefferson, with whom he shared Lockian concepts of government and its role in human affairs, Campbell had great hopes for the perfectibility of society in the United States.[11] Note has already been made (chapter 4) of Campbell's effort to lay the groundwork for the amelioration of the slave problem by providing for extension of suffrage in the new constitution of Virginia.

Campbell was fully aware of unsavory conditions in the political arena and discouraged Christians from entering it,[12] but his faith in the worth of the American democratic process did not waver. Patriotic themes abound in the *Harbinger*. Graduation at Bethany was always held on July 4 and was marked by patriotic celebration. Campbell shared the prevailing Enlightenment view of the basic goodness of the common man and his potential for improvement. He believed this would be realized through education and the influence of the simple gospel, both of which could be made available in the freedom of America. He was sure that his adopted nation provided mankind's best hope[13] for the realization of mankind's potential, a conviction that was reinforced by his visit to Great Britain in 1847-1848. However, this optimistic faith was severely shaken by the nation's drift toward war over the slavery issue. Campbell was a lifelong pacifist,[14] as were the co-editors of the *Millennial Harbinger*. The distress produced by watching the nation drift toward war and thus resort to barbarous methods of solving a problem that could only be adequately dealt with by rational means is often cited as one of the contributing factors to the deterioration of Campbell's mental faculties, a problem that became noticeable some months before his death in 1866.

Alexander Campbell: Biblical Preacher

As a preacher and an expounder of the sacred text, Alexander Campbell had few peers, according to the standards that prevailed in his day. Tributes to his pulpit effectiveness are lavish and numerous.[15] Among the better known is the comment of President James Madison, who heard Campbell preach in Richmond, Virginia, in 1829, and later recollected: "It was my pleasure to hear him very often as a preacher of the gospel, and I regard him as the ablest and most original expounder of the Scriptures I have ever heard."[16] Madison's tribute focused on the purpose of preaching, as Campbell perceived it, namely the exposition of the Scriptures. He insisted that the message of the Bible be the theme of every sermon. In the first volume of the *Millennial Harbinger,* he wrote, "Turning men to God is the great object and end of proclaiming the gospel."[17] He was repulsed by the wildly enthusiastic ranting that characterized the revivalism of frontier America. Quite naturally, Campbell's concept of preaching was shaped by his view of faith, which he associated with the mind of man rather than his emotions. The preacher's task was to appeal to man's understanding by setting forth facts and drawing reasonable conclusions. Much of the highly emotional preaching of the day obscured the facts of the gospel and tended to obstruct the generation of Christian faith, and it occasioned his bitter criticism. One student of Campbell's preaching has noted:

> It is probably safe to say that no religious practice of the time was more galling and abhorrent to him, or more regarded as a violation of human intelligence than the religious excitements engendered in these revivalistic procedures. Certainly on no other manifestation of contemporary religious practice were his strictures more scathing, his charges of crudity and ignorance more vehement, or his efforts at correction more continuous.[18]

Campbell exploded in indignation against some of the preaching of the contemporary Methodist revivalists. What they called "manifestations of the Holy Ghost" Campbell branded as "animalism" and observed:

> It is exceedingly vociferous and turbulent. It occasionally roars like a lion and screams like a panther. It seems rather to get into the lungs of the preacher than into his heart, and to reside in his throat rather than in his soul —Hence the rupture of so many lungs, and the laceration of so many bronchial vessels. Not one of the twelve Apostles died of bronchitis.—Hence I infer that the Holy Spirit of Paul essentially differed from the Holy Ghost of the Methodist martyrs.[19]

He also noted that the frenzied emotionalism that accompanied such preaching relied heavily on music that stimulated excitement.

> It is greatly under the power of music: nor is it fastidious whether it be the cornet, the sackbut, dulcimer, or psaltery. I have witnessed a hundred screams of agony and a hundred shouts of glory hushed by one blast of a conch shell, a ram's horn, or a tin trumpet. No animal is so much under the power of sound as this spirit of Methodism.[20]

By way of contrast, Campbell's sermons were closely reasoned discourses spoken in carefully chosen phrases that stimulated the mind more than the feelings. He often held audiences for several hours. Few of his sermons were ever written in full, and most of these were written after their delivery. He generally spoke extemporaneously, but the method of factual, logical, didactic style was scrupulously followed.

Campbell was shrewd in observing that the mere use of the Bible, and especially a short passage of the Bible, did not serve to make the sermon Biblical. The abuses of textual preaching and the folly of preaching from a brief phrase, common to every generation of preachers, came under Campbell's scrutiny. He castigated preachers who employed Biblical texts as mere camouflage, citing with approval a contemporary's condemnation of the practice:

> To display the fertility of their invention, they have selected for texts mere scraps of scripture language; which, so far from containing complete propositions, have not, in their dislocated state, conveyed a single idea. Upon these they have harangued, while the ignorant multitude have been greatly surprised that the preacher could find so much where common capacities perceived nothing. Sometimes these men of genius will choose passages of scripture expressive of plain historical fact, which have no connection with the great work of salvation by Jesus Christ; and handle them (not professedly by way of accommodation, for then it might be admitted) but as if they were *sacred allegories*. Such historical facts being "spiritualized," as they love to call it, doctrines, privileges, duties, in abundance, are easily derived from them. Nay, so ingenious are preachers of this turn, that it is no hard matter for them to find a great part of their creed in almost any text they take. Thus they allegorize common sense into pious absurdity.[21]

The importance that Campbell placed on Biblical preaching stemmed from his conviction that faith is generated by hearing the gospel rather than from some direct operation of the Holy Spirit. Opposed to both the Calvinist views of election and the revivalist practice of conversion by "enthusiasm" (the name given to emotional excitement), Campbell insisted that the Holy Spirit works through the preaching of the Word, a view shared by most of his associates and one that characterizes most Disciple thinking to this day.[22]

As a theologian, Alexander Campbell ranks with the leading thinkers of the nineteenth century, but he had a morbid dislike for theology. He would rather have been known as a reformer and apologist. He held that the enshrined theologies, the work of human minds, did untold damage to the unity of the church and thus to the cause of Christ. He set the simple message of the Bible against the crystallized dogmas of the church in the hope that the triumph of the former would overcome the divisions in the church that he believed the latter had produced. Consequently, he never attempted to produce a systematic theology,[23] and he expressly forbade the teaching of systematic theology at Bethany College by writing a prohibition into its charter. Nevertheless, Campbell held to clearly identifiable views about God, Jesus Christ, the Holy Spirit, man, the church, and other topics generally included in systematic theologies, and it is not difficult to arrange these convictions into a systematic pattern.[24] While Enlightenment and other influences led Campbell to reject certain aspects of Calvin's theology,[25] it is generally recognized that the Genevan reformer provides the basic framework for Campbell's theological structure.[26]

Professor Robert Handy calls Alexander Campbell a "rational supernaturalist." Campbell accepted the validity of rational argumentation, but he also regarded miracles as evidences of truth that is beyond the capacity of reason to discover. However, the Bible itself is to be understood and interpreted by the same rational processes that apply to all literature. Campbell frequently insisted upon this approach in opposition to the widely held revivalistic view that the Holy Spirit provided special insight to certain chosen persons who could perceive truths that were hidden from others. Campbell set forth seven rules for interpreting the Bible. These clearly reflect his rational, common-sense method of interpreting Scriptures.

I. On opening any book in the sacred scriptures, consider first the historical circumstances of the book. These are the order, the title, the author, the date, the place, and the occasion of it.

II. In examining the contents of any book, as respects precepts, promises, exhortations, &c. observe who it is that speaks, and under what dispensation he officiates. Is he a Patriarch, a Jew, or a Christian? Consider also the persons addressed—their prejudices, characters, and religious relations. Are they Jews or Christians—believers or unbelievers—approved or disapproved? This rule is essential to the proper application of every command, promise, threatening, admonition, or exhortation, in Old Testament or New.

III. To understand the meaning of what is commanded, promised, taught, &c., the same philological principles, deduced from the nature of language, or the same laws of interpretation which are applied to the language of other books, are to be applied to the language of the Bible.

IV. Common usage, which can only be ascertained by testimony, must always decide the meaning of any word which has but one signification; but when words have according to testimony,—(i.e. the Dictionary)—more meanings than one, whether literal or figurative, the scope, the context, or parallel passages must decide the meaning; for if common usage, the design of the writer, the context and parallel passages fail, there can be no certainty in the interpretation of languages.

V. In all tropical language ascertain the point of resemblance and judge of the nature of the trope, and its kind, from the point of resemblance.

VI. In the interpretation of symbols, types, allegories, and parables, this rule is supreme. Ascertain the point to be illustrated; for comparison is never to be extended beyond that point—to all attributes, qualities, or circumstances of the symbol, type, allegory, or parable.

VII. For the salutary and sanctifying intelligence of the oracles of God, the following rule is indispensable:—*We must come within the understanding distance.*[27]

These principles would be impressed on generations of preachers who studied under Campbell and his students in the many colleges that would be established.

Alexander Campbell: Religious Statesman

Alexander Campbell lived in a dramatically changing America. As one who was, despite the rural setting of his home, in constant touch with the developments taking place in a dynamic society, it is not surprising to note a variety of developments in his own thinking. While not given to calling attention to changes in his thinking, he displayed a mental resiliency that enabled him to alter his opinions in response to the demands of the time. The most conspicuous example is the contrast between the iconoclastic spirit of the *Christian Baptist* and the generally positive and more constructive attitudes seen in the the *Millennial Harbinger*. Without doubt, this change of attitude was due largely to the change of circumstances in which Campbell found himself as a result of forces he himself had set in motion. As a critic of the denominational system that he deplored, he was caustic. When, after

1830, he faced the task of guiding a movement that aimed to avoid the twin evils of perpetuating "human opinions" (creeds and theological systems) and entrenched clerical privileges while setting forth simple New Testament Christianity, it became necessary to shift the emphasis to a more constructive end. This not only gave the *Millennial Harbinger* a different tone from its predecessor, but it also thrust upon Campbell some very difficult problems and forced him to alter positions taken earlier. A case in point is the matter of church organization beyond the local congregation. Having felt the sting of ecclesiastical censure from both Baptist and Presbyterian tribunals, Campbell quite naturally sought and found refuge in Biblical primitivism and first-century congregational isolation. With his father, he could subscribe to the article in the *Declaration and Address* that held that "the New Testament is as perfect a constitution for the worship, discipline, and government of the New Testament church . . ." and could affirm in 1824 that "an individual church or congregation of Christ's disciples is the only ecclesiastical body recognized in the New Testament."[28] By 1830, however, he did not approve of the dissolution of the Mahoning Association and the substitution of an annual meeting for preaching and fellowship. He would thereafter call for meetings of "messengers" from the churches and move toward the view that the New Testament did not mandate any particular form of church organization.[29] Perhaps on no other point did Campbell's thinking develop in a direction so different from that of his readers and followers. As he traveled widely and observed problems that emerged in a growing, dynamic religious fellowship, Campbell inclined more and more toward a formal church structure beyond the local level. However, the Disciples, very much a part of the culture of the frontier, which stressed independency and individualism, effectively rejected any effort to invest an extra-congregational assembly with churchly authority.[30] Nevertheless, after 1830, Campbell became the unceasing advocate of inter-congregational cooperation. But the frontier spirit that guarded its independence was also sufficiently creative and practical to devise the operational means sufficient to the accomplishment of the task at hand. That task was understood to be evangelism, and the means was the formation of state and district "cooperations" through which the resources were directed that supported evangelists to establish new congregations in the rapidly expanding West.[31] The expedient worked well, and Disciples shared fully in the growth that marked Protestant expansion in the nineteenth century.[32] These "cooperations" fell short of Campbell's idea of church order, but, on the other hand, they were viewed with suspicion and alarm by many of his contemporaries.

Alexander Campbell's genius as a Christian statesman and his leadership of the Disciples never faced a more serious challenge than that provided by the perennial issue of slavery. Slaves had been found in American colonies since colonial times. Slave-holding was legal in the British Empire until 1833, and thus it was legal in all of the colonies that formed the Union. However, it was not profitable to own slaves except for agricultural purposes on large plantations; hence slavery was not widespread in the Northern colonies. But Northern shipowners profited handsomely from the slave trade. After the Revolutionary War, the institution was outlawed in the Northern states. Its perpetuation in the South was held to be guaranteed by the U.S. Constitution, which protected the right to hold property, and slaves were legally classified as "property." A public conscience on the moral wrong of slaveholding began to emerge in both North and South after the turn of the century, resulting in the prohibition of further slave imports after 1808. At that time, most Americans thought that slavery would gradually disappear in the United States. The trend was reversed, however, when Eli Whitney invented the cotton gin. This made it profitable to utilize short-fiber cotton of the type that could be produced with slave labor in the Southern states. The result was an economic boom to the South, or so it seemed. New plantations opened in the Louisiana Purchase area and westward. The price of slaves rose dramatically,[33] and the attitude of the Southern peoples toward slavery underwent a significant modification. Pulpits North and South reflected the interests of their respective regions and contributed considerably toward the formation of a pro-slave or anti-slave mind-set.[34] The press intensified the ideological conflict that threatened the unity of the nation. Nobody could escape the conflicts of the 1850s or the trauma of the 1860s.

Alexander Campbell disliked slavery, though he had owned several slaves who had been presented to him for differing reasons.[35] All of them he ultimately set free. As has been noted (chapter 4), his involvement in the Virginia Constitutional Convention in 1829 was motivated by his desire to rid the Old Dominion of slavery. Though frustrated by Eastern Virginia plantation owners, he continued to urge the legislature of his state to rid itself of the "curse." In 1832, he put forth what would have been considered a radical suggestion, namely, that the United States treasury should use part or all of its $10,000,000 annual surplus to redeem slaves and resettle them in Liberia. He calculated that within fifteen or twenty years, this "would rid this land of the curse, and bind the union more firmly than all the rail roads, canals, and highways which the treasury of the union could make in half a century."[36] In 1849, he urged the citizens of Kentucky to include in their new constitution a provision for the gradual emancipation of all slaves in the state.[37]

But Campbell's dislike of slavery was matched by his distaste for abolitionism. Aside from the very contentious attitude of most abolitionists, two considerations turned him away from the position of the radicals: (1) He could not condemn as immoral and ungodly what the Bible did not condemn.[38] Rather, he urged that the slave-master relationship be maintained on the kindly level set forth in the apostolic teaching. (2) He recognized that immediate emancipation would throw a large number of slaves on their own resources before they had been adequately prepared to fend for themselves. This could result in cruelties and suffering that would be every bit as onerous as that of servitude. This fear proved to be prophetic as the plight of many former slaves during the Reconstruction era amply demonstrated. Campbell recognized that the economy of the South was heavily dependent on slavery and would be ruined unless some system of indemnification was devised to ease the transition from slave to free labor. Such an insight into economic reality long before the science of economics was ever recognized was unusual for his times. Campbell's suggestion of an annual federal appropriation to indemnify slave holders would have aided an orderly transition to a free labor economy. The cost would have been only a fraction of the cost of the war and it would have spared lives, property, and the economy of the South.

It must be noted that Campbell's approach to the difficult problem of slavery was a rational one.[39] It had less and less appeal as the nation moved steadily from a rational to an emotional frame of mind with each passing year. His refusal to condone either of the developing extreme positions evoked criticism and brought cancellations of subscriptions to the *Millennial Harbinger*. He grieved to see the nation drift toward war, which he considered barbarous and anti-Christian.

Alexander Campbell: International Influence

While the Campbell-Stone movement may properly be understood as an American religious enterprise inasmuch as it was initiated and developed in the United States, we would be remiss to overlook similar and fraternal efforts in other portions of the English-speaking world that acknowledge kinship with their American counterpart. Here the thinking of Alexander Campbell influenced the formation and development of the Churches of Christ through the circulation of the *Millennial Harbinger*. Readers in Great Britain, New Zealand, Australia, and Canada would ponder the reforms advocated by the editor in Bethany.

British Churches of Christ are understandably sensitive against being seen as an appendage of the larger American body. David M. Thompson, whose history of the British Churches of Christ is the most current, observes:

There was no common founder figure for Churches of Christ in Great Britain in the sense that John Wesley was for Methodism, or even in the sense that Alexander Campbell was for the Disciple movement in the United States. Certainly Alexander Campbell's writings were the focus for the new movement, but he only ever made one visit to Britain after his emigration in 1809, and by then (1847) the British Churches were already established. Leaders in the British Churches never accepted everything that Campbell said, and they never accepted anything he said simply because he said it. His writings were accepted because they were felt to express certain convictions of the early British leaders, particularly on the need to restore the ancient order of things in church life.[40]

He admits, however, "there was no comparable native-born figure with the same influence as Campbell in the early days."[41]

While British Churches of Christ do not trace their origins from American sources, it is obvious that they rose from similar influences. The efforts of Glas, Sandeman, and the Scottish Baptists led by Archibald McLean resulted in the gathering of small independent congregations in England and Scotland. These churches practiced believer's baptism by immersion and weekly closed Communion. Additionally, there were new independent churches associated with the Haldane brothers. Although isolated from each other, all of these bodies were interested in restoring New Testament Christianity as they understood its meaning.

The earliest known contact between Alexander Campbell and the British Baptists came in 1825, through Robert Smyth, of Dungannon, North Ireland. He corresponded with Campbell, who sent him several sets of his published materials. By 1830, an independent congregation in Scotland was in contact with Alexander Campbell, and, in 1834, its minister, John Dron, visited Bethany. By this time, many of these independent churches had taken the name Church of Christ.

It was a Scotch Baptist pastor in London, William Jones, who did more than anybody else to create awareness in Great Britain of the American movement. In 1833, a visitor in his congregation told him about the similarity between his understanding of Christianity and that of the American Churches of Christ. Upon inquiring about leaders in the American church, he was surprised to hear first the name of Alexander Campbell, a name he had recently encountered when he read with pleasure the account of the debate against the British socialist, Robert Owen.

Jones, a bookseller, immediately opened correspondence with Campbell and received copies of the *Christian Baptist* and the *Millennial Harbinger*. In 1835, Jones began publication of the *Millennial Harbinger and Voluntary Church Advocate*. Although this was discontinued after sixteen months, it had circulated sufficiently among Scotch Baptists in England, Scotland, and Wales to create considerable interest in the writings of Alexander Campbell. Immediately, James Wallis began publication of the *Christian Messenger and Reformer.*

Although the emerging Churches of Christ in Great Britain were few and small, they were sufficiently anxious to meet Alexander Campbell that they responded generously to a plea in the *Christian Messenger* to share in the expense of a trip to Britain by Campbell. Twenty-seven congregations gave one hundred seventy pounds. In 1847, Campbell visited Britain. Large halls were secured, and he spoke to good audiences. This gave public visibility to the small churches in Britain, but it also created an unpleasant situation. While many hailed Campbell as the opponent of Robert Owen, the radical secretary of the Anti-slave Society in Edinburgh attacked him in every town as a slaveholder. He finally succeeded in having Campbell arrested in Glasgow on a ridiculous charge of libel, which the judge threw out of court.

While in Chester, Campbell presided over a "cooperation meeting" of twenty-six congregations. This was the second of the annual meetings of the British Churches of Christ.[42] A close organizational relationship has continued to characterize British Churches of Christ.

Because of differences in origin and background, certain differences in doctrine and practice between British and American Churches of Christ are quite obvious. One of these differences is the much greater aversion to a formalized ministerial office among the British. They practiced a "mutual ministry" of laymen in the place of a specially trained ministry. Campbell warned against this, but his warning went unheeded for more than a century.[43] Some of the British churches were so committed to a very literal interpretation of the New Testament that they found in Acts 2:42 a pattern of worship that mandated preaching, offering (a curious interpretation of "fellowship"), Communion, and prayers in that order. This reflects a degree of Biblical literalism hardly ever encountered in American churches of the movement.

Emigration from Great Britain to Canada, Australia, and New Zealand accounts for the spread of the influence of the Bethany reformer to these portions of the British Empire (see chapter 19). Among the possessions that some settlers carried to their new homes were copies of the British *Millennial Harbinger.* Subsequently, some of the readers would establish contact with the editor. The many references to, and reports from, Churches of Christ in Britain and her colonies bear witness to the sustained interest Alexander Campbell maintained in the progress of the movement on three continents. It was Campbell who established the links that would find expression a century later in the World Convention of Churches of Christ.

As the unrivaled leader of the Disciples prior to the Civil War, Alexander Campbell was an olympian figure. At times, he could be difficult to work with personally. However, his second wife, who survived him, paid tribute to Campbell's kindness and thoughtful concern for his large family.[44] His home life, though marked by several tragic deaths, seems to have been a happy one. His passing on March 4, 1866, was mourned by thousands. The Campbell home at Bethany, West Virginia, has been restored and is being preserved as a brotherhood monument.

The voice from Bethany had, for all practical purposes, been stilled from the onset of the Civil War. An inevitable leadership vacuum faced the churches as they sought to return to normalcy following the chaos of civil conflict. Lacking an ecclesiastical structure, it was not possible to pass the mantle of leadership to a designated successor in a formal manner that would be recognized by all of the churches. From among the several voices that would be raised in the postwar stress, only time would disclose which would speak effectively to point the course and give direction to the Churches of Christ in America. Few could have foreseen the conflicts that lay ahead.

End Notes

[1]W.E. Garrison, "Pioneer in Broadcloth," in Perry E. Gresham, ed., *Sage of Bethany* (St. Louis: Bethany Press, 1960), pp. 46, 47.

[2]In Campbell's early anti-clerical days, he wrote disparagingly of the clergy. His hostility is well summarized by Granville T. Walker, op. cit., pp. 141-148. But this initial hostility was abandoned and Campbell's mind changed considerably as he saw the need to provide a more orderly form of leadership for the churches on the developing frontier (pp. 148-191).

[3]Louis Cochran observes (in Gresham, op. cit., p. 72):
Without the financial independence of Alexander Campbell and his resultant ability for fifty years to preach the gospel of apostolic Christianity without interference, there probably would have been no reformation, or Restoration Movement, no Disciples of Christ, Christian Church, or Church of Christ, as we speak of them today, and no Bethany College. The cause of Christian unity based upon the Holy Scriptures alone might yet be waiting for a world spokesman.

[4]Original editions of the *Millennial Harbinger* may be found in both college and private libraries. A century after the periodical ceased publication, the entire series was republished by College Press, Joplin, Missouri, 1976. Subsequently, a very useful index to the series was compiled by David I. McWhirter, Director of Archives of Disciples of Christ Historical Society, Nashville, Tennessee, and published by College Press, 1981.

[5]*Millennial Harbinger*, 1846, p. 3.

[6]The study was built in 1836. A small addition to the rear of the original study incorporated a fireplace and window that provided a view of the house.

[7]For a student's description of the nature and the effect of Campbell's daily lecture to the whole student body, see Alexander Campbell, *Familiar Lectures on the Pentateuch* (Rosemead: Old Paths Book Club, 1958 reprint), pp. 36, 37.

[8]Alexander Campbell, "New Institution—No. III," *Millennial Harbinger*, 1840, pp. 157, 158.

[9]For additional information see John L. Morrison, op. cit. Particularly interesting is Morrison's comparison of Campbell and John Dewey.

[10]An excellent analysis of Campbell's intellectual background and thought is found in Richard Phillips, *Differences in the Theological and Philosophical Backgrounds of Alexander Campbell and Barton W. Stone and Resulting Differences of Thrust in Their Theological Formations* (Vanderbilt University: unpublished Ph.D. thesis, 1968).

[11]Richard Hughes notes that Campbell's optimism was grounded in his hope for a restored Christianity until 1841, when he seemed to transfer the basis of this hope to the American democratic nation. ("From Primitive Church to Civil Religion," op. cit.). Hughes bases his contention largely on an affirmation Campbell made in a speech at Cannonsburg, Pennsylvania, found in the *Millennial Harbinger,* 1852, p. 482.

[12]Having been repulsed by the excesses of the 1840 presidential campaign (Harrison—Van Buren), Campbell wrote: "Ought Christians to take an active part in politics—in the present politics of this country? . . . I am decidedly of opinion that they ought not. One of my reasons is, American politics are full of avarice and ambition. They are national and mammoth forms of pride and cupidity." ("Morality of Christians—No. XXI: Politics," *Millennial Harbinger,* 1840 p. 414.) This aversion to political involvement would be reinforced by David Lipscomb and characterized the thinking of the greater part of the Disciples (notably those who opposed instruments) until World War II. See Earl I. West, "Churches of Christ and Civil Government from 1900-1908" (Bethany College Restoration History Conference: unpublished address, 1976).

[13]For a good analysis of Campbell's political views, see Lunger, op. cit.

[14]Campbell's views are best summarized in his 1848 "Address on War," *Popular Lectures,* op. cit. pp. 342-366. It was printed in full in the *Congressional Record,* November 22, 1937.

[15]A listing of major tributes may be found in Fitch, op. cit., pp. 132-134.

[16]Richardson, op. cit., Vol. II, p. 313.

[17]*Millennial Harbinger,* 1830, p. 367.

[18]Granville T. Walker, op. cit., p. 29.

[19]Alexander Campbell, "Aspects of Methodism," *Millennial Harbinger,* 1843, p. 462.

[20]Ibid.

[21]Abraham Booth, "Essay on the Kingdom of Christ," quoted in *Millennial Harbinger,* 1830, p. 512.

[22]For a summary, see Walker, op. cit., pp. 50-61. This view has sometimes been criticized as tending to reduce the Holy Spirit to paper and ink and to produce cold and heartless sermons. In recent years, sermon content generally has tended to focus more on psychological than Biblical and doctrinal themes.

[23]*The Christian System* comes immediately to mind as a violation of this position. However, an examination of its content soon reveals that its scope is quite different from what would be considered systematic theology. Furthermore, such a role is disclaimed in the preface to the second edition, published in 1839.

[24]See W.E. Garrison, *Alexander Campbell's Theology: Its Sources and Historical Setting* (St. Louis: Christian Publishing Company, 1900) and Royal Humbert, ed., *A Compound of Alexander Campbell's Theology* (St. Louis: Bethany Press, 1961).

[25]For example, the doctrine of election. Richard Phillips (op. cit., p. 151, footnote) observes: "Campbell's rejection of Calvin in *Christian Baptist* (Burnet ed.) p. 172, is not so much a rejection of Calvin as the Calvin*ism* Campbell faced."

[26]"To fail to see Campbell's Calvinism is to fail to understand properly many of Campbell's acts and ideas, particularly those of the later period of his life." Ibid., p. 152. See also Royal Humbert, op. cit., p. 11.

[27]Alexander Campbell, "Tracts for the People—No. III: The Bible—Principles of Interpretation," *Millennial Harbinger,* 1846, p. 23.

[28]Alexander Campbell, "Essays on Ecclesiastical Characters, Councils, Creeds, and Sects—No. III," *Christian Baptist,* July 5, 1824 (p. 224 in Gospel Advocate reprint).

[29]See Wrather, op. cit., for a resumé of Campbell's thinking on church order.

[30]There are marked differences in ecclesiological patterns that prevail in each of the three religious bodies that emerge from the Campbellian heritage, and all can quote Alexander Campbell to reinforce their particular understanding of the church. Anti-organization champions find much satisfaction in quotations from the *Christian Baptist.* So completely did Campbell abandon this position in his later years that David Lipscomb suggested that he had suffered severe mental decline. See Earl I.

West, *The Search for the Ancient Order* (Nashville: Gospel Advocate, 1964), Vol. I., pp. 181-195.

31For a state-by-state resumé of this growth, see Garrison and DeGroot, op. cit., pp. 324-329.

32In 1853, Campbell wrote a new series of essays on "Church Organizations." He concluded the fifth installment thus, "To the perfection of the church and the success of the gospel ministry, organization is indispensable. Organization is both life and strength. Disorganization is death." *Millennial Harbinger,* 1853, p. 492. It is obvious that Campbell conceived of an organization much more comprehensive than simply a missionary society. Regulation of ministers to protect the churches from rogues and imposters was a frequently-mentioned goal.

33Between 1820 and 1860, the price of a good field hand increased from about $300 to $1,000 or more, and the number of slaves in the South grew from 1.5 million to nearly 4 million. The high price of slaves encouraged slave smuggling and placed freed slaves in the North in peril of being kidnapped and sold in the South. An immoderate portion of Southern wealth was invested in slaves, although only one Southern family in four owned slaves and three-fourths of these owned less than ten slaves each. J. Hicks, G. Mowry, and R. Burke, *The Federal Union* (Boston: Houghton Mifflin Co., 1964), pp. 520, 521.

34For a good resumé of the respective arguments, see *American Christianity,* Vol. II, pp. 157-212.

35For a discussion of the slavery issue among Disciples, see David E. Harrell, *Quest for a Christian America* (Nashville: Disciples of Christ Historical Society, 1966), pp. 91-138. A discussion of Alexander Campbell on slavery may be found in Robert O. Fife, *Alexander Campbell and the Christian Church in the Slavery Controversy* (Bloomington: University of Indiana, unpublished Ph.D. thesis, 1960).

36Alexander Campbell, "The Crisis," *Millennial Harbinger,* 1832, p. 88.

37Alexander Campbell, "Tract for the People of Kentucky," *Millennial Harbinger,* 1849, pp. 241-252.

38In 1845, he wrote, "The cardinal question affecting us, then, is,—*What does the Bible teach on this subject?*—not what natural reason, natural conscience, or the opinions of men may dictate, or what human prudence and expedience may allow" ("Our Position to American Slavery," *Millennial Harbinger,* 1845, p. 53).

[39]Campbell's most detailed discussion of the slave issue is found in a lengthy series of articles in 1845 on the theme, "Our Position to American Slavery," *Millennial Harbinger,* 1845, pp. 49-53, 67-71, 108-113, 145-149, 193-196, 232-236, 236-240, 257-264.

[40]David M. Thompson, *Let Sects and Parties Fall* (Birmingham, England: Berean Press, 1980), p. 7

[41]Ibid., p. 8.

[42]Ibid., p. 42.

[43]Ibid.

[44]See Selina Campbell, *Home Life and Reminiscences of Alexander Campbell* (Joplin: College Press, reprint, n.d.). See also R. Edwin Groover, *the Well-ordered Home: Alexander Campbell and the Family* (Joplin: College Press, 1988). A strange practice of the family was the celebration of the anniversary of Campbell's first marriage throughout the period of his second marriage. He considered his second wife, Selina, a worthy successor to the deceased Margaret (cf. *Homelife,* pp. 349-352).

Chapter Eight

The Civil War & Tragic Aftermath (1860-1874)

The Civil War is unequaled as a tragic chapter in American history. When brother took up arms against brother, either to preserve state sovereignty or to preserve the Union as the case may have been, there was unleashed a fury of destruction, a blood bath, and a whirlwind of sectional hatred that would leave wounds requiring decades to heal and scars that would be permanent.

At the outbreak of hostilities, most of the Disciples were pacifists. The two most widely-circulated periodicals, the monthly *Millennial Harbinger* and Benjamin Franklin's Cincinnati-based weekly *American Christian Review,* were antiwar. Because the strength of the movement lay in the border states, most of the preachers were reluctant to witness a recourse to arms, and some counseled their young men to have nothing to do with the war.[1] However, few were able to maintain their pacifism throughout the bitter conflict. When the drums began to roll, many of the young men rode off to fight.

There were conspicuous partisans in the movement. Though a minority, they were both loud and irritating at times. Foremost among the pro-slave advocates was the colorful and brilliant James Shannon. A graduate of the University of Belfast, this preacher-educator was a professor at the University of Georgia and successively president of the College of Louisiana, Berea College, the University of Missouri, and Christian University in Canton, Missouri, until his death in 1859. He preached, argued, and debated vigorously in behalf of slavery as part of the divine plan, fortifying his views with a host of proof texts. Insisting that blacks were created inferior and that freedom for them would be a curse, he openly advocated armed revolution if any attempt were made to deprive citizens of their right to property in slaves. There were other pro-slavery advocates among the preachers and editors—much more moderate in their positions—including W.K. Pendleton, Tolbert Fanning, and Benjamin Franklin.

Radical abolitionism was represented in the stormy career of Pardee Butler, who threw himself wholeheartedly into the perilous task of keeping slavery out of the Kansas Territory after 1855. Never one to shy away from a confrontation, he narrowly escaped death on more than one occasion. He precipitated a crisis for the newly-formed American Christian Missionary Society by seeking its aid for the prosecution of his "mission." When Isaac Errett, the corresponding secretary of the society, replied that any missionary enterprise in the Kansas Territory would have to ignore the question of slavery, Butler and his fellow radicals were furious. They set out to organize a new, abolitionist society to raise funds for their Kansas effort, which they dubbed the Christian Missionary Society. Its strength centered in the Indianapolis area, where Northwestern Christian University had been established in 1850. Ovid Butler was chairman of the board and chief benefactor of this institution, which was avowedly abolitionist. In 1856, Northwestern Christian University incurred the wrath of Alexander Campbell for admitting several students who had been dismissed from Bethany College for organizing an abolitionist demonstration.[2] Another abolitionist, John G. Fee, founded Berea College in Kentucky in July, 1859, as an interracial college. Not long afterwards, he was mobbed and driven from the state.

Most of the members of churches of the movement should be classified as moderates. There were some good reasons that this was the case. It has already been noted that the movement was centered in the border states where extreme positions were more difficult to maintain. The strong Biblical emphasis of the movement tended to result in a moderate position on slavery, such as is reflected in the epistle to Philemon, which sets forth an ideal of humane slavery. The crusading tendency was generally restrained by the attitude that pro- or anti-slavery views were not a matter of "faith" and should not be a hindrance to the unity that is in Christ.[3] Since views about slavery were deemed to be "opinion," liberty should be permitted for different points of view. David E. Harrell notes that with Campbell, "American slavery was not a religious problem but a political one and the fundamental principle of the Reformation which recognized the right to differ on non-essential, non-religious matters ought to prevent division."[4]

The commencement of hostilities in 1861 all but rendered untenable the moderate position. The sectional spirit was hard to resist in the face of lengthening casualty lists and widespread destruction. Walter Scott wrote a powerful pro-Union article, which Campbell, his lifelong friend, refused to publish in the *Millennial Harbinger.* W.T. Moore claimed credit for preserving Kentucky for the Union by

preaching a sermon in his church in Frankfort with forty to fifty legislators present on the Sunday before the vote was taken to determine that state's future. Five of the six uncommitted legislators,
whose votes were crucial to the decision, were members of Moore's
church.[5] James A. Garfield was commissioned a colonel in the Union
army and proceeded to recruit a regiment consisting of many Hiram
College students.[6] L.L. Pinkerton was a surgeon in the Union army.
"Raccoon" John Smith was an ardent pro-Union advocate, as was
David S. Burnet. Isaac Errett and his brother were pro-Union, the
latter serving as a major in the Union army.

Some illustrious names could also be found among the Confeder-
ates. Though Alexander Campbell favored the Union, his eldest son
was a Confederate cavalry man, Barton W. Stone, Jr. commanded
the Sixth Texas Cavalry, whose chaplain was Dr. Benjamin F. Hall, a
preacher of the movement whose enthusiasm for killing shocked his
brethren. Confederate chaplain Thomas W. Caskey of Mississippi
came to be known as "the fighting parson" for his readiness to shoul-
der a rifle and take his place in the front lines.[7]

Throughout the war, the American Christian Missionary Society
met annually in Cincinnati, Ohio. With access to the convention cut
off from the South, the body represented a decidedly pro-Union bias.
Some of the delegates came determined to obtain a pro-Union resolution. One was introduced in 1861, but it was ruled out of order by a
vote of the convention. A ten-minute recess was called, and David S.
Burnet called an *ad hoc* meeting to order, which proceeded to pass
the resolution with only one dissenting vote. The meaning of this
ambiguous action was in dispute for only two years. In 1863, the convention met in Cincinnati. State conventions in Indiana and Ohio
had already passed strong loyalty resolutions, and the determination
to do the same at the society's meeting was not to be denied. A resolution was introduced that said, among other things:

> *Resolved,* That we tender our sympathies to our brave soldiers in
> the fields, who are defending us from the attempts of armed traitors
> to overthrow our Government, and also to those bereaved, and ren-
> dered desolate by the ravages of war.[8]

Isaac Errett, presiding, ruled the motion out of order but was over-
ridden and the motion passed by a solid majority. It was to produce a
bitter reaction when published in the South, creating an anti-society
bias that could never be overcome and focusing Southern animosity
against many who would emerge as brotherhood leaders in the
decades to follow. It contributed immensely to the division that was
to come. David Lipscomb of Nashville, Tennessee, reflected Southern
reaction when he wrote that "that society committed a great wrong
against the church and the cause of God."[9] The pro-Union loyalty

resolution explains why very few friends of the society could be found in the South following the war.

On April 7, 1865, the guns were silenced, and a bleeding nation began the task of binding up its wounds. The sickening sights of war could be seen in many sections of the South. Cities had been burned and sacked, railroads had been torn up, bridges destroyed, harbor facilities demolished, farms laid waste, and livestock destroyed. The economy of the South was crippled. It had relied too heavily on one commodity, and the means for producing that one commodity had been wiped out. Southern currency was worthless, and Southern state governments were in the hands of carpetbaggers. Nothing comparable to the later Marshall Plan, through which the U.S. assisted in the economic recovery of the nations that were devastated in World War II, had been conceived to aid the crippled South. Unable to provide an adequate tax base, financially prostrate Southern states were forced to extreme measures—like discounting state bonds—to raise the funds needed to restore essential facilities. This placed a heavy burden on the region's economic future and insured the relative impoverishment of the South for decades. Widespread hunger prevailed in Tennessee, Georgia, Alabama, and Mississippi. The periodicals published appeals in behalf of the suffering South and offered to act as clearinghouses for money and clothing. A Nashville business firm received and distributed an enormous quantity of money and articles.[10] But this outpouring of benevolence from the North did nothing to assuage the sectional hatred that had seized the South.[11]

The postwar situation in the North was markedly different. A war-inspired prosperity launched the victors into a period of unprecedented expansion. Railroads had prospered from war business and soon, with generous federal subsidies, spanned the continent. Factories were turning out goods, and farms were producing commodities for market. The final third of the century saw nine new states come into the Union, all in the West. New inventions and technologies transformed the life-style of the Northern half of the nation. The South shared only marginally in these dramatic developments. The widening difference in the Southern and Northern economies exacerbated the bitter residue of the war and produced abundant opportunities for the development of dissension.

The Missionary Society Problem

It was inevitable that the American Christian Missionary Society would become the focus of hostilities that rose ultimately from regional bias. This was so partly because the society was the only extra-local meeting that brought the leadership together in one body. It would have been difficult, at best, for brethren North and South to come together in 1865 and pick up the work of missions where this had been left in 1860. The task was rendered impossible by the resolution of 1863, which had labeled the southerners as "armed traitors." Foremost among those opposed to the society was Tolbert Fanning of Tennessee, founder and editor of the *Gospel Advocate*.[12] Although Fanning was elected as one of the original vice presidents of the A.C.M.S., he developed serious reservations after 1852.[13] He urged the churches to meet together for "consultations" but cautioned against the development of more formal organizations. Fanning held that the church itself is the adequate missionary society, and anything else is superfluous at best. Fanning was patient and irenic, continuing to attend the meetings of the society and hoping for a reversal of developing trends, but the war took its toll. He was able to resume the publication of the *Gospel Advocate* in 1866, David Lipscomb sharing editorial responsibilities with him. Thenceforth, the journal would be unyielding in its opposition to the society. It would be joined by Benjamin Franklin's *American Christian Review*.[14] The barrage of criticism of the A.C.M.S. that followed may be summarized under five categories:

(1) The society was without Scriptural precedent,

(2) it did not represent the churches,

(3) membership was on a money basis,

(4) it "apes the sects," and

(5) it was inconsistent with the earlier position of the movement, a position unequivocally set forth in the *Christian Baptist*.

The *coup de grace* was administered when Benjamin Franklin declared his opposition to the A.C.M.S. His *American Christian Review* was, at the close of the Civil War, the most popular and influential paper in the brotherhood. When Franklin added his voice to those opposing the society, its doom was certain. Franklin's support was never wholehearted, although he had served the society as corresponding secretary. Earl West suggests that Franklin had given his support to the society because he wanted to avoid any threat to the unity of the movement. But, by 1867, qualms about the Scriptural sanction for such a device had triumphed, and Franklin concluded that unity was less important than fidelity to the Scriptures as he understood them. A lively debate ensued between Franklin and the editors of the *Millennial Harbinger*, W.K. Pendleton and C.L. Loos.[15] The ensuing arguments disclosed a serious divergence of opinion about the meaning of the slogan: "Where the Bible speaks, we speak; and where the Bible is silent, we are silent." Pendleton insisted that the silence of the Scripture was not to be interpreted as prohibition. Franklin spoke for a considerable core of Southern, anti-society sentiment when he insisted that it was.[16] Franklin and his associates looked upon the society as a human expedient created to do the work that the Lord had assigned to the church. The work of missions could only be done by the local congregation. Pendleton agreed that the task of converting the world belonged to the church, but the church was free to adopt any *method* it deemed expedient.

The situation confronting the society was so critical that the convention, in 1867, determined that something would have to be done to alter it. Accordingly, a committee of five was appointed to consider amending the constitution. The proposed amendments were adopted in 1868 but were destined to be short-lived. A midyear meeting of the society in St. Louis came to grips with the problem of faltering support by appointing a committee that redesigned the whole structure. The committee of twenty included, along with such society proponents as Isaac Errett, W.K. Pendleton, and W.T. Moore, the chief critic and opponent of the society, Ben Franklin. The proposal advanced by this committee eliminated individual memberships and omitted the word *society* altogether. The plan was submitted to the convention meeting in Louisville, Kentucky, in 1869 and was henceforth known as the Louisville Plan. It met Franklin's demand that missions is the responsibility of the church by creating what was in reality a representative churchly structure on a national level. Local congregations were to be represented in district conventions to which they were to send appointed delegates and their missionary monies. One-half of the funds were to be kept for use in the district while the other half was to be sent to a state convention consisting of messengers appointed by the constituent districts. These, in turn, were to send one-half of their receipts to the General Convention, which was no longer a society mass meeting because it was composed of representatives of the states. The whole structure was seen to be unitive, comprehensive, and Scriptural because it was representative of the churches.[17] But it met instant opposition. All who considered the local congregation as the only manifestation of the church to be found in the New Testament immediately saw this elaborate scheme as a reversion to denominational hierarchy and a menace to congregational independence.[18] Financially, the plan was a failure from the start. The constitution provided that donors could specify the disposition of their contributions and the Report to the Convention of 1874 complained that "so little [was] sent to the State Boards that they have for the most part been wholly unable either to keep up their own work or to send the proper dividends to the General Treasury."[19] No missionaries were sent out, and a committee recommended a resumption of the practice of selling life memberships and directorships.[20] The controversy that the whole issue had created was only relieved when a group of women, tired of the flow of words and impatient for results, seized the initiative to launch out on their own. Meanwhile, the missionary controversy became so inextricably interwoven with the sectionalism confronting the churches as to reinforce the tendency to fracture the fellowship. As has been noted, the loyalty resolution insured that support for the society was largely from the North and the border states, while the states of the old South were mostly anti-society.

The A.C.M.S. was not without defenders. Wearied by the negative, nonprogressive policy of the *American Christian Review* and the *Gospel Advocate,* a group of Northern Disciples met in Newcastle, Pennsylvania at the home of T.W. Phillips, Sr., on December 22, 1865. They decided to launch a new weekly journal, one that would reflect the progressive spirit which they shared.

The Christian Standard

The *Christian Standard* was organized when fourteen men gathered in the home of T.W. Phillips, Sr., in Newcastle, Pennsylvania, and formed the Christian Publishing Association. They were convinced that a weekly journal was needed, one with a broader base of interest than the *Millennial Harbinger* and a more generous and positive spirit than the *Gospel Advocate.* The aims of the new journal were set forth in a "Prospectus" published in the first issue of Elijah Goodwin's *Christian Record:*

> 1. A bold and rigorous advocacy of Christianity, as recorded in the New Testament, without respect to party, creed, or theological system.
> 2. A plan for the union of all who acknowledge the supreme authority of the Lord Jesus on the apostolic basis of "one Lord, one faith, one baptism."
> 3. Particular regard to practical religion in all the broad interests of piety and humanity. . . .
> 4. A Christian institution, involving a review of books and such discussions of literature, science, and art as may serve to invite inquiry and promote the intelligence and taste of its readers.
> 5. A faithful record of the important religious monuments in the old world and the new. . . .
> 6. Such a summary of political, commercial, and general intelligence as is suitable for a family paper.

A corporation was formed and was capitalized at $100,000. W.S. Streator was named its president, W.J. Ford, secretary, and J.P. Robinson, treasurer. Other directors were T.W. Phillips, C.M. Phillips, G.W.N. Yost, and James A. Garfield. Isaac Errett, who had recently accepted a faculty position at Hiram College, was persuaded to accept the editorship of the paper, which was named the *Christian*

Standard. The choice of editor was a fortunate one. Isaac Errett was to have a long and distinguished career and profoundly influence the development of the movement. Reared in Pittsburgh, Pennsylvania, where he had personal contact with the early leaders of the movement, Isaac Errett was thoroughly familiar with its aims. He began preaching in Pittsburgh and later ministered in New Lisbon and Warren, Ohio. Following a brief business interlude in Michigan, Errett was called to a ministry in Detroit. While there, he incurred the wrath of the more conservative Moses E. Lard by publishing *A Synopsis of the Faith and Practice of the Church of Christ,* which aimed to acquaint the community with the purposes of the church and the movement. Lard condemned Errett's synopsis as a "creed" and an "offense against the brotherhood."[21] From 1857, Errett served as corresponding secretary of the missionary society, a position that did not endear him to southern readers. Organized by Northern businessmen, the *Christian Standard* would reflect a different point of view from that seen by its southern counterpart, the *Gospel Advocate.*

Originally published in Cleveland, the new journal soon faced fiscal problems. By 1867, the situation was so severe that the incorporators were willing to turn the assets of the corporation over to Isaac Errett if he would be willing to assume the debts. Hoping that the income from the paper would be sufficient to carry the publication cost, Errett accepted the presidency of Alliance (Ohio) College to support his family. The dual responsibilities proved too much, and Errett cast about for a solution to the problem of saving the journal. It came when W.T. Moore of Cincinnati persuaded R.W. Carroll, a publisher in Cincinnati, to publish the paper if Errett would move to Cincinnati and continue as editor. The move was made in 1869 and, in the next few years, *Standard's* financial fortunes so improved that Errett was able to indemnify his patron and secure sole ownership. The wide acceptance of the *Christian Standard* was due in part to the fact that it was a new type of religious journal. It included something of interest to almost everybody in the family. Well-illustrated, it carried many essays, news of churches and of missionary activities, special features like poetry, political news, and comments, financial news, and scientific features. Nothing like it had appeared in the brotherhood before, and it soon won a solid base of appreciation and support in that part of the movement that was adjusting to the demands of a nation that was opening new frontiers and looked forward to the expansion of the movement. The editor possessed a deep conviction of the validity of the Restoration plea, a broad vision of its potential, and the ability to articulate both very clearly. As Alexander Campbell was the unquestioned leader of the movement prior to the Civil War, Isaac Errett is, in the opinion of most historians of the movement, the major influence in the last third of the

nineteenth century. His distaste for heresy hunting and his dislike of
pointless controversy caused him to embrace every new measure
that could advance the cause of New Testament Christianity, including missionary societies, better education, more adequate buildings,
and every other positive measure. His vigor was only curtailed by
failing health. When he died in 1888, he left no successor. His
funeral was conducted by James H. Garrison, the admiring editor of
The Christian Evangelist. W.E. Garrison has summarized Errett's
contribution in a classic statement: "More than to any other journal
and person, it was to the *Christian Standard* and Isaac Errett that
the Disciples were indebted for being saved from becoming a fissi-
parous sect of jangling legalists."[22]

The Christian Evangelist

The ministry of the *Christian Standard* was augmented by *The
Christian Evangelist.* J.H. Garrison had merged the *Gospel Echo*
(Macomb, Illinois) and the *Christian* (Kansas City, Missouri) and
began publishing the united paper, which retained the name of the
Christian, as a weekly from Quincy, Illinois, in 1872. In 1874, he
organized the Christian Publishing Company and moved to St.
Louis. In 1882, he merged the *Christian* with the Chicago-based
Evangelist, edited by B.W. Johnson. Subsequently, the subscription
lists of a number of smaller, failing journals were added, giving *The
Christian Evangelist* an increasingly larger influence. Johnson and
Garrison shared the editorship until 1894. Garrison was sole editor
until his retirement in 1912. He died in 1931.

Garrison's irenic editorial policies closely paralleled Isaac Errett's.
He supported the work of the missionary agencies, insisting that the
churches had the right to adopt whatever expedients would increase
their usefulness.[23] He never lost his passion to promote Christian
unity so far as he perceived the bounds of the New Testament would
permit. As the publishing interests of Errett and Garrison enlarged,
the two men became competitors in business, but always remained
partners in promoting the goals of the movement. Their joint influence was a powerful factor in counterbalancing the sectarian spirit of
the postwar period.

Issues Leading to Division

The controversy over the missionary society was soon accompanied
by other issues of contention. Growth in numbers and in prosperity

was enabling some congregations to call full-time, salaried preachers. The frontier churches had generally been led by elders who preached on Sundays for little or no compensation. Campbell had created a hostility toward clerical "hirelings" who preached for pay and had himself set the example of never taking any pay for preaching. But this frontier system was breaking down with growing urbanization. Congregations were demanding more competence in preaching and in management in the churches' affairs. The increased availability of education created a supply of trained leaders. Congregations found that "one man who knew how could accomplish what a plurality of amateurs could not."[24] Eventually, most of the congregations would call "ministers," but the transition from the lay ministry would not be an easy one. Fanning lamented the "pastor system" and "the idea of theological schools to manufacture preachers." He opined:

> But the times have changed and many have changed with the times. We witness these things in deep sorrow, but we have long been satisfied that many in this country, in addition to becoming influential with the world, have become worldly wise and are strongly inclined to conform to denominational service.[25]

Closed Communion was another issue that contributed its share of dissension. In 1863, Moses E. Lard, in the very first issue of his quarterly, wrote: "The subject of communion has been, for some time, engrossing much of the attention of our brotherhood." Lard proceeded to define the nature of Communion in such terms as to conclude that the unimmersed could eat and drink but could not commune because they are not of the kingdom.[26] Response was both negative and positive, causing Lard to observe: "It is high time the loose and ill-digested views of our brethren on the subject of communing with the sprinkled sects of the day were subjected to criticism."[27] He tended to see the increasing adoption of open Communion as symptomatic of a whole package of errors that he regarded as dangerous innovations. In an oft-quoted and impassioned essay, he wrote:

> Let us agree to commune with the sprinkled sects around us, and soon we shall come to recognize them as Christians. Let us agree to recognize them as Christians, and immersion, with its deep significance, is buried in the grave of our folly. Then in not one whit will we be better than others. Let us countenance political charlatans as preachers, and we at once become corrupt as the loathsome nest on which Beecher sets to hatch the things he calls Christians. Let us consent to introduce opinions in politics as tests of fellowship, and soon opinions in religion will become so. Then the door of heresy and

schism will stand wide open, and the work of ruin will begin. Let us agree to admit organs, and soon the pious, the meek, the peace-loving, will abandon us, and our churches will become gay worldly things, literal Noah's arks, full of clean and unclean beasts. To all this let us yet add, by way of dessert, and as a sort of spice to the dish, a few volumes of innerlight speculations, and a cargo or two of *reverend* dandies dubbed pastors, and we may congratulate ourselves on having completed the trip in a wonderfully short time. We can now take rooms in Rome, and chuckle over the fact that we are as orthodox as the rankest heretic in the land.[28]

The controversy that was to become the harshest and most divisive in the period following the Civil War involved the growing practice of introducing an instrument of music into the churches. Churches on the frontier were almost universally devoid of musical instruments. Organs were not among the items carried over the mountains by wagon. So long as instruments were not available, they posed no problems. But with the coming of the railroads, small pump organs and melodeons became part of the culture of the developing region. The distinction of introducing the first musical instrument to the worship service probably belongs to the physician-preacher, Dr. L.L. Pinkerton of Midway, Kentucky, shortly before his departure for medical service with the Union army. That it was an innovation nobody could deny. But was such an innovation permissible? Did its introduction vitiate the plan to restore New Testament Christianity, or was it an expedient that may be employed without affecting the nature of faith or the validity of worship? No unanimous answers could be found for these questions. Nor were they new questions for Protestants. The Swiss Reformers, Zwingli and Calvin, were adamantly

L.L. Pinkerton, (1812-1875) M.D., minister of the Church in Midway, Kentucky. He was the first to utilize a musical instrument in worship and the first to advocate what later became open membership. He has been called the first liberal of the Restoration Movement.

opposed to organs. The Puritan churches of New England engaged in a series of controversies relating to music in worship, beginning with the introduction of hymns of human authorship in place of "inspired Psalms" and continuing through a convulsion over the propriety of printing musical notes as well as words for the hymns. When musical instruments made their appearance in the region west of the Appalachians, it caused a strain in many congregations, but it failed to result in a division anywhere except among the churches of the Disciples. Why this was the case is a very interesting and important question, and it demands serious examination.

The reaction to the question of the propriety of using an instrument in the service of worship was varied, and several years lapsed before polarization could be discerned. The matter had not yet become an issue prior to Campbell's decline; hence, he never conceived of it as an issue capable of dividing the brotherhood.[29] William K. Pendleton, Campbell's co-editor and son-in-law, counseled deference to the conscience of the brethren in order to preserve harmony and unity.[30] Benjamin Franklin early declared himself opposed to instruments.[31] The colorful Moses E. Lard was quick to expose the perils. In 1864, he wrote an editorial essay on "Instrumental Music in Churches and Dancing" and openly advised separation from churches using an instrument. Lamenting the fact that several congregations had introduced the "infamous box," he asked:

> But what shall be done with such churches? Of course nothing. If they see fit to mortify the feelings of their brethren, to forsake the example of the primitive churches, to contemn [sic] the authority of Christ by resorting to will worship, to excite dissension, and give rise to general scandal, they must do it. As a body we can do nothing. Still we have three partial remedies left us to which we should at once resort. 1. Let every preacher in our ranks resolve at once that he will never, under any circumstances or on any account, enter a meeting house belonging to our brethren in which an organ stands. We beg and entreat our preaching brethren to adopt this as an unalterable rule of conduct. This and like evils must be checked, and the very speediest way to effect it is the one here suggested. 2. Let no brother who takes a letter from one church ever unite with another using an organ. Rather let him live out of a church than go into such a den. 3. Let those brethren who oppose the introduction of an organ first remonstrate in gentle, kind, but decided terms. If their remonstrance is unheeded, and the organ is brought in, then let them at once, and without even the formality of asking for a letter, abandon the church so acting; and let all such members unite elsewhere. Thus these organ-grinding churches will in the lapse of time be broken down, or wholly apostatize. And the sooner they are in fragments the better for the cause of Christ. I have no sympathy with them, no fellowship for them, and so help me God never intend to knowingly put my foot into one of them. As a people we claim to be engaged in an effort to return to the purity, simplicity, freedom from ostentation and pride, of the ancient apostolic churches. Let us,

then, neither wink at any thing standing in the way, nor compromise aught essential to this end. The moment we do so our unity is at an end, and our hopes are in the dust.[32]

J.W. McGarvey joined in disapproval of the use of the instrument in the following year. He questioned whether the silence of Scriptures can be understood to imply consent. He asked, "Is not the silence of the Scriptures the limit which God himself has assigned to the expression of his will?"[33] In the same issue of the Millennial Harbinger, Charles Louis Loos noted that Jewish synagogue worship was devoid of instrumental accompaniment, and concluded:

> We must introduce no innovation. But if absolutely some other music must be had, then, according to my opinion, it ought to come from trumpets and flutes, as it was heard in the Temple of Solomon.[34]

Although McGarvey and Loos agreed that organs ought not to be utilized, there is an interesting divergence. Loos could countenance those instruments used in Temple worship, while McGarvey insisted that the Old Testament could provide no authorization for Christian worship. The claim could easily be advanced that practices were permitted under the Old Covenant that were not allowable under the New.

The position of the various editors would be determining factors in molding the attitude of church members on issues such as this. Not until 1870 did Isaac Errett express himself on the growing concern over the introduction of the instrument. Then he wrote: *"It is a difference of opinion. . . . no man has a right to make it, on either side, a test of fellowship or an occasion of stumbling."* The following week, he stated his position more explicitly: "The real difference among us is a difference of opinion as to the *expediency* of instrumental worship in public worship, and therefore, *it is wrong to make this difference a test of fellowship,* on one hand, *or an occasion of stumbling,* on the other." [Italics in original.][35] Thus, to Errett, the unity of the brotherhood was vastly more important than either strict adherence to customs of the New Testament times or adaptation to the customs and tastes of modern, Western culture. But such a position as the one he took undermined those who insisted that the use of an instrument in worship was not a matter of "opinion" or "expediency," but a violation of a divinely ordered pattern. Moses E. Lard had expounded this point a year earlier when he wrote: "When we plead expediency to justify practices unknown to the apostolic age, we are not within the limits of the expedient. We are then violating the word of God."[36] The question of the nature and limits of "expediency" would be given a thorough journalistic thrashing.

David Lipscomb did not commit the *Gospel Advocate* on the matter of the instrument until 1873, and, when he did, he based his position squarely on the principle that what the Bible did not expressly permit was prohibited in the church. Lipscomb rejected the whole notion of expediency as a dangerous device for the introduction of a host of undesirable things, preferring the "safe ground" of strict adherence to first-century practice. No voice carried greater influence in the southern states than that of the *Gospel Advocate*.

As editors and journals debated the issues, congregations tended to align in support of one or the other opinion. Many congregations experienced inner tensions when some of the members began to request an instrument. More often than not, these tensions resulted in schism, especially in the border states of Kentucky and Tennessee. The musical instrument had readier acceptance in the Northern states for reasons that will soon be pointed out; however, even in the North, it did not gain universal acceptance. A notable event occurred on August 18, 1889, in Shelby County, Illinois. At a mass meeting of some 6,000 persons, a resolution of excommunication was submitted by the elders of the Sand Creek congregation and heartily endorsed by the mass. This "Sand Creek Address and Declaration," as it came to be known, listed several "corrupt practices," including missionary societies, musical instruments, choirs, and "the one-man imported preacher-pastor" as grounds for concluding that henceforth "we can not and will not regard them (i.e., the innovators) as brethren."[37] Three years later, Daniel Sommer reissued the Sand Creek address in the *Octagraphic Review* and strongly advised every church to insert a clause in its deed insuring that no instrument could ever be used.

These developments were applauded by Daniel Sommer and the staunchly conservative *Octographic Review*[38] and were condemned by the *Christian Standard*.[39] David Lipscomb and the *Gospel Advocate* approved the Declaration's proposed course as did the influential *Christian Messenger* of Dallas, Texas. A good case may be made for fixing the date for the division in the ranks of the movement in 1889 or 1892 because of the frank espousal and widespread acceptance of schism as the means of dealing with the problem. The commonly accepted date for the division is 1906, the date when the noninstrument Churches of Christ sought and obtained separate listing in the federal census. But by that date, the schism was manifestly well-advanced. Actually, it is very difficult to fix a date with any degree of satisfaction because this division was a process rather than an event. The selection of any particular event to symbolize what was in reality a lengthy development is somewhat arbitrary.

Individuals have often been heard to remark incredulously, "How could a brotherhood that went through the Civil War without dividing fracture over the use of an instrument in the worship service?"[40]

The question reflects the confidence expressed in Moses E. Lard's 1866 editorial, "Can We Divide?" in which Lard used glowing terms that were mistakenly optimistic:

> But further, we, as a nation and as Christians, have just passed the fierce ordeal of a terrible war, a war in which passion ran to its hight [sic], and feelings became as ferocious as feelings ever get. We had many brethren on both the opposing sides. Many of our churches stood precisely where the carnival raged most. Yet not a rent in our ranks did the war produce. True, for the time being it cooled many an ardent feeling, and caused old friends to regard one another a little shyly. Still it effected no division. And now even those kindly feelings are obviously beginning to flow back; and brethren from the two hostile sides are meeting each other as brethren should ever meet. They even seem to vie with each other in acts of magnanimity and high Christian bearing. The war is never mentioned but in accents of sorrow; crimination and recrimination are never heard; the cause of Christ is the constant topic of conversation; while all noble hearts are beating high with joy that our unity is left to us perfect. If now we have triumphantly come through this storm, and still gloriously stand an undivided people, have we not reason to count with confidence on the future? May we not boldly say, trusting in God to help us, we can never divide?[41]

Contemporary historiography does not reach such an easy conclusion. Viewing the whole unhappy sequence of events leading to tragic schism in the movement, it becomes increasingly clear that it was the consequence of a series of forces that were set in motion by the tensions leading up to the war and the consequences rising out of the war. This is clearly reflected in the geographic distribution of the churches electing to withdraw from the Disciples. The heavy concentration of the dissenting churches was in the region of the Old Confederacy.[42] It is especially interesting to note that, in Tennessee, the lines of separation correspond exactly to the North-South wartime division. East Tennessee, which remained with the Union during the war, found no problem in accepting musical instruments or missionary societies. Middle and West Tennessee, which joined the Confederacy, chose overwhelmingly to withdraw from the Disciples. It is no longer possible to consider this as mere coincidence. Rather, it has become increasingly apparent that the polarization that was largely sectional was the result of a series of developments that can best be seen as a change in the culture of a part of the nation and a resistance to such a change in other parts of the nation. The changes were more pronounced in the North, largely because of victory in the war and subsequent urbanization and industrialization—such changes were delayed half a century in the

South. Even the rural areas of the North shared in the post-war prosperity, but none of the South did. A decisive factor was the influence of the *Christian Standard,* which was acceptable to the North but not to the South. The resulting difference produced a genuine culture gap.

One symptom of change can be seen in a new attitude toward church buildings. In the early days of the movement, the frontier church was a simple log structure, often with no provision for heat or light, and shutters in the place of glazed windows. In 1832, Alexander Campbell was admonishing:

> It is most devoutly to be wished that all who plead for reformation would carry out their principles in the plainness, convenience, and cheapness of the buildings which they erect for the assemblies of christians. No greater satire could be inscribed on marble against the religion of Jesus Christ, than are many of the houses called churches, whenever the people have the means of gratifying the spirit which is in them. . . . Let there be only a regard to convenience and durability; let all that is merely to gratify the lusts of the eye and the pride of life be left to them who seek to gain influence on the children of the flesh by reducing Christianity to the taste and fashion of this world, and we can build two, three, and sometimes four meeting houses for the price of one of the same dimensions.[43]

The passing of time made it difficult to maintain this simplicity. Crude log cabins were replaced by more adequate, permanent homes. Railroads brought new products, newspapers multiplied, and books became more readily available. Schools were established, lectures were heard, and musical concerts were given. Gas lights, cook stoves, sidewalks, and a host of other innovations were transforming the life-style of the frontier so that the backwoodsman became a rare if not queer sight. When these changes came in the life-style of people, they could not but affect the churches. Where change occurred in society, it was bound to appear in the life and attitude of the church. But, where society remained largely unchanged, it would be too much to expect that change in the life of the church would be easily accepted. It was not.

Staunchly opposing "progress" in the churches was Ben Franklin, Moses E. Lard, and David Lipscomb. Moses E. Lard raised the flag of alarm immediately following the war. In a survey of the brotherhood under the title "The Work of the Past—Symptoms of the Future," he lamented the fact that the old ways were being altered.

> He is a poor observer of men and things who does not see slowly growing up among us a class of men who can no longer be satisfied with the ancient gospel and the ancient order of things. These men

must have changes; and silently they are preparing the mind of brotherhood to receive changes. Be not deceived, brethren, the Devil is not sleeping. If you refuse to see the danger till ruin is upon you, then it will be too late.[44]

A conspicuous example of such change came to the attention of Ben Franklin in 1872. Central Christian Church in Cincinnati, Ohio, built a new structure at a cost of $140,000 and, to make matters worse, installed an $8,000 pipe organ. Such conformity to the extravagance of this world horrified Franklin, who "stood as a living symbol of the past."[45] It could presage nothing but the abandonment of the plea of restoration and a wholesale surrender to the world, the flesh, and the devil. But the future in the prosperous North was in the direction that Franklin abhorred as, one by one, the old log churches were replaced with brick structures having stained glass windows, gas lights, and often equipped with choir lofts. The congregations, increasingly made up of better-educated members, some of whom had studied music in the proliferating colleges, were no longer satisfied with the very simple ways of worship that had characterized the frontier. In such cases, the demand for an organ was very pronounced, often irresistible.

Quite otherwise was it in most of the South. The war had wrought physical destruction and economic devastation. But the refusal of the Southern churches to accept the changes that the organ symbolized is not to be explained primarily on economic grounds. To do so would be serious oversimplification. More significant is the total mentality found in the states of the Confederacy, where resentment over the war, the hardship of reconstruction, unrelieved financial burdens, and the loss of pride prevailed. This made it extremely difficult to maintain a charitable attitude toward the Northern brethren, especially in view of the pro-Northern war resolution of the missionary society. Baptists, Methodists, and Presbyterians had separated before the war and felt no obligation to maintain fraternal contacts with their Northern counterparts. Disciples had suffered from the war fully as much as Baptists, Methodists, and Presbyterians. They shared equally the deep resentments and the sectional spirit. It would probably have been asking too much to expect that Disciples preserve intersectional fraternity when the other communions could not. The process of division would be different; the causes would be the same. Martin E. Marty, well-known historian of American religion, notes that the slavery controversy itself inclined Southern churches of all types to become more literalistic in their understanding of Scripture because such literalism gave them proof texts to justify slavery. No particular reference to the Disciples is implied when he notes: "Southern churchmen were more and more convinced to resist religious change," and consequently they tended to become the "most rigidly orthodox Protestants in America."[46] Commenting on the problem that the Southern churchmen confronted following the war, Marty notes:

> For Southerners, the recovery of pride was essential. . . . Making devils of the Northerners was not by itself a sufficient basis for new self-esteem. The religious people of the South had a more difficult problem. They had seen their cause to be a moral one, chartered by Providence himself. God had led them to slavery as a peculiar institution, to secession as a policy, and to battle as a means for defense of both. Now they had been defeated. Had they been wrong? Had God failed them, or had they failed him? There were varieties of answers to these questions, but few answers led to the kind of soul-searching out of which new concord with the North, including with Northern Protestants, could have come.[47]

The process whereby a body lacking a hierarchical structure undergoes division is quite different from that in which a more structured body like the Presbyterian Church, for example, divides. A General Assembly can formally divide, but a widely scattered fellowship of autonomous congregations cannot separate so readily. And when a schism develops in a body of this type, the real causes are often obscured by secondary causes that are more useful only because they are more highly visible. Such visible secondary causes readily become symbolic and thus tend to conceal the dynamics that are actually producing schism. D.E. Harrell has noted:

> The process of division was a bewildering unknown to the Disciples in the 1850's. It took most of the remainder of the nineteenth century to demonstrate the localized, time-consuming process necessary for a permanent schism in the loosely knit movement. The basic ingredients which proved necessary were the solidification of factions around opposing sets of institutions such as papers, schools, and societies and the development of an "issue" of sufficient importance to be regarded as a "test of fellowship." By 1860, abolitionist Disciples were rapidly uniting around separate institutional loyalties and many of them were prepared to make the slavery issue a "test of fellowship."[48]

The Civil War put the slavery issue to rest. In the context of southern resentment, following the war, the use of an instrument of music in worship became the "test of fellowship" needed to facilitate division. As such, it was admirably suited to the purpose. This issue was concrete and highly visible. Furthermore, although a number of motives (some of them very unlovely) could lead to its use or its nonuse, this whole issue was capable of being expressed in terms of fidelity to the Bible. And the issue had the additional merit of being insoluble except on the basis of examination of the hidden premises upon which the arguments, pro or con, rested. This was almost never done. Consequently, the issue of musical instruments became the touchstone upon which division would be predicated. But the fact that numerous other factors were involved is immediately apparent to those who undertake a serious examination of the matter after the passage of more than a century.[49]

The process of polarization was a gradual one. With the passing years, individual congregations would come to identify with one or the other of the emerging groups. In this process, the role of the various papers, as usual, was very significant. It has often been noted that "Disciples don't have bishops, they have editors."[50] Probably the role of the various papers has never been more critical than at this time, due largely to the fact that the printed page was the major communication medium beyond the local church. The dominant influence in the South was the *Gospel Advocate*, which was openly sectional in its outlook and a guardian of the old ways.[51] It became "the nucleus which the Churches of Christ gathered around."[52] Its position was augmented by the *Firm Foundation* of Austin, Texas, the *Apostolic Times*, Lexington, Kentucky, the *American Christian Review*, Cincinnati, Ohio, and its successor, the *Octographic Review*, of Indianapolis, Indiana, together with a number of smaller periodicals. All were unfriendly to cultural changes and feared what was often and ambiguously termed "progress."[53]

Preaching

No item is of greater significance to the development of a Protestant religious body than preaching, and none is more difficult to assess. Generalizations at this point are exceedingly precarious and should be made with great caution. Not only does the quality of sermonizing vary widely in any given period of the history of the church, but the criteria on which judgments are made undergo change from one generation to the next. Compared with prewar preaching, one observer holds that preaching became more emotional, the preachers being American frontiersmen who knew and used the local idiom effectively despite limited education. This kind of preaching was very different from that of the university-trained preachers like the Campbells and Walter Scott.[54] Emphasis was placed on a few "revealed essentials" and a very simple "New Testament plan" for the church. J.H. Garrison, who heard many sermons in his long life, comments as follows about the sermonizing of this period and the doctrinal structure upon which it was based:

It was a very simple theology, and a very rigid one so far as concerned the "revealed essentials." Theoretically it stressed the intellectual process of believing testimony on adequate evidence
addressed to the senses and the overt acts of obedience to clearly
stated divine commands. But how did they preach? Not, we may be
sure, with any such sole reliance upon proofs, evidences, and
authority as would be suggested by this theory. However they might
decry the abuses of religious experience and the dependence upon
"feeling," every successful preacher among them knew how to over-
lay his argument with an emotional appeal.[55]

In 1867, W.T. Moore published a volume of sermons by the better-
known preachers of that day.[56] It is enlightening to study these sermons, but they must not be seen as "typical" or "average." The two
most prominent characteristics of the last third of the nineteenth
century were growth and controversy, and the surviving sermonic
material reflects an abundance of both evangelistic and polemic
themes, at least by comparison to later Disciple preaching.[57] But
these emphases were wholly consistent with the spirit of the day,
which saw a vigorous and expanding nation fully enjoying a freedom
of expression little known in human history hitherto.

Lest the impression be formed that the acrimony generated by the
war was all-pervasive, and that the desire for a broader unity was
totally obscured by sectarian interests, note should be taken of a
four-day conference held in Richmond, Virginia, April 24-27, 1866,
between Baptists and Disciples to reach "a better understanding
between the two bodies, and to determine, if possible, whether the
time for proposing a union between them had come."[58]

The highly respected Dr. W.F. Broadus took the initiative to call
the conference and led the Baptist delegation, which included Dr.
Jeremiah B. Jeter, whose book, *Campbellism Examined,* had generated hostility toward him among the Disciples. Even so, he spent the
last years of his life urging the union of Baptists and Disciples. The
Disciple group was led by J.W. Goss. W.T. Moore observed:

> When it became evident that the union of the states would be pre-
> served, men began to ask questions about the union of God's people;
> and one question was, if a union of the states is important, is not a
> union of the churches of greater importance?[59]

After four days of courteous and respectful dialogue, the conference found, according to Dr. Jeter's report in the *Religious Herald,*
which he edited:

> The desirableness of the union all must concede. We are agreed on
> certain important points in which we differ from the rest of the

world. We believe that only immersion is Christian baptism; that only believers are entitled to the ordinance; and that churches are constituted only of immersed believers. Our views, too, of the great, vital evangelical duties, repentance and faith, as disclosed by the conference, are identical. On various points we differ; but some of these differences relate to terminology; some to matters of comparatively little moment and some may yet be the offspring of misconception; but still there are differences between us, the most serious of which, perhaps, concerns the design of baptism. It would be a bright day for the principles which we hold in common if these differences could be removed or overcome, so that their advocates, instead of wasting their time and energies in fruitless controversies, could heartily combine all their influence and efforts for their wider diffusion. It is our plain solemn duty to pray, not merely for the union of all Christians, but especially for the union of those Christians whose approximation to each other affords ground to hope for their harmony.[60]

This would not be the last dialogue with the Baptists, although none has occurred with the Southern Baptist body since this date.

In general, the years following the Civil War have been aptly described as "The Dark Ages of Controversy and Stagnation."[61] More positively, it can be seen as a time when latent possibilities within the general thrust of the Disciples were being explored and exploited in behalf of an ever-widening divergence of perspective that national events were imposing upon the growing fellowship.

End Notes

[1]For a discussion of the attitudes of many of the leaders of the movement toward the war, see D.E. Harrell, op. cit., chapter 5. See also the "Address" signed by fourteen prominent ministers urging no participation in warfare, reproduced in W.T. Moore, op. cit., pp. 494, 495.

[2]Alexander Campbell, "Reported Troubles at Bethany College," *Millennial Harbinger*, 1856, p. 111-117. Campbell had noted the "sectional" character of the school at the time of its opening "Christian University," *Millennial Harbinger*, 1850, p. 331.

[3]This was Campbell's conviction. After noting in 1845 that the rising sectional hostility had already fractured the Methodist church and threatened other bodies, Campbell wrote: "We are the only religious community in the civilized world whose principles (unless we abandon them) can preserve us from such an unfortunate predicament" ("Our Position to American Slavery," *Millennial Harbinger*, 1845, p. 51).

[4]Harrell, op. cit., p. 106.

[5]W.T. Moore, "Reformation of the Nineteenth Century," *The Christian Evangelist*, May 18, 1899, p. 617.

[6]Woodrow Wassom traces the change in Garfield's thinking from a pacifist and a moderate Campbellian attitude toward slavery to a militant, anti-slave pro-Unionist. He sees the change beginning in Garfield's study at Williams College in Massachusetts, where he came under the influence of Mark Hopkins. *James A. Garfield: His Religion and Education* (Nashville: Tennessee Book Co., 1952), pp. 82, 83.

[7]Herman A. Norton, *Rebel Religion* (St. Louis: Bethany Press, 1941), p. 89.

[8]*Report of Proceedings of the Fifteenth Annual Meeting of the American Christian Missionary Society* (Cincinnati: E. Morgan and Sons, 1863), p. 13.

[9]David Lipscomb, "I Did Wrong," *The Gospel Advocate*, March 13, 1866.

[10]The firm was Metcalf & Bros. V.M. Metcalf, David Lipscomb, and Philip S. Fall, all of Nashville, constituted a committee that disbursed thousands of dollars in money and provisions, mostly from Northern churches.

[11]Harrell notes: "Ironically, the massive relief from northern churches probably strengthened the influence of the conservative preachers who became the leaders of southern separation in the decades that followed." *The Social Sources of Division in the Disciples of Christ, 1865-1900* (Atlanta: by the author, 1973), p. 57.

[12]A fine biography of Fanning is James R. Wilburn's *The Hazard of the Die* (Austin: Sweet, 1969).

[13]Ibid. pp. 171ff. Wilburn suggests that Fanning's earlier enthusiasm for organization seen in his labors on behalf of cooperation in Tennessee was cooled in 1852 when Alexander Campbell suggested that the state meeting formally censure Jesse B. Ferguson for his advocacy of post-mortem repentance (p. 178). Sensing the possibilities for mischief in organization, Wilburn notes that Fanning "never again took part in an organized cooperation by holding office, as he had done for several years."

[14]David E. Harrell (*Social Sources,* op. cit., p. 17) suggests that the *American Christian Review* was the leading journal of the movement at the end of the war, but that its firm opposition to the missionary society, Franklin's "anti-progressivism," his "old-fogeyness," and "his stand against 'innovations' soon placed him outside of the mainstream of the movement."

[15]A good summary of the respective positions may be found in Earl I. West, op. cit. Vol. II, pp. 45-72.

[16]West comments: "Upon this interpretation of the motto was based every innovation which was brought into the church." He speaks approvingly of the segment of the movement "to whom the call for divine authority still meant something. They believed that whatever was not authorized by the word of God was wrong."

[17]Benjamin Franklin was of this opinion, but he forthwith changed his mind and classed it as a "human scheme . . . organized in *human wisdom* and not in the *wisdom of God*" (*American Christian Review,* 1876). W.K. Pendleton (*Report of Proceedings,* [Cincinnati: Bosworth, Chase and Hall, 1874], p. 28) reflected that the plan
> was a sacrifice on the part of many to the feelings and judgment of others, in the desire to satisfy their theoretical objections and to conciliate their prejudices. . . . The whole theory of this plan was clearly grasped, and every detail was analyzed, criticized and adjusted, till the whole stood before us clear, consistent, scriptural, and satisfactory. It was an earnest and a careful work.

[18]W.K. Pendleton (ibid., p. 22) cited Jacob Creath Jr. as foremost among those who opposed conventions. He cited Creath's article in the *Millennial Harbinger* of 1850, pp. 637-641, as typical of the mentality that would forbid the brotherhood "to consult and cooperate in any representative way about anything."

[19]Ibid., p. 15. See also p. 29.

[20]Ibid., p. 39.

[21]M.E. Lard, "Remarks on the [Synopsis]," *Lard's Quarterly* (September, 1863), Vol. I, pp. 100-107.

[22]Garrison and DeGroot, op. cit., p. 358.

[23]*The Christian Evangelist* (November 29), 1888, p. 739.

[24]Garrison and DeGroot, op. cit., p. 340.

[25]*Gospel Advocate* (March 14), 1862, p. 217.

[26]M.E. Lard, "Do the Unimmersed Commune?" *Lard's Quarterly* (September, 1863), Vol. I, p. 41.

[27]M.E. Lard, "Review of 'Theta' on Communion," *Lard's Quarterly* (March, 1864), Vol. I, p. 299.

[28]M.E. Lard, "The Work of the Past—Symptoms of the Future," *Lard's Quarterly* (April, 1865), Vol. II, p. 262.

[29]Campbell expressed an opinion that instruments belonged to the worldly, nonspiritual worship of the older denominations but could only be "as a cow bell in a concert" to the spiritual ("Instrumental Music," *Millennial Harbinger*, 1851, p. 582).

[30]W.K. Pendleton, "Pew-Renting and Organ-Music," *Millennial Harbinger*, 1864, p. 127.

[31]Benjamin Franklin, "Instrumental Music in Churches," *American Christian Review*, January 31, 1860, p. 19.

[32]M.E. Lard, "Instrumental Music and Dancing," *Lard's Quarterly* (March, 1864), Vol. I, pp. 332, 333.

[33]J.W. McGarvey, "Instrumental Music," *Millennial Harbinger* (February), 1865, p. 88.

34C.L. Loos, "Music in Churches," *Millennial Harbinger* (February), 1865, p. 92.

35Isaac Errett, "Instrumental Music in Our Churches," *Christian Standard* (May 7, 14), 1870, pp. 148, 156.

36M.E. Lard, "Innovations in Divine Worship," *Apostolic Times*, April 29, 1869, p. 20.

37The text of the Sand Creek Address may be found in the *Christian Leader*, Sept. 10, 1889, p. 2. It has been reproduced and is more readily available in E.I. West, op. cit., Vol. II, p. 431.

38Daniel Sommer, *Octagraphic Review*, May 24, 1892. The *Octographic Review* was the name given to the old *American Christian Review* in 1866 when it was purchased by Daniel Sommer. It was published in Indianapolis, Indiana, after 1883. See, also, James S. Wolfgang, *A Life of Humble Fear: the Biography of Daniel Sommer* (Indianapolis: Christian Theological Seminary, unpublished M.A. thesis, 1975), p. 89.

39Russell Errett, "A Divisive Work," *Christian Standard* (June 25), 1892, p. 521.

40The Disciple historian A.T. DeGroot titles a section of *The Disciples: A History*, "Through Civil War Without Division," p. 333.

41M.E. Lard, "Can We Divide?" *Lard's Quarterly* (April, 1866), Vol. III, p. 335, 336. A similar confidence was expressed in 1909 by W.T. Moore, *History*, op. cit., p. 495.

42See Edwin S. Gaustad, *Historical Atlas of Religion in America* (New York: Harper and Row, 1976), p. 65. Gaustad notes that, in 1906, almost half of the membership of the Churches of Christ were in Tennessee and Texas. Alabama also claimed a large fraction of this body (p. 66).

43Alexander Campbell, "Building Houses for Christian Worship," *Millennial Harbinger*, 1832, p. 229.

44M.E. Lard, "Work of the Past," loc. cit.

45E.I. West, op. cit., Vol. II, p. 133. Isaac Errett criticized Franklin for being an "alarmist" and generally approved of the progress and the growing stature of the movement. A journalistic conflict followed.

46Martin E. Marty, *Righteous Empire* (New York: Dial Press, 1970), p. 65.

[47]Ibid., pp. 134, 135.

[48]D.E. Harrell, *Quest,* op. cit., p. 132. For a fuller discussion, see H.E. Webb, "Sectional Conflict and Schism Within the Disciples of Christ," in *Essays on New Testament Christianity,* op. cit.

[49]Harrell comments:
Many factors are involved in the schisms of the restoration movement in the late nineteenth and early twentieth centuries. The role of economics has already been discussed. It is also obvious that sectionalism was an important factor in these divisions. The Church of Christ—Disciples of Christ rupture was basically a North-South division (Ibid, p. 132).

[50]This observation, oft-repeated, is generally attributed to W.T. Moore.

[51]D.E. Harrell (*Social Sources,* op. cit., p. 21) comments on the editorial influence of the journal: "Stubborn, caustic, and plodding, the editor of the *Advocate* virtually defined conservative Disciple orthodoxy."

[52]Ibid.

[53]Harrell (ibid, p. 47) insists that "genuine lower-class prejudice was everywhere apparent in the writings of southern and midwestern theological conservatives" and that "David Lipscomb was the most important Disciples figure with decided lower-class prejudice." J.S. Lamar notes that Benjamin Franklin of the *American Christian Review* attempted to "make the impression that the 'Review' was the paper of the *people,* the 'Standard' was that of a silent and aristocratic *class*" [italics in original]. Obviously sociological factors were beginning to reinforce other prejudices (J.S. Lamar, *Memoirs of Isaac Errett* [Cincinnati: Standard, 1893], p. 308).

[54]Garrison and DeGroot, op. cit., p. 337.

[55]J.H. Garrison, *Religion Follows the Frontier* (New York, Harper Brothers, 1931), p. 223.

[56]W.T. Moore, *The Living Pulpit of the Christian Church* (Cincinnati: R.W. Carroll, 1867). In addition to the volume by Moore and the numerous sermons found in the periodicals, the three-volume series edited by Z. T. Sweeney and titled *New Testament Christianity* (Columbus, 1926), will serve to illustrate the matter.

[57]W.T. Moore published a volume of sermons, *The New Living Pulpit of the Christian Church* (1918), and Hunter Beckelhymer has compared

the sermons of the two volumes, especially as they relate to Christology. He found that the earlier sermons were more legalistic and dogmatic than those of half a century later ("Representative Preaching about Jesus," Ronald Osborn, ed., *The Reformation of Traditions* [St. Louis: Bethany Press, 1963], pp. 78-97). Earl West notes this trend and considers it as symptomatic of the abandonment of the plea (op. cit., Vol. II, p. 143).

[58]W.T. Moore, *Comprehensive History,* op. cit., p. 589.

[59]Ibid., p. 589.

[60]Ibid., p. 591.

[61]J.H. Garrison, op. cit., p. 246.

Chapter Nine

Bold
New Strides
(1874-1900)

Four decades after the 1832 union of the Christians (B.W. Stone) and the Disciples (Campbell), the movement had grown to the point where it was a noticeable force in the religious life of the newer states being formed in mid-America. Religious statistics are always difficult to establish, and, for this period, they are little better than educated estimates. By the war's close, the total membership of the church was probably around 300,000[1] and growing. The nation was young and exuberant. Commerce was expanding, and the remarkable industrial growth that was to transform the nation into the world's leading producer within a half century was getting under way. The vigor that inspired growth in commerce and industry also was evident in the churches. D.L. Moody and Ira Sankey were embarking on their evangelistic efforts that were destined to shake many cities and convert scores of thousands of the unchurched. The Sunday-school Movement was emerging on an organized basis with the formation of a national convention that created the "Uniform Lesson Plan" in 1872. The YMCA and YWCA Movement shared in the enthusiasm of these years and sought to establish facilities in every major city. All of this energy in behalf of Christian expansion had its effect on the foreign missionary efforts of the various denominations. The British Empire, on whose flag the sun never set, controlled vast reaches of the world's surface and was generally friendly toward missionaries. American missionaries were pouring into other nations in record numbers, often under the motivation of the "white man's burden."[2]

The Disciples lagged behind as far as the missionary enterprise was concerned. While the various denominations were enthusiastically planning and promoting foreign missions, the Disciples were debating whether or not a New Testament people could utilize an organization beyond the local church to enable them to do missionary work. While the discussions were being carried on in the several periodicals, giving to the program of the society was suffering a steady decline. After the adoption of the Louisville Plan, income was so low that not a single missionary was sustained.[3] Words flowed in abundance, but no missionary work was done. In 1872, the General Convention (successor to the Annual Meeting of the A.C.M.S.) urged a resumption of foreign work and the convention passed a resolution to that effect the following year. But without the means to accomplish the desired objective, the words were of little avail.[4] If the Louisville Plan had won the support of the churches, it would have provided that only one fourth of the offerings of the churches would have been used for foreign work. As it was, this scheme seemed too much like a denominational hierarchy to recommend itself to individualistic majority in the average Christian church. There seemed to be no way to overcome the paralysis when a solution appeared from an unexpected quarter.

The Christian Women's Board of Missions

The last quarter of the nineteenth century would witness the emergence of an expanded role of women as an important factor in American society. Opportunities for education, employment outside the home, and a determination to have some influence upon the character of society would gradually but inevitably enlarge the role of women in American life. Some of the Protestant churches had developed women's missionary auxiliaries, and several were effectively organized on local, district, state, and national levels. In 1870, a committee of the General Convention had reported on the potential for a similar contribution by the women of the Restoration Movement, but the convention did nothing to implement the committee's input.[5]

It was a minister's wife in Iowa City, Iowa, Mrs. Caroline Neville Pearre, who initiated the movement to create a women's society. When this came to Isaac Errett's attention, he wrote what proved to be a very helpful editorial endorsement: "Help Those Women."[6] The 1874 Convention in Cincinnati, Ohio, passed a resolution of encouragement. Then and there, the Christian Women's Board of Missions was organized with Mrs. Love Jameson (daughter of Ovid Butler), president; vice presidents from each of nine states represented; Mrs. O.A. Burgess, treasurer; Mrs. William Wallace (daughter of Mrs. Jameson), recording secretary; and Mrs. C.N. Pearre, corresponding secretary. The headquarters was located in Indianapolis, home of several of the officers. The whole organization was to be under the control of women. Their first project was to reopen the Jamaican mission, which they were able to undertake in 1876 when they sent the W.H. Williams family to revive the old work. In 1881, work was begun among the blacks in Mississippi, and, in 1882, two couples (Mr. and Mrs. S.L. Wharton and Mr. and Mrs. Albert Norton) and four single women began work in India. In 1895, the C.W.B.M. began work in El Paso, Texas, among Mexican peoples. This work was subsequently transferred to Monterrey, Mexico, where it later became the center of bitter controversy. (See chapter 10.) Puerto Rico was entered in 1900, Liberia was reentered in 1905, Argentina also in 1905, and Paraguay in 1918. The C.W.B.M. was organized by women and supported by women in hundreds of congregations. They organized local societies to study missionary activities and gather the monies they could spare from their meager household funds. This money was sent to Indianapolis for deployment on the mission field. In the four decades of its history, the C.W.B.M. became the largest agency of the Disciples of Christ.

The formation of the Christian Women's Board of Missions was the beginning of a new era in the history of the Disciples. It not only meant the substitution of action for discussion but, by their very action, these women demonstrated a contempt for all of the discussion and arguments that others marshaled in behalf of inaction. It signified a determination by some to press forward even if that meant separation from those who chose to remain with the old ways. In this sense, it signified a preference for action and achievement over unity, and an abandonment of some of the brethren in behalf of the pursuit of new goals. None personified this new mentality or expressed this disposition more adequately than W.T. Moore, who wrote the following in the *Christian Quarterly* for October 1874, immediately following the formation of the C.W.B.M.

> The Disciples have spent twenty-five years in considering the plan of general co-operation. This consideration was doubtless necessary: but it has, in some respects, greatly retarded their work. The time has come when they ought to have something settled with regard to this matter, and if they cannot settle anything, they had better stop the discussion at once, and give up the whole case as hopeless. Organization is certainly the normal state of the Church, but active work is essential to its life. Almost anything is better than the present uncertainty. What is needed is a little brave *doing*. There has been brave *talk* long enough. If the days of babyhood are passed, let the Disciples put away their playthings, and assume the responsibilities of a true manhood. We think the time for decisive action has come. No matter what the result may be, *something must be done*. True, there may be danger ahead. There is danger in everything. But the worst danger is now to hesitate. To go backward is impossible; to stand still is eternal disgrace;

to go forward has at least the promise of victory, with all the inspirations of a glorious contest. Let every faithful disciple of Christ at once determine as to where the future shall find him. [Italics in original.][7]

W.T. Moore reflected the new spirit that has been described as a renaissance. It produced new agencies as well as new tensions.[8] The events of 1874-1875 might, with equal propriety, be seen as the beginning of the division that was recognized in 1906. Henceforth, the policy would be full-throttle ahead while ignoring the opposition. The ever-widening gulf separating those who were left behind soon stretched beyond compassion, concern, or communication. The actual division of the Disciples was a *fait accompli* long before 1906.

The Foreign Christian Missionary Society

The example set by the women was not long in being followed by men who were frustrated by the paralysis of the General Missionary Convention. When a motion in the Cincinnati Convention to instruct the General Board to establish a foreign mission during the year was voted down by the convention, a discouraged W.T. Moore retired to the basement of the Richmond Street Church to contemplate and pray. He shared his disappointment with a few like-minded individuals and suggested that they meet on the next day. About twenty-five gathered to hear W.T. Moore declare that "the time had come, in his judgment, when steps for the organization of a Foreign Christian Missionary Society should be taken."[9] The suggestion met instant approval, a committee to draw up a constitution was appointed, and a conference date was set for the next General Convention in 1875 at Louisville, Kentucky. There the society was organized and Isaac Errett was chosen to be its first president, a position he held for many years. The society provided for life memberships ($100) and life directorships ($500). The latter, with the elected officers, comprised the board of managers. The organization was modest; for years, the society had no office. Its board meetings were held in Mr. Errett's office in Cincinnati. In reality, the organization of the C.W.B.M. and the F.C.M.S. marks the triumph of individual, independent initiative over the collective decision of the convention organization.

The first missionary to be sent to a foreign land was Dr. A. Holck, a native of Denmark who was sent to his homeland, where he labored until his death thirty-one years later. A second representative of the society, H.S. Earl, was sent to Southampton, England. He initiated a relationship between the society and some of the British Churches of Christ that was to last for many years and set the British churches on a new course.[10]

A mission to France was undertaken in 1877, when Jules de Launcy was sent to Paris. After a decade, this work was discontinued, owing to opposition from Roman Catholic authorities.

The Foreign Society came under criticism from some of its friends because all of its efforts were directed toward European nations long regarded to be in the Christian tradition. So the society accepted the offer of G.N. Shismanian, an Armenian who was converted in Dallas, Texas, to begin work in Constantinople. An Isaac Errett Memorial Chapel was erected in Smyrna, but the work was given up in 1904. In 1882, the society's efforts extended to India, and the next year George T. Smith and C.E. Garst were sent to Japan. Increasing resources permitted opening of work in China, the Congo, Cuba, Honolulu, the Philippines, and Tibet. At the time of the Centennial Celebration in 1909, 167 missionaries were being sustained by the F.C.M.S. From its inception, the society sought to be international, and contributions to its work were received from Canada, England, and Australia.

The old A.C.M.S., which had maintained a paper existence during the years of the Louisville Plan, was revived as a home mission society, although the C.W.B.M. also sponsored home mission work. The income of all three societies was supplied by individual memberships, offerings from churches—the latter coming largely through "special day" offerings—and emotional appeals at the annual convention. All three promoted their work through publications. Most popular was *Missionary Tidings,* published by the C.W.B.M. The F.C.M.S. published *Missionary Intelligence,* and the A.C.M.S. put out *American Home Missionary.*

Other perceived needs of the churches soon caused national organizations to be created to serve their interests. The influx of immigrants and the westward flow of population in the expanding nation provided opportunities to open new congregations in new communities. In 1888, it was estimated that there were 1,628 mission churches appealing to the societies for aid in erection of buildings, a need the societies felt they could not undertake to fill. Consequently, the convention of 1888 created a Church Extension Fund to be administered by a board located in Kansas City, Missouri, a city chosen because it was in the geographic center of the growth area. This agency, which became the Board of Church Extension, has had continual existence to this day, although it was briefly merged into the United Christian Missionary Society (1920-1934).

Colleges

Protestantism in America has always considered the founding of colleges and the maintenance of some form of higher education as one of the important tasks of the church. While the Disciples' first efforts at Bacon College, in Georgetown, Kentucky, did not survive as such, Campbell's Bethany College was such a success as to encourage similar efforts in other parts of the nation. Following the Civil War, colleges were established in rapid succession. It must be borne in mind that recognized educational standards did not exist in the nineteenth century, and the terms *college* and *university* were used quite carelessly and did not convey the meaning that they do today. The Disciples were largely rural people, and most rural areas lacked public high schools. As late as 1890, not a single state in the Union had required school attendance through high-school age, and not one of the states of the South had any compulsory school attendance requirement whatever. The college student who had completed high school was exceptional. Classroom instruction centered on basic education to serve the rudimentary needs of frontier culture. But the genuine sacrifice by faculty and patrons and the heroic struggle of many of the institutions to render the best service of which they were capable must not be denigrated by a later generation whose resources are much better but whose level of achievement, in view of their improved resources, probably falls below that of the earlier period.

A listing of the more significant colleges founded by Disciples prior to the close of the century follows.[11]

*	Add-Ran-Jarvis College	Thorp Springs, Texas
	Berkeley Bible Seminary	Berkeley, California
	Bethany College	Bethany, West Virginia
	Bible College of Missouri	Columbia, Missouri
	Butler College	Indianapolis, Indiana
	Carlton College	
	Christian University	Canton, Missouri
	Drake University	Des Moines, Iowa
**	Eugene Bible University	Eugene, Oregon
	Eureka College	Eureka, Illinois
	Hiram College	Hiram, Ohio
	Kentucky Female Orphan School	Midway, Kentucky
	Milligan College	Milligan College, Tennessee
	McLean College	
	Nebraska Christian University	Bethany, Nebraska
+	School of the Evangelists	Kimberlin Heights, Tennessee
*	Texas Christian University	N. Waco, Texas
	Hamilton College	Lexington, Kentucky
	Transylvania University	Lexington, Kentucky
	College of the Bible	Lexington, Kentucky
	West Kentucky College	Mayfield, Kentucky
	William Woods College for Girls	Fulton, Missouri
	Sinclair College	St. Thomas, Ontario

Missouri Christian College for Girls	Camden Point, Missouri
Washington Christian College	Washington, D.C.
Louisville Christian Bible School	Louisville, Kentucky
Campbell-Hagerman College	Lexington, Kentucky
Carr-Burdette College	Sherman, Texas
Christian College	Sherman, Texas
Disciples' Divinity House	Chicago, Illinois

* Merged to become Texas Christian University, Ft. Worth, Texas.
** Presently Northwest Christian College.
\+ Renamed Johnson Bible College in 1909.

In addition to the above named colleges, the Disciples pioneered a new kind of educational effort, the Bible Chair in a state university. Because it was widely believed that the teaching of religion in a university supported by public funding was a violation of the principle of separation of church and state, the curriculum of state institutions were devoid of religious studies. Several universities, however, did not deem it inappropriate for outside funding to provide teaching of religion on the campus at an academic level. Disciples were quick to take advantage of this kind of opportunity and established a Bible Chair at the University of Michigan in 1893 and the University of Virginia in 1896. Subsequently, Bible chairs were established in other state universities.

A similar scheme to provide Biblical instruction to students at the state university was developed in the early Bible college. Built adjacent to the campus of the state university, the Bible college sought to supplement the offerings of the university where the students were matriculated. Conceived on the European model of a college, these

James A. Garfield (1831-1881), one-time president of Hiram (Ohio) College, colonel in the Union Army in the Civil War, and twentieth President of the United States.

schools originally did not plan to offer degrees. Eugene C. Sanderson pioneered this type of college when he established Eugene Divinity School next to the University of Oregon in 1895.[12] The following year a similar effort began adjacent to the University of Missouri at Columbia.

The educational philosophy advocated by Alexander Campbell and incorporated into Bethany College did not provide for specialized courses for ministers. In fact, a provision in the charter specifically forbids the teaching of theology. Hostility toward a professional clergy rendered special clerical education unacceptable. It was widely held that a good foundation in literature, history, and rhetoric, coupled with a greater emphasis on the Bible, should suffice for any person entering the preaching ministry. Hundreds of preachers were educated in this fashion at Bethany.

It was J.W. McGarvey who changed this pattern when he called for more emphasis on the Bible.[13] He had been called to the faculty of Kentucky University in 1865. He became professor of sacred history in the College of the Bible and designed its curriculum to insure a greater emphasis on the content of the Bible. Lexington soon displaced Bethany in influence, and a generation of preachers bore the imprint of the distinguished faculty that McGarvey gathered about

him, which included I.B. Grubbs, C.L. Loos, S.M. Jefferson, and Robert Graham.[14]

An educational effort specifically aimed at providing preachers for the impoverished postwar southern churches was begun by Ashley S. Johnson. While ministering in Augusta, Georgia, Johnson began instruction by correspondence. He was encouraged by the response. Sensing the limitations of instruction by correspondence, Johnson purchased a large farm a few miles from Knoxville, Tennessee, and opened the School of the Evangelists. (This school was renamed Johnson Bible College in 1909, after President Johnson's death.) Johnson's intention was to provide an opportunity to any young man, regardless of economic circumstances, to prepare for ministry by working on the farm while studying. This provided the preparation for hundreds of young

John W. McGarvey (1829-1911), president of the College of the Bible until 1911 and prolific writer. Through his "Biblical Criticism" column (1883-1911) in the *Christian Standard*, he took the lead in efforts to combat Biblical criticism, which he held to be destructive of Christian faith.

men who otherwise would have been denied the opportunity of serving in the ministry of the church.

Note must be taken of the considerable segment of the movement that was moving away from the larger body of Disciples. They, too, were faced with the need to educate their people. Their strictures against missionary societies did not apply with equal force against colleges. Evidently, preaching the gospel had to be under the direct supervision of a local church, but teaching the gospel could be done under private auspices in a college.[15] Tolbert Fanning, whose Franklin College (1842) was forced to close during the Civil War, was unable to revive the college after the war. The many churches in the Nashville area were repulsed by the "innovations" that had been introduced at Bethany, and the much closer College of the Bible was unacceptable to them because President McGarvey, who opposed use of instrumental music in the churches, found the missionary society acceptable. This disaffection mandated the establishment of a new school, a need that David Lipscomb and James A. Harding convenanted to fulfill.[16] The Nashville Bible School opened in the fall of 1881. Lipscomb's reservations, reflecting his Campbellian heritage, had been expressed four years earlier when he wrote:

> Our objection to Bible Colleges had been that they were especially to make preachers. The evil of the churches, the corrupting influence is found, we are sure, in the position of the churches to the work of the preachers. . . .
> If the brethren will just teach the Bible to all who will attend whether they intend to be preachers or follow any other calling in life, they will do a good work and none will more heartily rejoice than I.[17]

A college in west Tennessee, at Henderson, gradually came into the hands of the churches of Christ there and was named West Tennessee Christian College.[18] Earl I. West notes four colleges in California by 1876.

The proliferation of colleges in this period was generally accomplished without serious regard for the cost involved in developing and maintaining them. Too many were projected as "real estate" ventures. A conspicuous, but by no means solitary, example was Garfield University, launched by the State Convention of Kansas. A bold venture of the booming 1880s, the ambitious plans called for a building not to exceed $100,000 in cost and an endowment of $100,000. The former was to be supplied by the sale of city lots in Wichita, the land for which had been donated by two patrons. A "magnificent building" was constructed, which involved heavy cost overruns. The subsequent collapse of land values prevented the accumulation of enough resources to pay for the building. The institution, opened in 1887, graduated its only class in 1890, at which time the property was lost. A private receiver, who tried in vain to reopen the college, sold the building to the Quakers. They established Friends University at the location. The experience did not prevent other colleges from adopting the same financial measures, some successfully but others with the same unfortunate results.

In 1894, the General Convention authorized the formation of a Board of Education to coordinate the work of the colleges that would cooperate with such an efort. No offices or financial means were provided for the work of the board, and by no means were all of the colleges cooperative.

The National Benevolent Association

The tendency to organize, so characteristic of this period, did not fail to touch benevolence. While local church people have generally been responsive to local community needs, there were no institutions designed especially for sustained benevolent activity. The initiative to establish a home for orphans developed in St. Louis, Missouri, among a group of women in First Christian Church. In 1887, a charter was secured for the National Benevolent Association (N.B.A.), and two years later a home was opened for children. In 1899, the work was reorganized by the General Convention, and, in 1900, the first home for the aged was opened, also in St. Louis. The N.B.A. published *The Christian Philanthropist* and appealed for assistance from the churches through Easter offerings.

Once again, this means of reaching out to the needy was rejected by many, who held that this work was committed by God to the local churches (James 1:27). Such institutions were deemed to be human devices created to usurp the responsibility of the churches. Thus, another "innovation" was added to the growing list of issues serving to widen the breach that was increasingly discernable since the end of the Civil War.

Ministerial Relief

A new concern began to emerge when the plight of the growing number of aged, destitute ministers came to the attention of some of the churches. As long as the churches were served by the pious farmer-preacher, the needs of advancing age were met from the family farm. The growth of village and town churches with full-time ministers created a problem of support for the man who had given his life to preaching the gospel and had grown "too old for our church." Few ministers were independently wealthy, and fewer still were handsomely paid. Some were resourceful enough to invest wisely, but the greater portion faced genuine privation with advancing years unless their children were prepared to pick up the burden. The General Convention in 1895 recognized that the church had some measure of responsibility to meet the needs of the old warriors of the cause, and the Board of Ministerial Relief was organized. Two years later, the board was incorporated in Indiana and the convention designated Christmas offerings for its use. It should be noted that this was only "relief," and such meager funds as were collected were in far greater demand than the supply could satisfy. Systematic provision through an adequate pension arrangement was still some years ahead.[19]

The last quarter of the nineteenth century, which witnessed the formation of two new societies and several national boards, all of which reported to the General Convention, was the "period of organization" for the movement that began on the frontier at the beginning of the century. Furthermore, it is quite apparent that these organizations had close parallels to those of other religious bodies in the United States. This gave credibility to the charge that the movement was becoming "another denomination."[20] The charge was reinforced by the growing trend to replace simple and primitive buildings with more elaborate edifices. A cry of outrage was raised in 1872 when Central Christian Church in Cincinnati dedicated a "cathedral" costing $140,000, and insult was added to this injury when a grand organ concert featuring classical selections was advertized in the local papers.[21] It is understandable how people in rural areas contending with postwar impoverishment would be unable to adjust readily to such change. The charge of trying to imitate the denominations never settles well with people who oppose the denominational structure. It would be raised again in the future and whenever it was leveled, it involved certain presuppositions that were almost never stated, namely, what a denomination essentially is and precisely what must be done in order to become a denomination. When pressed for a definition, which was rarely done, the person making the charge usually advanced a definition that was in his own particular interest. In the absence of a satisfactory definition, the ambiguity of this charge continued to fuel misunderstandings.

The Influence of Editors

The development of agencies in this period made no provision for a publication board. From the beginning of the movement, extensive use was made of the press. Scores of interested individuals sought to extend the range of their influence by publishing periodicals. The formidable task of listing and classifying the plethora of Disciple publications has been undertaken by Claude Spencer.[22] Each of these publications was a private enterprise. None claimed to speak for anybody but himself and every editor-publisher assumed the financial risks and absorbed the losses that forced most to be short-lived. But in so doing, a tradition was established that journals should be privately owned. Advertizing revenue became an important means of survival as the gap between subscription revenues and production costs widened. Interestingly, it was those publishers who were successful in expanding into the new markets provided by the growing Bible-school movement that were able to absorb the losses sustained in publication. Isaac Errett became sole owner of Standard Publishing Company when the trustees assigned their stocks to him in return for his assumption of the debts of the company. After several years of financial struggle, the company's fortunes were turned around by the volume of Bible-school material that was produced. It was not different with the Christian Publishing Company of St. Louis, which was owned by J.H. Garrison, nor ultimately with the *Gospel Advocate.*

In the absence of a national ecclesiastical authority, the editors of papers with wide circulation exercised great influence. W.T. Moore's wry comment aptly describes the situation: "This government by journalism has perhaps been unavoidable in view of the fact that the Disciples have never had any organization of the churches that could speak for this whole brotherhood."[23] Among the publications of this period, four are especially notable, and a fifth developed quickly. Note has already been taken of the launching of the *Christian Standard* and the revival of the *Gospel Advocate* in 1866. These papers represented divergent sectional interests and their respective editors came to wield enormous influence. David Lipscomb had no rival as leader of the conservative churches that rejected missionary societies and any other innovation, especially instrumental music in worship. His twentieth-century counterpart, B.C. Goodpasture, described Lipscomb's role accordingly: "Perhaps he did more than any other man to keep the churches of Christ faithful to the teachings of the New Testament. Wherever *The Gospel Advocate* was read the churches as a whole remained steadfast in the truth."[24] A similar appraisal from a completely different perspective is made for Isaac Errett. W.E. Garrison observed, "There was no more able or more conspicuous advocate of the more liberal side in opposition to the policies of the strict constructionists."[25]

The strict constructionist position was well represented among the Disciples at this time by the *American Christian Review*, edited by Benjamin Franklin. During the 60s, it was the leading journal in the movement. As the first weekly publication, it outstripped its rivals in circulation, and, at the end of the Civil War, Franklin was the most widely-read editor. He was committed to the conservative views of the Southern churches, but his vacillation on the missionary issues and internal disputes between John F. Rowe, his successor, and the publisher, inclined many subscribers to transfer their confidence to the *Gospel Advocate*, which spoke with an unequivocal voice on the major issues of the day. In 1886, the *American Christian Review* was

Restoration Editors

Benjamin Franklin (1812-1878), editor of the *American Christian Review*, voice of the conservative opposition to musical instruments and missionary agencies. This was the leading journal in the movement at the end of the Civil War.

Isaac Errett (1820-1888), first editor of the *Christian Standard* (1866-1888), gave leadership to the progressive wing of the movement after the Civil War. He was the first president of the Foreign Christian Missionary Society.

David Lipscomb (1831-1917), editor of the *Gospel Advocate*, co-founder of Nashville Bible School (now David Lipscomb University), and a leader among the Southern conservative churches following the Civil War.

James H. Garrison (1842-1931) combined several journals to form *The Christian Evangelist*, which he edited (1869-1912). His Christian Publishing Company became the Christian Board of Publication in 1911.

purchased by Daniel Sommer, and the next year merged with his *Octograph* to become the *Octographic Review*. Indianapolis was chosen as the place for publication, but the stormy events of the period had effectively killed its influence. The new publication maintained a wavering influence until its demise in 1915.

When polarization develops, it is not unusual for a mediating position to emerge. It is not surprising that the border state of Kentucky would be the center of such a mediating viewpoint, one that would accept the missionary society as the best means of doing missionary work while rejecting the musical instrument as without warrant in the New Testament. This group of leaders could not be comfortable with any of the existing papers, so they launched the *Apostolic Times* in Lexington, in 1869. Its five editors, Moses E. Lard (whose *Quarterly* had expired the previous year), J.W. McGarvey, Winthrop H. Hopson, Lanceford B. Wilkes, and Robert Graham, presented as imposing an array of editorial talent as could be mustered in that day. Both Isaac Errett and David Lipscomb lamented the appearance of the *Apostolic Times;* nonetheless, the position of "the *Times* represented a large bulk of the brotherhood."[26] But the times changed and polarization advanced to the point where its illogical middle ground was untenable. The *Apostolic Times* "faltered under the weight of its own inconsistencies and succeeded in antagonizing just about everyone."[27] It died in 1885.

In contrast to the declining influence of the *American Christian Review* and the *Apostolic Times* in the final quarter of the nineteenth century was the rapid growth of the *Christian-Evangelist*. In 1874, James Harvey Garrison moved the *Christian* to St. Louis, the geographical heart of the movement. In 1882, he merged this weekly with the *Evangelist,* publishing under the joint name and sharing editorial responsibility with Barton W. Johnson until 1894. Garrison followed the same policies as Isaac Errett, whom he greatly admired, and the Cincinnati and St. Louis journals reinforced each other in their advocacy of the progressive trends.[28] The survival and development of the three missionary societies and the national boards were due largely to the dedication of Errett, Garrison, and the journals they edited.

Growth of the Movement

At the same time that separation was becoming division, the Disciples were growing. Their plea for the unity of believers on a platform of the Bible alone had a genuine appeal to the settlers in the expanding West. They trekked to Oregon in large numbers, were well represented in Southern California, shared fully in the Kansas and Oklahoma booms, and were very strong already in Missouri.

This was a period of intense activity by state missionary societies, whose primary function was to establish churches wherever possible in their respective states. State evangelists held meetings in courthouses, schoolhouses, and occasionally in tents. They organized small groups of "Christians only" who thereafter committed themselves to enlarge the infant congregations and support the work of evangelism. The papers of the period are filled with exuberant reports of baptisms and new church enterprises. It was a time of unparalleled growth.

In 1870, Disciple membership was reported as 350,000; ten years later, it was 475,000; in 1890, it was 641,000, and at the century's end it stood at 1,120,000. This impressive increase could hardly be matched by any of the religious bodies of the time. Since it was strictly an American movement, none of its growth came from immigration. It is important to note that the growth was almost entirely in the rural areas of the nation, a factor that had considerable bearing on Disciple understanding of issues that were rising in a nation that was rapidly becoming industrialized and urban.

It is hazardous to attempt to characterize the general thought patterns of the Disciples during this or any period in history. However, certain observations and general impressions can be reached by examining the literature of the period. It is a safe conjecture that, despite harangues over "innovations" to the plea, there has probably never been a period before or since when the mind of the movement was so uniform with regard to the basic tenets of the movement, *viz.* that there is a basic New Testament pattern for the church and that it is possible to restore this church short of its man-made accretions and that this restoration is the only logical, viable, and realistic platform for the greatly-to-be-desired unity of the people of God.[29] The Bible "plan of salvation" symbolized by the five-finger exercise was powerfully and effectively proclaimed. The waves of higher criticism and a new theology had not yet broken on the shores of Disciple consciousness, so the presuppositions of the message were not questioned. These troublesome issues would shatter the peace of the twentieth century, but they did not belong to this period, except in embryonic form. The conservative churches had withdrawn to such a distance as no longer to affect those who were united around a progressive understanding of the Disciple message and mission. None, at the threshold of the new century, could foresee the violent controversies that would fracture the fellowship in another quarter-century.

However, even then some widely divergent views were apparent in this fellowship that held "no creed but Christ." At no time have Disciples sought, much less attained, theological or doctrinal uniformity. Because the more liberal thinkers of this period advanced personal opinions, they were tolerated by the people whose motto often included the phrase, "in opinions—liberty." When, in the next century, persons advancing views different from the majority opinions threatened to gain control of the societies and agencies created in the late nineteenth century, there was a serious struggle.

Dr. Lewis L. Pinkerton has been called "the first true 'liberal' among the reformers."[30] A medical doctor who chose instead the ministry of the church in Midway, Kentucky, he was an outspoken Union sympathizer during the Civil War. He was the first to introduce the organ into the service of worship. He became the first to advocate the practice of receiving the pious unimmersed into membership in the church. He also abandoned the doctrine of Biblical infallibility. With John Shackleford, he edited the *Independent Monthly,* which has been described as "the stormy petrol of those somewhat turbulent days . . . a sort of Ishmaelite magazine."[31] Pinkerton's "heresies" seemed to present no cause for serious alarm. It was quite otherwise with Dr. R.C. Cave, minister of Central Christian Church in St. Louis, Missouri, who created a sensation in both his congregation and the whole city when, in a sermon in December 1889, he denied the virgin birth and the bodily resurrection of Jesus, held that the Bible was evolution rather than revelation, rejected any plan of salvation, and denied that the Great Commission involves water baptism.[32] Cave was forced to resign his pulpit. A shocked J.H. Garrison led the opposition to Dr. Cave and ran a series of doctrinal articles that were published in 1891 in book form as *The Old Faith Restated.*[33] Seventeen respected men contributed articles that reaffirmed the orthodox faith of the Disciples. So long as the Cave heresy was only that of an individual, it could be dealt with handily. It was quite otherwise when this type of thought came to be associated with institutions. This was about to happen. The introduction of Modernist theology into the stream of Disciple thought actually began in the final decade of the nineteenth century but its impact is so much a part of the problems of the twentieth century that it will be treated in the next chapter.

In summary, the final third of the nineteenth century must be recognized as a critical time for the movement. It was a period of vigorous growth and expansion. It was also a period when the process of division occurred, separating permanently the majority of the congregations of the old Confederacy from the main body of churches in the North. It was a period of organiztion and internal development. The period opened with missions in a state of confusion. Benevolence and education existed only on very primitive levels. By the end of the century, missionary activity was vigorous and sustained, an impressive number of educational institutions had been launched, new agencies had been organized to care for benevolence, church extension, and ministerial relief. But new forces were abroad in the nation, forces that would wreak havoc in the new century. Evolution, Modernism, and related ideologies were beginning to impact on a movement whose largely rural and small-town isolation could no longer be maintained.

End Notes

[1]J.H. Garrison, op. cit., p. 223. There was no federal census listing at this time.

[2]The expression derives from Rudyard Kipling's poem of this title written in 1899. It was an aspect of manifest destiny and suggests that the West is under obligation to extend the blessings of its advanced civilization to the "silent, sullen peoples" of the colonial areas of the world.

[3]Receipts that had been $10,000 per year prior to the adoption of the Louisville Plan averaged less than $4,000 per year under its program.

[4]R.M. Bishop—President of the 1873 Convention in Indianapolis, Indiana—expressed the frustration felt by many when he declared,
> We had just as well make up our minds to the fact that we can not conciliate the men who have opposed our missionary organization. They opposed the old plan because it was not a cooperation of churches, and now they oppose the new because it is. In fact, they mean to oppose us no matter what plan we adopt, and I really believe that if we had no plan at all, they would oppose us because we had none (*Report of Proceedings of the Convention,* microfilm, p. 6).

[5]*Minutes of the A.C.M.S., 1879,* microfilm (Indianapolis: United Christian Missionary Society).

[6]Isaac Errett, "Help Those Women," *Christian Standard,* July 11, 1874, p. 220.

[7]W.T. Moore, *Christian Quarterly,* 1874, p. 576. See also p. 622. Earl West (op. cit., Vol. II, p. 112) confirms, noting:
> The decision to abandon the Louisville Plan in 1875 and establish the Foreign Christian Missionary Society was significant in that it was also a decision to abandon all attempts to please the element opposing societies in the brotherhood. Henceforth all efforts to promote the society were to be exerted among its friends, and no attempt would be made to even notice the opposition.

[8]For contrasting evaluations of this period, compare J.H. Garrison, op. cit., pp. 246-274 with Earl I. West, op. cit., Vol. II, pp. 128-240.

[9]Moore, *Comprhensive History,* op. cit., p. 618.

[10]For details, see Moore, *Comprhensive History,* op. cit., pp. 626-631. See also chapter 19 in this work.

[11]Moore, op. cit., p. 684.

[12]R.C. Sanderson would later establish similar type schools in Seattle, Washington; Manhattan, Kansas; Ft. Collins, Colorado; Minneapolis, Minnesota; and San Jose, California.

[13]See W.C. Morro, *Brother McGarvey* (St. Louis: Bethany Press, 1940).

[14]In the next century, the College of the Bible underwent a considerable transformation, became a graduate seminary, and was the first such Disciple institution to gain full graduate accreditation. It is known today as Lexington Theological Seminary.

[15]Earl I. West (op. cit., p. 387) comments: "For a quarter of a century, it did not occur to the opponents of the Missionary Society to measure their principle against the Colleges." Lipscomb justified a distinction, at least to his own satisfaction, on the grounds that preaching was a task committed by God to the whole church, but teaching was the work of every individual Christian (see West, p. 389). David Sommer attacked colleges as contrary to the divine purpose and expressed a viewpoint later widely held, that a church cannot use its monies to support a college. A periodical war raged between *The Gospel Advocate* and the *Octographic Review* at the turn of this century.

[16]West, op. cit., Vol. II, pp. 372, 373.

[17]David Lipscomb, "Teaching The Bible" *Gospel Advocate,* Vol. No. 32, p. 505. At its inception, the school opposed the granting of degrees, considering them empty titles and presenting an inscribed book at the end of four years study in the place of a degree. In 1901, with the departure of Harding, the college conformed to established practice and began to offer degrees. Lipscomb's earlier hostility to endowments also gave way to practical needs. In 19—, the name of this school was changed to David Lipscomb College.

[18]Ultimately, this college would be named Freed-Hardeman College (cf. West, op. cit., pp. 361-364).

[19]See William Martin Smith, *For the Support of the Ministry* (Indianapolis: Pension Fund of the Disciples of Christ, 1956).

20Earl I. West (op. cit., Vol. II, p. 240) cites this trend as one of the causes leading to division. He observes:
> That there were Christians in all denominations now began to be openly advocated. [Both of the Campbells and Stone can be quoted to this effect.] The term, Disciples of Christ, was now elevated to the dignity of a denominational appellation, and the Disciples of Christ denomination, with its "reverends" and "pastors," a royal sect among sects, was now a reality.

21Benjamin Franklin (*American Christian Review*, February 20, 1872, p. 60) wrote: "This worldly and carnal display will send grief home to many hearts of the old saints. Many thousands now living will grieve."

22Claude E. Spencer, *Periodicals of the Disciples of Christ and Related Religious Groups* (Canton: Disciples of Christ Historical Society, 1943). See also Major James Brooks, *The Role of Periodicals in the Development of the Disciples of Christ* (Nashville: Vanderbilt University, unpublished Ph.D. thesis, 1966).

23W.T. Moore, *Comprhensive History*, op. cit., p. 702.

24B.C. Goodpasture, *The Gospel Advocate Centennial Volume*, (Nashville: Gospel Advocate, 1956), p. 15.

25W.E. Garrison, *Religion Follows the Frontier: a History of the Disciples of Christ* (New York: Harper and Brothers, 1931), p. 242.

26West, *Comprhensive History*, op. cit., p. 80.

27The opinion is that of Tucker and McAllister, op. cit., p. 22. Years earlier, W.T. Moore (op. cit., p. 558), had observed, "The paper turned out to be *nearly all editor*. It was made up chiefly of editorials on controversial questions and was virtually killed by the weight of its own talent."

28When Isaac Errett died in 1888, J.H. Garrison was asked to deliver the funeral message. The ill will that emerged between the two papers and their respective publishing firms began a few years later and developed in the twentieth century.

29This is easily discerned in a volume of testimonies published in 1907 under the title *From Darkness to Light* (Cincinnati: Standard; subsequently reprinted by College Press, Joplin, Missouri).

30Garrison and DeGroot, op. cit., p. 390.

[31]W.T. Moore, op. cit., p. 577.

[32]See *St. Louis Republic,* December 8, 1889. See also *Christian Evangelist,* January 9, 1890, p. 23.

[33]J.H. Garrison, ed., *The Old Faith Restated* (St. Louis: Christian Publishing Company, 1891; subsequently reprinted by College Press, Joplin, Missouri).

Chapter Ten

New Issues in a New Century

The first two decades of the new century were a period of increasing unrest for the Christian Churches. The old conflicts were a distant echo as the Churches of Christ had developed their own separate fellowship centering in a very conservative orthodoxy and focusing in assemblies, journals, and colleges distinctly their own. Growth continued both at home and abroad as the centennial anniversary of the publication of the *Declaration and Address* approached. But new forces were at work in the religious world, and these would produce new issues among Disciples of Christ. Before two decades had passed, a new polarization appeared that, within another decade, would strain the cohesive forces of brotherhood to the point of rupture. Three items stand out as major factors in the process of polarization. While they are discussed as separate issues, it should be understood that they were not unrelated. Those in favor of one of the controversial items tended to favor all three, and those opposing one generally rejected all. The issues were the rise of a new theology (Modernism), the Federated Church controversy, and open membership. Each of these issues must be examined to ascertain precisely how they affected the Disciples. In the process, it will become apparent that the issues could have been avoided had it been possible for the Disciples to remain in isolation from the religious world at large.[1] But this was hardly possible since science, industry, and technology were transforming American society and were raising issues that had significant implication for the churches. The response of the churches to these issues varied widely, and therein lies the problem of the twentieth century.

Modernism

The term *Modernism* refers to a particular theological perspective that was widespread in the first half of the present century. It is often called "liberalism," but that term is much too broad and ambiguous to be meaningful.[2] The kind of liberalism that troubled American churches in this century is that which is known specifically as Modernism.

Modernism is defined by one of its chief advocates as "the use of the methods of modern science to find, state and use the permanent and central values of inherited orthodoxy."[3] This admirable-sounding definition becomes a real threat to inherited orthodoxy itself when "modern science" is understood to be evolution, which, in turn, becomes the primary factor in determining religious truth.

The origin of theological Modernism is complex. It combines historical criticism of the Bible with an evolutionary viewpoint. Canons of literary criticism that were applied to other ancient writings, when applied to the several books of the Bible, seemed to mandate a radical revision of traditional views of date and authorship. Philosophic idealism was also an important factor in the theological development of the time. This combination had great appeal to many intellectuals because it seemed to place religion on a scientific base, freeing it from unacceptable traditions and superstitions. The Modernist approach to Christianity found ready acceptance in the older eastern universities and seminaries in the United States. It now appears that Modernism may best be understood simply as an acculturation of the Christian faith to the prevailing scientific climate, an acculturation that seemed inevitable to many of those who lived within the climate but one that would be largely destroyed by the impact of World War II, which obliterated the naive optimism that characterized Modernistic thought.

Modernism created enormous tensions and conflicts in all of the leading denominations. Its traumatic effects were somewhat late in reaching the Disciples primarily because Disciples were a midwestern people with few congregations in the eastern states where Modernism first took root. When it burst upon the movement, the impact was particularly severe. The Disciples' plea, based on the "Bible only," unsustained by a systematic theological structure supported by an accepted creed, was especially vulnerable to any approach that appeared to attack the Bible. By the turn of the century, many young men preparing for ministry began finding their way to eastern universities, particularly Yale, for graduate studies. They returned with a different understanding of the Bible, of the mission of the Disciples, and of the meaning of the "ordinances," particularly baptism.

J.W. McGarvey was the first to call wide Brotherhood attention to the new theological trends. In January of 1893, he initiated a department in the *Christian Standard* entitled simply "Biblical Criticism." It appeared with great frequency for almost nineteen years, until McGarvey's failing health stilled his pen. The subjects treated occupied anywhere from a single column to a whole page. Normally, one

would consider such a topic as Biblical criticism to be highly technical
and generally uninteresting for the average reader, but McGarvey's
column was anything but that. He wrote on a popular level and
spiced his essays with humor, sarcasm, and ridicule. In the earlier
years, McGarvey's barrages were aimed chiefly at European critics,
although a few professors from eastern seminaries came in for comment. Names such as Wellhausen, Driver, Dillman, T.K. Cheyne,
Harper, and Briggs appear frequently. The documentary approach
to the Pentateuch and the authorship of Deuteronomy occupied
McGarvey's attention for many months. He ridiculed the critics seeking to reduce their theses to absurdities. A typical example from an
early volume is a review of a sermon preached by T.K. Cheyne in
London:

> The *Christian Commonwealth,* London, publishes a sermon by
> some of the leading English preachers every week. The sermon in a
> recent number is from the pen of Prof. T.K. Cheyne, who is the
> acknowledged leader of the most advanced wing of the English crit-
> ics. So radical is he in his critical theories that I was curious to see
> how he would handle the Word of God in preaching to the people; so
> I read the sermon with eagerness. I must furnish my readers with a
> few extracts from the sermon, so as to afford them the same gratifi-
> cation which it has given me. Remember, that the gratification
> which I mean is gratification of curiosity. I would be ashamed to
> spend the preaching hour on the Lord's day in hearing a sermon for
> curiosity, but to read one in a day of the week for that purpose may
> not be wrong. The text for this sermon is Matthew v.4, 5, the second
> and third of the beatitudes. It begins with these sentences:
>   It is a beautiful tradition preserved for us by Matthew, and in
> itself historically probable, that when the Lord Jesus first opened
> his mouth in public teaching he uttered the sweet words, "Blessed
> are the poor, for theirs is the kingdom of heaven." Suppose that the
> devout disciple Matthew, or some other who compiled the great ser-
> mon, had given the first place to a saying like this, "Except your
> righteousness shall exceed the righteousness of the scribes and
> Pharisees, ye shall in no wise enter unto the kingdom of heaven,"
> what a different effect would have been produced!
>   Notice how uncertain this preacher is about the source of his text.
> First, it is a "beautiful tradition" that Jesus used the words referred
> to at the beginning of his teaching. Second, this "beautiful tradition"
> is "preserved for us by Matthew." Third, it was preserved by
> Matthew, or "some other who compiled the great sermon." How
> strengthening to the faith of his auditors it must have been to hear
> this scholarly preacher thus throw uncertainty on the source of this
> "beautiful tradition." How much more precious to them must
> Matthew's gospel have appeared as they listened to such preaching![4]

The *Christian Standard* was the most widely-read journal of the Disciples at this time, and McGarvey's reputation as protector of the Bible and defender of the faith was unmatched in his day. Questions were frequently directed to him, and his answers were forthright and convincing. The following sets forth the nature of McGarvey's orthodoxy:

> The fact that the only confession of faith which can be rightly required of a candidate for baptism, is Peter's notable confession, has caused many careless thinkers to run wild. Sometimes it has been demanded, Suppose that a man says, "I believe that Jesus is the Christ, the Son of God, but I don't believe in immersion," how can you refuse to receive him? And if you do not receive him, are you not making belief in immersion a part of your creed? Again, a man comes and wishes to make the confession, but says, "I don't believe that Jesus arose from the dead." If you reject him, do you not make belief in the resurrection an article in your creed? Many similar questions have been raised. And now comes the same old question in another form suggested by recent destructive criticism: "Suppose that a man comes to you desirous of making the good confession and being baptized, but saying at the same time: 'I don't believe those old stories in Genesis, nor such tales as that about Jonah,' would you baptize him?"
>
> I answer, "I would not." I would say to him, "My friend, your faith in Christ is not sufficient to justify baptizing you into his name. If you really believe in him, you can not refuse to believe anything that he believed, and you can not deny any fact which he declared real. He has declared true the very stories in Genesis which you say you do not believe, and he has endorsed as a reality the story told of Jonah. You must learn the way of the Lord more perfectly before I can baptize you."[5]

Here McGarvey was reflecting the convictions of many within the Brotherhood while, at the same time, shaping the thinking of others.

It would be difficult to overestimate the effect of McGarvey's column on the Disciples of Christ in his day. It influenced not only preachers, but also elders, deacons, and Bible teachers both in colleges and in churches. It created a vigilant mind-set that provided a basis for strong, hostile reactions to the new theology that questioned the historicity of not only many traditional views about the Bible, but of much in the Bible itself.

Modernism Among Disciples

It was inevitable that the new theology would enter the Disciple ranks as it did the ranks of all other major religious bodies of the day. As early as 1894, McGarvey noted that one of his former students had adopted the new views:

> P.O. Powell, now of Missouri, but formerly of Oregon, is one of the few graduates of the College of the Bible who have gone to eastern theological schools to extend their education, and to become perverts to rationalistic criticism.[6]

J.H. Garrison called McGarvey's attention to the liberal views of H.B. Cake, minister of the Maysville, Kentucky, Christian Church and a recent graduate of the College of the Bible. Cake's views were set forth in a series of "Half Hour Talks" in which he discussed the allegories and legends of Genesis and the folklore of Exodus and advocated an expurgated edition of the Bible. President McGarvey reviewed Cake's opinions and concluded that Cake had

> deserted and repudiated the religious body with which the Maysville church has been identified hitherto, and he has neither the moral nor the civil right to occupy that pulpit another Lord's day.[7]

Except for isolated cases, the critics whom President McGarvey excoriated in the "Biblical Criticism" column were men of other religious bodies, often of other lands. But events of far-reaching significance were taking place among some of the Disciples pursuing graduate studies at Yale. The idea of a fellowship of Disciple scholars was born. Soon, some of these Disciples would be in Chicago leading in the establishment of the Disciples Divinity House at the University of Chicago. They proceeded to create the Campbell Institute.

At the beginning of the new century, Chicago was the hub of the nation's railroads and a busy center of trade. It was considered to be a strategic site for a great university that could profoundly influence the nation's development. These views were reinforced by the spectacular Columbian Exposition held to commemorate the four-hundredth anniversary of the discovery of America. John D. Rockefeller was enlisted to lend his support to a plan to convert a small Baptist college into a major university. Leadership in the effort, which was to create the University of Chicago, was entrusted to Professor William Rainey Harper of Yale. An important part of the university plan was the development of a divinity school, which was to consist of distinguished professors from various denominations. An invitation was extended to the denominations to establish cooperating institutions. Herbert Lockyer Willett, one of Harper's students at Yale, began to urge the Disciples of Christ to undertake such a graduate-level enterprise. Early in 1893, he wrote in *The Christian Evangelist,*

Is it not also time that we provided a school of such an advanced grade that it should both meet the demand of those who go to higher schools, other than our own, and should likewise encourage many others in our colleges to undertake further work at the completion of their present studies?

Such a school can be established with comparatively small outlay. Overtures are being made to us by leading institutions already fully equipped or prepared for all theological work. They would welcome the establishment of a seminary in connection with their present plan. Such a plan would give us, at small expense, a high grade school, which is fast becoming a necessity to us, and is already the possession of nearly every other religious body, and such as would be a credit to Disciples of Christ.[8]

The Disciple's Divinity House was established in 1894 (actually there was no building until 1928). Willett was soon joined by Edward Scribner Ames, who would become distinguished as professor of philosophy at the university, and Winfred E. Garrison, also subsequently distinguished as professor of church history. Associated with these men was Charles Clayton Morrison who, though not a member of the university faculty, did more than any of them to extend the influence of the type of modern thought that the university represented through his long years as publisher and editor of the *Christian Century*. A more talented quartet of Disciples was never gathered in one place and time. At the risk of overlooking some differences between them, it may be said that they epitomized the very peril against which McGarvey's "Biblical Criticism" column in the *Christian Standard* was warning the Brotherhood. The "Chicago School" proceeded to interpret Alexander Campbell as a liberal theologian of their kind. They pointed approvingly to Campbell's insistence on a literary and historical interpretation of the Bible. They found common ground in Campbell's rejection of religious tradition as a source of truth. They discovered that Campbell was a pioneer in pointing to a progression in revelation from a primitive to a more spiritual covenant. And particularly appealing was Campbell's positive view of the future, which seemed to be quite similar to the Modernist's faith in progress.[9]

Herbert L. Willett was the most controversial of all the Chicago Disciples. He was a popular exponent of modern theology both in the classroom and on the lecture circuit. He was featured at conventions and ministerial meetings, and his addresses were often given extensive press coverage. Some of his lectures were printed in a book entitled *Our Plea for Union and the Present Crisis*.[10] J.A. Lord, editor of the *Christian Standard*, commented, "The book is vitiated with false teaching from cover to cover."[11] Widely diverging theological views were becoming visible in the Brotherhood of the Disciples.

As the time drew near for the observance of the centennial anniversary of *The Declaration and Address,* a great convention was planned for Pittsburgh, Pennsylvania, in October, 1909. A joint committee representing all of the agencies prepared an attractive program, and special trains from many parts of the nation brought enthusiastic delegates by the thousands to what would be the largest gathering to date in the history of the movement. When the program was released, it included the name of Professor Herbert L. Willett as one of the speakers. A storm of protest ensued, including demands that the program committee rescind the invitation.[12] Willett's address avoided controversial issues, but, when Standard Publishing published the volume of *Convention Addresses* and proceedings, it expressly disclaimed responsibility for including Willett's speech.

In 1906, McGarvey learned that a textbook incorporating higher critical views[13] was being used at the Disciples College in St. Thomas, Ontario, and also at Hiram College near Cleveland, Ohio. His comment that "the book is thoroughly rotten"[14] provoked a reply by Principal W.O. MacDougall, which was published in the *Christian Standard* of March 17, 1906. The Canadian educator wrote,

> While we all honor and love Bro. McGarvey for the work that he has done in the days that are gone, it is becoming increasingly evident that he no longer represents the best thought of the brotherhood on the question of historical criticism of the Bible.[15]

He included in his reply the text of letters from G.A. Peckham, professor of Hebrew in Hiram College, James H. Garrison, the editor of *The Christian Evangelist,* and Burris A. Jenkins, the president of Kentucky University (Transylvania University), who was one of McGarvey's colleagues. These letters were written at MacDougall's request and generally endorsed the book in question as a valuable aid to the study of the Old Testament. Further, the letters stated that most of the leaders and educators of the Brotherhood had adopted the modern, historical method of Biblical approach, and that this method of Biblical study would not endanger the faith of anybody.

McGarvey required several issues of the *Christian Standard* to publish his reply. The letters of Peckham and Garrison had come as no surprise, but that of President Jenkins struck a bitter blow. McGarvey wrote,

> The third [letter] was from a young man with almost no experience as an educator, and who, though a brilliant speaker, is scarcely yet a leading minister. . . .
> The letter of President Jenkins is the only one of the three that surprised me; for this is the first avowal by him of such views that

has come to my knowledge; and while I regret both for his sake, and for that of Kentucky University [now Transylvania] that he holds these views, he has, of course, the right to express them, and I the right to defend my own against them. I sincerely regret, as I have said to him, that he has become one of my antagonists.[16]

A subsequent article attempted to call the roll of the institutions of Biblical instruction affiliated with the Disciples of Christ. McGarvey found that all were opposed to the "historical criticism" except Hiram, Disciples Divinity House, St. Thomas College, and the president of Kentucky University. The latter was alone in his stand, for his faculty opposed him, McGarvey asserted.

McGarvey, though reluctant to do so, felt compelled to focus attention on the views of President Jenkins because his answer was the most radical of the three. The Lexington, Kentucky, institution thus became a center of interest until President Jenkins resigned in 1907 and was succeeded by R.H. Crossfield in 1908.

A new source of anxiety to the conservative Disciples of that day came into being as the Campbell Institute. The Campbell Institute came to the attention of President McGarvey in 1906 when a copy of *The Scroll*, the Institute publication, came into his possession.

The Campbell Institute was organized as a fellowship of college- and university-trained men who purposed, according to its constitution, Article II,

(1) To encourage and keep alive a scholarly spirit and to enable its members to help each other to a riper scholarship through the free discussion of vital issues. (2) To promote quiet self culture. . . . (3) To encourage positive productive work with a view to making contributions of permanent value to the literature and thought of the Disciples of Christ.[17]

Such an organization as the Campbell Institute was first discussed in 1892 by four or five young men who were pursuing graduate studies at Yale University. In 1895, three of these men went to the Disciples Divinity House of the University of Chicago to continue their studies, and there they interested other men in their project. Prior to the 1896 annual convention of the Disciples of Christ in Springfield, Illinois, "some twenty university trained men were invited to meet there to hear and discuss appropriate papers and to consider plans for future work."[18] The Campbell Institute was then organized with fourteen[19] or twenty[20] charter members.

The Institute began publishing the *Quarterly Bulletin* in October of 1903, edited by Edward Scribner Ames. This was expanded to ten issues yearly in 1906, and the name was changed to *The Scroll*. The journal consistently represented the most advanced liberal thought among Disciples of Christ. When a copy of *The Scroll* came to the attention of President McGarvey, he was shocked, and he challenged the editor to publish the names of the members of the Campbell Institute. The Campbell Institute was ten years old and had a membership of seventy-five, but its existence was little known in the Brotherhood. For this reason, it was accused of being a secret society, a charge it repudiated. The charge evidently grew out of the semi-clandestine character of the Campbell Institute that characterized its early years and is expressed in the first issue of the *Quarterly Bulletin* under the caption of "A Suggestion":

> The Campbell Institute is not a secret society. Neither does it seek publicity. It seeks to do a work for its own members and for others of like spirit. In the nature of the case the number is limited who meet the requirements of membership and would care to participate in the organization. In order to avoid misunderstandings or the temptation to any controversy concerning the Institute, its principles, or the work of individual members it is considered best to treat these matters as confidences not to be discussed with outsiders. For the same reasons, the *Bulletin* is not for general circulation, and it will be possible to make it of more value and interest if this restriction is observed.[21]

The editor did not indicate what the matters were that should be held in confidence. If subsequent issues of the *Quarterly Bulletin* are any indication, they are (1) "the attitude of the Disciples toward the pious unimmersed,"[22] and (2) "Christian Union."[23] It was suggested that members in various cities should "meet occasionally to cultivate each other and 'the cause.'"[24] A further suggestion was this:

> Why not concentrate Institute pastors so far as possible in Illinois and Indiana and make concerted action in these, or other selected states, on behalf of modern methods and ideas? It is refreshing to see what has already been accomplished in Indiana and Chicago by a few men in recent years. By a little forethought much more could be done.[25]

In the light of language of this character, it is curious to note that Stephen J. Corey laments,

> The paper [the *Christian Standard*] has constantly claimed that the members [of the Campbell Institute] attempted to dominate our missionary organizations, our colleges, our international Convention, and all the cooperative work that we have. The often reiterated claim that the Campbell Institute has tried to divert our Brotherhood from its main genius apparently has been an obsession—with this periodical.[26]

In 1906, a copy of *The Scroll* came to President McGarvey's attention, and he obtained a list of Campbell Institute members. He could hardly believe what he saw when he read the list, for it included the names of many college professors, some from institutions that McGarvey listed earlier in the year as being opposed to the higher critical views.[27]

From this point on, the pages of the *Christian Standard* were filled with letters and articles expressing alarm and protest over what was happening in the Brotherhood. The names of President E.V. Zollars and Professor Charles Louis Loos appear frequently over articles that stood opposed to the new theology. J.H. Garrison, editor of *The Christian Evangelist,* was much more friendly to the new approach to Biblical studies, being himself an honorary member of the Institute, although he admitted he did not share all of its views.[28]

Ironically, the most intense controversy provoked by the Modernist theology occurred at McGarvey's institution, the College of the Bible in Lexington. Having left an indelible impression on his people, the aged warrior passed from the scene in 1911. R.H. Crossfield, who had succeeded the ousted Jenkins as president of Kentucky University in 1908, assumed the office of president of the College of the Bible on January 17, 1912. By this time, the older faculty members, who had made the school famous, were either retired or dead, so that the period from 1910 to 1915 saw almost a complete change of faculty. The new faculty consisted of younger men whose training had been received in eastern theological institutions that were sympathetic to the type of thought the older faculty had opposed. J.W. McGarvey, S.J. Jefferson, C.L. Loos, and I.B. Grubbs were succeeded by A.W. Fortune, W.C. Morro, W.C. Bower, G.W. Henry, and E.E. Snoddy. To anyone remotely familiar with the history of the Disciples, the wide differences in points of view between these two groups are apparent. A single exception to the liberal outlook of the younger faculty was Dean H.L. Calhoun, whom S.J. Corey regards as "extremely conservative."[29]

Hall Laurie Calhoun, (1863-1935), protege of J.W. McGarvey and dean of the College of the Bible in Lexington, Kentucky. In 1917, he became the center of a fierce conflict surrounding the introduction of Biblical criticism into the curriculum of the college. He subsequently identified with the Churches of Christ.

Suspicions were aroused about the views of Dr. A.W. Fortune as soon as he was appointed to the faculty. John T. Brown, an evangelist of Louisville, Kentucky, accused Professor Fortune of being utterly sympathetic with everything his predecessors of the college opposed. In a series of six articles entitled: "What Will the Newly Elected Teacher of Theology in the College of the Bible Teach?"[30] he noted Fortune's membership in the Campbell Institute and quoted him as endorsing open membership and the liberal view of the Scriptures. Brown then sponsored a letter-writing campaign demanding that the Board of Trustees of the College of the Bible reconsider the summons of Dr. Fortune.

The Board of Trustees investigated the charges (although in a manner wholly unsatisfactory to the accuser)[31] and cleared Professor Fortune. But the issue burst into flame again when the *Christian Standard* for March 31, 1917, carried a letter written by B.F. Battenfield, a senior in the College of the Bible, charging that President Crossfield and the four professors he had been instrumental in placing on the faculty held advanced critical views and stood opposed to Professors Calhoun and Deweese, who held to the old principles of the college. The letter was signed by nine other students (five of whom later withdrew their signatures) and included a list of statements to prove their point. The letter also charged that there was an effort to rid the college of Dean Calhoun, and it concluded with an observation and an appeal.

> This strongly indicates that plans have been formed to convert the College of the Bible into a destructive critical seminary. Are you willing that this should be done?
>
> A number of students are today presenting a petition to the Executive Committee of the Board of Trustees. Will you join us in demanding the removal of the divisive teachers?
>
> Mark Collis, Lexington, is Chairman of the Board. Write him. Respectfully, I am yours in Christ,
>
> BEN F. BATTENFIELD.[32]

The editor of the *Christian Standard*, George P. Rutledge, called for an investigation on the threefold grounds that (1) the College of the Bible was training the leadership of the brotherhood for the next quarter-century, (2) the College of the Bible was created to support the plea of the brotherhood, and (3) the College of the Bible and Transylvania were about to receive $350,000 from the "Men and Millions Movement," which should be withheld if the institution was not sympathetic to the position of the people who were being asked to contribute the funds. Rutledge concluded:

Therefore, an investigation should be made; and it should be speedy, thorough, and out in the open. If there is treachery in the College of the Bible, it should at once be located and lifted to the gaze of the entire brotherhood; if the men suspected are sinned against, they should be speedily vindicated.[33]

The Executive Committee of the Board of Trustees of the College of the Bible issued a call for a meeting of the board on May 1, 1917. Hearings were conducted throughout the week. At the close of the hearings, Dean Calhoun resigned in protest over the manner in which the hearings were conducted.

The Board of Trustees submitted a report on the investigation in which they declared:

> The Board has found no teaching in this college by any member of the faculty that is out of harmony with the fundamental conceptions and convictions of our brotherhood which relate to the inspiration of the Bible as the divine Word of God, divinely given, and of divine authority, or to the divinity of Jesus Christ, or to the plea of our people.[34]

The report was signed by Mark Collis, chairman of the board, and R.N. Simpson, secretary. A statement denying the charges was also made by each of the five professors involved.

A statement endorsing the five accused professors of the College of the Bible was drawn by the faculty of Transylvania College, also under the presidency of R.H. Crossfield, and was signed by every member of the faculty except Professor Ralph L. Records, a chemistry professor.

Disciples were perplexed over the events in Lexington. Many were convinced that changes were taking place that threatened cherished convictions. Others believed that inquiries, such as the Board of Trustees was asked to conduct, bordered on "heresy trials," something repugnant to Disciples ever since the experience of Thomas Campbell with the Presbyterian Synod in 1808. The board was at a loss to know how to conduct the proceedings because Disciples had had no experience in such matters. It surely comes as no surprise that the findings of the board did not please everyone. *The Christian Evangelist* was noncommittal except for supporting the board, while the *Christian Standard* printed hundreds of letters of protest and the *Christian Century* defended the accused faculty. Churches were sharply divided.

Hostilities generated by this controversy did not abate for half of a century, until the two parties drifted so far apart as no longer to have any bearing on each other's interests. The conflict is sometimes represented as primarily a difference over pedagogy.[35] However, although it is true that McGarvey and the older men employed a teaching method characteristic of their day and teaching patterns were shifting, it is obvious that more substantive issues—hermeneutical and theological differences—were at the bottom of this upheaval. The issue has close parallels in other institutions of this type. The theology of Modernism was creating a formidable reaction.[36] In time, the issue would polarize American Protestantism.

The Federated Church Controversy

Concurrent with the controversy over Modernism was a closely related issue: the Federated Church movement. For almost a century, the Disciples had been advocating Christian unity by replacing the denominations with "simple, New Testament Christianity." In the movement for federation, they were confronted with a different formula to achieve what some considered to be substantially the same goal. It called for a limited degree of cooperation among the denominations in those areas of activity about which there was no disagreement, and there were many such areas in the life of a nation that was becoming industrial and urban. Many earnest seekers for the unity of Christ's people believed that such a limited degree of working together would lead eventually to the kind of mutual understanding that would permit denominations to fade into insignificance, thereby realizing the ultimate aim of the movement. In 1902, J.H. Garrison was approached by E.B. Sanford, the original force behind what was soon to emerge as the Federal Council of Churches, to place the matter of federation before the annual convention scheduled to convene in Omaha, Nebraska. Garrison arranged for Sanford to appear before the convention, following a moving sermon by E.L. Powell, of Louisville, Kentucky, on Christian union. Sanford's statement included the following:

> The movement this federation seeks to aid and foster is, at its heart, a missionary movement, spiritual and evangelistic in its spirit and purpose. It desires to bring believers of every name who recognize their oneness in Christ into such cooperative relations that along lines of practical service and counsel they will most effectively advance the Kingdom of God. This movement contemplates a vital linking together of forces that hold to Christ as the head with forces that inscribe upon their banners these supreme convictions.
>
> First: That the gospel affords a remedy for all evil: furnishing as it does the redemptive power that can save both the individual and the society.
>
> Second: The Church, of which Christ is the Head, composed of those who, in loyalty of purpose, trust, love, and serve Him, is the

chief instrumentality by and through which the gospel is to be brought in saving power into the life of men and the world.

Holding these convictions, federation is the recognition, on the part of those who enter into it, of the essential unity that underlies denominational and all other differences.[37]

Following Sanford's speech, J.H. Garrison introduced a resolution expressing approval of the proposed federation,

as the best means of promoting that complete unity for which our Lord prayed, and we pledge our hearty cooperation with this, and every other movement that has for its object the unification of believers, to the end that the world may be converted and the kingdom of righteousness established on the earth.[38]

J.A. Lord, editor of the *Christian Standard*, was immediately on his feet to raise the question as to whether the motion was a recognition of denominationalism. W.E. Garrison replied that "it would be recognizing that denominations exist and that there are Christians in them, but not that they ought to exist."[39] After an excited discussion, the motion passed, though not without considerable opposition. From this point, the battle lines for the next few years were drawn. Reflecting on the matter, J.H. Garrison later wrote,

Perhaps for no other position I have ever taken have I received more abuse and misrepresentation than for my defense of federation, nor have I ever taken a position about the correctness of which I was, and am, more absolutely certain.[40]

Some of the Disciples were beginning to be troubled that the denominational world was not accepting its platform for union as rapidly as they would have liked, and this measure served as a welcome relief to an otherwise hopeless impasse. Others looked upon it as being in perfect harmony with the spirit of the movement and a necessary preliminary step toward a more complete union in future decades. They were eager to project the Disciples' New Testament Church emphasis into the new movement.[41] J.H. Garrison had expressed this contention eight years earlier in an editorial:

There is no good reason why we should wait until such full, organic unity is possible before we recognize each other as Christian bodies, holding the vital truths and the essential faith, in spite of more or less error in doctrine and practice, and cooperate as far as practicable, in missionary and benevolent work, and in all moral reforms. This degree of union is called federation. We have often expressed ourselves in favor of it.[42]

But the vocal minority at the Omaha Convention felt otherwise. They feared lest the proposed federation would lead to a repudiation of the historic plea of the Disciples. Their sentiment was expressed in the pages of the *Christian Standard* by its editor, J.A. Lord, who commented,

> The object of these federations as generally stated is "the promotion of acquaintance, fellowship, and effective cooperation among the several churches of all denominations *in order that their essential unity may be manifested,*" [italics Lord's]. . . .
>
> Here is the basis of federation, and hence no disciple of Christ, at once intelligent and loyal to the divine plea, can take part in it. To say that denominational churches, and churches simply Christian have "essential unity" is to say that the plea of the Campbells and Stone was much ado about nothing.[43]

The controversy boiled in the church papers for years with the basic positions of the respective journals unmodified by the dispute, although both journals lost heavily in subscriptions in the general reshuffling of sympathies behind one or the other editors. Plans for the federation went forward without interruption.

A large delegation was appointed at the 1902 Omaha Convention to consider the matter further. This group of more than thirty members finally convened with similar groups from other religious bodies in historic Carnegie Hall, New York, in November, 1905, to plan for the formation of the Federal Council of Churches. When the council was chartered and a constitution adopted, the Disciples' group faced the serious problem of how to get the Disciples into the movement inasmuch as there was no official body to speak for the Brotherhood as a whole.

Meanwhile, the federation program was having a difficult going on the local and state level. Typical of the furor it created was the situation in Oregon, where the "Principles of State Federation" provided in part as follows:

> II. That church extension in neglected communities be conducted, as far as practicable, according to the following considerations:
>
> 1. No community, in which any denomination has any legitimate claim, should be entered by any other denomination through its official agencies, without conference with the denomination or denominations having said claims.
>
> 2. A feeble church should be revived, if possible, rather than a new one organized, to become its rival.
>
> 3. The preference of a community should always be regarded by denominational committees, missionary agents and individual workers.

4. Those denominations having churches nearest at hand should, other things being equal, be recognized as in the most advantageous position to encourage and aid in a new enterprise in their vicinity.

5. In case one denomination begins work in a neglected community, it should be left to develop that work without other denominational interferences.[44]

An Oregon minister, J.M. Morris, objected strenuously. He stated that he was heartily in favor of local church cooperation, but complained that:

1. Principle 1 in the proposed basis for federation requires that we consult some denomination, perhaps a hostile one, before we obey orders [i.e., the Great Commission].

2. Principle 2 requires that we co-operate in reviving a feeble denominational church rather than to establish a Church of Christ.

3. Principle 3 requires that we must be the preference of a community, perhaps a non-Christian community, before we may enter.

4. Principle 4 demands that we consult the nearest denominational church before we go.

5. Principles 5 and 6 [Principle 6 defined when a church had "abandoned" a field] are modified forms of the first.[45]

J.A. Lord attacked the federation idea bitterly in the *Christian Standard,* and the columns of the paper in 1906 and 1907 were ablaze with contributed articles supporting his stand. Their position, reiterated frequently for years, can be summarized as follows: (1) Federation is a tacit denial of the Restoration plea, a working with denominational bodies rather than a protest against the whole concept of denominationalism. (2) It offers an organizational union that does not touch, but rather relegates to the realm of the unimportant, the vital matter of unity in faith. (3) No committee of Disciples has any right to "represent" anybody but themselves. Since the Disciples are strictly congregational in government, no group within the Brotherhood can bring the local congregation into the council (essentially the position which the Southern Baptists hold to this day). The opposition to the Federal Council was so forbidding that the issue was not placed on the floor of the 1906 Buffalo Convention.

A committee was appointed at an ad hoc meeting in Cincinnati in March, 1907, to recommend Disciple participation in the Federal Council of Churches to the upcoming national convention in October, at Norfolk, Virginia. F.D. Power, of Washington, D.C., was chairman. The issue was not placed on the convention floor but was considered at a special mass meeting held separately. Here the entrance of the Disciples into the Federal Council was approved. Thus, by a rather anomalous method, the Disciples of Christ became an organic part of the Federal Council of Churches from its beginning. But the churches were so opposed to the measure that it was years before the Disciples were able to raise their portion of the council's budget. Hence they were not awarded an influential or conspicuous place in the council during the early years, so the issue became a chronic, festering sore spot while other issues came into the limelight.

Inter-church cooperation did not begin with the federated church movement. Ministerial alliances and the Sunday-school movement had produced cooperation activities, but never on such a comprehensive scale. At this point in time, the most fruitful area for denominational cooperation, and probably the most needed, was the matter of Christian social action. And precisely on this matter, modern theology reinforced the concern for cooperative efforts in behalf of social reform. Emphasis on the historical context of the Biblical writings, especially in the case of the prophets, brought a new awareness of the social injustices in contemporary society. Thus, social justice came to be a matter of concern to most of those who ascribed to Modernist theology. The career of Walter Rauchenbush—the father of the Social Gospel—best illustrates this emphasis;[46] however, he was by no means a solitary example of the link between Modernism and advanced social views. As the Federal Council came to be identified more and more with Modernism and the Social Gospel, conservative and traditional Christians tended to abandon it. As they did, the influence of the more liberal elements increased accordingly. Support of the Federal Council of Churches thus became a matter of contention between the churches that were opposed to the liberal theology that often fortified such an awareness.

The first application of the federation principle on the foreign field came in 1908, when the Foreign Christian Missionary Society approved a merger of schools operated in Nanking, China, by the Disciples, Presbyterians, and Methodists. This federation move had been led by F.E. Meigs, the Disciple missionary. The Methodists did not join until 1910, but, when they did, the federated school was chartered as the Union Christian University of Nanking. It ultimately developed into an influential school, though dominated by the liberal, positivistic rationalism that was hardly representative of the Disciple mind in the land from which it received its support.

This federated enterprise was viewed with alarm by the conservatives at home. C.B. Titus, one of the Disciple missionaries in China, wrote an article for the *Christian Standard* titled, "What Are We Here For?" In this article, he complained that $20,000 worth of property and years of toil were to be vested in an enterprise in which the Disciples had only one-third control; furthermore, the product of such a union enterprise would not be representative of the Disciple traditions nor of the people in the States who were furnishing the support for the work.[47]

New Issues in a New Century

Titus's sharp opposition to the union work led to his recall on the ground that he was "out of harmony" with the Foreign Christian Missionary Society.[48] The fact that this discharge came at the same time as the Guy W. Sarvis (to be discussed subsequently) appointment had the effect of adding insult to injury and left the conservatives smarting.

Peter Ainslie, Minister of Christian Temple, Baltimore, Maryland, had for years been an ardent advocate of Christian union. He presided over the national convention of the Disciples of Christ at Topeka, Kansas, in 1910, and issued a call for a special mass meeting at this time because he felt that "'the unfinished task of the Reformation' ought to be more seriously and prayerfully undertaken."[49] At this meeting, a committee was appointed to recommend a form of organization. This committee proposed that the convention establish a Commission on Christian Union, and they offered a simple constitution that was approved by the convention. The constitution stated the purpose of the organization to be:

> First: To create and distribute literature bearing on Christian Union among the people of our own and other religious bodies, and to solicit and hold in trust funds for this purpose.
>
> Second: To arrange conferences in important centers on the subject of Christian union.
>
> Third: To prepare and send to all religious peoples an address reciting the great cardinal principles of our movement, and urging the vital importance of Christian Union if we are to conquer the world for Christ.[50]

The convention appointed a commission of nine members, with Peter Ainslie as president. A meeting was held in New York City in February, 1911, with similar commissions of the Congregational, Presbyterian, and Episcopal Churches. In July of 1911, the commission published the first issue of what was later called the *Christian Union Quarterly*. Ainslie edited this journal until his death in 1934. C.C. Morrison and, later, H. Paul Douglas became editors, and the name of the publication was changed to *Christendom*. This publication was the organ of the commission until 1925.

The convention in Portland, Oregon, in July, 1911, enlarged the commission to twenty-five members, which included several of a conservative mind, such as E.V. Zollars, Z.T. Sweeney, Frederick Kershner, and C.S. Medbury. In 1914, the commission was incorporated under the laws of Maryland, and the name was changed to The Association for the Promotion of Christian Unity. It was allotted time at all national conventions. In 1918, H.C. Armstrong, minister of the Harlem Avenue Christian Church, Baltimore, became the full-time executive secretary.

By action of the International Convention in Atlanta, Georgia, in 1914, this commission, as it was called at that date, was given authority to represent the Disciples in the Federal Council of Churches and to represent the Federal Council among the Disciples. This act of the convention caused S.S. Lappin, the editor of the *Christian Standard*, to resign from the Executive Committee of the Federal Council. He had been appointed a delegate to the Second Quadrennial Convocation of the Federal Council at the Louisville Convention in 1912, and he accepted the appointment on the condition that he represented only himself. The Federal Council's convention met in Chicago in December, 1912, and Lappin's conscientious scruples against the ecclesiastical menace to a congregationally-governed church involved in "official representatives" was respected by the Federal Council at the time that he was seated as a delegate. He was appointed a member of the council's Executive Committee by President Shailer Matthews. But he felt that his own Brotherhood did not respect this conscience by their action in designating the Commission on Christian Union as the official liaison group. It furthermore presented the rather anomalous picture of the Disciples' being officially represented by a group in which one of the Disciples of the Council's Executive Committee was, himself, not a member. Furthermore, Lappin was keenly aware of, and utterly out of sympathy with, the theological complexion of the leaders of the group in which the Atlanta Convention had vested the Disciples' official representation. The situation was not a happy one, and Lappin resigned in protest.[51]

The second application of the federation principle (the first having been Nanking University) in the missionary work of the Disciples of Christ began in 1914 when a series of conferences was initiated by the Foreign Christian Missionary Society that led to a comity agreement by which the Disciples withdrew from their work that had been conducted in Northern Mexico at Monterrey by the Christian Women's Board of Missions. Although this agreement was actually reached by the United Christian Missionary Society, and falls in the next period, it will be treated here since the agreement was concluded in the year between the time when the first Restoration Congress was called (1918) and the time when it could be held (1919), the delay owing to the influenza epidemic.

By the terms of the comity agreement entered into by the Christian Women's Board of Missions for the Disciples with a number of mission boards already at work in Mexico, the Disciples became party to a sort of three-way trade. For twenty years, the Christian Women's Board of Missions had conducted work in Monterrey, where they had a school and several churches. The Methodists were also working there. The Presbyterians had a weak work in Central Mexico, and a large area of Mexico was wholly untouched. The agreement called for the Disciples to surrender their Monterrey work to the Methodists and take over the Presbyterian work in Central Mexico, leaving the latter body free to pioneer in the untouched region. The whole thing was done with a view to covering this Roman Catholic nation more thoroughly with Protestant Christianity; and, to those who sub- scribed to the federation principle, it made good sense. Moreover, the Disciples felt they had made a very good "bargain" since they had traded a small, competitive field for a large one in which they were guaranteed freedom for unhampered development. But the project called for the abandonment of an established mission to a paedobap- tist group. The school was sold to the Methodists, and the churches were abandoned to native leadership with the privilege of continuing as autonomous Christian Churches. It was urged that, after twenty years, these churches (seven or eight) should be self-supporting if they were ever going to be.[52]

E.T. Westrup, a Mexican teacher, objected bitterly to the with- drawal by the Christian Women's Board of Missions. He maintained that the titles to the church buildings were held by the Christian Women's Board of Missions, and that the members of the churches were advised to affiliate with the Methodists. He further observed that the Mexican churches had been accustomed to turning their offerings over to the mission, which administered all funds; thus, the churches were in no position to know how to carry on alone.[53] Westrup, therefore, organized a group of nationals into the Mexican Society for Christian Missions, and appealed to the churches in the United States for help.

The *Christian Standard* took up the cause. In an editorial, "To the Rescue of the Mexican Mission," the editor said,

> They are not Methodists; they can never be Methodists; they declare, by their united action [forming the Mexican mission soci- ety], that they will never be Methodists—even though a million offi- cial "decisions" are registered at headquarters.

After commending some who had sent in offerings, the editor went on to say,

> They [the people of the American churches] will decide that the official "decision," against the inclination of the Mexican brethren, to turn the Monterrey work over to the Southern Methodists *shall not stand*. And they will decide that a least a part of the money set aside for the Lord's work shall go into the treasury of the Mexican Society for Christian Missions. . . .
>
> All contributions for this cause sent to us will be acknowledged through the STANDARD and sent promptly to the treasurer of the Mexican Society for Christian Missions.[54]

Thus the Mexican Society for Christian Missions took its place among the earliest independent agencies. As the abortive child of the Christian Women's Board of Mission's comity agreement, it naturally caused the C.W.B.M. a measure of embarrassment when they faced the Southern Methodists, who occupied the field. This led to bitterness between the Mexican Mission and the society at home, bitterness that was reflected on both sides for many years. However, in spite of all the reasons that can be listed in favor of this move, the Mexican Christians' opposition to a transfer of their religious faith arranged by officials in the U.S. is not at all difficult to understand.

Open Membership

The third major controversy of the period under consideration was the issue of open membership, or the practice of admitting unimmersed believers into membership in the churches. The Disciples' position on baptism was largely fixed in 1812 when Alexander Campbell faced the question whether he should baptize his child. As a result of serious study of the Scriptures, he concluded that it was he who needed to be immersed. Ultimately, this led him into fellowship with Baptists, involved him in debates on the subject of baptism, and caused him to write extensively on the subject over many years. Barton W. Stone and the Christians had adopted the same practice, thereby facilitating the merger of the two groups in 1832. At the time of Alexander Campbell's death, Disciples were unanimous in their practice of baptism by immersion of believers.

Not everybody was happy with the prevailing practice of baptism. Dr. L.L. Pinkerton of Midway, Kentucky, always the foe of anything that he believed could be interpreted as legalism, began to advocate open membership as early as 1869, and R.C. Cave, of the Central Christian Church in St. Louis, Missouri, urged his congregation to adopt the practice in 1889, resigning when they refused to do so.[55] In 1890, J.H. Garrison, editor of *The Christian Evangelist*, commented to Dr. Cave, "I know of no preacher in our ranks who holds your views as to baptism and church membership."[56]

W.T. Moore, who had been sent to England to minister to the West London Tabernacle by the Foreign Christian Missionary Society, was probably the first to receive the unimmersed as church members. The first church in America to adopt the practice was the Lenox Avenue Church of New York, of which J.M. Philputt was pastor. This group received the unimmersed into the "congregation," but not into the church.[57] The Cedar Avenue Church of Cleveland, Ohio, adopted the practice in 1895, and its pastor, Harris R. Cooley, was censured by the Ohio Minister's Association for introducing the custom.[58]

270 New Issues in a New Century

The man who, more than anyone else, is responsible for the unwearied promotion of open membership among Disciples of Christ is Edward S. Ames. He came to the ministry of the Hyde Park Church of Chicago, Illinois, which was sponsored by the American Christian Missionary Society, in 1900. In accord with Campbell's ideal of Christian union, but rejecting Campbell's platform for achieving the desired unity through the reestablishment of Biblical Christianity as it was then being advocated, Ames came to the conclusion that baptism was a hindrance to Christian union. He immediately began an agitation in the Hyde Park Church to admit the unimmersed as "associate members." He preached a series of sermons on the subject in 1903,[59] and in the fall of the same year the Hyde Park Church adopted the practice. At the same time (October, 1903) the Campbell Institute, of which Ames was the secretary, began to publish *The Quarterly Bulletin,* edited by Ames. The very first editorial was the following:

A Perennial Question

From the days of Thomas Campbell the plea for Christian union has fundamentally involved the attitude of the Disciples toward the pious unimmersed. Whenever a serious effort is made to state the problem of union or to take steps toward its solution this question inevitably arises. Last year it was the crux in the discussion of church federation. Just now it appears again in the sincere effort to really do something toward Christian union in local churches.

The following churches are receiving persons from other denominations into some sort of fraternal relationship: South Broadway, Denver, B.B. Tyler, pastor; Monroe Street, Chicago, E.A. Ott, pastor; Austin, Chicago, G.A. Campbell, pastor; Hyde Park, Chicago, E.S. Ames, pastor. The Cedar Avenue Church in Cleveland, E.P. Wise, pastor, has practiced it for several years. Other churches also reported as favoring it, while the pastors who approve it are not a few.

According to the plan suggested by the Pennsylvania Evangelical Alliance the letters of "fraternal associates" are received and held by the pastor or clerk, and if the parties remove, their original letters are returned to them with the pastor's endorsement to the effect that they have stood in this relationship. They are not granted regular letters and therefore no confusion concerning their standing could arise in the churches to which they remove. These associates do not vote nor hold offices such as those of elder or deacon. The plan has as yet had slight trial, but it gives promise of good things.

It is, of course, always difficult to know when, where, and how to test plans like this. Many men say, "it is probably intellectually and spiritually right," but the practice, or at least the avowed practice, is "a strategical error," "inexpedient at this time." Every man, church, and paper interested must decide such questions for themselves. But it cannot be forgotten that the question at issue after all is the question of the Christian character of Congregationalists, Methodists, Presbyterians and others. If they are Christians, then the Disciples should unite, federate, associate with them in every possible way. If they are not then the plea for union is absurd and every attempt to work with the aliens is wholly pernicious.[60]

Ames was assisted in his advocacy of open membership by C.C. Morrison. As publisher, and later editor, of the *Christian Century*, he took peculiar delight in goading the Disciples about "the immersion dogma." So flamboyant was his propaganda that, by 1912, W.R. Warren, editor of *The Christian Evangelist*, was complaining:

> With tiresome iteration, painful reiteration, and wearisome monotony, *The Christian Century* has been trying to impose upon our churches the practice of receiving into our congregations unimmersed Christians.[61]

Morrison led the Monroe Street Church of Christ (later to be called the Monroe Street Church of the Disciples and later still, following a merger with the California Avenue Congregational Church in 1919, the Monroe Street Federated Church) to adopt the "London Plan" of open membership advocated by W.T. Moore. This provided for the practice of immersion for those not previously affiliated with any church, but otherwise it permitted church membership on the same basis as admission to the Lord's Table. Thus, this church was the first in America to admit unimmersed into full membership, doing away with the device of dual membership (which the Hyde Park Church retained until 1919).

From this point, the practice grew among the churches until, at the present time, most churches among the Disciples admit the unimmersed. The majority of those churches practice a modified form of open membership, which recognizes sprinkling as valid baptism but calls for immersion as the only form of baptism that can be administered by the church. The inconsistency of this position has been repeatedly exposed in the course of the long controversy. A few churches have adopted full-blown open membership, which provides that the church will sprinkle or immerse, or the candidate may become a member by merely stating his desire to do so.[62]

So long as individual congregations elected to practice open membership, there was little that could be done about it. It was a different matter when the agencies and institutions became involved. This happened in 1911 when Guy W. Sarvis, associate minister of the Hyde Park Church of Chicago (where E.S. Ames was pastor), was appointed by the Foreign Christian Missionary Society to serve in China. Since Sarvis was to be the living link of the Hyde Park Church, there was concern over whether he would attempt to introduce the Hyde Park practice into the China Mission.[63] The executive committee of the F.C.M.S. was challenged to declare its position unequivocally on the subject of open membership.[64] But the suspicions of many were confirmed when, at a later date, Sarvis wrote the executive committee:

> There is probably not a missionary in China who has any conscientious scruples against extending the fullest fellowship to unimmersed Christians. If this is open membership, we believe in it.[65]

Charles Clayton Morrison became the most articulate advocate of open membership through the pages of the *Christian Century*. A struggling periodical, the *Christian Oracle,* published in Des Moines, Iowa, had moved to Chicago in 1888. The publishers were convinced that the twentieth century would be the time when the missionary movement would win the world to Christ, so they changed the name of the periodical in 1900 to the *Christian Century*. Morrison purchased it in 1908, and, in 1916, he changed the nature of the paper to an interdenominational journal of religion. It subsequently became by far the most influential voice of liberal Protestantism.

Morrison held very explicit views of baptism, which he expounded in a series of articles titled "The Meaning of Baptism" and later published in book form under the same title. Morrison maintained (1) that it is doubtful if Jesus ever commanded immersion (he rejected the "Great Commission" on critical grounds), (2) that "immersion" and "baptism" are two different things, the former a legalistic, physical act, and the latter a spiritual experience,[66] (3) and that immersion was originally an ablution, signalizing a transition for an old life to a new one, and that,

> the outward sign of immersion in water lent itself happily to the influence of the poetic and mystical mind of Paul, who gave it a distinctive Christian symbolism. It is not too much to say that Paul *Christianized* baptism.[67]

Thus, in Morrison's view, baptism was, prior to Paul, only a customary initiatory religious rite, but Paul fixed it as a symbol of the death, burial, and resurrection of Christ.

During the publication of his articles, Morrison was challenged by Z.T. Sweeney, prominent preacher of Columbus, Indiana, who represented the conservative views of most of the Disciples. In the course of the debate, Morrison deplored the "legalism" of the Disciples, which he believed Sweeney represented, observing,

Our answer is that a legalistic mode of thought has organized and established itself in the minds of this body of pleaders for Christian unity, the effect of which is to poison their plea at its root, and to blight its fine flower whenever it bursts forth into practice.[68]

The bitterness increased until Morrison closed the columns of the *Christian Century* to Sweeney. It was a matter of only a few weeks, however, before Morrison was embroiled in a another controversy over the same issue with J.H. Garrison, editor emeritus of *The Christian Evangelist*.

The Disciples Congress (promoted by the Campbell Institute; not to be confused with the later Restoration Congresses promoted by the *Christian Standard*) for 1912 was held in the Linwood Boulevard Christian Church of Kansas City, Missouri, April 16-18. These congresses were for the discussion of doctrine. C.C. Morrison was assigned a paper on the topic "The Essential Plea of the Disciples in the Light of Their Origin and Aim." In this paper he took the position that the *Declaration and Address* represented the genius of the Disciples, but that its intent was destroyed when Alexander and Thomas Campbell, and the Brush Run Church, adopted immersionist views. He declared,

> The fact is, and it can hardly be disputed by anyone who will face the full content of the *Declaration and Address*, that the Brush Run Church in adopting the policy of immersionist exclusiveness lapsed back that far into sectarianism.
>
> Their lapse consisted not in the practice of immersion, but in the adoption of a basis of membership narrower than the living Church of Christ, which necessarily barred the large majority of those to whom their plea was addressed, and whose working was dramatically illustrated in the actual excision of a considerable company of those who had hitherto walked with them.[69]

Such an assertion was a virtual repudiation of the very basis of the program for unity that had called the Disciples of Christ into existence, and it could not go unchallenged. J.H. Garrison was appointed to review the paper, and his criticism met the issue squarely. He commented:

> So far as I can recall, it [Morrison's paper] is, in its relation to our religious position, the most radical paper ever submitted to a Congress of the Disciples of Christ. It is a clear and distinct repudiation of a cardinal feature of the religious movement urged by the Disciples of Christ as that movement developed under the leadership of Thomas and Alexander Campbell, Walter Scott and others, and as it is understood and practiced by the great body of Disciples today.

The ground upon which the great body of our sane, sound-thinking ministers and workers have stood for a century is that our religious reformation does not claim that we are the only Christians and our Churches the only Churches entitled to wear the name of Christ, but that Christian union is impossible on these denominational bases, and that we are here to promote the cause of Christian union by a return, both in faith and practice, to the New Testament basis of unity, and to establish congregations illustrating, in their faith and practice, the efficiency and sufficiency of this basis. If that is not solid ground for any intelligent and self-respecting body of people to stand on, then a religious reformation is an impertinence, and our whole movement has been a colossal mistake.[70]

The *Kansas City Journal*, reporting on this congress, said,

> Discussion as to admitting the "pious unimmersed" into Christian fellowship occupied the major portion of this session of the Congress, the object of which is to discuss subjects most affecting church harmony. The issue shows there is discord among the Disciples on the subject of baptism. The outcome of the battle between the two factions will be watched with interest.[71]

The aforementioned controversies would have sufficed to imperil the unity of the Disciples had it not been for a fourth unfortunate issue, the Rockefeller gifts dispute. This controversy was not related to the theological issues.

Rockefeller Oil Money Controversy

John D. Rockefeller, Sr., of the Standard Oil Company, was a noted philanthropist whose gifts were widely distributed among many causes. Upon solicitation from F.M. Rains of the Foreign Christian Missionary Society, he had made a series of gifts to the society that totaled $25,000 by 1907. This money was looked upon as unacceptable by some of the Disciples because of questions concerning the business ethics of the Rockefeller organization. As early as 1905, the time of the first gift, J.A. Lord, editor of the *Christian Standard*, expressed the view that such benefactions were really bribes to purchase the sanction of Christian people for the objectionable methods that Rockefeller employed to obtain his wealth. Lord wrote:

> Now, the charge against Mr. Rockefeller—a charge established by indisputable proof, in many public trials—is that he has reduced his peculiar methods of plunder to a system . . . so secret, so far-reaching

and so relentless that he has placed the business of thousands and tens of thousands at his mercy, and that he continues this system of plunder to this day. These things are not even denied. Wherever his secret transactions are brought to light, they are of this character. How anyone can accept money so acquired as a gift without sanctioning this system of rapine and oppression, is a mystery to us. And it is evident that it is just this *sanction* that the gentleman seeks. He does not need the *assistance* of any missionary society in the distribution of funds. There is nothing in the way of his "returning" the money to the Lord without the intervention of any missionary society. He has the means of establishing the greatest missionary fund on earth. Let him do that and see what comes of it. But it will be observed in all his public "benefactions" he is careful to provide for the sanction of Christian people, the very thing which it is our contention should be withheld. [Italics in original.][72]

Undoubtedly, Russell Errett and J.A. Lord, respectively owner and editor of the *Christian Standard,* were acutely aware of the evils of the Rockefeller combine because of their close personal friendship with Thomas W. Phillips, owner of the Phillips Petroleum company, a competitor of the Standard Oil Company. Phillips's interests were threatened by Rockefeller's expansionist tactics. He reacted by running for and being elected a Congressman from Pennsylvania and subsequently led the fight to enact legislation to curb unethical corporate business practice.

When the Rockefeller gifts of 1906 and 1907 were received, the controversy became sharp. T.W. Phillips wrote a series of articles in the *Christian Standard* protesting against receiving this money; and he was supported by a series of editorials by J.A. Lord, who severely criticized the officials of the Foreign Christian Missionary Society. The controversy then degenerated into personal invectives. The *Christian Standard* of September 21, 1907,[73] carried a blistering attack by Archibald McLean, the president of the society, against Russell Errett and J.A. Lord. The attack was returned blow for blow by Errett.[74] When McLean made a reply, Errett refused to allow it to be published in the *Christian Standard.* McLean subsequently published it at his own expense in tract form. It bore the title, *Debarred from the Standard,* and copies of the tract were mailed to the Disciple ministers.

The 1907 International Christian Convention was held in Norfolk, Virginia, in October. The strife between McLean and Errett had torn the Disciples of Christ for many months, and the issue demanded some kind of settlement. After heated debate, the convention decided to accept no more Rockefeller money, but a motion to return the $25,000 already accepted was defeated. The action of the convention ended the Errett-McLean controversy.

This tragic, fratricidal war had incalculable consequences. McLean and Errett never were reconciled, and the name of Archibald McLean is seldom thereafter found in the pages of the *Christian Standard*. These two able men were of much the same mind, theologically, and had they pulled together at the time when the brotherhood faced a changing doctrinal emphasis, the outcome might have been very different. It should be observed that such affairs as this, involving bitter personal strife, serve to set subjective attitudes that, in a way that defies measurement, influence points of view on issues of a far more important nature.

The Centennial Convention

Although the first two decades of the present century were marked with increasing acrimony that would build to a mighty crescendo in 1919, they were also a time of growth. Total membership increased from 1,120,000 in 1900 to 1,450,000 in 1925. However, the most visible index of the vitality of the Disciple movement is found in the events leading up to, and changes taking place as a result of, the great Centennial Convention in 1909, marking the one-hundredth anniversary of the publication of the *Declaration and Address*. Advance planning for the event began with the appointment of a committee at the Minneapolis, Minnesota, Convention in 1901. J.H. Garrison was named chairman, and the members were Helen E. Moses, Benjamin L. Smith, Archibald McLean, and C.P. Kane. In 1905, a local committee from the Pittsburgh area was named, which included T.E. Cramblet, Wallace Tharp, R.S. Latimer, George T. Oliver, John G. Slayten, William H. Graham, W.R. Warren, O.H. Phillips, M.M. Cochran, and T.W. Phillips, Sr., with the latter serving as chairman of an executive committee. A Centennial Campaign was developed that included goals for all of the agencies, for congregations, and for individuals.[75] Both the *Christian Standard* and *The Christian Evangelist* promoted the goals and the convention itself. In spite of the problems being faced, the whole Brotherhood was being rallied as it never had before and never has since. The experience of all of the agencies working closely together in a unified effort through the Centennial Committee would recommend permanent unification to many Disciples and set in motion plans that would come to fruition ten years later in the United Christian Missionary Society.

The convention session, October 11-19, 1909, was a huge success. More than 25,000 persons crowded Pittsburgh. Railroads granted special rates for chartered trains, and these arrived in such numbers as to crowd the siding facilities. Every available hotel was booked (the World

Series there at the same time further strained housing accommodations), and local committees canvassed neighborhoods to ask people to rent unused bedrooms. No convention auditorium could hold the crowd, so simultaneous sessions were scheduled in the largest available auditoriums. On Sunday, two hundred fifty congregations welcomed Disciple preachers into their pulpits, and, in the afternoon, 20,000 people assembled in Forbes Field to share in the largest Communion service ever held on American soil.[76] The convention theme was "The union of all believers, on a basis of holy Scriptures, to the end that the world may be evangelized," a succinct but accurate statement of the plea of the movement.[77] The religious world took note that the Disciples were on the march. The reports of the agencies bore this out. The C.W.B.M. reported that it was maintaining fifty-nine schools in the homeland and abroad, and property had been secured to open several more. Most exciting was the anticipated opening of the College of Missions, located adjacent to Butler College in Indianapolis. This would provide a unique educational facility for the preparation of missionaries for the Disciples. Seven orphanages, four hospitals plus eleven medical dispensaries, and 256 missionaries were being sustained overseas. In addition, 244 served in the United States.[78] Archibald McLean reported for the Foreign Society that the work was flourishing in India, Japan, China, the Philippines, Cuba, and Africa. A special event at the convention was the launching of the steamer *Oregon* at a Pittsburgh shipyard. Following its dedication, the ship was dismantled and taken to the Belgian Congo, where it served the mission there for many years, plying the Congo River and its tributaries.[79] The A.C.M.S. reported that, in cooperation with the state boards, 584 missionaries (evangelists) were being supported. These had reported more than 15,000 baptisms and 13,000 additions to churches otherwise. They had organized 158 new congregations in the previous year and had assisted 1,179 churches otherwise.[80]

The Board of Ministerial Relief reported record but inadequate income.[81] The Board of Church Extension was filling loan requests as fast as funds would permit. The National Benevolent Association, less than a quarter century old, reported two hospitals, three homes for the aged, and seven homes for children, including one under construction in Denver as part of the Centennial program. In its twenty-three years it had assisted 21,634 persons.[82] The Board of Education report called attention to thirty-six educational institutions of all kinds enrolling 7,658 students.[83] A Temperance Board was functioning. Christian Endeavor Societies were being organized for youth in many churches, and there was much enthusiasm for Bible-school development.

Among the board reports to the convention, there is no mention of a publication board. All of the papers were published as private enterprises. Some believed that a brotherhood-owned press would be desirable. Efforts were initiated to that end in 1907, at Norfolk. J.H. Garrison, heavily in debt and approaching retirement, was willing to

sell the stock in the Christian Publishing Company of St. Louis, and
R.A. Long, a wealthy lumberman and committed Disciple, purchased
it and vested it in a Christian Board of Publication in 1910. A self-
perpetuating board managed the company and was mandated to distribute the profits to missionary, benevolent, or other service agencies
of the churches. This enabled the company to claim an official status,
which increased tensions with its rival in Cincinnati.

Men and Millions

The unified planning and concerted efforts of the various agencies
that was so effective in promoting the great Centennial Convention
created enthusiasm for cooperative action that next manifested itself
in the Men and Millions Movement. This originated as an effort to
raise funds for missions and grew to include a comprehensive stewardship effort in behalf of all of the agencies and boards. R.A. Long
offered a challenge gift of $1,000,000, provided that the rest of the
brotherhood contribute $5,300,000. Abram E. Cory was named
national chairman. A slogan, "We seek not yours but you," was
adopted, and the massive stewardship campaign was launched in
1913. In addition to a financial goal of $6,300,000, one thousand
young people were sought for enlistment in ministry at home or
abroad. Never before had a religious body engaged in such a comprehensive, well-organized effort, which included an every-member can-
vass in every congregation. Although the time schedule was
interrupted by the nation's participation in World War I, by the end
of the war, the goals had been over-subscribed. A single effort in
behalf of all of the agencies seemed preferable to the many special-
day offerings on which these agencies had been dependent. Once
again, the successful prosecution of the united effort seemed to point
to the wisdom of combining the agencies into one organization. In
1917, the Kansas City Convention created a joint committee of representatives of several boards to consider unification.

A New Type of Convention

From the beginning, the role of conventions has been an anomaly
among the Disciples. When a delegate-type convention was rejected
in 1849, the convention became in reality the annual business meeting of the missionary society. The Louisville Plan tried to change this
to a delegate plan, but the organization of the C.W.B.M. in 1894 and
the F.C.M.S. in 1875 upset this, and the annual gatherings were

once again business meetings, although they functioned as rallies and fellowship occasions as well. The addition of other agencies later in the nineteenth century made these assemblies what they came to be called—a General Missionary Convention—although several of the boards holding annual business meetings and reporting to their constituencies were engaged in activity not directly related to missions. The tempestuous Louisville Convention in 1912 attempted to revive a delegate plan, but it met with such little success that it had to be abandoned. Clearly, the Disciples did not want this type of a convention.

A committee was appointed in 1916 to revise the constitution adopted in Louisville in 1912. The new constitution, which was the work of a committee consisting of Z.T. Sweeney, F.D. Kershner, Charles S. Medbury, Judge Frederick Henry, and B.A. Abbott, was a compromise. It provided for a mass meeting convention and a smaller Committee on Recommendations to be composed of delegates from the state societies. All reports and recommendations were mandated to this committee before being introduced to the convention. The committee would recommend action to the mass body. After discussion, the convention could approve, disapprove, or remand the item to the committee. The convention did not have power to alter the recommendation on the floor.

The 1917 convention in Kansas City, Missouri, adopted the proposed constitution for the International Convention (United States and Canada) of Disciples of Christ without a dissenting vote.[84] This constitution remained in effect for half a century, until it was replaced by the Provisional Design adopted in 1968. The Kansas City Convention also set into motion procedures aimed at merging the missionary organizations. At the very first convention under the new constitution, the question of merging the existing agencies into a single organization was faced. The merger of these agencies into the United Christian Missionary Society opened a new era in the history of the Disciples of Christ.

End Notes

[1]The fact that such controversies are not found among the newly-separated Churches of Christ is often explained by their cultural-religious isolation from the mainstream of American religious life. See William Banowsky, *Mirror of a Movement* (Dallas: Christian Publishing, 1965), pp. 45-50.

[2]While all Modernists may be classified as Liberals, certainly all Liberals were not Modernists. See "The Christocentric Liberal Traditions," Smith, Handy, Loetscher, op. cit. Vol. II, p. 255.

[3]Shailer Matthews, *The Faith of Modernism* (New York: Macmillan, 1924), p. 23. The great popular exponent of Modernism was the nationally famous preacher of Riverside Church in New York City, Henry Emerson Fosdick. See *The Modern Use of the Bible* (New York: Macmillan, 1925).

[4]J.W. McGarvey, "Biblical Criticism," *Christian Standard,* January 20, 1894, p. 9. Essays of the first ten years were subsequently published in one volume: *Biblical Criticism* (Cincinnati: Standard, 1910).

[5]J.W. McGarvey, "Biblical Criticism," *Christian Standard,* February 8, 1902, p. 14.

[6]J.W. McGarvey, "Biblical Criticism," *Christian Standard,* November 10, 1894, p. 11.

[7]J.W. McGarvey, "Biblical Criticism," *Christian Standard,* April 20, 1895, p. 11.

[8]H.L. Willett, "Higher Ministerial Education," *The Christian Evangelist,* 1893, p. 55.

[9]E.S. Ames, "A New Epoch in the History of the Disciples," *The Christian Quarterly,* II:1 (January, 1898), p. 73.

[10]Herbert L. Willett, *Our Plea for Union and the Present Crisis* (Chicago: Century Publishing Company, 1901).

[11]J.A. Lord, Editorial, *Christian Standard,* March 1, 1902, p. 22.

[12]See the *Christian Standard,* issues for September, October, and November, 1908.

[13]The text was Charles F. Kent, *The History of the Hebrew People* (New York: Scribner, 1904).

[14]J.W. McGarvey, "Biblical Criticism," *Christian Standard,* February 10, 1906, p. 5.

[15]W.C. MacDougall, "Trouble in Canada," *Christian Standard,* March 17, 1906, p. 9.

[16]J.W. McGarvey, "Biblical Criticism," *Christian Standard,* March 31, 1906, p. 6.

[17]"Constitution," *The Quarterly Bulletin of the Campbell Institute,* October, 1903, p. 1.

[18]E.S. Ames, "The Campbell Institute," ibid., p. 3.

[19]Garrison and DeGroot, op. cit., p. 381.

[20]Ames, loc. cit. There is a question as to the number and identity of the charter membership of the Campbell Institute.

[21]E.S. Ames, "A Suggestion," ibid., p. 5.

[22]E.S. Ames, "A Perennial Question," *Quarterly Bulletin,* January, 1904, p. 1.

[23]E.S. Ames, "Christian Union," *Quarterly Bulletin,* April, 1904, p. 1.

[24]E.S. Ames, "Notes," *Quarterly Bulletin,* January, 1904, p. 2.

[25]*Quarterly Bulletin,* July, 1904, p. 10.

[26]Stephen J. Corey, *Fifty Years of Attack and Controversy* (St. Louis: Bethany Press, 1946), p. 19. (Corey's original manuscript was entitled *Fifty Years of Heresy Hunting,* and a copy may be found in The Disciples of Christ Historical Society. This manuscript was revised and published under the title cited above.)

[27]J.W. McGarvey, "Biblical Criticism," *Christian Standard,* November 24, 1906, p. 7.

[28]J.W. McGarvey, "Biblical Criticism," *Christian Standard,* January 20, 1907, p. 96.

[29]Corey, op. cit., p. 49.

New Issues in a New Century

J. T. Brown, "What Will the Newly Elected Teacher of Theology in the College of the Bible Teach?" *Christian Standard*, 1912, July 27, p. 6; August 3, pp. 5, 6; August 10, p. 12; August 17, p. 6; August 31, pp. 5, 6; September 14, p. 5.

J.B. Briney, "The Lexington Situation," *Christian Standard*, April 7, 1917, p. 9.

Ben F. Battenfield, Letter of March 12, 1917 (copy on file at Disciples of Christ Historical Society, Nashville, Tennessee). Reproduced in the *Christian Standard*, March 31, 1917, p. 4.

George P. Rutledge, Editorial, "Three Reasons for the Proposed Investigation," *Christian Standard*, April 7, 1917, p. 10.

"Report of the Board of Trustees," *The College of the Bible Quarterly Bulletin*, May, 1917, p. 3.

Corey, op. cit., p. 48.

Generally, this reaction would take the form of Fundamentalism. At this point, however, it would be incorrect to see the conservative reaction as Fundamentalist. The character of Fundamentalism was not yet defined and, subsequently, conservative Disciples would have serious difficulty identifying with Fundamentalism.

E.B. Sanford, quoted by J.H. Garrison in letter of May 3, 1909, to W.T. Moore. See Moore, *Comprehensive History*, op. cit., p. 704.

Ibid.

Garrison and DeGroot, op. cit., p. 407.

Moore, *Comprehensive History*, op. cit., p. 705.

Ibid., p. 710.

J.H. Garrison, "Compromise Christian Union," *The Christian Evangelist*, 1894, p. 386.

J.A. Lord, "Federation Once More," *Christian Standard*, December 6, 1902, p. 8. (The first paragraph quotes a letter Lord received from "the secretary of Church Federation." The second is Lord's comments on it.)

"Statement of the Principles of State Federation," quoted by J.M. Morris, "It is Denominational Federation: Open Letter to the Brethren of Oregon," *Christian Standard*, February 17, 1906, p. 3.

[45]Morris, loc. cit.

[46]There is extensive literature on this subject. See two important works by Rauchenbush: *Christianity and the Social Crisis* (New York: Macmillan, 1907) and *A Theology for the Social Gospel* (New York: Macmillan, 1917). See also C. Howard Hopkins, *The Rise of the Social Gospel in American Protestantism 1865-1915* (New Haven: Yale University Press, 1940).

[47]C.B. Titus, "What Are We Here For?" *Christian Standard,* June 11, 1910, pp. 6, 7.

[48]C.B. Titus, "Out of Harmony with F.C.M.S.," *Christian Standard,* January 20, 1912, pp. 4, 5.

[49]F.W. Burnham, *Second Annual Report of Commission on Christian Union* (copy on file at Disciples of Christ Historical Society, Nashville, Tennessee), p. 1.

[50]"Constitution of Commission on Christian Union," ibid., p. 2.

[51]S.S. Lappin, "Time to Withdraw," *Christian Standard,* October 31, 1914, p. 8.

[52]Corey, op. cit., p. 61.

[53]E.T. Westrup, "Facts About the Mexican Mission," *Christian Standard,* September 6, 1919, p. 5.

[54]George P. Rutledge, "To the Rescue of the Mexican Mission," *Christian Standard,* June 14, 1919, p. 9.

[55]Garrison and DeGroot, op. cit., pp. 386-388.

[56]J.H. Garrison, "An Open Reply to Bro. Cave," *Christian Evangelist,* 1890, p. 23.

[57]Garrison and DeGroot, op. cit., p. 393.

[58]Henry K. Shaw, *Buckeye Disciples* (St. Louis: Christian Board of Publication, 1952), pp. 288, 289.

[59]E.S. Ames, *Associate Church Membership,* pamphlet (Chicago: E.S. Ames, 1903). Copy on file at Disciples of Christ Historical Library, Nashville, Tennessee.

[60]E.S. Ames, "A Perennial Question," *The Quarterly Bulletin of the Campbell Institute,* January, 1904, pp. 1, 2.

[61]W.R. Warren, "Misrepresenting the Disciples," *The Christian Evangelist,* 1912, p. 437.

[62]The history of open membership in the churches of Christ has been ably traced to 1940 in a B.D. thesis by Carl S. Ledbetter (Indianapolis: Christian Theological Seminary, 1940).

[63]J.A. Lord, "Two Boards Speak" *Christian Standard,* April 29, 1911, pp. 9, 10.

[64]J.A. Lord, "The Statement of the Executive Committee," *Christian Standard,* June 10, 1911, p. 8.

[65]Quoted by John T. Brown, *The United Christian Missionary Society Self-Impeached* (Louisville: printed by author, n.d.), p. 4.

[66]C.C. Morrison, "The Meaning of Baptism," *Christian Century,* 1912, p. 1176.

[67]Ibid., p. 127.

[68]C.C. Morrison, "The Essential Plea of the Disciples," *Christian Century,* 1912, p. 79.

[69]Ibid., p. 393.

[70]J.H. Garrison, ibid., pp. 656, 657.

[71]News item in the *Kansas City Journal,* quoted in *Christian Standard,* May 18, 1912, p. 10.

[72]J.A. Lord, "Tainted Money," *Christian Standard,* September 30, 1905, p. 13.

[73]Archibald McLean, "Rockefeller Gift and the Standard's Insincerity," *Christian Standard,* September 21, 1907, pp. 1-10.

[74]R. Errett, "And Still, Why Did They Solicit Rockefeller?" *Christian Standard,* September 21, 1907, pp. 11-15.

[75]For an account of this campaign, which involved twenty-eight goals, see the *Centennial Convention Report* (Cincinnati: Standard, 1909), pp. 9, 10.

[76]This has since been exceeded by the World Council of Churches Communion in 1954 in Evanston, Illinois, and by public Papal masses on the occasion of the visit of Pope John Paul II, although the latter did not have nearly as many actual communicants.

[77]W.T. Moore's ponderous *Comprehensive History of the Disciples of Christ,* op. cit., was a centennial volume.

[78]*Centennial Convention Report,* (Cincinnati: Standard, 1909), p. 41.

[79]Ibid., p. 169.

[80]Ibid., p. 172.

[81]Ibid., p. 247.

[82]Ibid., p. 287.

[83]Ibid., p. 109.

[84]For a report of this action, and a copy of the constitution, see *The Christian Evangelist,* 1917, pp. 1214, 1230. M.C. Kurfees, Editor of the *Gospel Advocate,* in a very cordial letter to Z.T. Sweeney, criticized the constitution because it transferred "control in ecclesiastical affairs from the local church organization, where God has placed it, to a general organization, where it is placed by man" (Ibid.).

Chapter Eleven

Organized Opposition

The International Convention of the Disciples of Christ for 1918 was scheduled to meet October 9-13 in St. Louis, Missouri. The unresolved issues of the extent that Modernist theology had entered into the educational institutions, the meaning of participation in the work of the Federal Council of Churches, and the strategy of the missionary societies threatened the tranquility of future gatherings. The *Christian Standard* took the initiative to summon a pre-convention rally, called a "congress," for October 8. However, the national influenza epidemic of 1918 had reached such threatening proportions that the mayor of St. Louis forbade assemblies of more than six people. This postponed organized opposition for another year, inasmuch as both meetings were called off. The Campbell Institute, however, was able to meet, holding their meeting in a hotel dining room where "the members sat in groups of not more than six at a table."[1]

The issues smoldered until convention time of the following year. Again, a congress was called, this time being endorsed by hundreds of laymen and ministers whose names were printed in the *Christian Standard*. The objects of the congress were announced in the summons appearing in the July 26, 1919, edition of the paper under the caption, "To the Rescue of the Restoration Movement."

> *Objectives of the Proposed Congress:*
> Our deliberations will be addressed:
> 1. To a renewal, on the widest possible scale, of the New Testament evangelism, which is the crowning glory of the Restoration.
> 2. To the repudiation of the materialistic philosophy which discredits the Scriptures.
> 3. To the repudiation of the methods of compromise which would substitute a variety of human creeds for the simple creed of the New Testament.

4. To take such action as may be found necessary to reassert the New Testament plea with clearness and increased vigor, and to insure its perpetuation unimpaired.[2]

The nature of this proposed congress was described by the editor of the *Christian Standard* in the following graphic language: "It is a call to battle between the loyal advocates of the Restoration cause and the propagandists who are endeavoring to swing the Restoration movement away from its mission."[3]

The Odd Fellows Hall in Cincinnati was secured for the meeting, but its seating capacity of eight hundred proved inadequate for the initial gathering on Monday morning. The afternoon session was moved to Emery Auditorium, which was filled to its capacity of more than two thousand.

This significant meeting, on the eve of the convention that was to merge the agencies of the Brotherhood into the United Christian Missionary Society, set a pattern for future congresses. The issues were thrashed on the platform, and fourteen resolutions were drafted. These were presented to the convention and referred to the Resolutions Committee of the convention by Edgar D. Jones, the president. On Saturday afternoon, after the convention had acted to form the United Christian Missionary Society, the Convention "approved" the resolutions proposed by the congress.[4]

This is about all the action that could have been taken at the time. It was not long, however, before those submitting the resolutions felt that the approval was only formal. S.S. Lappin, who wrote a resumé of the congress for the *Christian Standard,* said,

> One wonders if boards of management who are responsible for the Sarvis fiasco, for endorsing as a substitute for union the "Community Church," for abandoning our property and people in Mexico, for exploiting rationalistic teachers on convention programs—if boards, or their agents, who have done these things will be able to recognize the day of visitation. The brethren will hear and watch with interest what the outcome will be.
>
> Many who came for the Congress were deeply disappointed that "nothing was done," meaning that no new missionary agency was launched and no plan put forward to go into and control the Convention now in session. For myself, I am glad the Congress confined itself to the four objects for which it was called. There is time yet, we hope, for stones if those who have trespassed upon the rights of their brethren and betrayed our common cause would be disposed to laugh at the turf with which we have sought to bring them down.[5]

The United Christian Missionary Society was launched at the Cincinnati Convention of 1919. Many voted for the merger in spite of misgivings, realizing that the very issues they opposed might be more firmly entrenched in the new, more-closely-knit organization. While many were uneasy over the creation of the United Christian Missionary Society and the character of its officialdom, the editor of the *Christian Century* rejoiced (although he lamented the convention's adoption of the fourteen points of the congress). He viewed the election of the new leaders as "the decisive answer to the campaign of detraction and opposition." Asserting that the time for timidity was past, Morrison felt that the new leadership had been "given a mandate to open a new era in the history of the brotherhood."[6]

Through the whole fracas, *The Christian Evangelist* maintained a judicious neutrality, lamenting extreme views in both directions, and condemning the bitterness that was manifest. But the *Christian Standard* and the *Christian Century* represented irreconcilable points of view. Eventually, some sort of fragmentation was inevitable.

Six agencies were merged into the United Christian Missionary Society. They were the American Christian Missionary Society, the Christian Women's Board of Missions, the Foreign Christian Missionary Society, the Board of Church Extensions, the Board of Ministerial Relief, and the National Benevolent Association.[7] The society was to be governed by a Board of Managers, half of whom were to be women because the Christian Women's Board of Missions was, by far, the largest of the component agencies. The U.C.M.S. headquarters was located in St. Louis until 1928, when it was transferred to the College of Missions building in Indianapolis, Indiana, the college having been merged with the Kennedy School of Missions in

Charles Clayton Morrison (1874-1966), publisher and editor of the *Christian Century,* the influential voice of liberal Protestantism in America.

Hartford, Connecticut.[8] Archibald McLean, whose life had been given to promoting the cause of missions, was too advanced in age to assume the heavy responsibilities of consolidating the agencies into a working unity. The task was given to Frederick W. Burnham, president of the American Christian Missionary Society. McLean and Anna R. Atwater, of the Christian Women's Board of Missions, served as vice presidents. A year earlier, the journals of the agencies were merged into a new publication known as *World Call,* edited by W.R. Warren.

The Cincinnati Congress of 1919, and those following, were ineffective so far as influencing the policies of the agencies was concerned. The need to hold such a congress can best be appraised as a symptom of a very serious condition within the ranks, a symptom that was generally treated with contempt by the officials of the new United Christian Missionary Society. Whether the course of subsequent years would have been altered had more consideration had been given to the problems causing the confusion is hard to say. But it is certain that neither the size of the congress nor the fact that some of the most distinguished ministers of the Disciples were numbered among the ones voicing dissatisfaction seemed to impress the leadership of the new United Christian Missionary Society very much. It is not surprising, therefore, that a similar congress was called for the following year at St. Louis, Missouri.

A significant event took place at the Cincinnati Congress that should not pass unnoticed here. E.T. Westrup, of Monterrey, Mexico, who had refused to abide by the comity agreement by which the Christian Women's Board of Missions had withdrawn from the territory, was introduced to the audience and was accorded an ovation. The Tabernacle Christian Church of Columbus, Indiana, which had withheld offerings from the mission societies, presented Westrup a large sum, and others followed suit. Commenting on this action, the editor of the *Christian Standard* wrote:

> Those of us who wish the Restoration message proclaimed in its purity, and without compromise, have waited long for reform from within. The reform, however, has gone glimmering. Recent events have put the lid on and clamped it down tight. Therefore, there seems to be only one course left—that of turning to the agencies that ring true.[9]

This was the policy of the *Christian Standard,* and also of many churches, from this time forward.

The second congress was called for St. Louis, Missouri, October 15-18, 1920. During the year, the *Christian Standard* conducted a preferential straw vote for the United Christian Missionary Society presidency. There were 10,684 votes cast. While any straw vote of this nature is capable of several different interpretations, the editor of the *Christian Standard* understood its result as follows:

> The ballot shows simply that in a cross-section of one hundred thousand disciples of Christ chosen without knowledge of sympathies, out of the ten per cent., or 10,684 interested sufficiently to vote according to the printed instructions, 9,399 preferred a change in administration, and the bringing in of new blood in the form of a man of unquestioned loyalty to New Testament principles, while 865 endorsed the men now in official position.[10]

E.L. Powell, minister of the First Christian Church of Louisville, Kentucky, strongly in favor of the society and usually opposed to much that the *Christian Standard* stood for, was aware of the weakness of the new organizational structure and proposed that the second congress fight for a more democratic method of control of the agencies.[11] The issues for the St. Louis Congress were sharply defined in debates carried in the *Christian Standard* between E.L. Powell and Russell Errett (owner of Standard Publishing Company), and between Mark Collis and Archibald McLean.

The China Mission Controversy

During the months since the first congress, Robert E. Elmore had brought to light startling disclosures of open membership in China. Ten points of protest were enumerated by Elmore in the *Christian Standard* prior to the St. Louis Congress. They included a protest against the following: The United Christian Missionary Society's act of enrolling the Disciples in the Interchurch World Movement, assistance given to disloyal colleges, practice of open membership in the foreign field, comity agreements, duplicity of society officials, and the organizational structure of this society that rendered the officials immune from democratic responsibility.[12] But the big item at the congress was the China controversy. This issue was touched off by the disclosure by R.E. Elmore, who had served as secretary of the Executive Committee of the Foreign Christian Missionary Society prior to its merger into the U.C.M.S., of correspondence with Frank Garrett, secretary of the China Mission. In this exchange, Garrett had asked the advice of the Executive Committee relative to the proposed Union Church of Christ. Garrett's lengthy letter contains the following item:

> As we see it, the only point of difficulty is the question of open membership. We are writing this letter to you to put the situation before you, and to tell you that in our Convention we quite thoroughly discussed this question, and there was no one who opposed the introduction of this practice. Our committee was asked by a unanimous vote to present to your committee this question for your consideration, with the understanding that the step has the approval of the China mission.[13]

Elmore drafted an unequivocal answer to Garrett's letter, but a substitute resolution by L.N.D. Wells was adopted in its stead. Elmore then moved for "the recall of Mr. Garrett, and thereafter all missionaries who favor this unscriptural practice," but the motion was not seconded. Elmore then felt duty-bound to disclose the situation, saying, "In bringing to the brotherhood evidences of broken faith on the mission field, I am performing a sorrowful duty."[14]

The congress assembled with two thousand persons present. P.H. Welshimer, minister of the largest of the Disciple churches, the First Christian Church of Canton, Ohio, presided. Archibald McLean, the former president of the Foreign Christian Missionary Society, appeared on the platform to defend the China Mission against the charges of open membership proffered by R.E. Elmore and by the *Christian Century*, the former with alarm, the latter with joy. The sessions of both congress and convention were marked by some of the bitterest controversy and invective in all of Disciple history. Z.T. Sweeney had attempted to get the Board of Managers of the United Christian Missionary Society to adopt the policy of the old Foreign Christian Missionary Society, which stated that "certainly they would not appoint, and, indeed, would recall, any one known to be not in such accord"[15] with the practice of receiving only immersed, penitent believers in Christ into church membership. But his resolution was tabled by a thirty-six to sixteen vote. At the convention that immediately followed the congress, Mark Collis introduced a resolution for the recall of Frank Garrett, the missionary who disclosed the practice of open membership in the China Mission. A special committee, which was chaired by Charles Medbury, minister of the University Church of Des Moines, Iowa, and a member of the Executive Committee, considered the resolution, disapproved it, and recommended in its place what has since been called the "Medbury Peace Resolution." This provided that the Executive Committee does not approve the practice of open membership and that this statement of the Foreign Christian Missionary Society be distributed to all missionaries in question,

Robert E. Elmore (1878-1968), the corresponding secretary of the Executive Committee of the Foreign Christian Missionary Society, he disclosed open membership practices in China and precipitated a furious controversy. He later became editor of *The Touchstone* (1925-1927) and of *The Restoration Herald* (1938-1960).

> to the end that their open avowal of loyal support of such an expression of the thought and life of the brotherhood may restore, in the

hearts of all, complete confidence in them, or, if in the liberty of conscience such avowal is impossible, may indicate the wisdom of a
prompt cessation of service as representatives of the Disciples of
Christ.[16]

This resolution contained no provision for any recall, and, as such,
it was ineffective beyond the inclinations of any missionary to resign.
S.J. Corey, at that time secretary of the United Christian Missionary
Society, comments, "This resolution was sent to all the fields of work
and there was no dissent from it."[17] But Z.T. Sweeney erred badly
when he expressed the hopes of the congress constituency in a letter
to George P. Rutledge, remarking, "As you will remember, the board
is under obligation to make a full and impartial investigation, and
discharge those who are in favor of open membership."[18] What Z.T.
Sweeney had in mind was never done.

A regrettable incident occurred at the St. Louis convention, which
was indicative of the mentality of some of the advocates of the new
United Society. The chairman of the committee on buildings, with
police protection, carried the literature of four agencies not affiliated
with the United Christian Missionary Society out into the alley. The
agencies were the Christian Women's Benevolent Association (whose
nurses from Christian Hospital were on duty at the convention), the
Yotsuya Mission in Japan, the Mexico Christian Mission, and the
International Christian Missionary Association. This led to questions such as those raised by S.S. Lappin:

Is the United Society a monopoly and the field shut up to its constituent agencies? Is the International Convention an ecclesiasticism, with power to expel all not so included, and silence all others
who would get the ear of our people?[19]

The congress adjourned in time for the convention. Among its resolutions was one calling for an annual congress to emphasize evangelism and New Testament Christianity; and that such congresses be
held in the various states where practical. After the convention had
been in session for several days, the congress reconvened. The consensus of opinion was that the congress had accomplished what it
had set out to do and would therefore adjourn. The convention
passed a resolution that no more congresses be held in connection
with the convention; instead, the convention agreed to devote time
on its program for discussion of doctrinal matters. Both assemblies
adjourned in a cordial spirit, the dissatisfied element confident that
the society would rectify its policy in accord with the Medbury Peace
Resolution. The day of strife seemed to be giving way to a day of harmony, and the *Christian Standard,* which had opposed the United
Society's participation in the Interchurch World Movement, issued a

plea for the churches to pay the society's $600,000 "debt of honor" after the collapse of that movement.[20]

State congresses were held throughout the year, the first being held at Broadway Christian Church, Lexington, Kentucky. Others followed in Terre Haute, Indiana; Minneapolis, Minnesota; and Columbus, Indiana. The purpose of these congresses was largely to stress doctrine and evangelism.

The 1921 convention was held at Winona Lake, Indiana. No congress was held, in accordance with the resolution to that effect passed at St. Louis. Instead, a day was given to the discussion of doctrinal matters, as per the same resolution. But this convention was not devoid of conflict. Frank Garrett of the China Mission was present and was questioned. E.S. Ames loudly extolled open membership from the platform, a gesture that contributed nothing to the harmony of the gathering. Those who were uneasy over the China Mission were disappointed at the failure of the United Christian Missionary Society to do more than to make a gesture of compliance with the Medbury Peace Resolution.

The Louisville Congress

Lacking any plan for a congress, nothing was done toward calling a protest assembly. However, the disappointment was so keen that a regional congress was called for midwinter, to be held in Louisville, Kentucky, at the Broadway Church of Christ (now the Douglas Boulevard Christian Church). This assembly was preceded by a series of seven articles by R.C. Foster in the *Christian Standard,* stating the issues to be faced in Louisville. These articles, under the general heading of "Programs and Protests," presented an analysis of the "issues facing the Brotherhood."[21]

The Louisville Congress, though only a regional one, is of utmost importance for the fact that it was the first to conclude that its constituency could not hope for a change in the existing order, and that it would have to explore new areas of outlet for it energies. Just prior to the convocation of the congress, the First Christian Church of Canton, Ohio, the largest church of the Disciples of Christ, passed a resolution to withdraw all financial support from the U.C.M.S. until such time as the Executive Committee would go on record as opposing the reception of the unimmersed and indicate their sincerity in this by recalling all missionaries who practiced open membership. The statement went on to declare that the church differed with the society in matters of *policy,* not *plan,* did not favor the organization of another society, and looked forward to the day when full support could be resumed. Regret was expressed that the church could not designate offerings so that it could continue sending aid to the many worthy missionaries in the society's employ, but that henceforth the church would assume responsibility for the direction of its own missionary funds, anxiously awaiting the day when it could resume support of the United Society.[22] This action, coming when it did, had a profound effect on the Louisville Congress.

The Louisville Congress assembled about seven hundred persons from nearby states. It is significant because it reviewed the situation among the Disciples and then turned its interest in the direction of mission and benevolent work outside the regular, organized channels. Accomplishments of the congress were summarized by the editor of the *Christian Standard* as,

1. Organization of New Testament Tract Society. . . .

2. Resolution passed urging all churches to discontinue fellowship with the United Christian Missionary Society and the General Convention until present abuses are rectified. This resolution was arrived at with reluctance, but with surprising unanimity and determination.

3. The launching of an organization to provide for a chain of state and regional conferences all over the country.

4. Recommendation that all free agencies issue annual printed reports, properly audited, and that their properties be placed under such trusteeship as will guarantee their being kept safe.

5. Provision for a committee to investigate and report on all free colleges and agencies willing to be investigated.

6. Attainment of the best clearing of the atmosphere and the

P.H. Welshimer (1873-1957), minister of the First Christian Church in Canton, Ohio, then the largest church in the Brotherhood. A re-spected leader in opposition to open membership, he was the first president of the North American Christian Convention.

most satisfactory mutual understanding those standing for preservation of the Restoration movement against rationalism have yet enjoyed.

7. Demonstration that those who are opposed to the present rationalistic propaganda are able to handle a delicate situation without bitter invectives and personalities.[23]

A resolution was also passed urging another national congress to convene immediately preceding the next International Convention.

F.W. Burnham, the president of the United Christian Missionary Society, and several other officers were present and were allowed to speak. They denied knowledge of open membership in the society's work. Z.T. Sweeney, a member of the society's board, rose to tell how he and Archibald McLean had attempted to get a resolution denouncing open membership through the Board of Managers of the United Society, but had failed. Sweeney declared that he was not ready to quit the society, but that he chose to pursue his efforts further within the Board of Managers.

An important address at the Louisville Congress was that of Ralph L. Records, former professor of chemistry at Transylvania College, Bethany College, and, at that time, of Franklin College. He discussed ministerial training. After surveying the unsatisfactory situation of the day, he described a Bible college governed by a board of trustees that was not a closed corporation, led by a faculty "loyal" to the Scriptures and the Restoration plea, with a curriculum geared not to the requirements of "standardization" but to the training of the ministry. He pointed out that "such an institution could be put in operation with little expense and maintained without the raising of a great sum to endow and equip it."[24] The suggestions of this paper were soon to take form in the McGarvey Bible College, established in Louisville in 1923 with Ralph L. Records as president. R.C. Foster and H.F. Lutz, both congress speakers, were also on the faculty. The following year would see McGarvey Bible College merge with the Cincinnati Bible Institute to form The Cincinnati Bible Seminary.

This congress demonstrated the great weakness in the course that was to be pursued by the proponents of its cause. Some who assembled in Louisville were for breaking away from the organized work immediately, and a resolution was passed to that effect. The nucleus of what would emerge as an independent program is clearly discernable in the Louisville gathering. But others were present who sought to reform the existing organizations. While there was notable strength in the dissatisfied group, the lack of clear objectives for united action by the group as a whole proved to be a major handicap for this group.

John T. Brown, a conservative member of the United Christian Missionary Society Board of Managers, appeared on the floor of the congress to declare that he was going to make a worldwide tour of inspection to ascertain the truth of the charges against the various missionaries. He was sent, as a member of the Executive Committee, largely at the expense of E.M. Bowman, of New York City. Stephen J. Corey, the secretary of the society, later indicated that the Board of Managers was not too pleased with the proposed trip of Brown. He comments, "There was considerable feeling in the group that it might be unwise for him to go since he was connected with the *Christian Standard* in his attitudes and sympathies."[25] Brown appealed to the congress constituency to wait another year before abandoning the society.

The Sweeney Resolution

Z.T. Sweeney went from the congress to a Board of Managers' meeting in St. Louis in January of 1922. He was a member of the Committee on Foreign Work, and, although he failed to get this committee to go on record in its policy resolution as opposed to the practice of open membership in the foreign field, he succeeded in getting the board to adopt a substitute resolution that contained the following statement:

> In harmony with the teaching of the New Testament as understood by the Board of Managers, the United Christian Missionary Society is conducting its work everywhere on the principle of receiving into the membership of the churches at home and abroad, by any of its missionaries, only those who are immersed, penitent believers in Christ.
>
> Furthermore it is believed by this Board of Managers that all of the missionaries appointed and supported by this Board, are in sincere accord with this policy, and certainly it will not appoint and indeed it will not continue in its service any one known by it to be not in such accord. It disclaims any right, and disowns any desire to do otherwise.[26]

C.M. Chilton resigned at the adoption of this resolution, but his resignation was not accepted. In the following issue of *World Call*, F.W. Burnham, president of the United Christian Missionary Society, stated that the Executive Committee had investigated the China affair and found no evidence of open membership there, and that it hoped the Sweeney Resolution would "quiet the fears of any friends of the Society who may have been unduly agitated regarding it."[27]

The editor of the *Christian Standard* was outraged, regarding Burnham's statement as a repudiation of the Sweeney Resolution. He polled the Board of Managers, which generally did not extend him their sympathies.

Meanwhile, "Restoration Congresses" were being held throughout the country, encouraged by the *Christian Standard*. Ira Boswell and R.C. Foster traveled in behalf of these gatherings, and a large number of churches took action to withhold financial aid from the United Christian Missionary Society.

The *Christian Standard* carried a debate on missionary methods during the year. Edwin Errett championed the cause of independency, citing Paul's method as exemplary, and Stephen J. Corey, vice president of the United Christian Missionary Society, championed the society's method.

At this point in the Brotherhood development, it is good to note what schools were sympathetic to the protest movement. The Bible colleges in Minneapolis, Minnesota, and Eugene, Oregon (which were affiliated with the International Christian Missionary Association), and Johnson Bible College, Kimberlin Heights, Tennessee, had declared themselves openly to be in the independent stream of thought. The liberal arts colleges usually were noncommittal, although most of them were affiliated with the Board of Education. Milligan College in East Tennessee was an exception.

Zachary T. Sweeney (1849-1926), minister of the church in Columbus, Indiana, leader of the conservative opposition within the mission organization, and author of the "Sweeney Resolution."

The International Convention met at Winona Lake again in 1922. Many of the dissatisfied group did not attend this convention. The *Christian Standard* boycotted it,[28] and promoted instead the third National Restoration Congress, held six weeks later in St. Louis.

Meanwhile, John T. Brown had returned from his world tour of Disciples' mission stations. He filed his report with the Board of Managers of the United Society and was given a place on the convention program. He praised the missionaries for their devotion to their tasks, but he reported his dissatisfaction with what he found in China and in the Philippines with regard to E.K. Higdon. The latter acknowledged practicing open membership in the Taft Avenue Church in Manila, where he had three deacons who were unimmersed.

Higdon had written the Society's Board of Managers for an interpretation of the Sweeney Resolution, particularly the statement regarding "being in sincere accord" with the policy of opposition to open membership. The Foreign Department of the society wrote Higdon as follows:

> We interpret the statement with regard to "being in sincere accord" with the policy pronounced to mean that the missionary should be

willing to earnestly carry on the work in the manner suggested. We feel that this was not meant in any sense to infringe upon private opinion or individual liberty of conviction so long as none judges his brother, or insists on forcing his own opinions upon others or on making them an occasion of strife.[29]

The Sweeney Resolution was introduced on the floor of the Winona Lake Convention, along with the "Higdon interpretation." The liberal element called for its rejection by the convention, and there was heated debate as to whether or not the resolution was "creedal." When the question came to vote, the enraged convention passed the Sweeney Resolution by a large majority, but with it also passed the Higdon interpretation, which virtually abolished the intent of the conservative element in the original resolution. The result was wholly unsatisfactory to some conservatives, encouraging to others, and puzzling to still others.[30]

The liberal wing of the Disciples was enraged at the passage of this "creedal" resolution. C.C. Morrison cited the huge debt of the United Society ($400,000) and the dire financial consequences to the society should a split occur in the Disciple ranks as basis for his caustic criticism that the convention's action was merely a camouflage to replenish the society's depleted treasury.[31]

The congress, which convened six weeks after the International Convention, featured what was called a "constructive" program. William Jennings Bryan, who had been denied a place on the program of the International Convention, was invited to deliver one of his well-known orations against evolution. A Bible-school institute was also featured.

This congress appointed a number of commissions to set forth positive aims. The lengthy reports advocated a renewed emphasis in evangelism, Bible-institute training for preachers, and an effort to acquaint the membership of the churches with the historic aims of the Restoration Movement and create an awareness of the disloyal areas in the Disciples of Christ. "Loyalty" was largely the theme of all of the reports.[32]

Hitherto the congresses were protest assemblies held in connection with the International Convention. It should be noted, however, that the 1922 congress partook more of the nature of a competitive assembly than a protest. It was held at a different time and place, and the *Christian Standard* virtually overlooked the International Convention while it vigorously promoted the congress. The eleven-month period from the Louisville Congress to the St. Louis Congress was significant for turning the dissatisfied energies into channels of their own. But the larger cleavage was still several years away, and further efforts were yet to be made to reform the United Christian Missionary Society.[33]

The John T. Brown Report

John T. Brown, whose tour has been previously noted, filed a report with the Board of Managers of the U.C.M.S. There was a demand that Brown's report be made public, but Brown disclosed nothing until October of 1922. Feeling that the Brotherhood was "entitled to see my *full* report,"[34] he asked the journals to publish it. The editor of *The Christian Evangelist* told him that it was too long, while the editor of the *Christian Century* advised him not to publish the full report at all. The *Christian Standard* carried the full report in its issue of October 28, 1922. The report carried charges of open membership in China and the Philippine Islands and also an indictment of the society's Board of Managers for being unwilling to remedy the situation. Brown felt that the society's interpretation of the Sweeney Resolution (the "Higdon interpretation") required only loyalty to the society's policies rather than actual personal "accord" with its resolution of opposition to open membership. He noted that the board had recalled none of the missionaries in question, though two had resigned.

R.E. Elmore shortly afterward began a series of articles in the *Christian Standard* called "The United Society Has Broken Faith."[35] The articles were strong recriminations of the society's policies, work, and management. Elmore's thesis was that the society was hopelessly beyond redemption and that the conservative brethren should cease supporting it in any way (since "designation" was a hoax) and turn their energies to those Brotherhood enterprises that were independent, and "loyal."

Z.T. Sweeney published an article in the *Christian Standard* in 1923, on "The Missionary Crisis." In it, he described the missionary situation as "a mess" and concluded that there were three courses of possible action, which can be summarized as follows: (1) pull out and let the society alone (R.E. Elmore's position), (2) pull out of the society but still fight to save it, a course Sweeney felt to be dishonorable, or (3) stay in and fight for what the conservative element believed was right. Sweeney advocated the third course, saying, "I don't like this 'pack up and get out motto.' I personally shall stay in the Society and *watch it*. Wherever evil raises its head, I shall 'strike.'"[36]

In the same issue of the *Christian Standard,* the editor protested that the United Christian Missionary Society had no right to represent itself as *the* missionary agency of the Brotherhood. It was his contention (and has been the contention of the *Christian Standard* consistently ever since) that the United Christian Missionary Society was *a* missionary agency, but not *the* agency. He urged that the Brotherhood was not identical with the society (faith, not organization, as the basis of unity has always been urged by the *Christian*

Standard), and that to withdraw from the society was not to forsake the Brotherhood. Therefore, he urged that the society be abandoned, asserting that the only other possible option

> must be the dissolution of the society into its original elements, which can then separately take up the task of freeing themselves from the accumulated encumbrances that afflict them.[37]

The Executive Committee of the United Christian Missionary Society met in St. Louis in May, 1923. Brown had tendered his resignation in February, but had been asked to meet with the board and was persuaded to withdraw his resignation. The 1923 International Convention met at Colorado Springs, Colorado, September 3-9, and Brown was not reelected to the Executive Committee, although he remained a member of the Board of Managers.

Brown published a series of twelve articles on "Three Years a Member of the Executive Committee [United Christian Missionary Society], and Why I Resigned" in the *Christian Standard* issues of November 17, 1923, through February 23, 1924. The eleventh article was also published in tract form under the title, *An Experiment That Failed*. It listed "Twenty-seven Ways in Which the United Christian Missionary Society Has Broken Faith."[38]

The Executive Committee answered the charges in a booklet entitled *Facts About the Visit of John T. Brown to Some of the Mission Fields and Answers to His Statements in the Christian Standard*.[39] This reply sought to explain the "perilous circumstances" that led to Brown's charges, and it severely criticized him for the manner in which he conducted his "investigation." Brown countered with a lengthy booklet in which he reviewed both his original charges and the replies of the Executive Committee. This booklet, published by the Standard Publishing Company, was called *The United Christian Missionary Society Self-Impeached*,[40] and enjoyed a tremendous circulation over a period of several years. The Brotherhood was aflame with civil war.

The International Convention met in Cleveland, Ohio, October 14, 1924, and was boycotted by the *Christian Standard* and many individuals who were of the opinion that further attempts to "reform" the society were vain. But Z.T. Sweeney spearheaded a group of conservative Disciples who were determined not to abandon the cause. The 1924 convention was relatively free from conflict. The most noteworthy item, so far as this study is concerned, was the introduction of a resolution calling for the convention to sever its ties with the Association for the Promotion of Christian Unity because of the open membership pleas of its president, Peter Ainslie. This matter was referred to a commission (which had been authorized but not appointed) to adjust disagreements among the brethren.[41]

The convention at Cleveland proved to be the calm before the storm. W.H. Mohorter, the editor of the *Christian Standard,* commenting on the convention, wrote,

> Nothing was more evident at Cleveland than a smouldering, uneasy dissatisfaction with conditions as they are, but everywhere there was a marked hesitation about coming out into the open where all states of mind could be known, and each man could be located as to his point of view. While the log-rolling tactics of the few who manipulated the machinery continued to set up the word "unity" in larger type on the front page, and give more lung power to the declaration that everything is all right, the conviction settled more heavily upon the hearts of practically all that everything is not all right, and never can be without some kind of upheaval.[42]

The editor went on to note three areas of trouble: (1) the open membership question, which was becoming more acute than ever, (2) the convention's failure to voice the plea of restoration of primitive Christianity for the union of Christendom, and (3) the convention machinery had been captured by the liberal few. He then expressed this conclusion:

> The time for silence, courteous consideration, and watchful waiting is past, and those who have all along been faithful to the Restoration movement must take charge of it, or see it vanish in the dust of a "a disappearing brotherhood."[43]

Here is noted a significant change of policy on the part of the *Christian Standard* editorial staff. The next few years would witness an intensity of conflict unparalleled before or since. The opposition would make a last desperate effort to influence the direction of the United Society. The language employed on both sides of this conflict would seem unjustifiably harsh to any who were not caught up in the struggle.

The Oklahoma City Convention

The zenith of conservative influence in this period was reached at the Oklahoma City Convention in 1925. A new organization, the Christian Restoration Association, born in the heat of controversy, sponsored a series of nine regional Restoration rallies in different parts of the nation. The enterprise was hailed as a "New Cooperative Program" of "a dozen 'free agencies.'" The cooperating agencies were as follows:

African Christian Missionary Society
Christian Normal Institute
Christian Restoration Association
Christian Women's Benevolent Association
Christian Bible College of Colorado
Christian Witness to Israel
Cincinnati Bible Seminary
Eugene Bible University
International Bible Mission
Indiana Christian Hospital
Mexican Society for Christian Missions
Minneapolis Bible College
National Home Finding Society
Osaka Christian Mission
Southwest Virginia Evangelizing Association (later called Appalachian Evangelizing Association)
Yotsuya Mission[44]

The *Standard* also announced that a new "missionary journal" would appear: *Facts* (monthly, the name was changed in 1925 to the *Restoration Herald*), which would be the organ of the Christian Restoration Association. James DeForest Murch was the first editor. A six-point platform for the rallies which it sponsored was outlined:

The Christian Restoration Association, and associated agencies:

1. Stand four-square for the old Jerusalem gospel in its letter and spirit, and will press it to the four corners of the world with renewed vigor. We challenge the brotherhood to choose between modernism and the old paths.

2. Champion the Restoration plea, instead of the shameful compromises of men, for the unity of Christ's church in the world. We challenge the brotherhood to choose between the "Bible plan" and "open membership."

3. Exalt the local church as the fullest flower of the kingdom of God on earth, free and untrammeled by any agency of men's making. We challenge the brotherhood to prove whether it will be bond, or free.

4. Present an all-inclusive program of Christian service which will, on sheer merit, enlist the support of brethren everywhere. We challenge the brotherhood to choose between merit and privilege.

5. Do all in a spirit of aggressive loyalty and challenging love, believing that principles, not personalities or organizations, are the issue of the hour. We challenge the brotherhood to choose between loyalty and diplomacy.

6. Promote a spirit of Christian fellowship on the basis of like faith and order, and not because of organizational affiliations. We

challenge the brotherhood to choose between friendly cooperation and dictatorial consolidation.[45]

Within a month, the *Christian Standard* announced the appearance of another new monthly journal, the *Spotlight*. The purpose of this journal, according to the editor of the *Christian Standard,* was to make a "speciality of exposure and rebuke, to be done with a freedom and thoroughness denied to us, but which alone can be made effectual."[46] The *Christian Standard* henceforth would give itself to "constructive work." The task of editing *The Spotlight* was given to Robert E. Elmore, and the paper made its first appearance on September 1, 1925. Henceforth it was to be "The 'Standard' for Advancement" and "'The Spotlight' for Defense,"[47] and pages of statements of approval were printed in the *Christian Standard.* After its first issue, the name of *The Spotlight* was changed to *The Touchstone,* as it was learned that another periodical used the former name.

All things were pointing toward the Oklahoma City Convention, October 6-11, 1925. The programs of the nine regional rallies gave widespread publicity to the problems of the day, while the personnel of these rallies was marked by independent missionaries and Bible college teachers.[48] These rallies, plus the vigorous program of the *Christian Standard,* plus the campaign of *The Touchstone,* plus a Church Life Institute, which the *Christian Standard* called to meet in Oklahoma City on October 7, added up to a well-calculated effort to get the conservative element of the Disciples of Christ out to the Oklahoma City Convention in sufficient numbers to take action of some kind.

The program worked, and a large gathering came together in Oklahoma City. A "Peace Commission," consisting of Claude Edgar Hill, chairman; Thomas C. Howe, Mrs. R.C. Latshaw, M.M. Amunson, and Will R. Shaw, was appointed after the Cleveland Convention. This committee called a conference for September 15, 1925, at Indianapolis, Indiana, and asked five men representing the agencies and five men representing the opposition to meet with them. The five who represented the agencies were Stephen J. Corey, Robert Hopkins, H.C. Armstrong, Milo J. Smith, and H.O. Pritchard. The five who represented the opposition were John T. Brown, Z.T. Sweeney, W.R. Walker, P.H. Welshimer, and S.S. Lappin. The Peace Commission prepared a resolution to be submitted to the International Convention containing the following provisions:

1. That no person be employed by the United Christian Missionary Society as its representative who has committed himself or herself to belief in or practice of the reception of unimmersed persons into the membership of Churches of Christ.

2. That if any person is now in the employment of the United Christian Missionary Society as representative who has committed himself or herself to belief in or practice of the reception of unimmersed persons into the membership Churches of Christ, the relationship of that person to the United Christian Missionary Society be severed as an employee.[49]

This resolution was referred to the Committee on Resolutions for consideration. A.E. Cory made a plea to this committee that such a resolution was really a creed, since it dealt with a matter of belief. The committee returned the Peace Commission's resolution to the floor of the convention with the recommendation that the questionable article be rejected and a substitute article be included.

There was considerable debate, which ran over into the second day. The chairman, J.H. Goldner, did a masterful job of handling a difficult situation in a very fair manner. Speakers in behalf of the original resolution were George A. Miller, Z.T. Sweeney, Claude E. Hill, J.B. Briney, P.H. Welshimer, Samuel J. Smith, C.S. Medbury, and R.A. Long. Those speaking against adoption of the original resolution were H.O. Pritchard, A.D. Rogers, E.D. Jones, C.M. Chilton, Mrs. W.H. Hart, F.W. Burnham, and Edwin Marx. The latter group held that the resolution was a creed and should be rejected as such. The former group held that it was a statement of policy for the agency that the churches were employing to handle their missionary activity.[50] The intense debate carried over into a second day. Finally, R.A. Long, the wealthy benefactor whose gifts spurred the Men and Millions Movement and who purchased the Christian Publication Company and gave it to the Brotherhood,

Robert A. Long (1850-1934), wealthy industrialist whose benefactions included a large gift to the Men and Millions Movement and the purchase of the Christian Publishing Company, which became the Christian Board of Publication.

ended the debate by moving the original question. This meant that a vote had to be taken, and, when it came, it was overwhelmingly in favor of the Peace Resolution. Writing in the *Christian Standard* fifteen years later, F.D. Kershner calls this "one of the few occasions in Disciple history when the organizational forces were defeated in a clear-cut battle on the floor of the convention."[51] It was a dark hour for the liberal element of the Disciples. Stephen J. Corey, vice president and foreign secretary of the society at that time, wrote out his resignation that night, but was persuaded to withhold it until the Board of Managers could interpret the Peace Resolution.

The Board of Managers of the United Christian Missionary Society met in St. Louis, Missouri, December 2 and 3, 1925, to consider the Peace Resolution. The discussion centered about the phrase *committed to belief in* the practice of admitting unimmersed in the fellowship. After long consideration, the Board of Managers agreed to interpret the phrase as follows:

> The Board of Managers interprets the expression, "committed to belief in" as not intended to invade the private judgment, but only to apply to such as open agitations would prove divisive.[52]

Thus, the letter of the resolution was kept by interpreting away its purpose. It is little wonder that those who had hoped that Brotherhood peace could be restored through restoring confidence in the management of the United Christian Missionary Society cried out at this "interpretation," which nullified their efforts.

Terrified that Brotherhood leadership might be taken over by "reactionaries," the liberal Disciple leaders met the week following the Board of Managers' meeting to map out a strategy.[53] Meeting in Columbus, Ohio, they appointed a Continuation Committee consisting of E.M. Bowman, chairman; R.A. Doan, Mrs. Ida W. Harrison, E.S. Ames, Peter Ainslie, and W.C. Harding. They began publication of a *Bulletin* to spread their point of view, and they issued a call for a "Committee of One Thousand"[54] to join their cause.

The columns of the *Christian Standard* are free from controversy for the next several months, *The Touchstone* carrying this task. To combat the latter, the United Christian Missionary Society began publishing *The United Society News,* edited by W.M. Williams, the next month. It was published spasmodically, and it rivaled its Cincinnati opponent in the use of invective. The conservative elements were called "a garrulous bunch of tomcats"[55] who should be at home catching mice in their own backyard instead of disturbing the peace of the neighborhood; a "Restorationist" denomination with headquarters in Cincinnati where "the Cincinnati pope's toe has been kissed too many times for the good of the brotherhood."[56]

The Commission to the Orient

The Board of Managers could not permit the John T. Brown Report to remain unchallenged as the only on-site report of the explosive

China Mission situation, so it appointed a Commission to the Orient at the conclusion of its December 3, 1925, meeting. In so doing, the society was investigating itself. The commission consisted of Cleveland Kleihauer, Robert N. Simpson, and John R. Golden. The men sailed on January 22, 1926, to investigate matters in the Philippines, Japan, and China. The commission was the focal point of Brotherhood interest for the next year, since its mission was to carry out the Peace Resolution (interpreted away by the Board of Managers). It spent five weeks in the Philippines, where it investigated a controversy, already months old, between Leslie Wolfe and E.K. Higdon. Higdon had advocated open membership and had succeeded in winning most of the missionaries to his support. Wolfe strenuously opposed, and a large element of the native leadership stood with him. Higdon had succeeded in getting the missionaries to petition for the recall of Wolfe on the grounds of incompatibility, and Wolfe contended that his incompatibility was his refusal to acquiesce in the open membership and comity policies of the other missionaries.[57] Final disposition was left in the hands of the commission, and the commission wired recommending the immediate recall of Wolfe.

The *Christian Standard* came back into the area of the controversy when this happened. It related Wolfe's story, and his willingness to work as an independent missionary with the churches in Manila that stood with him, which was virtually all of the churches of the Tagalog district.[58] The *Christian Standard* and the Christian Restoration Association appealed to the churches to send missionary support to the Wolfes, and the Christian Restoration Association acted as forwarding agency. Funds that had been withheld from the United Christian Missionary Society were immediately sent to the Wolfes, sustaining and giving permanency to their work.

The commission went on to China, where, it reported, it found that there had been some irregular practices at Luchowfu, but that they had been corrected.[59]

The Memphis Convention

The International Convention was scheduled to meet in Memphis, November 11-17, 1926. A "Committee on Future Action" was formed in June by the conservatives following a conference in Indianapolis. This committee, consisting of W.E. Sweeney, Mark Collis, W.R. Walker, P.H. Welshimer, and S.S. Lappin, planned a congress for Memphis to be held on November 10, and they engaged the auditorium of the First Methodist-Episcopal Church South for their assembly. When these plans were published, Walter M. White, minister of the Linwood Avenue Christian Church, and chairman of local arrangements for the International Convention, brought local pressure to bear that resulted in the church's canceling its agreement and forcing the congress to meet six blocks away in the Pantages Theater.[60] This greatly reduced its effectiveness.

Leslie Wolfe and two Philippine nationals who were associated with him in the Manila Bible Seminary were brought to Memphis.[61] But this time, the organized element in the Brotherhood had things well in hand; and the convention president, A.D. Harmon, president of Transylvania University and the College of the Bible, made no attempt at showing the impartiality characterized by J.H. Goldner the previous year. His keynote address was regarded as the espousal of the liberal cause in every controversial question.[62]

The crucial hour of the convention came on Saturday afternoon when the report of the Commission to the Orient came up for action. On the evening before the day when the report was to be given, John R. Golden approached P.H. Welshimer and asked for an informal meeting with the leaders of the congress. In this meeting, Golden advised the congress leaders that the report to be given the following day was accurate to the extent of what it contained, but there was incriminating evidence not included that would be reported if the proper questions were raised. A series of six questions were formulated, each to be asked by a different person during the floor discussion. At the next day's session, the first question was posed by Mark Collis. But the answer that he was given from the platform was directly contradictory to what had been indicated the previous evening by Golden. Collis, who was deaf, was wholly unaware that he had been made to appear ridiculous. Ira M. Boswell, who was to raise the second question, refused to do so on the ground that the whole procedure was a setup.[63] The commissioners reported what had been previously denied; namely, that there had been some irregularities in Manila, and in China, but that these practices had stopped and everything was as it should be when they were there. (In contrast, the editor of the *Christian Century* cited reports from the society to the effect that "every Disciple mission in China except one is practicing 'open membership.'"[64]) Leslie Wolfe and Juan L. Baronia objected to this clean bill of health for the Philippine mission, but the convention sustained the commission, and those who objected were laughed out.

The Memphis Convention is quite a contrast to that of Oklahoma City. The dissatisfied element was without definite policy, confused, and outwitted from the start. Part of the strategy of the pro-society leadership was to hold a youth convention simultaneously with the convention. The president of the convention, who appealed in his presidential address for a delegate convention to prevent the manipulation of decisions by large local attendance,[65] ruled that the young people were registered and entitled to vote in the main convention's business sessions. Although they had separate sessions, they were brought in to the main session at strategic times to add their voices to the voting procedure. The convention was a ringing triumph for the organized forces and a defeat for the opposition that was so crushing and thorough that they never again attempted to make themselves heard in the International Convention. As such, Memphis marks the end of an era. Edwin R. Errett, reporting the convention for *Christian Standard,* called it "A Convention of Bad Faith," and concluded his report by observing:

> Many devout disciples of the simple Nazarene went away declaring it the last International Convention they would attend; at least, until they could see evidence of a genuine "clean up." . . .
> In short, if we had to believe that this gathering at Memphis represents the disciples of Christ in the Restoration movement, then we must conclude that we don't belong.[66]

In his report, Errett was reflecting the conclusion that thousands shared. Having believed that they had made their voices heard the year before in Oklahoma City, the disaffected component was stunned to realize that their efforts had been nullified by the strategy of an official body that they were powerless to control. The frustration created such a reaction to organizations *per se* among those who abandoned the International Convention that they would never allow a similar consolidation of resources to evolve in their fellowship. Until 1926, the protest had been directed against specific policies of the organization and a determined effort was directed toward changing such policies. However, experiences between 1919 and 1926 led many to conclude that a strong organization creates entrenched authority that does not yield to popular mandate. From this point forward, a strong distrust of any central organization of any type or purpose would characterize the dissenting portion of the movement. Such a framework of thinking is congenial to a people who still hold to individualism and free enterprise, strong traits in the regions where Disciples were numerous. From this date, those who could not endorse the program of the organizations turned their energies elsewhere and developed their own religious activities and institutions according to their own preferences.

The Memphis Convention in 1926 stands as a watershed, the beginning of a slow process of separation that required a quarter of a century to be fully realized. Few who were present at this convention could have foreseen its consequences for the Disciples of Christ. For many years, the *Yearbook of the Disciples of Christ* would list all of the congregations as part of the same religious fellowship, and fraternal relations were usually maintained on the local level. The *Christian Standard* also took the position, until 1944, that the

Brotherhood was one, even though there were multiple missionary agencies and conventions.[67] However, this was not the viewpoint of the *Restoration Herald,* especially after 1934, when Leon Myers became editor. Nor was it the view of the leaders of the U.C.M.S. and the International Convention. Memphis may be seen as a tragic event that, given better statesmanship, should not have happened the way it did; or it can be viewed as the inevitable result of the breakdown of relations and the erosion of trust that had been in process for a decade or more.

End Notes

[1]George P. Rutledge, "The Campbell Institute," *Christian Standard,* October 26, 1918, p. 9.

[2]"To the Rescue of the Restoration Movement," *Christian Standard,* July 26, 1919, p. 1.

[3]"The Challenge of the Cincinnati Convention," *Christian Standard,* August 2, 1919, p. 9.

[4]"Action of General Convention in Regard to Congress Resolutions," *Christian Standard,* October 25, 1919, p. 6.

[5]S.S. Lappin, "Story of the Restoration Congress," *Christian Standard,* October 25, 1919, p. 3.

[6]C.C. Morrison, "Carry On," *Christian Century,* October 30, 1919, p. 6.

[7]The boards withdrew in 1933 and 1934.

[8]For an account of the history of the College of Missions see Ray Stites, *The College of Missions, Indianapolis, In., 1910-1927* (Milligan College, TN: Emmanuel School of Religion, unpublished B.D. Thesis, 1974).

[9]George P. Rutledge, "To the Rescue of the Mexican Mission," *Christian Standard,* November 1, 1919, p. 119.

[10]George P. Rutledge, "Result of the Preferential Ballot," *Christian Standard,* October 16, 1920, p. 13.

[11]E.L. Powell, "E.L. Powell Suggests Program for Congress," *Christian Standard,* July 10, 1920, p. 5.

[12]R.E. Elmore, "The Year of Trial," *Christian Standard,* October 16, 1920, p. 1.

[13]Frank Garrett, letter to Executive Committee, United Christian Missionary Society, reproduced in the *Christian Standard,* August 7, 1920, p. 4.

[14]R.E. Elmore, "Does China Mission Endorse Open Membership?" *Christian Standard,* August 7, 1920, p. 3.

[15]Z.T. Sweeney, "Resolution Tabled by Board of Managers of U.C.M.S.," *Christian Standard,* November 6, 1920, p. 1.

[16]"A Resolution Approved by the Committee on Recommendations and Adopted by the Convention," *Christian Standard,* October 30, 1920, p. 1.

[17]Corey, op. cit., p. 84.

[18]Z.T. Sweeney, Letter of October 27, 1920, to George P. Rutledge, *Christian Standard,* November 6, 1920, p. 1.

[19]S.S. Lappin, "St. Louis Congress and Convention," *Christian Standard,* November 13, 1920, p. 6.

[20]George P. Rutledge, "Let's Clear Away the United Society's Interchurch Debt," *Christian Standard,* November 20, 1920, p. 13.

[21]See *Christian Standard,* 1921: October 22, pp. 5, 6; October 29, pp. 5, 6; November 5, pp. 5, 6; November 12, pp. 5, 6; November 19, pp. 5, 6; November 26, pp. 4, 5; December 3, pp. 4, 5.

[22]P.H. Welshimer, "Canton (O.) Church Withdraws Financial Support from U.C.M.S.," *Christian Standard,* December 3, 1921, pp. 1, 2.

[23]George P. Rutledge, "Louisville Congress Makes History," *Christian Standard,* December 17, 1921, p. 1.

[24]R.L. Records, "Training for the Ministry," *Christian Standard,* February 4, 1922, p. 6.

[25]Corey, *Fifty Years,* op. cit., p. 84.

[26]*Second Annual Report of the United Christian Missionary Society* (St. Louis: United Christian Missionary Society, 1922), p. 20.

[27]F.W. Burnham, "The Board of Managers Speaks Again," *World Call,* February, 1922, inside front cover.

[28]W.H. Mohorter, "We Can Not Participate," *Christian Standard,* August 19, 1922, p. 9.

[29]"'Sweeney' Resolution with Higdon Interpretation, as Endorsed by the Winona Convention," *Christian Standard,* September 30, 1922, p. 8.

[30]P.H. Welshimer, R.E. Elmore, and *Christian Standard* editors, "What Attitude Shall We Take Toward the United Society?", *Christian Standard,* September 30, 1922, pp. 8, 9, 15.

[31]C.C. Morrison, "Apparent Reaction, Real Progress," *The Christian Century,* 1922, p. 1119.

[32]"The Commissions Report to the Congress," *Christian Standard,* November 4, 1922, pp. 6, 7, 17.

[33]The determined efforts of a small minority of the conservative brethren to effect a cleavage in the Disciple ranks are obvious from this date. Henceforth they were to capitalize on every failure of their brethren to influence the organizations toward a more conservative policy.

[34]John T. Brown, *The United Christian Missionary Society Self-Impeached* (Cincinnati: Standard, 1924), p. 17.

[35]R.E. Elmore, ed., "The United Society Has Broken Faith," *Christian Standard,* one page a week appearing under this title from December 9, 1922, through March 31, 1923.

[36]Z.T. Sweeney, "The Missionary Crisis," *Christian Standard,* LVIII:41 (July 14, 1923), p. 4. This article was the last in a series on "Crises in Restoration History."

[37]W.H. Mohorter, "Is There a Remedy?" *Christian Standard,* July 14, 1923, p. 10.

[38]John T. Brown, *An Experiment That Failed* (Cincinnati: Standard, 1924).

[39]*Facts About the Visit of John T. Brown to Some of the Mission Fields and Answers to His Statements in the Christian Standard* (St. Louis: U.C.M.S. Executive Committee, 1924).

[40]Brown, *U.C.M.S. Self-Impeached,* op. cit.

[41]"The Story of the Golden Jubilee Convention," *The Christian Evangelist,* October 30, 1924, p. 1407.

[42]W.H. Mohorter, "The Gathering at Cleveland," *Christian Standard,* October 25, 1924, p. 8.

[43]Ibid.

[44]Horace W. Vaile, "Nine Great Restoration Rallies," *Christian Standard,* July 18, 1925, p. 17.

[45]Ibid.

[46]"A New Adjunct to 'Standard' Journalism," *Christian Standard,* August 8, 1925, p. 2.

[47]"The 'Standard' for Advancement," *Christian Standard,* August 15, 1925, p. 8; "'The Spotlight' for Defense," *Christian Standard,* August 15, 1925, p. 9.

[48]"Programs, Regional Restoration Rallies," *Christian Standard,* August 22, 1925, p. 13; August 29, 1925, pp. 14, 18.

[49]"Report of the Peace Conference Committee," *Christian Standard,* October 24, 1925, p. 9.

[50]Ibid., pp. 13-15; October 31, 1925, pp. 19, 23.

[51]F.D. Kershner, "Stars," *Christian Standard,* October 19, 1940, p. 32.

[52]"Peace Resolution Policy Adopted," *United Society News,* December 3, 1925, p. 2.

[53]C.C. Morrison, "For the Freedom of the Disciples," *Christian Century,* 1925, p. 1533.

[54]*Bulletin of Continuation Committee of Columbus Conference* (copy on file at Disciples of Christ Historical Society, Nashville, Tennessee), inside back cover.

[55]W.M. Williams, "Those Theological Tomcats," *United Society News,* December 8, 1925, p. 4.

[56]W.M. Williams, "No Further Dictation from New Denomination," *United Society News,* December 15, 1925, p. 1.

[57]Leslie Wolfe, *Supplement to the Christian Standard,* October 9, 1926, p. 6. Stephen Corey (*Fifty Years,* op. cit., pp. 109-111) notes that Wolfe had been party to a comity agreement with the Presbyterian mission in 1918. It was a three-year agreement that obviously did not prove satisfactory to Wolfe.

[58]Edwin R. Errett, "Refuse Denominational Yoke," *Christian Standard,* April 3, 1926, pp. 1, 6, 7. See also Edith W. Allison, *Prisoner of Christ* (Joplin: College Press, 1960) for biographical information.

[59]"Report of Commission to Orient," *The United Society News,* July 23, 1926, p. 1.

[60]S.S. Lappin, "Interference at Memphis," *Christian Standard,* November 6, 1926, p. 7.

[61]An effort was made by U.C.M.S. officials to intimidate one of the Philippine nationals by representing to the congress leaders that he was guilty of moral infractions (see S.J. Corey, op. cit., p. 120). However, no evidence was ever produced and no subsequent charges ever emerged.

[62]W.H. Mohorter, "The Memphis Convention," *Christian Standard,* November 27, 1926, p. 10.

[63]Reported to the author by J.H. Dampier; confirmed by O.A. Trinkle, who was one of the six selected to raise questions.

[64]"The Freedom of Missionaries," *Christian Century,* September 30, 1920.

[65]"International Convention of the Disciples of Christ," *Christian Century,* 1926, p. 1468.

[66]Edwin R. Errett, "A Convention of Bad Faith," *Christian Standard,* November 27, 1926, p. 8.

[67]The date marks the editorial change from Edwin R. Errett to Burris Butler, a change that involved a radical change in policy.

Chapter Twelve

The Widening Gulf

The International Convention at Memphis, Tennessee, in 1926, was a watershed in the history of the Restoration Movement. It marked the climax of a decade of accusations, denials, policy shifts, and organizational realignments. For too long, the conventions had been arenas for confrontation between divergent and widening ideologies. There were those who sought to perpetuate the plea to base a broad Christian fellowship on a model derived from careful examination of the church in the New Testament. They would offer such a model to the larger Christian world as the only viable basis for Christian unity. There were others, equally sincere and determined, who began with the contemporary religious situation and held that certain accommodations would produce the desired unity on a less doctrinal and more practical basis, and that the latter was the only option that provided any real possibility for success. The second point of view was growing, especially among those who occupied leadership positions in the centralized organizations of the Disciples. This idea of a federated unity had expressed itself in the Disciples' entry into the Federal Council of Churches, the comity agreement at Monterrey, Mexico, the introduction of open membership in China and the Phillipines, and the activities of the Commission on Christian Unity. The efforts that were made to check or alter these trends reached their climax in the Peace Resolution adopted by the convention in Oklahoma City in 1925. But this was interpreted away by the organization, in the judgment of many delegates, and covered over by an official investigation often described as a "whitewash" by those who disagreed with its findings.

The disillusioned at Memphis left with several conclusions taking shape in their minds. One was that centralization of organizations was a mistake because it made discrimination in support of the various enterprises all but impossible. More importantly, a basic change in methodology was gaining acceptance, namely, that organization was itself unnecessary and unacceptable for Christian service because of the virtual impossibility of effectively modifying policies that became entrenched behind organizational ramparts. A strong aversion to any kind of organization beyond the local congregation was developing in reaction to the events at Memphis. The road ahead was confusing, and the best course to take was unclear to many who left Memphis uncertain about the future. Thenceforth, for two more decades, the *Christian Standard* would give news coverage to the International Convention but never again would it give enthusiastic endorsement. There would be no more efforts to influence the direction that the organizations would take.

All religious fellowships require a variety of extra-congregational institutions if they are to sustain inter-congregational fellowship and activity. Among such activities are conventions, assemblies or some such gathering for inter-group fellowship and encouragement, mission activity, benevolent institutions, educational agencies, and publications. Of these, only the last existed to any significant degree outside of the organized agencies that were abandoned in 1926. Within the next twenty-five years, all the kinds of activities necessary to sustain a totally separate religious fellowship would be developed. Persons and congregations functioning independently of the old agencies were thenceforth called "Independents." This is the origin of the identifying term that, although disliked for reasons previously noted,[1] has become firmly attached to those who no longer care to be identified as Disciples of Christ, a denomination with national headquarters in Indianapolis, Indiana.

The story of the developments within the Independent fellowship in the period 1926-1950 can best be understood if the agencies and institutions that came to serve the needs of these people are treated separately. All of the activities and agencies through which Christian mission and service were expressed arose out of individual initiative, did not seek any kind of official recognition, and appealed to congregations directly. Thus, many of the congregations became the focus of competing efforts between the old agencies and new ones. The issues that once created conflict in the conventions were transferred to the local congregations, causing innumerable splits and resulting in shifts of membership. As a result, individual congregations were generally forced to choose whether to align with the old agencies of the Disciples of Christ or with the new enterprises that insisted they were more representative of the historic position of the movement.

The North American Christian Convention

The International Convention of 1926 voted to have no convention at all in 1927. Instead, one was planned for the spring of 1928. Those who resented what they considered to be treacherous official maneu-vering assembled ad hoc in the Pantages Theater in Memphis to con-sider a course of action. Generally, they were tired of strife and convinced that it would be futile to attempt further to influence the policies of the International Convention. Instead, they appointed a Committee on Future Action, consisting of P.H. Welshimer, chair-man, Mark Collis, W.E. Sweeney, W.R. Walker, Robert F. Tuck, O.A. Trinkle, and F.S. Dowdy. This committee issued a call for a conven-tion to meet in Indianapolis, Indiana, in October of 1927.

The purpose in the mind of the leadership of the North American Christian Convention was not schismatic. In fact, it was the very opposite. For a decade, the International Convention had been marked by conflicts over agency policies. But the new convention leadership insisted that agencies were not the basis of the unity of the Brotherhood. Instead, they came to be seen as a threat to the unity that really consisted in a common faith and purpose. Could an assembly that emphasized matters of faith while giving no endorse-ment to any agency be the means of preserving the unity of the Brotherhood? Would it not be possible to come together on common grounds of a shared heritage while permitting complete freedom of choice to churches and individuals in regard to the agencies they preferred to support and utilize? Such a possibility seemed reason-able, and many considered this to be the only viable formula for pre-vention of another schism. The Brotherhood was deemed to be broader than either the supporters or the critics of any of the agen-cies. Consequently, the early programs of the North American Chris-tian Convention were broader than its constituency. Men of pronounced organizational preference appeared on every program of the convention during this period.[2] However, despite the intentions that the convention should help to maintain the unity of the Brother-hood, the effect was quite the opposite, as the Commission to Restudy the Brotherhood would note.[3] Perhaps it was naive to think that two conventions could be other than divisive. The dynamics at work in the Brotherhood, coupled with the practical difficulties most people found in attending two national conventions in a given year, caused individuals and congregations to align with one or the other meeting. The two leading journals promoted one or the other conven-tion and, after 1927, each gave little coverage to the other assembly.

The first North American Christian Convention met at Cadle Tabernacle in Indianapolis, October 12-16, 1927. More than three thousand attended. It was primarily a preaching and fellowship gathering. The major emphases of this "Grand Reunion to Honor the Plea" were to be fourfold: "(1) The Deity of Jesus, (2) The Inspiration and Integrity of the Scriptures, (3) The Church, and (4) Christian Evangelism."[4] Mark Collis, a member of the committee, forecast the nature of the proposed convention in March, 1927, saying,

Neither rationalism, nor Unitarianism, nor any form of unbelief, should have place in this convention. No modernist should be invited to a place on the program. I would not call it a "fundamentalist convention," but, in the strictest sense of the word, it should be a Christian convention. Let such questions as the deity of Christ and His authority in the church be discussed. . . . The Bible should be exalted. There are men who can show us that this blessed Book can be trusted, that it is free from errors and contradictions, that it is a safe guide, and that the time has not come that we should discard the slogan: "Where the Scriptures speak, we speak, and where the Scriptures are silent, we are silent."[5]

No business was transacted other than to select a continuation committee charged with responsibility to call another convention the following year. The second North American Christian Convention met in 1929 in Canton, Ohio. Thereafter, for two decades, because of depression and World War II, the Convention met only seven times, usually in Indianapolis.[6] In 1950, however, the convention became an annual assembly, and a policy was adopted to make it a genuinely national gathering by moving it to all sections of the country.

The North American Christian Convention met the needs of the Independent Churches well during the period. It furnished needed cohesion and fellowship on a wider level. This was critical during formative years. It provided inspiration, *esprit de corps,* and a platform for expression of the central core of the heritage of the constituency. This influence prevented fragmentation at the very time when congregational autonomy was given a high degree of emphasis in the churches. During the period under consideration, no sustained regional conventions developed, although a Southwest Christian Convention and a Midwest Christian Convention appeared briefly, largely because the North American Convention seemed to be anchored in Indianapolis. There was no inclination to develop Independent state conventions. The existing state conventions were all integrated into the Disciple programs, with the exception of Arizona and Wisconsin. Oregon recognized both types of activity. However, in the absence of state or regional gatherings, the need for personal contact and fellowship was filled by several rallies sponsored by institutions. The oldest and largest of these gatherings was the Conference on Evangelism sponsored annually by The Cincinnati Bible Seminary. Attendance at times rivaled that of the North American Christian Convention, and the program format was quite similar. Minnesota Bible College developed a similar Midwinter Conference on Evangelism, and occasionally other Bible colleges became sites for area rallies.

Note should be taken at this time of an agency that played a very influential role in molding the opinions and attitudes of the developing Independent efforts, the Christian Restoration Association

(C.R.A.). It was organized in 1922 as the Clarke Fund, incorporated in Cincinnati, Ohio. It evolved out of the Clarke Estate, founded in 1894 to establish churches of Christ "in destitute fields." It was incorporated as a home missionary agency; the original trustees were James DeForest Murch (chairman), Horace Vaile, and C.D. Saunders. The C.R.A. sponsored rallies in strategic cities, which gave visibility to Brotherhood issues and reinforced efforts for a new direction in missionary activity. R.C. Foster and Ira M. Boswell traveled extensively conducting these Restoration Rallies.[7] However, no attempt was made to establish them as regular, annual events.

Missionary Activity

Since the tension and ultimate frustration of the Brotherhood was directly related to missionary policy and practices and the organized structures that protected such practice, it was a foregone conclusion that a new and different method of missionary operation would be developed. In reality, however, what developed was not really new at all. Mission activity sustained on resources derived directly from local congregations or personal interest had probably always existed to some extent, although the missionary activity sustained by the agencies was by far the more visible. But, when congregations began to look for more satisfactory outlets for their missionary interests, they were quick to discover them. As funds were withheld from the United Society, they became available for new enterprises conducted independently of the society. By 1926, there were some conspicuously successful examples that gave credibility to the independent method of doing missionary work.

The Yotsuya Mission is the oldest Independent mission of the Christian Church still in operation. It was established by Mr. and Mrs. W.D. Cunningham in 1901. Committed to missionary activity, Mr. and Mrs. Cunningham were appointed by the Foreign Christian Missionary Society for work in Japan with C.E. Garst. A week before their scheduled departure in 1899, Mr. Cunningham contracted what proved to be poliomyelitis. As soon as he was sufficiently recovered, he was examined by the society's doctor and advised to wait a year. After repeated examinations and postponements, the society's doctors pronounced him unfit for foreign service.[8] Application was then made to the Christian Women's Board of Missions, but that group felt that it could not open a work in Japan at that time.[9] This was a severe blow, but gradually the idea grew that they could go to Japan without the assistance of the society. After securing support from their friends, they sailed for Japan, arriving on October 1, 1901. In Tokyo, they were met by M.B. Madden and F.E. Hagin, both working under the society, who entertained them until they were able to locate a house.

Among the few things that the Cunninghams took to Japan with them was a small printing press, from which came the first issue of the *Tokyo Christian* on November 1, 1901. This monthly paper is still published and is probably the oldest Independent mission journal in the entire Brotherhood. The first editorial in the paper carried the following statement:

> Most of our friends understand why it is that we are not receiving any support from our Foreign Mission Board. We have entertained none but the kindliest feelings for all the members of the Board and desire that our friends should do the same.
>
> All our expenses in connection with our coming to Japan were paid by some of our friends who agreed with us that it was our duty to come. We are here to do the work to which we believe the Lord has called us. . . .[10]

Cunningham found part-time employment as a teacher of English in the school for the Japanese nobility. A Bible class was organized, and, after two years on the field, Cunningham had developed this class into a church with its own building and a Bible school of 221 pupils. A second church was opened in 1905, and a third was organized in 1906, both of them having grown out of previous Bible schools.[11] It was Cunningham's policy to press the Japanese converts into service in an effort to put the churches on a self-sustaining basis as soon as possible. For that reason, he concentrated his efforts upon training native preachers, to whom he would then turn over the preaching responsibility as soon as they were able to assume it.

W.D. Cunningham (1864-1936), pioneer Independent missionary. He published The *Tokyo Christian,* presently the oldest mission paper in the movement.

Mr. and Mrs. Cunningham took their first furlough in 1908. Their cordial reception in the churches and conventions of America was such as to insure their continued support in Japan. George A. Miller, of the Ninth Street Christian Church in Washington, D.C., opened his pulpit to W.D. Cunningham. Following the sermon, Miller said,

I was one of the Executive Committee that refused to send Brother Cunningham to Japan. We made a mistake. God has overruled that mistake for good, for Brother Cunningham has done a better work than he could possibly have done if he had gone out under the direction of the Society.[12]

Cunningham was aggressive, resourceful, and diligent. Every November, the annual report of the mission appeared in the *Tokyo Christian*. These reports reveal the steady growth of the mission and the expanding vision of Cunningham. In 1909, he translated Herbert Monninger's *Training for Service*[13] into Japanese to assist in training native Christians. At the time of Cunningham's second furlough in 1916, there were five churches, and a report of 1919 lists, in addition, ten Bible schools, five outstations, one kindergarten, and a total of 592 baptisms.[14]

The early years of the history of the Yotsuya Mission are not marked by any animosity toward the missionaries of the Foreign Society who also worked in Tokyo. The promotional resourcefulness of Cunningham sufficed to keep the mission in operation without aid from the society. It was one of several mission enterprises that were operating successfully under independent initiative. The *Christian Standard* kept the churches informed of these independent enterprises, as well as the works of the various societies, because it was felt that they were all a part of the greater work of the Brotherhood as a whole.

When the period of crises arose in 1919, the very nature of the case worked to the advantage of the independent missionaries. The criticism aimed at the societies, and later at the United Society, and the intransigence (in the opinion of a great many Disciples) of the organizations to take steps to remedy the problems, left the dissatisfied churches no recourse but to turn their energies toward the independent agencies. The successful operation of the Yotsuya Mission in Japan for more than two decades demonstrated the feasibility of the independent principle of operation. Therefore, there were not only churches that abandoned the society, there were also missionaries. The decade from 1919 to 1929 saw six missionaries who were formerly affiliated with the societies launch independent enterprises, and a seventh enterprise grow out of the society's abandonment of a mission station. Whereas previous independent endeavors had been largely indifferent toward the societies, these seven missions were militantly independent and anti-society. The story of resignations or dismissals of these missionaries from the United Christian Missionary Society is a sad episode in the history of the movement. The following is a resumé of these independent efforts, all of which proved to be permanent enterprises that would endure through depression and wars.

An account has already been given of the comity agreement that
led to the abandonment of the Monterrey, Mexico, Mission by the
United Christian Missionary Society and of the formation of the
Mexican Society for Christian Missions, led by E.T. Westrup. Appeal
for financial support through the *Christian Standard*[15] and the large
offering made at the 1919 Congress in Cincinnati insured the success and continued support of this venture.

Mr. and Mrs. M.D. Madden, who had been sent to Japan by the
Foreign Christian Missionary Society in 1895, resigned from this
service in 1914 because of a misunderstanding, the details of which
have never been disclosed. Mr. and Mrs. Madden returned to Japan
as independent missionaries in 1919 and located in Osaka.[16]

The Independent mission to South Africa was organized through
the initiative of W.H. Book and the Columbus Tabernacle Church.
Thomas Kalane, an American-educated national, was sent to South
Africa in 1920. British regulations required white supervision of the
mission, so O.E. Payne, at sixty-three years of age, was sent to the
field in 1923. Kalane died in 1922, and Payne died in 1925. Charles
Butts Titus, who had spent twelve years in China as a missionary
under the Foreign Christian Missionary Society and had resigned
because of differences with the United Christian Missionary Society,
was sent to supervise the work in 1925. Titus remained until ill
health and depression forced him home in 1930.[17]

Mr. and Mrs. Leslie Wolfe were sent to the Philippine Islands in
1907 by the Foreign Christian Missionary Society. Wolfe was given
several responsible positions there during the first two terms of service, but the introduction of the open-membership and comity issues
by E.K. Higdon brought about a crisis in 1926 that led to a petition
for the recall of the Wolfes on the ground of "incompatibility."[18] They
remained on the field as Independent missionaries and established
one of the largest mission works of the Christian Churches.

In 1921, the United Christian Missionary Society sent Mr. and
Mrs. Russell Morse to the Tibetan field. However, the Morses
resigned from this commission in 1926 because they felt that the
society's policy restricted their evangelistic work, so the society
brought them back to America. The following two years were spent
in the United States making preparation for their return to the Lisu
tribes of China-Tibet in 1929. This work was maintained despite
incredible hardships during World War II, but was later destroyed by
the Communist occupation.

The Central Provinces India Mission was launched by Mr. and
Mrs. Harry D. Schaefer, Sr., in 1928. They spent two terms in India
previously, one under the Christian Women's Board of Missions
(1913-1919), and one under the United Christian Missionary Society
(1920-1927). The second term was marked by disagreeable clashes
with some of the missionaries over the new policies of the United

Society, and Schaefer's recall was requested. As with the Wolfes before them, the Schaefers' recall was also on the grounds of "incompatibility."[19] They returned to India as Independent missionaries and established a work that was carried on through World War II by their son.

Mr. and Mrs. Sterling G. Rothermel served as missionaries in India under the Christian Women's Board of Missions from 1914-1920. The United Christian Missionary Society was organized during their first term and, when their furlough was ended, abruptly informed them that they could not return, despite the fact that their missionary colleagues had requested their return. They then sent out a circular letter relating that they had dedicated their lives to mission work and asking their brethren for advice.[20] In 1926, they sailed for India as Independent missionaries and established the United Provinces Christian Mission, locating in Ragaul, Hamirpur. U.P. Rothermel insisted that the grounds for their dismissal was their conservative theological convictions, which the society's Board of Managers felt would cause them to oppose the new policy of the United Christian Missionary Society.[21]

The decade of the "roaring twenties" closed with the practice of doing missionary work on an independent basis well-established. The decade that followed was the period of the Great Depression. This would test the stability of the Independent enterprises. It would demonstrate whether missionaries supported directly by congregations could weather severe economic crises. During this period, the United Society was forced to curtail its work, recalling a number of missionaries and closing several stations. This led to the opening of a new Independent mission. Dr. and Mrs. Norton H. Bare, who had served a term in Tibet under the United Society and were recalled in 1931 when the Society was forced to close its Tibetan work, returned to the field in 1933 as Independent missionaries. They worked in Batang with Mr. and Mrs. Morse for two years before pushing on to establish their own work at Atuntze.[22] But the Thomas Evangelistic Mission in South Africa, which was being operated as an Independent enterprise by Basil Holt after Kellems, its founder, became involved in marital difficulties, was closed down for lack of funds, and C.B. Titus was recalled to America in 1930 because of lack of funds. All of the other missionaries remained on their fields through the difficult days of the Depression, and several expanded their forces.

Aside from the work of Bare, four other new missions were established during the decade of the thirties. In 1934, Misses Grace Farnham, Ruth Schoonover, and Vivian Lemmon resigned from the Yotsuya Mission and began a new work in the Mabashi district, a poorer district of Tokyo.[23]

Mr. and Mrs. John T. Chase resigned from the Yotsuya Mission in 1935 because of a disagreement with Cunningham. In 1936, they went to Seoul, Korea, to give leadership to a work that had been conducted since 1923 by natives sent out by the Yotsuya Mission. The Chases were joined by Mr. and Mrs. John Hill in 1939, but both couples were forced home in 1940 by the international crisis. They left six churches, six Bible schools, a Bible institute, and several hundred Christians. The work was resumed after the war.[24]

The Jamaica Christian Mission, as an American enterprise, dates from 1938, when Luke D. Elliott went to Jamaica. Before that, a Lieutenant C. Vincent Hall, of the British army, had worked in Jamaica to establish churches there. His work, beginning in 1935, met with a good response, and he toured the United States in 1938 appealing for funds and missionaries for the island. Elliott answered Lieutenant Hall's plea to go to Jamaica and establish a Bible college. Shortly after Elliott's arrival, Lieutenant Hall dropped out of the work, presumably because of Britain's involvement in World War II.

The fourth mission field outside the continental United States to be entered in the decade of the thirties was Alaska. The first Independent work there was begun in 1936, when Franklin Smith and his family settled at Ekwak. In 1939, Charles Railsback and Harry Parsons began a separate work in Ketchikan, Alaska's largest city.[25]

A survey of the foreign missionary situation as of 1940 indicates that there were forty-eight missionaries distributed among eight foreign countries, as follows: Jamaica, two; India, three; Tibetan Border of China, eleven; Korea, four; Japan, fourteen; Philippine Islands, eight; and Alaska, four. Within the next year, war conditions forced several of this number to return to the United States, and others were located in Japanese prison camps.

The decade from 1940 to 1950 witnessed a rapid growth of missionary activity. During World War II, the Japanese ravished the Philippine and Japanese missions, and the restrictions that the war placed on travel prevented any of the mission enterprises from expanding. The single exception was Alaska. A survey of foreign missionary work made by the *Christian Standard* in 1944 indicated that there were sixty-three foreign missionaries on the field, or waiting to return as soon as hostilities ended.[26] The increase from forty-eight in 1940 to sixty-three in 1944 was due almost entirely to the growth of the Alaska enterprises, which accounted for an increase in the number of missionaries from four to seventeen in this period.

With the close of hostilities, missionaries and their eager recruits were zealous to journey to their places of service. Scores of young men returned from the armed services ready to devote their lives to carrying the gospel of Christ to the places where they formerly carried arms and ammunition. Former chaplains, like Guy Mayfield and Mark Maxey, returned immediately to the places where they had been stationed during war times. A few missionaries were dislocated during the war and began work where they were located only to remain in these places when the way was opened to return to their original fields. This is what happened in the case of the Cebu Mission and the Hawaiian Mission.

In 1927, when the abandonment of the United Society began on a significant scale, there was no way to predict the shape that the new missionary effort would take. It was by no means a certainty that total autonomy of the missionary effort would be the acceptable form of missionary operation. The Standard Publishing Company had, from time to time, offered its services as a clearinghouse/forwarding agent for various missionary and benevolent efforts, but this was clearly not a function it enjoyed or intended to fulfill on a permanent basis. Much more ambitious plans were projected by two other organizations. In 1925, the Christian Restoration Association announced that it would act as forwarding agent to receive and disburse funds for missionaries. It also offered to publicize the work of the missionaries. It disavowed any desire to control the associated missionaries.[27] At this time, it also supported home missionaries and subsidized two full-time and ten part-time instructors in The Cincinnati Bible Seminary.[28] The Christian Restoration Association published the *Restoration Herald* and anticipated publishing tracts and establishing a fund for church building and another for ministerial relief. But these plans were aborted by the economic recession and an internal shake-up. The Cincinnati Bible Seminary was separated from the Christian Restoration Association and reorganized in 1928. Another internal crisis arose over a policy change in 1933,[29] when J.D. Murch was replaced as president and editor of the the *Restoration Herald*. After a brief tenure by Leon Myers, Robert E. Elmore became editor of the C.R.A. journal, and all efforts to function as a disbursing agency ceased.

A second agency with a multiple purpose was the short-lived International Bible Mission. In 1895, Eugene C. Sanderson established Eugene (Oregon) Bible University, which expanded into a school of nursing and a hospital in Eugene, a Bible college in Seattle, Washington, and a graduate school of divinity. In 1923, all of these were incorporated into the International Bible Mission, which embraced departments of education, benevolence, religious literature, business, and American Christianization (evangelism). It published *World Evangel*. The next year it absorbed the International Christian Missionary Association[30] with its college in Minneapolis, Minnesota, and shortly opened Bible colleges in Manhattan (Kansas), Ft. Collins (Colorado), and Camden Point (Missouri), as well as several benevolent homes. But this elaborate structure was built on shaky fiscal foundations, and it collapsed with the onset of the Depression in 1929. Thereafter, Independent ventures would be single purpose activities and institutions.[31] After World War II, the Independent missionary enterprises proliferated in a way that few could have anticipated.

Educational Institutions

Colleges have always held a prominent place of interest in the movement. Because they tend to be heavily dependent upon outside resources for survival, the existing colleges were understandably cautious about cutting existing ties to the Board of Education of the Disciples of Christ. The foremost concern of the congregations that were prepared to abandon the United Society and the International Convention was to provide a ministry for the future that would avoid the pitfalls that had created the rupture. The answer to this problem was the Bible college. Several Bible colleges already existed[32] but they were not specifically aligned with either of the developing polarities. The Bible colleges established during the period under study were very much concerned with addressing the needs of Independent churches and missions.

Note was taken in the previous chapter that Ralph L. Records outlined plans for a college for ministerial training in 1921 at the Louisville Congress. In 1923, the McGarvey Bible College opened in Louisville, Kentucky, and the Cincinnati Bible Institute opened in Cincinnati, Ohio, largely through efforts of the Christian Restoration Association. The two schools merged in 1924 to form The Cincinnati Bible Seminary (now Cincinnati Bible College & Seminary).

In 1925, Atlanta Christian College was launched along much the same lines. Judge T.O. Hathcock, who had been disappointed in a previous venture with Josephus Hopwood to establish Lamar College in Atlanta, was the guiding influence and chief benefactor of Atlanta Christian College.[33] In 1927, Manhattan, Kansas, was the site chosen by Eugene Sanderson for a Bible college, and 1928 saw Pacific Christian Seminary opened in Long Beach, California.

Thereafter, the Depression effectively stopped the opening of more Bible colleges. In the entire decade of the thirties, only Alberta (Canada) Bible College and San Jose (California) Bible College were launched, both in 1932. Sixteen Bible colleges were organized in the forties, some with pitifully small enrollments. By 1950, the following colleges were identified with the Independent movement. More would be established later:

College	Date founded
Alberta Bible College	1932
Atlanta Bible College	1937

Boise Bible College	1945
Cincinnati Bible Seminary	1924
Colegio Biblico	1945
College of Scriptures	1945
Dakota Bible College	1942
Dallas Bible College	1950
Eastern Christian Institute	1946
Great Lakes Bible College	1949
Intermountain Bible College	1946
Johnson Bible College	1893
Kentucky Christian College	1919
Lincoln Bible Institute	1944
Louisville Bible College	1948
Manhattan Bible College	1927
Mexican Seminary	1950
Midwest Christian College	1946
Mid-West School of Evangelism	1947
* Milligan College	1881
Minnesota Bible College	1913
Nebraska Christian College	1945
Ozark Bible College	1942
Pacific Seminary	1928
Puget Sound Bible College	1950
Platte Valley Bible College,	1951
Roanoke Bible College	1948
San Jose Bible College	1939
Southern Christian College	1947
Southwest Christian College	1947
Winston-Salem Bible College	1950
+ Northwest Christian College	1895

* Milligan College is not a Bible college. It is included in the above list because it is affiliated with the Independent Mission enterprise.

+ Affiliated with the Board of Higher Education of Disciples of Christ after 1950.

The Bible colleges provided ministers for the congregations that became alienated from the organized agencies of the Disciples of Christ. None of the Bible colleges manifested any inclination to expand into liberal arts institutions. Milligan College in Tennessee was loosely identified with the Disciples prior to World War II. Taken over completely by the Navy Department during the War, Milligan reopened in 1945 as the only liberal arts college in the Independent Movement.

During the period under consideration, some of the Bible colleges began to consider accreditation by the accrediting association that was organized in 1947 by educators who were involved with the National Association of Evangelicals.[34] Some of the colleges were reluctant to accept membership in the association because it involved subscription to a creed, which was deemed to be contrary to their heritage, although many of them published a "statement of faith" in their catalogs. Others considered subscription to a creed to be no obstacle for a college since an institution is not a church.[35] Manhattan Bible College and Minnesota Bible College were first to join the association. In time, others concluded that the requirements imposed by accreditation were beneficial and accordingly sought membership. In later years, the Bible college accrediting association would gain recognition by the regional accrediting associations, thereby enhancing the status of its member institutions.

Publishing Facilities

If the churches of the Independent persuasion were required to develop new convention, mission, and education agencies, it was quite otherwise with publication resources. Standard Publishing had provided Sunday-school literature, young people's materials, books, and other printed materials for many years. Standard Publishing was already at the forefront in technology among publishers of religious materials. It was the first religious publisher to introduce full color production. Its Sunday-school materials found acceptance well beyond Christian Churches. Standard was able to meet all of the publishing needs of the Independent churches adequately.

Beyond simply providing publications, Standard filled a leadership role that was both applauded and criticized. The *Christian Standard* had a long history of journalistic leadership. The positions taken by the successive editors were carefully considered by ministers and lay leaders alike. *The Lookout,* published since 1894,[36] was read weekly by students in thousands of Bible schools. The *Christian Endeavor Quarterly* and other youth publications from Standard Publishing, as well as books about the movement, met the literature needs of the churches and also provided a much-needed cohesive factor in the period from 1927 to 1950. The company was owned by Russell Errett, the son of the founder, who managed it until his death in 1929. Russell Errett's will provided that ownership of the company should pass to a committee that would hold it in the name of the churches, indemnifying the family over a period of years. The family contested the will, which was found to have been improperly executed, and thereby retained ownership of the company until 1955, when it was sold to John Bolton, who later incorporated it into Standex International.

The guiding influence at Standard Publishing Company during the period following Memphis was Edwin R. Errett, who edited the *Christian Standard* from 1929 until his death in 1944. Edwin R. Errett was a second cousin of Russell Errett. He had been educated at Bethany and Yale and knew personally many men who were leading the organizations in a direction that he could not endorse. Errett was committed to the whole Brotherhood and was an enthusiastic supporter of the Pension Fund, the Board of Church Extension, and the National Benevolent Association. However, he strongly disapproved of the United Christian Society and staunchly maintained that the United Society was not the Brotherhood, but was only one agency within the whole Brotherhood. He regretted a tendency to allow this, or any other, agency to divide the Brotherhood. He stated his position clearly:

> In our judgment, the peril we always face is not merely the continued existence of "a United Society denomination," but the creation of an anti-United Society denomination, if you please. . . .
> For that reason the CHRISTIAN STANDARD is following a policy of recognizing as brethren all who give evidence of being sincere believers in Christ as Lord and Saviour and seekers for New Testament Christianity, regardless of their position on the United Society. We refuse to make the United Society a test of fellowship.[37]

Errett was interested in the ecumenical efforts that led to the formation after World War II of the World Council of Churches. He believed that advocates of New Testament Christianity had something to contribute and ought to be heard. He was a delegate to the World Conference on Faith and Order in Denmark in 1935 and again in Edinburg in 1937. He maintained a heavy speaking schedule and still found time to teach evening courses in The Cincinnati Bible Seminary.

Youth Activities

The rise of the Christian Endeavor movement at the turn of the century tended to focus the attention of all churches on the importance of youth in the life of the church. Local societies of Christian Endeavor were linked in interdenominational conferences and conventions. The various mainline denominations were quick to capture their own youth in denominational organizations, which eventually brought about the decline of Christian Endeavor. However, Christian churches, of both Disciple and Independent leanings, generally participated in Christian Endeavor during the twenties and thirties.

The distinctive feature of youth activity that was developed by the churches that turned away from the older organized agencies during this period was the Christian Service Camp. The story of the origin of the camp movement is best told by Mildred Welshimer Phillips, who was actively involved from the beginning.

> A group of young people met in 1924 for the first Christian Service Camp under the leadership of Judge T.O. Hathcock and Jerry Johnson. Following a youth session in an evangelistic rally in the Richmond Street Church in Cincinnati, Ohio, December 6 through 10, 1926, James DeForest Murch presented a plan for a nationwide series of Christian Service Camps. The gathering gave the plan its endorsement.
>
> Mr. Murch and his associates used the Georgia camp for their pattern in laying their plans for the summer of 1927. Five Christian Service Camps were held that year. The largest and most successful of the group was the one held at Erieside, near Willoughby, Ohio.
>
> While Mr. Murch and his group were pleased at the progress made, they realized there were many problems to be solved. There was no general plan of organization which could be furnished churches and groups who desired to start new camps. Accordingly, a call was issued for a meeting of interested parties to convene in the Hotel English, Indianapolis, Indiana between the sessions of the first North American Convention held in that city, October 12, 1927. After much discussion, the following committees were appointed to meet in Cincinnati, November 29, their findings to be final: General Committee—James DeForest Murch, Chairman: Robert S. Tuck, J. Merle Applegate, John S. Raum and Guy P. Leavitt. Curriculum Committee—W.R. Walker, Chairman; Edwin R. Errett and Henrietta Heron.
>
> The name "Christian Service Camp" was not lightly chosen. The leaders did not want it to be called "Leadership Training Camp" for they want the young people to return to their local churches not feeling they have more authority than others and therefore may dictate, but want them to return as real servants of Christ. The local church has always been held up in the camps as the place for the young people to begin to work.
>
> The Christian Service Camps did not come into existence in opposition to the conferences already sponsored by the United Christian Missionary Society, but rather because a need was felt by many for the type of teaching which the conferences were not giving.
>
> Each individual camp has come into existence because the leaders in the vicinity wanted a camp where the young people's faith would be strengthened and where they would be indoctrinated. They feel that our young people have a great challenge, but they need help to restore the New Testament Church, therefore they want the young

people to understand the plan of it and to be enthused in helping to bring about the unity for which Christ prayed.

Every student who attends a Christian Service Camp must take so many Bible courses and have an understanding of the history of the Restoration Movement.

There is no central board. Each camp is a unit in itself yet there is great similarity among them all, but this has all been spontaneous.[38]

Christian Service camps continued to grow and develop throughout the period under examination and into subsequent years. They followed a different line of development from the Leadership Conferences for Youth, sponsored by the Disciples of Christ. The effect was to separate the youth of the churches into two groups that were mutually unacquainted with each other.

Benevolence

Note has already been taken of the establishment of the National Benevolent Association (chapter 9). This agency was amalgamated into the U.C.M.S. in 1919 and separated from it in 1933. It was never directly involved in the doctrinal controversies that centered in the missionary enterprise, so the churches that separated from the United Society generally had little reason to cease support of the N.B.A. Consequently, relatively few benevolent agencies that were outside the National Benevolent Association came into being in the period from 1926 until 1950.

The oldest of the benevolent institutions outside the N.B.A. is the Christian Women's Benevolent Association. Located in St. Louis, Missouri, it was organized in 1911 and is operated by a board of directors consisting mostly of women. This association operates three institutions in St. Louis: the Christian Mother's and Babies' Home (established in 1899), Christian Hospital (established in 1903), and Christian Old People's Home (established in 1910).

The Mountain Mission School was founded in 1921 by Sam R. Hurley, in Grundy, Virginia. It has served orphaned and needy children of the Appalachian area ever since by providing shelter and school facilities. The school is governed today by a board of trustees.

The Turner Memorial Home was founded in Turner, Oregon, in 1933 to care for the aged. It is operated on the cottage plan and preference is given to ministers and missionaries.

Children's homes were opened in Boise, Idaho, and Elizabethton, Tennessee, in 1946. Both of these institutions came into being through the initiative of the local church in these cities, and both appealed for assistance from nearby congregations.

The Kentucky Christian Widows and Orphans Home was established in Louisville in 1884 by action of the state convention and
was never affiliated with the N.B.A. It was supported during the
period under study by the churches of the state regardless of their
position on the missionary and other issues, and it served all of the
congregations of the state.

Evangelistic Associations

Evangelism has always been a high-priority concern among the
churches that lost confidence in the organized enterprises of the
Disciples of Christ. Indeed, one of the complaints often heard was
that the agencies of the Disciples were no longer interested in evangelism, this despite the fact that there came into being a National
Evangelistic Association that met annually on the day preceding the
opening of the International Convention. But Independents, who no
longer attended the International Convention and were not involved
in the National Evangelistic Association, quite naturally joined in
common efforts in their communities to establish new congregations
and strengthen weaker ones. These initiatives took the form of associations for evangelism and new church establishment. The oldest of
these evangelistic associations still in existence is the Chicago District Evangelistic Association, which was organized in 1922 through
the efforts of C.G. Kindred and C.J. Sharp.[39] This association
employs evangelists and raises building funds for congregations in
northern Indiana and Illinois.

The Christian Evangelistic Association of Allegheny County
(Pittsburgh), Pennsylvania, was organized in 1929, and the
Appalachian Mountain Evangelizing Association began its work in
1930. Then came the Virginia Evangelizing Fellowship, organized in
1939; the Coal Belt Evangelistic Association (Southern Illinois),
1943; KYOWVA (Kentucky-Ohio-West Virginia) Evangelizing Association, 1943; New Churches of Christ Evangelism (Michigan),
1948; Go Ye Chapel Mission (New York City), 1948; and NOAH
(Northeastern Ohio Association of Helpers), 1948. An era of proliferation of evangelistic associations came in the period after 1950.[40]

The period under scrutiny, 1927-1950, was a turbulent period in
American history. It includes the Roaring Twenties, the Great
Depression, the Second World War, and the postwar adjustments.
This period witnessed dramatic changes in American religious life.
The period opened with the Modernist-Fundamentalist controversy
in full fury. The outbreak of war and dreadful atrocities that came
to public attention brought about a marked change in the nature of

religious thinking. The rise of neo-Orthodox theology and the general revival of interest in religious values created a religious climate by midcentury that was challenging and exciting. Christian Churches shared fully in the renewed vitality of post-World War II religious activity. Because they had developed all of the needed institutions and agencies for carrying on a separate churchly program utterly independent of the old agencies and institutions of the Disciples, it was easy for Independents to ride the crest of the wave of popular religious enthusiasm while at the same time completing their separation from the Disciples with little discomfort, save in a number of local congregations. By 1950, the dream of preserving the unity of a people who half a century earlier had been so confident of their future was fading away.

End Notes

[1]See the Introduction above.

[2]See James B. Hunter, *A History of the North American Christian Convention* (Indianapolis: Butler University School of Religion [Christian Theological Seminary], unpublished Bachelor of Divinity thesis, 1950).

[3]See discussion in the next chapter.

[4]"A Grand Reunion to Honor the Plea," *Christian Standard*, February 26, 1927, p. 1.

[5]Mark Collis, "The Convention Proposed for This Fall," *Christian Standard*, March 19, 1927, p. 5.

[6]For a listing of dates, places, and presidents of the North American Christian Convention, see Appendix 1.

[7]For an account of the activities of the C.R.A. at this time, see James DeForest Murch, *Adventuring for Christ* (Louisville: Restoration Press, 1973), pp. 69-95.

[8]Mrs. W.D. Cunningham and Mrs. Owen Still, *The Flaming Torch* (Tokyo: Yotsuya Mission, 1939), p. 28.

[9]Minutes of Executive Committee Meeting of Christian Women's Board of Missions, July 17, 1901, *Missionary Tidings*, September, 1901, p. 138.

[10]Cunningham and Still, op. cit., p. 33.

[11]Ibid., pp. 36-44.

[12]Ibid., p. 49.

[13]Herbert Monninger, *Training for Service* (Cincinnati: Standard Publishing, 1907).

[14]W.D. Cunningham, "An Enterprise That Has Proved Its Worth" *Christian Standard*, November 8, 1919, p. 149.

[15]George P. Rutledge, "To the Rescue of the Mexican Mission," June 14, 1919, pp. 8, 9; November 1, 1919, p. 11.

16James B. Carr, *The Foreign Mission Work of the Christian Church* (Manhattan: published by the author, 1946), p. 141.

17Guy Humphries, *African Christian Mission,* pamphlet, (Cincinnati: African Christian Mission, n.d.), pp. 12-16.

18Mark Maxey, "History of the Christian Mission in the Philippine Islands" (Cincinnati: Cincinnati Bible Seminary, unpublished Bachelor of Divinity thesis, 1943), pp. 60-107. The issue of the Wolfes is also discussed in the previous chapter of the present work.

19Harry Schaefer, "Christ Is All Sufficient," *The Restoration Herald,* January 1944, p. 11.

20S.G. and L.S. Rothermel, *Open Letter to the Churches,* 1926 (copy on file at the Butler University School of Religion Library, Indianapolis, Indiana).

21Carr, op. cit., p. 123.

22*Biography and History of Independent Missionaries and Agencies* (Angola: Lake James School of Missions), pp. 7, 8.

23Ibid., p. 32.

24Carr, op. cit., p. 144.

25Fred Hoy, ed., *Bulletin of All Alaskan Mission Committee,* Inglewood, December, 1944.

26"Missions: Evangelism Plus Geography," *Christian Standard,* December 16, 1944, pp. 1, 5-7, 16.

27*Christian Standard,* January 3, 1925.

28The work of the Christian Restoration Association is thus described in a thirty-two-page booklet on file in Disciples of Christ Historical Society, Nashville, Tennessee.

29See J.D. Murch, "A Change of Policy," *Restoration Herald,* October, 1933, p. 2.

30The International Christian Missionary Association was a home mission agency organized to evangelize the various national groups, largely Scandanavian, that were to be found in Minnesota.

[31]An exception is the Christian Missionary Fellowship. Although it was incorporated in 1949, it did not engage in multiple-field operations until several years after this date.

[32]Johnson Bible College, 1893; Eugene Bible University, 1895; Minnesota Bible College, 1913, originally intended to train workers for evangelism among immigrants.

[33]For further details see R. Edwin Groover, "T.O. Hathcock: The Judge and His Work" (Milligan College, TN: Emmanuel School of Religion, unpublished Master of Divinity Thesis, 1972).

[34]See *United Evangelical Action,* June 15, 1953, p. 19.

[35]In 1912, Phillips Bible Institute opened in Canton, Ohio. It published a "Statement of Faith," which was immediately labeled a "creed" and condemned as a departure from the heritage of the Disciples. A considerable controversy followed. See *The Christian Evangelist,* April 2, April 30, 1914; *Christian Standard,* April 18, April 25, 1914; *Christian Century,* July 30, 1914.

[36]Previous to this date it had been published as *Young Peoples Standard,* 1884-1894.

[37]Edwin R. Errett, "Editorial Response [to 'A Letter from R.E. Elmore']," *Christian Standard,* June 6, 1936, p. 4.

[38]Mildred W. Phillips, Letter to Leon Kidd. The full text of this letter is available in Henry E. Webb, *A History of the Independent Mission Movement of the Disciples of Christ* (Louisville: Southern Baptist Theological Seminary, unpublished Ph.D. thesis, 1954), pp. 223, 224.

[39]The C.D.E.A. was the heir of an earlier cooperative known as the Chicago-Calumet Evangelistic Association. Between 1922 and 1928, the C.D.E.A. established fifty-five churches in the Chicago area. See Alan J. White, "The Chicago District Evangelistic Association," *Restoration Papers,* Vol. 17 (Milligan College Library).

[40]A study of the formation and work of evangelistic associations was made by Seth Wilson. Some of his findings were published in three parts in the *Christian Standard,* September 2, 1973, pp. 8, 9; September 9, 1973, pp. 15, 16; September 16, 1973, pp. 13, 14.

Chapter Thirteen

Efforts to Preserve Unity

As tensions long rife within the Brotherhood were creating obvious polarities, the more sensitive leaders of both groups became increasingly aware of the baneful possibilities for outright schism. Since the turn of the century, the noninstrument Churches of Christ had been charting their own course with decreasing concern for the larger body, and they were manifesting considerable growth. Each passing year saw fewer contacts between these churches and the others in the larger segment of the movement. Many committed Disciples genuinely lamented this breach in the fellowship.

Meanwhile, the reactions to the Memphis Convention in 1926 gave increasing reason to believe that the gathering was to be a fork in the road that would cause congregations to go in one of two separate directions. Two different kinds of missionary activities were practiced. Two different kinds of college programs were being promoted. The two leading Brotherhood journals were supporting one or the other of these differences. Many thoughtful persons recognized that, unless these tendencies were checked, an outright division in the Brotherhood was inevitable. They demanded that the International Convention make an effort to analyze the problem and attempt to cope with the difficulties involved. Consequently, a resolution was introduced into the 1934 International Convention at Des Moines, Iowa, authorizing the appointment of a Commission to Restudy the Disciples of Christ. The resolution said:

> In view of the passion for unity which gave birth to the brotherhood of Disciples of Christ; in view of the irenic spirit which characterized our early movement; in view of the many union movements arising in Protestant Christianity; in view of the need of an aroused passion for unity among ourselves and in further view of the new frontiers and of the new challenge which the world is giving to the

church for a deeper spiritual interpretation of God and the Gospel faced not only by the Disciples of Christ but by all other communions;

It is hereby recommended that after a century and a quarter of history the convention, by its regularly constituted methods, appoint a commission to restudy the origin, history, slogans, methods, successes and failures of the movement of the Disciples of Christ, and with the purpose of a more effective and a more united program and closer Christian fellowship among us.

The Commission, which will be appointed shall be composed of twenty members, proportionately representing the varied phases and schools of thought in the institutional life among us.

It is recommended that this committee proceed at once to restudy our whole Disciple movement and, if possible, to recommend a future program.[1]

The original membership consisted of the following men:

E.S. Ames	Edgar DeWitt Jones
L.D. Anderson	F.D. Kershner
H.G. Armstrong	C.E. Lemmon
F.W. Burnham	R.H. Miller
George A. Campbell	C.C. Morrison
Homer W. Carpenter	William F. Rothenburger
C.M. Chilton	Willard E. Shelton
A.E. Cory	George H. Stewart
Edwin R. Errett	W.E. Sweeney
A.W. Fortune	L.N.D. Wells
Graham Frank	P.H. Welshimer

Subsequent additions were as follows:
1936
W.E. Garrison
Dean E. Walker

1939*
Claude E. Hill
Robert S. Tuck

1942
Eugene C. Beach   Orval Morgan
R.M. Bell   James DeForest Murch

*T.K. Smith and George W. Buckner were also added to the commission sometime after its beginning. Both are listed in the 1938 *Yearbook of Disciples of Christ*. Precisely when they joined is not clear, however, as the yearbook did not list the members prior to 1938.

1942 (continued)

J.H. Dampier	M.E. Sadler
Virgil Elliot	O.L. Shelton
Stephen J. England	G. Gerald Sias
Henry G. Harmon	J.J. Whitehouse
Hugh B. Kilgour	

Officers of the commission were as follows:

F.D. Kershner, chairman	1935-1943
R.H. Miller, chairman	1943-1946
O.L. Shelton, chairman	1946-1949
T.K. Smith, vice chairman	1946-1949
William F. Rothenburger, secretary	1935-1949
William F. Rothenburger, treasurer	1935-1945
Dean E. Walker, treasurer	1945-1949

The commission that this resolution established worked long and conscientiously. It met three times each year. Two of these meetings were devoted to study and the third was given largely to business matters. Serious differences of opinion surfaced during these meetings, and much effort was given to refining understanding and defining positions with a view toward isolating the differences and bringing to the fore issues of genuine substance. It was obvious that there were basic philosophic conflicts within the movement and these differences soon became apparent in the membership of the commission.[2] Very wisely, the commission proceeded to focus attention upon points of agreement prior to elucidating points at variance. Extensive deliberation was given to insure the accurate representation of divergent views.

The committee made its first substantive report to the International Convention in 1946 in Columbus, Ohio. This report is sufficiently relevant to the events of this crucial period to warrant extensive reproduction and careful reading. Note that the format recognizes the matters of contention and then discerns areas of agreement before proceeding to a careful definition of the opposing positions. Seldom had such a carefully reasoned survey been produced. Any attempt to understand the issues that were crucial to the events leading to ultimate division in the movement must carefully consider this report.

I. Denomination or Movement?

It is agreed that in our inception we were a movement rather than a denomination; that historically we have endeavored to avoid denominational status; and that to be content with occupying a status as one among many denominations is to abandon our attempt to realize unsectarian Christianity.

Some of us hold that we must therefore refuse to accept any denominational status, and rather seek to occupy non-partisan and ultimate ground in all points of faith and order.

Others hold that we are compelled by the existing order of Protestant denominationalism to be a denomination, while at the same time testifying against denominationalism and exploring all possibilities of finding common ground on which all Christians may stand.

Still others, in the judgment of this commission few in number, hold that we have in the processes of history become a denomination, possessing peculiarities and identity in a manner similar to the denominations round about us.

II. Local Church Autonomy

We are agreed that from the beginning we have emphasized the autonomy of the local church.

Some among us hold that there is a tendency on the part of the agencies and conventions to assume and to exercise authority over the local churches.

Others interpret the utterances and policies of the agencies and conventions as, in the main, the exercise of the responsibility of leadership which the churches desire them to undertake and to which the churches respond voluntarily with no sense of constraint by official authority.

III. The New Testament Church

We are agreed that the New Testament affords the sufficient basis and norm of evangelism and church life. But there are differences of understanding at certain points as to what the New Testament requires. The differences arise largely from two considerations. The first has to do with the bearing of the New Testament upon the structure of the local church.

Some among us find in the New Testament the divinely authoritative pattern for the form and organization of the local church, and affirm that, historically, we set out to restore this New Testament pattern and that our local churches essentially represent its restoration.

Others among us recognize in the New Testament certain *principles* which inherently belong to any local church that calls itself Christian, but they do not find any evidence that the particular *forms* of organization or procedure prevailing in the primitive church, were authoritatively prescribed as a pattern which the Christian church is obligated to reproduce in detail, everywhere and throughout all time.

The second consideration has to do with the relations among local churches. We are agreed that the New Testament distinctly discloses a clear conception of the *Church* as distinguished from the local churches and a profound sense of interdependence among all the churches. But the New Testament gives no clear evidence of an organization of local churches in a general or connexional relationship. From these facts two alternative conclusions are drawn.

Some believe that our churches would therefore deviate from the New Testament norm should they (1) recognize such a relationship, or (2) consent to create a recognized agency as their exclusive instrument for the united administration of their missionary or benevolent enterprises, or (3) create a single representative convention or council for the formation and expression of their united convictions on (a) matters which concern the churches and their agencies, or (b) our witness to Christian unity, or (c) our witness to the gospel in relation to the moral and human problems of our time. But they would leave to the brethren freedom to create any number of agencies for the expression of any or all of these above ends, as may seem to them expedient.

Others believe that the absence of an authoritative pattern leaves the churches free, and their relation to each other in the *Church* renders it their duty, (a) to create such agencies or organs as may be needed in order unitedly to carry on their missionary and benevolent enterprises and their plea for Christian unity in the most adequate and responsible manner; and (b) to constitute a genuinely representative convention or council through which the united voice of the brotherhood may be expressed—provided, always, that such agencies or organs and such convention or council shall not be clothed with nor allowed to assume any independent authority over the churches, but shall operate only under the consent of the churches whose rightful duty it is to participate in the democratic process by which their consent is enlisted and expressed.

IV. Conventions

We are agreed that our conventions have a highly important place in the life of our churches. As occasions for fellowship and witness-bearing, they have served to enlarge the vision of the local churches by exchange of views and experiences and by keeping the churches conscious of belonging to one another. We are also agreed that our people have not yet found a type of convention which fully satisfies their tradition, their convictions and their sense of obligation to give united expression to the interests of Christ's kingdom. The dissatisfaction which we all share has, however, in recent years, found expression in the holding of other conventions sponsored by those who desire to protest against certain features of the existing International Conventions, as well as to exemplify, by contrast, a convention of a different type.

This development is an expression of the dissatisfaction and is also a cause of tension and of possible peril to the unity of our brotherhood. We believe that the sponsors of the North American Convention deplore what seemed to them, in good conscience, the necessity of holding another type of assemblage. In view of the dissatisfaction, not only on the part of dissenters, but of supporters also, it seems evident that the brotherhood has a clear call to provide itself with a convention that will unite our people wholeheartedly, instead of tending to divide them.

V. Unity and Restoration

We are agreed that from our beginning we have cherished no purpose more steadfastly than to exercise a potent influence on behalf of Christian unity. Our movement began under this impulsion, and the passion for the unity of the whole church has never been lost. We are agreed, however, that we stand in need of Christ's forgiveness that our witness on behalf of this great consummation has not been more consistently proclaimed and, especially, more appealingly exemplified. We are embarrassed in our testimony and humbled in our hearts by the divisions that have already occurred in our own fellowship, and by the present tensions which gave rise to the creation of our commission.

Our study of the history and ideals of our people has led us to the conclusion that a basic cause of our divisions and our serious dissensions, both past and recent, lies in a difference of understanding with respect to the fundamental purpose of our movement.

Our commission agrees that the two concepts of unity and restoration have been, from the beginning, held together in a parity of mutual dependence. The fathers believed that they had discovered in the New Testament the pattern of the true church, that this pattern was authoritative for the Church of Christ in all time, and that Christian unity could be attained only by its restoration. Throughout our history this conception of our plea has persisted. During the past half century, however, in the thinking of a considerable section of our people, the ideals of union and restoration have tended to fall apart as two concepts that are not coordinate or mutually dependent. This, the commission believes, is a principal cause of the major dissensions which disturb us.

Some among us maintain that these two conceptions of union and restoration must be held together, essentially unchanged, in the form in which we traditionally conceived them. It is affirmed that Christian unity is possible only on the basis of the restoration of the primitive church in this form.

Others among us are content to abandon the concept of the restoration of the primitive church and center our emphasis upon union.

Still others believe that a new synthesis of these two concepts of unity and restoration is possible which would avoid, on the one hand, the too dogmatic claim that we alone have restored the New Testament church and, on the other hand, the indifferentism that regards the restoration concept as irrelevant to Christian unity.

VI. Baptism

Our churches have from the beginning administered the ordinance of baptism by the immersion in water of a penitent believer. Our study discloses no appreciable tendency among our churches to abandon or modify this practice. It has also been our practice, in the case of unimmersed members of other churches who sought membership with us, to receive them only on condition of their acceptance of immersion. A considerable number of our churches have, however, modified our traditional procedure at this point by receiving such applicants into membership without raising the question of baptism. This practice, commonly called "open membership," is one of the causes of tension among us.

Some hold that, under the authority of Christ we have no right to receive any who have not been scripturally baptized, and that we are bound to apply this principle to the penitent believer and the unimmersed Christian without discrimination. It is maintained that any such discrimination is a surrender of the witness which we have been called to bear with respect to the scriptural action of baptism.

Others hold that in making the distinction between a penitent believer and one who brings credentials from a sister church of Christ, they are acting under the authority of Christ. They believe that inasmuch as Christ has received such a person into the membership of his church, they would be disloyal to Christ in not recognizing the full status of such a person as a Christian, a member of the Church of Christ, and receiving him as such without re-baptism, unless he desires to be re-baptized.

Among those who hold this view and practice it, are many who testify that, instead of surrendering or weakening our witness to immersion, it enhances it.

VII. In Faith, Unity

Our brotherhood has from the beginning rested upon a broad basis. It represented a revolt against the divisive use of human creeds as terms of admittance into the church and as authoritatively bound upon its ministers and members. In place of such creeds, there was adopted a simple, scriptural and truly catholic creed, namely, faith in Jesus Christ as the Son of God and man's Savior. A declaration of faith in the divine Lordship of Christ was the only confession required for membership in the Church or for ordination of ministry. This faith represented not a belief about Him in terms of the historic creeds, but was a simple acceptance of the fact of His divinity and a spiritual and moral attitude toward Him. In our study of contemporary thought among our people, we have found two tendencies in the matter of faith which are a cause of tension and a peril to our unity.

Some among us seem to have abandoned the theological implications in the simple confession of Christ, and have come to regard His Lordship chiefly and essentially in ethical terms. He is the supreme moral and spiritual leader of mankind, and the confession of faith in Him is essentially a decision to follow His way of life.

Others go to the other extreme and seem to confound faith with doctrine. They insist that the Lordship of Christ must be interpreted theologically, and that their particular interpretation must be made explicit in the confession as the basis of our fellowship and unity.

Thus the traditional simple formula of faith which was to guarantee our unity as a people is challenged from two sides. From one side, by those who would abandon its implicit theological connotation; from the other, by those who would make their own particular theological connotation explicit as a basis of unity. Between these two schools of thought the main body of our people continue to use the scriptural confession without specific interpretation.

VIII. In Opinions, Liberty

The breadth of our conception of unity on the basis of the Lordship of Christ left a large place for diversity in the realm of opinion—both as to creedal opinion and practical or procedural opinion. In this field, the fathers hoped that a common loyalty to Christ would produce such "charity in all things" that disagreements and diversity of opinion would not impair the unity and complete fellowship of our churches. Our study of the past and the present has led us to the unhappy conclusion that we have, in practice, fallen far below their high hopes and the standard under which they summoned us to march together.

Our commission is unanimous in affirming the soundness of the two principles of unity in faith and liberty in opinion. That these principles were wrong or mistaken is, to us, unthinkable. But the divisions that have already taken place, and the dissension that exists among us today, plainly call for a re-examination of the principles upon which our movement was launched and of the spirit in which we have proclaimed and exemplified them. Such a re-examination we have been making in the deliberations of our commission.

Conclusion

In view of the situation as thus analyzed and summarized in this report, we recommend to the International Convention that our commission be continued in order that it may further explore the matters referred to herein and extend its studies into other areas in which the unity of our people may be threatened. We recommend also that the commission be authorized to incorporate the results of its study in an extended report, the precise nature and form of which would be detemined by the commission in the light of its further study.

We also recommend and invite a general and open discussion in our press, on our convention platforms and in the boards of our agencies, of the questions indicated in our present report, and any other questions relevant to our unity. We wish the brotherhood to know that the spirit of mutual considcration, respect and brotherly trust has drawn the members of our commission, representing the diversities of opinion existing among us, into an exceedingly precious fellowship. It is our highest desire and our prayer that the spirit which characteizes the fellowship within our commission might be spread throughout the entire brotherhood as it pursues the discussion of these matters to which we have given, and if so ordered, will continue to give, our best thought and devotion.

Unanimously adopted by the commission at its meeting in Indianapolis, July 11, 1946.[3]

The following year, the report of the commission to the International Convention listed a number of significant points of agreement between the differing groups.

We find that the great body of Disciples agree that:

1. The acknowledgment of Jesus Christ as Lord and Saviour is the sole affirmation of faith necessary to the fellowship of Christians.

2. The New Testament is the primary source of our knowledge concerning the will of God and the revelation of God in Christ, and is the authoritative scripture by which the will of God is conveyed to men.

3. Each local church is, under Christ, a self-governing unit; that organizations and agencies are in no sense governing bodies but may be useful instruments in carrying on Christian work and in fostering and expressing fellowship; that likewise congregations and individuals have the inherent right to initiate and carry on Christian work through directly supported enterprises without breach of the wider fellowship; and that the unity of the whole church in faith, fellowship and service is to be earnestly sought.

4. In the proclamation of the gospel of Christ as the message of salvation to the affection and intelligence of men, we have found our largest unity. The Great Commission demands that to make this "one world" we must first make it God's world, by the universal acceptance of Christ as Saviour. This acceptance of Christ can be attained only by the recovery of the apostolic passion for the proclamation of the message, regarding the method as incidental. "That the world may be saved" is our only hope of unity. The message of salvation in Christ is the only business of the Church.

5. The unity of Christians according to the program and prayer of our Lord, with Christ Himself the center of that unity, by the restoration of New Testament Christianity, is necessary to the realization of God's program for human redemption.

6. Their historical position has given them practical insight into the New Testament fellowship which they desire to share with the whole divided body of Christ.

In the light of this body of unifying principles and sentiments of faith and practice, the Commission has come to the conclusion that we ought to take courage, and address ourselves to active endeavors to magnify our unity and rally our people to ardent advocacy of these central agreements. The Commission therefore proposes:

1. That, recognizing that the unity of the Church must be maintained by constant care, all who occupy positions of trust in both congregations and general work, might well examine their work in the light of the above unifying center.

2. That we all seek opportunities of expressing our conviction that diversity of methods in Christian activities is no barrier to the fellowship of Christian men.

3. That we all magnify our agreement in belief of the Gospel—"in faith unity": here there must be unity; and all grant freedom in opinions and methods—"in opinions liberty": here there must be liberty; and in charity and Christian love each must seek to excel the other.

4. That, since the Word of God transmitted to us in the New Testament is of primary significance to the Church, we all give ourselves to a continuous study of the New Testament Church in respect to its origin and nature, its structure and function, its mission and hope.

In loyalty to Jesus Christ, we believe, lies the hope of unity for the whole Church of Christ. To accept, let alone advocate division, would be, we believe, supreme disloyalty to our Lord. To give ourselves to advocacy of unity as encompassed above is, we believe, our mission in loyalty to our Lord.[4]

Although acutely aware of serious differences that existed within the fellowship of the movement, the members of the commission were persuaded that the continued unity of the Brotherhood was not only possible but highly desirable and desperately urgent. Having refocused their attention on the basic genius of the movement, which provided a breadth of liberty based upon a common conviction of the lordship of Jesus Christ, the members of the commission felt that the divisive differences in the Brotherhood were challenges to be met and overcome rather than impossible obstacles that could result only in a severance of fellowship. The commission's report to the 1948 Convention reflects genuine concern and desperate urgency.

The Commission would record its judgment that the most immediate problems requiring our attention in order to the preservation and development of our unity may be reduced to the following statements:

Our first major problem is to distinguish carefully the nature of our agreements and differences.

We are forced to recognize in the analyses of 1946 and 1947, that our differences deal with matters of relative emphasis, and our agreements with matters of basic importance. The differences lie in the realm of history, of theology, of application of principles to the problems of the church, of methods in labor and co-operation. The agreements are in the area of fact, of faith, and of doctrine. The differences touch only the periphery of the Christian life, but the agreements are at its center.

We hold that the divisive differences are obstacles to be overcome, while our agreements are foundations on which to build. These agreements speak of the person of Jesus Christ, confession of whom as Son of God, Lord and Savior, is the sole affirmation of faith necessary to the fellowship of Christians; of the definitive place which the New Testament holds in our personal religious lives and in the work of the Church; of the Church itself as Christ's body, making a reality on earth of the fellowship of those who are Christ's; of the unfinished business before the Church in the persons of those who have not heard or have not heeded the Gospel of Christ; and of the absolute necessity of unity among Christians as a condition to the answer of Christ's prayer that the world may believe. These matters of agreement are neither few nor trivial. They lie at the center of the faith that constitutes us a people, and a people of God.

Our second major problem is to discover, maintain and enjoy fellowship.

The discord, hatred and bitterness which evidences the alienation of this age from God, the desolation of this present world, would seem to be warning enough that God abandons to their destruction those who live in strife. We would, therefore, that our brethren seize quickly upon whatever fellowship we may have, that by cultivation we may enrich it; and that under the healing rays of the light of Christ it may be purified; so that we may exemplify the reconciled community of him whose ministry was the breaking of the walls of partition among men.

Fellowship among Christians is based on the relation they sustain to Christ. It is, therefore, personal, not organizational; religious—personal commitment to Christ—not theological; moral, not legal. The sole element of constraint is the love of Christ. Nothing must be permitted to obscure this high view of fellowship. At the same time, we may rightly appropriate all practical means of expressing this fellowship. Among such means we may note the various agencies for

Christian work; direct participation by a local church in work beyond its own community; and attempts to make Christianity "one community" in fact, such as the "ecumenical movement." Each such activity may be interpreted on a subpersonal level, and so be evil; each may express an extension to personality, and so be Christian.

Our third major problem lies in educating our people to the realization, intellectually and practically, of the nature of our movement.

We cannot think of our brotherhood as a sect, but think of it rather as a demonstration of that unity to which Christ has called his whole Church. The historic distinctiveness of our people is not of our will, but has been made necessary in order that we may appropriate unto salvation the instruments of Christ's appointment for his Church. To these appointments, of belief, of ordinance, of doctrine, of polity, we lay no exclusive claim. Within these appointments we seek the unity of his Church and the salvation of men.

When we plead for the unity of the Church, it is not alone unity for unity's sake; when we plead for the Good Confession of Christ as the sole creedal requirement, it is not merely for the abolition of human creeds; but this plea for unity in faith is in order that Christ may be unobscured and that the world may believe in him, and be saved.

We are therefore persuaded that at no time has the demand been more imperative than now for a demonstration of the sufficiency and catholicity of the New Testament Church as the divine agent in human redemption.

We Therefore Sound a Call to All Disciples

That we sink into oblivion the particularisms which divide us as a people, and rally ourselves to a supreme and common effort for the realization of Christian unity, beginning each one with himself. Let each examine himself in respect to the teachings of the New Testament in his personal and corporate life. Let each one hear again the Gospel, and judge again his attitudes and sentiments, his programs and procedures, his thoughts and deeds—whether these things flow from the preaching of Christ and him crucified. Let us be no less concerned that our co-operative life shall relate itself to these same standards. Let each agency and congregation examine its stewardship, and so form and declare its policies and activities that all may rejoice in their manifest loyalty to the spirit and mandate of Christ's New Covenant.

That we evaluate our differences by treating them for what they really are, opinions which are subjects for free and open discussion, and which all are free to accept or to reject, answering only to Christ. To make these divergences from our central agreements more than this is to fall into the sin of sectarianism, and by overvaluing, actually devalue the silences of the Bible wherein we find liberty.

That we rise to a new sense of our mission to the Church and our mission to the world, noting their essential interdependence; for only if the Churches hear our Lord's prayer for unity may we expect the world to believe. Let us remember the holy purpose calling our movement into existence—the nations must wait in ignorance and destruction for Christians to unite. How can we today, standing under the impending world tragedy, do less than throw ourselves unreservedly into the one divinely commissioned business of the Church—and, using whatever means and methods may commend themselves to our Christian intelligence, seek to reach all this generation's unreached with the Gospel of our blessed Lord. We mean not alone the first proclamation of the Gospel to those who have not heard—but the continued preaching to those who have not heeded. We would reach with the Gospel those in the Church "who having ears, hear not"; we would reach the architects of our social order; we would reach all the people in all their affairs, that they may all pass under the judgment of the Gospel. Let us not be preoccupied with the dangers of disunity, but lift our eyes from the deadly concern we have for our particularistic preferences, and take to a desperate world the Gospel of its redemption! We live in this hour as men on borrowed time. Can we expend it, under God, on less than the most urgent work? Cannot we as a people point the way by our agreements to the unity of a Church resurgent, consecrated only to the Gospel of reconciliation with God through Christ Jesus, furnished in the grace of God with power to win the whole world? To do less, as we judge, is to forfeit our heritage as Disciples; nay, is to be found false stewards of the mystery of the faith.

In a time of sectarian strife, we were called into being as a people to bear witness to the unity of the Church without which its divine task could not be accomplished. Now again in a critical time of confusion we see the Church recognizing the impotency of division and seeking the power of unity. The Church will hear us now, and be restored to her might, if we but give clear voice to that plea to "unite for the conversion of the world." This is the dynamic of our mission.

We close with a fervent prayer, that God may grant us the grace of his Providence, that our concern for lost men may so burden our souls that we shall find no rest until the Church is united for the world's redemption, through the Gospel of Jesus Christ as proclaimed in the New Testament.[5]

One could reasonably conclude that this report, in which such a great amount of time, energy, and resources had been invested, would have merited extensive circulation and consideration in every sector of the wider Brotherhood of Disciples. Unfortunately, such was not to be the case. In fact, it was largely ignored. By the time that the differences had been carefully and meticulously defined and the call for unity constructed, the total climate had changed radically. Ironically, a series of events had been set in motion by the commission itself some years earlier that would destroy the intention and work of the commission. Not only were there to be found leaders in both groups who were anxious to preserve the unity of the fellowship; there were also leaders who were equally convinced that outright division was the preferable option. The decade of the 1940s witnessed a struggle between the divisive and the cohesive forces within both groups that saw the will to remain united effectively sublimated to partisan causes.

Defining the causes of tension in the movement was a relatively harmless activity. Repairing the breach that had appeared was an entirely different matter. Concrete suggestions to reverse the trend appeared to be a threat to some on both sides of the rupture. The initial event in a long series of moves and countermoves occurred in 1941 when the commission took the first concrete step toward healing the breach of 1926. In its meeting on July 8, 1941, the commission adopted the following recommendation, which it addressed to the Executive Committee of the International Convention:

> That the president and the executive committee of the International Convention invite representatives of the North American Christian Convention to collaborate in preparing the program for a unitary Convention in 1942.[6]

The report of the commission for 1942 also referred to the effort that was subsequently made to implement this recommendation.

> It was suggested that this plan be given a three-year trial during which time but one convention be held, looking toward conclusions based on actual experience.
>
> In keeping with this recommendation, President W.A. Shullenberger, of the International Convention, with the cordial cooperation of President Dean Walker of the North American Christian Convention, called such a joint meeting in Indianapolis on September 18, 1941, prior to the drafting of the 1942 convention program. Both of these leaders are to be congratulated upon their sincere efforts in carrying out the Commission's recommendation as above. Unfortunately, for the time being at least, this attempt has not been fraught with success. However, it is the abiding belief of your commissioners, representing a wide variety of different opinions, that further efforts should be made in the interest of unity.[7]

In 1941, the presidents of both conventions, Dean E. Walker and W.A. Shullenberger, lived in Indianapolis. Both taught on the faculty of Butler School of Religion and were personal friends. They shared the conviction that the Brotherhood ought to make every effort to avoid schism.

The reactions to the proposal were quick and decisive. There were those on both sides of the fracture to whom the prospect of reunification of the Brotherhood was frightening; they frankly preferred to see the movement divide. The proposal was not only rejected by the Executive Committee of the International Convention, the opposition in that body made their rejection emphatic by electing, for the first time, an avowed advocate of open membership to be president of the 1942 convention. Such an act was an affront to the efforts of the commission and a major block to future efforts looking toward reunification. It came as a stunning blow to all those who were laboring toward Brotherhood reconciliation. Edwin R. Errett responded by insisting that the action of the convention was not representative of the thinking of the Disciples, nor was the interpretation placed upon it by two prominent editors of the more liberal wing that "this indicates that the brotherhood regards the practice of open membership as no longer disqualifying a person for election to a key office in brotherhood agencies."[8] The *Christian Standard* sought to substantiate Errett's conclusion by conducting a straw vote among all the ministers listed in the *Yearbook of Disciples of Christ.* A total of 7,443 ballots were mailed to the ministers, asking: "Do you approve the election of those who practice open membership to key positions in organizations offering service to the

Dean Everest Walker (1899-1988), advocate of unity as set forth by the Commission on Restudy, he held many positions of leadership among Christian Churches and was founding president of Emmanuel School of Religion.

brotherhood?" Of the 3,708 that were returned, 3,193 were considered efficacious. The results were a resounding "no" by a ratio of more than three and a half to one.

If the commission's resolution for a healing of the latent breach by uniting the conventions aroused a stiffened resistance to reconciliation within the leadership of the International Convention, the consequences were no less dramatic within the North American Convention's Continuation Committee. President Dean E. Walker and all of the members of the commission were subjected to heavy criticism in some quarters, and the unlovely term "compromise" was frequently heard. Edwin R. Errett, editor of the *Christian Standard* and a member of the commission, fully shared in the criticism and became the focal point of a furious conflict that ended with his untimely death in January of 1944.

Edwin R. Errett was a grandnephew of Isaac Errett. He graduated from Bethany College and pursued graduate studies at Yale Divinity School. He was deeply committed to the Restoration Plea, and his active role in the conflicts of the 1920s had thoroughly acquainted him with the issues confronting the Brotherhood and the leadership of the various schools of thought. He became editor of the *Christian Standard* in 1929. His broad and generous attitude was coupled with an intelligent understanding of the issues of the day so that he commanded the respect of almost all who knew him. His opposition to some of the agencies was not based on methodology but on his conviction that they had forsaken the plea that they were charged to represent. He never yielded to those who insisted the Brotherhood was coterminous with either those who supported or those who

refused to support any or all of the agencies. He attended and commented on the international conventions and promoted almost all of the agencies of the convention. In 1937, he became a delegate to the World Faith and Order Conference in Edinburgh, Scotland, and, when that assembly took action to join in the conversations that eventuated in the World Council of Churches, he accepted a place on the continuing committee on Faith and Order. He was convinced that the Restoration Movement had a contribution to make to worldwide concern for Christian unity, and he felt an obligation to attempt to make that contribution.

Edwin R. Errett (1891-1944), editor of the *Christian Standard* (1929-1944), champion of unity within the movement, he was interested and active in early ecumenical efforts.

Intensely loyal to the cause that had claimed the energies of his family for three generations, Edwin Errett was possessed of the gift to articulate the fundamental substance of the plea in such a way as to win the serious attention of the learned and cultured both at home and abroad. He was motivated by a passion for unity that caused him to reach out to both liberal and conservative. He longed to heal the ruptures of both 1906 (Churches of Christ) and 1926 (Disciples of Christ) and gave himself unstintingly to every hopeful enterprise in either direction. The wide range of Errett's activities, the broad spectrum of his associations, and the thoughtful, courteous, and irenic manner in which he always conducted himself, whether in the conference hall, on the platform (he maintained a heavy speaking schedule), or in his editor's chair, earned him the ill will and suspicion of extremists of all kinds.

Meanwhile, those who were alarmed at the prospect of Brotherhood reunification were not idle. In the autumn of 1943, a series of rallies was held in the chapel at The Cincinnati Bible Seminary. Out of these rallies came an ad hoc Committee on Action that issued a "Call for Enlistment"[9] in a five-point program that looked toward a militant stand against conciliation. Burris Butler, minister of South Side Christian Church in Kokomo, Indiana, was named chairman of a Committee of Fifty. An executive committee included Lester Ford, treasurer, Fred Smith, secretary, R.C. Foster, Ard Hoven, S.S. Lappin, Orval Morgan, Harry Poll, T.K. Smith, W.R. Walker, and P.H. Welshimer. When the militant aims of the committee became apparent, the executive committee disintegrated. However, the effort had the support of W.H. Mohorter, the manager of Standard Publishing Company.

The December 4, 1943, issue of the *Christian Standard* announced a "change in policy" by which, "instead of continuing chiefly as a home paper of general religious information and instruction," the *Christian Standard* would be "a rallying center for all who believe implicitly in the authority of Christ as revealed to us in the divinely inspired New Testament Scriptures." The announcement included the declaration that the journal would "vigorously protest every instance of the substitution of human expediency for the authority of Christ." This was generally understood to mean an abandonment of the policy of conciliation and the adoption of an aggressively militant policy. The announcement was made by Willard Mohorter, the manger of the company, rather than by Edwin Errett, the editor of the *Christian Standard*, who was resisting the change. There were serious differences within the company.

The next issue of the *Christian Standard* contained a statement by Burris Butler that made it quite obvious that the focus of the effort was not only against those who were deemed to be Modernist, but equally against those who sought to preserve the fellowship of the whole Brotherhood. Referring to those who supported the call, Butler noted,

> A great loyal group feels that we can no more temporize, compromise, and placate the forces that would destroy the freedom of Christian ministers and churches than we can appease totalitarian forces in the political realm [a reference to Hitler during World War II]. It seems to be their belief that a "middle-of-the-road" policy is as

dangerous to the future of the Restoration movement as is the actual perfidy of its modernistic saboteurs.[10]

Henceforth, "Middle of the Roader" was a term applied to the center position that sought to preserve the unity of the Brotherhood along lines delineated by the Commission on Restudy. The label became increasingly pejorative as the unitive position came under attack from leaders of both extremes. The future would force the moderates to take one side or the other as the center position was squeezed out of existence.

With the change of policy by the *Christian Standard*, Edwin Errett believed that his dismissal was imminent and began to consider the possibility of launching a new journal that would continue to plead for Brotherhood unity. The financial obstacles to such an effort were enormous, to say nothing of other problems associated with the contemporary war economy. Errett laid the problem before his friends on the Board of Directors of the Christian Foundation. He was encouraged by their interest, but he was unable to act on his dream. Evidently, the pressure he was under proved too great for his physical stamina; he died suddenly on January 29. The reaction at the Christian Foundation was decisive.[11]

The editorial chair at the *Christian Standard* office was not long vacant. In April, 1944, Burris Butler was named managing editor. A year later, he was promoted to editor. The policies he had promoted through the call were now fully on. However, there were many within Standard Publishing who were very much opposed to the new direction, so a purge was held and a number of editors were either fired (J.D. Murch) or convinced of the necessity to resign (Aldis Webb, J. Vernon Jacobs, Harry Boll, Woodford Boebinger, Mildred Welshimer). Several of the above, along with others, sought to carry out Errett's intention to begin a new publication but were unable to arrange financing.

Meanwhile, the new policy was taking effect. Issues that had formerly been thrashed out in conventions were now projected into many congregations,[12] causing divisions and resulting in a rash of litigation.[13] In such a context, the work of the commission became futile. Neither Brotherhood paper was willing to print its report and pleas of 1946 and 1947. The commission died a quiet death, making its final report to the International Convention in 1948. A new policy of militancy had stilled the voices of conciliation. The consequences would be swift, decisive, and irreversible. The Call to Enlistment was quickly eclipsed by a "Committee of One Thousand," headed by Willis Meredith, an attorney in Jefferson City, Missouri.[14] The names of the committee were never published, but its efforts were encouraged by the editor of the *Christian Standard*. The zenith of the Committee of One Thousand's activity was reached in 1946, when the International Convention met in Columbus, Ohio. The committee purchased a full page ad in the *Ohio State Journal* of August 7, 1946, indicting the International Convention, the U.C.M.S., and the Christian Board of Publication for attacking the Bible, usurping authority over the Brotherhood, wasting the church's money, and dividing the Brotherhood. It issued a challenge offering publicly to defend the Bible as "God's holy word" against any whom the convention would officially appoint to "attack" the Bible. When word of this unfortunate action reached the churches, many hitherto sympathetic people were scandalized.

Conflicts quickly developed in local congregations that had hitherto managed the problem of two types of missionary practice in amiable ways. Local strife was exacerbated when the *Christian Standard* launched a new program: "Stand Up and Be Counted," in its issue of June 7, 1947. It urged congregations to "Cast off the fetters" of the organized agencies and promised to publish the names of those that did in an "Honor Roll of the Faithful."[15] As aconsequence of such forcing of the issues, many congregations split and the resort to litigation over property rights became epidemic. In 1951, following several distressing suits, Burris Butler wisely cautioned that "no good end can be achieved by this method of settling disputes."[16]

As the troubled decade of the forties drew to a close, division of the Brotherhood was a reality. What had first appeared as an undesirable possibility a decade earlier had become an accomplished fact. Several incidents may be cited to substantiate this conclusion. In 1949, the International Convention was held in Cincinnati, celebrating the centennial of the first convention that formed the American Christian Missionary Society in 1849 in Cincinnati. The *Christian Standard* ignored the gathering and, when questioned about it, the editor replied: "There is no more reason for us to devote time and space to a detailed report of the recent gathering in Music Hall than there would be for our giving a report of any other denominational gathering."[17] In fairness to Burris Butler, it should be observed that there was no evident disposition on the part of the leadership of this convention to grant any recognition to any person or institution in the area that was not associated with its agencies.

Until this time, the Christian Board of Publication had always been invited to share exhibit space at the North American Christian Convention, along with the Pension Fund, the National Benevolent Association, and the Board of Church Extension. This fraternizing came to an end in 1951 in Springfield, Illinois. Thus, by mid-century, it was obvious that the divisive tendencies would prevail, resulting in a permanent fracture of the movement that sought the unity of the body of Christ. The previous year, the North American Christian Convention voted to become an annual gathering of those who were operating wholly independently of the old agencies.

During the period when Disciple-Independent ties were being severed, the matter of fraternal relations with Churches of Christ were not completely ignored. James DeForest Murch and Claude I. Witty, minister of the Westside Central Church of Christ in Detroit, Michigan, organized a series of unity meetings.[18] The effort had the support of the *Christian Standard* but received a cool reception from the *Gospel Advocate* and the *Firm Foundation,* the two leading journals of the Churches of Christ. Nonetheless, a *Christian Union Quarterly* was launched, and a hymnbook, edited by E.L. Jorgenson of the Church of Christ, was published by Standard Publishing and widely used by Christian Churches.[19] The effort came to naught in 1943 due to the increasing acrimony of the meetings, restrictions of wartime travel, and Murch's employment by the National Association of Evangelicals following his dismissal from the Standard Publishing Company.[20] The decade of the forties, with the world embroiled in war and its difficulties, was not conducive to unity and reconciliation in the religious sector. Christian unity, which had so effectively motivated the movement at its beginning, was proving to be an elusive goal for its second-century heirs.

End Notes

[1]*The Report of the Commission on Restudy of the Disciples of Christ* (Indianapolis: International Convention, 1948), p. 263.

[2]J.H. Dampier, a member of the commission, observed in lectures to the author's classes on the history of the movement, that three distinct groups could be discerned within the commission's membership. One, of whom C.C. Morrison was general leader and spokesman, was theologically liberal and pro-agency. Opposed was a group that, in the later years of the commission's life, was led by Dean Walker, which was theologically conservative and critical of the agencies. A third group was theologically conservative and pro-agency. Claude E. Hill generally spoke for this group on ecclesiological issues.

[3]"Commission on Restudy of the Disciples of Christ, Annual Report," *Yearbook of Christian Churches (Disciples of Christ)*, 1946, pp. 116-120. The report can also be found in the program booklet of the 1946 International Convention, pp. 124-128. A series of studies by members of the commission may be found in *The Shane Quarterly* (Indianapolis: Butler University), Vol II, No. 2 & 3, April—July, 1941.

[4]*Yearbook of Christian Churches*, 1947, pp. 116, 117.

[5]*Yearbook of Christian Churches*, 1948, pp. 120-122.

[6]*Yearbook of Christian Churches*, 1942, p. 87.

[7]*Yearbook of Christian Churches*, 1941, p. 87.

[8]See Harold E. Fey, "Disciples Reprove Reaction Policy," *Christian Century*, August 12, 1942, p. 989. Also Herbert Minard, *Front Rank*, (St. Louis: Christian Board of Publication), 1942, p. 797.

[9]"A Call for Enlistment," *Christian Standard*, Nov. 27, 1943, pp. 1-3.

[10]Burris Butler, "The Enlistment Opens," *Christian Standard*, December 11, 1943, p. 1.

[11]The Christian Foundation was established in 1920 by Frederick D. Kershner, Marshall Reeves, and Will Irwin to promote New Testament Christianity by assisting institutions of higher learning. It was a major source of funding for Butler School of Religion and The Cincinnati Bible Seminary and gave generous subsidies to other enterprises as well.

After 1944, its interests shifted to Disciple agencies exclusively. When Butler School of Religion began a shift of emphasis under O.L. Shelton's leadership, it gained almost exclusive claims on the foundation's benefactions. In 1964, its assets of approximately $6,000,000 were turned over to Christian Theological Seminary. See Edwin Hayden, "Shifting Emphasis," *Christian Standard,* January 18, 1964, p. 2.

[12]As editorials in the *Christian Standard* became more inflammatory, *The Christian Evangelist* took the unusual step in 1945 of copyrighting its publication. *The Christian Evangelist,* January 2, 1946, p. 2. For Butler's response, see *Christian Standard,* January 19, 1946, p. 2.

[13]For a resumé of the litigation at this time, see Henry E. Webb, op. cit., pp. 258-269. Generally speaking, attorneys for the agencies contended that support of the agencies was part of the "fundamental faith, immemorial customs, usages, and practices" of Christian churches, and any change in agency support was tantamount to a change in denominational status. Uniformly, they were unable to sustain such a contention, although this often demanded resort to appellate processes.

[14]See *Christian Standard,* August 3, 1946. The leaders of the agencies were charged with "'Organized' Infidelity." The committee was formed at a Restoration Congress in Rolla, Missouri, in April, 1946. These congresses were sponsored by the C.R.A. The committee's demise was noted in the *Restoration Herald,* September 1949, p. 7.

[15]Burris Butler, "Stand Up and Be Counted," *Christian Standard,* June 7, 1947, p. 2.

[16]Burris Butler, "Christianity on Trial in the Civil Courts," *Christian Standard,* September 29, 1951, p. 3.

[17]Burris Butler, "No Blast," *Christian Standard,* Nov. 12, 1949, p. 10.

[18]For details, see J.D. Murch, *Christians Only* (op. cit.), pp. 273-276. Also by the same author, *Adventuring for Christ,* op. cit., pp. 126-132.

[19]*Great Songs of the Church.*

[19]Following his separation from Standard Publishing Company, Murch became editor of the NAE (National Association of Evangelicals) Journal. In his opinion, such involvement with an interdenominational enterprise compromised his credibility with the churches of Christ, so he withdrew from the unity effort. His place was taken by Peyton Canary, who quickly lost the confidence of Claude E. Witty, hastening the end of the efforts. See Murch, *Adventuring for Christ,* op. cit., p. 132.

Chapter Fourteen

Making Division Permanent

It is something of an irony that the session of the International Convention that received the Report of the Commission on Restudy urging that Brotherhood differences be sublimated to the unity that the Disciples' plea provided should be the very convention that was confronted with the inflammatory full-page ad in the of the *Ohio State Journal*. (See chapter 13.) The effect of this ad was to give credibility to the divisive elements in both groups. Events of the next several months rendered the commission's works anticlimactic.

Within the next few years, the body divided. It is not possible to fix a precise date for this division. A number of events can be cited as indications of division,[1] but none of these taken alone was decisive. Together, they were symptomatic of the growing breach. Nothing illustrated the breach more clearly than a series of local church splits that resulted in trials at law during the decade of the 1950s. A uniform theme is found in these unfortunate suits, namely, that refusal to support the agencies of the International Convention placed one in a different denominational affiliation than the Stone-Campbell heritage. Needless to say, this was an impossible claim to sustain in the courts, but the adversarial relationships generated in this period facilitated the division in ranks and insured its permanent nature.

Still, there were some who found it difficult to surrender the conviction that, deep down beneath the disputes over agencies and philosophies, there remained a fundamental unity in the movement. As late as 1955, W.E. Garrison wrote:

> It is a painful admission for Disciples that, as regards unity, "our own vineyard have we not kept." But nothing is to be gained by closing our eyes to the facts. We are badly divided. Yet there is still a sufficient substratum of unity so that we can say that "we" are divided. To speak of the whole company as "we" is to imply that

there is some bond that unites them. The bond is partly historical. We are all sprung from the same root. But it is more than that. We are at one in refusing to be complacent about a divided Church and in cherishing the goal of a universal Christian fellowship. We are at one in the conviction that unity can be attained only upon the basis of what is indisputably essential to loyalty to Jesus Christ our Lord. We are in agreement that liberty of opinion is the right of every Christian man, and that therefore concurrence of opinions cannot be any part of a platform for a united Church.

The "we" who hold these salutary principles include not only the supporting constituency of the International Convention, but all the "independents" who have seceded from it, and the Churches of Christ as well.[2]

With commendable candor, Lin Cartwright, the editor of *The Christian Evangelist,* commented in 1957:

It would seem that all are included in [the brotherhood] who have accepted the Lordship of Jesus Christ and possess a brotherly spirit.

Since it is a basic term with universal connotations, it runs beneath all type of organization among us. The support, or lack of support of agencies, methods of doing the work of the Lord, theological differences or practices cannot affect it. It is a mood and a spirit and travels only in the realm of the spirit.

There must be room within it for all shades of honest opinion among us. It should be all-inclusive, as broad as the Kingdom of God and as wide as the gates of heaven.

If you are a member of "the brotherhood" according to Disciple thought and practice, there is no one who can read you out of it. However, it would seem reasonable that if one is to remain in "the brotherhood" one must show a brotherly attitude toward others in it.[3]

Internal Unity Consultations

A renewed concern for "internal unity" manifested itself in 1959. James B. Carr, a professor of missions at Manhattan Bible College and chairman of one of the discussion groups at the Consultation on Ecumenical Christian Unity sponsored jointly by the Council on Christian Unity and Phillips University in Enid, Oklahoma, stirred considerable interest within his discussion group by his insistence that whatever principles are urged for ecumenical concern must also be applied within the larger Brotherhood of the Disciples of Christ. This insistence tested the sincerity of the group's commitment to unity in a very realistic fashion. The group spent most of its allotted time trying to face up to problems of unity within the Restoration Movement. A suggestion was made in the course of the discussion that a Consultation on Internal Unity might be desirable. This led the chairman to send letters of inquiry to representative ministers and professors in the Oklahoma and Kansas area. An *ad hoc* committee was formed to plan for such a consultation, and a sincere effort was made to maintain a balance on this committee between Disciples of Christ and Independents. The committee consisted of James B. Carr (chairman), Dyre Campbell, Ting Champie, John Greenlee, Charles Gresham, Clifford Hauxwell, W.L. McEver, and Thomas O. Parish. This committee summoned a mass meeting, the Consultation on Internal Unity, for June 2 and 3, 1959, at Friend's University in Wichita, Kansas. Over two hundred people attended, and Disciples and Independents were nearly equal in number.

Enthusiasm for this effort was sufficient to suggest that a second consultation would be desirable. The Broadway Christian Church, Wichita, Kansas, hosted this second gathering, February 8-10, 1961. Among those addressing the consultation were Cecil K. Thomas, George Earl Owen, Charles R. Gresham, Woodrow Phillips, Fred P. Thompson, Tom O. Parish, Robert Tobias, James D. Murch, A. Dale Fiers, and Donald McGavran. Such topics as "Independent Versus Cooperative Mission Methodology," "Local Church Autonomy," "Nature of Church Membership," "Possibilities and Problems of the Ecumenical Movement," and the "Restoration Plea in an Ecumenical Era" were discussed. A. Dale Fiers, then president of the United Christian Missionary Society, gave voice to a persistent theme when he insisted that unity must manifest itself in one organization. After noting that unity is first given of God, second manifested in spirit, and third expressed in work, he declared:

> Fourth, we must strive for the structure of unity. A unified Brotherhood implies some structure. A common structure for the administration of inter-congregational responsibility is absolutely necessary.[4]

Fiers thus repeated the policy long held by the adherents of the agencies, namely that brotherhood is signified by support of certain organizations. This insistence by the cooperative leaders that unity within the Brotherhood must be organizationally structured foredoomed future consultations to frustration. Wichita was the first and last consultation that involved high-level participation by agency officials.

The third Consultation on Internal Unity was held in 1962 at the Wheeling Avenue Christian Church in Tulsa, Oklahoma. Here it was evident that unity within the Disciples was not a high priority with the leadership in Indianapolis. They were in pursuit of other goals, which internal unity could only threaten. The issues confronting the movement were faced frankly and discussed irenically. W. Carl Ketcherside, of the Churches of Christ, was invited to deliver the Bible lectures at this consultation.

The fourth Consultation on Internal Unity met at the Disciples of Christ Historical Society in 1963. Attendance from the Disciples sector of the Brotherhood was disappointing, and it was apparent that the interest of the leadership of the Disciples of Christ in Christian unity was focused primarily on groups outside of the movement.

A fifth consultation was held at the Christian Board of Publication in St. Louis, Missouri, February 27-29, 1964. It was hoped that holding the consultation at this location would encourage involvement from agency leadership. The predominant themes for discussion were "Church Structure" and "The Restoration Ideal." Despite the location, attendance from the Disciples of Christ sector was again disappointing. The leadership of the Disciples of Christ was absorbed in the effort to restructure the Disciples.

A sixth Consultation on Internal Unity of Christian Churches was held in February, 1965, at the Overland Park Christian Church, near Kansas City, Kansas. Severe weather conditions caused attendance to be far below expectation.

Enid, Oklahoma, was the site of the final Consultation on Internal Unity, February 28-March 2, 1966. By this time, the leadership of the Disciples of Christ was vigorously promoting Brotherhood Restructure, and internal unity could only impose an impediment on the goals these leaders had in view. Internal Unity Consultations died for want of interest and hope of achievement.

Directing Division

In the same year that the internal unity consultations were being conceived (1959), another force was gathering momentum that was to subvert the ends the consultations sought to serve. The Denver International Convention adopted *"Resolution 52, Urging Cooperative Strategy."* The provisions of Resolution 52 were implemented in 1960 at Louisville, Kentucky, by the appointment of a *Commission on Cooperative Policy and Practice,* with George Earle Owen as chairman. The commission conceived its purpose to be to "keep abreast with current developments in the field of cooperation," to "survey the problem," to "lift up the major issues in the light of historical developments and present trends," to "create a climate of understanding," and to "recognize that there is a real division in our Brotherhood life."[5] In its 1962 report, the commission announced that it was in the process of "the creation of literature" dealing with "the problems."[6]

The first major work of this commission was to publish a twenty-page booklet: *What Brotherhood Cooperation Means*. Its aim was to delineate more clearly the *differences* between the "Cooperative" and "Independent" groups so that "marginal congregations" would be led to become partisan, an aim not basically different from the previously noted "Call to Enlistment." The pamphlet's first statement was an affront, not only to those who were exploring avenues of expanded Brotherhood fellowship and good will, but to the historic thrust of the movement that had understood Christian unity to be based in a community of faith in Jesus Christ. It defined *Brotherhood* in terms of allegiance to certain agencies.

> "The Brotherhood" is a familiar term used to designate the fellowship and cooperation that characterizes the Christian Churches or Disciples of Christ which are affiliated with the International Convention of Christian Churches (Disciples of Christ).[7]

The pamphlet then proceeded to characterize "Independents" in a most negative and unfavorable manner while extolling the virtues of those who supported the Disciple agencies as those who manifested "integrity, oneness in Christ, acceptance of and trust in one another, love and good will."[8]

This unfortunate piece of religious propaganda in behalf of separation came at an inopportune time, and it was followed shortly thereafter by a second pamphlet: *We Disciples*. Simultaneously, Dr. A.T. DeGroot, a member of the commission, published a small book that carried the endorsement of the commission and presented a sharply critical account of the history of "Church of Christ Number Two."[9] None of these publications was designed to promote the cause of internal unity. The Commission on Cooperative Policy and Practice continued its watchdog role until 1971, financed by the convention, magnifying differences and focusing attention on what it considered to be an inevitable schism.[10]

Restructure

While some ministers and other leaders of the Disciples of Christ and the Independent segments of the Brotherhood were nostalgically struggling to reinforce the bonds of internal unity that were still viable, other forces were at work planning for a major new development. Known as "Brotherhood Restructure," it was the most ambitious and controversial project undertaken by Disciples of Christ in the present century. The initiative for this move came from within the United Christian Missionary Society (Willard M. Wickizer is often dubbed "The Father of Restructure" in informal conversation) and the Board of Higher Education. These agencies created a carefully selected panel of scholars in 1956. In the opening statement of the panel's three-volume report, published in 1963, Wickizer relates:

> After extended consideration the United Christian Missionary Society and the Board of Higher Education of Disciples of Christ came to the conviction that the time was ripe for Disciples of Christ to re-examine their beliefs and doctrines in a scholarly way. The tenets held by our fathers in the faith needed to be restudied and validated or modified in the light of modern scholarship. New light and understanding should be sought. A new and firmer base of Christian doctrine should be laid. A new certainty concerning what we believe and why we believe it should be achieved.
>
> As one step in the direction of bringing a new certainty and clarity of thought to Disciples of Christ the two agencies decided to join in the creation of a Panel of Scholars that would be asked to restudy the doctrines of Disciples of Christ, justifying their conclusions on the basis of the best available scholarship. It was agreed that the Panel would have complete freedom, deciding for themselves the areas they would consider and how they would proceed with their studies, but it was hoped that the Panel would see fit to consider theologically some of the more practical issues and problems confronting Disciples of Christ.
>
> In the spring of 1956 the creation of such a Panel of Scholars was authorized and in January of 1957 the first meeting of the Panel was held. Originally it was thought that the Panel would work for three years but its life was extended for an additional two and a half years. The Panel has met twice a year and its members have shown both dedication and zeal.[11]

Howard E. Short, professor of church history at the College of the Bible in Lexington, Kentucky, served as chairman of the panel from 1956 until September of 1958, when he resigned to become editor of *The Christian Evangelist.* He was succeeded by W.B. Blakemore. Other members of this panel were William R. Baird, Paul Hunter Beckelhymer, James A. Clague, Stephen J. England, Frank N. Gardner, Virgil V. Hinds, J. Phillip Hyatt, Clarence E. Lemmon, D. Ray Lindley, Ronald E. Osborn, Eugene H. Peters, Glen C. Routt, Dwight E. Stevenson, William G. West, and Ralph G. Wilburn.

It must be noted that this panel was not appointed by the International Convention and thus did not represent the "Brotherhood," but only two of its agencies. The criteria for selection was never disclosed, but the omission of several of the eminent conservative scholars among the Disciples raised questions in the minds of many as to the basis of inclusion.

Willard M. Wickizer, of the U.C.M.S., first formally proposed the idea of restructuring the Disciples at a meeting of the Council of Agencies at Culver Stockton College, Canton, Missouri, July 8-12, 1958.[12] Four months later, the Board of Directors of the International Convention created a Committee on Brotherhood Restructure, with Wickizer as chairman. The charge was to "explore the magnitude and complexity of the task of restructuring the Brotherhood" and "formulate a proposal . . . for action which would set forth in detail how a broadly representative Commission on Brotherhood Restructure can best be constituted."[13] In 1960, the International Convention authorized the enlargement of the committee into a 120-person Commission on Brotherhood Restructure,[14] and Granville T. Walker, minister of University Christian Church, Ft. Worth, Texas, was named chairman, a post he continued to hold until the commission finished its work. The same convention approved Resolution 30, which provided an official rationale for restructuring. After noting that the Disciples of Christ held an aversion to "official" organizations and feared ecclesiasticism, the resolution found that:

> Much of the problem that the Disciples of Christ have had with organization stems from the fact that as a religious body we have had almost no theology of Church beyond the local congregation. The Church was only the sum total of autonomous congregations and it was thought congregational autonomy should be protected at all cost.

The resolution then suggested the aims of the commission in the following words:

> Furthermore the conviction has come to us that the Church is something more than the sum total of local congregations, that it has a very real and vital total entity that should be reflected in its corporate structure. . . .
> Such an over-all restructuring does not mean a turning back from our historic concern for Christian unity. It merely means a realistic appraisal of where we are at this point to negotiate with other religious bodies that may be interested in discussing union with us.[15]

From the outset, there was confusion over the intention of the wording in the above resolution. Many Disciples were convinced that the agencies needed to be integrated in a more functional official pattern and they thus viewed restructure in terms of a reevaluation of the role of each of the agencies with reference to the whole. They were repulsed by intentions of others who saw the task of restructuring as primarily theological, requiring a new definition of *church*, which clearly transformed the inherited congregational polity into a well-defined supra-congregational structure.[16] The term *church* was no

longer to be confined to a local body of believers. It was claimed that
such a restriction obscured the wholeness of the Brotherhood. Furthermore, the term *agency* failed to convey the concept that the service being performed was really the work of the church. A proper
understanding of *church*, it was argued, must embrace the work of
the church at all levels and in its broadest dimension. Thus, the gathering of Christians at a state convention is not properly understood as
a "convention" but rather as "the church" functioning at the state
level. Similarly, the International Convention of Disciples of Christ is
improperly conceived as a mass meeting of disciples and a reporting
body for the separate agencies; it is more properly a manifestation of
the "church" functioning at the national or international level. This
being the case, it was only appropriate that these bodies be designated as "church" (assemblies) and that the former "state secretary"
of a society become the "minister" to the church at this level. The
General Secretary of the International Convention would be designated as the General Minister of the Christian Church (Disciples of
Christ). All of these conceptual changes, representing quite a variance from the historic heritage of the Disciples, were incorporated in
A Provisional Design for the Christian Church (Disciples of Christ),
which was submitted to the International Convention at Dallas,
Texas, in 1966. The Convention "received" the document and called
for a "Provisional Assembly" to be convened at St. Louis, Missouri, in
1967, to take final action.[17]

Meanwhile, an important change had taken place in the International Convention. Conceived as a mass meeting at which every registered person was allowed to vote, the convention was judged by
some to be less representative of the churches than should be the
case. The Mahoning Association of Baptists had been dissolved in
1830 because of dislike of the official nature of a delegate-body, and
twice since Disciples had resisted efforts to reinstate conventions
composed of official delegates[18] that made decisions above the level
of the congregation. However, as the first critical step toward effect-
ing restructure, a resolution was introduced at the International
Convention in Detroit, Michigan (1964), to amend the bylaws of the
convention in such a way as to convert it into a delegate assembly.[19]
The debates were harsh, and time was inadequate to discuss the
issue in depth. The majority voted to "receive" this recommendation
with final approval to come in 1966. There was significant opposition
to this move. The effect of this action at Detroit was to eliminate the
votes from all those congregations that feared to certify official delegates to subsequent conventions on the ground that they would be
legally bound by the future action of such assemblies. A host of court
cases involving parallel situations in other religious communions
gave ground for these concerns. Some congregations sought legal
advice only to find that the opinions of attorneys differed.

The elimination of the voting rights of those Disciples who opposed restructure, combined with the heavy voting representation that the amended bylaws gave to the agency officials,[20] assured a favorable response to restructure. In a very real sense, the issue of restructure was settled in Detroit in 1964.

There was a second item in Resolution 30 of the 1960 Louisville Convention that produced serious concern for many Disciples. This was the statement in the rationale indicating that the proposed restructure would be "placing us in a stronger position to negotiate with other religious bodies that may be interested in discussing union with us." Disciples had been discussing union with the United Church of Christ and would shortly be entering into the Consultation on Church Union. Memories of the litigation in which those congregations of the Congregational Christian Church opposed to the merger with the Evangelical Reformed Church to form the United Church of Christ became involved were fresh in the minds of some Disciples. They were naturally uneasy as to whether the proposed delegate assembly would be able to commit them legally to a denominational fusion against their will. The language often employed by restructure enthusiasts was anything but reassuring at this point. There was wide diversity of opinion within the leadership on whether restructure was calculated to put the Disciples in a position to effect a merger by action of one of the "autonomous" levels of "the church" or not. Heated discussions of this question erupted in informal gatherings where ministers and others met. When confronted with this question, some of the officials denied such intent while others declared that there would be no point at all to restructure if it did not facilitate mergers.[21]

The unremitting advocacy of restructure on the part of commission members, agency officials, and members of the panel of scholars generated a furious opposition. The decisive step was to be taken at the convention in St. Louis in 1967, as time was critical if the movement toward a new and different structure were to be stopped. There was no official structure through which opposing views could be presented. An expression in opposition would have to be *ad hoc*. Ministers and leaders of non-cooperating (Independent) churches were in no position to influence developments within the Disciples and remained uninvolved. But a group of eminent ministers, educators, and laymen from cooperating Disciple congregations gathered in Atlanta, Georgia, in May of 1967 to explore possible ways of altering the course being pursued by the advocates of restructure. George C. Stuart, of Jacksonville, Florida, was chairman. The secretary of this group was Robert W. Burns, minister of Peachtree Christian Church of Atlanta, Georgia, and a former president of the convention. The group issued what they called "The Atlanta Declaration," expressing three basic concerns about the proposed Provisional Design:

1. The basis of voluntary cooperation in which we have worked up until the proposed Restructure is being replaced by an authoritarian, connectional system which may endanger our freedom in Christ.

2. The complex nature of what has been presented in the Provisional Design requires us to request that no final action be taken on this at the St. Louis convention.

3. The effect of the present Provisional Design will be, in our opinion, to exclude many who have been cooperative in the past.[22]

The document expressed the basic viewpoint of this group in the following terms:

> We find that we are of one mind in the belief that an institutional and organizational unity does not make Christ's followers "one." Instead, we would declare that it is "oneness in faith and belief" that glorifies Him.
>
> Our concerns have led us to the unanimous conclusion that action must be taken to persuade Agency leaders to change their course. We wish to convey to the Commission on Brotherhood Restructure, and others, our unanimous belief that the whole basis of the Design must be changed so that any restructure will affect only the agencies that need restructuring, leaving local congregations and basic individual responsibility unrestricted.[23]

The Atlanta group saw the basic issue of restructure as essentially a matter of control of local congregations.

> What is at stake in the proposal to Restructure the Brotherhood is the issue whether the Christian Faith is a free, inclusive, evangelistic, witnessing fellowship of Christian Believers, in personal relationship with each other through their personal relationship to Jesus Christ, facing each other responsibly in free congregations, the structure of whose Faith is Biblically given: Or whether the Christian Faith can be constituted as *The* Christian Church by the majority decision upon hundreds of congregations who may not even send delegates to the convention, thereby erecting a system of authoritative connections extending downwards from the President and the Executive Council through the General Council and General Assembly to the regions, congregations, and ministers.[24]

A second *ad hoc* effort to stem the tide toward restructure was made by the anonymous "Committee for the Preservation of the Brotherhood." Two carefully prepared documents were drawn up and mailed to all persons listed in the Disciples' yearbook.[25] In addition, some other less ambitious efforts were made in behalf of halting or delaying the move toward restructure. One of these was by a group known as "Christians Concerned," which voiced its opposition by mail from Macon, Georgia.

Actually, the struggle against the program to restructure the Disciples was rather pathetic because the advocates had control of all of the media and the organizational resources of the Disciples while the opposition was bereft of adequate communication media to give effective representation to its position. The Commission on Brotherhood Restructure was funded by the convention, and its recommendations were generously publicized in the official press and advocated in scheduled assemblies by agency personnel. But the voice of the opposition had no organization, no effective access to the official publications, no fair provision for representation on district, state, or national conventions, and, of course, no agency officials promoting it. A sense of frustration and despair gripped those who were convinced that the Disciples of Christ were cutting loose from their historic moorings.

St. Louis was the scene for the fateful decision in 1967. Opponents of restructure approached the convention with little hope. Many were unable to vote because of the 1964 action limiting voting to certified delegates. All were convinced that they had been denied opportunities to articulate their views. Robert W. Burns pleaded the cause of the Atlanta Committee in an impassioned address before a tense meeting of the Campbell Institute at the convention, saying,

> The Atlanta Declaration Committee hopes that the years ahead will be the most creative and exciting in all our history. We ask for the joy of sharing face to face in meaningful discussion all across our brotherhood in many colloquium meetings, of at least three days each, where these issues may be considered patiently and by which we may achieve a consensus which will enlist the voluntary cooperation of the vast majority of our people.
>
> I am not here to try to win an argument or to change your minds. What I do ask for is the opportunity, before the Design is approved, of dialogue with dignity, and in brotherhood, with equal time allowed for the various differences to be expressed and with access to our magazines, *The Christian* and *World Call*, for articles other than the official "party line."
>
> Brothers, make room for those of us who cannot accept the narrow confines of the Provisional Design. Let us discuss our convictions within the framework of our loyalty to Christ and our continuity with the effort to renew in our generation authentic Apostolic Christianity.
>
> I believe in the brotherhood of Disciples of Christ. I love our history. I cherish every congregation. I long for our spiritual renewal in evangelism, in establishing new churches, in personal devotion of

our members, in cooperation with all others who love Christ, in offering ourselves to God for Him to use us in establishing justice and mercy with love for all mankind. May God continue to bless you.[26]

But careful preparation by the restructure advocates paid dividends at St. Louis. The convention's accredited delegates registered approval of Resolution 29 incorporating the Revised Provisional Design. Following this action, the document was to be accepted by two-thirds of the area assemblies and two-thirds of the agencies reporting to the International Convention to become fully in force. All of this was accomplished by the time the convention met in 1968 in Kansas City, Missouri. Following action on Report 54, which included the Revised Provisional Design, a Provisional General Assembly was declared in session and the actual process of restructuring began under the skillful management of A. Dale Fiers, the President and General Minister of the Christian Church (Disciples of Christ).[27] The report included the significant statement:

> The Commission submits the Design for action by this Assembly. The adoption of the Design here might well be for the future as historically significant as the general acceptance by Disciples of the *Declaration and Address* of Thomas Campbell.

The aftermath of the whole effort is disconcerting. The bulk of the opposition to restructure came from older ministers whose roots were deep in Disciple traditions. Many were disillusioned and declared that they would "fold their tents," or "retire soon." A wave of actions by congregations to withdraw from listing in the *Yearbook* removed about 3,000 congregations from this registry. But Disciple leaders pointed out that most of these churches were not previously participating in the "Brotherhood" anyway. Restructure seemed to have consolidated the Disciples into what one of their historians termed "a tight little denomination of higher maneuverability."[28] Having thus crystallized into a clearly defined denomination, the possibility of the reunion of all of the Disciples as envisioned in the 1945 report of the restudy commission had effectively vanished.

The effort to restructure the Disciples of Christ was accomplished at a very heavy cost. A rather loosely identified body of Christians and churches was thereby transformed into a clearly defined denomination of approximately two-thirds its earlier size. Those justifying the change point out that the loss was more apparent than it was-real and that the increased involvement in the decisions and activities of the church by a more responsible body would ultimately be more desirable and effective. Furthermore, advocates of restructure had long complained that mass conventions were not democratic or representative because they were subject to disproportionate influence from the sections of the country in which they were held. It was claimed that restructure would insure a representation of the Brotherhood as a whole. That this is the case is questioned, even after almost two decades of practice. A regular columnist in *The Disciple*, the journal of the denomination, observed:

> Disciples may talk about representative government, but the rhetoric is window dressing for what turns out to be a closed system. Denominations from the Southern Baptists to the Unitarians have found ways to practice what we preach. Democracy has its risks, but so does rule by a few which poses as democratic. The alternative is to give up the illusion that the General Assembly has any power, and simply recognize openly that the General Board really makes all the decisions.[29]

Those congregations of the Disciples of Christ that did not accept restructure did not elect to create a schismatic body. While restructure thinned the ranks of the Disciples of Christ, it did not cause a split. Some of the congregations wanting nothing to do with restructure aligned with Independent Christian Churches, finding that the Christian Missionary Fellowship offered the kind of structured mission work they desired. A few others became independent congregations with very limited relationships to any outside body. The rest, including the majority of the Atlanta Declaration group, eventually called new ministers who led the congregations back into the Disciples of Christ.

Independent Christian Churches were not affected by the restructure effort, and many were hardly aware that such a development was taking place. No effort was made by Christian Churches to exploit the division in the Disciples of Christ, which is probably a reflection on how far the two bodies had already drifted apart.

Disciples of Christ conformed readily to the new organizational structure. A certain excitement marked the process of adjusting to a new nomenclature, new procedures, and new relationships. Fears that the leadership, fortified with greater authority, would lead Disciples into merger with another denomination have to date proved to be unfounded, partly because of the decline of enthusiasm for denominational merger that accompanied the collapse of the Consultation on Church Union noted in the next chapter.

End Notes

[1]Some of these are as follows: 1949, Burris Butler's editorial comment that the Centennial Convention celebrating the founding of the A.C.M.S. was no different from "any other denominational gathering" ("No Blast," *Christian Standard,* November 12, 1949, p. 10). 1950, the decision of the North American Christian Convention to become an annual gathering. 1955, the publication of a separate, independent yearbook.

[2]W.E. Garrison, *Christian Unity* (op. cit.), pp. 219, 220.

[3]*The Christian Evangelist,* February 13, 1957.

[4]Printed addresses, *The Second Consultation on Internal Unity* (Oklahoma City), p. 145.

[5]*Yearbook of the Christian Churches (Disciples of Christ),* 1962, p. 26.

[6]Ibid.

[7]*What Brotherhood Cooperation Means,* tract published by the Commission on Brotherhood Polity and Practice, International Convention of Disciples of Christ.

[8]Ibid, pp. 18, 19.

[9]A.T. DeGroot, *New Possibilities For Disciples and Independents* (St. Louis: Bethany Press, 1963). This polemic work bears the endorsement of the Commission on Cooperative Policy and Practice of the International Convention of Disciples of Christ.

[10]After eleven years of activity, Dr. Fiers announced that the commission was "abolished in the church's restructuring" and the "task originally given to the Commission is now being reassigned so the effective work of the Commission will be continued." *The Christian,* February 13, 1972, p. 22.

[11]W.M. Wickizer, "A Statement Concerning the Panel of Scholars," *Panel of Scholars Reports,* Vol. I (St. Louis: Christian Board of Publication, 1963), p. 8.

[12]Ibid, Vol. 3, p. 112.

[13]*Yearbook of Disciples of Christ,* 1959, pp. 26, 27.

[14]*Yearbook of Disciples of Christ,* 1960, pp. 26-28.

[15]Ibid.

[16]See W.B. Blakemore, *Panel of Scholars Reports,* Vol. III, pp. 52-81, where the author acknowledges that he is playing semantic tricks with the word "congregation." Loren E. Lair took the same semantic liberties in an address to a district convention in Adel, Iowa, September 19, 1965, referring to the state convention as "state congregation."

[17]*The Provisional Design for the Christian Church (Disciples of Christ),* with revisions by the commission, may be found in the "Report of the Commission on Brotherhood Restructure (Resolution 29) to the 1967 Convention." See the 1967 convention program, p. 292 (Indianapolis: International Convention of Christian Churches, 1967).

[18]The Louisville Plan in 1869, abandoned by 1875; and a subsequent attempt in 1912 when the General Convention of Disciples of Christ was adopted in 1917.

[19]Amendment 34, 1964, International Convention of Christian Churches, *Program Book,* p. 271.

[20]Ibid., Section 2: b, c, d.

[21]See George W. Beazley, *Midstream* (Indianapolis: Council on Christian Unity, March, 1964), p. 108.

[22]*The Atlanta Declaration of Convictions and Concerns* (Atlanta: Progress Committee), p. 2.

[23]Ibid.

[24]Ibid., p. 5.

[25]The cost was underwritten by B.D. Phillips, of Butler, Pennsylvania. The publications were *Freedom or Restructure,* and *The Truth About Restructure.* Also, J.D. Murch was engaged to write a book, *The Free Church,* which was widely circulated.

[26]Robert W. Burns, "Why the Atlanta Declaration?" *Atlanta Declaration,* op. cit., p. 3.

[27]In anticipation, Dr. Fiers had been ordained to the post of General Minister of the Christian Church at an ecumenical service held as part of the 1964 Convention in Detroit (cf. *Convention Program,* pp. 46-48).

[28]A.T. DeGroot, *"Apologia Pro Vita Sua"* (Ft. Worth: published by the author), p. 3.

[29]Charles H. Bayer, *The Disciple,* January, 1984, p. 38.

Chapter Fifteen

The Restoration Movement and the Larger Religious Community

The theme of Christian unity has been too much a part of the heritage of the Restoration Movement to be forgotten amidst the trauma of internal problems of the twentieth century. Pride is often expressed in the effectiveness of the union of the followers of the Campbells and Barton W. Stone, which began in 1832. However, since that date, no union has occurred and two schisms have developed. It could well be asked: have the people who came into being to address the problem of the divided body of Christ completely lost their interest in Christian unity? The answer to this question depends upon the branch of the broader movement to which the question is addressed. The Disciples of Christ in the twentieth century have far outstripped both the Independent Christian Churches and the Noninstrumental Churches of Christ in pursuit of Christian unity. The activity of the Commission on Christian Unity—created by the International Convention in Topeka, Kansas, in 1910—is the primary manifestation of this interest.

Baptist-Disciple Union

Efforts to explore the possibility of organic union with Baptists have been made on several occasions since the separation that occurred in 1830. Since both Baptists and Disciples are practitioners of believer's baptism by immersion, this would seem to be a likely possibility. A congress of Baptists and Disciples met regularly until forces within the Northern Baptist Convention closed the door in 1930 by rejecting the prospect of union with those who held a doctrine of "baptismal regeneration," a term that harshly characterized the Disciple position. But, despite this reversal, negotiations were soon resumed and a joint commission was appointed by the Northern Baptist Convention and the International Convention in 1946, which led to holding simultaneous conventions in Chicago in 1952. A tangible result of these efforts was the publication of a new hymnal by a joint committee of Baptists and Disciples. But these efforts came to an abrupt halt in 1955 when doctrinal issues centering mainly on the meaning of baptism were again raised in the Northern Baptist Convention. Since 1955, no further efforts have been made for union with any portion of the Baptist fellowship, except in a very few local congregations in the northeastern part of the United States.

The Ecumenical Movement

When the religious history of the twentieth century is placed in perspective with all the rest of church history, it will very likely be designated as the century of ecumenical interest. It witnessed the rise of the Ecumenical Movement and its extension worldwide. By mid-century, a World Council of Churches had been organized, which soon embraced not only Protestant bodies but orthodox churches as well, and observers were exchanged between it and the Roman Catholic Vatican II Council. This movement, with its growing awareness of the problems of a divided Christendom and its aim of enhancing Christian unity, bears some striking similarities to, along with some significant differences from, the Restoration Movement of the Campbell-Stone tradition. Consequently, any account of the latter is grossly incomplete unless it not only notes these similarities and differences, but also notes the impact of the one upon the other.

A century before the early stirrings of ecumenism were discernible on the religious scene, the frontier efforts of Barton W. Stone and the Campbells were solitary voices crying for Christian unity in the midst of a sectarian wilderness. The *Declaration and Address* pleaded for Christians to forsake Old World loyalties and unite on the Bible alone. The Christians held out the hope that a united Christendom would marshall its resources behind a dynamic effort for world mission. Hope that the reconstitution of the apostolic church would rejuvenate mankind and usher in the millennium seemed to be well within the optimism with which the frontiersmen viewed the future.

With the passing of the frontier, these hopes did not materialize. American denominations did not lose their opportunity to organize, crystallize, and evangelize. The Restoration Movement had indeed swept across the frontier, but so had the Baptists, the Methodists, and the Presbyterians. Subsequently came waves of Lutheran and Roman Catholic immigrants. By the end of the nineteenth century, the American religious scene presented Christendom's most complex pluralism. To the great number of Old-World religious loyalties American freedom of worship was to contribute a generous supply of new ones. Aggressive sectarianism manifested itself all too frequently in American religious history. In its wake was left the sad spectacle of a seriously divided body of Christians and, too often, an unreasoning bigotry that was incapable of either the conversion of the sinners or the edification of the saints. The statistics for the growth of the denominations are impressive for two decades before and after the turn of this century. But this record of denominational growth must be seen against the background of some very real social and ethical ills that force one to the conclusion that denominational growth must not be identified with either the health or the influence of the Christian body.

At the turn of this century, many sensitive churchmen became increasingly aware of the sinful nature of the divisions among the followers of Christ. A new concern for the unity of all Christians arose from sources wholly outside the Restoration Movement. The initiative came largely from the Episcopal Church, but others soon manifested similar concern over a divided Christendom, and gradually there emerged the Ecumenical Movement, which has been so prominent in Christian circles in the twentieth century.

It is apparent at a glance that the motives and objectives of the Restoration and the Ecumenical Movements are similar. Both regret sectarian divisions, and both seek the unity of Christian peoples. Serious divergence between the two movements appears primarily at the point of the precise means to be employed in the quest of their desired ends. The Restoration Movement seeks to restore a genuinely Biblically based faith and practice as the only viable foundation for the unity of all who follow Jesus Christ. It begins with the Bible. The Ecumenical Movement begins with the fact of denoiminational divisions. The implications of this difference are enormous. To understand this divergence more clearly and to note its impact on the Restoration Movement, it will be necessary to take a brief look at the rise of the Ecumenical Movement.

The General Convention of the Episcopal Church, held in 1886 in Chicago, Illinois, set forth a platform for the union of all churches on the basis of four points that the delegates deemed to be "the substantial deposit of Christian Faith and Order committed by Christ and His apostles to the Church unto the end of the world, and therefore incapable of compromise or surrender. . . ." Slightly modified by the Lambeth Conference in 1888, this four-point platform came to be known as the Chicago-Lambeth Quadrilateral. It is fundamental to the Ecumenical Movement and is involved overtly or covertly in every ecumenical endeavor. The four points are listed below:

1. The Holy Scriptures of the Old and New Testaments, as "containing all things necessary to salvation," and as being the rule and ultimate standard of faith.

2. The Apostles' Creed as the Baptismal Symbol; and the Nicene Creed as the sufficient statement of the Christian Faith.

3. The two Sacraments ordained by Christ Himself—Baptism and the Supper of the Lord—ministered with unfailing use of Christ's words of institution and of the elements ordained by Him.

4. The Historic Episcopate, locally adapted in the methods of its administration to the varying needs of the nations and peoples called of God into the unity of His church.[1]

The kind of unity anticipated in the Quadrilateral could not come about abruptly. A much less ambitious proposal was put forth that

Peter Ainslie (1867-1934), early ecumenist and controversial president of the Council on Christian Union.

envisioned a limited degree of cooperation among the various denominations without asking any of them to surrender its distinctiveness or autonomy. Such a proposal was the Federal Council of Churches,[2] already discussed in chapter 10. From the outset, the question of whether or not the Disciples should participate was highly controversial. Some believed that involvement as one of the denominations was a repudiation of the heritage that aimed at elimination of denominational distinction. Others believed that the century that had elapsed since publication of the *Declaration and Address* had seen the denominational system so firmly established that the only realistic hope for Christian unity would be through a growing-together of the denominations in some scheme similar to a Council of Churches. Chief spokesman among Disciples for this view was Peter Ainslie,[3] minister of Christian Temple in Baltimore, Maryland, and the president of the International Convention that met in Topeka, Kansas, in 1910. He took the initiative that led to that convention's authorization of the Commission on Christian Union. The following were appointed at Topeka: Peter Ainslie, A.C. Smither, F.W. Burnham, E.M. Bowman, Hill M. Bell, W.T. Moore, M.M. Davis, J.H. Garrison, and I.J. Spencer. The number was increased to twenty-five the next year at the Portland convention. This organization and its successors have served as the rallying ground for those among the Disciples who champion the Ecumenical Movement. In 1914, the Atlanta, Georgia, convention gave to this commission the authority to represent the Disciples in the Federal Council and to represent the council to the Disciples.

The Federal Council of Churches was ardently supported by the officials of the International Convention, but it never did win the support of the Brotherhood at large. As a result, the Disciples had continuing problems raising their portion of the council's budget. The F.C.C.'s espousal of social goals resulted in the early defection of the conservative and Fundamentalist bodies, which meant that its posture was much more liberally oriented than was true of American Protestantism as a whole. Its position on several social issues was considered radical by many conservative Christians. In 1950, the Federal Council was merged with twelve other interdenominational agencies to form the National Council of Churches of Christ. Its headquarters are located in a multi-storied building at 475 Riverside Drive in New York City.

Disciples were active in the National Council of Churches from its inception. Three Disciples were almost immediately given positions of high authority. Roy G. Ross was made executive secretary of the N.C.C.; Mrs. James D. Wyker was named chairman of the United Church Women; and Raymond F. McLain became director of the Commission on Christian Higher Education. Scores of Disciples were given positions of importance in divisions, departments, commissions, and committees. J. Irwin Miller, of Columbus, Indiana, became the first layman elected president of the N.C.C. in 1961.

The Ecumenical Movement is one of worldwide significance. Its beginnings are generally traced to the International World Missionary Conference in Edinburgh, Scotland, in 1910. A disposition was manifested to address frankly the various aspects of a divided Christendom on a worldwide level. Two of the obvious problems involved differences in doctrinal viewpoints and in understanding of the nature and role of ministry. A Conference on Life and Work was held in Stockholm, Sweden, in 1925, followed by a second such conference in Oxford, England in 1937. Another concern was addressed in a Conference on Faith and Order, held in Lausanne, Switzerland, in 1927. A second Conference on Faith and Order was held in 1937 in Edinburgh. These two conferences, in 1937, passed resolutions calling for integration into a World Council of Churches. Realization of these plans was delayed by World War II until 1948, when the World

Council of Churches (W.C.C.) was launched in Amsterdam, Holland, with 145 churches from forty-four countries participating. Since 1948, the number of churches has increased, and the W.C.C. has set up headquarters in Bossey (near Geneva), Switzerland.

Disciples were not prominent in Edinburgh in 1910, but they have been represented since in all the worldwide gatherings of the Ecumenical Movement. Their representatives, appointed through the International Convention and its successor, the General Assembly, have served in many capacities within the W.C.C. structure. Disciples pride themselves in being in the vanguard of the Ecumenical Movement and, even though they do not represent a large denomination, their dedication has not been excelled by any.

Advocates of cooperation with the National and World Councils contend that these bodies are composed of churches that accept Jesus Christ as Lord and Savior and believe in "one Lord, one faith, one baptism, one God and Father of all." They insist that Christians of different denominations ought not to ignore or oppose one another; rather, they must try to manifest their unity in Christ by cooperating in witness and service. They point out that the councils are a working fellowship of churches—not a centralized ecclesiastical authority apart from and superior to the churches constituting them.

Answering the critics of the councils, their advocates insist that they have no "superchurch" characteristics since they cannot legislate for their member churches nor act for them unless permitted to do so. The councils do not seek to enforce conformity or uniformity, do not negotiate mergers of churches, and do not advance any specific theology of the nature of the church or any particular plan for the church's unity. The councils, they say, are merely fellowships of churches in which Christian cooperation is practiced so that churches mutually advance the cause of Christ. In such fellowship, the churches unite to meet human needs; common witness is rendered to the lordship of Christ over the world and the church. The churches in the council enter into serious discussions about their differences in creed, practical emphases, message, ministry, church government, and the missionary task in the world. It is believed by many Disciples that such cooperative activity is a practical, initial step toward the unity and renewal of the Church of Christ.

The major Protestant denominations, with the notable exception of Southern Baptists, hold membership in the National and World Councils of Churches. The newer, more evangelical church bodies do not belong; in fact, most are very much opposed to the councils, especially to the National Council. James DeForest Murch, who maintained close ties with the evangelical church bodies, summarized their objections in the following indictment:

(1) The Council steadfastly refused to adopt as a basis of fellowship the hard core of generally accepted Biblical Christian doctrine. (2) It admitted into its membership a host of liberals who denied these doctrines and gave them preferred status in Council leadership. (3) It had created an ecclesiastical oligarchy which might easily develop into a superchurch. (4) Non-Council churches were forced to take protective measures to insure unfettered liberty in preaching the gospel. (5) It refused to state its acceptance of the Bible as the authoritative Word of God. (6) It considered man's need and not God's grace as motivation for social action and the amelioration of the social order as of greater concern than the salvation of souls. (7) It seriously threatened a distinctly evangelistic thrust in foreign missionary work. (8) It encouraged social revolution to displace capitalism and condoned communism. (9) Its relations with the Eastern Orthodox Catholic churches and its general attitude toward Roman Catholicism threatened to weaken its Protestant testimony. (10) It deliberately omitted to include provisions for the preservation and perpetuation of all the values and liberties inherent in Protestantism.[4]

Neither the Independent Christian Churches nor the Churches of Christ have ever manifested any desire to be identified with either the National or World Council of Churches. In general, they have remained aloof from the Ecumenical Movement as a whole.

Meanwhile, a greater enthusiasm for ecumenicity centered in activity that was generated outside the councils of churches, which remain "councils" and at best are only the first step toward one church.[5] As such, they can never represent the end product of the Ecumenical Movement. Real ecumenists seek mergers and are not satisfied with councils.

In 1949, a conference was held in Greenwich, Connecticut, in response to an invitation issued by Congregational Christian Churches and Disciples of Christ, to explore possibilities of merging those American denominations that recognize one another's ministers and sacraments. Eight groups participated. A second meeting was held in Cincinnati, Ohio, in 1951, where a blueprint for union was presented. Out of this, after prolonged discussions, came the 1957 merger of the Congregational Christian and Evangelical and Reformed Churches to form the United Church of Christ. The International Convention, through its Council on Christian Unity, was an interested observer in the conversations leading to the formation of the United Church of Christ and immediately entered conversations with that body looking toward possible union. But before these conversations could produce concrete results, developments in the National Council of Churches once again captured eccumenical interest.

Consultation on Church Union

On December 4, 1960, at one of the sessions of the triennial meeting of the National Council of the Churches of Christ, which was held in Grace Cathedral of the Episcopal Church in San Francisco, Dr. Eugene Carson Blake, stated clerk of the Presbyterian Church U.S.A., preached a sermon on the subject, "Toward the Reunion of Christ's Church." He proposed that four bodies (the Methodist Church, the Episcopal Church, the Presbyterian Church, and the United Church of Christ) meet to form "a plan of church union both catholic and reformed." He added, "Any other churches which find that they can accept both the principles and plan would also be warmly invited to unite with us."[6]

The four bodies responded affirmatively in 1961. Ominously, the enabling legislation by the Episcopal Church charged its Joint Commission on Approaches to Unity to "conduct these conversations on the basis of the Chicago-Lambeth Quadrilateral on behalf of the Protestant Episcopal Church."[7] Thus, it was clear from the beginning that the Episcopal position on the four matters of Scripture, Creeds, Sacraments, and the Historic Episcopate were not open to negotiation. This predetermined the pattern that subsequent negotiations would take before the first meeting was held.[8]

Duly appointed delegates met in April, 1962, in Washington, D.C., for the first Consultation on Church Union (hereafter known as COCU). To the initial invitation to explore the establishment of a church "truly catholic and truly reformed" were added the words "truly evangelical." The Disciples of Christ and Evangelical United Brethren were invited to join the consultation and accepted forthwith. Subsequent consultations were held in Oberlin, Ohio (1963), Princeton, New Jersey (1964), Lexington, Kentucky (1965), and in Dallas, Texas (1966).

The Dallas consultation adopted *Principles of Church Union,* designed to "become the basis from which to formulate a 'Plan of Union.'"[9] These set forth COCU's general position on (1) the Faith of the Church, (2) the Worship of the Church, (3) the Sacraments of the Church, (4) the Ministry of the Church. No attempt to summarize these positions is necessary since the document is readily available. Suffice it to say that, while the position on baptism (infant or believers, to be performed by immersion, pouring, or sprinkling) posed difficulties for some Disciples, it was the position on the ministry that was to evoke the most serious objection. The principles provided for a threefold ministry of bishops, presbyters, and deacons. In keeping with the nonnegotiable requirements of the Quadrilateral, the episcopal office was advanced as the "symbol and means of continuity and unity of the Church."[10] A precedent had been set in South India in 1947 when the United Church (Presbyterian and Congregational) and the Methodist Church, after long negotiations, agreed to accept episcopal ordination and were fused with the Anglican Church into the Church of South India.[11] Acceptance of episcopal ministry paved the way to union.

Some Disciples could not accept this capitulation to episcopacy. Years earlier, W.E. Garrison had summarized the attitude of many Disciples toward the Chicago-Lambeth Quadrilateral when he observed that "it included as essentials of the Church, and so of Christian fellowship, some things which were not essential to salvation according to the New Testament and omitted one thing that was."[12] Alfred T. DeGroot, known to all as a supporter of ecumenical goals, published a scholarly review of the doctrine of the historic episcopate that was sharply critical of the disposition of Disciple delegates to COCU.[13]

When COCU met in 1970 in St. Louis, Missouri, it issued *A Plan of Union for the Church of Christ Uniting,*[14] which was recommended to the churches for study and response. By this time, the consultation had grown to nine participating bodies with the addition of the African M.E. Church, the African M.E. Church Zion, the Christian Methodist Church, and the Presbyterian Church U.S. (the Methodist and the E.U.B. Church had merged since the consultation began). Also in 1968, the consultation engaged Dr. Paul Crowe, professor of church history at Lexington Theological Seminary (Disciples of Christ), to be its full-time executive secretary. Offices were established in Princeton, New Jersey.

Internal difficulties began to appear for COCU at the Princeton meeting in 1964. It was evident that serious resistance was being encountered within both the Methodist and Episcopal bodies. The Methodist Church did not like the image of the bishop that seemed to be emerging in this *Plan.* Much unrest focused on the proposal to organize congregations into parishes designed to insure racial and socioeconomic wholeness. This frightened some who were reminded of the contemporary issue in the public schools in which courts ordered busing to achieve racial balance. A short time after the release of the *Plan of Union,* there was a distinct decline in interest in COCU. In 1972, the United Presbyterian Church withdrew from COCU, and other bodies were obviously cool.

But the Disciple participants remained devoted to the goals of COCU. George Beazley, of the Disciples, was made chairman of the consultation in 1972. Referring to the study given to the *Plan of Union,* the report of the Disciples' Council on Christian Unity for 1972 pointed out, "All observers of this process seem to agree that our members are carrying a share of this work that is all out of proportion with our size. This is certainly in accord with our commitment to Christian unity."[15]

Future prospects for COCU do not appear to be encouraging. The Chicago-Lambeth Quadrilateral has proved to be a heavy burden, predisposing the whole effort to a particular pattern. Even more difficult was the problem of merging vested institutional interests of the various denominations. By 1975, interest in COCU had declined and Paul Crowe resigned to become the chief administrative officer of the Commission on Christian Unity of the Christian Church (Disciples of Christ). As an effort to achieve the desired unity of the followers of Jesus Christ, the *Plan of Union* seemed to offer little promise.

Union With the United Church of Christ

As prospects for church union through COCU diminished, interest in union between the United Church of Christ and the Christian Church (Disciples of Christ) was revived. The two denominations, through their representative assemblies, entered into a six-year "covenant" to explore the possibilities of union (1979-1985). This anticipated a decision by 1985, and a national steering committee was created with membership divided between the two denominations. Convinced that the work of bringing about church union "has to do with the essential message of God's reconciling action in Jesus Christ," the committee was forced to recognize that "hesitancy abounds in many corners of both churches."[16] The program of the national steering committee was incorporated into a working paper, *Shared Life: a New Approach to Church Union,* which was submitted to the two denominations for reaction. Dissatisfaction quickly surfaced in the United Church of Christ, and it proved to have a chilling effect on the program for union.[17] By 1985, neither denomination was ready for merger; instead a concept of "Ecumenical Partnership" was adopted, which shifted the focus of unity from organizational and structural merging to celebrating the unity that already exists in mission, theology, and worship and seeking new ways to augment this unity.[18] This decision was disappointing to some, encouraging to others, and confusing to yet others.

The National Association of Evangelicals

Meanwhile, there were other efforts at inter-church cooperation that were not a part of the Ecumenical Movement itself, which should not be ignored, especially since these efforts touched some of the Independent Christian Churches. In 1943, some of the leaders of the evangelical Protestant community, who were convinced that the

Federal Council of Churches was not representative of the true Protestant spirit, launched the National Association of Evangelicals in Chicago. The N.A.E. has now grown to a constituency of some forty denominations with ten million members. Some Christian Church ministers were attracted to the N.A.E. because of its strong Biblical position and its similarity to the world Evangelical Alliance that Alexander Campbell had so generously endorsed. Among the early leaders of the association was James D. Murch, who in 1945 was appointed editor of its official organ, *United Evangelical Action.* For fourteen years, Murch edited this journal, which became "the voice of evangelical Christianity in America" until it was eclipsed by *Christianity Today,* which was launched in 1956. Murch was active in the association and served in several evangelical enterprises. He served as president of the National Religious Broadcasters (which included in its membership 150 of the major evangelical radio and television broadcasters in America), of the National Sunday School Association, and of the Evangelical Press Association.[19]

As an organization that brings many denominations together, the N.A.E. has never been accorded the slightest recognition by the International Convention or by its successor body, the General Assembly. Its acceptance by numerous Christian Church ministers and churches has been on a purely voluntary basis. The N.A.E. has also met opposition among Christian Churches. James G. Van Buren took a strong stand against cooperation with the N.A.E. He identified the organization with "fundamentalism," deplored its "creedal basis" for membership, rejected its claim that the Bible is "the only infallible, authoritative, Word of God," noted its superchurch potentialities, and indicated that membership in the N.A.E. automatically condoned denominationalism.[20] J.D. Murch, in defense, insisted that the N.A.E.

> (1) was "evangelical" and not committed to narrow "fundamentalists" views; (2) was neither a church nor council of churches with a creedal test of fellowship, but required its members for purposes of organizational solidarity to sign a statement of belief; (3) held the same view of the Scriptures as that held by the Campbells; (4) was a service organization; and (5) had many members from undenominational churches and organizations.[21]

Independent Christian Churches have been attracted by several of the evangelistic and youth programs that have emerged from the N.A.E. through its affiliated organizations. Some work with Youth for Christ, Campus Crusade, and Evangelism Explosion. Fred P. Thompson served on the N.A.E. Board of Advisors and contributed regularly to the N.A.E. Quarterly, *Action.* Key 73, an evangelistic effort of nationwide scope, was conceived by evangelical churchmen at a meeting in 1967 in Arlington, Virginia. While not directly connected with the N.A.E., Key 73 found its most enthusiastic support from the evangelicals of this body. Many Independent Christian Churches joined the Key 73 effort, and there was hearty support from the *Christian Standard* and *The Lookout*. Ralph Small served on the central committee and Paul Benjamin on the executive committee of Key 73. As might be expected, some ministers held that the evangelistic programs generally identified with Key 73 could not be reconciled with the Restoration Plea and hence refused to participate. The *Restoration Herald* published negative views by ministers opposed to Key 73, and Churches of Christ were not involved in Key 73 at all.

Generally speaking, the heirs of the Stone-Campbell Movement in each of its component parts have been uncomfortable with the evangelical community for several reasons. The creedal basis of cooperation is contrary to the Stone-Campbell heritage even when there is no disagreement with the contents of the creed. In addition, the heavy influence of Calvinist doctrine runs counter to the doctrinal emphasis in the movement. The evangelical emphasis on experiential grace is strange to the thinking of all branches of the movement. On the other hand, the Restoration Movement heirs have placed an importance on baptism and the Lord's Supper that few in the evangelical community accept.

Cooperation in inter-church activity on a local level is quite naturally consistent with attitudes on the national level. Disciples of Christ ministers are usually hearty supporters of local councils of churches. Independent ministers vary in their involvement in such activities, usually remaining aloof from councils of churches, but very often sharing in ministerial associations. Church of Christ ministers have nothing to do with either. These differences can easily be traced to insights expressed in the early development of the movement in the nineteenth century. Precisely how such emphases as "the restoration of the ancient order" and "the union of all Christians" are to be realized in the changing environment of the twentieth century is the critical issue out of which radically divergent viewpoints arise. The problem has been well stated by one of the historians of the Ecumenical Movement:

> The paradox in the Campbellite position, as viewed from the standpoint of the 20th-century union efforts, is that this organic union was to be accomplished through voluntary associations of individuals, who were to "come out" from their denominations and unite on the Bible. The Campbells placed the problem of Church Union on the individual personal level, forcing those who felt as they did to break with their old denominations, rather than building a new Christian Church out of the co-ordinated denominational machin-

ery of several merging Churches. At least the Campbells, in announcing their own positive programme for union, saved themselves the ecclesiastical carpentry which 20th century organic mergers between denominations have so often involved.[22]

This insightful observation from the vantage of one outside the movement itself points directly to the dilemma which has exacted a heavy toll on the heirs of Stone and Campbell in the present century. The plea for Christian unity, which is heard both in Churches of Christ and in Christian Churches, still is addressed to individuals who are urged to "come out" from their denomination and unite with a Bible-only congregation. On the other hand, Disciples of Christ have concluded that experience has shown that unity, left to individual initiative, is unattainable. Thus they have chosen the "ecclesiastical carpentry" option as the more realistic means of attaining the desired unity. This fundamental difference, which appeared at the beginning of the century when the issue of the Federal Council was first introduced at the International Convention in Omaha, Nebraska, in 1902, remains a major barrier to the unity of the movement at the close of the century.

End Notes

[1]Reprinted in W.E. Garrison, *Christian Unity* (op. cit.), pp. 47, 48.

[2]The idea for a Federal Council of Churches was first suggested by the great historian Philip Schaff in his last speech given at the World's Parliament of Religions in connection with the Chicago World's Fair in 1893. Schaff projected a

> voluntary association of different churches in their official capacity, each retaining its freedom and independence in the management of its internal affairs, but all recognizing one another as sisters with equal rights and co-operating in general enterprises, such as the spread of the gospel at home and abroad, the defense of the faith against infidelity, the evaluation of the poor and neglected classes of society, works of philanthropy and charity, and moral reform. (Quoted in Rouse and Neill, op. cit., p. 256.)

[3]Donald Herbert Yoder holds that it was Ainslie who "more than any other single man was responsible for recalling the Disciples to a sense of ecumenical mission." (Rouse and Neill, op. cit., p. 240.)

[4]Murch, *Christians Only* (op. cit)., p. 349.

[5]For a note on the limits of federation, see Yoder, op. cit., pp. 257, 258.

[6]George L. Hunt and Paul A. Crowe, eds., *Where We Are in Church Union* (New York: Association Press, 1965), p. 13.

[7]Ibid., p. 14.

[8]For a contemporary Disciple reaction to the Quadrilateral, see G. Plattenberg, "The Unity of the Church," *The Old Faith Restated,* J.H. Garrison, ed., (St. Louis: Christian Publishing Co.), pp. 334-340. Plattenberg finds the idea of basing Christian union on the historic episcopacy "wholly inconsistent with the nature of Christianity" (p. 335).

[9]*Principles of Church Union* (Cincinnati: Forward Movement Publications, 1966), p. 9.

[10]Ibid., p. 48.

[11]Rouse and Neill, op. cit. pp. 473-476.

[12]W.E. Garrison, *Christian Unity and Disciples* (op. cit.), p. 48.

[13]Alfred T. DeGroot, *Episcopacy in Succession* (Fort Worth: published by the author).

[14]*A Plan of Union for the Church of Christ Uniting* (Philadelphia: COCU Distribution Center, 1970).

[15]*Yearbook and Directory of the Christian Church (Disciples of Christ)*, 1972, p. 101.

[16]Ibid., 1984, p. 142.

[17]Ibid., 1985, p. 150.

[18]Robert K. Welsh, "Ecumenical Partnership: Its Meaning and Mandate for Church Unity," *Lexington Theological Quarterly*, October, 1985, pp. 123-129.

[19]For the story of the National Association of Evangelicals, see J.D. Murch, *Cooperation Without Compromise* (Grand Rapids: Eerdmans, 1956).

[20]James G. Van Buren, "Views and Reviews," *Christian Standard*, October 6, 1951, pp. 14, 15.

[21]Murch, *Christians Only* (op. cit.), p. 350.

[22]Yoder, op. cit., p. 239.

Chapter Sixteen

Approaching the Twenty-first Century: Disciples of Christ

When the twentieth century opened, plans were under way for a great celebration of the centennial anniversary of the publication of the *Declaration and Address,* the symbolic origin of the Restoration Movement. The convention poster, circulated nationwide to advertise the great Pittsburgh assembly, described the Stone-Campbell Movement as "an American Movement for Christian Union." But the enthusiasm and optimism of the event was beclouded by the fact that one fracture had already occurred and early symptoms of another could be discerned. At the end of the twentieth century, three separate religious communions can be identified. Each of the bodies claims to be the true heir of the movement, and each is partially correct. Each of the groups has evolved distinct characteristics, interests, and sense of purpose. Each has developed its own agencies, institutions, and resources. The three groups exist at present as totally separate, self-sufficient bodies composed of very different types of people. Despite a common heritage, the events that have impinged upon the movement in the past century and a half have evoked differing responses that have created differing and often antithetical points of view. When such differences become sufficiently numerous and important, the bonds of prior unity inevitably give way to more immediate concerns and new bonds of unity are created that supplant older identities. The three religious communions that derive their heritage from the Stone-Campbell efforts may be easily identified by their separate and disparate understandings, interests, and objectives. Each of these bodies faces problems and opportunities unique to itself; thus, considereation will be given to each in the order of its historic identity.

393

Distinguishing Characteristics
of Disciples of Christ

The Christian Church (Disciples of Christ) is the primary advocate of the unity theme of the movement. The Disciples' commitment to Christian unity is based on their understanding of the nature of the church[1] and is manifest in their literature, assemblies, and participation in ecumenical activities at all levels. Disciples take pride in their energetic participation in various councils of churches because they are convinced that Christ's church is larger than their denomination, and they believe that this larger dimension finds expression in cooperative ventures with other denominations. Disciples are much less assured that they represent the true Christian way than are the other two branches of the movement; hence they are less reluctant to enter into contact with denominational bodies.[2] Furthermore, Disciples appreciate the practical value of cooperative enterprises and enter wholeheartedly into ecumenical activities. Most concur with Walter R. Naff, of Brite Divinity School, Texas Christian University, who affirms,

> The purpose of any council of churches, whether on the world, national, or community level, is to do better together what we cannot do as well alone.
> Disciples of Christ have always believed in a strong church, but most of us have been forced to recognize the insufficiency of ours or any other denomination and are ready to acknowledge a mutual concern that can give effectiveness to our common mission.[3]

Disciples of Christ differ from the other heirs of the movement in another understanding of the nature of the church. While Christian Churches and Churches of Christ tend to confine their understanding of the church to local congregations, Disciples have adjusted theirs to include extra-congregational gatherings on a regional and general (U.S. and Canada) level as "manifestations of church." This concept is seen in restructure (see chapter 14) and is summarized by Keith Clark:

> Disciples have a tradition of congregational autonomy that has matured to an understanding of *one* Christian Church (Disciples of Christ) rather than an International Convention of Christian Churches, and association of independent fellowships.[4]

Accordingly, Disciples regard persons formerly known as agency secretaries as "regional ministers" or "area ministers." Because such "ministers" have responsibility for overseeing the work of congregations, it is suggested that they have a de facto "ministry of oversight" *(episcope)*, and thus they ought to be regarded as bishops. A recent study, *Ministry Among the Disciples*, concludes that a ministry that includes the three offices of *diaconate* (service), *presbyterate* (word and sacraments), and *episcopate* (oversight)

> appears to be in line with the emerging consensus within the ecumenical movement and is the current pattern accepted by many churches throughout the world, e.g., Anglican, Methodist, Roman Catholic, Orthodox, Lutheran, and United Churches. It thus appears to offer a strong possibility for wider ecumenical relations in the future.[5]

This concept of the episcopal ministry is recommended because it acknowledges the wholeness of the church. Such an understanding, which tends to see the wholeness of the church in a ministry of *episcope* (oversight), finds no sympathy in the other two branches of the movement, which view it as more Cyprianic than Biblical. Disciples, however, view the idea of unity in faith as important but impractical when seen as the sole basis or expression of unity. Disciples are heirs of the tendency to organize, an impulse that can be traced at least as far back as to the formation of the American Christian Missionary Society in 1849. This tendency advanced to the demand for a unified organization in 1919 (the United Christian Missionary Society) and to a unified structure for the whole church in 1968 (restructure). The view that such structure "is absolutely necessary"[6] to the well-being of the church finds no agreement in either Christian Churches or Churches of Christ.

Another important distinction in the Disciples' concept of the church and its ministry is found in the role of women. Disciples have welcomed women in ministry at all levels. The number of women enrolled in seminaries of Disciples of Christ approaches the number for men. It is common among churches of the Disciples of Christ for women to serve as elders, and a growing number of women serve as pastors and as regional and area ministers. This is not the case in Christian Churches or Churches of Christ.

A second distinction between the Disciples of Christ and the other heirs of the movement is found in the way Disciples view the Bible. The impact of Biblical criticism on the Stone-Campbell movement has been noted (chapter 10) as one of several divisive factors. As a whole, have not shared the hostility to Biblical criticism found in the other segments of the movement. It is not accurate to suggest that Disciples do not respect apostolic authority. It is correct to note that Disciples' Biblical scholars see the message and authority of the Bible from a very different perspective than is the case with scholars from Christian Churches and Churches of Christ. Disciples view the Bible as a reflection of the faith of the early church but not necessarily as a pattern for what the church ought to be in the culture of contemporary society. Occasionally an objection is registered that "we have swung too far,"[7] but Disciple Biblical scholars are generally uncomfortable with what they regard as the proof-texting exegetical methodology found elsewhere.

A third distinction that is unique to the Disciple heirs of the Stone-Campbell tradition is the almost universal acceptance of open membership, the practice of admitting by transfer unimmersed persons into full membership of the church. Note has already been taken of the divisive nature of this practice (chapter 10). Until recently, all Disciple churches administered baptism only by immersion. Logical inconsistencies in this arrangement have led a few Disciple churches a step further, as Charles H. Bayer noted,

> Open membership seems to be a closed issue for many of us; at least one seldom hears it discussed. Most of us now receive the unimmersed without the indignity of re-baptism. But what about their children? What is the meaning of the grace of God in baptism, and how does that grace operate beyond our rationality? Is our fixation on the age of accountability a Lockean trap into which we have long since fallen?
>
> We have thought about that question in congregation and we now baptize as many infants as we dedicate. Not only that, but we baptize those who request it as adults with far less than the 700 gallons of water it takes to fill our baptistry.[8]

Both of the other bodies of the movement reject any semblance of open membership and consider it a rejection of Biblical example and teaching as well as a repudiation of the heritage of the movement.

A fourth distinction between Disciples of Christ and the other two bodies deriving from the Stone-Campbell Movement is found in mission philosophy. The United Christian Missionary Society, heir to eight decades of mission endeavor by Disciples, set forth its mission aims in a major publication in 1928 as follows:

> to establish Churches of Christ in sufficient number so located and so imbued with missionary and evangelistic passion as to make possible the Christianization of the territory for which they have assumed responsibility and to conduct such other lines of activity as may contribute to this end.[9]

Several factors contributed to a change in policy in the half century that followed. The Great Depression forced a curtailment of the number of missionaries sent to foreign fields. Increased involvement with other denominations in union activities and institutions, and the rise of national churches in nations that were once mission fields encouraged a change in policy. The Division of Overseas Ministry (successor body to the U.C.M.S.) is no longer primarily engaged in converting peoples of other cultures. It now conceives its role as one of assisting national churches in their quest to develop as the national bodies deem wise within their own culture. It is believed that the work of evangelism is best carried out by nationals. The role of the D.O.M. is to respond to requests from national churches to send persons with particular skills (such as physicians, teachers, engineers, and hygienists) for limited-term service. For Disciples, the day of the long-term professional missionary is past.

In contrast to this mission philosophy, both Christian Churches and Churches of Christ understand missionary efforts primarily in terms of evangelism. Medical and educational efforts are not neglected, but they are deemed ancillary to the primary goal of making converts.

Disciples of Christ differ from the other branches of the Stone-Campbell Movement in the importance that they attach to the social dimension of the gospel. The nature of the intense congregationalism of Christian Churches and Churches of Christ prevents these churches from addressing social problems of national and international significance. Issues such as unemployment, war and peace, and the nation's economic structure cannot be addressed effectively by single congregations. Consequently, thoroughgoing congregationalist churches tend to focus on the ethic of the individual. This is not to infer that such churches are indifferent to the larger problems; rather, it means that they vest the matter of social action in other community organizations in which Christians are urged to participate and to make their influence felt.[10] This position holds that the church, *per se,* should not be involved in social action because (a) it is extraneous to its major purpose and (b) the church is ill-equipped to make pronouncements and create policies of a social nature, as numerous examples from the past seem to indicate.

Disciples of Christ are not content with the attitude toward social issues that leaves action up to individual inclination.[11] They believe that the weight and influence of the whole church is necessary to produce the change needed in society. The temperance issue produced the first organization designed to address a problem in society. The American Temperance Board was created by the Centennial Convention in Pittsburgh, Pennsylvania, in 1909.

The creation of the Federal Council of Churches aroused new interest in the relevance of Christianity to social problems, especially after the council adopted a "Social Creed of the Churches" at its first Quadrennial in 1912. The Disciples' General Missionary Convention, meeting in Louisville, Kentucky, in 1912, created a committee within the American Christian Missionary Society and charged it to address social concerns and work in all possible ways with the Social Service Commission of the Federal Council of Churches. The next year, in Toronto, this committee became the Commission on Social Service and the Rural Church. The "rural church" aspect was soon separated, and the commission became the first of several successive boards changed in title but not in purpose as the structure of the Disciple organizations has been altered. A glance at proceedings of the International Convention of Disciples of Christ and its successor, the General Assembly, will provide abundant evidence of Disciples' continuing concern for social issues.[12]

Characteristics distinguishing Disciples of Christ from the other two branches of the Stone-Campbell heritage that have been noted thus far are theological in nature. There are also some important sociological differences that help to explain why the distinctions noted above prevail. Historians have understood for decades that sociological factors are very significant in predisposing attitudes and reactions in religious communities; but it is only recently that serious attention has been directed to the sociological differences among the three branches of the Stone-Campbell heirs. Lawrence C. Keene, associate professor of sociology at Pepperdine University, has made the most thorough study to date of the differences among these groups. Keene's research led him to characterize the beliefs and attitudes of Disciple ministers and lay leaders as "significantly more 'liberal' than the responses of the Independents and Churches of Christ."[13] As a result, Disciples are much less doctrinaire on such issues as women's role in the church, abortion, social drinking, divorce, and homosexuality. He noted that the wide divergence of beliefs entertained by Disciples unwittingly creates the impression that Disciples can believe anything they want.[14] He warns, "The more Disciples differ from one another and the *stronger* these differences become among us, the *less viable* and *stable* Disciples will be!" and he concludes, "We have leaders who in many ways have 'outgrown' the constituency."[15]

Disciple leadership quite naturally resists the idea that they are theologically vacuous or that just anything goes. John O. Humbart, president and general minister of the Christian Church (Disciples of Christ), expressed his hope that the Disciples will be able to move toward being "a confessing church rather than just an anti-creedal one,"[16] citing the affirmation of faith stated in the preamble to the *Provisional Design of the Christian Church (Disciples of Christ)* as a "sure word."

The absence of ideological cohesion among Disciples of Christ may be compensated for by the structural cohesion that is provided by the Provisional Design. While restructure has not measured up to everybody's full expectations, there is general satisfaction among Disciples as to the results it has produced and little inclination can be found to make serious modification of the design.

Resources of the Disciples of Christ

The Disciples are the heirs of the accumulated resources of more than a century. Each of the groups that separated from the Disciples was faced with the task of developing its own resources and creating new agencies and institutions.[17] Trust funds, endowments, and extensive property holdings were brought into the United Christian Missionary Society and other agencies that reported to the International Convention of Disciples of Christ. After Restructure, these resources were incorporated into the Christian Church (Disciples of Christ) or held by one of the colleges or agencies that maintains a "covenant relationship" with the church. Among these are the eighteen colleges and universities and seven seminaries and divinity schools that are member institutions of the Division of Higher Education.[18] This involvement in higher education is augmented by sixty campus ministers serving in ecumenical campus ministries in state universities. Disciples also operate forty-eight summer camps and conference programs.

The National Benevolent Association, chartered in 1887, maintains sixty-five homes for the elderly and for children. The Pension Fund of the Christian Church, successor to the Board of Ministerial Relief established in 1895, offers a fully funded pension service to ministers and agency personnel of all three branches of the movement, although the services are utilized by few other than Disciples. Dues paid by ministers and churches or institutions insure continuing income for members whose working years have terminated. The Board of Church Extension manages assets of sixty million dollars and provides counsel and fund-raising assistance as well as moderate-cost loans to congregations and institutions involved in building programs. In addition to Disciple churches, its services are usually extended to Independent Christian Churches when requested.

The Christian Board of Publication, located in St. Louis, Missouri, is wholly owned by Disciples of Christ. Purchased by R.A. Long in 1910, it was given to the Disciples to be operated as a not-for-profit enterprise. It has published Sunday-school and other literature, periodicals including the influential *The Christian Evangelist* and its successor publications, and books relating to Disciples of Christ, under the Bethany Press imprint. But limitations imposed by the government on nonprofit publishers, plus the high cost of sophisticated new presses, have made it difficult for these publishing efforts to be cost effective. Decline in subscriptions resulted in the merging of *World Call* and the *Christian* (successor journal to *The Christian Evangelist)* into *The Disciple* in 1974. At first published semi-weekly, the *Disciple* became a monthly journal in 1975, with the loss of frequency compensated by expanded proportions.

Increased costs of publication and diminished demand forced the Christian Board to join with other denominational publishers to supply Sunday-school literature on a cooperative basis. Eventually, the decision was reached to sell the printing plant and terminate this phase of publishing. While the sale of the press may be viewed as a retrenchment, it was fiscally wise and hence considered to be good stewardship of Disciple resources.[19] Presently, all of the printing of the Christian Board of Publications is done on contract.

A developing resource of the Christian Church (Disciples of Christ) is the Christian Church Foundation. It receives gifts, bequests, and assets from churches that close, and it aims to distribute income derived therefrom to the various ministries of the Christian Church (Disciples of Christ). Theodore P. Beasley, a Disciple layman and founder of the fund, also initiated a project to build a new office center for the Christian Church. It will provide a central location in Indianapolis for offices now scattered in several separate locations.

Disciples have made a serious effort to preserve historical materials relating to the movement. In 1941, Claude E. Spencer, librarian at Culver-Stockton College, Canton, Missouri, launched the Disciples of Christ Historical Society. A collection of materials was housed in the library of this college for a decade. Largely through the efforts of Forrest F. Reed, who shared Spencer's vision of locating the society near a major university, the collection was moved to Nashville, Tennessee, adjacent to Vanderbilt University. In 1951, T.W. and B.D. Phillips, of Butler, Pennsylvania, provided the society with a modern, adequate building facility in memory of their father, T.W. Phillips, Sr. The society attempts to preserve materials of historic significance related to all three branches of the movement. The archives are made available to scholars and interested persons of all branches of the heritage, but the management and the financial burden of the society rest mainly with Disciples of Christ.

The oldest important historical sites also are maintained largely by the Disciples of Christ. The old Cane Ridge Meeting House, erected in 1791, served to house a congregation until 1921. By that date, people in the rural area of Cane Ridge preferred to attend churches in nearby towns, and the building began to deteriorate. In 1922, a Cane Ridge Memorial Fund was established, which made possible periodic repairs to the old structure, built of native blue ash logs. In 1949, under auspices of the Department of Men's Work of the United Christian Miossionary Society, a series of annual men's retreats at the old meeting house kindled an interest in its preservation. The Cane Ridge Preservation Project was launched, providing in 1957 a beautiful superstructure over the old building. A curator's residence and the Barton Warren Stone Memorial Building, housing a museum, have since been erected on adjoining sites.

The Campbell home at Bethany, West Virginia, was for decades the responsibility of Bethany College to maintain. Recently, however, a Campbell Home Association was organized to assume responsibility for maintenance and preservation of this historic place.

The old Bethany church, site of many of Alexander Campbell's later sermons, fell into a tragic state of disrepair in the years following the removal of the congregation to an expanded and more modern facility. It has been restored through the generosity of an interested individual.

Challenges Facing Disciples of Christ

The future confronts every denomination with a variety of problems, both internal and external. The Christian Church (Disciples of Christ) is no exception. The most serious challenge is found in the consistent membership decline experienced by the denomination over the past two decades. In the years immediately following restructure, declining statistics were attributed to the withdrawal of many congregations from the denomination. More recent declines cannot be so easily dismissed. The problem of declining membership among Disciples of Christ has been forcefully called to their attention by Herb Miller, executive director of the Disciples' National Evangelistic Association.

> The Christian Church (Disciples of Christ) is dying. At the present rate of membership decline, the Disciples will cease to exist in the year 2027.
>
> During the 1985 calendar year, Disciples suffered net participating member losses of forty-four persons each day—or 1.6 percent of North American membership . . . Net participating member losses in our 4,251 congregations totaled 13.5 percent during the past ten years. Participating membership has dropped more than thirty percent during the past twenty-two years. If we counted entire congregations lost during restructure, the decline totals sixty percent. Membership losses slowed down during the early 1980's, but decline is now speeding up again. Why? Too few young adults are coming into our congregations to compensate for the higher median age of Disciple members.[20]

Miller described the situation as a "crisis" mandating immediate action. He concluded, "If Disciples do not reverse this death march by 1990, the rapidly rising median age level of our members will create a terminally ill denomination." Lawrence Keene, in a study already noted, discovered that Disciple ministers and elders are "significantly older than ministers and elders in the other two Stone-Campbell groups."[21]

The concern expressed by Herb Miller is shared by many in the Disciple fellowship. Faculty and students at Christian Theological Seminary in Indianapolis took the initiative to hold a conference in March, 1987, on the theme: Reappraising the Disciples' Tradition for the Twenty-first Century.[22] The motivation was "a nagging sense that we have 'lost' part of our identity and purpose" and a frank recognition that "our membership continues to decrease; our worship seems lethargic; our theological debates are often superficial and divisive."[23] A response of 150 to 200 participants was expected. The fact that more than 550 persons registered for the conference indicates how great is the level of concern. A wide range of topics was given careful consideration, mostly by scholars. However, no major conclusions were reached that would point the way to significant future action.[24]

Nonetheless, some Disciples are making a serious effort to reverse the trend of decline. Eight of the thirty regions of the church have engaged in a five-year program called GROW that has registered positive results.[25] The Board of Church Extension and the Division of Homeland Ministries have sponsored a project to start 100 new Disciple churches in the decade of the eighties. Known as CAN (Church Advance Now), the project achieved its goal in 1987. However commendable such a project is, a goal of ten new congregations per year does not keep pace with normal attrition.

The problem of declining membership is not unique to Disciples of Christ; it is shared by several other mainline denominations, such as Methodists, Presbyterians, and the United Church of Christ. Part of this decline is due to the phenomenal growth of charismatic denominations in recent years. However, unless some way is found to halt the trend toward membership decline, the outlook for Disciples is not encouraging.

A second challenge facing Disciples of Christ will arise if the hopes of some in the denomination to effect a merger with another denomination should be realized. The history of denominational mergers is that, more often than not, they produce schism simply because the compromises required to merge prove unacceptable to parties within one or both of the existing denominations.[26] The history of restructure has demonstrated that the Disciples of Christ can adjust to new conditions, but it also warns that such adjustments are not without cost in terms of defections. Whether the denomination can accommodate the adjustments required to enter into union with another religious body remains to be seen. Should the union conversations now in progress (see chapter 14) prove fruitful, this challenge becomes critical for Disciples of Christ.

It should be noted that success in achievement of the perceived mission of the Disciples of Christ in promoting Christian unity is not contingent upon numerical growth. As consistent advocates of the unity of all Christians in ecumenical efforts of both national and international scope, Disciples of Christ have exercised influence well beyond the relative size of the denomination. Through their hearty support of world, national, and local councils of churches, through the commitment of the Division of Overseas Ministries to ecumenical missionary activity, and through the structure of their seminaries, Disciples of Christ continue to promote the cause of the unity of Christians. As they face the future, there is no evidence of decline in their commitment to that ideal.

End Notes

[1]Disciples of Christ have an active Commission on Theology, which, for several years, has focused on the nature of the church. It has issued a series of booklets treating various aspects of this subject. The booklets were published by the Council on Christian Unity, Indianapolis, Indiana.

[2]Lawrence C. Keene, "Disciples of Christ on the Pacific Slope: a Sociological Approach," *Impact* (Claremont: Disciples Seminary Foundation, 1984), pp. 5-91.

[3]Walter R. Naff, "We Need the Church Councils," *The Disciple,* September, 1986, p. 18.

[4]Keith E. Clark, "Where God's People Gather," *The Disciple,* October, 1987, p. 17.

[5]D. Newell Williams, *Ministry Among the Disciples* (St. Louis: Bethany Press, 1985), p. 49.

[6]A. Dale Fiers, *The Second Consultation on Internal Unity,* Charles Gresham, ed. (Oklahoma City: private publication, 1960), p. 145.

[7]Dale Patrick, "We've Swung Too Far on the Bible," *The Disciple,* January, 1986, p. 52. The General Board of the church rejected a resolution submitted by one of the churches affirming that the Bible is inspired and "infallible." It substituted "important" and "central" (*Yearbook,* 1986, p. 244). Prof. Patrick considered this "a vague affirmation . . . open to a wide variety of positions."

[8]Charles H. Bayer, "Do We Care About Theological Issues?" *The Disciple,*, June, 1986, p. 54.

[9]*Survey of Service* (St. Louis: Christian Board of Publication, 1928), p. 517.

[10]An exception is found in Churches of Christ. The view that Christians should not participate in the political process was urged by David Lipscomb in the *Gospel Advocate* and continues to have wide acceptance. See Earl I. West, *op cit.,* Vol. II, pp. 212ff.

[11]The futility of assuming that an individual ethic would apply effectively to social problems was pointed out by Reinhold Niebuhr in *Moral Man and Immoral Society* (New York: Scribner's, 1932).

[12]The history of Disciples' concern for social action has been ably written by James H. Crain, *The Development of Social Ideas Among Disciples of Christ* (St. Louis: Bethany Press, 1969).

[13]Keene, op. cit., pp. 46-50. See also same author, "Our Definite Differences," *The Disciple,* December, 1987, p. 24.

[14]Disciples have not been indifferent to the need to express their faith. Vol. II of the *Panel of Scholars Reports* (op. cit.) is given to "A Reconstruction of Theology." On a more popular level see Colbert S. Cartwright, *People of the Chalice: Disciples of Christ In Faith and Practice* (St. Louis: Christian Board of Publication, 1987).

[15]Keene, "Definite Differences" (op. cit.), p. 24.

[16]John O. Humbart, "The Design's Affirmation of Faith Provides the Disciples with a 'Sure Word,'" *The Disciple,* July, 1988, p. 30.

[17]Of the older Disciple institutions, only Milligan College and Johnson Bible College are identified with Independent Christian Churches. None is identified with the Churches of Christ.

[18]For a listing, see Appendix A.

[19]*The Disciple,* June, 1986, p. 30.

[20]Herb Miller, "Voting on Our Future," *The Disciple,* October, 1986, p. 8.

[21]Keene, "Differences," loc. cit.

[22]The addresses were published in *Midstream* (Indianapolis: Council on Christian Unity), July, 1987.

[23]Michael Kinnamon, "Introduction to a Conference," *Midstream,* July, 1987, p. 261.

[24]For a resumé, see Keith E. Clark, "An Identity for the Future," *The Disciple,* September, 1987, pp. 22-25.

[25]Herb Miller, "Contemporary Disciples' Evangelism," *Mainstream,* July, 1987, p. 355.

[26]For example, when the majority of British Churches of Christ voted to merge with the United Reform Church in 1970, twenty-seven congregations declined to unite with the URC. Instead, they formed the Fellowship of Churches of Christ following the dissolution of the Conference.

Chapter Seventeen

Approaching the Twenty-first Century: Churches of Christ

Churches of Christ (noninstrument) became a separate religious body as the result of a process of withdrawal that covered several decades beginning with the end of the Civil War and culminating at the close of the nineteenth century. No single event or series of events can be cited as the point when the fellowship was ruptured. The separation was more of a process than an event. In a few instances, congregations did not choose their affiliation until well into the twentieth century. Formal recognition of the division came with the request from Churches of Christ not to be included with Disciples of Christ in the federal census, a request that was honored in the census of 1906. Actually, fellowship between the two bodies had ceased in most regions of the nation many years before this date. Contacts between the two (later three) bodies in the twentieth century have been very limited.

Distinguishing Characteristics of Churches of Christ

Churches of Christ are distinguished from the other two segments of the Stone-Campbell heritage in a number of ways. The most obvious is the refusal of this body of people to use any form of instrumental accompaniment in their congregational singing. Failing to find sanction or precedent in the New Testament for singing to the accompaniment of an instrument in public worship, Churches of Christ conclude that such a practice is not acceptable to God and, thus, must not be permitted in the church. They deem the use of an instrument to be an "innovation" of sufficient nature as to justify a schism in the ranks of the church.

As has been noted (chapter 8), the roots of this schism go back to the decades immediately following the Civil War. Originally, the issue of instrumental music was only one of several matters of tension. The most serious issue concerned the missionary society, whose loyalty resolution in 1863 deeply offended the Southern churches. Other issues included the tendency of the larger, more affluent congregations to "hire" their "one-man minister," the tendency of congregations to abandon the single cup for Communion (the dreaded tuberculin bacillus made individual cups preferable), and the adoption of Sunday schools with classes for various age groups. All of the above were considered to be innovations without sanction in the New Testament and, therefore, grounds for separation from the innovators. To this day, there remain champions of each of these positions.[1] The numbers of those who make the single Communion cup, the paid preacher, and the separate Sunday school a test of fellowship have declined until they are only a tiny minority of Churches of Christ today. The vast majority of Churches of Christ now employ one or more professional ministers, use individual Communion cups, and sponsor Sunday schools. Opposition to the musical instruments and to any missionary organization continues to be characteristic of all Churches of Christ. The anti-instrument feature is, of course, the most visible.

Beyond these two characteristics, other generalizations are more precarious. Most Churches of Christ do not have choirs nor do they permit solos, quartets, or any other type of "special music" in their worship services. Such performances are deemed to be exhibitionist and non-edifying. Music for wedding ceremonies poses a problem that is solved in various ways by different congregations. Some weddings of a large nature are held in denominational church buildings where instruments are utilized. Some are held in rented halls. Occasionally organs are brought into the building for the wedding only, on the grounds that a wedding is not a worship service. Otherwise, the music for a wedding is a cappella vocal.

Churches of Christ, like Christian Churches and unlike Disciples of Christ, understand the church to be found only in the local congregation. Each local church is understood to be a kind of a microcosm of the church universal. All of the work supported by a local church is under the supervision of the elders of that local church, of which it is considered an extension. Missionaries, for example, are accountable to and may be discharged by the elders of a congregation.[2] Congregations that are too small to support their own missionary send funds to the church that sponsors a missionary whose work they deem to be worthy; funds are not sent directly to the missionary.

This practice has posed a serious problem for some congregations, particularly with reference to supporting institutions that cannot be supervised by a local church, such as a college or university or homes for children or the aged. The issue of whether or not a congregation may send financial support to an institution over which it cannot exercise direct supervision has created the largest schism within the Churches of Christ at the present time. Approximately fifteen percent of the congregations of Churches of Christ deny that the church can "use the Lord's money" to support an agency or institution that is not "church" (although they admit the propriety of individuals contributing to such institutions). Accordingly, they do not have fellowship with churches that are willing to engage in such "compromise" (as they conceive it) of the New Testament practice. Noninstitutional churches can be found in forty-eight of the fifty states.[3] They are more numerous in Texas and in Florida. Florida College, in Tampa, is associated with the noninstitutional churches.

Another characteristic of Churches of Christ is that they are uniformly postmillennial, except for 101 congregations (.8%) that were influenced by R.H. Boll, who was front-page editor of the *Gospel Advocate,* 1909-1915, and later minister of the Portland Avenue Church of Christ in Louisville, Kentucky, and a publisher of *Word and Work.* Boll had been impressed by millennial views set forth by the Plymouth Brethren, and he subsequently influenced these churches to adopt a premillennial position. In bitter controversy running over several decades, these congregations were ostracized and now have no contact with the main body of Churches of Christ.

It must be noted that the postmillennialism of mainstream Churches of Christ is strictly of the nineteenth-century variety. In the twentieth century, most postmillennialism inclined toward the social gospel or some alternate form of social involvement. But Churches of Christ, probably because of their isolation from other religious influences and because of the rural location of most of their congregations,[4] hold firmly to the view often advocated in the nineteenth century that the preaching of the gospel would convert the world, thus ushering in the millennium.

This form of postmillennial theology, in contrast to later forms, does not countenance direct involvement of the church in social issues. The postmillennial Churches of Christ eschew such involvement. Seldom is a member of a Church of Christ found in a political office or position.[5] Their confidence in the future is not related to any type of social action of either a religious or secular nature.

The extreme congregationalism of the Churches of Christ makes it difficult to treat them as one body. In reality, various subgroups may be identified that have no fellowship with the others. The *Directory of Churches of Christ* designates twelve different doctrinal issues that have divided Churches of Christ.[6] However, about seventy-five percent of all Churches of Christ are part of the mainstream. Since almost none of the activity of Churches of Christ depends upon inter-congregational cooperation, they are able to accommodate a wide range of divisions of this type with less consequence than would be the case with more structured denominations.

Churches of Christ are characterized by very conservative attitudes toward the Bible. Higher criticism has found almost no sympathizers in any of the colleges and universities associated with Churches of Christ. Exegetical methods employed in Churches of Christ, as found in sermons and Bible lessons, are literalistic. Textual justification is sought for every aspect of church activity, which is consistent with the widely held conviction that the New Testament provides a pattern for the church. This disposition toward a very literal Biblical interpretation accounts for much of the schism previously noted and has led Leroy Garrett to conclude that an emphasis on restoration is divisive by nature.[7]

The role of women in Churches of Christ is more restricted than in either of the other branches of the movement. Women are never permitted to serve as elder, deaconess, or preacher. Generally, they are not permitted to speak in the worship service or to teach men in a Sunday-school class. Interestingly, however, the wearing of a head covering, once mandated as a sign of women's status (1 Corinthians 11:6-10), has undergone silent modification as the custom has disappeared in the larger society. This explicit apostolic injunction pertaining to worship no longer carries much force in practice among Churches of Christ. Similarly, most Churches of Christ have not been different from the majority of Protestant denominations in their quiet abandonment of the practice of church discipline, for which 1 Corinthians 5:1-8 provides apostolic precedence.

A noticeable characteristic of Churches of Christ is their uniform aversion to ecumenical activity, either of the liberal or of the evangelical variety. Involvement with any of the denominations is generally viewed as a compromise of the ideal of the one church established by Christ and fashioned by examples and precedents found within the New Testament. Pragmatic reasons that are advanced by many Protestant bodies to recommend interdenominational cooperation in behalf of evangelistic or social ends are ineffective on Churches of Christ, who do not subscribe to either the social objectives and methods of the church councils or the evangelistic formulas of the evangelicals. Consequently, Churches of Christ follow a policy of isolation except for fellowship with those of their own group or subgroup.

Sociological studies have disclosed several interesting characteristics of Churches of Christ. Having begun as a movement in the post-Civil War South, these churches continue to be predominantly Southern. Slightly over half of the churches and 884,498 of their 1,277,004 members, or 69.2%, are found in the churches in fourteen

Southern states.[8] Somewhat surprisingly—considering the strong Southern orientation of these churches—Churches of Christ have had more success working with ethnic minorities than has been the case with the other two branches of the Stone-Campbell heritage.[9]

Elders in Churches of Christ in nine Western states examined by Lawrence Keene were found to be predominantly rural in background, and 89.4% were convinced that the Church of Christ is "closer than any other to the complete truth."[10] Elders in Churches of Christ were more likely than not to have parents who were also members of their church, and they were much more likely to be second-generation members of their church than is the case with their counterparts in the other two fellowships.[11] Elders also have a much more significant and active leadership role in the church than is the case with elders in the other parts of the movement. Elders in Churches of Christ generally hold lifetime tenure in contrast to term tenure in the other branches of the movement, although this situation may be changing.

Resources of Churches of Christ

Churches of Christ enter the twenty-first century as a body of more than 13,000 listed congregations in the United States, plus 139 congregations in Canada. Membership is 1,227,004 in the United States, and Canada adds 5,898.[12] This makes it the largest of the three bodies of the movement. The needs of Churches of Christ are served by a variety of institutions that have been developed over the past century. Beyond the institutional structure is a very real though intangible resource, namely, the aggressive evangelistic spirit that marks most of the Churches of Christ. This is due, in part, to the conviction, previously noted, that the Church of Christ is the "true church," the only one that is acceptable to God. Thus, when members of the church move into a community where there is no Church of Christ, they are encouraged to start one in their own home rather than to associate with any of the denominations. An examination of the *Directory of the Churches of Christ* discloses that many of the churches have fewer than twenty members, and some have only three or four. Without doubt, some of these "churches" in time grow to become self-supporting congregations. The simple worship pattern of Churches of Christ is well suited to house-church expression. However, the question must be faced as to whether a family of three persons worshiping separately in a community where no others accept the noninstrument position can actually be understood to constitute a "church" in the sense in which the concept is found in the New Testament.[13] Such a question cannot easily be dispensed with by a body that places primary emphasis on restoring the church as it is found in the New Testament. On the other hand, the commitment to what many of the members of Churches of Christ perceive to be the church of the New Testament cannot be questioned, and it accounts in part for the growth of this segment of the movement in the last century.

In recent years, the evangelistic nature of the Churches of Christ has taken on a new dimension in the development of the Crossroads Movement. Originating in a student ministry led by Chuck Lucas at the University of Florida in Gainesville, efforts to reach out and incorporate the lost in discipling groups spread to other college and university campuses. Kip McKean adapted the Crossroads methods to a congregation in Boston, Massachusetts. This church has developed scores of house meetings and now has thousands of members in the Boston area. Sixty-two house churches led by "evangelists" are tightly linked to the Boston Church of Christ and operate under the direction of two elders.[14] The whole church meets on an average of once a month, when it is able to rent the Boston Garden. The church has projected similar efforts in an ambitious evangelistic program that targets several U.S. cities as well as a number of foreign countries. Its nontraditional methodology and its pyramidal, authoritarian structure of leadership has provided cause for concern in the mainline churches. Mac Lynn, editor of the *Directory of the Churches of Christ,* notes that "The 'movement' is still finding its place and continues in a state of development."[15]

The strong sense of mission in Churches of Christ is reinforced by nineteen colleges and universities and ten degree-granting Bible colleges.[16] Churches of Christ have maintained a liberal arts approach to education while still maintaining the strong church relationship. A graduate school of religion is found in Memphis, Tennessee, and two universities are now offering graduate degrees in the field of religion. Sixty-five adult schools of preaching that train lay preachers and church leaders provide additional leadership. Churches of Christ maintain eighty-three homes for children in twenty-seven states. They support forty-six homes for the aged, which are located in fifteen states.[17]

More than Disciples of Christ or Christian Churches, Churches of Christ have utilized the printed word to set forth their position. All publications are privately owned. Several have attained national significance. The *Gospel Advocate,* owned and published by the McQuiddy family of Nashville, Tennessee, ranks as the oldest and one of the more influential publications that circulate among Churches of Christ. The Gospel Advocate Publishing House also publishes books and Sunday-school literature.

Ranking with the *Gospel Advocate* as a journal of wide influence is *The Twentieth Century Christian,* also published in Nashville. *Firm*

Foundation, published in Pensacola, Florida, is read by many in Churches of Christ. A newer journal, *Image,* is published in West Monroe, Louisiana, and has gained broad acceptance. R.W. Sweet Company, of Austin, Texas, is a major publisher of books and other religious literature utilized by Churches of Christ. It is noteworthy that all of these journals and publishing companies are located in the South.

Many smaller journals of lesser circulation may also be found among Churches of Christ, reflecting the previously noted importance that Churches of Christ attach to the printed word. No publication may be considered official or representative of the position of the whole church.

Churches of Christ have no "conventions" on either national or state levels. Aversion to gatherings of this type may be traced back to the Civil War, when the convention of the American Missionary Society adopted an anti-Southern loyalty resolution. As Churches of Christ separated from the rest of the Disciples following the Civil War, conventions were too reminiscent of the despised missionary society to be tolerated. Even those of the type found today among Christian Churches, which exist only for preaching and fellowship, carry too much of a suggestion of denominational organization to be acceptable to Churches of Christ. However, college lectureships serve much the same purpose that conventions fill for Christian Churches. These gatherings satisfy the need for cohesive personal fellowship without which a larger body cannot long survive. At the same time they provide a platform for discussion of issues and contribute to the formulation of an ideological consensus that is equally vital to group identity. The oldest and largest of these annual gatherings is the one sponsored by Abilene Christian University, Abilene, Texas. William Banowsky holds that this lectureship has provided, over the decades since its inception in 1918, the most complete reflection of the issues and attitudes found among Churches of Christ in America.[18] The value of lectureships for needed fellowship and discussion has led other colleges to sponsor similar gatherings. Although they serve much the same purposes as do the conventions in the Christian Churches, they operate under a different sanction.

Challenges Facing Churches of Christ

Beyond doubt, the gravest challenge facing Churches of Christ as they enter the twenty-first century is the matter of preserving their particular identity, especially as that particular identity pertains to the issue of instrumental music in worship. A century ago, when the culture of the postwar South was rural and relatively simplistic, and the economy in the South was suffering from postwar impoverishment, it was not difficult to maintain the view that denied the use of any instrument in the service of the church. An unsophisticated service of worship in a simple, unadorned building was perfectly consistent with other aspects of the culture in general. So long as this type of cultural milieu prevailed, no serious threat to the noninstrumental position was found. But social conditions are never static, and change is inevitable. Churches of Christ, once predominantly rural, are now found in urban communities. Furthermore, rural culture is no longer isolated to the degree that marked pre-World War II times. The mobility of American society and the breadth and intensity of media coverage has made cultural isolation very difficult to maintain.

The problem of cultural modifications has been exacerbated by the upward social mobility of many members of Churches of Christ. Once a church of the relatively poor, it has become in four generations a church of solid middle-class members with a share of affluent professional and business types.[19] This sociological transition bespeaks significant change in point of view in numerous attitudes relating to the culture in general. One tangible reflection of this upward social mobility of Churches of Christ may be seen in the types of buildings that have been erected by Churches of Christ since World War II. It is no longer considered apostate to build structures that are relatively elaborate.[20] Modesty and simplicity are no longer signs of fidelity to the gospel, nor is relative affluence a matter to excite suspicion. Church buildings often exhibit sophisticated architectural taste and incorporate the latest in technological and aesthetic features.

But therein lies a problem for many of the members, particularly those in urban congregations who sense a cultural incongruity in the type of worship that is devoid of organ and choir. A primitive worship service is difficult to maintain in a building that is, in itself, somewhat elaborate. This cultural anomaly has called into question the doctrinal basis for the anti-instrument position. Many ministers are encountering increasing difficulty in maintaining the doctrine and admit privately that half or more of the members of their congregations would have no objection to the installation of an organ.[21] Arguments in behalf of exclusion of the instrument are not so persuasive as they once were. Many of the arguments are based on analogy, which is a recognized logical fallacy. Others rest on conclusions drawn from the silence of Scripture. These are convincing only to those otherwise persuaded. A scholarly explanation of the position against the use of an instrument in worship was made by Everett Ferguson of Abilene Christian University. He expressed his conclusion, after carefully surveying the linguistic and patristic evidences on the issue, as follows:

There are good historical, theological, and musicological grounds to engage only in *a cappella* music in public worship. This is safe, ecumenical ground that all can agree is acceptable. Instrumental music cannot be confirmed or authorized in the New Testament. It did not exist for centuries after the New Testament. Vocal music is more consistent with the nature of Christian worship . . . [instrumental music] introduces into man's relationship to God an act lacking specific apostolic authorization.[22]

There are few outside the Churches of Christ who would find a problem with these conclusions, except for the value judgment that "vocal music is more consistent with the nature of Christian worship." Singing with an instrument is also "vocal music." If vocal music *only* is meant, the conclusion can be challenged by a careful examination of the presuppositions on which it rests. Otherwise, there is a serious hiatus between the above conclusion and the position that everything that lacks "specific apostolic authorization" is thereby forbidden and constitutes a valid basis to justify schism. It is this hiatus that is causing serious problems in Churches of Christ. Observing that "many of our preachers don't talk about the music issue any more," Walter Yancey candidly acknowledges:

Our position on the music issue has probably done more to damage our reputation than has any other single thing. By taking a position which is so obviously false (to everyone but ourselves) we have destroyed the credibility of our whole approach to Bible study. It has ruined our reputation throughout Christendom. We have much Bible truth to offer the world, such as the importance of baptism, in connection with faith and repentance, for the forgiveness of sins, but people won't take us seriously; largely, I think, because we have destroyed our credibility with the music issue.[23]

It is not unusual in the history of the church for Christians to find that they are in opposition to the prevailing culture. Indeed, the more thrilling and heroic eras in church history are those in which the church was forced to struggle against the culture in order to maintain its Christian integrity. A serious cultural disjunction may indicate courageous fidelity to the Lord of the church. But the question facing Churches of Christ is whether singing with instrumental accompaniment is a matter sufficiently central to Christian faith as to warrant maintaining the cultural disjunction that many of its members sense. The problem is exacerbated by the popularity of religious music in contemporary society. The young are particularly attracted to popular religious music, which does not adapt readily to noninstrumental performance. The result has been a serious erosion of young people from membership in Churches of Christ, a matter that has understanably aroused concern among some of the leaders of the churches.[24]

Membership erosion is not a new problem for Churches of Christ.[25] In past decades, the growth rate of the churches has more than offset the loss when individuals slowly departed. Presently, however, the growth rate has declined and the disposition to modify the position regarding instrumental music is now found among members who have no inclination to abandon the church they love. Continuing in fellowship, they are asking serious questions about the validity of the method of interpretation of Scripture employed to sustain the anti-instrument position. Attention to this hermeneutical problem was often cited in *Mission,* a publication that often called into question presuppositions that were unconsciously and uncritically assumed.[26] One scholar from the fellowship points out that this methodology presupposes that an exact "pattern" for the church can be found in the New Testament, a "pattern" that provided a rigid norm for every detail of the church's life in every century of history. He points out that the construction of such a rigid "pattern" depends on many "necessary inferences" in order to supply those details that lack specific definition in Scripture. Despite the fact that the historic position of the movement, stated clearly in the *Declaration and Address* (Proposition VI), is that such "necessary inferences" can never be binding on Christians as matters of faith, he notes that, for those who are inclined to construct a "pattern," such inferences become "matters of faith."[27]

> For the rigid patternist *all* [italics in original] biblical instruction, whether explicit or implicit, is a matter of faith. It may be argued that we have departed from the early ideal of the movement: "In matters of opinion, liberty" becomes meaningless when there are no matters of opinion. When "necessary inference" and "implicit revelation" are seen as matters of faith, there are virtually no matters of opinion.[28]

The consequence of imposing such a methodology of Biblical interpretation (hermeneutics) on the Scriptures is a disastrous "impasse." This scholar laments, "The great advances pioneered by the early restorers have been lost by an arid Restorationist scholasticism that set in as Churches of Christ retrenched following the controversies of the past century."[29] This conclusion is representative of some of the restless self-examination that is current within Churches of Christ.

Meanwhile, concern for a more fraternal relationship with the Christian Churches, largely dormant since the collapse of the Murch/Witty efforts (chapter 13), were kept alive through the personal efforts of Carl Ketcherside of St. Louis, Missouri. His *Missions Messenger* magazine was unequivocal in its repudiation of the sectarian spirit that perpetuated division. More recently, a renewal of interest in more fraternal relations was initiated by the joint efforts of Don DeWelt of Christian Churches and Alan Cloyd and Dennis Randall of Churches of Christ. Beginning in 1984, annual meetings of interested leaders have continued to explore possibilities of closer fellowship, but specific measures that would generate closer fellowship have proven to be elusive.

Along with Disciples of Christ and Christian Churches, the Churches of Christ are concerned about the problem of membership decline. Aside from the cultural incongruity already noted, another contributing factor to this decline is cited by Lawrence Keene:

> Our movement was rooted in the rationalism of the eighteenth century where the idea and notion of a "meeting of the minds" forged much of the thinking of our movement's leaders. This cerebral orientation continues to this day, finding its expression in the worship services and day-to-day personality of each of the three groups in our movement. The theological positions of each of the three groups is admittedly different but the cerebral, intellectual spirit of each of the three groups is the same. All three groups have an implicit (and sometimes not so implicit) disdain for the emotional and demonstrative worship and life style characteristic of many of the growing denominations today. We need to give more careful consideration to the emotional content of our message to see if it is congruent or at least compatible with the emotional needs of our times. The presence of "warmth" in the leadership and the membership seems to be the one ingredient and component of growing churches![30]

The plea that lies at the heart of the Restoration Movement is addressed primarily to the mind, and the tendency to understand faith as belief of testimony is primarily an intellectual approach to religion. Here, again, a widening gap with the culture is encountered. The society at large seems to be in search of religious values that address deep personal anxieties and minister to alienation and insecurities that beset individuals. A number of developments in post-World War II decades can be cited as contributing to the breakdown of the sense of individual well-being. The phenomenal expansion of scientific knowledge and the adjustments in life-style mandated by developments in technology have had a bewildering impact on many individuals. Contemporary mankind confronts threats that dwarf those of pre-World War II times. Among the most obvious are the ever-present threat of nuclear war, unstable international situations compounded by terrorism, environmental and chemical pollution, economic uncertainties stemming from the growth of multinational megacorporations, the breakdown of traditional moral and family values, and increasing secularization of the values of society and culture. The result of these conditions is widespread social and individual frustration and anxiety, and those religious bodies that seem to speak more effectively to individual needs are growing. Such bodies tend to sublimate doctrine to personal satisfaction and emotional expression, a tendency that is clearly seen in the phenomenal expansion of Pentecostal-type denominations and also in the charismatic subgroups that can be found in virtually all of the older denominations. The trend is discernable also in the extent to which psychology has replaced theology in contemporary preaching, as a comparison of representative sermons of today with those of fifty years ago will readily disclose.[31]

Churches of Christ do not fit easily into the religious pattern that is in demand in today's society. While Keene has described all three branches of the Stone-Campbell Movement as manifesting a "cerebral orientation," the description is much more appropriate to the Churches of Christ where a much higher premium is placed on doctrinal correctness than is the case with Disciples of Christ or Christian Churches. The emphasis in Churches of Christ on conformity to a "New Testament pattern" has diminished appeal in today's religious climate. On the other hand, the popular quest for a sense of the imminent presence of the Holy Spirit (usually experienced subjectively) finds little understanding in Churches of Christ. At no point is the doctrinal emphasis found in Churches of Christ at greater variance with the religious interests of the times than in understanding the nature of the presence and work of the Holy Spirit. Generally, Churches of Christ see the work of the Holy Spirit in the canonical Scriptures and believe that the Spirit speaks to today's world only through the Scriptures.[32] All subsequent manifestations of the Spirit are rejected as inauthentic. Accordingly, Churches of Christ do not tolerate charismatic sectors in the membership and generally deplore the subjective dimension of contemporary religious bodies. The few congregations that have been affected by the charismatic renewal that is part of contemporary religious life are no longer recognized as legitimate Churches of Christ.[33] For this reason, Churches of Christ are sometimes accused, perhaps unjustly, of being cold and legalistic because of the absence of a noticeable emotional dimension in worship and preaching. There can be no doubt that the "cerebral orientation" places Churches of Christ outside the main focus of current religious interests and compounds the problem of growth. As such, the Churches of Christ face no challenge more serious than that of developing the capacity to address meaningfully the emotional emptiness and personal frustrations of contemporary society while retaining the doctrinal emphases that fidelity to their particular heritage requires.

End Notes

[1]Mac Lynn, ed., *Where the Saints Meet: a Directory of the Churches of Christ* (Pensacola: Firm Foundation Publishing House, 1987), notes that more than 1,000 congregations oppose the Sunday school, 554 congregations are listed as one-cup churches, and 150 oppose a designated minister (p. ix).

[2]For a discussion of mission methodology of Churches of Christ, see Philip W. Elkins, *Church Sponsored Missions* (Austin: Firm Foundation, 1974).

[3]Lynn (op. cit.) finds Churches of Christ in every state except Delaware and Rhode Island.

[4]For an analysis of the rural nature of Churches of Christ and the impact of this characteristic on their general viewpoints in the critical state of Tennessee, see D.E. Harrell, "The Disciples of Christ and Social Force in Tennessee, 1865-1900," *The East Tennessee Society's Publications* (No. XXXVIII, 1966), pp. 30-47.

[5]For a discussion of changing attitudes toward political involvement by members of Churches of Christ, see Royce Money, "Recent Developments of Religious Nationalism Among Churches of Christ" (Bethany: unpublished Restoration History Conference address, July 23, 1977).

[6]Lynn, op. cit., pp. x, xi.

[7]Garrett (op. cit., p. 11) holds that "Restorationism . . . has always been divisive and always will be, and when it gained sufficient influence within the Movement it divided it."

[8]Lynn, op. cit., p. xii.

[9]See ibid., p. x, for notations that indicate ethnic witness. See also Keene, *Impact*, op cit., p. 36.

[10]Keene, *Impact*, op. cit., pp. 38, 75.

[11]Ibid., p. 40.

[12]Lynn, op. cit., p. xii.

[13]For a discussion of the meaning of the terms found in the New Tes-

tament that are translated "church," see K.L. Schmidt, *Theological Dictionary of the New Testament,* G. Kittel, ed. (Grand Rapids: Eerdmans, 1966), pp. 502-536.

[14]Information on this particular work may be found in *Boston Church of Christ* newsletter (Boston: Boston Church of Christ).

[15]Lynn, op. cit., p. ix.

[16]See Appendix B.

[17]Lynn, op. cit., pp. 399-403.

[18]Banowsky, op. cit, pp. x, xi.

[19]Lawrence Keene (*Impact,* op. cit., p. 33) discovered that the average family income of elders and ministers in Churches of Christ in nine Western states exceeded that of their counterparts in the Disciples of Christ and Christian Churches.

[20]For a discussion of this attitude among Churches of Christ see Harrell, *Sources of Division,* op. cit., pp. 46-49.

[21]See Charles Turner, "The Pain of Breaking Free," *Christian Standard,* March 13, 1988, p. 15. Also Walt Yancey, *Endangered Heritage: an Examination of Church of Christ Doctrine* (Joplin: College Press, 1987). These voices come from within the Church of Christ fellowship.

[22]Everett Ferguson, *A Cappella Music in the Public Worship* (revised edition, Abilene: Biblical Research Press, 1972), p. 95.

[23]Walt Yancey, op. cit., p. 161. Yancey is a chemist and has no institutional bias.

[24]Keene expanded to a national level the study cited earlier (*Impact,* op. cit.), which had been confined to the Pacific Slope. Details of this four-year effort were published privately by Dr. Keene. (A copy is on file at the library of the Emmanuel School of Religion, Milligan College, TN.) Keene actually notes a decline in membership in Churches of Christ between 1980 (1,600,000) and 1985 (1,250,000). This decline may reflect somewhat the difficulty in gathering reliable statistical information.

[25]See Robert Myers, ed., *Voices of Concern, Critical Studies in Church of Christism* (St. Louis: Mission Messenger, 1966).

[26]For example, see "Restoration and the Cultural Task," *Mission Jour-*

nal (June, 1987), pp. 11-13. For a summary of the mission of the publication, see Walther Burch, "The Birth of Mission" (September, 1986), pp. 10, 11.

[27]Russ Dudrey, "Restoration Hermeneutics Among Churches of Christ: Why Are We at an Impasse?" *Restoration Quarterly* (Abilene: Restoration Quarterly Corporation), Vol. 30, No. 1, 1988, p. 37. Dudrey's study on the hermeneutic of Churches of Christ was funded by a grant from the National Endowment for the Humanities in 1984.

[28]Ibid., p. 37. Dudrey further observes (p. 28) that "adherence to hardline patternism . . . has been elevated not merely to our method, but our *raison d'etre.*"

[29]Ibid., p. 38.

[30]Keene, private study (op. cit., see note 23, above), "Summary and Conclusions," p. 1.

[31]Examples of preaching with major psychological emphasis may be seen in the sermons of Norman Vincent Peale and Robert Schuller. They are typical in this respect of many TV evangelists and are widely copied.

[32]See T.W. Brents, *The Gospel Plan of Salvation* (Nashville: Gospel Advocate, 1984), pp. 571-662, for an exposition of this position, which continues to be characteristic of Churches of Christ.

[33]For example, the large Belmont Church of Christ in Nashville, Tennessee, is no longer listed as a Church of Christ because, among other things, it incorporates charismatic features in its services of worship.

Chapter Eighteen

Approaching the Twenty-first Century: Christian Churches

All three of the branches of the Stone-Campbell heritage have been conditioned by events and issues that mark their history. Among the distinguishing features of Christian Churches, several clearly relate to issues and controversies out of which this fellowship of Independent congregations emerged, and, apart from their history, it is not possible to understand or appreciate these characteristics.

Distinguishing Characteristics of Christian Churches

Much of what distinguishes Christian Churches stems from the theology of the church that this body holds. This theology maintains that the local congregation is the only manifestation of the "church" found in the New Testament and hence the only one that may be accepted. The Biblical references to the "church" generally apply to a congregation in a specific location. Where generic references occur, as may be found in Ephesians 1:22; 5:23; Colossians 1:24, they refer to the totality of Christ's followers, which is never manifested by any organization, synod, or body of clergy. It is a term that, when employed in a universal sense, refers to the faith and commitment of Christians everywhere. This faith and commitment finds its only concrete manifestation in the body of believers that assembles regularly for the purpose of the proclamation of the Word and the celebration of the sacraments. It is this conviction that lies at the base of the deep commitment to local church autonomy found in Christian

Churches, a characteristic that has roots in the earliest history of the Campbell efforts. Such a conviction is reflected in the dissolution of the Mahoning Baptist Association in 1830, in the structure of the American Christian Missionary Society in 1849 as a body composed of individuals rather than representatives of churches, and in the rejection of the Louisville Plan after 1869. Following the merger of the missionary agencies into a unified organization in 1919, the series of disappointments associated with efforts to influence the policies adopted by this organization (ante, chapter 11) has led Christian Churches to conclude that an organization on a large and unified scale is uncontrollable and hence dangerous. They note that the early church had no extra-congregational organization, and yet the most outstanding evangelistic and missionary results in the history of Christianity were accomplished in this period. Thus, the churches that had fought energetically but unsuccessfully to reclaim an organization concluded by 1926 that following a New Testament precedent meant forming no unifying organization that would in any way infringe on the complete freedom and self-determination of the local congregation. To this day, the idea that "the church" could be manifested on state, national, or international levels finds no acceptance in the Christian Churches.

This being the case, one might be surprised at the plethora of organizations of every kind that are found within the fellowship of Christian Churches. Three points should be noted in this regard:
(1) none of the organizations claims to be "church" in any sense of the word,
(2) none of the organizations represents churches, though they may receive contributions from churches, and
(3) none claims to be the sole legitimate means through which the work of the churches is done. (A single exception would be the Commission on the Chaplaincy, which certifies chaplains for military and institutional appointment.)

The many organizations are understood to be agencies created to perform specific ministries through which individuals or churches may elect to extend their ministry and outreach. There exists no sentiment for merging these organizations into a unified structure. In fact, any suggestion to that effect would be met with fierce and passionate opposition. Even the North American Christian Convention, which functions somewhat as an umbrella organization for the Christian Churches and derives the major part of its support from churches, scrupulously avoids any appearance of acting in an official capacity.

Consistent with the concept of the church as a local congregation, Christian Churches vest responsibility for ordination of ministers with local congregations. While it is obvious that some congregations fail to take this responsibility with the degree of gravity found in others, the strong emphasis placed on the priesthood of all believers in Christian Churches means that relatively less emphasis is given to ordination. Whereas most Protestant bodies, including Disciples of Christ, utilize ordination as a means to regulate its ministry and to define ministerial eligibility, it is a rare Christian Church that inquires into the ordination of a candidate for its ministry.

Ordination by a single congregation has sometimes been criticized on the ground that, when one is set aside for ministry, it is to the ministry not of a single congregation but rather to the ministry of any or all congregations that would engage his services. In other words, ordination is not to the ministry of the church local but to the ministry of the church at large; hence, the argument goes, it ought to be administered by representatives of a wider body. But those who hold to a local understanding of the church cite baptism as a parallel. The act of baptism, which is performed in the local church, is valid for the church at large.

The concept of local church autonomy has led some to refer mistakenly to Christian Churches as "non-cooperatives."[1] The designation is both pejorative and ambiguous. Sometimes it refers to the fact that Christian Churches do not cooperate with the agencies of the Disciples of Christ. Sometimes it refers to extreme congregational polity in which congregations become self-centered and indifferent to concerns of the brotherhood of churches. This is a peculiar peril for some "super-churches" that have developed in urban centers. Congregations of several thousands of members develop such complex programs that they sometimes tend to become self-sufficient. While there undoubtedly are congregations that have little interest beyond their own affairs, this condition is probably not more widespread than is the case in any other religious body; in fact, it may be less prevalent because of the constant appeals from missionaries, Bible colleges, youth camps, and other organizations that keep such extra-congregational activities highly visible. Despite their strong bias toward total congregational independence, Christian Churches cooperate in 123 evangelistic associations for new-church planting, in more than 100 youth camps, and in a growing number of retirement homes. Such agencies are genuinely cooperative ventures operated by boards of directors that are mostly self-perpetuating but required by the nature of maintaining a broad fiscal base of support to be closely in touch with the churches.

Christian Churches do not differ from Churches of Christ in the perceived purpose of missions. Missionaries are sent out with the purpose of converting non-Christians and building churches that ultimately will become self-supporting and autonomous. But, in the matter of support structure, Christian Churches differ from both Disciples of Christ and Churches of Christ. The former commission and direct all missionaries from a central agency, the Division of

Overseas Ministries. Missionaries from Churches of Christ are sent out by, and remain accountable to, a local congregation. Christian Church missionaries may claim one or more congregations as a "living-link church," but most claim accountability to an advisory body that generally consists of persons from several, often widely-scattered, congregations. Funds to support Disciples' missionaries are sent from churches to the Department of Overseas Ministries, which makes distribution to the missionaries. Funds for missionaries from Churches of Christ are usually sent to the sponsoring congregations, which administer them. Moneys for Christian Church missionaries are sent by individuals and churches to a forwarding agent who sends them on to the missionary. Since neither the advisory committee nor the "living-link church" has any measurable control of funds, the level of accountability is questionable in many cases, and abuses have sometimes gone unchecked. This condition prompted a group of concerned persons to form the Christian Missionary Fellowship in 1949. As an organization that exercises a measure of supervision over its missionaries, it has satisfied the concerns of those in Christian Churches who were uncomfortable with the support structure otherwise found in Independent missions.

Another distinguishing characteristic of Christian Churches that must be noted is the complete liberty within the fellowship that permits any person or combination of persons to take the initiative for any type of Christian endeavor that, in their judgment, would serve to advance the cause of Christ. Total freedom is given to appeal to individuals and churches for support of same, and no official approval is needed. All that is required to win support is the ability to make a good claim. Support is given on the basis of perceived merit. In no other religious body of comparable size is there greater freedom of initiative. The visitor to the annual North American Christian Convention is overwhelmed by the bewildering array of exhibits by agencies and institutions of a wide variety. Such could be considered as evidence of confusion, or it may reflect a creditable level of religious vitality and activity.[2]

A sociological study of Christian Churches done by Lawrence Keene in 1986 revealed some interesting characteristics. The heavy concentration of membership in midwestern states is reflected in the finding that both ministers and elders are overwhelmingly identified with the Republican Party. There is general subscription to the work ethic and a cool disposition toward public welfare. Ministers and elders "agreed very strongly that 'the death penalty is suitable for (some) criminal offenses.'" They also registered socially conservative views on other issues such as divorce, race, and others. Keene was surprised to find that ministers in the Christian Churches were much younger than among Disciples of Christ. Most (82%) are less than fifty years old. Half of this number are between twenty and thirty-five, whereas half of Disciple ministers are fifty years old or older. Keene notes that such a preponderance of young ministers indicates a serious attrition rate among ministers in Christian Churches. This may be related to the fact that these ministers have the lowest incomes of the three groups, and that 70% have only a four-year Bible college education (in contrast, 90% of Disciple ministers were found to hold either a Masters or Ph.D. degree).[3] Despite this attrition, Christian Churches do not experience a shortage of ministers, which may be an indication of the effectiveness of their methods of ministerial recruitment.

Keene's study noted that a wide diversity of opinion exists in different sections of the nation, and between ministers and elders on the way the churches are operated. He concludes:

> We have *always* been a diverse people! We still are! We must be careful that we do *not* send the message that we are a group that requires a rigid conformity in a great many things for fear that our "freedom" in Christ be lost.[4]

Resources of the Christian Churches

Most of the resources of Christian Churches have been developed since the abandonment of the International Convention of Disciples of Christ that began in 1919. An important exception is the Standard Publishing Company. Although the Standard Publishing Company has always been a privately-owned company, it has aimed to serve the publishing needs of the movement through providing Sunday-school literature, youth programs, books, tracts, and other types of publications. In 1955, the descendants of founder Isaac Errett sold the corporation to John Bolton, whose intention was to operate the company as a nonprofit foundation. However, federal regulations governing foundations made this intention unfeasible, so Mr. Bolton subsequently merged Standard with other corporations that he controlled and formed the Standex International Corporation. The editorial chairs of the company continue to be occupied by Christian Church members, and the editorial policies are directed by a publishing committee that consists of leaders of Christian Churches. Religious literature published by Standard is used by a wide range of evangelical churches.

The North American Christian Convention functions as the great cohesive force to which all Christian Churches and institutions relate. It is often referred to as the "umbrella" under which the disparate components find identity and community. The convention met irregularly until 1950, when annual meetings were inaugurated. In

1963, a permanent office was located in Cincinnati, Ohio, and Leonard Wymore was engaged as its first full-time director. Upon his retirement in 1986, he was succeeded by Rod Huron.

The North American Christian Convention is a gathering of individuals for education, inspiration, and fellowship. A continuation committee of one hundred men (plus ten women who serve in a nonvoting capacity) meets annually in St. Louis, Missouri, in October to plan the following year's convention. No other official business is transacted. Activities and meetings are provided for all ages, and thousands of Christians attend what is essentially a family gathering that far outnumbers any other assembly in either of the other branches of the movement.

Leonard C. Wymore (1921-   ), first permanent director of the North American Christian Convention (1963-1986).

Additionally, an annual National Missionary Convention has met since 1951. This has provided the missionary cause a level of visibility that many missionaries had felt was missing in the North American Christian Convention.

Some states have state conventions, most of which are of rather recent origin. Included are Arizona, Florida, Colorado, Ohio, Illinois, Indiana, Kansas, Michigan, Missouri, and Wisconsin. Eastern states cooperate in the Eastern Christian Convention. Southern states support a Southern Christian Youth Convention.

The distinctive educational institution of Christian Churches is the Bible college. Only a few of these colleges antedate the period of abandonment of the older educational institutions affiliated with the Disciples of Christ.[5] Most of the Bible colleges were established during or shortly after World War II. Sixteen were begun in the decade of the forties and six more in the fifties. The relative ease with which a Bible college may be established and the generous provisions of the G.I. Bill of Rights, which created a large number of potential students, resulted in overly ambitious enterprises that did not take account of long-term needs. The inevitable decline in the number of available students coupled with rising costs forced several of these schools to cease operation.[6] Others expanded their curricula to attract students with vocational interests other than church-related careers.[7] As the twentieth century nears its close, thirty-three Bible colleges serve Christian Churches in the United States and three in

Canada. Three graduate seminaries have been established.[8] Milligan College in Tennessee is the only college of liberal arts that is related to the Christian Churches.

As the Bible colleges have developed, several trends may be discerned. Foremost is the improvement in faculty competence. Earned doctorates, once rare, are fairly commonplace. Expanded and modern facilities are found on many campuses. A noticeable trend has been to abandon the name "Bible college" and replace it with "Christian college." Most Bible colleges are accredited by the Association for Accreditation of Bible Colleges. Regional accreditation, once spurned, is now sought after. Four Bible colleges have attained such accreditation and others are in process.[9]

Bible colleges provide undergraduate education for the vast majority of the ministers of Christian Churches, but the conviction that graduate education is vital for serious ministerial service is a growing one. In addition to the seminaries noted, three Bible colleges provide programs leading to the Masters degree.[10]

Christian Churches have not been indifferent toward students on campuses of state universities. Seventy-eight campus ministries are provided to give support to students on state university campuses.[11]

Christian Churches have found the Christian Service Camp to be an invaluable resource in ministering to youth. Since the first such camp was held in Georgia in 1924, the movement to hold summer youth gatherings of this type has grown until hundreds of weeks of camps are held annually in the eighty-five camp sites that are located in thirty states (plus two more in Ontario, Canada).[12] Most camps are regional in nature and draw their support from nearby congregations. Most own their own facilities, which range all the way from the very primitive to highly developed operations with full-time staffs. In recent years, many have developed facilities for year-round retreats and other activities. Investments in these properties reflect the belief of the supporting churches that they make a significant contribution to the evangelization and conservation of the youth of the churches.

Christian Churches have established thirty-nine children's homes in the United States, twenty-eight homes for retired persons, fifteen nursing homes, and two ministries for the physically handicapped.[13] Eighty-six day schools are operated in twenty-five states.[14]

Foreign missions remains an important interest of Christian Churches. The origin of the Independent mission methodology has been noted in chapter 12.[15] Organization-guided mission work reappeared with the founding of the Christian Missionary Fellowship in 1949. One thousand fifty-two missionaries were serving on foreign fields in 1989.[16]

Commitment to mission service and support shows no sign of slackening among Christian Churches. A popular feature in many congregations is the annual faith-promise rally, a weekend of mission emphasis that is climaxed by an effort to secure pledges to underwrite the year's mission budget of the church. A recent study found that the average Christian Church devotes sixteen percent of its annual budget to missions.[17]

Home evangelization is conducted on an extra-congregational level by evangelistic associations, which concentrate on establishing new congregations. A recent study[18] disclosed the fact that 123 evangelistic associations operate in forty-four states and two provinces in Canada. These associations study sites, gather funds, enlist leadership, and nurture new congregations until they are self-supporting.

Other resources of the CHristian Churches include the Christian Church Pension Plan, located in Joplin, Missouri, which offers financial planning and pension services to ministers and others. The Christian Church Extension Foundation of Denver, Colorado, assists churches and institutions in building programs. Some states also maintain their own loan funds. Statistical information pertaining to the Christian Churches is compiled and published by Specialized Christian Services, which has published an annual *Directory of the Ministry* since 1955.

Challenges Facing Christian Churches

Christian Churches look to the future with confidence that is tempered with concern about church growth. Overall, the churches are growing, but not at a rate that gives cause for rejoicing. Statistics published by the *Directory of the Ministry* at five-year intervals since 1965 reveal:

	Churches		Membership	
Year	United States	Canada	United States	Canada
1965	4,381	58	921,267	7,258
1970	4,693	65	915,255	4,318
1975	5,449	65	1,041,879	4,795
1980	5,566	66	1,058,465	4,718
1985	5,487	66	1,051,469	5,272
1990 (1989[19])	5,579	69	1,070,616	5,997

The above statistics are compiled on the basis of responses to mail-survey requests. Accuracy may vary from year to year.

The growth rate seen in the above statistics does not equal the growth rate of the general population. Recognition of this fact came forcefully to the attention of an ad hoc meeting of 100 churchmen in St. Louis, Missouri, in March of 1983. This led to the calling of annual Open Forums, out of which emerged, among other results, a church-planting program known as Double Vision. Alan Ahlgrim, of Longmont, Colorado, was named chairman of a committee that created an ambitious program to challenge Christian Churches to double the number of churches and the membership by the end of the century. Leonard Wymore, on retirement from years of service as director of the North American Christian Convention, became the national director of Double Vision. The goals of the effort may be overly ambitious, but to the extent that it generates renewed effort for increased growth, it will be considered worthwhile.

A continuing challenge to a religious community that is as loosely structured as the Christian Churches is that of maintaining internal unity. To be sure, a number of cohesive factors such as the common heritage, common interest in agencies, institutions, and missions help to bind the fellowship together. On the other hand, unity is threatened by issues that are potentially divisive. Foremost among such issues is the matter of the doctrine of Biblical inerrancy. While this does not seem to be an issue of much interest to the average person in the pew, it has been raised to prominence by several professors in some of the Bible colleges.[20] As an issue, it is peculiar to Christian Churches. Disciples of Christ are not uncomfortable with critical views about the Bible. Churches of Christ, while holding conservative views about the Bible, have not been influenced by Fundamentalism due to their self-imposed isolation from the mainstream of American religious controversies.[21] But Fundamentalism has made some inroads into the Christian Church segment of the Stone-Campbell heirs, as the stress on Biblical inerrancy clearly illustrates.[22] The heritage of the movement requires that this issue be understood as a matter of opinion about which liberty should prevail. As a matter of fact, a wide range of opinion on the issue can be found from the earliest days of the movement.[23]

A third challenge facing Christian Churches as the century draws to its close concerns the altered role of women in the culture. Traditionally, women have not served as ministers of churches, although their service as missionaries has not been questioned. In rare situations, they have served as deaconesses, but not on church boards as deacons or elder. Women serve as teachers in Sunday schools, but often only in children's classes. Some churches do not permit women to teach men. However, in a society where women are more involved in prominent roles in the media, in business, and in the professions, it is difficult to deny to women a more active role in the churches. In 1985, ten women were added to the one-hundred-man continuation committee of the North American Christian Convention in an advisory, nonvoting capacity. The number of women in teaching positions in the colleges has increased, but women are not admitted to the pulpit ministry of any of the churches. Only a relatively few Christian

Churches admit women to membership on their board, and women are rarely found on boards that govern Bible colleges or other agencies.

Unlike those denominations whose ecclesiastical policy is fixed by a body above the congregation, Christian Churches feel compelled to establish their church polity on Biblical teaching or precedent. Both the defenders of the status quo and those who seek an enlarged role of women in the leadership of the church find an abundance of proof texts to sustain their positions. Like other issues confronting the churches, this one will test the viability of the time-honored slogan: "In faith, unity; in opinion, liberty; in all things, charity."

A fourth challenge facing the Christian Churches is that of developing effective leadership for a body that is decentralized and intensely local-autonomy oriented. Only the *Christian Standard* and the North American Christian Convention have national leadership influence, and both are sensitive to any intimation of the exercise of authority. Consequently, regional centers of influence develop and permit agencies and institutions to promote objectives in their own special interest. It is exceedingly difficult to enlist the entire Brotherhood in behalf of any effort simply because effective leadership channels that would produce results do not exist. Beyond doubt, many benefits have accrued to Christian Churches because the absence of precast programs from outside the congregation have focused responsibility and generated initiative within the local leadership. Still, Christian Churches face the challenge to develop a strategy of planning and leadership that will make possible the marshaling and application of greater resources to achieve more ambitious goals while at the same time preserving intact the cherished freedom of the local congregation. The solution to the problem of declining growth is not unrelated to the challenge of effective leadership.[24]

There is great theological and sociological diversity within the Christian Church fellowship. Inevitably such diversity places strains on the unity of the fellowship. The future for Christian Churches will offer new opportunities to test the validity of the claim that fellowship of faith within a loosely structured community can survive the strains that a widening diversity inevitably imposes.

End Notes

[1]See *What Brotherhood Cooperation Means,* op. cit.

[2]The *Directory of the Ministry* (1989, p. F-38) lists 1,037 agencies.

[3]Lawrence C. Keene, "Counting Noses: An 'Independent' Profile," *Christian Standard,* October 18, 1987, pp. 7, 8.

[4]Lawrence C. Keene, "A Sociological Analysis of Beliefs and Attitudes Among Ministers and Elders," *Christian Standard,* Oct. 25, 1987, p. 14.

[5]For a listing of the Bible colleges and the dates of their founding, see Appendix C.

[6]See Appendix C for a list of Bible colleges that have ceased operation.

[7]Several Bible colleges have established cooperative degree programs with nearby colleges to enable students to gain certification for public school teaching. Kentucky Christian College is able to offer certification for elementary teachers. It also offers a degree in business.

[8]Graduate seminaries are Cincinnati (Ohio) Bible Seminary, Lincoln (Illinois) Christian Seminary, and Emmanuel School of Religion (Milligan College, Tennessee).

[9]Pacific Christian College, Kentucky Christian College, Johnson Bible College, and Cincinnati Bible College & Seminary have regional accreditation.

[10]Pacific Christian College, Kentucky Christian College, and Johnson Bible College offer Masters degrees.

[11]*Directory of the Ministry,* 1989, p. F-38.

[12]Ibid.

[13]Ibid., pp. F-25, 27.

[14]Ibid., p. F-38.

[15]For a history of this phase of missions, see David Filbeck, *The First Fifty Years: a Brief History of the Independent Mission Movement* (Joplin: College Press, 1980).

434   *Approaching the Twenty-first Century: Christian Churches*

[16]*Directory of the Ministry,* 1989, p. F-36.

[17]The most complete analysis of mission support by Christian Churches is *An Assessment of the Mission Support of Christian Churches/Churches of Christ,* Sherman Pemberton, ed. (an unpublished report of the Missions Task Force of the Open Forum of the Christian Churches, 1987—Rondall Smith, chairman). See p. 19.

[18]This study was conducted by Seth Wilson, Ozark Christian College, Joplin, Missouri, and published by Mr. Wilson.

[19]Figures for 1990 are not available at this writing. Figures from 1989 cited.

[20]See, for example, Jack Cottrell, "Dedicated to Scriptural Inerrancy," *The Seminary Review,* September, 1984, pp. 93ff. Also Donald Nash, "What About Inerrancy?" *The Restoration Herald,* April, 1987, pp. 4, 5.

[21]Banowsky, loc. cit.

[22]Woodrow Phillips, president of San Jose (California) Bible College: "The direct support mission movement has been correctly labeled 'The Fundamentalist Segment' of our brotherhood" (*Second Consultation on Internal Unity,* op. cit., p. 75).

[23]Contrast the views of Isaac Errett (outlined in James G. Van Buren, "Isaac Errett's View of Biblical Inspiration," in Wetzel, op. cit., pp. 128-141) with those of Jack Cottrell (*Solid* [Cincinnati: Standard, 1978]).

[24]For a discussion, see Henry E. Webb, "Our Future Requires An Honest Self-Appraisal," *Christian Standard,* July 28, 1985, pp. 6, 7. Also, four addresses to the North American Christian Convention Committee, October, 1980 (Cincinnati: N.A.C.C., 1980).

Chapter Nineteen

Great Britain, Canada, New Zealand, & Australia

Great Britain

The beginnings of the movement in Great Britain that later came to be associated with the Restoration Movement in America have already been noted in relating the account of Alexander Campbell's visit to Britain in 1847. (See chapter 7.) It is important to note that, whereas the early leaders of the American movement rose out of Presbyterian backgrounds, the origins of the British efforts are found among Scotch Baptists. These were a people who were distinguished from English Baptists by their dislike of emotional revivalism and their unwillingness to place emphasis on a "conversion experience."

In 1833, a young American portrait painter, Peyton Wyeth, from Pennsylvania, visited a Scotch Baptist chapel in London and introduced one of the elders to the writings of Alexander Campbell. Thus began an association that was to be very fruitful. David Thompson, historian of the British Churches of Christ, observes: "It is always necessary to remember that in Britain Alexander Campbell's ideas were grafted on to Scotch Baptist roots."[1]

The London elder, William Jones, was a bookseller. In 1835, he began publication of *The Millennial Harbinger and Voluntary Church Advocate*. Although disagreements with Alexander Campbell caused Jones to discontinue publication after only one year, the journal served to introduce Campbell's writings to many Scotch Baptists. Significant similarities were immediately discernible, such as congregational government, plurality of elders, and weekly Communion.

Differences also surfaced, such as questions about the significance of baptism (although both practiced believer's baptism by immersion) and questions as to whether the Lord's Supper could be celebrated without the presence of an elder.

Meanwhile, Campbell's writings were being introduced into Great Britain through another channel. Scotch Baptist churches in the English cities of Liverpool, Manchester, and Nottingham were learning about the American reformer through some of his relatives in Northern Ireland.[2] James Wallis, a draper in Nottingham, was impressed that, in Campbell's writings, "the religion of Jesus is founded altogether upon the knowledge and belief of facts instead of abstract influences and mystic operations."[3] He made direct contact with Mr. Campbell in 1835 and was sent one of the first editions of *The Christian System* (the first edition was published under the title *Christianity Restored*).

In 1837, Wallis began publication of *The Christian Messenger, A Voice From America,* which filled the void that had been left by the termination of Jones's *Millennial Harbinger.* Wallis's publication was a unifying factor among those Scotch Baptist churches that found themselves in a measure of agreement with Campbell's views. In addition to publishing a British version of *The Christian System,* Wallis also published Campbell's debates with Owen and McCalla. The *Messenger* also contained articles by Walter Scott. Thus the message of the reformers on the American frontier was reaching into Great Britain.

By 1842, it seemed that it would be possible to convene a meeting of church representatives, and the first cooperation meeting was held in Edinburgh. Fifty congregations were represented or otherwise accounted for with a combined membership of 1,233,[4] about equally divided between England and Scotland. The first resolution, which was adopted unanimously, affirmed "that this meeting deem it binding upon them, as disciples of Jesus Christ, to cooperate for the maintenance of evangelists to proclaim the Gospel."[5] This was a step which Scotch Baptists would normally never have taken, and it thereby marks the formal breach of many congregations from the Scotch Baptists and the formal beginning of a new body subsequently known as British Churches of Christ.

The composition of the churches was largely from the artisan and small business strata of society. Public debate was a favorite activity, and the congregations would be considered quite contentious by later standards. James Wallis is credited with nurturing the spirit of cooperation among the congregations that were otherwise troubled and in danger of dividing over such questions as whether the bread of the Lord's Supper should be leavened or unleavened, whether the wine should be fermented or unfermented, and whether the unimmersed should be permitted to share in the Supper. The report that the

Campbells in America permitted the unimmersed to commune was disturbing to many of the churches.

A second cooperation meeting was not held until October 1 and 2, 1847, in Chester. Alexander Campbell addressed this meeting, urging the congregations to work together. It was determined at that time that there were eighty-five congregations with a total membership of 2,553, an encouraging increase over the number in the report five years earlier. But trouble was immanent. A Dr. John Thomas, one-time friend of Alexander Campbell, arrived shortly following the meeting. His thinking had been influenced by the Millerites in America, and he advocated a premillennial adventism. His followers took the name Christadelphians, and the inroads Thomas made into the membership of the churches stifled growth for a decade.

The Chester Cooperation of 1847 established a fund for support of an American evangelist, but none was forthcoming. The following year, the cooperation meeting was held in Glasgow, and eighty-four churches reported a membership of about 2,300, the decline probably reflecting the Christadelphian problem. This year also saw James Wallis change the name of his periodical to *The British Millennial Harbinger.*

The year 1854 marked something of a new beginning for the British churches. In that year, J.B. Rotherham, a scholarly Welsh Baptist preacher, impressed by the understanding of the meaning of baptism he found in the literature of the Churches of Christ, joined the movement. In the same year, a young preacher named David King kindled a spirit of evangelism through a successful evangelistic tour, and the first large-scale cooperative effort to establish a new congregation in Manchester, supported by contributions from several congregations, proved to be fruitful. This marked the beginning of a period of aggressive expansion, which included a renewed appeal for evangelists to come from America, albeit with the exclusion of anybody who was "in any way entangled in the subject of slavery."[6]

For the next several years, J.B. Rotherham and David King cooperated in evangelistic efforts. In 1861, James Wallis turned over *The British Millennial Harbinger* to David King, who then became the dominant figure among the churches for the next thirty years. King was less generous and more hard-line doctrinaire than Wallis, following policies similar to those of Benjamin Franklin in America. The churches and the total membership continued to grow, more in England than in Scotland. Half of all the churches were located in the industrial midlands. Conversions came mostly from Methodists, who were of the same social class and were otherwise "Bible oriented." Evangelistic activity was organized by district associations. The first *Yearbook of the Churches of Christ* was published in 1866, growing out of the *Annual Meeting Supplement* published in the *Christian Advocate.*

The most vexing issue troubling the churches in the latter third of the nineteenth century was "open Communion." This was part of the "American question," another dimension of which was the role of the "evangelist" in the services of the church. The American pattern was quite different from what developed in Britain. American involvement in British evangelism effectively began in 1875 with Henry S. Earl, an Englishman who had graduated from Bethany College and had worked successfully in both New Zealand and Australia. Earl was present that year at the Louisville, Kentucky, Convention when the Foreign Christian Missionary Society was organized, and he volunteered to serve as its first missionary. He was engaged to return to England under the society's auspices. He went to Southampton, engaged the Philharmonic Hall, preached to thousands, and organized a church that soon numbered more than a hundred members. Impressed by American evangelistic methods, Timothy Coop, a layman from Wigan and the corresponding secretary of the cooperation, offered to give one thousand pounds if the F.C.M.S. would match it with two thousand pounds to recruit American evangelists for Britain. Marion Todd was sent to Chester, and William T. Moore, minister of the large Central Christian Church in Cincinnati, Ohio, resigned his work to go to Southampton.

Moore represented the more progressive wing of the American churches and was an irritant to the conservative British churches. After successful work in Southampton, Moore moved to Liverpool and then went to London, where he settled at the West London Tabernacle. Sensing the hostility of the more conservative British churches and subject to King's criticisms in the *Harbinger*, Moore founded the *Christian Commonwealth*, a journal that served to articulate the views of the pro-American churches, which formed themselves into their own "Christian Association." A disastrous division followed that lasted for thirty-five years. While "open Communion" appeared to be the issue, David King attacked such other innovations as instrumental music, open collections (allowing the unimmersed to contribute in the offerings), and choirs that were not limited to members of the churches.

David Thompson contends that "the real difference between the British and the Americans was not communion but preaching."[7] Sunday-morning services in the old British churches were given to the celebration of the Lord's Supper and to "mutual edification." The "evangelist" was permitted to preach only at the Sunday evening "evangelistic service," which was held for the purpose of addressing non-Christians. But the churches under American influence allowed a much more vigorous style of leadership on the part of the "evangelist." This leadership, though it proved to be quite effective, compromised the power and authority of the elders. Furthermore, it was wanting for Biblical precedent. (A similar controversy over the one-man pastor was going on in some parts of the United States at the same time.)

Meanwhile, a younger generation, unimpressed by the wrangling over the "American question," was coming on the scene and generating pressures for new concerns. Less provincial in outlook, the younger leaders began publication of *The Young Christian* "to give a forward impetus to Apostolic Christianity." The new voices championed a "Forward Movement" in evangelism and social reform at home, as well as a renewed overseas mission effort. They were willing to grapple with new theological issues rising out of Biblical criticism, and they wanted reconciliation with the Christian Association and the establishment of a college for theological education. The future belonged to this group, especially after the death of David King in 1894.

Some of the British churches had sent aid to Dr. Barkley and the American mission in Jerusalem. Subsequently, there was some aid given to the A.C.M.S. mission in Jamaica. The first distinctly British mission effort was made in 1892 in Burma. The following year, a work was begun in South Africa in cooperation with the Australian churches. India was entered in 1910.

It was not possible, despite the isolationist mentality of many of the British Churches of Christ, for them to remain unaffected by the events of the Edinburgh Missions Conference in 1910. The pro-American Christian Association leaders were actively involved. From 1910 on, Christian unity would be an important part of the climate within which Protestantism lived. The conference papers for the 1914 Annual Conference of British Churches of Christ (often referred to simply as "Conference") dealt with the theme: "What Churches of Christ Might Do to Promote Unity Among Baptized Believers."[8] Conference appointed a Committee for Christian Unity. The division with the pro-American Christian Association was healed in 1917.

The desire to have a college was not easily realized. Traditionally, Scotch Baptists opposed colleges because they held that colleges created "clergymen." But, by the turn of the century, the need for an educated ministry was obvious to many of the churches.[9] William Robinson was sent to Mansfield College, Oxford, for theological study to prepare him to become principal of Overdale College, which was opened in 1920 in Birmingham. In 1931, Overdale was accepted as a member of the Selly Oak College consortium.

British churches, as a whole, suffered a disastrous decline following World War I. The causes for this decline are complex. A major factor is to be found in the general disillusionment and widespread social cynicism that took root in British society following the devastating conflict. Churches of Christ, however, continued to grow until 1930, when membership peaked at 16,596.[10] Thereafter, decline set in, slowly at first, accelerating following World War II. By 1964, membership had been reduced to half its 1930 level. In the face of this situation, some of the leadership began to look to merging with another body as a viable option, a solution that was made attractive by the current popularity of the ecumenical movement. But this was distinctly a small minority opinion. In 1960, the World Convention of Churches of Christ was held in Edinburgh. The question was posed in one of the discussion groups: "What would be the impact on the British churches if a sizable portion of the Disciples in America would enter into organic union with the United Church of Christ?" James Gray, chairman of the Union Committee, responded instantly, "It would mean schism."[11] This point of view was given further explanation in a book issued on the occasion of the convention by the Union Committee entitled *Towards Christian Union.* The section on baptism, always a critical item in considering Christian unity, concludes as follows:

> Churches of Christ today find themselves keenly interested in the ecumenical debate about Baptism and willing to share in that debate, concerned about their own position and practice and willing to improve in every way possible, yet at the bottom of the matter still defending the position of their forefathers. This is not out of loyalty to a past tradition or to cherished arguments, but out of a deep conviction that Believers' Baptism is both the New Testament practice and that which accords with the Gospel. So far we have not felt it right to change; indeed, much as we desire unity, it would be wrong for us to abandon our convictions. Rather our hope is that we and those from whom we differ will be led to a common understanding of the will of God, in obedience to Whom alone true unity lies.[12]

But James Gray underwent a radical change of mind the next year when he was sent as the Churches of Christ delegate to the 1961 assembly of the World Council of Churches in New Delhi. Henceforth, he would champion a different position and lead the Churches of Christ on a different course. Gray explained the transformation in this way:

> At New Delhi I reached a painful conclusion that the Churches of the world are not going to abandon Infant Baptism. The battle of scholarship on the question of Baptism is not being won for "our side." Some of the greatest scholars and theological leaders of the world who have spoken most strongly against the present practice of Infant Baptism, and who believe that New Testament Baptism was solely for believers, are not yet prepared to abandon Infant Baptism today. Therefore, if we are to move closer to Infant Baptist Churches we must make up our minds to accommodate to this situation; it is

the real situation and it is likely to remain so for the foreseeable future.[13]

Henceforth the Union Committee began urging the churches to adopt "ecumenical membership" (known as open membership in the U.S.A.) and, by about 1971, about twenty percent of the churches had adopted the practice.[14]

Meanwhile, the ecumenical spirit was at work among the Congregational and the Presbyterian churches. Concrete steps to merge the two denominations were initiated in 1968, and these efforts culminated in the formation of the United Reformed Church in 1971. Churches of Christ manifested an interest in this development from its beginning when Conference authorized the Union Committee to negotiate on its behalf. By 1976, a proposal for unification of the United Reformed Church and the Churches of Christ was ready for consideration. The following year, it was approved by the URC. A substantial majority of the membership of Churches of Christ voted in favor of the merger; however, the vote failed because advocates of the merger were unable to win the seventy-five-percent majority in two-thirds of the congregations, which is required by British law for a denomination to alter its status. Conference then opted for a rather extreme measure in order to circumvent the legal requirement. The churches were asked to dissolve the Conference and vote as individual congregations to unite with the URC. By a vote of fifty-four to twenty, the 1979 Conference dissolved itself.[15] Immediately a Reformed Association of Churches of Christ took steps to join the United Reformed Church.

Twenty-four churches unwilling to merge with the URC organized the Fellowship of Churches of Christ. By 1988, the number had grown to thirty-seven as other churches that had previously withdrawn from Conference joined the Fellowship. A half-dozen other churches whose distrust of organization precludes formal affiliation cooperate with the Fellowship.[16]

Alan Robinson, a businessman in the great Francis Street Church in Birmingham, took steps to organize the Christian Renewal Trust in order to accumulate resources to perpetuate the original movement. (Overdale College was closed in 1976.) Dr. C. Robert Wetzel, a professor from Milligan College on sabbatical leave at Cambridge University, became very interested in the cause of the surviving churches and appealed for American assistance, organizing the British-American Fellowship. In 1980, Springdale College was launched. Subsequently, property was secured in Birmingham, and Springdale College has been accepted into the Selly Oak consortium. Several American ministers have been sent to assist the surviving churches, and the Christian Missionary Fellowship has made plans to send ministers to new locations to begin new congregations in

Britain. As the century draws to a close, there is a spirit of hopeful optimism among the surviving Churches of Christ in Britain.

Canada

The Scotch Baptist roots of the British Churches of Christ are clearly seen in the Churches of Christ in Canada. Reform movements that eventually led some congregations to become Churches of Christ erupted in several locations in Canada quite independently of each other. Little is known of one of the pioneers, John McKellar, who migrated from Argyllshire, Scotland, to Aldborough, Ontario (south of Rodney), in 1818. He preached reform among Baptist churches and preferred to be known as a "disciple of the Lord" rather than as a Scotch Baptist. Later, he was identified with a congregation at Mosa Township.

Another immigrant, James Black, also of the Aldborough congregation, migrated eastward to the region of Niagara and organized a congregation in his home. It later came to be known as the East Eramosa Church. Nearby, in Dundas, David Oliphant, Sr., was preaching reform views. Black and Oliphant united their efforts, recruited fellow Scots, and formed a nucleus that led to the establishment of nine more congregations consisting of 858 members by 1861.[17] The *Millennial Harbinger* found its way to these churches and influenced their thinking on some of the vexing questions facing them, such as whether the Lord's Supper could be celebrated in the absence of an ordained minister. Barton W. Stone's influence also reached Ontario. In 1833, through the "Christian" or "New Light" movement, an Anglican minister was led to accept immersion. Reuben Butchart, historian of the Canadian movement, notes that "the Campbells and Stone enlarged, qualified, and to a large extent developed what had already begun. Especially did they add soul and breadth to what was sometimes rigid, legalistic, and literalistic."[18]

Inter-congregational contacts led to the calling of a meeting of delegates in 1843 in Equesing. Sixteen congregations were represented or accounted for, according to a report sent by James Menzies and published in the *Millennial Harbinger*.[19] James Black and Alexander Anderson had been engaged "to travel as evangelists." They reported twenty-five immersions. They were directed to continue and were to be supported by freewill offerings from the churches. But efforts to develop closer cooperation of the churches in Ontario were not without opposition. "The idea that 'nothing but what was used, mentioned, or approved in the Book should constitute any part of Christian endeavor either within or without the church'"[20] was extensive. A year later, an American visitor, W.W. Eaton, noted that the little congregations were so "fearful that their yearly meeting might grow into a *calf,* an *ox,* or something *worse* [Exodus 32], they concluded that in future such meetings shall be for the alone purpose of cultivating Christian union [i.e., fellowship between congregations]."[21] However, the urge to create the cooperative means to provide for preaching and church-planting was not to be denied. A "cooperation" was organized at Eramosa East in February, 1846, and a treasurer appointed to receive funds to undergird the evangelistic labors of James Black and James Menzies in Wellington County. A year earlier, in 1845, David Oliphant, who had attended Bethany College, began publication of the *Witness of Truth.*

Simultaneously, a more ambitious plan emerged in churches to the east, namely, to organize a provincial cooperation. After a few years of frustration, during which it became apparent that "the number of disciples of Christ was small and the field too large for such ambitious plans as 'provincial,'"[22] this cooperation was moved and merged into the Wellington Cooperation. The efforts of the latter cooperation eventually extended beyond Wellington with the result that, by 1886, delegates from thirty-two churches reorganized the body into "The Cooperation of Disciples of Christ in Ontario." The same meeting encouraged the women of the churches to organize the Ontario Christian Women's Board of Missions.[23] A constitution was adopted in 1889 and, in 1892, was certified to conform to the appropriate Act of Parliament governing such religious. It provided for "messengers" delegated by constituent churches, a method of organization that is common in churches of British background.

The beginnings of the movement in the maritime provinces (Nova Scotia, New Brunswick, and Prince Edward Island) are quite independent of the movement in Ontario. Surviving records are scarce, and the origins are shrouded in obscurity, but it is quite apparent that the initial influences were also Scotch Baptist. The River John, N.S., church dates from 1815, and Halifax dates at least from 1832. Other churches of "Christian Baptists" came into being in Daultry, Newport, Upper Rawdon, West Gore, and Cornwallis. W.H. Harding and Donald Crawford were respected leaders of these churches. In 1855, a "cooperation" was formed, and Crawford was engaged as evangelist.

The first churches in New Brunswick were formed on Deer Island at Lord's Cove. Other churches came into being, but the potential of this field was not realized because of inadequate leadership. However, it was otherwise with Prince Edward Island, the smallest of the Canadian provinces. An independent-minded Scotch Baptist preacher named Alexander Crawford came to the island in 1811. He organized several churches, one of which eventually became the first of the "reform" churches of the island under the leadership of Dr. John Knox, an Anglican minister whose study of the New Testament led him to adopt baptism by immersion as the New Testament position. Through the efforts of Donald Crawford, other churches came into existence. They were founded in New Glasgow, Charlottetown, Greenmount, Summerside, and Montague. Until 1855, these churches worked together in an "association." In that year, a "cooperation" was organized.

Religious conviction ran deep in these hardy Scots, and their dedication to the cause resulted in the entry of scores of young men from Prince Edward Island congregations into ministerial service. Some of them sought education at Bethany College and, in later years, at the College of the Bible in Lexington, Kentucky. Names such as Archibald McLean, C.B. Titus, J.A. Lord, Hugh B. Kilgour, Maitland Watterworth, O.E. Payne, and Malcom Outhouse suggest the disproportionate contribution that this small province made to the movement in the United States.

The vast expanse of western Canada was the last region of the dominion to be developed. Some efforts began in Portage La Prairie, Manitoba, as early as 1881. Little is known of the earliest years of this, the mother church of the west. This congregation called together scattered disciples in western territories and formed the Western Canadian Missionary Association in 1901. The American Christian Missionary Society rendered assistance and encouragement and, in 1902, sent J.A. Romig to initiate a work in Winnipeg, which eventually became a leading church. In 1903, a congregation was organized at Swan River, and, in 1905, a church was established at Riding Mountain. Meanwhile, two other congregations were established through efforts of the Ontario churches.

From Manitoba, the work spread to Saskatchewan through the efforts of William G. Kitchen, a pioneer preacher who had studied at Kentucky University (Transylvania) and Eureka College. Romig preached in homes where he could gather interested persons. A church was established at Milestone following an evangelistic meeting led by Romig. Subsequently, churches were organized in Yellow Grass and the university center of Sascatoon, the latter a cooperative effort of the Saskatchewan Christian Missionary Board and the American Christian Missionary Society. Assistance from the latter also helped start the church in Regina, the provincial capital.

Alberta proved to be the most fruitful of the western territories for Churches of Christ. At the turn of the century, thousands of immigrants from the United States, many from Missouri, in search of good farmland, moved into western Canada. The church in McLeod was established by the Montgomery family. M.B. Ryan was a tireless laborer in shepherding scattered Disciples in this vast area and encouraging them to form nucleus-congregations. In this sparsely settled region, the earliest efforts were often "union" Sunday schools, out of which a church would eventually be formed. Alberta Christian

Missionary Society was organized in 1909, and churches were formed in Erskine (1909), Clyde (1911), Lethbridge (1911), Calgary (1913), and the capital city of Edmonton (1913), to name the earliest. The influx of settlers from midwestern United States insured the interest and involvement of the A.C.M.S., without whose help the progress in Alberta would have been less vigorous.

Far-west British Columbia saw its first Church of Christ gather in 1905 when A.H. Cowherd preached in a public hall in Vancouver to Disciples who had migrated from Ontario. Support for this effort came from the Ontario Cooperation and the A.C.M.S. The following year, a second congregation was organized in Vancouver.

Canadian Churches of Christ have come under the influence of the larger movement in the United States. Note has been taken of the circulation of the *Millennial Harbinger* among the Ontario churches. Personal contacts have also been numerous and fruitful. Alexander Campbell made a tour into Canada in the summer of 1855.[24] In 1868, Benjamin Franklin visited churches in eastern Canada, and Isaac Errett did likewise in 1875. It cannot be rightly said that the issues that troubled the churches in the United States were exported to Canadian churches, but it must be admitted that the same attitudes of rigid literalism vs. progressive expansion that were vexing the churches in the States were to be found in Canada and were exacerbated by the influence of leaders from the United States. W.H. Harding maintains that Benjamin Franklin's influence was greatly enhanced by the enthusiastic reception accorded his visit to Prince Edward Island in 1869, so that the conservative influence of his *American Christian Review* greatly hindered the work of the churches on the Island. Harding observes:

> The trouble with the *American Christian Review* was not that it proclaimed a wrong doctrine, but it circumscribed the methods of work to be used in the promulgation of the gospel. Women must keep silence in the church; young people were to be seen and not heard; Sunday Schools were not scriptural; missionary societies were contrary to the Bible; preachers had to trust the Lord and the people for their support, etc. This non-progressive policy was hammered into the people every week. Sectarian churches were harlots, an organ was unscriptural, and until fifty years ago, the Coburg St. Church in St. John was the only church in the Maritime provinces that used an organ. Then the *Christian Standard* came along, but it was tabooed; Erret [sic] was an anti-Christ, and to have a copy of the *Christian Standard* in the house was a sign of heresy. We are asking the question, "Why have we not grown in Canada like they have grown in the U.S.?" Here is the answer. The Church in the provinces came to the crossroads, and took the wrong turn under the influence of the weekly visits of the old *Review,* and the non-progressive policy

crushed all the life, and the Reformation and the Plea for New Testament Christianity was turned into a hard and fast legality.[25]

Many of the congregations in Canada have retained characteristics of noninstrument Churches of Christ[26] in the U.S., but there was no bitter breach of fellowship such as developed in the States. The majority of noninstrument churches are found in Ontario.

A serious problem for the Canadian churches is that of isolation in a nation of vast distances and relatively sparse habitation. Even within individual provinces, great distances make it difficult to develop and maintain a sense of brotherhood. Formation of cooperative activity within the provinces has been noted. Joint efforts between these cooperatives and the American Christian Misionary Society has linked the churches in the neighboring nations. When the International Convention of Disciples of Christ was organized in 1917, it was given the name "International" to indicate inclusion of the Canadian churches, and occasionally the convention met in Canada. The International Convention of 1922, at Winona Lake, Indiana, encouraged the Canadian churches to send delegates to a conference at Guelph, Ontario, in October of that year, where a proposal was put forth to form an All-Canada Organization. George H. Stewart of Winnipeg, Ontario, was the driving force behind this move. He led a team that visited thirty-eight locations and addressed more than fifty churches, receiving almost unanimous endorsement for the proposed organization. In 1922, the All-Canada Organization was launched with George H. Stewart as chairman and John Stuart Mill (of St. Louis, Missouri) as secretary. Resolutions called for creation of a Bible-school literature "having a Canadian atmosphere and emphasis," merging of the Ontario and maritime papers into an All-Canada publication, establishment of a Bible Chair or an All-Canada Bible College, and creation of a church extension fund.[27] Women's organizations were integrated into the All-Canada Conference in 1927. Canadian churches sent a disproportionate share of their members into missionary service through the Foreign Christian Missionary Society, the Christian Women's Board of Missions, and the United Christian Missionary Society. Charles T. Paul, from Ontario, became president of the College of Missions in Indianapolis, an institution sponsored by the C.W.B.M.

Efforts to establish a college that would provide a ministry for Canadian churches antedate the formation of the All-Canada Committee. A school named Maritime Bible College opened in West Gore, Nova Scotia, in 1908. It functioned until 1915, when it was forced to close because of problems arising out of World War I. Efforts in Ontario began as far back as 1892 and 1893 when lectures were held in the Cecil Street Church attended by students at the University of Toronto. These efforts were transferred to the St. Thomas Church, where the college took shape. St. Thomas College occupied its own quarters in 1897. Its second principal, Dr. W.C. Macdougall (1903-1906), had earned his Ph.D. at the University of Chicago, and his theological perspectives were evidently at variance with those of a good portion of the college constituency. The ensuing controversy forced Dr. Macdougall's resignation in favor of a missionary career in India, but the college did not long survive. Its assets were liquidated and placed in a trust that was subsequently made available to the new Toronto college.

Careful plans were made for the opening of the College of the Churches of Christ in 1926. In 1927, this college occupied its own premises; in 1928, W.C. Macdougall was recalled to serve as principal. The program of the college was integrated with the University of Toronto, which awarded the degree. Extension courses were offered in such distant cities as Halifax, Edmonton, and Winnipeg, and correspondence courses were also made available. Total enrollment in all departments reached 156 in 1929.[28] But the Great Depression forced the college to close during most of the 1930s. It managed to reopen in 1939. However, a change of interest among the Canadian Disciples caused a decline in enrollment, and that forced the college to close permanently in 1956.[29] The assets were placed in trust to provide financial assistance to students who were preparing for ministry in "approved colleges and seminaries."[30]

Part of the cause of the decline in interest in the Toronto college may be assigned to the fascination with ecumenism that engrossed the leadership of the churches in these years. In 1948, Reuben Butchart wrote: "Christian union as leaven in a measure of meal is quickening the Christian world. Great religious leaders in Canada today are sounding forth pleas and prophecies looking towards union in Christ, that were undreamed of even twenty-five years ago."[31]

The Disciples of Christ in Canada were invited to join the efforts of the United Church (Methodist and Presbyterian) and the Anglican Church aiming at union. The All-Canada Convention gave hearty approval to the efforts in 1969 and appointed delegates to the negotiations.[32] Within two years, a plan of union was drafted and submitted to the respective churches.[33] It provided for an ecclesiastical structure quite different in many respects from that which Disciple churches had known. Those willing to make adjustments received the draft document sympathetically,[34] but this response was by no means universal. The following years saw some serious introspection, internal stress, and serious membership erosion. Total membership of the Canadian Disciples in 1975 had been reduced to slightly more than half that of 1965.[35] One of the issues involved surrender of the position on believer's baptism, which constitutes a significant part of the Scotch-Baptist heritage.[36] After years of dissent, the plan of union was abandoned because submissions from the churches indicated that "by far most felt that the directions were not promising."[37] By 1985, membership had declined by another one-third from that of ten years earlier.

Part of the decline in membership can be attributed to the fact that churches that were once part of the All-Canada work withdrew from it because of disagreement over the policies of the leadership of the All-Canada Committee. They came to be numbered among the Independent Christian Churches. Separation of churches from the All-Canada fellowship cannot be dated specifically. As in the United States, the separation was more of a process than an event.

Distance from Toronto and the need for ministers among the western churches were factors that led C.H. Phillips to establish Alberta Bible College in Lethbridge in 1932. Subsequently, the college was moved to the city of Calgary. It maintains a theological position that is more aligned with Christian Churches than with Disciples. It is listed among the Bible Colleges in the *Directory of Ministry* of the Christian Churches.

The churches of the maritime provinces have also established a Bible college on Prince Edward Island. Additionally, several attempts have been made to establish a college in Toronto, but with limited success. Ontario Christian Seminary struggles to fulfill its ministry amid formidable odds.

Churches of Christ in Canada have suffered the trauma of separation in much the same way as the churches in the United States. Sixty-nine churches with an estimated membership of 5,997 are listed in the Christian Church *Directory of Ministry* for 1989, while forty-one congregations with a membership of 4,006 are listed in the 1989 *Yearbook of Disciples of Christ.*[38] However, the smaller population of Canada and the vast distances between population centers has made schism in Canada much more devastating than is the case in the United States.

New Zealand

The first Church of Christ in New Zealand came into being through the dilligent efforts of Mr. and Mrs. Thomas Jackson, who arrived in Nelson from Glasgow, Scotland, in 1843. Within a year, Jackson was able to report to the *Christian Messenger* in Great Britain that he had established a small congregation according to the New Testament order.[39] He was joined by George Taylor in 1844, who brought a quantity of literature from Great Britain and also wrote to Alexander Campbell appealing for more literature.[40] In 1845, the Jacksons moved to Auckland, where they began a new work that resulted in a church of about fifty members within the next decade. Meanwhile, a new convert in Nelson, Thomas Magarey, left for Adelaide, where he planted the first church in Australia.

Another beachhead was established when about twenty-five persons from the church in Cupar, Fife (Scotland), migrated to Dunedin. They stayed together and formed the first Church of Christ in Dunedin. One family, the James Butlers, sailed to Otago and began a church there. The "Reformed Baptist Church of Dunedin," whose members were called "Disciples," built the first church building of the movement in New Zealand. In the same year that this group migrated from Fife, Mr. and Mrs. John Taylor arrived in Invercargill, the southernmost city in New Zealand. By 1863, a regular meeting of fifteen Disciples was holding forth, and the cause spread to nearby Mataura in 1868.

Thus far, the establishment of churches in New Zealand was entirely a layman's effort; all the members were priests and ministers. The members were convinced that they had found their way out of denominationalism and that others would follow. The regular weekly observance of the Lord's Supper in homes or in rented halls was the distinguishing bond that linked these remote congregations in a common endeavor. Growth in membership was aided by immigration, especially during the 1850s and 1860s when gold was discovered in several areas of New Zealand.

Henry S. Earl, an Englishman who had studied at Bethany, was the first "educated minister" to come to New Zealand. Coming in 1867, he served briefly in Dunedin before moving on to Adelaide, Australia. Another American-educated minister, G.L. Surber, came to Dunedin, where he introduced the practice of "open confession" following the sermon as preferable to the older practice of examination of the prospective members by the elders. The cause flourished in Dunedin with the coming of T.H. Bates, an American evangelist who rented a tabernacle seating 1,000 persons and preached to capacity audiences. Several new congregations were organized from this effort.

A church was organized in the capital city of Wellington in 1869, and in Christchurch in 1879. Discipline in the churches was strict, and, at this time, there were no musical instruments. When they were subsequently introduced, there was no schism. Noninstrument Churches of Christ list no congregations in New Zealand and only recently have undertaken mission work there.

Inter-congregational activity began with a primitive "conference" organized in 1865 for "consultation and encouragement." Important to the work in New Zealand was *The British Millennial Harbinger*, edited by James Wallis. The ministry was almost entirely "lay," except for those who came from the United States. F.W. Greenwood was the first of the New Zealand students who came to America for education to return to New Zealand.

The earliest statistics date from 1885 and disclose that there were at that date twenty-five churches, thirteen chapels, and 1,238 members. By 1905, the number had doubled to fifty churches with 2,463 members. Annual Dominion Conferences date from 1901.[41] In 1906, mission work was begun in Rhodesia, a field where persistent effort has produced much fruit. *The New Zealand Christian* began publication in 1920.

By 1924, membership in the churches had reached 3,269. In 1929 E.C. Hinrichsen began an extensive evangelistic effort among the churches that added 1,600 members in eighteen months.[42] Membership peaked in 1938 at 4,962. Since then there has been steady decline and the membership of forty-two churches reporting in 1987 was 2,503.[43]

The need for a college to educate a ministry was discussed in the churches' annual conference as early as 1920. A college was opened at Glen Leith, Dunedin, in 1927, and A.L. Haddon was brought from Sydney to serve as principal. Although located far from the geographic center of this two-island nation, the college grew because Haddon was a good organizer and fund raiser. When he was made editor of *The New Zealand Christian* he enjoyed greater visibility and additional influence. From these two positions, Haddon gave leadership to the churches for a generation.

Arthur Haddon was a dedicated ecumenist. He was one of the organizers of the National Council of Churches of New Zealand and served on its executive committee.[44] He was a delegate to the World Council in New Delhi in 1961. His course on ecumenics was the first of its kind in any college in the South Pacific area. Many of Haddon's students were enthusiastic participants in the earliest ecumenical discussions with Methodist, Congregational, Presbyterian, and later Anglican delegates in the 1960s. It was almost a foregone conclusion that Churches of Christ would merge into some type of a united body.[45] The college at Glen Leith, which had suffered a decline in enrollment, was merged with Knox College (Presbyterian), and Churches of Christ participated to the extent of supplying a faculty post. Gavin Munroe, who succeeded Haddon as principal at Glen Leith, was appointed "Haddon Lecturer" at Knox College.

With the passing of Haddon, ecumenism lost its most ardent champion. When the 1970 World Convention of Churches of Christ met in Adelaide, Australia, a number of younger New Zealand ministers in attendance became aware of the American "Independent" branch of the movement and of the viewpoints espoused by the fellowship involved in the North American Christian Convention. As a result, they formed a "Restoration Fellowship" to oppose merger and to reinvigorate the historic position of the Churches of Christ.[46] Simultaneously, the American ministers whose acquaintance with the situation in New Zealand moved them to provide assistance organized the South Pacific Evangelizing Fellowship. American ministers were sent to serve New Zealand churches that were unable to find or provide suitable ministers. The closure of the Glen Leith Bible College forced New Zealand ministerial candidates who disliked studying at Knox to seek education either in Australia or the U.S. American interest was also responsible for building a youth ranch near Nelson for the purpose of developing a new type of youth program. The result of this infusion of interest from America was to provide the churches with an option to merger. Consequently, the schism that occurred in Britain has been avoided. With the decline of the merger issue, the conference has become much more united and the churches are closing ranks behind their earlier position.

While tensions over denominational merger were at their height in the early 1980s, another issue threatened the unity of the churches. The Charismatic Movement, which touched many denominations worldwide, found a ready reception in many of the congregations. A few churches experienced splits, but most learned to accommodate this influence and to profit by the renewed vigor that accompanied this phenomenon.

Australia

Churches of Christ in Australia, like those in Britain and Canada, trace their roots to Scotch Baptist sources. Thomas Magarey, who migrated from North Ireland to Nelson, New Zealand, met Thomas Jackson in Nelson and was converted to simple New Testament Christianity by Jackson in 1841. A massacre of Europeans by Maori natives in the same year impelled Magarey to move on to Adelaide, Australia, where he came to be associated with a Scotch Baptist group in which the writings of Alexander Campbell were already being discussed. Obtaining thirty copies of *The British Millennial Harbinger,* Magarey distributed them among the congregation. A lively debate over Calvinist doctrines followed, and a division ensued, a part of the congregation leaving to organize a more traditional Baptist church. In 1847, Jackson arrived from New Zealand and a building was erected. Also in 1847, a small group of immigrants arrived from Ayrshire, Scotland, and constituted a Church of Christ in nearby MacLaren Vale. From these two churches, others were organized, and prospects for the work were so promising that Magarey wrote James Wallis appealing for an evangelist to serve full-time in Victoria.[47]

The movement developed otherwise in New South Wales. Albert Griffin, the pioneer of the movement in Sydney, was Methodist. He was troubled over the doctrine that held that a sinner desiring to become a Christian had to wait in agony until God was disposed to relieve his distress through an experience. His brother in London, a member of a Church of Christ, sent him a box containing several books, among which were copies of *The British Millennial Harbinger* and the *Bible Advocate*. When he read in these journals that sinners who wanted to become Christians could do so simply by following directions given by the apostles, he requested baptism from a local Baptist preacher. He also learned from an 1852 *Harbinger* that a Mr. and Mrs. Henry Mitchell of one of the churches in Scotland were living in Sydney. He established contact with them, and they met to observe the Lord's Supper. In 1853, they were joined by four Methodists, two of whom were preachers. A veterinary surgeon nearby, who sought to reclaim the group for the Methodist Church, was also won. As the cause spread in New South Wales in the next several years, the bulk of the converts were of Methodist background, which gave the churches in New South Wales a slightly different character from those in Victoria and South Australia.

The Victoria churches were established largely by immigrants from Britain who came as part of the gold rush in the 1850s. A church was organized at Prahran in 1855 and one in Melbourne the next year.

Thomas Magarey was a tireless worker in behalf of the cause. Not an effective speaker himself, he was an intrepid distributor of literature. *The British Millennial Harbinger* was a potent influence, especially inasmuch as its editor, James Wallis, showed a keen interest in the cause in Australia. Inevitably, the churches developed along British lines. As in England, the Sunday-morning service was devoted to the Lord's Supper and mutual edification, usually by one of the elders. Discipline was strict, and Communion was restricted to members. Nonmembers were welcome to attend the evening "evangelistic service."

A new phase in the life of the Churches of Christ in Australia began in 1864 with the arrival of Henry S. Earl. As previously noted, Earl was an Englishman who graduated from Bethany College in 1858. His superior preaching soon attracted crowds in excess of 1,000, which seemed to confirm the suggestion then being advanced that the best interest of the cause would be served by an educated ministry. An appeal was made to the British churches to send more men like Henry Earl, but none came. A similar appeal to America brought G.L. Surber to Melbourne and T.J. Gore to Adelaide. They were soon followed by J.J. Haley, W.H. Martin, H.H. Geeslin, and O.A. Carr. Carr initiated the work in Tasmania. The results of this new thrust was that the membership of the churches in Victoria and South Australia tripled in the decade following 1865. New South Wales, where there were no American evangelists, showed little increase. Graeme Chapman, historian of the Australian Churches of Christ, offers the following explanation:

> Varied factors were responsible for the success of the Americans. First, they were college-educated. Second, they were careful, though adventuresome, strategists, hiring in cities or country towns, the largest buildings available. Third, their presentation of the message differed from that of the pioneers. Their addresses were well-structured. They confined themselves to a few points, cultivated an expansive oratorical approach, and injected the Restoration logic with an emotional warmth. Fourth, they made it easier for individuals to respond by substituting for the usual examination by elders, the making of an open "confession," that is, walking to the front of the building to indicate repentance for sin and confession of Christ. Fifth, to draw attention to their message and presence, and to concentrate their appeal, they held "protracted meetings." These intensive missions, running over one, two, or more weeks, were supported by well-attended prayer meetings [an American technique developed by Charles G. Finney]. Finally, speaking frequently of "Our Position," they were less afraid to acknowledge a distinctive identity. If more successful, they appeared less underhanded in their evangelism.[48]

But along with the American success came a serious problem. The great number of new converts tended to look to the "evangelist" for leadership, especially as these men began to settle in with one congregation. Their presence constituted a challenge to the rule of the elders. A case in point, and one that was by no means unusual: T.J. Gore clashed with the elders of the Grote St. congregation over who should occupy the pulpit on Sunday mornings, the elders wishing to limit the "evangelist" to the Sunday-evening evangelistic service. Another item of contention arose from the American's practice of accepting offerings from all present at the service. The British practice was to permit only members to contribute. On this matter, the American practice was eventually to prevail. It was otherwise in the matter of organization. American suspicion of any organization above the local congregation found little reception among Australians. The beginnings of a Conference in Victoria date from 1873. Twelve churches in New South Wales began to cooperate for evangelism in 1875; the annual Conference there dates from 1885. Queensland organized a State Conference in 1883, Tasmania in 1894, and Western Australia in 1898. An Intercolonial Conference was held in 1889, followed by a second in 1898, mainly as acquaintanceship meetings. The first Federal Conference was held in 1906.

Aaron B. Maston came to Australia from America to pursue a ministry of printing and publishing. In 1891, he established the Austral

Printing and Publishing Company, initially producing Restoration tracts. In 1898, he was able to combine two smaller papers into *The Australian Christian,*[49] which became the national journal of the Australian Churches of Christ.

As the nineteenth century came to a close, there was increasing conviction that the need for adequate ministry meant that a college was a necessity, although there was a vocal residue of the earlier bias against "a parson manufactory." Henry S. Earl had attempted, without success, to raise funds on a tour of America in 1870 for a college in South Australia. In 1903, an evening school was conducted in affiliation with Texas Christian University. But the fact that most of the young men seeking education for ministry went to the United States, and few returned, moved the churches to act on the matter of establishing a college. The first Federal Conference set this as its goal, and the college was opened in 1907. The close association of this school with the College of the Bible in Lexington, Kentucky, where several Australians studied and where Australian-born Mark Collis became chairman of the trustees, is reflected in the name taken by the new college—College of the Bible. The site at Glen Iris was occupied in 1910. A.R. Main was named principal.

The first three decades of the twentieth century saw the population of Australia almost double. Membership in Churches of Christ doubled to 33,095. The College of the Bible produced preachers, and vigorous evangelistic efforts produced results. American evangelist John T. Brown conducted a successful evangelistic tour in 1906, followed by Charles Reign Schoville in 1912 and Jesse Kelleums in 1923. But the most fruitful evangelistic leadership was given by E.C. Hinrichsen, described as "the most spectacular and consistently successful evangelist in Churches of Christ over a longer period of time than anyone else."[50] Chapman notes that a novel feature of many Hinrichsen missions was the locating of the mission in an area where a handful of members met in a private home. During the period of the mission, up to 100 and sometimes 200 decisions for Christ were made, a building erected, and a full-time minister placed in charge of a church large enough to be self-supporting.[51]

Unquestionably, the leader of the period was A.R. Main, who in addition to serving as principal of the College of the Bible was also editor of *The Australian Christian.* From this dual position, Main influenced a whole generation of preachers and churches. Possessed of a keen, logical mind, Main was always ready to enter into ecumenical dialogue (he participated in the ecumenical conferences in Lausanne, Oxford, and Geneva), but he was unwilling to compromise what he considered to be "fundamentals," and he was terribly disappointed that a large segment of the American churches and colleges had been infected with what he termed "the Liberal disease." But some of the newer views of the Bible entered the college through other faculty, and an open rift ensued, which resulted in Main's retirement in 1938 in favor of T.H. Scambler. The Conference in New South Wales resisted what they perceived as unfortunate changes in the college at Glen Iris and established a college at Woolwich, a suburb of Sydney. Main was called from retirement to serve as the first principal. Largely through the diplomatic skill of A.W. Stephenson, who succeeded Main as editor of *The Australian Christian,* a rupture was averted and amicable relations between the two institutions have been maintained. A third college, located in Brisbane, was established in 1965 by the Queensland Conference.

Beginning with the Great Depression, membership began a slight decline. World War II dislodged many people in Australia and created new social problems. Churches of Christ have responded by developing a series of homes for the elderly and the needy that witness admirably to the Christian commitment of the membership. Likewise, the youth emphases in most of the churches gives indication of vitality and of a promising future. Enrollment in the three colleges for ministerial education increases. While there have been theological tensions, these have not proven to be disruptive, and the removal of the issue of denominational merger has eliminated a troublesome theme. Almost all of the churches (more than 400 in 1987, embracing more than 30,000 members)[52] work together through the Federal Conference. As a whole, Churches of Christ in Australia have demonstrated a more viable sense of brotherhood and unity than has been the case in Great Britain, Canada, New Zealand, or the United States. Remarkable growth has been achieved in the 1980s in New South Wales and Queensland, where a confident optimism about the future prevails. Australian Churches of Christ maintain significant missionary activity among the aborigines and in India and Papua, New Guinea, the latter field reporting over 5,000 members.

End Notes

[1]Thompson, op. cit., p. 17.

[2]Ibid., p. 22.

[3]*Christian Messenger,* Vol. I, p. 204.

[4]Thompson, op. cit., p. 31.

[5]Ibid.

[6]See *The British Millennial Harbinger,* 1855, pp. 359, 410-412, 452-457. Cited in Thompson, op. cit., p. 51.

[7]Ibid., p. 79.

[8]Ibid., p. 207. The subjects of the conference papers reflect the issues current among the Churches of Christ in much the same way that William Banowsky (op. cit.) has shown that the Abilene Lectures reflect issues in the American Churches of Christ.

[9]See excerpts from the presidential address of Lancelot Oliver (A.C. Watters, *History of the British Churches of Christ* [Indianapolis: Butler School of Religion, 1948], p. 114).

[10]Philip Morgan, *Churches of Christ Yearbook (Great Britain),* cited by Thompson, op. cit., p. 204.

[11]The author was present. This position is affirmed in James Gray, ed. *Toward Christian Union* (unpublished report of the Union Committee of Churches of Christ, 1960), pp. 24-31.

[12]Ibid., p. 30.

[13]*Yearbook,* 1964, p. 61. Cf. Thompson, op. cit., p. 189.

[14]Thompson, op. cit. p. 189.

[15]The figures in behalf of merger are misleading. An undetermined number of churches opposing merger had already abandoned Conference.

[16]Additionally, there are an undetermined number of churches that never affiliated with Conference. These are known as "Old Path"

churches and bear resemblance to the anti-instrument churches in the United States.

17Reuben Butchart, *History of the Disciples of Christ in Canada Since 1830* (Toronto: Churches of Christ, 1949), p. 60.

18Ibid., p. 61.

19James Menzies, *Millennial Harbinger*, 1843, p. 377.

20Butchart, op. cit., p. 77.

21W.W. Eaton, *Millennial Harbinger*, 1844, p. 380.

22Butchart, op. cit., p. 80.

23Ibid., p. 88.

24Campbell published his impressions of the Canadian movement in the September and October, 1855, issues of the *Millennial Harbinger*.

25W.H. Harding, in Butchart, op. cit., p. 105.

26Mac Lynn (op. cit., pp. 347-351) lists 120 congregations. Many of these are very small; only 13 report 100 or more members. Interestingly, there are no churches in Prince Edward Island.

27"Resolutions." See Butchart, op. cit., p. 180. (Butchart was Editor of *The Canadian Disciple.*)

28Butchart, op. cit., p. 160.

29"The College—Present Status," *The Canadian Disciple*, January, 1957, p. 6.

30"College of Churches of Christ in Canada: What Is It?" *The Canadian Disciple*, November, 1971, p. 1. Statement of policy is found in "Another New Day for Disciples," *The Canadian Disciple* October, 1976, p. 1.

31Butchart, op. cit., p. 280.

32"All Canada Resolution Regarding Church Union," *The Canadian Disciple*, October, 1969, p. 1.

33"The Plan of Union—First Draft" found in *Church Union Report*, Vol. II, No. 3 (Toronto: The General Commission on Church Union, 1971).

[34]Elmer S. Stainton, "You and Church Union," *Canadian Disciple*, March, 1971, p. 1.

[35]Compare *Yearbook of Christian Churches (Disciples of Christ)*, 1965 (8,909 members), with the 1975 *Yearbook* (4,718 members).

[36]See Russel Legge, "Mutual Recognition of Members," *Canadian Disciple*, Spring, 1982.

[37]Neil Bergman, "Joint National Commission Dissolved," *Canadian Disciple*, Summer, 1985, p. 5.

[38]See 1989 *Directory of the Ministry*, p. F-37 and *Yearbook of Christian Churches (Disciples)*, 1989, p. 284.

[39]See A.L. Haddon, *Centennial Souvenir Book: Being a Brief History of the Associated Churches of Christ in New Zealand* (Wellington, N.Z.: Deslandes, Ltd., 1944), p. 16.

[40]*Millennial Harbinger*, 1846, p. 331.

[41]T. Graeme Todd, ed., *Handbook of Associated Churches of Christ in New Zealand* (Nelson, N.Z.: Associated Churches of Christ, 1987), p. 58.

[42]Haddon, op. cit., p. 42.

[43]Todd, op. cit., p. 66.

[44]Savage, op. cit, p. 68.

[45]Ibid., p. 75. Also see Ron O'Grady, "Down Under," *The Disciple*, May, 1988, p. 26.

[46]Although merger was never adopted by Conference, eleven congregations entered into merger with Methodist or Presbyterian churches on a local basis. O'Grady, op., cit., p. 27.

[47]A.B. Maston, *Jubilee History of Churches of Christ in Australia* (cited by A.G. Elliott, *Bridge Builders in Restoration* [Sydney, NSW: Churches of Christ Christian Unity Committee], p. 31).

[48]Graeme Chapman, *One Lord, One Faith, One Baptism* (Melbourne: Federal Literature Department of Churches of Christ, 1979), p. 63.

[49]Ibid., p. 85.

50Ibid., p. 112.

51Ibid.

52Richard Phillips, "The Restoration Movement in Australia," *Christian Standard*, September 6, 1987, pp. 1, 4-6. Statistics supplied by Keith Farmer, principal of the Theological College of NSW, Sydney, Australia.

Division of Higher Education Disciples of Christ

Member Institutions

Colleges and Universities

Atlantic Christian College
Wilson, NC

Bethany College
Bethany, WV

Chapman College
Orange, CA

Columbia College
Columbia, MO

Culver-Stockton College
Canton, MO

Drake University
Des Moines, Iowa

Drury College
Springfield, MO

Jarvis Christian College
Hawkins, TX

Lynchburg College
Lynchburg, VA

Midway College
Midway, KY

Northwest Christian College
Eugene, OR

Phillips University
Enid, OK

Texas Christian University
Ft. Worth, TX

Tugaloo College
Tugaloo, MS

Eureka College
Eureka, IL

Hiram College
Hiram, OH

Transylvania University
Lexington, KY

William Woods College
Fulton, MO

Seminaries

Brite Divinity School
Texas Christian University
Ft. Worth, TX

Christian Theological Seminary
Indianapolis, IN

Lexington Theological Seminary
Lexington, KY

The Graduate Seminary
Phillips University
Enid, OK

Seminary Foundation Houses

Disciples Divinity House
University of Chicago
Chicago, IL

Disciples Divinity House
Vanderbilt University
Nashville, TN

Disciples Seminary Foundation
School of Theology at Claremont
Claremont, CA

Schools and Universities Affiliated With Churches of Christ

Liberal Arts Colleges and Universities

Abilene Christian University
Abilene, TX

Amber University
Garland, TX

Columbia Christian College
Portland, OR

Crowley's Ridge College
Paragould, AR

David Lipscomb College
Nashville, TN

Faulkner University
Montgomery, AL

Florida College
Tampa, FL

Lubbock Christian University
Lubbock, TX

Michigan Christian Center
Rochester, MI

Northeastern Christian Junior
College, Villanova, PA

Ohio Valley College
Parkersburg, WV

Oklahoma Christian College
Oklahoma City, OK

Pepperdine University
Malibu, CA

Southwestern Christian College
Terrell, TX

Freed-Hardeman College
Henderson, TN

Western Christian College
North Weyburn, Saskachewan, Canada

Great Lakes Christian College
Beamsville, Ontario, Canada

York College
York, NE

Harding University
Searcy, AR

Bible Colleges and Other Degree-Granting Schools of Religion

Alabama Christian School of Religion
Montgomery, AL

Magnolia Bible College
Kosciusko, MS

American Christian Bible College
West Monroe, LA

Oconee Bible College
Eatonton, GA

Harding University
Graduate School of Religion
Memphis, TN

Southwest Bible Institute
San Angelo, TX (non-class)

The Institute for Christian Studies
Austin, TX

Tennessee Bible College
Cookeville, TN

International Bible College
Florence, AL 35630

White's Ferry Road of
Biblical Studies
West Monroe, LA

Colleges and Seminaries of the Christian Churches

Bible Colleges

College	Location	Founded
Alberta Bible College	Calgary, Alberta, Canada	1932
Atlanta Christian College	East Point, GA	1937
Bluefield College of Evangelism	Bluefield, WV	1971
Boise Bible College	Boise, ID	1945
Central Christian College of the the Bible	Moberly, MO	1957
Cincinnati Bible College	Cincinnati, OH	1924
Colegio Biblico	Eagle Pass, TX	1945
College of the Scriptures	Louisville, KY	1945
Dallas Christian College	Dallas, TX	1950
Eastern Christian College	Bel Air, MD	1946/60
El Paso School of Missions	El Paso, TX	1982
Florida Christian College	Kissimmee, FL	1976
Great Lakes Bible College	Lansing, MI	1949
Iowa Christian College	Des Moines, IA	1978
Johnson Bible College	Kimberlin Heights, TN	1893
Kentucky Christian College	Grayson, KY	1919
Lincoln Christian College	Lincoln, IL	1944
Louisville Christian College	Louisville, KY	1948
Manhattan Christian College	Manhattan, KS	1927
Maritime Christian College	Charlottetown, PEI, Canada	1960
Mid-South Christian College	Memphis, MS	1959
Minnesota Bible College	Rochester, MN	1913

Nebraska Christian College	Norfolk, NE	1945
Ontario Christian Seminary	Toronto, Ontario, Canada	1958/72
Ozark Christian College	Joplin, MO	1942
Pacific Christian College	Fullerton, CA	1928
Platte Valley Bible College	Scottsbluff, NE	1951
Puget Sound College of the Bible	Seattle, WA	1950
Roanoke Bible College	Elizabeth City, NC	1948
St. Louis Christian College	Florissant, MO	1956
San Jose Bible College	San Jose, CA	1939
Winston-Salem Bible College	Winston-Salem, NC	1950

Liberal Arts College

| Milligan College | Milligan College, TN | 1881 |

Seminaries

Emmanuel School of Religion	Johnson City, TN	1961
Cincinnati Bible Seminary	Cincinnati, OH	*
Lincoln Christian Seminary	Lincoln, IL	*

*Graduate divisions at Cincinnati and Lincoln were established some time after the undergraduate schools, but precise dating is difficult to determine since they granted Masters degrees before they had clearly established graduate schools with separate deans and faculties.

Bible Colleges That Have Closed

Christian College of the Rockies	Longmont, CO	1981-1984
Dakota Bible College	Huron, SD	1942-1988
Gulf States Christian College	New Orleans, LA	1953-1959
Intermountain Bible College	Grand Junction, CO	1946-1988
Lexington Bible College	Lexington, KY	1954-1960
Midwest Christian College	Oklahoma City, OK	1946-1985
New York Christian Institute	Clarence, NY	1971-1981
Ohio Valley Christian College	Hardin, KY	1975-1981
Paducah Bible College	Paducah, KY	1962-1964
Southern Christian College	San Antonio, TX	1947-1963
Southwest Christian Seminary	Phoenix, AZ	1947-1963

Bibliography

The following bibliography is selective and aims to be representative of the historical development of the movement. It is regrettable that space does not permit the inclusion of many other items. The categories in which titles appear have been chosen somewhat arbitrarily in hopes they will assist the reader in locating books of particular interest.

Contents

Basic Documents and Anthologies

Campbell, Thomas. *The Declaration and Address.* 1809. Several editions available, including St. Louis: Bethany Press, 1955.

Dickinson, Hoke S., ed. *The Cane Ridge Reader.* 1972.

Haggard, Rice. *An Address to the Different Religious Societies on the Sacred Import of the Christian Name.* Nashville: Disciples of Christ Historical Society, 1954.

Humbert, Royal, ed. *A Compound of Alexander Campbell's Theology.* St. Louis: Bethany Press, 1961.

Kershner, Frederick. *Christian Union Overture (Commentary on the Declaration and Address).* St. Louis: Bethany Press, 1923.

Neth, John W. *Walter Scott Speaks.* Milligan College, TN: Emmanuel School of Religion, 1967.

Stone, Barton W. *The Last Will and Testament of the Springfield Presbytery.* 1804. Several editions currently available, including St. Louis: Bethany Press, 1955.

Warren, W.R., ed. *Centennial Convention Report.* Cincinnati: Standard Publishing, 1909.

Young, Charles A. *Historical Documents Advocating Christian Union.* Chicago: Christian Century, 1904.

Yearbooks and Directories

Lynn, Mac, ed. *Where the Saints Meet: a Directory of the Churches of Christ.* Pensacola: Firm Foundation Publishing House, 1987.

McLean, Ralph, ed. *Directory of the Ministry: a Yearbook of Christian Churches and Churches of Christ.* Springfield: Specialized Christian Services, 1955ff.

Morgan, Philip. *Churches of Christ Yearbook (Great Britain).* Churches of Christ, 1845ff.

Todd, T. Graeme, ed. *Handbook of Associated of Churches of Christ in New Zealand.* Nelson: Associated Churches of Christ, 1922ff.

Yearbook of Christian Churches (Disciples of Christ). Indianapolis, 1885ff.

General Histories

Banowsky, William S. *Mirror of a Movement.* Dallas: Christian Publishing, 1965.

Brown, John T. *Churches of Christ.* Louisville: John P. Morton, 1904.

Cochran, Louis, and Bess White. *Captives of the Word.* Garden City: Doubleday, 1969.

Davis, Morrison M. *How the Disciples Began and Grew.* Cincinnati: Standard Publishing, 1915.

Ford, Harold. *A History of the Restoration Plea.* Joplin: College Press, 1952.

Fortune, Alonzo W. *Adventuring With Disciple Pioneers.* St. Louis: Bethany Press, 1942.

Garrett, LeRoy. *The Stone-Campbell Movement.* Joplin: College Press, 1981.

Garrison, James H. *The Reformation of the Nineteenth Century.* St. Louis: Christian Publishing, 1901.

Garrison, James H. *The Story of a Century.* St. Louis: Christian Publishing, 1909.

Garrison, Winfred E. *An American Religious Movement.* St. Louis: Bethany Press, 1945.

Garrison, Winfred E. *Heritage and Destiny: an American Religious Movement Looks Ahead.* St. Louis: Bethany Press, 1961.

Garrison, Winfred E. *Religion Follows the Frontier.* New York: Harper & Row. 1931.

Garrison, W.E., and A.T. DeGroot. *The Disciples: A History.* St. Louis: Christian Board of Publication, 1948.

Gates, Errett. *The Disciples of Christ.* New York: Baker & Taylor, 1905.

Harrell, David Edwin. *Quest for a Christian America.* Nashville: Disciples of Christ Historical Society, 1966.

Harrell, David E. *The Social Sources of Division in the Disciples of Christ 1865-1900.* Atlanta: author, 1973.

Hayden, Amos S. *The Early History of the Disciples in the Western Reserve, Ohio.* Cincinnati: Chase & Hall, 1875.

Jennings, Walter W. *Origin and Early History of the Disciples of Christ.* Cincinnati: Standard Publishing, 1919.

Moore, William T. *A Comprehensive History of the Disciples of Christ.* New York: Revell, 1909.

Morrison, Charles C. *The Unfinished Reformation.* New York: Harper, 1953.

Murch, James D. *Christians Only: a History of the Restoration Movement.* Cincinnati: Standard Publishing, 1962.

Tucker, William E., and Lester G. McAllister. *Journey in Faith.* St. Louis: Christian Board of Publication, 1975.

Tyler, Benjamin B. *A History of the Disciples of Christ.* New York: Christian Literature, 1894.

Walker, Dean E. *Adventuring for Christian Unity.* Birmingham, England: Berean Press, 1935.

Whitely, Oliver Read. *Trumpet Call of Reformation.* St. Louis: Bethany Press, 1959

Interpretations

Ainslee, Peter. *The Message of the Disciples for the Union of the Church, Including Their Origin and History.* New York: Revell, 1913.

Allen, C. Leonard, and Richard T. Hughes, *Discovering Our Roots: the Ancestry of Churches of Christ.* Abilene: Abilene Christian University Press, 1988.

Anderson, L.D. *What We Believe.* Ft. Worth: author, 1957.

Beazley, George W., Jr. *The Christian Church (Disciples of Christ): an Interpretive Examination in the Cultural Context.* St. Louis: Bethany Press, 1973.

Blakemore, W.P., et. al., eds. *The Renewal of the Church* (3 vols.). St. Louis: Bethany Press, 1963.

Crowe, Paul A., ed. *Reappraising the Disciples Tradition for the 21st Century.* Indianapolis: Council on Christian Unity, Disciples of Christ, 1987.

DeGroot, Alfred T. *Disciple Thought: A History.* Ft. Worth: author, 1965.

DeGroot, Alfred T. *The Grounds of Division Among the Disciples of Christ.* Chicago: author, 1940.

Garrison, Winfred E. *Alexander Campbell's Theology: Its Sources and Setting.* St. Louis: Christian Publishing, 1900.

Gresham, Perry E., ed. *The Sage of Bethany: a Pioneer in Broadcloth.* St. Louis: Bethany Press, 1960.

Hughes, Richard T., and C. Leonard Allen. *Illusions of Innocence: Protestant Primitivism in America, 1630-1875.* Chicago: University of Chicago Press, 1988.

Keene, Lawrence. "Disciples of Christ on the Pacific Slope: a Sociological Approach," *Impact.* Claremont: Disciples Seminary Foundation, 1984.

Leggett, Marshall. *Introduction to the Restoration Ideal.* Cincinnati: Standard Publishing, 1986.

Lunger, Harold L. *The Political Ethics of Alexander Campbell.* St. Louis: Bethany Press, 1954.

Moore, W.T. *The Plea of the Disciples of Christ.* Chicago: Christian Century, 1906.

Osborne, Ronald. *Experiment in Liberty.* St. Louis: Bethany Press, 1978.

Phillips, Thomas W., Sr. *The Church of Christ.* New York: Funk & Wagnalls, 1905.

Robinson, William. *What Churches of Christ Stand For.* Birmingham, England:Berean Press, 1959.

Short, Howard E. *Christian Unity Is Our Business: Disciples of Christ Within the Ecumenical Movement.* St. Louis: Bethany Press, 1953.

Short, Howard E. *Doctrine and Thought of the Disciples of Christ.* St. Louis: Christian Board of Publication, 1951.

Tristano, Richard. The Origin of the Restoration Movement: an Intellectual History. Atlanta: Glenmary Home Missions, 1988.

Walker, Dean E. *Adventuring for Christian Unity.* Birmingham, England: Berean Press, 1935.

Wetzel, C. Robert, ed. *Essays on New Testament Christianity.* Cincinnati: Standard Publishing, 1978.

Thesis and Dissertation Lists

Roberts, R.L. "Dissertations on Alexander Campbell," *Restoration Quarterly*. Vol. 30, Nos. 2 and 3, 1988, pp. 169-175.

Spencer, Claude E. *Theses Concerning Disciples of Christ and Related Religious Groups*. Nashville: Discisples of Christ Historical Society, 1964.

Doctrinal Works

Campbell, Alexander. *The Christian System*. Cincinnati: Standard Publishing, 1910.

Crowe, Paul, A. ed. *Reapapraising the Disciple Tradition for the 21st Century*. Indianapolis: Council on Christian Unity, Disciples of Christ, 1987.

England, Stephen J. *One Baptism*. St. Louis: Bethany Press, 1960.

Garrison, James H. *The Old Faith Restated*. St. Louis: Christian Publishing, 1891.

Gray, James. *The Authority of the New Testament in Relation to Christian Union*. Birmingham, England: Churches of Christ Publishing Committee, 1967.

Hawley, Monroe. *The Focus of Our Faith*. Nashville: 20th Century Christian, 1985.

Humbert, Royal, ed. *A Compound of Alexander Campbell's Theology*. St. Louis: Bethany Press, 1961.

Lamar, J.S. *First Principles and Reflections*. Cincinnati: Standard Publishing, 1891.

Lard, Moses E. *Review of Campbellism Examined*. Shreveport: Lambert Book Co., 1857.

Lunger, Harold L. *The Political Ethics of Alexander Campbell*. St. Louis: Bethany Press.

Milligan, Robert. *An Exposition and Defense of the Scheme of Redemption as It Is Taught in the Holy Scriptures*. Cincinnati: W.R. Carroll, 1869.

Morrison, Charles C. "The Meaning of Baptism," *Christian Century*, 1912.

Robinson, William. *The Biblical Doctrine of the Church*. Birmingham, England: Berean Press, 1948.

Robinson, William. *The Shattered Cross: the Many Churches and the One Church*. Birmingham, England: Berean Press, 1945.

Scott, Walter. *The Messiahship, or the Great Demonstration.* Cincinnati: H.S. Bosworth, 1859.

Teegarden, Kenneth L. *We Call Ourselves Disciples.* St. Louis: Bethany Press, 1975.

van Kirk, Hiram. *The Rise of the Current Reformation: a History of the Theology of Christian Churches.* St. Louis: Christian Publishing, 1907.

Wetzel, C. Robert. *Essays in New Testament Christianity.* Cincinnati: Standard Publishing, 1978.

Polemic Works

Brewer, G.C. *Contending for the Faith*. Nashville: Gospel Advocate Press, 1941.

Corey, Stephen J. *Fifty Years of Attack and Controversy: the Consequences Among Disciples of Christ*. St. Louis: Bethany Press, 1946.

DeGroot, Alfred T. *Extra Ecclesiam Nulla Salus Est (or Restructure Problems)*. Ft. Worth: author, 1968.

DeGroot, Alfred T. *The Restoration Principle*. St. Louis: Bethany Press, 1960.

Ferguson, Everett. *A Capella Music in the Public Worship of the Church*. Abilene: Biblical Research Press, 1972.

Johnson, Ashley S. *The Great Controversy*. Cincinnati: F.L. Rowe, 1939.

Kurfees, M.C. *Instrumental Music in the Worship*. Nashville: Gospel Advocate Press, 1950.

Matsler, W.R. *The Independent Movement Within the Christian Church: an Historical Study*. Canyon: author.

McGarvey, John W. *Biblical Criticism*. Cincinnati: Standard, 1910.

Meyers, Robert, ed. *Voices of Concern Critical Studies in Church of Christism*. St. Louis: Mission Messenger, 1966.

Milburn, J.H. *Origin of Campbellism*. Chicago: Regan House, 1913.

Whitsitt, W.H. *Origin of the Disciples of Christ*. New York: A.C. Armstrong & Son, 1888.

Yancey, C. Walter. *Endangered Heritage, an Examination of Church of Christ Doctrine*. Joplin: College Press, 1987.

Debates

A Debate Between Rev. A. Campbell and Rev. N. L. Rice on the Action, Subject, Design, and Administrator of Christian Baptism. Pittsburgh: Thomas Carter, 1844.

A Debate on Christian Baptism (the Campbell-McCalla Debate). Bethany: Alexander Campbell, 1824.

A Debate on the Evidences of Christianity (the Campbell-Owen Debate). Bethany: Alexander Campbell, 1829.

A Debate on the Roman Catholic Religion (the Campbell-Purcell Debate). Cincinnati: J.A. James, 1837.

Infant Sprinkling Proved to Be a Human Tradition; Being the Substance of a Debate on Christian Baptism Between Mr. John Walker, a Minister of the Secession, and Alexander Campbell, V.D.M., a Regular Baptist Minister. Steubenville: James Wilson, 1820.

Major Periodicals

American Christian Review. Cincinnati, 1856-1887.

Apostolic Times. Lexington, 1869-1885.

Christian Baptist. Alexander Campbell, ed. Bethany, 1823-30.

Christian Century (originally called *Christian Oracle*). Chicago, 1884ff.

Christian Messenger. Barton W. Stone, ed. Georgetown, 1826-1844.

Christian Standard. Cincinnati: Standard Publishing, 1865ff.

The Evangelist. Walter Scott, ed. Carthage, 1832-38.

Gospel Advocate. Nashville: Gospel Advocate Press, 1855ff.

Lard's Quarterly. Moses E. Lard, ed. Georgetown & Frankfort, 1863-1868.

Midstream. Indianapolis: Council on Christian Unity, 1961ff.

Millennial Harbinger. Alexander Campbell, ed. Bethany, 1830-70.

Restoration Herald. Cincinnati: Christian Restoration Association, 1925ff.

Riley, E. C. *A Classified and Annotated List of the Periodicals of the Christian Church Prior to 1900.* Lexington: unpublished M.A. thesis, University of Kentucky, 1941.

Spencer, Claude. *Periodicals of Disciples of Christ and Related Religious Groups.* Canton: Disciples of Christ Historical Society, 1943.

Biographies

Allison, Edith Wolfe. *Prisoner of Christ: the Life Story of Leslie and Carrie Wolfe.* Joplin: College Press, 1960.

*Ames, Edward S. *Beyond Theology.* Chicago: Chicago University Press, 1959.

Arant, Francis M. *"P.H.": the Welshimer Story.* Cincinnati: Standard Publishing, 1958.

Baxter, William. *The Life of Knowles Shaw, the Singing Evangelist.* Cincinnati: Central Book Concern, 1879.

Baxter, William. *The Life of Walter Scott.* Cincinnati: Bosworth, Chase and Hall, 1874. Centennial edition: *Life of Elder Walter Scott,* condensed by B.A. Abbott, St. Louis: Bethany Press, 1926.

Boles, H. Leo. *Biographical Sketches of Gospel Preachers.* Nashville: Gospel Advocate Press, 1932.

*Book, William H. *Real Life and Original Sayings of W.H. Book.* Richmond: Wade and Duke, 1900.

Brown, Alva Ross. *Standing on the Promises* (Ashley S. & Erma E. Johnson). Knoxville: author, 1928.

Campbell, Selina. *Home Life of Alexander Campbell.* St Louis: John A. Burns, 1882.

Choate, J.E. *The Anchor that Holds: a Biography of Benton Cordell Goodpasture.* Nashville: Gospel Advocate Press, 1971.

Clark, Richard L., and Bates, Jack W. *Faith Is My Fortune: a Life Story of George Pepperdine.*

Cochran, Louis. *The Fool of God.* New York: Duell, Sloan, & Pearce, 1958.

Cochran, Louis. *Raccoon John Smith.* St. Louis: Bethany Press, 1963.

*Asterisk indicates autobiography

Combs, George H. *I'd Take This Way Again.* St. Louis: Bethany Press, 1944.

Cunningham, Mrs. W.D., and Mrs. Owen Still. *The Flaming Torch: Life Story of W.D. Cunningham.* Tokyo: Yotsuya Mission, 1939.

Dahlberg, Edwin, ed. *Herald of the Evangel (Jesse M. Bader).* St. Louis: Bethany Press, 1965.

Donan, P. *Memoir of Jacob Creath, Jr.* Indianapolis: Religious Book Service.

Franklin, Joseph, and J.A. Headington. *Life and Times of Benjamin Franklin.* St. Louis: Christian Board of Publication.

Fuller, Corydon E. *Reminiscences of James A. Garfield.* Cincinnati: Standard Publishing, 1887.

*Garrison, James H. *Memories and Experiences.* St. Louis: Christian Board of Publication, 1926.

Goodnight, Cloyd, and Dwight E. Stevenson. *Home to Bethphage (Robert Richardson).* St. Louis: Christian Board of Publication, 1949.

Gray, James. *W.R., the Man and His Work.* Birmingham, England: Berean Press, 1978.

Green, F.M. *The Life of James A. Garfield.* Chicago: Central Book Concern, 1882.

Gresham, Perry, ed. *The Sage of Bethany: Pioneer in Broadcloth.* St. Louis: Bethany Press, 1960.

Groover, R. Edwin. *The Well-Ordered Home (Alexander Campbell).* Joplin: College Press, 1988.

Haley, J.J. *Makers and Molders of the Reformation Movement.* St. Louis: Christian Board of Publication, 1914.

Hall, Colby D. *Rice Haggard: the American Frontier Evangelist Who Revived the Name Christian.* Ft. Worth: University Christian Church, 1957.

Hannah, W.H. *Thomas Campbell: Seceeder and Christian Union Advocate.* Cincinnati: Standard Publishing, 1935.

Hooper, Robert D. *Crying in the Wilderness: a Biography of David Lipscomb.* Nashville: David Lipscomb College, 1979.

*Hopwood, Josephus. *A Journey Through the Years.* St. Louis: Bethany Press, 1932.

Idleman, Finis S. *Peter Ainslee: Ambassador of Good Will.* Chicago: Willett Clark Co., 1941.

Keith, Noell. *The Story of David Burnett: Undeserved Obscurity.* St. Louis: Bethany Press, 1954.

Kellems, Jesse R. *Alexander Campbell and the Disciples.* New York: R.R. Smith, 1930.

Lamar, C.P. *The Life of Joseph Rucker Lamar.* New York: G.P. Putnams, 1926.

Lamar, J.S. *Memoirs of Isaac Errett* (2 vols.). Cincinnati: Standard Publishing, 1893.

*Lappin, S.S. *Run, Sammy, Run.* St. Louis: Bethany Press, 1958.

MacLean, John P. *A Sketch of the Life and Labors of Richard McNemar.* Franklin, OH: author, 1905.

Mathes, J.W. *Works of Elder B.W. Stone.* Rosemead: Old Paths Book Club, 1953.

McAllister, Lester. *Thomas Campbell: Man of the Book.* St. Louis: Bethany Press, 1954.

McAllister, Lester. *Z.T. Sweeney: Preacher and Peacemaker.* St. Louis: Christian Board of Publication, 1968.

*McGarvey, John W. *The Autobiography of J.W. McGarvey.* Lexington: College of the Bible, 1960.

Miller, Raphael H., ed. *Charles S. Medbury: Preacher and Master Workman for Christ.* St. Louis: Christian Board of Publication, 1932.

Moore, William T. *The Life of Timothy Coop.* Cincinnati: Standard Publishing.

Morro, W.C. *Brother McGarvey.* St. Louis: Bethany Press 1940.

*Murch, James D. *Adventuring for Christ in Changing Times.* Louisville: Restoration Press, 1973.

Murch, James D. *B.D. Phillips: Life and Letters.* Louisville, 1969.

Osborne, Ronald. *Ely Vaughn Zollars: Teacher of Preachers, Builder of Colleges.* St. Louis: Christian Board of Publication, 1947.

Peters, H.H. *Charles Reign Scoville.* St. Louis: Bethany Press, 1924.

Phillips, Dabney. *Restoration Principles and Personalities.* Birmingham: University of Alabama, 1975.

Power, Fredrick D. *The Life of William Kimbrough Pendleton.* St. Louis: Christian Publishing, 1902.

Rains, Paul. *Francis Marion Rains.* St. Louis: Christian Board of Publication, 1922.

Richardson, Robert. *Memoirs of Alexander Campbell.* Philadelphia: J. Lippincott, 1868.

Rogers, John. *The Biography of Elder Barton W. Stone, Written by Himself; With Additions and Reflections by Elder John Rogers.* Cincinnati: J.A. & U.P. James, 1847.

Savage, Murray. *Haddon of Glen Leith: an Ecumenical Pilgrimage.* Dunedin, New Zealand: Associated Churches of Christ, 1970.

Smith, Benjamin L. *Alexander Campbell.* St. Louis: Bethany, 1930.

Stevenson, Dwight E. *Walter Scott: Voice of the Golden Oracle.* St. Louis: Christian Board of Publication, 1946.

Tucker, William. *J.H. Garrison and Disciples of Christ.* St. Louis: Bethany Press, 1964.

Wallace, William. *Daniel Sommer, 1850-1940.* author, 1969.

Warren, W.R. *The Life and Labors of Archibald McLean.*

Wasson, Woodrow W. *James A. Garfield: His Religion and Ed* tion. Nashville: Tennessee Book Co., 1952.

West, Earl I. *The Life and Times of David Lipscomb.* H Religious Book Service, 1954.

West, J.W. *Sketches of Our Mountain Pioneers.* Lynchburg: author, 1939.

West, William G. *Barton Warren Stone: Early American Advocate of Christian Unity.* Nashville: Disciples of Christ Historical Society, 1954.

Wilburn, James R. *The Hazard of the Die: Tolbert Fanning and the Restoration Movement.* Austin: Sweet Publishing, 1969.

Williams, John A. *The Life of Elder John Smith.* Cincinnati: Standard Publishing, 1904.

Mission Histories

Buckner, George Walker, Jr. *Concerns of a World Church.* St. Louis: Bethany Press, 1943.

Burnet, David S. *The Jerusalem Mission Under the Direction of the American Christian Missionary Society.* Cincinnati: American Christian Missionary Society, 1853.

Burnham, Frederick W. *Unification: the How, What and Why of the United Christian Missionary Society.* St. Louis: United Christian Missionary Society, 1927.

Carpenter, Vere C. *Puerto Rican Disciples.* Tampa: Christian Press, 1960.

Carr, James B. *The Foreign Mission Work of the Christian Church. Manhattan: author, 1946.*

Filbeck, David. *The First Fifty Years: a Brief History of the Independent Mission Movement.* Joplin: College Press, 1980.

Gallagher, Mark. *A Critical History of the Mission and Ministry of the Christian Church (Disciples of Christ) in Hawaii.* Honolulu: Ph.D. thesis, University of Hawaii, 1977.

Garst, Laura D. *A West Pointer in the Land of the Mikado.* New York: Revell, 1913.

Green, F.M. *Christian Missions and Historical Sketches.* St. Louis: John Burns Publishing, 1884.

History of the Foreign Christian Missionary Society: by the Missionaries. Cincinnati: F.C.M.S., 1917.

Lewis, Grant K. *The American Christian Missionary Society.* St. Louis: Christian Board of Publication, 1937.

McLean, Alexander. *The Foreign Christian Missisonary Society.* New York: Revell, 1919.

McLean, Archibald. *A History of the Foreign Christian Mission Society.* New York: Revell, 1921.

Montgomery, J. Dexter. *Disciples of Christ in Argentina.* S Bethany Press, 1956.

Savage, Murray J. *Forward Into Freedom (New Zealand Missions in Zimbabwe and Vanuatu)*. Dunedin, NZ: Associated Churches of Christ in New Zealand.

Shelton, Albert L. *Pioneering in Tibet: a Personal Record of Life and Experience in Mission Fields*. New York: Revell, 1921.

Shelton, Flora B. *Shelton of Tibet*. New York: Doran, 1923.

Slate, Philip, ed. *Perspectives on Worldwide Evangelization*.

Smith, H.G. *Fifty Years in the Congo*. Indianapolis: United Christian Missionary Society, 1949.

They Went to India: Biographies of Missionaries of the Disciples of Christ. Indianapolis: United Christian Missionary Society, 1954.

Warren, W.R., ed. *Survey of Service*. St. Louis: Christian Board of Publication, 1929.

Webb, Henry E. *A History of the Independent Mission Movement Among Disciples of Christ*. Louisville: Ph.D. Thesis, Southern Baptist Theological Seminary, 1954.

Institutional Histories

Blakemore, William Barnett. *Quest for Intelligence in Ministry.* Chicago: Disciples Divinity House, 1970.

Cornwell, Cindy. *By the Waters of the Buffalo.* Johnson City: Overmountain Press, 1989.

Cummins, D. Duane. *The Disciples Colleges: a History.* St. Louis: C.B.P. Press, 1987.

Dickinson, Elmira J. *A History of Eureka College.* Eureka: Eureka College, 1984.

Giovannoli, Harry. *Kentucky Female Orphan School: a History.* Midway: 1930.

Green, Francis M. *Hiram College and Western Reserve Eclectic Institute: Fifty Years of History, 1850-1900.* Cleveland: Hubbell Printing, 1901.

Hale, Allean. *Petticoat Pioneer: Christian College Story, 1851-1951.* Columbia: Columbia College, 1956.

Hamlin, Griffith A. *In Faith and History: the Story of William Woods College.* St. Louis: Bethany Press, 1965.

Jennings, Walter W. *Transylvania: Pioneer University of the West.* New York: Pageant Press, 1955.

Lee, George R. *Culver Stockton College: the First 130 Years.* Canton: Culver Stockton College, 1984.

Marshal, Frank, and M. Powell. *Phillips University's First Fifty Years* (3 vols). Enid: Phillips University, 1967.

Moore, Jerome A. *Texas Christian University: a Hundred Years of History.* Ft. Worth: T.C.U. Press, 1974.

Ritchey, Charles. *Drake University Through 75 Years.* Des Moines: Drake University, 1956.

Seale, James M. *A Century of Faith and Caring (Christian Chu Homes of Kentucky).* Christian Church Homes of Ken* 1984.

Smith, William M. *For the Support of the Ministry.* Indianapolis: Pension Fund of the Disciples of Christ, 1956.

Stevenson, Dwight E. *The Bacon College Story: 1836-1865.* Lexington: College of the Bible, 1962.

Stevenson, Dwight E. *Lexington Theological Seminary.* St. Louis: Bethany Press, 1962.

Trendley, Mary B. *Prelude to the Future: the First Hundred Years of Hiram College.* New York: Association Press, 1950.

Ware, Charles C. *A History of Atlantic Christian College.* Wilson: Atlantic Christian College, 1956.

Woolery, W.K. *Bethany Years.* Cincinnati: Standard Publishing, 1941.

Wright, John D. *Transylvania: Tutor to the West.* Lexington: Transylvania University, 1975.

Young, M. Norval. *A History of Colleges Established and Controlled by Members of the Churches of Christ.* Kansas City: Old Paths Book Club, 1949.

State Histories

Burlingame, M.G., and Hartling, H.C. *Big Sky Disciples: a History of the Christian Church (Disciples of Christ) in Montana.* Great Falls: Christian Church in Montana, 1984.

Cauble, Wesley. *Disciples of Christ in Indiana.* Indianapolis: Meigs Publishing, 1930.

Cole, Clifford C. *The Christian Churches of Southern California.* St. Louis: Christian Board of Publication, 1959.

Cramblet, Wilber H. *The Christian Church (Disciples of Christ) in West Virginia.* St. Louis: Bethany Press, 1971.

Darst, H. Jackson. *Ante-Bellum Virginia Disciples.* Richmond: Virginia Christian Missionary Society, 1959.

Eckstein, Stephen D. *History of the Churches of Christ in Texas.* Austin: Firm Foundation Publishing, 1963.

England, Stephen J. *Oklahoma Christians.* St. Louis: Bethany, 1975.

Forster, Ada. *History of the Christian Church and Churches of Christ in Minnesota.* St. Louis: Christian Board of Publication, 1953.

Fortune, Alonzo W. *The Disciples in Kentucky.* Christian Churches in Kentucky, 1932.

Haley, Thomas P. *Dawn of the Reformation in Missouri.* St. Louis: Christian Publishing, 1888.

Hall, Colby D. *Texas Disciples.* Fort Worth: Texas Christian University Press, 1953.

Harmon, Marion F. *A History of the Christian Churches in Mississippi.* Aberdeen, 1929.

Hayden, Amos S. *Early History of the Disciples in the Western Reserve, Ohio.* Cincinnati: Chase and Hall, 1875.

Haynes, Nathaniel S. *History of the Disciples of Christ in Illinois, 1819-1914.* Cincinnati: Standard Publishing, 1915.

Hodge, Frederick A. *The Plea and the Pioneers in Virginia.* Richmond: Everett Waddy Company, 1905.

McPherson, Chalmers. *Disciples of Christ in Texas.* Cincinnati: Standard Publishing, 1920.

Mosley, Edward J. *Disciples of Christ in Georgia.* St. Louis: Bethany Press, 1954.

Nance, Elwood C. *Florida Disciples.* Joplin: College Press, 1941.

Norton, Herman A. *Tennessee Disciples.* Nashville: Disciples of Christ Historical Society, 1971.

Peters, George L. *The Disciples of Christ in Missouri.* Columbia: Centennial Commission of Missouri Convention of Christian Churches, 1937.

Peterson, Orval. *Washington-Northern Idaho Disciples.* St. Louis: Christian Board of Publication, 1953.

Shaw, Henry K. *Buckeye Disciples: a History of Disciples of Christ in Ohio.* St. Louis: Ohio Christian Missionary Society, 1952.

Shaw, Henry K. *Hoosier Disciples: a Comprehensive History of Christian Churches (Disciples of Christ) in Indiana.* Indianapolis: Association of Christian Churches in Indiana, 1966.

Swander, Clarence F. *Making Disciples in Oregon.* Portland, 1928.

Tyler, J.Z. *Disciples of Christ in Virginia.* Richmond, 1879.

Updegraff, John C. *The Christian Church (Disciples of Christ) in Florida.* Anna Publishing, 1981.

Ware, Charles C. *North Carolina Disciples of Christ.* St. Louis: Christian Board of Publication, 1927.

Ware, Charles C. *South Carolina Disciples of Christ: a History.* Charleston: Christian Churches of South Carolina, 1967.

Ware, Elias B. *History of the Disciples of Christ in California.* Healdsburg: F.W. Cooke, 1916.

Watson, George H., and Mildred B. Watson. *History of the Christian Church in the Alabama Area.* St. Louis: Bethany Press, 1965.

Wilcox, Alanson. *History of the Disciples of Christ in Ohio.* Cincinnati: Standard Publishing, 1918.

Representative Sermons

Book, William H. *Columbus Tabernacle Sermons.*

Briney, J.B. *Sermons and Addresses.* Cincinnati: Standard Publishing, 1922.

Fitch, Alger M. *Alexander Campbell: Preacher of Reform and Reformer of Preaching.* Cincinnati: Standard Publishing, 1975.

Franklin, Benjamin. *The Gospel Preacher* (2 vols). Nashville: Gospel Advocate Press (reprint of 1896 ed.), 1947.

Jones, Edgar D. *Sermons I Love to Preach.*

McReynolds, A.B. *Soul-Winning and Stewardship Sermons.* St. Louis: Christian Board of Publication, 1931.

Moore, William T. *The Living Pulpit of the Christian Church.* St. Louis: Christian Publishing, 1867.

Moore, William T. *The New Living Pulpit of the Christian Church.* St. Louis: Christian Board of Publication, 1919.

Stevenson, Dwight E. *Disciple Preaching in the First Generation: an Ecological Study.* Nashville: Disciples of Christ Historical Society, 1969.

Sweeney, Z.T., ED. *New Testament Christianity* (3 vols). Columbus: editor, 1933.

Walker, Granville T. *Preaching in the Thought of Alexander Campbell.* St. Louis: Bethany Press, 1954.

British Commonwealth

Butchart, Reuben. *History of the Disciples of Christ in Canada Since 1830.* Toronto: Churches of Christ (Disciples), 1949.

Chapman, Graeme. *One Lord, One Faith, One Baptism: a History of Churches of Christ in Australia.* Melbourne: Federal Literature Department, Churches of Christ, 1979.

DeGroot, Alfred T. *Literature of the Churches of Christ in Great Britain and Ireland.* Ft. Worth: author, 1950.

Elliott, Allen G. *Bridge Builders in Restoration.* Great Britain: Gowans & Son.

Gray, James, ed. *Towards Christian Union, Twenty-five Years of Thought and Action in Churches of Christ, 1935-1960.* 1960.

Haddon, A.L. *Centennial Souvenir Book: a Brief History of the Associated Churches of Christ in New Zealand, 1844-1944.* Wellington: Deslandes, Ltd., 1944.

Hudson, John A. *The Church in Great Britain.* Rosemead: Old Paths Book Club, 1948.

Muir, Shirley. *The Disciples in Canada.* Indianapolis: United Christian Missionary Society, 1966.

Robinson, William. *What Churches of Christ Stand For.* Birmingham, England: Berean Press, 1959.

Roper, David. *Voices Crying in the Wilderness: a History of the Lord's Church ... Emphasis on Australia.* Salisbury: Restoration Publications, 1979.

Thompson, David. *Let Sects and Parties Fall.* Birmingham, England: Berean Press, 1980.

Watters, Archibald C. *History of the British Churches of Christ.* Indianapolis: Butler School of Religion, 1948.